Short Stories
for Stories
for Students

National Advisory Board

Short Stories for Students

**Presenting Analysis, Context, and Criticism on
Commonly Studied Short Stories**

Volume 17

David Galens, Project Editor

GALE®

THOMSON

™

GALE

Detroit • New York • San Diego • San Francisco • Cleveland • New Haven, Conn. • Waterville, Maine • London • Munich

Short Stories for Students, Volume 17

Project Editor
David Galens

Editorial
Anne Marie Hacht, Michelle Kazensky, Ira Mark Milne, Pam Revitzer, Kathy Sauer, Timothy J. Sisler, Jennifer Smith, Carol Ullmann

Research
Nicodemus Ford, Sarah Genik, Tamara Nott

Permissions
Lori Hines

Manufacturing
Stacy Melson

Imaging and Multimedia
Lezlie Light, David G. Oblender, Kelly A. Quin, Luke Rademacher

Product Design
Pamela A. E. Galbreath, Michael Logusz

ISBN 0-7876-4269-X
ISSN 1092-7735

Printed in the United States of America
10 9 8 7 6 5 4 3 2 1

Table of Contents

Why Study Literature At All?

Short Stories for Students is designed to provide readers with information and discussion about a wide range of important contemporary and historical works of short fiction, and it does that job very well. However, I want to use this guest foreword to address a question that it does *not* take up. It is a fundamental question that is often ignored in high school and college English classes as well as research texts, and one that causes frustration among students at all levels, namely—why study literature at all? Isn't it enough to read a story, enjoy it, and go about one's business? My answer (to be expected from a literary professional, I suppose) is no. It is not enough. It is a start; but it is not enough. Here's why.

First, literature is the only part of the educational curriculum that deals directly with the actual world of lived experience. The philosopher Edmund Husserl used the apt German term *die Lebenswelt*, "the living world," to denote this realm. All the other content areas of the modern American educational system avoid the subjective, present reality of everyday life. Science (both the natural and the social varieties) objectifies, the fine arts create and/or perform, history reconstructs. Only literary study persists in posing those questions we all asked before our schooling taught us to give up on them. Only literature gives credibility to personal perceptions, feelings, dreams, and the "stream of consciousness" that is our inner voice. Literature wonders about infinity, wonders why God permits evil, wonders what will happen to us after we die.

Literature admits that we get our hearts broken, that people sometimes cheat and get away with it, that the world is a strange and probably incomprehensible place. Literature, in other words, takes on all the big and small issues of what it means to be human. So my first answer is that of the humanist—we should read literature and study it and take it seriously because it enriches us as human beings. We develop our moral imagination, our capacity to sympathize with other people, and our ability to understand our existence through the experience of fiction.

My second answer is more practical. By studying literature we can learn how to explore and analyze texts. Fiction may be about *die Lebenswelt*, but it is a construct of words put together in a certain order by an artist using the medium of language. By examining and studying those constructions, we can learn about language as a medium. We can become more sophisticated about word associations and connotations, about the manipulation of symbols, and about style and atmosphere. We can grasp how ambiguous language is and how important context and texture is to meaning. In our first encounter with a work of literature, of course, we are not supposed to catch all of these things. We are spellbound, just as the writer wanted us to be. It is as serious students of the writer's art that we begin to see how the tricks are done.

Seeing the tricks, which is another way of saying "developing analytical and close reading skills," is important above and beyond its intrinsic literary educational value. These skills transfer to other fields and enhance critical thinking of any kind. Understanding how language is used to construct texts is powerful knowledge. It makes engineers better problem solvers, lawyers better advocates and courtroom practitioners, politicians better rhetoricians, marketing and advertising agents better sellers, and citizens more aware consumers as well as better participants in democracy. This last point is especially important, because rhetorical skill works both ways—when we learn how language is manipulated in the making of texts the result is that we become less susceptible when language is used to manipulate us.

My third reason is related to the second. When we begin to see literature as created artifacts of language, we become more sensitive to good writing in general. We get a stronger sense of the importance of individual words, even the sounds of words and word combinations. We begin to understand Mark Twain's delicious proverb—"The difference between the right word and the almost right word is the difference between lightning and a lightning bug." Getting beyond the "enjoyment only" stage of literature gets us closer to becoming makers of word art ourselves. I am not saying that studying fiction will turn every student into a Faulkner or a Shakespeare. But it will make us more adaptable and effective writers, even if our art form ends up being the office memo or the corporate annual report.

Studying short stories, then, can help students become better readers, better writers, and even better human beings. But I want to close with a warning. If your study and exploration of the craft, history, context, symbolism, or anything else about a story starts to rob it of the magic you felt when you first read it, it is time to stop. Take a break, study another subject, shoot some hoops, or go for a run. Love of reading is too important to be ruined by school. The early twentieth century writer Willa Cather, in her novel *My Antonia*, has her narrator Jack Burden tell a story that he and Antonia heard from two old Russian immigrants when they were teenagers. These immigrants, Pavel and Peter, told about an incident from their youth back in Russia that the narrator could recall in vivid detail thirty years later. It was a harrowing story of a wedding party starting home in sleds and being chased by starving wolves. Hundreds of wolves attacked the group's sleds one by one as they sped across the snow trying to reach their village. In a horrible revelation, the old Russians revealed that the groom eventually threw his own bride to the wolves to save himself. There was even a hint that one of the old immigrants might have been the groom mentioned in the story. Cather has her narrator conclude with his feelings about the story. "We did not tell Pavel's secret to anyone, but guarded it jealously—as if the wolves of the Ukraine had gathered that night long ago, and the wedding party had been sacrificed, just to give us a painful and peculiar pleasure." That feeling, that painful and peculiar pleasure, is the most important thing about literature. Study and research should enhance that feeling and never be allowed to overwhelm it.

Thomas E. Barden
Professor of English and
Director of Graduate English Studies
The University of Toledo

Introduction

Purpose of the Book

The purpose of *Short Stories for Students* (*SSfS*) is to provide readers with a guide to understanding, enjoying, and studying short stories by giving them easy access to information about the work. Part of Gale's "For Students" Literature line, *SSfS* is specifically designed to meet the curricular needs of high school and undergraduate college students and their teachers, as well as the interests of general readers and researchers considering specific short fiction. While each volume contains entries on "classic" stories frequently studied in classrooms, there are also entries containing hard-to-find information on contemporary stories, including works by multicultural, international, and women writers.

The information covered in each entry includes an introduction to the story and the story's author; a plot summary, to help readers unravel and understand the events in the work; descriptions of important characters, including explanation of a given character's role in the narrative as well as discussion about that character's relationship to other characters in the story; analysis of important themes in the story; and an explanation of important literary techniques and movements as they are demonstrated in the work.

In addition to this material, which helps the readers analyze the story itself, students are also provided with important information on the literary and historical background informing each work. This includes a historical context essay, a box comparing the time or place the story was written to modern Western culture, a critical essay, and excerpts from critical essays on the story or author. A unique feature of *SSfS* is a specially commissioned critical essay on each story, targeted toward the student reader.

To further aid the student in studying and enjoying each story, information on media adaptations is provided (if available), as well as reading suggestions for works of fiction and nonfiction on similar themes and topics. Classroom aids include ideas for research papers and lists of critical sources that provide additional material on the work.

Selection Criteria

The titles for each volume of *SSfS* were selected by surveying numerous sources on teaching literature and analyzing course curricula for various school districts. Some of the sources surveyed include: literature anthologies, *Reading Lists for College-Bound Students: The Books Most Recommended by America's Top Colleges*; *Teaching the Short Story: A Guide to Using Stories from around the World*, by the National Council of Teachers of English (NCTE); and "A Study of High School Literature Anthologies," conducted by Arthur Applebee at the Center for the Learning and Teaching of Literature and sponsored by the National Endowment for the Arts and the Office of Educational Research and Improvement.

Input was also solicited from our advisory board, as well as from educators from various areas. From these discussions, it was determined that each volume should have a mix of "classic" stories (those works commonly taught in literature classes) and contemporary stories for which information is often hard to find. Because of the interest in expanding the canon of literature, an emphasis was also placed on including works by international, multicultural, and women authors. Our advisory board members—educational professionals—helped pare down the list for each volume. Works not selected for the present volume were noted as possibilities for future volumes. As always, the editor welcomes suggestions for titles to be included in future volumes.

How Each Entry Is Organized

Each entry, or chapter, in *SSfS* focuses on one story. Each entry heading lists the title of the story, the author's name, and the date of the story's publication. The following elements are contained in each entry:

- **Introduction:** a brief overview of the story which provides information about its first appearance, its literary standing, any controversies surrounding the work, and major conflicts or themes within the work.

- **Author Biography:** this section includes basic facts about the author's life, and focuses on events and times in the author's life that may have inspired the story in question.

- **Plot Summary:** a description of the events in the story. Lengthy summaries are broken down with subheads.

- **Characters:** an alphabetical listing of the characters who appear in the story. Each character name is followed by a brief to an extensive description of the character's role in the story, as well as discussion of the character's actions, relationships, and possible motivation.

  Characters are listed alphabetically by last name. If a character is unnamed—for instance, the narrator in "The Eatonville Anthology"—the character is listed as "The Narrator" and alphabetized as "Narrator." If a character's first name is the only one given, the name will appear alphabetically by that name.

- **Themes:** a thorough overview of how the topics, themes, and issues are addressed within the story. Each theme discussed appears in a sepa-

rate subhead, and is easily accessed through the boldface entries in the Subject/Theme Index.

- **Style:** this section addresses important style elements of the story, such as setting, point of view, and narration; important literary devices used, such as imagery, foreshadowing, symbolism; and, if applicable, genres to which the work might have belonged, such as Gothicism or Romanticism. Literary terms are explained within the entry, but can also be found in the Glossary.

- **Historical Context:** this section outlines the social, political, and cultural climate *in which the author lived and the work was created.* This section may include descriptions of related historical events, pertinent aspects of daily life in the culture, and the artistic and literary sensibilities of the time in which the work was written. If the story is historical in nature, information regarding the time in which the story is set is also included. Long sections are broken down with helpful subheads.

- **Critical Overview:** this section provides background on the critical reputation of the author and the story, including bannings or any other public controversies surrounding the work. For older works, this section may include a history of how the story was first received and how perceptions of it may have changed over the years; for more recent works, direct quotes from early reviews may also be included.

- **Criticism:** an essay commissioned by *SSfS* which specifically deals with the story and is written specifically for the student audience, as well as excerpts from previously published criticism on the work (if available).

- **Sources:** an alphabetical list of critical material used in compiling the entry, with bibliographical information.

- **Further Reading:** an alphabetical list of other critical sources which may prove useful for the student. It includes bibliographical information and a brief annotation.

In addition, each entry contains the following highlighted sections, set apart from the main text as sidebars:

- **Media Adaptations:** if available, a list of film and television adaptations of the story, including source information. The list also includes stage adaptations, audio recordings, musical adaptations, etc.

- **Topics for Further Study:** a list of potential study questions or research topics dealing with the story. This section includes questions related to other disciplines the student may be studying, such as American history, world history, science, math, government, business, geography, economics, psychology, etc.

- **Compare and Contrast:** an ''at-a-glance'' comparison of the cultural and historical differences between the author's time and culture and late twentieth century or early twenty-first century Western culture. This box includes pertinent parallels between the major scientific, political, and cultural movements of the time or place the story was written, the time or place the story was set (if a historical work), and modern Western culture. Works written after 1990 may not have this box.

- **What Do I Read Next?:** a list of works that might complement the featured story or serve as a contrast to it. This includes works by the same author and others, works of fiction and nonfiction, and works from various genres, cultures, and eras.

Other Features

SSfS includes ''Why Study Literature At All?,'' a foreword by Thomas E. Barden, Professor of English and Director of Graduate English Studies at the University of Toledo. This essay provides a number of very fundamental reasons for studying literature and, therefore, reasons why a book such as *SSfS*, designed to facilitate the study of litererture, is useful.

A Cumulative Author/Title Index lists the authors and titles covered in each volume of the *SSfS* series.

A Cumulative Nationality/Ethnicity Index breaks down the authors and titles covered in each volume of the *SSfS* series by nationality and ethnicity.

A Subject/Theme Index, specific to each volume, provides easy reference for users who may be studying a particular subject or theme rather than a single work. Significant subjects from events to broad themes are included, and the entries pointing to the specific theme discussions in each entry are indicated in **boldface**.

Each entry may include illustrations, including photo of the author, stills from film adaptations (if available), maps, and/or photos of key historical events.

Citing Short Stories for Students

When writing papers, students who quote directly from any volume of *SSfS* may use the following general forms to document their source. These examples are based on MLA style; teachers may request that students adhere to a different style, thus, the following examples may be adapted as needed.

When citing text from *SSfS* that is not attributed to a particular author (for example, the Themes, Style, Historical Context sections, etc.), the following format may be used:

''The Celebrated Jumping Frog of Calavaras County.'' *Short Stories for Students*. Ed. Kathleen Wilson. Vol. 1. Detroit: Gale, 1997. 19–20.

When quoting the specially commissioned essay from *SSfS* (usually the first essay under the Criticism subhead), the following format may be used:

Korb, Rena. Critical Essay on ''Children of the Sea.'' *Short Stories for Students*. Ed. Kathleen Wilson. Vol. 1. Detroit: Gale, 1997. 42.

When quoting a journal or newspaper essay that is reprinted in a volume of *Short Stories for Students*, the following form may be used:

Schmidt, Paul. ''The Deadpan on Simon Wheeler.'' *Southwest Review* Vol. XLI, No. 3 (Summer, 1956), 270–77; excerpted and reprinted in *Short Stories for Students*, Vol. 1, ed. Kathleen Wilson (Detroit: Gale, 1997), pp. 29–31.

When quoting material from a book that is reprinted in a volume of *SSfS,* the following form may be used:

Bell-Villada, Gene H. ''The Master of Short Forms,'' in *Garcia Marquez: The Man and His Work*. University of North Carolina Press, 1990, pp. 119–36; excerpted and reprinted in *Short Stories for Students*, Vol. 1, ed. Kathleen Wilson (Detroit: Gale, 1997), pp. 89–90.

We Welcome Your Suggestions

The editor of *Short Stories for Students* welcomes your comments and ideas. Readers who wish to suggest short stories to appear in future volumes, or who have other suggestions, are cordially invited to contact the editor. You may contact the editor via E-mail at: **ForStudentsEditors@gale.com.** Or write to the editor at:

Editor, *Short Stories for Students*
The Gale Group
27500 Drake Road
Farmington Hills, MI 48331–3535

Literary Chronology

1851: Kate Chopin (born Katherine O'Flaherty) is born on February 8 in St. Louis, Missouri.

1874: W. Somerset Maugham is born on January 25 at the British Embassy in Paris.

1889: Kate Chopin's "A Point at Issue!" is published.

1899: Jorge Luis Borges is born on August 24 in Buenos Aires, Argentina.

1899: Ernest Hemingway is born on July 21 in Oak Park, Illinois.

1904: Kate Chopin dies of a cerebral hemorrhage on August 22 in St. Louis.

1910: Paul Bowles is born on December 30 in New York City.

1919: Jerome David (J. D.) Salinger is born on New Year's Day in New York City.

1920: Isaac Asimov is born on January 2 in Russia.

1921: W. Somerset Maugham's "The Fall of Edward Barnard" is published.

1927: Ernest Hemingway's "The Killers" is published.

1931: Donald Barthelme is born on April 7 in Philadelphia.

1937: Mohamed El-Bisatie is born on November 19 in the Nile Delta in a place called el-Gamalia, Dakahlia, in Sharqiya Province, Egypt, a setting that dominates most of El-Bisatie's writings.

1937: Marlene Reed Wetzel is born on April 5.

1938: Joyce Carol Oates is born on June 16 in Millersport, New York.

1941: Anne Tyler is born on October 25 in Minneapolis, Minnesota.

1941: Isaac Asimov's "Nightfall" is published.

1945: Jorge Luis Borges's "The Aleph" is published.

1948: J. D. Salinger's "A Perfect Day for Bananafish" is published.

1951: Anne Devlin is born to a Catholic family in Belfast.

1956: Ha Jin (born Jin Xuefei) is born on February 21 in Liaoning, a province in northeast China.

1961: Ernest Hemingway commits suicide by shooting himself at his home in Ketchum, Idaho.

1962: Pam Houston is born in New Jersey.

1965: W. Somerset Maugham dies on December 16 at his villa on the French Riviera at the age of ninety-one.

1967: Joyce Carol Oates's "Four Summers" is published.

1968: Donald Barthelme's "The Indian Uprising" is published.

1976: Paul Bowles's "The Eye" is published.

1977: Anne Tyler's "Average Waves in Unprotected Waters" is published.

1986: Anne Devlin's "Naming the Names" is published.

1986: Jorge Luis Borges dies of liver cancer on June 14.

1989: Donald Barthelme dies of cancer on July 23 in Houston.

1992: Isaac Asimov dies of heart and kidney failure on April 6.

1994: Mohamed El-Bisatie's "A Conversation from the Third Floor" is published.

1998: Pam Houston's "The Best Girlfriend You Never Had" is published.

1999: Ha Jin's "In the Kindergarten" is published.

1999: Paul Bowles dies of a heart attack on November 18 in Tangier.

2000: Marlene Reed Wetzel's "A Map of Tripoli, 1967" is published.

Acknowledgments

The editors wish to thank the copyright holders of the excerpted criticism included in this volume and the permissions managers of many book and magazine publishing companies for assisting us in securing reproduction rights. We are also grateful to the staffs of the Detroit Public Library, the Library of Congress, the University of Detroit Mercy Library, Wayne State University Purdy/Kresge Library Complex, and the University of Michigan Libraries for making their resources available to us. Following is a list of the copyright holders who have granted us permission to reproduce material in this volume of *Short Stories for Students (SSfS)*. Every effort has been made to trace copyright, but if omissions have been made, please let us know.

COPYRIGHTED MATERIALS IN *SSfS*, VOLUME 17, WERE REPRODUCED FROM THE FOLLOWING PERIODICALS:

Arizona Quarterly, v. 42, Spring, 1986 for "Comanches and Civilization in Donald Barthelme's 'The Indian Uprising,'" by Walter Evans. Copyright © 1986 by the Regents of the University of Arizona. Reproduced by permission of the publisher and the author.—*Comparative Literature*, v. 40, Spring, 1988 for "Borges, Dante, and the Poetics of Total Vision," by Jon Thiem. © copyright 1988 by University of Oregon. Reproduced by permission of Comparative Literature.—*Explicator*, v. 52, Fall, 1993. Copyright © 1993 Helen Dwight Reid Educational Foundation. Reproduced with permis-

sion of the Helen Dwight Reid Educational Foundation, published by Heldref Publications, 1319 18th Street, NW, Washington, DC 20036–1802.—*The Hemingway Review*, v. 8, Spring, 1989. Copyright © 1989 by The Ernest Hemingway Foundation. Reproduced by permission.—*Papers on Language & Literature*, v. 25, Winter, 1989. Copyright © 1989 by The Board of Trustees, Southern Illinois University at Edwardsville. Reproduced by permission.—*Science Fiction Studies*, v. 8, March, 1981. Copyright © 1981 by SFS Publications. Reproduced by permission.—*Studies in Short Fiction*, v. X, Winter, 1973; v. 18, Spring, 1981. Copyright 1973, 1981 by Newberry College. Reproduced by permission.—*Twentieth Century Literature*, v. 45, Spring, 1999. Copyright 1999, Hofstra University Press. Reproduced by permission.—*Variaciones Borges*, v. 5, 1998. Reproduced by permission.

COPYRIGHTED MATERIALS IN *SSfS*, VOLUME 17, WERE REPRODUCED FROM THE FOLLOWING BOOKS:

Evans, Elizabeth. From *Anne Tyler*. Twayne Publishers, 1993. Copyright 1993 by Twayne Publishers. All rights reserved. Reproduced by permission.—Hibbard, Allen. From *Paul Bowles: A Study of the Short Fiction*. Twayne Publishers, 1993. Copyright © 1993 by Twayne Publishers. All rights reserved. Reproduced by permission.—Patrouch, Joseph F., Jr. From *The Science Fiction of Isaac Asimov*. Doubleday & Company, Inc., 1974. Copyright © 1974 by Joseph F. Patrouch, Jr. All rights reserved. Reproduced by permission.—Seyersted, Per. From *Kate Chopin: A Critical Biography*. Louisiana State University Press, 1969. Reproduced by permission of the author.—Whitehead, John. From *Maugham: A Reappraisal*, pp. 80–113. Vision Press Limited and Barnes & Noble Books, 1987. © 1987 by John Whitehead. All rights reserved. Reproduced by permission.

PHOTOGRAPHS AND ILLUSTRATIONS APPEARING IN *SSfS*, VOLUME 17, WERE RECEIVED FROM THE FOLLOWING SOURCES:

Asimov, Isaac, photograph. AP/Wide World Photos. Reproduced by permission.—Borges, Jorge Luis, photograph by Jerry Bauer. Reproduced by permission.—Bowles, Paul, photograph. AP/Wide World Photos. Reproduced by permission.—Chopin, Kate, photograph.—Cover of "New Yorker" Magazine from January 31, 1948, photograph. Original Artwork by Charles E. Martin. Copyright © 1948 The New Yorker Magazine Inc. Reprinted by permission. All Rights Reserved.—Hemingway, Ernest, photograph. Corbis-Bettmann. Reproduced by permission.—Lancaster, Burt, and Ava Gardner in the film "The Killers," 1946, photograph. The Kobal Collection. Reproduced by permission.—Map of Israel and neighboring countries prior to the 1967 Six Day War (left), map showing territory captured by Israel during the Six Day War (right). © Bettmann/Corbis. Reproduced by permission.—Maugham, W. Somerset, photograph. AP/Wide World Photos. Reproduced by permission.—Muslim woman, standing next to an enclosed cell where suspected militants wait for the opening of their trial in a military court in Haekstep, Egypt, photograph. AP/Wide World Photos. Reproduced by permission.—Oates, Joyce Carol, photograph. UPI/Corbis-Bettmann. Reproduced by permission.—Palace of Fine Arts in San Francisco, California, designed by Bernard R. Maybeck, photograph. © Art on File/Corbis. Reproduced by permission.—Policeman standing outside the Lion Bar, near a burning barricade on a street in Belfast during riots in Northern Ireland, photograph. © Hulton-Deutsch Collection/Corbis. Reproduced by permission.—Salinger, J. D., 1951, photograph. AP/Wide World Photos, Inc. Reproduced by permission.—Sun during eclipse, photograph. New York Pubic Library Picture Collection.—Tyler, Anne, photograph. Courtesy of Knopf. Reproduced by permission.—View of Tangier, Morocco, photograph. © Roger Wood/Corbis. Reproduced by permission.—Wetzel, Marlene Reed, photograph. Reproduced by permission.

Contributors

Bryan Aubrey: Aubrey holds a Ph.D. in English and has published many articles on twentieth-century literature. Entries on *The Fall of Edward Barnard* and *Naming the Names*. Original essays on *The Fall of Edward Barnard* and *Naming the Names*.

Allison DeFrees: DeFrees is a published writer and an editor with a bachelor's degree in English from the University of Virginia and a law degree from the University of Texas. Original essays on *A Conversation from the Third Floor*, *Naming the Names*, and *A Point at Issue!*

Joyce Hart: Hart has degrees in English literature and creative writing, and she focuses her writing on literary themes. Entry on *A Conversation from the Third Floor*. Original essays on *A Conversation from the Third Floor*, *In the Kindergarten*, and *Naming the Names*.

Carol Johnson: Johnson is an instructor of creative writing, composition, and literature. Original essay on *A Map of Tripoli, 1967*.

David Kelly: Kelly is an instructor of creative writing and composition. Entry on *In the Kindergarten*. Original essay on *In the Kindergarten*.

Lois Kerschen: Kerschen, a former teacher, is now the executive director of a children's charity and a freelance writer. Entry on *Nightfall*. Original essay on *Nightfall*.

Daniel Moran: Moran is an instructor of English and American literature. Entries on *The Aleph* and *A Perfect Day for Bananafish*. Original essays on *The Aleph* and *A Perfect Day for Bananafish*.

Candyce Norvell: Norvell is an independent writer who has published short fiction and often writes about literature. Original essay on *A Map of Tripoli, 1967*.

Wendy Perkins: Perkins is an instructor of American literature and film. Entry on *A Point at Issue!* Original essay on *A Point at Issue!*

Frank Pool: Pool has published poetry and reviews in a number of literary journals. He teaches Advanced Placement and International Baccalaureate English in Austin, Texas. Original essay on *Average Waves in Unprotected Waters*.

Susan Sanderson: Sanderson holds a master of fine arts degree in fiction writing and is an independent writer. Entries on *The Indian Uprising* and *A Map of Tripoli, 1967*. Original essays on *The Best Girlfriend You Never Had*, *The Eye*, *The Indian Uprising*, and *A Map of Tripoli, 1967*.

Chris Semansky: Semansky is an instructor of

English literature and composition who writes about literature and culture for various publications. Entries on *The Best Girlfriend You Never Had*, *The Eye*, *Four Summers*, and *The Killers*. Original essays on *The Best Girlfriend You Never Had*, *The Eye*, *Four Summers*, *The Indian Uprising*, and *The Killers*.

Erika Taibl: Taibl is an English instructor and a writer. Entry on *Average Waves in Unprotected Waters*. Original essays on *Average Waves in Unprotected Waters* and *The Best Girlfriend You Never Had*.

Carey Wallace: Wallace is a freelance writer and poet. Original essays on *A Conversation from the Third Floor*, *In the Kindergarten*, and *A Perfect Day for Bananafish*.

The Aleph

Jorge Luis Borges
1945

In his 1969 study *The Narrow Act: Borges's Art of Allusion,* Ronald J. Christ offers an important piece of advice to anyone reading Borges for the first time: "The point of origin for most of Borges's fiction is neither character nor plot . . . but, instead, as in science fiction, a proposition, an idea, a metaphor, which, because of its ingenious or fantastic quality, is perhaps best call[ed] a conceit." "The Aleph" certainly fits this description, for while it does possess the elements of traditional fiction, it is more concerned with exploring the "conceit" of infinity: if there were a point in space that contained all other points, and one could look at it, what would one see—and how would one describe what he or she saw to another person? Such are the questions raised by Borges's story.

"The Aleph" was first published in the Argentine journal *Sur* in 1945 and was included as the title work in the 1949 collection *The Aleph.* Like so many of Borges's other stories, essays, and poems, "The Aleph" is an attempt to explore and dramatize a philosophical or scientific riddle. To date, the story stands as one of Borges's most well-known and representative works.

In a 1970 commentary on the story, Borges explained, "What eternity is to time, the Aleph is to space." As the narrator of the story discovers, however, trying to describe such an idea in conventional terms can prove a daunting—even impossible—task.

Author Biography

Jorge Luis Borges was born on August 24, 1899, in Buenos Aires, one of Argentina's most famous cities. His father, Jorge Guillermo Borges, was a lawyer; it was in his father's large library that the young "Georgie" (as he was called) discovered his love of reading. When Borges was a young boy, his family moved to Palermo, a suburb of Buenos Aires. Surprisingly, Borges did not begin attending school until he was nine years old. Because of the fear of tuberculosis, which was being transmitted at a deadly rate among schoolchildren, his mother, his English grandmother, and an English governess tutored him. Both English and Spanish were spoken in the Borges house, and many of Borges's favorite authors were ones who wrote in English. H. G. Wells, Charles Dickens, Edgar Allen Poe, and Henry Wadsworth Longfellow were some of the authors he discovered in his youth for whom he held a lifelong enthusiasm. The first book he ever read from start to finish was Mark Twain's *The Adventures of Huckleberry Finn.*

In 1914, Borges traveled through Europe with his family. The outbreak of World War I forced them to stay for some time in Geneva, Switzerland, where Borges finished his secondary education. In 1919, he traveled to Spain and found himself one of the members of the *Ultraists,* a number of writers contributing to a vaguely defined literary movement that aimed to renew literature through radical techniques. As Borges explains in his *An Autobiographical Essay,* however, literature was "a branch of the arts of which they knew nothing whatever." Before leaving Spain in 1921, Borges published his first poem, "Hymn to the Sea," in the magazine *Grecia.*

Upon returning to Buenos Aires in 1921, Borges collaborated on the magazine *Prisma,* notable for its unusual method of delivery—it was pasted, mural-style, on the walls of the city. The next ten or so years saw Borges publishing a number of books, both collections of poetry and essays. His poetry collections include 1923's *Fervor of Buenos Aires,* 1925's *Moon Across the Way,* and 1929's *San Martin Copybook.* His essay collections were 1925's *Inquisitions,* 1926's *The Measure of My Hope,* 1928's *The Language of the Argentines,* 1930s *Evaristo Carriego* and 1932's *Discussion.* In 1935, Borges published his first attempt at prose fiction, *A Universal History of Infamy.* Two years later, he took a librarian's post at a small municipal Buenos Aires library.

During subsequent years, Borges remained in Argentina and perfected the techniques for his short, puzzling stories. In 1941, a collection of stories, *The Garden of Forking Paths,* was published to great acclaim. When Borges was not awarded the National Prize for Literature in 1942, the influential journal *Sur* devoted a special issue to protesting the award committee's decision. In 1944, *Ficciones,* one of his most popular and important collections, was published.

Despite his status, he was removed from his librarian's post in 1946 for political reasons. With the 1955 overthrow of the Perón government, he was appointed Director of the National Library in Buenos Aires. His reputation now confirmed, Borges enjoyed a life of travel, lecturing, honorary degrees, and worldwide recognition. In 1961, he shared the International Publishers' Prize with Samuel Beckett and lectured on Argentine literature at the University of Texas. The year 1962 saw Borges's first two English publications: the translation of *Ficciones* and *Labyrinths,* an anthology of stories, essays, and poems. As his fame grew, his eyesight worsened, and by 1964 he was totally blind. However, this did not affect his prolific output and he continued publishing books of verse, essays, lectures, and stories until his death (from liver cancer) on June 14, 1986.

Plot Summary

"The Aleph" begins in 1943 with Borges (the narrator) informing the reader of his love for Beatriz Viterbo, who (we are told) died in 1929. In an effort to devote himself "to her memory," Borges began visiting Beatriz's father and cousin, Carlos Argentino Daneri, every April thirtieth—Beatriz's birthday. These visits occurred every year, and Borges gradually ingratiated himself with Beatriz's father and cousin to the point where they began asking him to dinner.

At the conclusion of one such dinner (on Sunday, April 30, 1941), Daneri begins pontificating to Borges about subjects such as "the glorification of modern man" and the idea that, at this date, "actual travel was superfluous," since modern man enjoys a number of ways to experience the pleasures of the world without leaving his home. Thinking his host a fool but not wanting to insult him, Borges suggests to him that he record his observations for posterity;

Daneri explains that he has already begun to do so and then shows Borges the poem upon which he has been working for years. Simply titled *The Earth,* Daneri's poem is an attempt to encapsulate the entire planet into verse. He reads a passage to Borges and praises his own merits as a poet; Borges, however, finds the poem uninteresting and even thinks that Daneri's reasons for why his poem should be admired are actually more clever and artistic than the poem itself.

Two Sundays later, Daneri telephones Borges and asks him to meet at Zunino and Zungri's salon, located next to his house. After reading him some additional fragments of the poem and telling of his plan to publish some of its initial cantos, Daneri asks Borges a favor: will he use his influence as a writer to contact his fellow author Alvaro Melian Lafinur and ask him to pen an introduction? And will Borges himself offer to attach his name to a blurb (that Daneri himself had already composed) about the poem's greatness? Borges agrees, but thinks, on his way home, that he will do nothing, partly because of his own laziness and partly because he has found Daneri a self-important fool.

Borges expects Daneri to telephone him again and rail against his "indolence" in not securing Lafinur's preface, but Daneri never does. Months pass until one day in October Daneri telephones the narrator and complains that Zunino and Zungri are planning to expand their salon—and knock down his house in the process. This seems reason enough for concern, but Daneri further explains that the real reason he was so upset was that there was an Aleph in his basement. An Aleph, he explains, "is one of the points in space that contains all other points," and he needs the Aleph to help him compose his poem. Because the Aleph is "the only place on earth where all places are—seen from every angle, each standing clear, without confusion or blending," its loss will mean an end to Daneri's poem. Borges tells Daneri that he will come to see it, convinced that Daneri is a madman but also filled with "spiteful elation," since he and Daneri have, "deep down," always "detested each other."

Once there, Borges speaks tenderly to a portrait of Beatriz until Daneri interrupts, offering Borges a glass of cognac and leading him to the cellar, giving him instructions to lay on the floor at the base of the stairs and look at the nineteenth step. Daneri leaves and shuts the door; Borges worries that Daneri has poisoned the cognac and then locked him in the cellar to die. These fears, however, are dispelled

Jorge Luis Borges

once Borges sees the Aleph, a point of space no larger than an inch but which contains the entire universe.

Borges then breaks the narrative by describing the "despair" he faces in using language to replicate the experience of seeing the Aleph. Because language is apprehended sequentially, a reader cannot fully grasp the nature of seeing the Aleph, where all images are seen simultaneously. Having no tools other than words, however, Borges proceeds and offers a selective list of some of the things he saw in the Aleph: the sea, London, bunches of grapes, a Scottish woman, horses' manes, armies, tigers, Beatriz's "obscene" letters to Daneri, and his own face.

Daneri returns and asks Borges if he saw everything, but to spite him, Borges evades the question and advises Daneri to let his house be demolished so that he can "get away from the pernicious metropolis" and live in the fresh air of the country. Once on the street, Borges fears that "not a single thing on earth" will ever again surprise him; after a few "sleepless nights," however, he is "visited once more by oblivion."

The story then returns to the present (March 1, 1943), where Borges explains that Daneri's house was pulled down and that his poem was published to great acclaim, wining the Second National Prize for Literature. After a discussion of the etymology of the word "aleph," Borges states his belief that the Aleph he saw in Daneri's basement was a "false Aleph." Citing the author and traveler Captain Sir Richard Francis Burton, Borges tells of other "Alephs" throughout literature and concludes with the thought that "our minds are porous and forgetfulness seeps in." Because he can no longer say for certain whether or not he did, indeed, see all things in Daneri's cellar, he is doubtful of all human memory, including that of the face of his beloved Beatriz.

Characters

Borges

"The Aleph" is narrated by Borges, a fictional stand-in for the author, which allows him to foster a sense of realism. Like the author, the narrator is an Argentine writer who detests pretentious authors like Daneri and who was also passed by for the National Prize for Literature. The narrator is a man haunted by the memory of his beloved Beatriz; bereft and longing for her company, he visits her father and cousin, Daneri, each year on her birthday, thus mourning her death on the day of her birth. While at her cousin's, Borges studies photographs of Beatriz and (as if this were the price to be paid for such a visit to Beatriz's images) endures the foolish pontifications of her cousin.

As a rational and conventional man, the narrator is predictably bewildered at the sight of the Aleph—and angry that a fool such as Daneri should be in the possession of something so miraculous. As a jealous and spiteful man, however, the narrator lies to Daneri by pretending to offer sound advice: the country and fresh air are "the greatest physicians," he says, hoping that Daneri will abandon his house and allow the Aleph to be destroyed with it. Without the Aleph, the narrator reasons, Daneri will be unable to finish his poem. Daneri's being awarded the Second National Prize for Literature, however, only infuriates the narrator: "Once again dullness and envy had their triumph," he laments.

Carlos Argentino Daneri

Introduced in the story as the first cousin of Borges's beloved Beatriz, Daneri is described as a pompous, fatuous man who loves the sound of his own voice. At first, Borges does not take him seriously, calling him "pink-faced, overweight" and dismissing his "minor position in an unreadable library out on the edge of the Southside of Buenos Aires." Daneri delights in clichés (calling Paul Fort, for example, "the Prince of Poets") and overreaching pronouncements about "modern man," which Borges instantly dismisses. However, as Borges (and the reader) learns, Daneri has been recording his thoughts in a poem called *The Earth;* his speech to Borges concerning the merits of his own work mark him as unbearably pedantic. Concerned with his career, Daneri asks Borges to solicit a foreword to his poem from another author and even suggests that Borges offer himself as a "spokesman" for the "undeniable virtues" of the poem.

Daneri is a parody of a poet, a satire of the brand of literary pretentiousness that Borges obviously found ridiculous (yet also amusing). That something as wonderful as the Aleph and that an honor as coveted as the National Prize for Literature should both be conferred on such a fool suggests both the indiscriminate nature of the universe as well as the questionable taste of the judges who award literary prizes. Daneri's obnoxious letter to Borges, where he brags, "I have crowned my cap with the reddest of feathers," cements the reader's impression of Daneri as a bombastic opposite of the reserved and intelligent narrator.

Beatriz Viterbo

Although not a physical presence in the story, the deceased Beatriz propels the plot: because of the narrator's devotion to her, he visits her home each year. It is during these visits that he is taken into the confidence of her cousin, Daneri, and eventually learns of the Aleph.

Zungri

Zungri and his partner Zunino are the cafe owners who wish to demolish Daneri's home so that they can expand their business.

Zunino

Zunino and his partner Zungri are the cafe owners who wish to demolish Daneri's home so that they can expand their business.

Topics for Further Study

- Research the philosophical puzzles known as the paradox of Zeno and Pascal's sphere. How do stories such as "The Aleph" dramatize these paradoxes in narrative form?

- During his lifetime, Borges wrote extensively of other authors and gave numerous interviews where he shared his opinions on literature. Read some of his essays or interviews to learn about his tastes. To what degree are his tastes reflected in "The Aleph," in terms of both style and content?

- Part of what makes "The Aleph" a success is Borges's setting it in an everyday location and describing the fantastic event in everyday language. Compose a story in which a character discovers a fantastic object or event and use

Borges's style to describe it. How does the use of everyday language (rather than inflated diction) heighten the believability of the event for the reader?

- Research trends of thought among physicists and other scientists who seek to better understand the relationship between space and time. How does "The Aleph" reflect their ideas, such as the possibility of a "naked singularity" or the theoretical foundations of chaos theory?

- In 1946, Borges was removed from his librarian post by the Perón government. Research Borges's life to learn more of how he opposed the Peron government and eventually became a spokesperson for human rights.

Themes

The Nature of Memory

In his parable "The Witness," Borges imagines the last man to have witnessed pagan rituals dying in Anglo-Saxon England and remarks, "with him will die, and never return, the last immediate images of these pagan rites." Because of this, "the world will be a little poorer," since it will have lost its last link to a vanished historical era. Borges then wonders what images will die with him.

Similarly, "The Aleph" examines the fragile and faulty nature of memory. The story opens with Borges revealing his admiration of Beatriz Viterbo's never allowing her final agonies to "give way to self-pity or fear"; this admiration, however, is then seasoned by melancholy when he notices a new billboard advertising a brand of American cigarettes. While this detail may initially strike the reader as trivial, it helps Borges illustrate the subtle ways in which one's world is always changing and, by extension, the idea that when one dies, the memory of the world at that particular point in time

will die as well. "This slight change," Borges knows, "was the first of an endless series"—eventually, the last person to have seen Beatriz will die and, as Borges reasons in "The Witness," the world will be "a little poorer." At the end of the story, Borges acknowledges this sad fact by describing our minds as "porous" and admitting that he is "distorting and losing, under the wearing away of the years, the face of Beatriz." While a reader can empathize with the narrator's despair of using his "floundering mind" to recall what he saw in the Aleph, the story also reminds the reader that the effort to truly and accurately remember something as meaningful as the face of a loved one is doomed to fail because of the effects of time on human memory. Thus the reader is told that in the Aleph, Borges "saw the rotted dust and bones that had once deliciously been Beatriz Viterbo."

The Literary Problem of Infinity

Much of Borges's power as a writer comes from his having read so much for so many years. In his essay "The Fearful Sphere of Pascal," he examines the historical notion that God is a sphere whose center is everywhere and circumference is nowhere. In his own words, ''if the future and the past are infinite, there cannot really be a when,'' and ''if every being is equidistant from the infinite and infinitesimal, neither can there be a where.'' By this logic (he concludes), ''No one exists on a certain day, in a certain place.'' The difficulty in writing about such an idea is that language cannot hope to replicate the concept in words, for if a character really could see an Aleph, how could he or she hope to convey the sensation of seeing it to a reader or even to himself or herself?

Borges approaches this problem by first having his narrator apologize for being unable to ''translate into words the limitless Aleph.'' Because all language is ''a set of symbols'' that can only be understood sequentially, any attempt to replicate the experience of seeing every point in the universe *at once* is doomed to fail. His apology fresh in the reader's mind, Borges then offers a limited but selective catalog of some of the things he saw in the Aleph. To suggest the totality of what he saw, Borges includes images relating to nature (''the teeming sea,'' ''tides,'' ''deserts,'' ''shadows of ferns on a greenhouse floor,'' ''bunches of grapes, snow, tobacco''), animal life (''horses with flowing manes,'' ''tigers,'' ''bison,'' ''all the ants on the planet''), history (''a copy of the first English translation of Pliny''), geography (''a terrestrial globe''), astronomy (''a Persian astrolabe''), biology (''the delicate bone structure of a hand,'' ''my own bowels''), as well as a number of specific place names (America, London, Soler Street, Queretaro, Bengal, Fray Bentos, Inverness, Adrogue, Alkmaar, the Caspian Sea, Mirzapur, the Chacarita cemetery) to suggest the breadth of the Alpeh's contents. While the description of what he saw in the Aleph takes up only a fraction of the story, it does give the reader a sense of the sheer inconceivability of infinity. ''In the Aleph I saw the earth and in the earth the Aleph,'' Borges explains; if this language strikes a reader as vague or elusive, it is only because language is not up to the task of replicating infinity on the printed page.

Style

The Story's Epigraphs

The two epigraphs that precede ''The Aleph'' serve as introductions to the story's plot as well as short commentaries on its issues. The first, from

Shakespeare's *Hamlet,* is said by the title character to his friends Rosencrantz and Guildenstern: ''O God! I could be bound in a nutshell, and count myself a king of infinite space.'' Hamlet's meaning here is (as he later says), ''There is nothing good or bad but thinking makes it so.'' By this logic, Hamlet argues that ''Denmark's a prison.'' Here, however, Borges imagines Hamlet's lament literally: how *might* a man in a nutshell call himself ''a King of infinite space?'' Borges's story responds to (if not answers) this question through the idea of the Aleph, for its existence in the story forces the reader to consider the proposition that there are an infinite number of points in space and, therefore, that even a nutshell would contain an infinite number of points. This is perhaps why the Aleph in Daneri's basement is only an inch in diameter.

The second epigraph comes from Thomas Hobbes's *Leviathan* and suggests the impossibility of understanding what ''an Infinite greatness of Place'' would be like. This impossibility, of course, is what the story attempts to address; the difficulty inherent in understanding infinity is discussed by Borges before he begins his description of what he saw in the Aleph.

Setting

While ''The Aleph'' revolves around a fantastic element and plot, the setting is decidedly mundane: the streets and sights of Buenos Aires are depicted in unadorned language without romance, nostalgia, or wonder. Even more odd is that the Aleph is in a house like any other. Part of Borges's reason for placing the Aleph in Daneri's cellar has to do with the comic effect of the story: Daneri is a pompous fool (the likes of which Borges himself had undoubtedly met many times in literary circles), and the contrast of his lack of imagination with an object that lies beyond the bounds of imagination frustrates the narrator, who feels himself superior to Daneri (and thus bitter when reporting Daneri's literary accolades at the end of the story). Similarly, placing the Aleph in Daneri's cellar allows Borges to comically juxtapose the mind-blowing with the mundane, just as Daneri's explanations for why his verse is so good is thought (by Borges) to be superior to the verse itself.

A second reason for placing the Aleph in an ordinary cellar is that doing so grounds the story in reality. By first offering the conventions of a love story (''On the burning February morning Beatriz Viterbo died.''), Borges lulls the reader into thinking that the story will be a relatively routine one about common human emotions and experience. However, when Daneri first mentions the Aleph, the reader is jarred and must reconcile the seemingly "normal" plot (lamenting a lost love) and setting (a cellar) with Borges's wild and unpredictable element. Thus, the setting works as a kind of literary sleight-of-hand, allowing Borges to distract the reader before revealing the Aleph and thus making the impact of the Aleph on the reader much greater that it may have been had the Aleph been described at the beginning.

Historical Context

Argentine Politics and Art

In 1940, Roman Castillo replaced President Roberto Ortiz. Like many Argentines at the time, Castillo admired Hitler and Mussolini; like many citizens of Germany and Italy, many Argentines yearned for the order that fascism would presumably impose on their nation; like many of their European counterparts, many Argentines lacked the foresight to see the eventual, bloody results of such political movements.

The tide of fascist sympathy in Castillo's administration was felt by Borges in 1942, when the National Commission for Culture did not award his collection *The Garden of Forking Paths* the National Prize for Literature on the grounds that Borges's work was too "English"—a suggestion by the NCC that indirectly (but clearly) condemned Borges as one sympathetic to the Allied cause (which he was). Borges's indignant friends devoted a special issue of the influential journal *Sur* to what they saw as a clear example of a government attempting to shape the literary tastes of a nation according to its authors' political ideas. The issue was called "Amends to Borges" and its contributors feted the author at a restaurant, where the lights of the Argentine literary scene came to show their support.

Various short term governments then took turns strutting and struggling on the Argentine political stage. Castillo was ousted in a bloodless coup in 1943 and replaced by General Pedro Ramirez, who, in turn, was ousted in 1944 when he submitted to pressure from the United States to sever all ties with the Axis powers. *His* replacement, General Edelmiro Farrell, allowed the country to be run by the army

and figuratively opened the door for Juan Domingo Perón (then vice president) to come to power (which he would do in 1946). While the war in Europe was coming to a close, the rise of Perón's terror in Argentina was just beginning: when, in 1944, a crowd gathered in Buenos Aires to celebrate the liberation of Paris, the police broke up the demonstration with such force that several civilians were wounded and killed. While Argentina did declare war on the Axis powers in March of 1945, there was not much left for its military to do; Germany fell that May and, through a series of maneuvers and machinations, Perón was elected president on February 24, 1946. He was incredibly charismatic; many Argentines were likewise wooed by the charms of his wife, Eva.

Borges, however, stood apart from the crowd and considered Perón a thug. As James Woodall (in his biography *Borges: A Life*) quotes Borges as writing in a Montevideo newspaper, "a great number of Argentines" were "becoming Nazis without being aware of it." Borges's hatred of Perón eventually caused him to be removed from his municipal librarian's post and not reinstated (as the Director of the National Library) until after Perón's fall in 1955.

Composed in 1945, "The Aleph" reflects Borges's contempt for committees like the NCC, which ostensibly work for the promotion of art but actually serve as politically wayward slaves of the current regime. Carlos Daneri's winning the Second National Prize for Literature shocks both the narrator and the reader and is obviously a bitter joke about Borges's not being awarded the National Prize in 1942. "Once again," the narrator explains, "dullness" had had its "triumph"—a sentiment surely felt by Borges in 1942. The fact that Daneri also plans to compose an epic about General José de San Martín, the Argentine liberator, also reflects Borges's distaste for the marriage of politics and art: the reader is meant to assume that Daneri's poem will be a mindless piece of propaganda, much like the kind Borges saw plastered all over Buenos Aires during the rise of Perón.

Trends in Twentieth-Century Argentine Literature

The first half of the twentieth century saw an explosion of literary schools, styles, and attitudes espoused and practiced by Argentine poets, novelists, and short-story writers. By the time Borges wrote "The Aleph," his country had witnessed the birth and death of several literary movements, all of which surface in the whole of Borges's work.

Compare & Contrast

- **1940s:** Latin-American literature is not widely studied in North American high schools or universities.

  Today: Many universities sponsor whole departments devoted to Latin-American literature; works by writers such as Borges, Julio Cortazar, and Gabriel García Márquez are included in many high school curricula.

- **1940s:** Argentina's fascist Perón government grows in power; Borges is eventually removed from his post at the Miguel Cane Municipal Library for signing anti-Perón petitions.

  Today: Since the overthrow of Perón in 1955, Argentina has undergone a series of revolutions and suspensions of its constitution. The followers of Perón (the Perónists) are still a vigorous political party. Perón's story became more well known in 1978, when Andrew Lloyd Weber's *Evita,* a stylized musical about Perón and his wife, premiered.

- **1940s:** Scientists studying subatomic particles have discovered the strong and the weak nuclear forces in addition to the electromagnetic and gravitational forces. They continue to develop quantum theory as they discover a zoo of subatomic particles in addition to the proton, neutron, and electron.

  Today: Over a quarter century after the November Revolution of 1974, when evidence for the charmed quark was discovered at Stanford Linear Accelerator (SLAC) and at Brookhaven National Laboratory, the Standard Model of quantum field theory is still the leader in the field. This model suggests that all matter and energy is made up of quarks, gluons (particles that exchange forces between quarks), leptons (light-in-mass particles), and electromagnetic waves. However, because of the inability to test predictions requiring higher energies than current particle accelerators can produce, many physicists have turned towards Chaos Theory, a branch of physics that seeks to explain how the seemingly random behaviors of systems (such as the universe and the stock exchange) rely on mathematical laws.

- **1940s:** Science fiction is viewed as a well-established yet whimsical genre: science fiction writers are able to sell their work to vast audiences, but many are viewed by the critical establishment as trivial and derivative.

  Today: There is little doubt that science fiction writers are addressing some of the most pressing issues of our time. Authors such as David Brin, Orson Scott Card, and William Gibson stand as literary descendents of Borges, often exploring the same issues addressed by Borges in his work.

At the turn of the century, Argentine literature was grounded in realism, and writers attempted (as did their European and American counterparts) to create believable simulations of everyday life. Some of the first throbs of modernism (*modernista*), however, were found in the work of Ruben Dario, a poet who expanded the possibilities of verse and, by extension, what the Argentine writer could accomplish if he or she did not rely exclusively on traditional forms. Dario's presence in Buenos Aires—which had become a widely-used setting and subject of Argentine literature—reinforced the city's reputation as the cultural Mecca of its day. The enthusiasm of Argentine writers for exploring the history and people of their homeland grew and was epitomized in 1913, when the first Department of Argentine Literature was created in the University of Buenos Aires.

A number of journals and magazines devoted to Argentine literature also began taking shape and gaining popularity. The first major example, *Nosotros,* was founded in 1907 by Alfredo Bianchi and Roberto F. Gusti; its pages were the first place that several notable Argentine writers saw their work in print. A more novel (if less durable) journal was *Prisima:* its two editions (November 1921 and March 1922) were plastered on the walls of buildings throughout Buenos Aires. In 1921, Bianchi asked Borges to compose a piece that outlined the tenets of ultraism (*ultraismo*), a short-lived literary movement that stressed economy of language and a turning away from older and (as its founders believed) more stale forms of expression. Again, Argentine writers were seeking to reinvent their national literature. Other movements and literary groups followed, such as the Boedo group (which emphasized the importance of authors' devotion to social causes) and the Florida group (which practiced the avant-garde techniques of the time). Like their predecessors, these movements gave off more light than heat and fell out of favor with readers and intellectuals always on the lookout for the newest literary fashions. These readers had to look no further than *Sur,* a journal founded by Borges's friend Victoria Ocampo that still stands as an indication of sophisticated Argentine readers' tastes in the 1930s and '40s. Borges appeared in its pages many times; ''The Aleph'' was first published there in 1945.

By the time ''The Aleph'' was published, Argentine literature was again looking to avant-garde writers to steer the nation's literature in new directions. In the work of some writers, fiction and nonfiction seemed to meld to the point where authors were taking pains to make their work seem ''real'' by grounding it in actual events (something that Borges does throughout ''The Aleph''). This technique allowed Argentine writers to explore their nation's past through their art or (in Borges's case) to lull readers into believing that they were reading about ''real'' events. Such works also led to a heightened interest in surrealism and metaphysical fiction. As Naomi Lindstrom says in her essay on Argentine art (collected in David William Foster's *Handbook of Latin American Literature*), ''The results of the 1940s movement are still unfolding,'' and contemporary Argentine art still shows the influence of its cutting-edge predecessors.

Critical Overview

Borges is universally regarded as a major and powerful figure in twentieth-century literature; indeed, it is as difficult to find a negative critique of Borges's work as it is to find an essay on the failures of Shakespeare as a dramatist. Most critics agree with James E. Irby, who boldly states in his preface to the 1962 collection *Labyrinths* that Borges's work is ''one of the most extraordinary expressions in all Western literature of modern man's anguish of time, of space, of the infinite.''

''The Aleph'' is conventionally praised as one of Borges's most important stories. In her 1965 study, *Borges the Labyrinth Maker,* Ana Maria Barrenechea argues that ''the most important of Borges's concerns is the conviction that the world is a chaos impossible to reduce to any human law.'' She specifically praises ''The Aleph'' as an example of ''the economy of Borges's work'' in its ability to erase ''the limits of reality'' and create in the reader ''an atmosphere of anxiety.'' In his 1969 study, Ronald Christ contends that ''The Aleph'' stands as wholly representative of Borges's art and his attempts to ''abbreviate the universe in literature.'' To Christ, the Aleph of the story's title is a symbol of Borges's style and desire to compose another of his ''resumes of the universe.'' Martin S. Stabb, in his 1970 book *Jorge Luis Borges,* suggests that ''The Aleph'' is Borges's attempt to explore his dominant themes in a lighthearted fashion that may not possess the depth of his other work that reads as a ''half-philosophical, basically playful composition—generously sprinkled with Borgesian irony and satire,'' the story ''comes off rather well.'' Perhaps the most effusive praise of the story comes from George R. McMurray, who (in his 1980 study *Jorge Luis Borges*) states that the story not only reflects the ''mystical aura of magic that imbues so many of Borges's works,'' but also ''emerges as a symbol of all literature, whose purpose . . . is to subvert objective reality and recreate it through the powers of imagination.''

Other critics have examined the story from different angles. In his 1996 biography, *Borges: A Life,* James Woodall examines the ways in which ''The Aleph'' can be read as a piece of veiled autobiography containing references to Borges's discovery of a kaleidoscope (which becomes the Aleph in the story), his love affair with Estela Canto (who becomes the story's Beatriz) and his opinions of some fellow writers (who are mocked through the character of Carlos Daneri). According to Woodall, ''women, sex and love'' were ''preying'' on Borges's mind while he composed the story.

One of the most startling and cutting-edge approaches to the story, however, is found in Floyd

Merrell's *Unthinking Thinking: Jorge Luis Borges, Mathematics, and the New Physics* (1991). In this complex study that combines literary analysis with current scientific theories, Merrell argues that "The Aleph" dramatizes the discovery of what physicists call a space-time singularity: a point in the universe where a star collapses and "the limits of space and time have been reached." Like his fellow critics, Merrell praises Borges's work for its ability to illustrate abstract and difficult ideas.

Criticism

Daniel Moran

Moran is an instructor of English and American literature. In this essay, Moran examines the ways in which Borges's story reads like a prophecy of modern telecommunications technology.

In 1995, Bill Gates, the world-renowned founder of Microsoft and personal computing visionary, published *The Road Ahead,* his study of computing history and examination of the ways in which computers will transform the lives of people all over the world. His enthusiasm for what is now commonly called the Information Age is found on every page, particularly in those where he speaks (almost in a hushed awe) of the ways in which computers will surmount space and time—those two pesky and seemingly insurmountable barriers that humans have tried to dodge since time immemorial. Gates argues that the phrase "information highway" is an inadequate metaphor, since it suggests "landscape and geography, a distance between points, and embodies the implication that you have to travel to get from one place to another." Gates corrects this metaphor saying:

> One of the most remarkable aspects of this new communications technology is that it will eliminate distance. It won't matter if someone you're contacting is in the next room or the next continent, because the highly mediated network will be unconstrained by miles and kilometers.

Gates further argues that the speed of computer networks using fiber optics will deliver "streams of information at very high speeds—up to 155 million bits per second at first, later jumping up to 622 million bits per second and eventually up to 2 billion bits per second." Thus, video will be as easy to send across networks as the human voice is currently sent along telephone lines. Eventually (as Gates, cheerleader-like, imagines throughout his book), people will live in an age where "the network will draw us together" and "give us choices that can put us in touch with entertainment, information and each other."

"The Aleph" was first published in 1945, fifty years before *The Road Ahead* and before the first waves of enthusiasm for the personal computer crashed on the shores of the modern world. But who can read Borges's story and not sense the slightest hint of the embryonic Bill Gates? "Our twentieth century," Daneri explains, "had inverted the story of Mohammed and the mountain: nowadays, the mountain came to the modern Mohammed." Is this not reminiscent of Bill Gates's talk of eliminating distance? Consider also Daneri's vision of "modern man," alone in his "inner sanctum . . . supplied with telephones, telegraphs, phonographs, wireless sets, motion-picture screens, slide projectors, glossaries, timetables, handbooks, bulletins. . . ." Daneri's vision of modern man "as though in his castle tower" strikes the modern reader as very much like that of Bill Gates's modern American receiving his "2 billion bits per second" at his desk or in his living room. Borges (the story's narrator) dismisses Daneri as a fool, but who among us (like myself, who downloaded a copy of "The Aleph" before composing this essay, which I will then email to my editor) cannot sense in Daneri's musings a vision of modern life, where we regularly download Mohammed's mountain from remote servers?

If literary taste proves Daneri an awful and pedantic poet, the history of technology and communications has proven him a prophet. The narrator condescendingly calls Daneri's poem *The Earth* a "boring" attempt to "set to verse the entire face of the planet." While the poem might be not as clever as its author's reasons for why it should be admired, it is very much like the "virtual reality" which modern consumers have heard so much about in the media (and in the plots of numerous science-fiction films, such as 1990's *Total Recall* and 1999's *The Matrix*). At the time in which the story takes place (1941), Daneri has only partially completed his goal of simulating, in verse, the experience of seeing the whole planet. The reader in 1945 would have laughed

What Do I Read Next?

- Borges's story "The Garden of Forking Paths" (1941) does with time what "The Aleph" does with space. In it, a German spy during World War I learns about the multitudinous dimensions of time and the nature of eternity.

- Borges's essay "The Fearful Sphere of Pascal" (1951) explores the issue of infinity by addressing the philosopher Blaise Pascal's notion of God as a sphere whose center is everywhere and whose circumference is nowhere.

- Italo Calvino's 1965 collection *Cosmicomics* traces (through a series of humorous short stories) the evolution of the universe. Like Borges, Calvino enjoys meeting thorny matters such as the nature of space and time head-on and with subtle humor.

- James Joyce's 1916 novel *A Portrait of the Artist as a Young Man* features a long chapter in which a Jesuit priest attempts to explain (with horrifying results) the nature of infinity to a school of teenage boys. Like the narrator of "The Aleph," the priest must address the limitations of language to describe something beyond the scope of words.

- Borges's 1967 work *The Book of Imaginary Beings* is a catalog of mythical and literary creatures. As he does in "The Aleph," Borges treats the fantastic as if it were a part of everyday life.

- Like "The Aleph," Emily Dickinson's poem "The Brain Is Wider Than the Sky" (1890) explores the nature of infinity and eternity—in this case, the limitless nature of human thought.

- H. G. Wells was one of Borges's favorite authors; his story "The Crystal Egg" (1897) was one of Borges's inspirations for "The Aleph." In Wells's story, an antiques dealer finds an object that exists simultaneously on Earth and Mars.

- Like Daneri's poem *The Earth,* the American poet Walt Whitman's *Leaves of Grass* (1855) features a number of verses in which images and sensations are catalogued, producing a sometimes-hypnotic effect.

- The cognitive-science professor Douglas Hofstader's 1979 book *Godel, Escher, Bach: An Eternal Golden Braid* examines the mathematical theories of Kurt Godel, the drawings of M. C. Escher, and the music of J. S. Bach to explore (like all of Borges's work) the nature of matter, the composition of the universe, and the workings of the human mind.

---

at this fool's errand, but a modern one may call to mind video games where a person stands on a pair of skis while "virtually racing" through a projected slalom course or modern airline pilots, who train in incredibly sensitive and accurate flight simulators to hone their skills. What Daneri attempts in verse, modern man has achieved, in part, with the microchip.

The Earth is also reminiscent of the numerous multimedia encyclopedias or websites where one link leads to another and to another and to anothe. A fifth-grader writing a report on tulips, for example, could visit a website devoted to flowers, read a description of the tulip, follow a link to Holland's tourism page, have her eye caught by a link on *that* site that leads her to one detailing current trends in music of the Netherlands, and so on. In some ways, "the entire face of the planet" *is* available to "modern man," or at least any modern man with a modem.

An Aleph (Borges tells the reader) is a point in space that contains all other points. To replicate the experience of Borges the narrator seeing the Aleph was, understandably, a daunting task for Borges the author. In a 1982 interview (collected in *Jorge Luis Borges: Conversations*), Borges spoke of the scene as one that gave him "great trouble:" "I had to give

> Our world is not yet fully 'Alephed,' but with the seemingly daily innovations in speed, surely the day will come when the perfect computer network is created--and such a network will be very much like the Aleph."

a sensation of endless things in a single paragraph." The beauty of the paragraph where Borges sees the Aleph is indisputable and meant to contrast the dullness of Daneri's poem:

> I saw all the mirrors on earth and none of them reflected me; I saw in a backyard of Soler Street the same tiles that thirty years before I'd seen in the entry of a house in Fray Bentos; I saw bunches of grapes, snow, tobacco, lodes of metal, steam . . . I saw the delicate bone structure of a hand; I saw the survivors of a battle sending out picture postcards . . .

This passage is reminiscent of Walt Whitman, whose cadences are heard throughout Borges's description and whose musical qualities contrast with the forced metrics and rhymes of Daneri's *opus*. But if Daneri's poem lacks the beauty and splendor of Borges's paragraph, it does so only because Borges the narrator is a better writer. Both men see the same thing; one of them is just more skillful in describing it. This, too, has its technological counterpart: imagine the Aleph as a perfect and infinite network of computers, each capable of linking to an infinite number of websites without being slowed by the traffic of innumerable users or the limits of broadband, however wide.

If, as Walter Pater remarked, all art aspires to the condition of music, all computing and telecommunications innovations aspire to the condition of the Aleph. Our world is not yet fully "Alephed," but with the seemingly daily innovations in speed, surely the day will come when the perfect computer network is created—and such a network will be very much like the Aleph.

In his 1952 essay "Kafka and His Precursors," Borges notes the ways in which works written *before* Kafka (by writers as varied as Aristotle and Robert Browning) are notable for their Kafkaesque qualities. Because of Kafka, Borges argues, we read older works differently than we would have if Kafka had never written: "In each of these texts we find Kafka's idiosyncrasy to a greater or lesser degree, but if Kafka had never written a line, we would not perceive this quality; in other words, it would not exist." Borges's point here is that "every writer *creates* his own precursors" and "modifies our conception of the past." What Kafka does to our reading of Aristotle and Browning, modern computing has done to our reading of "The Aleph."

But perhaps the final word should go to Bill Gates, once dismissed by many as a Harvard dropout, just as the narrator dismisses Daneri. "New technology," he asserts, "will offer people a new means with which to express themselves." The information highway (or Aleph) will "open undreamed-of artistic and scientific opportunities to a new generation of geniuses." While Daneri's Aleph is destroyed with his house, modern computing companies have proven themselves more than ready to create newer, more permanent Alephs. These will, in turn, give rise to legions of Daneris. Emerson (one of Borges's favorite authors) famously said, "To be great is to be misunderstood," and it has taken the fifty years since "The Aleph's" publication for readers to understand (and newly appreciate) Daneri's ideas about moving the mountain to Mohammed.

Source: Daniel Moran, Critical Essay on "The Aleph," in *Short Stories for Students,* The Gale Group, 2003.

Nada Elia

In the following essay excerpt, Elia explores the influence of Islamic mysticism permeating Borges's work, particularly in "The Aleph" and "The Zahir."

Studies of Jorge Luis Borges's work invariably highlight the wealth of philosophical and theological influences that underlie his œuvre. Yet a search through the bibliography tracing these sources reveals disappointingly few titles elaborating on what strikes me as one of the major threads running through many of his works: Islamic mysticism. The paucity of such studies is especially surprising when one considers that Borges himself frequently referred to Islam and Islamic thinkers both in his written work and lectures at various academic fora. In *Seven Nights*, the series of public lectures originally given in Buenos Aires, he devotes a full chapter to a discussion of *The Thousand and One Nights,* claiming that the first translation of this collection was "a major event for all of European literature." In *Borges on Writing,* an edited volume based on lectures he gave at a graduate writing seminar at Columbia University in 1971, he unambiguously acknowledges his attempt at writing in the Arab Islamic tradition. Thus he says of his short story "The Two Kings and Their Two Labyrinths." that he wanted it to sound as "a page-overlooked by Lane and Burton-out of the *Arabian Nights.*" In his fiction, he makes direct references to aspects of Islamic mysticism, as well as demonstrates a familiarity with Islamic esoteric writing that goes beyond superficial, mundane information. That Borges should be familiar with Islam is in no way surprising. He is an extremely erudite writer steeped in metaphysical tradition, but also in the Spanish heritage. That heritage itself reflects eight centuries of close interaction with Arabs (the Moors), as Giovanna de Garayalde reminds readers and critics in *Jorge Luis Borges: Sources and Illuminations,* one of the very few works that foreground a link between the author and Sufism. "But eight centuries of coexistence," de Garayalde writes:

> are not easily eliminated from a country's past, least of all in the case of Spain, where the Arab influence is evident in the physical aspects, the habits and the arts in general. And Sufism, precisely because it is not tied to any dogma, seems to have been one of the main factors uniting the two cultures, separated though they were by politico-religious fanaticisms.

In this essay, I wish to further foreground the Islamic concepts Borges weaves into his writing, by focussing on two short stories, "The Zahir" and "The Aleph." I will also be referring to other works by Borges, in order to both support my thesis that Islamic references have permeated many of Borges's stories, and are thus not to be dismissed as haphazard or tangential, and because these various references also reveal the depth of Borges's knowledge of the Islamic cultural heritage. While I do not seek to suggest that Borges ever embraced the religious aspect of Sufism, I nevertheless would advance that his fascination with that sect's privileging of layered writing and multiple interpretations is a direct result of his own view that reading and writing are intimate companions, and that the best reading is a rewriting. (This view is best exemplified in "Pierre Menard, Author of the Quixote," an analysis of which falls outside the scope of this essay). The "burden of interpretation" is incumbent on the Sufis, as I demonstrate below.

> "'I saw all the mirrors on earth, and none of them reflected me,' Borges recalls, thus suggesting that, at least while his vision lasted, his individual existence was uncertain."

"Belief in the Zahir is of Islamic origin," wrote Borges, the narrator in Jorge Luis Borges's short story "The Zahir." This narrator is not absolutely sure who he is, nor what has happened to him, but he is sure something has happened to him, which has changed the course of his life. He has come across the Zahir. Borges, the narrator of "The Aleph," is at a loss for words: "And here begins my despair as a writer. All language is a set of symbols whose use among its speakers assumes a shared past." But his experience is unique, and therefore uncommunicable. For he has seen the Aleph.

"The Zahir" and "The Aleph," although written a number of years apart, are frequently paired by critics, as a number of stylistic and thematic parallels invite the comparison. The narrator in both stories is a man, Borges, who has had an experience that proves to be a revelation. This experience, in both cases, has left an indelible trace on him, left him a different person. In both cases, he finds himself questioning his sanity and unable to express what he has seen. In both cases, he becomes obsessed with his vision. Even minor, textual details correspond in the two stories: both begin with the death of a beloved woman and take place in Buenos Aires, as distinct from some abstract "universal" locale. The spiritual affinity, however, spans further back in time and space.

That belief in the Zahir should be of Islamic origin is not surprising, since *zahir* itself is not merely an Arabic word, it is, like all Arabic words contained in the Koran, ultimately an Islamic word: the Koran canonized the Arabic language of the seventh century A.D. (first century After the Hejira, or A. H.), and bound it forever to Islam. Today, even in countries where Arabic is not the native language, it is nevertheless acknowledged as the language of

Islam, and devout Muslims everywhere outside of the Arab world recite the Koran not in their own language, but in Arabic. Indonesia, the country with the largest Muslim population in the world, is a case in point: the official language there is Indonesian, with Arabic being the language of religious (Islamic) studies. Indeed, the better non-Arabic renditions of the Koran are appropriately called ''interpretations,'' for the language of Islam is held to be ''untranslatable.'' In the case of non-Muslim Arabs, I contend that these are influenced by Islam, since it is my belief that language and culture are inexorably linked.

Moreover *''zahir,''* as Borges points out, means visible or apparent, and is one of Allah's attributes, since Allah is ''apparent'' in all his creation. *Zahir* as a concept is traditionally coupled with, and opposed to, *batin,* thus making up a complete entity comprising thesis, antithesis, and synthesis. *Batin,* another Arabic word, is the antonym of *zahir* and means inner, innermost, concealed. The *zahir* and the *batin* are as inseparable as two sides of a coin, and the Zahir is indeed a coin in the short story by this title.

Who is qualified to look into the *batin* is at the root of a dispute in Islam dating back to the late second century A. H. For grasping the *batin* requires initiation if it is not to be detrimental to the seer. But seeing the *batin* is also mandatory for those who ''have vision,'' failing which they would be sinners. And Borges, our narrator, has seen the Zahir, Allah's apparent aspect. Let us examine his thoughts and feelings upon coming across this threshold to the *batin:*

> I stared at it for a moment, and went into the street, perhaps with the beginnings of a fever . . . As if in a dream, the thought that every piece of money entails such illustrious connotations seemed to me of huge, though inexplicable, importance . . .

> Sleepless, obsessed, almost happy, I reflected that there is nothing less material than money, since every coin whatsoever . . . is, strictly speaking, a repertory of possible futures.

Borges then goes on to say that he is a different man for having seen the Zahir, and that he cannot go back to his ''pre-Zahir'' state. This closely echoes the assertion of the Islamic thinker and mystic al-Ghazali that ''there is certainly no point in trying to return to the level of naive and derivative belief once it has been left, since a condition of being at such a level is that one should not know one is there. When a man comes to know that, the glass of his

naive beliefs is broken.'' This level, according to al-Ghazali, is lost as soon as one has had an insight into divinity.

An experience of the Zahir, according to Borges, leads to ''madness or saintliness.'' The two terms are also paired, almost equated, in the Koran: ''We know very well how they listen when they listen to thee, and when they conspire, when the evildoers say, 'You are only following a man bewitched!'.'' References to Islam and the linguistic aspects of the Koran itself also bound in ''The Aleph.'' The Koran is most difficult to read because, unlike the Bible, which contains considerable narrative stretches and can be read with the expectations readers bring to narrative texts, the Koran does not offer this familiar pattern: it was revealed as a whole to Muhammad, who merely had it transcribed. As such it is believed to be a pure expression of Allah, and one of his attributes. The Koran recounts universal creation in divine terms, and makes therefore no distinction between past, present, and future. The Aleph, Borges writes is ''the only place on earth where all places are seen from every angle.'' But Aleph is also the first letter of the Arabic alphabet, the language of Islam and its book. Further on Borges adds: ''What my eyes saw was simultaneous, what I shall transcribe is successive, because language is successive.'' He finds himself, however, utterly incapable of giving a coherent account of his vision.

Here, once again, we are confronted not with reluctance but with the impossibility of recounting an experience that does not belong to this world, or at least to the quotidian—a feeling most familiar to the Muslim mystics, or Sufis. Thus al-Ghazali refers us to Ibn-al-Mu'tazz who, after a mystic experience, told the uninitiated: ''Of the things I do not remember, what was, was,/ Think it good, do not ask an account of it.'' Nor is it insignificant, in the context of our study, that Islam alone of the three monotheistic religions is one where a revelation most frequently results in failure to communicate. In Judaism, Yahweh revealed himself to prophets so that they, in turn, might share what they have seen with their fellow-believers. Some Hebraic prophets, such as Ezra and Baruch, were expressly instructed in their mystical vision not to occlude that vision, but this implies that they would have otherwise been able to express it. In Christianity, the emphasis is on ''spreading the word.'' Moreover, both the Old and the New Testaments, with the exception of the Mosaic laws, are books about God. The Koran, on the other hand, is not a book about Allah as much as it is Allah's book. It is ''A Book We have sent down to thee." The Koran frequently refers to its own ambiguities, reminding the Muslims that some passages must be read at face value (literally, *zahir*), while others ought to be interpreted by "those who have been given knowledge in degrees," for the Koran is "a book whose verses are set clear, and then distinguished."

Yet a further digression is necessary here, before I move on to a discussion of Borges's style, which I shall try to show as a conscious attempt at *batini* writing. I had referred earlier to the *batin/zahir* dichotomy as the cause of a dispute in Islam. Although we cannot speak of a *batini* school as such, a group of thinkers, heralded by al-Ghazali (1058–1111), believe that with proper training, anyone can reach the *batin*. Al-Ghazali wrote two seminal books, *Deliverance from Error and Attachment to the Lord of Might and Majesty,* in which he presents Sufism as the only way to spiritual salvation, and *Tahafut al-Falasifa* (The Incoherence of Philosophy), in which he argues that Muslims should not be barred from attempting a *batini* reading of the Koran since, as he says, this allows for a greater grasp of the truth than philosophy will even make possible. Al-Ghazali supports his argument by citing the *sunna:* "There is the saying that the man who is mistaken in independent judgement receives a reward, but the man who is correct a twofold reward." One is rewarded simply for having tried, regardless of the outcome of the attempt. Moreover, the risk of leading a member of the masses astray is moot to al-Ghazali, since interpretation is undertaken by the Sufis, who "are not men of words." The word Sufi is believed to come from the Arabic "souf," meaning wool, since the Muslim mystics wore woollen garments. They traditionally withdrew from society, leading an ascetic, solitary life. Another etymological identification is with the root word *safa,* meaning purity. Some scholars argue that Sufi comes from Sophia, for wisdom. This would however imply that Greek "philosophy" influenced the Sufis, an untenable thesis, since Greek philosophy is grounded in the rational, an approach Sufism frequently disregards.

At the other end of the scale, the *zahirite* school, whose spokesperson is Ibn Rushd (Averroes, 1126–1198), believes that a member of the masses should not attempt to understand the inner (*batin*) meaning of ambiguous passages in the Koran, since this may lead to disbelief in the *zahir*—a sin under all circumstances—and will inevitably result in miscomprehension of the *batin*. For the masses, the Koran tells us, simply cannot understand, since God

has not given them "knowledge in degrees." "And those who interpret for the layman are calling him to heresy, and they are heretics themselves," warns Ibn Rushd. Thus a member of the masses, a person who has no vision or intuition, no practice in "learning," is saved if s/he believes in the *zahir* of the ayah (Koranic verse): "The Merciful sat upon the throne." But should s/he be told that God has no material body, and can therefore not sit, s/he will stop believing in the *zahir,* yet will still fail to grasp God's immateriality. "As to the one who is not versed in learning, he must take things at face value, for interpretation in his case is heresy, and will lead to heresy."

Ibn Rushd was highly disturbed by the growing influence and popularity of al-Ghazali's ideas, and set out to write *Tahafut al-Tahafut* (The Incoherence of Incoherence), an overt attack on al-Ghazali's book, in which he repudiates mysticism and *batini* reading, and *The Decisive Treatise, Determining the Nature of the Harmony between Religion and Philosophy,* in which he argues that reason, not mysticism, can help clarify the complexities of Islam.

Borges sets up an analogous set of dialectical counterpoints in his various essays on the Platonists and Aristotelians, or the Realists and the Nominalists. Thus, in the short story "Averroes' Search," Borges deals with the dispute between the Muslim thinkers, suggesting that Averroes will always fall short of full understanding. Both schools refer to interpretation as the "rending of the veil," that essential image in Islam, which Borges picks up twice in "The Zahir."

In this story, Borges the narrator has seen a most perplexing and disturbing aspect of Allah: "There was a time when I could visualize the obverse and then the reverse. Now I see them simultaneously," he says of the coin. Unable to comprehend this phenomenon, he struggles to forget or ignore it, but his attempts are all vain, and he begins to lose his own identity: "Before 1948, Julia's destiny will have caught up with me. I shall not know who Borges was." Julia is in a madhouse, for she too has had a vision, leading to "madness or saintliness," Borges says, to madness *and* saintliness, the Koran suggests. Clementina's sister Julia— and we shall soon see what these women symbolize— was thought to have lost her sanity: "Poor Julie! She got awfully *queer,* and they had to shut her up in the Bosch," laments one of her friends. "Why, she keeps on talking about a *coin,* just like Morena Sachmann's *chauffeur.*"

Borges himself sees no reason to fear such a destiny, should it befall him too: "To call this prospect terrible is a fallacy, for none of its circumstances will exist for me. One might as well say that an anesthetized man feels terrible pain when they open his cranium." Indeed, Borges is yearning for a yet greater obsession with the coin, for only then will he be fully anesthetized, self "unconscious." This he knows is a *sine qua non* for grasping the *batin,* and putting an end to his torment.

> In order to lose themselves in God, the Sufis recite their own names, or the ninety-nine divine names, until they become meaningless. I long to travel that path. Perhaps I shall conclude by wearing away the Zahir simply by thinking of it again and again. Perhaps behind the coin I shall find God.

The Aleph is not as material, as obvious a manifestation of Allah, hence the person who sees it must be closer to selflessness, to a total immersion into God's creation, to a loss of all that is proper to his/her individuality. "I saw all the mirrors on earth, and none of them reflected me," Borges recalls, thus suggesting that, at least while his vision lasted, his individual existence was uncertain. Immediately after this vision of "the inconceivable universe," Borges manages to "pick [him]self up and utter: 'One hell of a—yes, one hell of a—' The matter-of-factedness of my voice surprised me."

Borges the narrator and Carlos Argentino, in "The Aleph," were rivals, competing for Beatriz's attention. A *zahiri* reading of this passage would therefore refer to a reluctance on Borges' part to admit Carlos Argentino's clear advantage, for the latter is Beatriz' cousin, and the Aleph was seen under his own roof. A *batini* reading is much richer: Borges, having experienced a direct vision, grows indifferent to Beatriz, the mediator, the guide (who, moreover, was not sufficiently qualified to guide the visionary Dante through Paradiso, but abandoned him instead at the outer gates of Purgatorio). Borges' voice, his medium of expression and communication, becomes "matter of fact." But Borges and Carlos Argentino are also two writers competing for the same literary prize, which the latter wins, because Borges could not put, in "successive language," his vision of the universe. In this instance too, Borges is indifferent to Carlos Argentino's material, worldly, and wordly success, and to his own failure.

A very similar change had occurred in "The Zahir." Borges had gone to Clementina's house and, while there, inquired about Julia. Upon being told that she had been hospitalized, he reflects that this prospect is not terrible. "Clementina" means gentle, complacent, undemanding, yet Borges now thinks of "the arrogant image of Clementina, physical pain," hence his yearning to be "anesthetized." Julia, on the other hand, means "God's gift," hence "I long to travel this path . . . Perhaps behind the coin I shall find God."

But did Borges have a revelation, or was it just a dream, as he seems to suggest at the beginning of "The Zahir?" Again, the Muslims equate both: "God most High, however, has favoured His creatures by giving them something analogous to the faculty of prophecy, namely dreams. In the dream-state, a man apprehends what is to be in the future, which is something of the unseen; he does so explicitly or else clothed in a symbolic form whose interpretation is to be disclosed." Borges feels the same way. As the narrator of the "Zahir," he spoke of the coin as a repertory of possible futures," like a dream. As a nonfictional persona, he wrote in *Seven Nights:* "In a psychology book I greatly admire . . . Gustav Spiller states that dreams correspond to the lowest plane of mental activity—I would maintain that, at least for me, this is an error."

The Muslim mystics, al-Ghazali tells us, are "men who had real experiences, not men of words." Yet some of the most beautiful Arabic poetry is written by Sufis, probably because of their effort to find the words most apt to describe the ineffable. Borges, again, is aware of this:

> How, then, can I translate into words the limitless Aleph, which my floundering mind can scarcely encompass? Mystics, faced with the same problem, fall back on symbols . . . Perhaps the Gods might grant me a similar metaphor, but then this account would become contaminated by literature, with fiction.

But why is Borges writing at all, if literature contaminates the truth, and if words for him suffer from "the guilty condition of being mere metaphors?" One is tempted to venture a bold and ambitious suggestion. The Islamic mystics believed that they belonged to the elite who "had vision." They could, to put it in simpler terms, read between the lines of their own writings, and knew that their fellow-mystics could and would do the same. Moreover, as al-Ghazali points out, "whoever sits in their company derives from them this faith, and none who sits in their company is pained." None is pained because their literature, like the Koran, reads on a number of levels, has a *zahir* and a *batin.* For Sufi writing is, above all, esoteric writing.

Source: Nada Elia, "Islamic Esoteric Concepts as Borges Stategies," in *Variaciones Borges: Journal of the Jorge Luis Borges Center for Studies and Documents,* Vol. 5, 1998, pp. 129–44.

Jon Thiem

In the following essay excerpt, Thiem examines Borges's reluctance to acknowledge the influence of Dante in "The Aleph."

Readers and critics of Borges's "The Aleph" ("El Aleph,") 1945 have long recognized the Dante allusions, some subtle, some obvious, woven into the text of this intricate, famous tale. In various unmistakable ways Borges alludes to Dante Alighieri, to Beatrice, and to elements of the *Commedia.* Even so, he never refers directly to Dante or the *Commedia,* in spite of the fact that in "The Aleph" he cites numerous "precursors." Furthermore, in his 1970 "Aleph" commentary Borges virtually denied that the allusions to Dante were intentional:

> Critics . . . have detected Beatrice Portinari in Beatriz Viterbo, Dante in Daneri, and the descent into hell in the descent into the cellar. I am, of course, duly grateful for these unlooked-for gifts.

Although a number of critics have glossed the major Dante allusions in "The Aleph," few have tried to explain Borges's reluctance to recognize Dante as his precursor in this instance. Yet an awareness of Borges's curious method of appropriating Dante, one of his favorite poets, seriously affects how we read the story. It also reveals a puzzling moment in which Borges's practice as a writer seems to conflict with his own pronouncements on literary influence.

Such pronouncements, in defying critical platitudes about literary indebtedness, originality, and the autonomy of the author, have attracted the attention of contemporary writers and theorists, such as John Barth, Alain Robbe-Grillet, Gérard Genette, and Harold Bloom. Increasingly, Borges's ideas have become an obligatory touchstone for critics doubtful about more traditional ways of studying literary relations. The well-known 1951 essay "Kafka y sus precursores" offers a convenient summary of Borges's thinking in this respect. Here Borges would "purify" the term "precursor" of all of its polemical association. Echoing T. S. Eliot, he claims that "each writer *creates* his own precursors. His work modifies our conception of the past just as it will modify the future. In this interdependency the identity or plurality of men does not matter at all," . . . So, having read Kafka, for

> In 'The Aleph' Borges neglects to cite Dante in spite of conclusive evidence that the story owes much to Dante. Would not Bloom's concept of poetic anxiety better account for Borges's omission in 'The Aleph' than Borges's own notion of influence?"

example, we will reread Browning and Kierkegaard differently, more appreciatively than before. In the precursor we discover Kafkaesque features that we would have missed had Kafka not written. One suspects that Borges has inverted the usual order of poetic obligation: now the precursor owes a debt to the epigone, for the latter has caused the former to be read anew. In the end, literary debts between precursors and epigone cancel each other out. Elsewhere, Borges toys with the idea that all authors are ultimately avatars of one Universal Author, so that influence, plagiarism, priority—literary relations in general—are, strictly speaking, illusory. Indeed, Borges's delight in revealing his own precursors suggests that he suffers little from the anxieties of influence. Nor is it surprising that among the avant-garde critics who have taken Borges's ideas on influence seriously, the most critical has been Harold Bloom, who, though agreeing with Borges that writers create their own precursors, rejects Borges's "aesthetic idealism" in which the relation of poet to precursor is seen as "clean" rather than malign. Bloom holds that the new poet fashions his own precursors by misinterpreting them, a process that "malforms" the new poet. Poetic influence is a kind of disease that makes strong poets suffer an "anxiety of influence" Precisely the plurality, the agonizing individuality, of poets is what matters most.

From a Bloomian perspective interesting questions emerge concerning Borges's ideas and poetic practice. Is Borges's metaphysical rejection of literary relations itself a defense mechanism, a revisionary ratio in Bloom's terms, made to evade the psychological perils of influence? In "The Aleph" Borges neglects to cite Dante in spite of conclusive evidence that the story owes much to Dante. Would not Bloom's concept of poetic anxiety better account for Borges's omission in ''The Aleph'' than Borges's own notion of influence?

We know that Borges has worked a great deal with Dante. Like other twentieth-century writers—one thinks of Joyce, Mann, Eliot, Pound, Beckett, Flannery O'Connor, and Solzhenitsyn—Borges has shown an extensive, often penetrating, knowledge of the Italian poet (see the ''Estudio preliminar''). He claims to have read through English or Italian versions of the *Commedia* at least ten times; the first time he read Dante in the original was probably in the late 1930s, long before he wrote ''The Aleph'' His writings attest to an intense interest in Dante: the parable ''Inferno, I 23'' 1955; his introduction to a Spanish translation of the *Commedia* which includes short essays on Ulysses, Ugolino, and Beatrice in the earthly paradise; several occasional essays published between 1948 and 1962, never reprinted (e.g. ''El noble castillo'' and ''El verdugo piadoso''); and numerous references and allusions scattered not only through the stories collected in *El Aleph*, but also throughout his whole opus. Nor does Borges profess to hold any writer in higher esteem than Dante. As early as 1943, in ''Sobre el 'Vathek' de William Beckford,'' he wrote that *''La Divina Comedia* is the most justifiable and the most solid book of all literature,'' . . . And over thirty years later: ''Had I to name a single work as being at the top of all literature, I should choose the *Divina Commedia* by Dante.'' A Bloomian might well argue thus: if for Borges the *Commedia* is the paradigmatic poem, then it is possible that he would regard its shadow in ''The Aleph'' as an ''intolerable presence,'' one he could not acknowledge.

This does seem plausible since ''The Aleph'' is one of Borges's most ambitious stories. As the title story of one of Borges's two main collections it retains a strategic place in his oeuvre. Like the *Commedia,* it tries to elicit a total vision of the cosmos. The Aleph of the title, a bright sphere about an inch in diameter, is a magical microcosm, a point that contains all other points in the cosmos. The Aleph makes all things visible without diminishing them or making them overlap. As the epigraph from Hobbes suggests, the Aleph is to space what eternity is to time. The heart of the story is a partial listing of what the narrator saw in the Aleph. This listing, the description of the Aleph, and an inventory of various precursors of the Aleph constitute about a third of the account. The rest of the story sets down how

Borges, the narrator, is gradually drawn into the confidences of the Aleph's owner, the poet Carlos Argentino Daneri, in whose surname many readers have recognized an abbreviation of Dante Alighieri. Borges knows Daneri through the latter's cousin, Beatriz Viterbo, who was Borges's great, unrequited love, long deceased at the time of the main events of the story. After her death in 1929, Borges, on her birthday, would pay a nostalgic visit to her old house in Buenos Aires, still occupied by Daneri. In 1941 Daneri, now an intimate of Borges, reads to him sections of his topographico-encyclopedic epic *The Earth, La Tierra,* which, when finished, will include a complete inventory of every natural and artificial feature of the planet. About a third of the story involves a critical assessment of Daneri and his encyclopedic epic. Shortly after this reading a distraught Daneri notifies Borges that Beatriz's house is to be demolished and with it the Aleph, which is in the cellar and which Daneri has used to gather the vast materials for *The Earth.* Daneri leads Borges to the cellar where the latter experiences a total vision through the agency of the Aleph. But on returning, Borges spitefully refuses to recognize the existence of the Aleph and even implies that Daneri is deluded. In the postscript, where the narrator lists numerous earlier references to Alephs, we learn that Daneri's Aleph has been destroyed, that *The Earth* has received the Second National Prize for Literature, and that the narrator's own entry failed to get a single vote.

Of the numerous parallels between Dante's work and ''The Aleph'' the most significant for an interpretation of the poetics of Borges's story relate to the *Paradiso.* These in particular have been convincingly established in separate studies by Alberto Carlos, Roberto Paoli and Ruggiero Stefanini. Foremost is the striking similarity between Dante's God in the *Paradiso* and the Aleph, Borges's total point. Borges the narrator sees the Aleph as ''a tiny, iridescent sphere of almost intolerable brilliance,'' . . . Similarly, Dante the pilgrim sees God as a mere point of light which nevertheless makes the eye want to close because of its piercing brilliance. Just as Beatrice describes God as ''that place where every *ubi* and every *quando* is centered in a point'' . . . so too the Aleph is ''one of the points in space that contains all the [other] points,'' . . . The pilgrim in his final vision of the divine point of light sees confined in its depths ''all that lies scattered in pages throughout the universe,'' . . . Likewise Borges sees in the Aleph the whole ''unimaginable universe,'' ''el inconcebible universo.'' More important still, each work presents a spatial paradox that also involves a perceptual anomaly: not just a point that is all points, but a point in which all other points remain discernible to the human eye. Each work, in short, concerns itself with the nature and scope of total vision.

Other parallels suggest that Borges uses the *Paradiso* to set up a poetics of total vision, in other words a study of the principles and limits of expressing a total vision by means of verbal art. The first canto of the *Paradiso* states the well-known problem: ''through words it is not possible to signify transhuman matters,'' . . . Throughout the *Paradiso* Dante regrets his inability to remember or put into language his visionary experiences. These regrets reach a crescendo in the last canto where he repeatedly laments that the ultimate vision he has received exceeds a human's verbal and mnemonic capacities to set it forth, and he likens the evanescence of his vision to the ''unsealing'' of snow by the sun and to the scattering by the wind of the light leaves of the Sibyl so that the ''meaning,'' ''sentenza,'' of her oracle is lost. His difficulty lies not only in the magnitude or totality of the vision, but also in its remarkable concentration, for, as he says, he sees ''confined, / bound by love into a single volume, / all that lies scattered in pages throughout the universe,'' . . . Thus, though the pilgrim sees all-in-one, the poet cannot describe all-in-one by human means, except scatter-fashion, as a sort of sequence in which the all ceases to be all, and the one becomes several, presented in succession. Similarly, we learn from Beatrice that the spirits the pilgrim meets distributed among the planets are there only as appearances or signs (''per far segno''), put there as a concession to the pilgrim's human faculties, which at this point can only apprehend trans-spatial things in a spatial, sequential order. In fact these spirits reside in the first circle of the Empyrean, their seeming dispersal among the planets a kind of illusion engineered for the pilgrim's gradual introduction into the metaphysics of total vision. The reader nearly forgets, here, that it is the poet who has devised this spectacle for the reader, not the angels for the pilgrim, and that Dante's problem relates as much to poetics as to celestial metaphysics.

Like Dante, Borges the narrator shows a keen awareness of the limits that language and human cognition impose on the re-presentation of a total vision. Before he begins the ''ineffable center,'' ''inefable centro'' of his story, that is, the catalog of what he saw in the Aleph, he speaks of his ''des-peration as a writer,'' ''desesperación de escritor,'' and of the problem of how to ''convey to others the infinite Aleph, which my timorous memory can scarcely comprehend,'' . . . Writing must also fail to re-present the alephic vision because what he sees is simultaneous but its ''transcription [is] sequential, for such is the nature of language,'' . . . Just as Dante in the last tercets of the *Commedia* refers to his incapacity to grasp his vision for long, so too Borges gives the last sentences of his story to the failure of his memory to confirm that he even saw the Aleph or had a total vision. One might, of course, see in this correspondence merely the recurrence of a stock motif: the ineffability and evanescence of total vision. Yet the positioning of the motif in Borges and his use of it in conjunction with the Aleph, which almost certainly owes its main features to the God of the *Paradiso,* argue powerfully that this is a case of direct influence.

Generally, the Dante parallels in ''The Aleph'' are explained as instances of Borgesian parody, an indisputable finding, which, however, does not take us very far. In my view these parallels only begin to take on significance when the reader concentrates on Borges's ''sin of omission,'' namely, his not acknowledging Dante as his precursor . . .

Total enumeration by means of a comprehensive catalog or encyclopedia is, of course, a long-standing method for re-presenting a total vision. In fact it is Daneri's method in his encyclopedic epic *The Earth,* the poetics of which Borges takes such pains to discredit. The method does not work well because total inclusiveness in the arts, if not elsewhere, remains a chimera. Even if it were not, there would always remain a serious disjunction between a total enumeration and a total vision, for the former is sequential and encyclopedic whereas the latter is simultaneous and unified. Hence that ineffability of total vision which is the despair of mystical poets from Dante to Borges, and a central theme of ''The Aleph.'' The narrator himself makes this point when he complains that this alephic vision was instantaneous but that his means of expression is sequential. And in 1970 the author explained that his ''chief problem in writing the story'' was in ''the setting down of a *limited* catalog of *endless* things'' (my emphasis). Here, however, the discrepancy between total enumeration and total vision reflects the dichotomy limited/endless, that is, the inevitable incompleteness of a ''total enumeration'' rather than its sequential nature. Thus the narrator's omission of Dante references in an inventory of precursors illustrates a specific defect of total enumeration. Moreover, this ''sin of omission'' is ironic, for the defect in the telling of the story reflects the story's subject: the inadequacy of total enumeration . . .

In this context, a remark by Borges from an essay of 1949 is revealing about his view of Dante. Borges imagines a total picture, a magical engraving, ''lámina,'' of which he says that ''nothing on earth is not included there,'' . . . In this engraving one sees all that is, was and will be—the history of the past and that of the future. It is a ''microcosm,'' ''microcosmo.'' ''That engraving of universal compass,'' . . . he says, is Dante's *Commedia*. For Borges then, the *Commedia* is an anomaly, a human fabrication that miraculously achieves the quality of all-inclusiveness. In this respect Dante's masterpiece suspiciously resembles Borges's Aleph.

Given Borges's preoccupation with the inclusionary obsession, it is hard not to infer that in ''The Aleph'' Borges has excluded the mention of Dante so that the authorial audience will see reflected in the narrator/pseudo-author the pathos of unintentional omission. The Dante omission, which is at once conspicuous, supposedly unintentional, and broadly significant, offers a key to understanding Borges's own procedures in dealing with total vision. He knows that the law of unintentional omission invariably undermines the inclusionary process. Out of this knowledge he has drawn the paradoxical conclusion that a method of *significant* omission is essential to a modern poetics of total vision.

Thus the theme of total enumeration and the method of significant omission coexist in the story in a relation of ironic tension. They also have something in common: each points to the epic as a poetic vehicle of all-inclusive vision. The omission of Dante references in a parody of the *Commedia* calls to mind the fact that for Borges, as for many moderns, Dante's magnum opus is the paradigmatic epic. So too, total enumeration is one of the main procedures by which epic poems create the effect of all-inclusive vision. In this matter I follow Tillyard and a host of others who regard epics as long poems distinguished by their amplitude and inclusiveness. Tillyard's perspective is useful here because he differentiates the heroic poem from the epic, which need not have a ''heroic matter'' but which does give a ''heroic impression'' through the ambitiousness and comprehensiveness of its project. In fact, this accords well with medieval views of the epic poet as encyclopedist/polymath and of

the classical epic as a compendium of knowledge. The encyclopedia is ultimately the most comprehensive type of total enumeration. When critics refer to the epic as encyclopedic, they mean that its mode of narration, extended and digressive, tends to generate an enumeration of all things. In this sense, the major epics from the *Iliad* to *Paradise Lost* become the summas of their worlds.

Yet epic is not the only literary mode of all-inclusive vision, nor is total enumeration the only means to convey such a vision. The short poem or the prose meditation can also convey a total vision, usually through the mystical apprehension of the unity of all things in God. Here the mode is lyrical or meditative rather than encyclopedic. The rhetoric, depending as it does on the method of significant omission, employs oxymoron, apophasis, the *via negativa,* and the ineffability topos to communicate the experience, rather than the content, of total vision. The works of the Spanish mystics and the English metaphysicals are the best known examples of the lyric or meditative mode of total vision.

These divergent modes necessarily entail different versions of total vision: the one, extensional and objective, describing the contents of total vision; the other, intensive and subjective, centering on the paradoxical experience of total vision. It is perhaps yet another measure of its all-inclusiveness that Dante's epic incorporates both modes and both versions of total vision. As we have seen, this is especially evident in the *Paradiso* where the enumerative or sequential presentation of the cosmos is declared an enabling fiction and where the encyclopedic description of the heavenly order is ruptured by lyrical moments of significant omission, of blindness, muteness, and amnesia. Here paradox and oxymoron reflect the inadequacy of total enumeration in the face of the pilgrim's mystical experience of the unity of all things in God. In this way the *Paradiso* offers paradigms for both the encyclopedic epic of total vision and its lyrical, apophatic counterpart.

If taken too seriously as an evaluative principle, this neo-Crocean typology of visionary modes would not be very tenable. But it does serve as a helpful way of approaching both the theme and method of ''The Aleph,'' where it accounts for three models of poetic form for total vision offered by the story: Daneri's *The Earth* (an encyclopedic epic), Dante's *Commedia* (which uses both encyclopedic and lyric modes), and the story ''The Aleph'' itself, whose mode of total vision is lyric-meditative.

Borges presents *The Earth* as an encyclopedic epic. We learn, for instance, that *The Earth,* like Dante's epic, unfolds in cantos, that it has the epic aim of putting into verse "the whole wide world," "toda la redondez del planeta," and that it uses such epic conventions as the digression and the apostrophe. It is not surprising that Borges compares *The Earth* to the encyclopedic *Polyolbion,* a "topographical epic," "epopeya topográfica" by Drayton. And four of the quoted verses from *The Earth* allude to Homer's *Odyssey* and Hesiod's *Works and Days,* thereby signalling the encyclopedic range of Daneri's work. Yet the narrator rarely tires of pointing up the mediocrity of *The Earth,* in spite of the Dante legacy suggested in Daneri's name.

The second model, covertly present, is Dante's epic, especially the *Paradiso.* The Dante parodies, allusions, and parallels in the story continually bring the authorial reader back to Dante's own poetics of total vision as set forth in the *Paradiso.* Drawing on Borges's comments as well as his practice, one can infer three aspects of the *Commedia* that make it for Borges the paradigmatic long poem: it encompasses the medieval cosmos in a total vision ; it exploits the method of significant omission to give the impression that it is neither incomplete nor redundant ; and, also by this method, it enforces the illusion of its own unity and thereby the transcendental unity of all things . . .

Borges conveys the effect of amplitude within small compass by relying on suggestion, a mode of significant omission, rather than on total representation through total enumeration, the ponderous method of Daneri. For Borges, re-presentation, the extended, exhaustive description of objects, results in works that are "large," "considerable" but "limited," "limitado," to use the narrator's characterization of *Polyolbion,* and by implication *The Earth.* The results of encyclopedic re-presentation reverse or overthrow the alephic principle, which seeks to confine the unlimited in something small. Suggestion, as opposed to re-presentation or direct expression, is alephic. Suggestion draws on ellipsis, allusion, apophasis, *pars pro toto,* and veiling, all techniques of significant omission. An analogy from the visual arts illustrates well the power of suggestion through significant omission. As E. H. Gombrich has noted, Rembrandt and Leonardo deliberately blurred those features of the face that would be most expressive. Paradoxically, this partial omission of the most expressive features makes the face much more expressive than if they were fully expressed. This method foreshadows Borges's neo-Symbolist poetics, already enunciated in 1932 in his essay "Narrative Art and Magic." Here Borges speaks of blurring as a means of emphasis, citing William Morris and Mallarmé as examples. Thus omission, which is a serious defect from a re-presentational viewpoint, becomes a virtue in evocation. Through omission evocation is alephic: it encompasses more with less. Even so, Borges asserts that this method can never achieve the complete presentation of the essential object: "I think you can only allude to things, you can never express them."

Source: Jon Thiem, "Borges, Dante, and the Poetics of Total Vision," in *Comparative Literature,* Vol. 40, No. 2, Spring 1988, pp. 97–121.

Sources

Barrenechea, Ana Maria, *Borges the Labyrinth Maker,* New York University Press, 1965, pp. 39, 50.

Biguenet, John, and Tom Whalen, "An Interview with Jorge Luis Borges," in *Jorge Luis Borges: Conversations,* edited by Richard Burgin, University Press of Mississippi, 1998, p. 212.

Borges, Jorge Luis, "An Autobiographical Essay," in *The Aleph and Other Stories 1933–1969,* E. P. Dutton, 1978, p. 220.

———, "Commentaries," in *The Aleph and Other Stories 1933–1969,* E. P. Dutton, 1978, p. 263.

———, "The Fearful Sphere of Pascal," in *Labyrinths,* edited by Donald A. Yates and James E. Irby, New Directions, 1964, p. 191.

———, "Kafka and His Precursors," in *Labyrinths,* edited by Donald A. Yates and James E. Irby, New Directions, 1964, p. 201.

———, "The Witness," in *Labyrinths,* edited by Donald A. Yates and James E. Irby, New Directions, 1964, p. 243.

Christ, Ronald, *The Narrow Act: Borges's Art of Allusion,* New York University Press, 1969, pp. 11, 15.

Gates, Bill, *The Road Ahead,* Viking Penguin, 1995, pp. 6, 105, 134, 274.

Irby, James E., "Introduction," in *Labyrinths,* edited by Donald A. Yates and James E. Irby, New Directions, 1964, p. xxiii.

Lindstrom, Naomi, "Argentina," in *Handbook of Latin American Literature,* Garland Publishing, Inc., 1987, p. 22.

McMurray, George R., *Jorge Luis Borges,* Frederick Ungar Publishing Co., 1980, pp. 30, 173.

Merrell, Floyd, *Unthinking Thinking: Jorge Luis Borges, Mathematics, and the New Physics,* Purdue University Press, 1991, p. 146.

Stabb, Martin S., *Jorge Luis Borges,* Twayne Publishers, Inc., 1970, p. 111.

Woodall, James, *Borges: A Life,* BasicBooks, 1996, pp. 133, 148.

Further Reading

Borges, Jorge Luis, ''An Autobiographical Essay,'' in *The Aleph and Other Stories 1933–1969,* E. P. Dutton, 1978.
This essay, first published in the *New Yorker* magazine in 1970, offers a glimpse of Borges's childhood reading habits and life as an up-and-coming writer in Buenos Aires.

———, *Other Inquisitions 1937–1952,* University of Texas Press, 1988.
This volume contains over thirty of Borges's essays; the topics range from literature and history to the nature of time.

———, *A Universal History of Infamy,* Penguin Books, 1975.
Borges's first collection was originally written for the pages of an Argentinian newspaper. A reader of this entertaining volume will note Borges's trademark blending of fact and fiction.

Burgin, Richard, ed., *Jorge Luis Borges: Conversations,* University Press of Mississippi, 1998.
This collection features the text of sixteen conversations with Borges, ranging from 1966 to 1985. There is also a valuable index, so readers can quickly find Borges's opinions on a number of topics and writers.

Smith, Verity, ed., *Encyclopedia of Latin American Literature,* Fitzroy Dearborn Publishers, 1997.
This exhaustive reference work features comprehensive entries on the work of Borges and other Argentinian literature.

Average Waves in Unprotected Waters

Anne Tyler
1977

"Average Waves in Unprotected Waters," first published in the February 28, 1977, edition of the *New Yorker,* is one of Anne Tyler's most anthologized short stories. Themes that appear in all of Tyler's writing are encapsulated in the life of the story's protagonist, Bet Blevins, whom the reader meets on the day she is to institutionalize her mentally handicapped son. These themes include: the family and the role of the individual in relationship to the family, parenting, memory, absent fathers, and identity and self-discovery. Published the same year Tyler published her seventh novel, *Earthly Possessions*, the story grapples with the complex web of characteristics that define an ordinary life. Like many of Tyler's characters, Bet Blevins is an ordinary American. She endures the hardships she has been dealt and does so as a "normal" person may be expected to endure. Through Blevins and others, Tyler proves that most events in life are complex and nuanced, which often clouds the delineation between what is heroic and what is simply normal. Tyler is well known for her ability and propensity for writing about ordinary people, a trait she shares with one of her greatest literary influences, the southern writer Eudora Welty.

Tyler developed an affinity for the short story form in the early 1970s, as it allowed her to balance the demands of motherhood and writing while her children were young, and in the latter half of the decade, she published stories in many magazines, including the *Ladies' Home Journal,* the *New Yorker,*

and *McCall's*. Though there is not an edition of Tyler's collected short stories in which "Average Waves in Unprotected Waters" appears, the story can currently be found in several anthologies, including the ninth edition of *The American Tradition in Literature*, edited by George Perkins and Barbara Perkins and published by McGraw-Hill.

Author Biography

Anne Tyler was born on October 25, 1941, in Minneapolis, Minnesota. Her father, Lloyd Parry Tyler, a chemist, and mother, Mahon Tyler, a social worker, were committed Quakers and social activists. They raised Tyler and her three younger brothers in several Utopian communities throughout the United States, settling in the Celo Community in the mountains of North Carolina for five of Tyler's formative years. Robert W. Croft, in his book *An Anne Tyler Companion,* writes about Tyler's life at Celo, where Tyler was perceived as an outsider, a role she claims helped her learn to use her imagination. A voracious reader, Tyler often read favorite books twenty and thirty times. She and her brothers were primarily home schooled, which placed Tyler ahead of most students her age and allowed her to enter Duke University at the age of sixteen. At Duke, she majored in Russian. After graduating, she moved to New York to pursue a master's degree in Russian at Columbia University. Though she finished all the required coursework, she never completed her thesis. Instead, Tyler returned to North Carolina and worked as a Russian bibliographer in the Duke University Library. She met Taghi Modarressi, an Iranian psychiatrist and writer, and married him in 1963. Shortly after their wedding, the newlyweds moved to Montreal, Canada, where Modarressi completed his medical residency.

While in Montreal, Tyler's writing life began to take shape. She completed the manuscript for her first novel, *If Morning Ever Comes*, in 1963. Knopf published the book and all of her subsequent novels. In 1965, her first daughter, Tezh, was born, and two years later another daughter, Mitra, arrived. Tyler published her second novel, *The Tin Can Tree*, in 1965. In 1967, the family moved to Baltimore, Maryland, a city that has figured prominently in Tyler's later fiction. Between 1967 and 1977, when "Average Waves in Unprotected Waters" appeared in the *New Yorker,* Tyler published five novels and many short stories. Though she began to receive very favorable reviews beginning with her fifth book, *Celestial Navigation*, in 1974, her public following was still quite sparse. In 1982, with the release of *Dinner at the Homesick Restaurant*, that began to change. The book won the PEN/Faulkner Award for fiction and in 1983 was nominated for the Pulitzer Prize for fiction. In the same year, Tyler was elected a member of the American Academy and Institute of Arts and Letters. Her next book, *The Accidental Tourist*, won the National Book Critics Circle Award and was also nominated for the Pulitzer Prize for fiction. In 1988, *The Accidental Tourist* was made into an Academy Award–nominated motion picture, and the following year, her book *Breathing Lessons* won the coveted Pulitzer Prize for fiction. The success of these last books catapulted Tyler onto the list of America's bestselling authors and secured a large audience for her work. She continues to write novels, and her latest book, *Back When We Were Grownups*, appeared in 2001. Tyler lives a very private life in Baltimore with her family.

Plot Summary

"Average Waves in Unprotected Waters" begins at first light on the day Bet Blevins, the story's protagonist, is to institutionalize her mentally handicapped son, Arnold. At the age of nine, Arnold has become too difficult for Bet to manage. In the shabby, one-room apartment, Bet wonders, as she prepares Arnold's things and dresses him one last time, if he understands what is happening and if she is truly making the right decision. As they leave the crumbling apartment building, Mrs. Puckett, a kindly neighbor who is crying, stops Bet and gives her cookies for Arnold, but he runs off without acknowledging the woman who has baby-sat for him since his birth.

After taking a bus from their apartment, Bet and Arnold arrive at the train station. Bet has purchased gum, which she gives to a nervous Arnold. As the train leaves, he becomes calmer and falls asleep. While Arnold sleeps, Bet remembers him as a younger child. She remembers her husband, Avery, who left a few weeks after Arnold's mental disability was diagnosed. She determines that she and Avery married too young, against her parents' wishes. She wonders if the gene that caused Arnold's disability came from Avery or from her. She speculates that it came from her because, "she never could do anything as well as most people." She wonders why she was so eager to leave her home, which she now sees as "beautifully free and spacious." She realizes that she has had, and continues to have, one virtue: her steadfastness. She remembers herself as a child, at the shore with her parents, and how she used to stand in the waves and let them pound her. She draws a connection between the waves and her life with Avery, remembering that after Avery left, she even stayed in the old apartment for a while, because she "took some comfort from enduring." Arnold wakes up and she must entertain him. They both watch the conductor come through the train asking for tickets. Arnold laughs at an old woman whom the conductor is accusing of having no ticket. Bet imagines that she is the one the conductor is scolding.

At Parkinsville, Bet and Arnold find a cab to take them to the Parkinsville State Hospital. Arnold wants to eat a cookie, but Bet refuses to give him one. She is afraid that he will get messy, and she wants the people at the hospital to think highly of him and to see that "someone cherished him." She is afraid that Arnold will go into one of his rages. To appease him, she breaks off a little piece of cookie and gives it to him to eat. When they arrive at the hospital, she asks the cab driver, repeatedly, if he will stay and wait for her. He promises that he will stay.

Inside the hospital, a nurse gives Bet a tour and shows her where Arnold will sleep. As they look around, Bet tries to tell the nurse how to care for Arnold. The nurse assures Bet that Arnold will be well cared for and informs her that she will be not be able to visit Arnold for six months as he becomes acclimated to his new home. After leaving Arnold with his blanket, Bet says good-bye.

Rushing from the building in tears, Bet climbs into the cab and urges the driver to drive quickly to the train station. She has timed her departure so she will not have to wait very long for a train. When she arrives at the train station, she learns that the train has been delayed by twenty minutes. Bet becomes nearly desperate at this news and wonders how she will endure the interminable wait. Just then, the town's mayor enters the station and announces that he will be giving a twenty-minute speech. Bet is greatly relieved and believes that they have "come just for her sake," and that from now on, everything will be like that, "just something on a stage, for her to sit back and watch."

Anne Tyler

Characters

Arnold Blevins

Arnold Blevins is a nine-year-old boy with developmental disabilities who has been raised by his mother, Bet. The day portrayed in the story marks his transition from his mother's apartment to his new home at the Parkinsville State Hospital. Arnold is described as small though "strong, wiry" and "thin-skinned, almost transparent." He has "great glassy eyes" and looks that make him appear elderly, "pinched, strained, tired." He rarely alters his expression. The reader is told that he has fits, frequently violent tantrums that have become difficult for his mother to manage. He is easily bored, and when he becomes so, he often becomes unruly. He loves gum and sometimes swallows the gum even though he has been told not to. He often looks at familiar things as if they were unfamiliar or brand new. New things also "have no meaning for him." Though he is described in a way that suggests he forms no attachments, he does form attachments to some material items like his little "red duffel coat." He appears, however, oblivious to most human attachments, including the long-standing relationship with the Blevins's neighbor, Mrs. Puckett, who has baby-sat him since his birth.

Media Adaptations

- *The Accidental Tourist* was adapted as an Academy Award–nominated film and released by Warner Brothers in 1988. The film stars Kathleen Turner and William Hurt.

- Almost all of Tyler's novels appear as books on tape from Random House, including *Back When We Were Grownups,* which appeared in 2001. Other Random House audio books include *Breathing Lessons, The Clock Winder,* and *Dinner at the Homesick Restaurant.*

Avery Blevins

Avery Blevins is Bet Blevins's absent husband, who left her and their son, Arnold, a few weeks after learning that Arnold was mentally handicapped.

Bet Blevins

Bet Blevins is the struggling single mother of Arnold Blevins, a nine-year-old developmentally disabled boy for whom she can no longer care. Bet's viewpoint is prevalent throughout the story and shows her as a woman who, first and foremost, takes "comfort from enduring." Strength of character has facilitated her life with Arnold, without the support of family, for many years. Bet's choices have required that she endure. She withstood a rash marriage to Avery, who left her and Arnold a few weeks after the boy was diagnosed as mentally disabled, and she has endured the hardship of caring for Arnold by herself. Bet vacillates between believing that Avery was the genetic cause of her son's defect and placing the culpability on herself. She believes that she "never could do anything as well as most people," and this feeling of failure translates not only to her guilty belief in her role in her son's biological condition, but now, in her social role as Arnold's mother. Bet's thoughts are fixated on making Arnold appear acceptable, clean, and cherished on this day, when she is to take him to live in the state hospital. Though the place ultimately promises proper and ongoing care for him, many of Bet's actions during the day suggest her uncertainty about the decision.

Much of Bet's character is revealed through memory. Through Bet's memories, the reader becomes aware of the hardship and isolation she has had to endure. In many ways, Bet idealizes her past life, which was "beautifully free and spacious," though she recognizes how, even then, she was destined to live staunchly and endure, "as if standing staunch were a virtue." Her strength throughout these years of struggle takes a great toll on her, and ultimately, in order to endure the pain of loss, she chooses to disconnect and become an observer of life rather than a participant.

Mrs. Puckett

Mrs. Puckett is the Blevins's neighbor who baby-sat Arnold from his birth until he became too big for her to manage. She breaks down as she gives Bet cookies for Arnold and watches him leave his home for the last time.

Themes

Memory

Memory plays an important role in almost all of Tyler's fiction. In "Average Waves in Unprotected Waters," memory is a disconnecting as well as a connecting force, both allowing characters to make discoveries about themselves and serving as a means of alienation. The first acknowledgment of memory, or lack of memory, occurs when Mrs. Puckett gives Bet cookies for Arnold. The boy passes the older woman without acknowledging her. He does not seem to know her or have a memory of her. Bet has worried over Arnold's lack of memory for objects, but his inability to recognize the woman who baby-sat him from birth irritates her. Later, on the train, the act of remembering is an act of self-realization for Bet. As she remembers her childhood and marriage, she learns about herself and her ability to endure. Parts of her memory are idealized. She decides that "her old life had been beautifully free and spacious." In many ways, her memories

Topics for Further Study

- The story "Average Waves in Unprotected Waters" appeared in the *New Yorker* in the late 1970s during an important time in the feminist movement. What was happening in the feminist movement during the late 1970s? Using examples from the story, explain how the story portrays or does not portray the feminist values and objectives of the time. Would you call Tyler a feminist writer? Why or why not?

- In "Average Waves in Unprotected Waters," Bet's husband, Avery, has abandoned her and their son. What was life like for single mothers in the late 1970s? How does Bet's life compare to your findings? Use examples from the story to explain your conclusions.

- In the story, Bet questions whose genes caused her son's disability. What do geneticists say about genes and developmental disabilities? Are disabilities genetic? Explain your findings.

- In the story, how does Bet handle her son? What do her actions reveal about her attitude toward him? Does it appear that Bet loves her son? Explain and justify your answers using examples from the text.

- "Average Waves in Unprotected Waters" is told from Bet's point of view, in which a reader gains full access to the thoughts and feelings of Bet Blevins. Explain how the story might change if it were told from Arnold's perspective or Mrs. Puckett's point of view. What elements in the story present a bias that a reader may not trust as absolute truth?

---

are contradictory to her present situation. But, she realizes that she is the same person throughout her memory, and from that, she gleans comfort and understanding.

Family versus Individual

As the most constant theme in Tyler's work, the family provides a contradictory force in the characters of Tyler's fiction. On the one hand, family nurtures and sustains an individual and provides him or her with a basic identity. Family is also a unit of stagnation and can strip individuals of their identity. Bet Blevins defines herself as a mother throughout the story, and her role as a single mother in her family of two is complicated by the fact that she is the mother of a developmentally disabled boy. The traditional family and traditional motherhood, the idea of nurturing a child from birth to adulthood and then watching that child leave "the nest" and make his own life, is not a possibility for Bet. She must decide, perhaps before she is ready, to release Arnold into a life that is appropriate for him. Acting alone, Bet defies the traditional definition of the

successful family. Ultimately, she believes that her decision will save the family and herself. Her memories of her family serve as a catalyst to help Bet find herself and find in herself the ability to make a necessary decision.

Identity

In many ways, "Average Waves in Unprotected Waters" is a story about the search for self, from the most miniscule gene to the more intangible character traits that truly make a person unique. As Bet Blevins searches her son's unresponsive face and his spastic limbs for some sign of identity, she questions not only where his disability originated but the motivations for her own biological and emotional character. She wonders about the gene that she possibly gave him that caused his disability, which has, in a way, prevented Arnold from having a true identity. While questioning who her son is, she makes discoveries about herself, particularly her ability to endure hardship. One hardship she endures is seeing others interact with Arnold. As she watches, she is often induced to try and prove that Arnold is "real." Throughout the story, she projects personality traits onto Arnold, hoping to prove to those around him that he is like other children and that she has not failed, either through the passage of her genes to him or through her actions as his mother. She does define herself as a mother. Yet, at the conclusion of the story, she has given up her role as mother, and in doing so chooses a kind of lack of identity that is the result of passivity. Bet becomes a mere observer of ''something on a stage.''

Clean versus Dirty

Throughout ''Average Waves in Unprotected Waters,'' images of cleaning and the concern for tidy appearances prevail. The first reference to the apartment building in which Bet and Arnold live reveals that the place is ''crumbling'' and that there was nothing anyone could do to ''lighten its cluttered look.'' The building's degraded appearance is irritating and depressing to Bet as a physical manifestation of her poverty and hardship. With Arnold, Bet struggles between wanting him to be tidy and wanting him to appear more ''real.'' Arnold, whose jeans are unfaded, has a crooked collar. Bet does not fix it, because she thinks it makes him look more real, like other children. Later in the story, Bet is concerned that Arnold remain clean. She begs him not to get messy. She then tidies his collar. She wants anyone who meets him to see that he has been well cared for, ''cherished.'' Appearance is a clue to economic comfort and love, but it is contradicted by Bet's need for Arnold to appear ''real.'' Those elements that are not tidy in the story are manifestations of economic hardship, but they are also manifestations of real living and personality. Ultimately, Bet shuns this reality and the messiness of life. When the mayor's entourage arrives in their clean gray suits with their bunting and microphone, Bet feels she can surrender herself to them. The well-dressed government people represent comfort and an ease in life, both economic and emotional, that Bet is ready to embrace, even if, ultimately, it is a betrayal of her true identity.

Style

Setting

Throughout ''Average Waves in Unprotected Waters,'' the settings of different scenes augment the plot by mirroring Bet's feelings. Bet Blevins's apartment is crumbling and provides the ''feeling of too many lives layered over other lives, like the layers of brownish wallpaper.'' The description of the place mirrors Bet's feelings of suffocation and loneliness. Though there are ''too many lives,'' she is living hers alone and must act alone.

Later, in the train, the movement of the engine lulls Arnold and provides Bet with an opportunity to travel back into her memory. The journey motif occurs on two levels, on a physical level as Bet and Arnold travel to Parkinsville, and on a more symbolic level as Bet travels back in her own memory to find answers about herself and her life. When they arrive at the state hospital, everything is sterile and white and the story states that ''there wasn't a sign that children lived here except for a tiny cardboard clown picture hanging on one vacant wall.'' The environment elicits some action in Bet, who begins to tell the nurse that her son is a child who needs his ''special blanket'' and that he is not ''vacant'' but that ''there's a whole lot to him.'' The sterility of the environment mirrors Bet's perception of her son's personality. She finds him vacant and sterile, and she attempts to explain away these characteristics and prove that he is special and that he does have a personality.

At the conclusion of the story, the train station is described as ''bombed out—nothing but a shell.'' This mirrors Bet's life now that her son is gone. She has found identity as his mother and earlier as Avery's wife and her parents' daughter, but now, all these roles are completed and she is abandoned in a ''bombed out'' train station, without any of the roles that have defined her. Like the train station, she is empty, suddenly void.

Symbolism

Though on many levels setting plays a role as symbolism in ''Average Waves in Unprotected Water,'' by mirroring and representing characters' feelings and actions, the largest symbolic reference is expressed in the title of the story. The title, ''Average Waves in Unprotected Waters,'' speaks to Bet's memory of her childhood at the shore, when her father ''couldn't arrange his day till he'd heard the marine forecast. . . the height of average waves in unprotected waters.'' The marine forecast and the height of waves determined if the water was safe for swimmers. As a child, Bet's father tried to teach her to body surf in these average waves, but she couldn't do it. She just stood in the waves, ''as if standing staunch were a virtue.'' How does this tie into her life now? Instead of water, the ''average waves'' that appear in her life are the average troubles that appear in every life. They are the loss of a husband, the loss of parents, and ultimately, the institutionalization of her son. She is not the only one who has dealt with such troubles. Such troubles are "average waves" in the water of life. The symbol of "average waves in unprotected waters" acts as a metaphor. It simultaneously represents the true oceanic waves of her childhood memory and the rather ordinary troubles she faces in her current life.

Point of View

"Average Waves in Unprotected Waters" tells Bet's story from a third-person point of view. In "Average Waves in Unprotected Waters" this perspective accomplishes two things. First, it allows the reader to fully empathize with Bet's motivations and understand her position as she institutionalizes her son. Second, it allows Bet to suggest the motivation of the other characters. Bet's perspective induces the reader to believe that Arnold is both completely catatonic and potentially violent, that he has no personality and then that he may indeed have some distinguishing characteristics. Because of point of view, the reader is taken on a labyrinthine journey through Bet's psyche on this difficult day. The perspective provides unique insight for the reader into the inner workings of Bet's mind, while leaving doubts about Arnold, the nurse who is to care for him, and even the absent husband. Are their personalities and actions accurately portrayed as they are filtered through Bet's perception and memory? Tyler's choice of this point of view speaks about her motivations as a writer as well. She chose to look at the day through Bet's eyes and engage the reader through Bet's thoughts and feelings.

Historical Context

When "Average Waves in Unprotected Waters" appeared in the *New Yorker* in the winter of 1977, it arrived in a climate of economic instability and social sobriety. The 1970s, the post-Vietnam years in America, were marked by feelings of disillusionment. Working-class people lost faith in government, believing that their vote would not make a difference, and high unemployment created a sharp contrast between the wealthy and the poor.

Households headed by women, similar to Bet Blevins's in Tyler's story, were especially hard hit economically. Salary discrepancies for women and men working in similar jobs became a focus of the feminist movement, and efforts of the movement elicited slow change for economically disadvantaged female workers. The positive news for working mothers was a shift in social perspective that freed women to work and raise families without feeling social ridicule. More and more mothers entered the workforce out of financial obligation, but increasingly, women entered the workforce as they searched for self-fulfillment.

The search for self-fulfillment became a prominent theme in 1970s life, one that Bet shares in the story. She questions her identity and feels a palpable need to escape her current life and its hardships. Many Americans felt that need in the post-Vietnam era and, like Bet, were hindered in their quest by socioeconomic situations that greatly limited their possibilities.

The search for self-fulfillment led, for many, to a shift in priorities that placed personal needs ahead of family. This shift would ultimately mark the birth of the "Me Generation" that became prevalent in the 1980s. In the late 1970s, this growing attitude had a negative impact on marriages, resulting in a dramatic rise in the divorce rate. A society that had once admired marriages in which difficult circumstances were endured and obligations to others were placed ahead of personal happiness gave way to disillusionment and the normality of divorce and abandonment. Bet's absent husband, Avery, is an example of this trend and the relational wreckage that scarred many lives.

Self-fulfillment also led to rampant self-expression, which came in many forms, some of them unlikely, such as denim jeans. For rich and poor, the personalization of jeans in the 1970s provided contrast to the plain jeans and black, beatnik sweaters of the 1960s. Whereas only collegians and rebels wore jeans in the 1960s, jeans in the 1970s became a national uniform. In "Average Waves in Unprotected Waters," Bet worries that Arnold's jeans are not faded or worn enough, and that this makes him appear unreal. The use of jeans to symbolize her worries about her son's character is an apt one for the 1970s, an era when jeans helped defined the person.

The person of the president was defined in the decade first as Republican Richard Nixon, who resigned from office after the Watergate scandal and was later pardoned by his former vice president, Gerald Ford. In 1977, Ford relinquished his inherited presidency to a man many people called "the non-politician," Jimmy Carter. Formerly a peanut

Compare & Contrast

- **1970s:** The 1970 census reveals that three million women are raising families by themselves.

  Today: The 2000 census reports that over ten million women, many of them by choice, raise families as single mothers.

- **1970s:** Late in the decade, British scientists report that they have determined, for the first time, the complete genetic structure of a living organism.

  Today: Scientists from the Human Genome Project finish drafts of the human genome, one of the largest scientific undertakings of all time, and determine that the human genome contains between 26,000 and 40,000 genes.

- **1970s:** Post-Vietnam America, plagued by economic instability, widespread civic distrust of government, and an energy crisis, begins to rebound as government agencies concentrate on the domestic agenda.

  Today: Post–September 11, 2001, America, plagued by economic instability, concerns over national security, and threats of bioterrorism, focuses on a domestic agenda that strives to make America safe and economically stable once again.

- **1970s:** ''Let's talk about me,'' a line borrowed from author Tom Wolfe, becomes the unofficial slogan of America, creating an atmosphere in which people begin to publicly share personal history, strife, sacrifice, and turmoil. Complete disclosure becomes a distinctive national style.

  Today: American citizens tell their personal stories on daytime television programs and sell their stories to national magazines, while nightly news is criticized for featuring private glimpses into the lives of elected officials and celebrities.

---

farmer, then Governor of Georgia, Carter won the election as a Washington outsider. At the end of the decade, just as at the end of ''Average Waves in Unprotected Waters,'' an ambiguous view of government and patriotism took the stage. Bet is ''saved'' by the mayor in what she believes is a kind of act of fate. She believes that the government people ''had come just for her sake.'' As the decade came to a close, there was a similar public attitude toward government. The Democratic Party was leaving office and the country was welcoming Ronald Reagan and the Republican Party to Washington along with a new era of politics that promised to focus on individual needs.

Tyler's ''Average Waves in Unprotected Waters'' manifests 1970s ideologies, cultural phenomena, and values, but what is most notable about the story is that its time and place are relatively irrelevant. Tyler's story, and much of her other work, has a distinct universality about it that allows it to speak across generations. This is one reason this story, in particular, keeps cropping up in anthologies. Students of the text still find something relevant in its message and find the historical and cultural framework of the story easily adaptable to the current day.

Critical Overview

Like most of her short stories, Anne Tyler's ''Average Waves in Unprotected Waters'' has been largely ignored by literary critics. Though very little has been written about the text, the story does encapsulate the Tyler reading experience as it focuses on themes of family, self-discovery, and the elevation of the ordinary to writers' material. Broad criticism of Tyler's work is therefore relevant to the story and certainly pertains to the growth of Tyler's writing career.

Criticism began to really shape Tyler's literary success in the late 1960s, when her work was reviewed and praised by critics John Updike and Gail Godwin. John Updike, in particular, provided a certain amount of fuel for Tyler's career in his review of *Searching for Caleb,* as printed in *Anne Tyler as Novelist,* in which he says that Tyler is "not merely good, she is *wickedly* good." Charlotte Templin in her article "Tyler's Literary Reputation" in *Anne Tyler as Novelist,* says, "It seems safe to say that with one well-made phrase, Updike provided the nudge that raised Tyler to the rank of 'important writers.'" Templin suggests throughout her piece that Tyler's success has been influenced by critically timed reviews from literary giants and that her work's themes provide an "ideological and sociocultural 'fit'" for the American readership that makes them widely accepted and praised.

Tyler has been called a humanist, naturalist, and a romantic, whose influences are diverse. Alice Hall Petry, writing in her 1990 book, *Understanding Anne Tyler,* writes, "It would appear, indeed, that Tyler's true literary forebears, the figures within whose tradition she seems most clearly to be working, are the writers of the Concord circle, the great Russian playwrights and novelists of the nineteenth century, and the writers of the modern South." Petry also claims Tyler shares a connection to the romantics with her frequent focus on nurturance of self and self-reliance. The Anton Chekov connection that links Tyler to the Russian school of literature, says Petry, is apparent in Tyler's "skewed dialogue, non sequiturs, illogical trains of thought."

One of Tyler's self-acknowledged influences is the southern writer Eudora Welty. Robert W. Croft, in his book, *An Anne Tyler Companion,* recalls Tyler's essay "Still Just Writing," in which Tyler discusses Welty's influence on her work. Welty, "whose stories," Croft says, "taught her the importance of carefully chosen details and showed her the possibilities of writing about ordinary life," provided Tyler with a model for writing the ordinary that has become implicit in her work. Templin recalls a review by Brigitte Weeks in *Ms.*, in which Weeks made reference to Tyler's use of the ordinary and called Tyler's characters "Everyman" characters, or characters reminiscent of medieval morality plays in which the main character represented all humankind.

The realism and ordinariness of Tyler's work has been disputed by other critics. Templin writes, "Tyler has been charged with a tendency to present a false or sentimentalized view of reality and an inability to sound the depths of human experience."

Even Updike, one of Tyler's long-time supporters, posits that her books may lack substance. Templin discusses a Vivian Gornick review from the *Village Voice* in which Gornick attacks Tyler's lack of depth and calls attention to fear of experience in Tyler's work. She writes, "A pity: A good writer being rewarded for making virtue out of the fear of experience." At the same time, critic Frances H. Bachelder, in her article "Manacles of Fear: Emotional Affliction in Tyler's Works" in *Anne Tyler as Novelist,* defends the fear found in Tyler's work. She says, "Over and over, these people are driven by fear, and their adaptation to that fear is one of Tyler's central concerns."

For the most part, Tyler's work has become popular with critics, scholars, and recreational readers. Templin states that "Tyler is sometimes called an apolitical novelist, but it would be more accurate to say that she shares the politics of the American majority." Themes of ordinary life and broad political views have created a universal appeal and a mass popular audience for Tyler's work. From the academic and literary side, Tyler's psychology appeals to psychoanalytic critics just as her use of memory appeals to those critics writing about Jacques Lacan's treatment of the unconscious. Even anthropologists find something in Tyler's use of kinship to write about. The inclusion of "Average Waves in Unprotected Waters" in many high school and college anthologies is one example of how Tyler's fiction has been adopted by academic circles, and the thousands of paperbacks in print speak to her success with a general readership.

Criticism

Erika Taibl

Taibl is an English instructor and a writer. In this essay, Taibl discusses the difficulty of defining Tyler's work using traditional literary classifications.

Contemporary writers arrive on the literary scene with a force of history behind them. They arrive after major literary movements and eras and are sometimes compared to the romantics, the humanists, the southern school, or the Victorians. Sometimes a writer fits neatly into a category or the melding of a few categories. Anne Tyler, in a career that began in the 1960s and continues today, has been compared to all of these seemingly disparate schools and eras of literature. Not only can critics

What Do I Read Next?

- *Anne Tyler: A New Collection* (1991) contains three of Tyler's most critically acclaimed books published between 1976 and 1988: *The Accidental Tourist, Breathing Lessons,* and *Searching for Caleb.*

- In *Anne Tyler as Novelist,* David Salwak has collected seventeen essays by highly respected contemporary critics writing about the distinctive features that have earned Anne Tyler a body of devoted readers and critical admirers. The 1994 collection addresses major themes, characterization, and style in Tyler's work.

- Robert W. Croft's *An Anne Tyler Companion* (1998) provides a comprehensive look at Tyler's work and includes a listing of annotated characters, themes, and works. Croft also provides a comprehensive chronology of Tyler's life and influences.

- *The 1970s* (2000), a collection of essays written by respected historians and academics and edited by Mark Ray Schmidt, provides an overview of the major political, social, cultural, and environmental themes that shaped the 1970s.

- *The Misunderstood Gene* (2001), written by Michel Morange and translated by Matthew Cobb, provides a history of the gene. The book investigates what genes actually do and how they affect behavior and control life and death.

- *The Role of the State Hospital in the Twenty-First Century* (1999), edited by William D. Spalding, is a collection of critical essays that investigate the evolution of the state hospital and its future role in American society.

- *My Children, My Gold: A Journey to the World of Seven Single Mothers* (1994), by Debbie Taylor, discusses the experiences of single mothers from a cross-cultural perspective.

---

not agree on what category she belongs to, but they also cannot agree on how to read her work. Her prose has been called at once "brilliantly funny," by Robert McPhilips in his review of *Breathing Lessons* in *The Nation,* and "cute till it cloys . . . schmatlz," by John C. Hawley in his review of *Back When We Were Grownups* in *America.* Paul Gray, in his review of *A Patchwork Planet* in *Time,* calls Tyler's fiction "a fragile place sustained by hope and love," while Carol Iannone, in a review of Tyler's work in the *National Review,* calls her stories "faceless and thin." With so many conflicting adjectives used to describe Tyler's work, a reader may have a difficult time determining just where she fits. Alice Hall Petry, in her book, *Understanding Anne Tyler,* notes that critical attention "has consisted of efforts to fit her work into traditional literary classifications." She suggests that this is a difficult if not impossible task because of what many critics, including Laura Shapiro in her *Newsweek* review of *Ladder of Years,* call Tyler's

"literature of daily life." The widespread acknowledgement of Tyler's knack for portraying the ordinary is the complicating factor when trying to fit her into a category or even the amalgamation of a few. The ordinary, a focus Tyler shares with one of her major influences, Eudora Welty, can be all of the things mentioned above. It can be deep and it can lack substance. It can be schmaltzy and brilliantly funny.

Ordinary life in "Average Waves in Unprotected Waters" is the life of Bet Blevins, a single mother living with her son in a "rented room in an ancient, crumbling house." Really, there is nothing extraordinary here at all. Bet is simply dealing with a day in her ordinarily difficult life. Frances H. Bachelder, in her article "Manacles of Fear: Emotional Affliction in Tyler's Works" in *Anne Tyler as Novelist,* generalizes the roles of many of Tyler's characters, including Bet, as people "perpetually struggling to live decent lives despite the handicaps of a tormented inner world and a troubling outer one.'' At the beginning of the story, the reader knows only that something is happening on this day that is different than other days. Otherwise, Bet's concerns are normal, daily concerns. She is concerned that her son, Arnold, look clean. She worries that he not become agitated. She worries that they will miss their bus and frets over giving him gum on the train. All of these are the worries of an ordinary mother.

Most ordinary lives contain a twist, and it is not until Bet is on the train that the reader truly learns, though he or she may have suspected, that Arnold is handicapped. The twist in Bet's life is this burden, and the reader is meeting this ordinary woman on the day in which she is to institutionalize her son. Through characterization, or the way a character is portrayed, a reader may have guessed that there was something different about Arnold, but not until Bet begins to remember his birth is the full truth about Arnold revealed. Bet questions the ''evil gene'' that caused Arnold's disability. She wonders if it came from her or from her husband, Avery, who left when they found out Arnold was handicapped. Ultimately, in questioning the gene, Bet questions the beginning of life and identity. Throughout the story, Arnold's identity is vague. His jeans are too blue. Bet worries that he does not ''look real.'' It is his lack of identity and the origin of this lack that concerns Bet. Is it her fault? Did this handicap and vacancy come from her? As she recalls, ''she never could do anything as well as most people,'' and this revelation seems to include not only her biological contribution to Arnold's life but also her role as Arnold's caregiver.

As Bet wonders about her son and her worth as a mother, she also questions her own identity and the road she has taken to arrive at this time and place in her life. Bet recalls her ''old life'' that was ''beautifully free and spacious.'' The beauty and spaciousness of her remembered home is juxtaposed, or set in opposition, with her current life. As Croft states about many of Tyler's characters, ''the individual sometimes begins to feel restricted or even imprisoned.'' Because her life is restricted, Bet chooses memory as a way to understand. She recalls her father trying to teach her how to body surf, how before he could ''arrange his day'' he had to listen for the tides and the ''height of average waves in unprotected waters.'' Bet recalls being unable to body surf instead, just standing ''staunch'' and letting the waves ''slam into her.'' This whole series of images acts as an extended metaphor, or a

> Anne Tyler, in a career that began in the 1960s and continues today, has been compared to all of these seemingly disparate schools and eras of literature. Not only can critics not agree on what category she belongs to, but they also cannot agree on how to read her work."

story that ultimately illuminates another story. Here, Bet's past life illuminates her present life. Like herself as a child, Bet has yet to learn how to live flexibly, how to body surf over the waves, which are the ordinary problems that make a life. She stands staunch ''as if standing staunch were a virtue.'' She even stayed in the apartment after Avery, her husband, left her because she ''took some comfort from enduring.'' The average waves in unprotected waters are the ordinary problems and challenges that characterize every life. Instead of rolling over them and adapting to change, Bet lets these challenges hit her full force. Bet lets them ''slam into her.'' As Croft states, ''What to do in a world of change becomes a critical question for Tyler's characters.'' Bet's answer thus far has been to do nothing except to simply endure.

The act of remembering is critical for Bet as she deals with change. Croft says that Tyler rarely ventures far from themes of home and family, yet the journeys her characters make ''are nevertheless far-ranging, for they are journeys of self-exploration. During these journeys Tyler's characters attempt to learn more about themselves and their places in the world.'' Bet's journey through memory parallels the actual journey Bet and Arnold are taking on the train. As Bet's life literally changes, her memories help her determine how to live beyond this point. The journey on the train and the act of remembering are also necessary for the reader in understanding Bet's character and motivations. As Croft says,

''As she (Bet) rides along in the train, the reader becomes aware of the hardships and isolation that this brave woman has had to endure. Thus, Bet's decision to give up her son for his own good becomes more sympathetic and her action as an act of heroism.''

Ultimately, however, the action of institutionalizing her son paralyzes Bet. Arnold will finally get the care he requires from trained individuals, but Bet, who has identified herself as a mother and caregiver and has endured hardship, no longer has a son to raise or a hardship to endure. In one day, she has lost the things that define her, thus, it is her identity that is in peril.

At the conclusion of ''Average Waves in Unprotected Waters,'' Bet indicates that she is prepared to disengage from life. Life has become ''just something on a stage for her to sit back and watch.'' Bet's pivotal journey through memory has led her to a kind of understanding that does not initiate action but creates a kind of paralysis. Karen Levenback in her article ''Function of (Picturing) Memory'' in *Anne Tyler as Novelist,* says, ''The key to using memory wisely and well has less to do with realizing the significance of memories today than with what we do with this sense tomorrow.'' Bet's choice for tomorrow is to let go of life, to watch it rather than live it. For one who has defined herself in terms of endurance and standing staunch in adversity, the sudden freedom coupled with her perceived failure as a mother, creates paralysis. She idealized her ''old life'' as one that was ''spacious'' and free, but when provided with these very things, the decision to live spaciously and freely is too great a burden. She is the one, not her son, who ends up losing identity, because her identity has been so tied to the things she has just lost: her son, her family. Charlotte Templin, in her article ''Tyler's Literary Reputation'' in *Anne Tyler as Novelist,* cites a review by Vivian Gornick in the *Village Voice,* that talks about Bet's very decision to disengage. Gornick writes, ''A pity: A good writer being rewarded for making virtue out of the fear of experience.'' Gornick's reflection on Tyler's use of fear pertains to Bet, who finds the possibility of experience paralytic. But, the question about virtue remains. What is the reader to understand about Bet? Is she a hero? And is Tyler truly making virtue of Bet's fear?

What readers glean from this text has been and will continue to be a response to the elements of their own ordinary lives found within it. Gornick seems to suggest that literature should provide role models, or people from whom the ordinary person can model behavior. With Bet, Tyler seems to suggest that daily decisions are difficult decisions and sometimes they simply get the better of people. Through Bet, Tyler teaches that learning to surf through the difficulties of life is perhaps the only way to ensure a future in which a person has enough energy and hope to remain actively engaged. Bet never learned to live flexibly, or body surf. She stood staunch and took every slam life had for her, and the end of her story finds her in a bleak kind of nothingness. A reader may not find something in Bet to emulate or model but may empathize with her hardship and realize that her choice is not the choice to make and not the life to emulate, but to avoid.

Tyler has been criticized for being either too rosy or too bleak, opposites that ultimately must be resolved by her reading audience. Just as Bet can be read as a hero and coward, so can many of Tyler's characters. The reader is the final arbiter of truth, and hence literary categories, which have emerged to explain the writing of contemporary authors and place them in tidy categories, do not work for Tyler. Her work defies pre-defined categories and does so under the guise of writing about average life. The ordinary life, it seems, is a multifaceted, nuanced endeavor that thousands of readers have found and identified with in Tyler's fiction. Readers of her stories and novels meet in Tyler's words what Croft calls the ''typical Tylerian situation—a person attempting to endure the hand that life has dealt him or her.'' Critics are conflicted about the typical Tylerian situation, offering both praise and criticism, which Tyler seems to suggest, throughout all her work, is just one of ordinary life's complications.

Source: Erika Taibl, Critical Essay on ''Average Waves in Unprotected Waters,'' in *Short Stories for Students,* The Gale Group, 2003.

Frank Pool

Pool has published poetry and reviews in a number of literary journals. He teaches Advanced Placement and International Baccalaureate English in Austin, Texas. In this essay, Pool identifies themes and imagery in the short story which are characteristic of the author.

Anne Tyler is a prolific novelist who has developed a strong literary reputation. Writing in the *New York Times Book Review*, Gail Godwin has said,

''Her fiction is filled with displaced persons who persist stubbornly in their own destinies. They are 'oddballs,' visionaries, lonely souls, but she has a way of transcribing their personalities with such loving wholeness that when we examine them we keep finding more and more pieces of ourselves.''

The short story "Average Waves in Unprotected Waters," first published in 1977 in *The New Yorker*, centers on one episode in the life of Bet Blevins, a single mother who places her mentally disabled son in a public institution after having exhausted herself trying to care for the child. Although Tyler dramatizes only the trip to the institution, the reception Bet and Arnold experience there, and the wait in the station for the train to arrive, the author uses Bet's reminiscences to place the traumatic moments of the story in the context of her life and her character.

Most of the story consists of the mother's memories and reflections about her son, her marriage, her parents, and the anxiety and guilt she feels in having to institutionalize the boy who has grown too large and too wild for her to control. It is apparent from the outset that her son Arnold is profoundly different. In the initial paragraph Tyler, describes the boy as "a knobby child with great glassy eyes and her own fair hair," emphasizing both his distance from the world and his closeness to her. Unlike normal children, he never wears out his clothes, and he seldom changes his expression. Although the precise nature of Arnold's problem is never explained, it is evident that he is utterly incapable of growing into a self-supporting individual. Unaided by husband or family, Bet has been worn out by the efforts she has made to care for her son. Tyler typically shows Bet or other characters speaking or in action; then she makes a transition into Bet's thoughts and imagination, preoccupied as they are by her son's predicament.

Bet struggles both with her son and with a shabby, depressing poverty. They live in rented rooms in an old house, where "there was always the feel of too many lives layered over other lives." She wears a worn beige dress that visually echoes the brownness of the wallpaper that Arnold peels from the corner. The color brown also appears in the corduroy coat he wears, one he does not like, but which has set her back half a week's pay.

Tyler's imagery further reinforces the emotional bleakness of the piece. "She felt too slight and frail, too wispy for all she had to do today." This early in the story, it is still unclear to the reader what will happen, but Tyler foreshadows the outcome by portraying the emotional devastation of a neighbor, old Mrs. Puckett, who, with tears in her eyes, presents Arnold his favorite cookies, though

> **Perhaps her tragic flaw and her greatest virtue arise from the same source. She is a woman who 'took comfort from enduring.' . . . Tyler often writes of characters who manage to endure what life throws at them."**

he is too distracted to take them. Bet hopes Arnold might make his "little crowing noise" to the old woman. Bet immediately feels guilty again, but she tells herself that she has done the best she could, only giving up when the child grew to be too much for her to handle.

On the bus and train to their destination, Bet constantly worries that Arnold will make a scene. As Arnold becomes more quiet, fighting against sleep, Tyler explains that the child has never slept well, leading her to remember her husband's abandonment of the child soon after they learned of his disabilities. Bet alternates between guilt and resentment, alternately blaming herself, then her husband, for the boy's condition. This complex mix of emotions makes Tyler's story remarkable.

An author telling such a poignant tale must be careful to steer clear of sentimentality. If the reader comes to suspect that he or she is being manipulated into pity, then the story fails. In this story, Bet must be sympathetic but not pathetic. She has made some mistakes of her own, especially marrying too early, against her parents' wishes. She had wanted to get away from life at home with her parents, but now she remembers her parents, both dead, with a longing fondness she had not known as a girl. In retrospect, her life in a trailer near the harbor of Salt Spray, Maryland, seemed free and idyllic. Going far back into memory, Bet thinks of her father, who ran a boat that took tourists on fishing expeditions, and how for him "everything had been run by the sea."

It is at this point in the story that Tyler introduces the phrase that becomes the title. As a man who went out on the water, her father regulated his life by the weather forecasts, "the wind, the tide, the small-craft warnings, the height of average waves in unprotected waters." Good authors almost always choose titles that are significant to their stories, and this line is no exception. We may ask the significance of this phrase apparently unrelated to the main narrative of the exhausted mother and disabled child.

This central image, the key word being "unprotected," parallels the conflict of the story. Bet is utterly unprotected, having no husband, father, or mother to shelter or support her. Neither does she possess the financial resources that might partially alleviate the situation. She is a woman, presumably still fairly young and lacking advanced education, with a needy child and stuck in a low-paying job. She is average in all respects but one: her dogged devotion to her son. This determination proves to be in character, as Bet remembers her childhood, when her father tried to teach her to body surf. She failed to learn how, because she could not let the breakers take her away; instead she stood rigid against them, letting them slam into her "as if standing staunch was a virtue, really. She couldn't explain it. Her father thought she was scared, but it wasn't that at all."

Robert McPhilips, writing in *The Nation*, says, "Tyler's strongest card is her ability to orchestrate brilliantly funny set pieces and to create exasperating but sympathetic characters." There is certainly much that is sympathetic and admirable about Bet. She would never have left her husband, even before Arnold's birth, not even when the marriage had "turned grim and cranky." Her efforts to raise a profoundly disabled son, alone and unprotected, are nothing less than heroic. Additionally, though, Tyler suggests another side to Bet, a stubbornness of personality, a tenacious rigidity in the face of forces larger than herself. Perhaps her tragic flaw and her greatest virtue arise from the same source. She is a woman who "took comfort from enduring." It is difficult to fault her for her love and her determination to cherish and protect her child, and perhaps simple endurance might not have been her most fruitful strategy, but she acts according to the best that is in her. Tyler often writes of characters who manage to endure what life throws at them. In her novel *Saint Maybe*, the protagonist, Ian Bedloe, takes upon himself the burden of raising his brother's orphaned children. As he moves from a golden childhood to a harried middle age, he searches for redemption from his guilt over his small role in his brother's suicide. Bet Blevins also is consumed with guilt, yet she, like other Tyler characters, appeals to us through her humanity.

Following this passage of exposition, in which the author provides important information about the past, Tyler adroitly switches back to the present, dramatizing a little scene in which the conductor berates a small black woman in a purple coat for not paying her fare. This episode is simultaneously funny and sad and a bit grotesque, an illustration of Tyler's keen eye and ear for humor. Bet is mortified at the confrontation before her, but suddenly, inexplicably, Arnold starts to laugh. Something about what he has seen strikes him as funny, and he reacts the same way he does to "Sesame Street." This abrupt juxtaposition of embarrassment and laughter epitomizes the author's ear for the absurd and incongruous situations that make for off-beat humor in a very grim situation indeed.

Bet's plans, it seems, involve admitting her son to Parkinsville State Hospital and leaving just as quickly as she can. Something eccentric, even odd, emerges from her desperate attempts to flee. She nervously asks the taxi driver to wait for her outside the hospital, and she must reassure herself repeatedly that he will be there. Once at the institution, she is met by a nurse, who is brisk and polished though not particularly sympathetic. Bet lingers, trying to say things about her son. She adjusts a picture of a clown, the only evidence that the barracks-like room where her son will sleep was meant for children. The institution is cool and efficient, and Bet is conflicted and exhausted. On her way out the door, "she heard a single, terrible scream, but the nurse only patted her shoulder and pushed her gently on through." She rushes to the train station, expecting to get on the train at the last minute, only to discover that the train is twenty minutes late. She asks the ticket agent in despair what she will do for twenty minutes. Her obsession with getting away is not very rational, but she's a mother in extreme emotional pain. "'Twenty minutes!' she said aloud. 'What am I going to do?'"

She finds relief in an unexpected source. A crew comes in and sets up a lectern, some red, white, and blue bunting, and a public-address system so the mayor can make a twenty-minute speech. Bet is grateful for the diversion. The story ends poignantly. "They were putting on a sort of private play. From now on, all the world was going to be like that—just something to watch on a stage for her to sit back and watch." Tyler's protagonist has endured the unendurable. She has been so involved with watching out for Arnold for so long that now she disassociates herself from life, which becomes a thing to observe. She is still in unprotected waters, though the storm has passed, and she faces life with detachment and endurance.

Source: Frank Pool, Critical Essay on ''Average Waves in Unprotected Waters,'' in *Short Stories for Students,* The Gale Group, 2003.

Elizabeth Evans

In the following essay excerpt, Evans provides an overview of ''Average Waves in Unprotected Waters'' and explores the idea of the frailty of human safety in Tyler's works.

The Precarious State of Well-Being

When Tyler deals with the ever-precarious state of human safety and well-being, she shows how mysteriously disaster awaits us, whether in the genetic makeup of an infant or in the presence of a dangerous intruder. One of Tyler's best and most moving stories, ''Average Waves in Unprotected Waters'' (1977), confronts the problem of a mentally deficient child and follows the mother, driven to the limit of her resources, as she commits her son Arnold to the state institution. The disorder of agoraphobia is pervasive in Tyler's fiction, from the severe condition Jeremy Pauling suffers in *Celestial Navigation* to the somewhat lesser form of this disorder that Ira's sister, Junie, suffers in *Breathing Lessons.* Jeremy has not left his Baltimore street block for years; Junie will not step out of the Baltimore apartment unless she has dressed in full disguise, replete with a flaming red wig. As irritating and serious as their conditions are, they do not touch Arnold's severe malady, a tragedy for Bet, the anguished mother in ''Average Waves on Unprotected Waters,'' who ''felt too slight and frail, too wispy for all she had to do today.''

When Arnold's problem had become evident, Avery, the boy's father, abandoned the family. For a long time Bet agonizes over the reason for Arnold's condition: Was it from a bad gene her husband possessed? that she possessed? Was it because she and Avery married too young and against their parents' advice? No answers, of course, come, and she is left with the arduous daily routine of caring for Arnold and providing a living. On the day the story takes place, Bet dresses the child carefully and frets to keep him neat and clean during the train ride to the state institution—her gesture to show that Arnold *was* special, was cherished. As the nurse

> ''So, the title suggests, by arming ourselves we may avoid danger, may ensure safety. Bet, however, cannot protect herself or Arnold from the fate that was his from birth. Precaution cannot always guarantee safety.''

locks doors that will keep Arnold inside, Bet hears ''a single, terrible scream''—this unearthly sound is the last contact with her child.

With few exceptions, Tyler uses her story and novel titles within the texts themselves, thus deepening and layering the titles' significance. The title ''Average Waves in Unprotected Waters'' comes from Bet's childhood, when she lived with her parents in Salt Spray, Maryland. Her father operated a fishing boat for tourists and could not set out for the day until he received the pertinent weather information: ''the wind, the tide, the small-craft warnings, the height of average waves in unprotected waters.'' So, the title suggests, by arming ourselves we may avoid danger, may ensure safety. Bet, however, cannot protect herself or Arnold from the fate that was his from birth. Precaution cannot always guarantee safety. Tyler suggests by the conclusion of the story that Bet has suffered an extreme loss. As she waits out a 20-minute delay for her train home, local figures scurry about, setting up for the mayor's plan to take ''about twenty minutes of your time, friends.'' Bet watches, sensing that ''they were putting on a sort of private play. From now on, all the world was going to be like that—just something on a stage, for her to sit back and watch.'' Her real self was tied to Arnold, who is hers no longer.

Frequently in Tyler's fiction, characters must face the absurd twists of fate—those inexplicable chance moments that create an Arnold who, locked in his mental chaos, finally goes beyond his mother's reach. Or the irony of time that in ''A Misstep of the Mind'' causes what the rape victim, Julie Madison, describes as the worst minutes of her life. In this story Tyler exposes several layers of contemporary life in a world where neighborhood safety is no longer a fact and where the violation of rape is made worse by the indignity the police cause the victim, and even by the hapless blunders of neighbors.

Rape, the story insists, implies the total loss of innocence, an episode that opens and closes the story. Tyler begins, "Julie Madison was raped and robbed on a Tuesday, a warm and sunny noontime when you would least expect anything to go wrong," and ends, "Yet what she remembered, after everything else had gone, was the packed feeling that the air has when an intruder lies in wait, the capacity for betrayal in a cheerful world where dust floats lazily in sunbeams, the knowledge that it is possible to die." The private trauma is counterpointed by the public dilemma: the police bombard Julie with questions about the man's physical description and his gun, their concern less over her experience than in their capturing the intruder, "because Baltimore had recently had a plague of burglaries by someone fitting the same description: tall and black, very young, wearing a pale yellow windbreaker." The old problem of racial tension comes full circle after Julie identifies the man in a lineup (his scar had floated persistently in her dreams), because she must on leaving the police station pass "a black family all dressed up and sternly erect." If this is the rapist's family, they give a picture of dignity far removed from the crime that has occurred. The racial tension that society endures is manifest in the reality of city life, where each day someone like Julie Madison discovers that "safety had crumbled in a second, as if it had never been more than a myth."

In concrete detail Tyler describes the plight of a private citizen caught in the world of police investigation. Julie must examine mugshots as a bored policewoman, ignorant of manners, "sighed and cleaned her fingernails with a door key." Then closed in the booth alone to view the lineup, Julie must obey these instructions: "If you can positively identify any of these men as having done you harm, you have ten seconds to call out his number." The real world, Julie discovers in this moment, is a far cry from the world of television, where a victim viewing the lineup could, if she chose, just take all the time in the world. This experience has marked Julie's educated, dignified, and sensible family for life, and Tyler's point hits hard: Julie Madison's mother has worked with the Urban League to find better jobs for blacks. Now she can only say of Julie's ordeal, "Oh, it's ironic." Ironic indeed, and

regardless of the complicated social conditions that precipitate such crimes, for Julie Madison, the safety she had assumed and enjoyed had indeed crumbled in a second.

Source: Elizabeth Evans, "The Short Stories," in *Anne Tyler,* Twayne Publishers, 1993, pp. 21–43.

Sources

Bachelder, Frances H., "Manacles of Fear: Emotional Affliction in Tyler's Works," in *Anne Tyler as Novelist,* edited by David Salwak, University of Iowa Press, 1994, pp. 43–50.

Croft, Robert W., *An Anne Tyler Companion,* Greenwood Press, 1998, pp. 1–14, 28–29.

Godwin, Gail, "Celestial Navigation," in the *New York Times Book Review,* April 28, 1978.

Gray, Paul, Review of *A Patchwork Planet,* in *Time,* Vol. 151, No. 16, April 27, 1998, p. 80.

Hawley, John C., "The 'Wrong' Rebecca: Review of *Back When We Were Grownups,*" in *America,* Vol. 185, October 8, 2001, p. 33.

Iannone, Carol, "Novel Events," in *National Review,* Vol. 41, No. 16, September 1, 1989, pp. 46–48.

Levenback, Karen L., "Functions of (Picturing) Memory," in *Anne Tyler as Novelist,* edited by David Salwak, University of Iowa Press, 1994, pp. 77–85.

McPhilips, Robert, Review of *Breathing Lessons,* in the *Nation,* Vol. 247, No. 13, November 7, 1988, pp. 464–66.

Petry, Alice Hall, *Understanding Anne Tyler,* University of South Carolina Press, 1990, pp. 1–21.

Shapiro, Laura, Review of *Ladder of Years,* in *Newsweek,* Vol. 125, No. 17, April 24, 1995, pp. 60–61.

Templin, Charlotte, "Tyler's Literary Reputation," in *Anne Tyler as Novelist,* edited by David Salwak, University of Iowa Press, 1994, pp. 175–98.

Updike, John, "Family Ways," in *Anne Tyler as Novelist,* edited by David Salwak, University of Iowa Press, 1994, pp. 11–119.

Further Reading

Chekhov, Anton, *The Comic Stories,* edited by Harvey Pitcher, Ivan R. Dee, 1999.
    The Comic Stories includes forty of Chekhov's stories from the simple and unsophisticated to the sophisticated and complex. As a student of Russian, Tyler read Chekhov's work, and many critics have observed a connection between the two writers' styles.

Hicks, George L., *Experimental America: Celo and Utopian Community in the Twentieth Century,* University of Illinois Press, 2001.

> Hicks explores American utopian communities and the effort to revitalize America using these models in the 1930s and 1940s. His exploration largely revolves around the Celo Community in North Carolina, where Tyler spent five years of her childhood.

Welty, Eudora, *The Collected Stories,* Harcourt Brace Jovanovich, 1980.

> This volume includes work from *The Curtain of Green and Other Stories, The Wide Net and Other Stories, The Golden Apples, The Bride of the InnisFallen and Other Stories,* and two uncollected stories. Tyler has said that Welty's ability to write the lives of ordinary people was a tremendous influence on her own work.

Women Writers of the Contemporary South, edited by Peggy Whitman Prenshaw, University Press of Mississippi, 1984.

> Prenshaw has collected twenty-one essays from respected authors and critics about contemporary southern women writers, including an essay by Doris Betts about Tyler and her work.

The Best Girlfriend You Never Had

Pam Houston

1998

"The Best Girlfriend You Never Had" is the first story in Pam Houston's 1998 collection of stories, *Waltzing the Cat*, published by W. W. Norton. Houston won the Willa Award for Contemporary Fiction for the book. As in all of the collection's eleven interlocked stories, Lucy O'Rourke narrates "The Best Girlfriend You Never Had." O'Rourke is a thirty-one-year-old photographer obsessed with finding lasting love. Comprised of a series of anecdotes and reflections in which O'Rourke recounts traumatic childhood episodes with her parents and key events of past relationships—those of her friends and hers—"The Best Girlfriend You Never Had" meanders along rather than charging ahead, while musing on the near-impossibility of finding a suitable partner. In this sense, the story is more of a collage of various encounters and insights that comments on a theme rather than a single story with a unified beginning, middle, and end. O'Rourke introduces characters such as her best friend, Leo, a stand-offish "boyfriend" named Josh, and Lucy's girlfriend, Thea, all of whom appear in other stories in the collection. Houston established her reputation by writing about her attraction to men she knows are inappropriate for her, and this theme also permeates many of these stories. John Updike included the story in the collection *Best American Short Stories of the Century* in 2000.

Author Biography

When Pam Houston published her first collection of stories, *Cowboys Are My Weakness*, in 1992, she established herself as a promising young American fiction writer and a model for women who aspired to a life of outdoor adventure. Houston drew on her experiences as river guide, rafter, rock climber, skier, and extreme backpacker for the stories, and critics favorably compared her to writers such as Ernest Hemingway and Richard Ford, who similarly extol the joys of confronting the natural world head-on. Born in 1962 in New Jersey, the only child of a businessman and an actress, Houston grew up practicing to be a world-class tennis player, largely to please her father. After winning a tournament at thirteen, she gave up the sport for good. Houston pursued a life of adventure in earnest after graduating from Denison University in Ohio, bicycling through Canada and down to Colorado. After a series of odd jobs such as bartending, working on road crews, teaching skiing, etc., Houston entered the doctoral program in creative writing at the University of Utah. She left six months short of completing her degree.

Houston's second collection, *Waltzing the Cat* (1998), which contains her popular story "The Best Girlfriend You Never Had," was as popular as her first, and publications such as *Mirabella, Mademoiselle, The New York Times, Elle,* and *Vogue* solicited essays and stories from her. A licensed river and hunting guide and seasoned horserider, Houston created characters like herself: tough, daring women who fall in love easily and have their hearts broken. In addition to her story collections, Houston has edited *Women on Hunting: Essays, Fiction, and Poetry* (1994), and written the text for *Men Before Ten A.M.* (1997), a collection of photographs by French photographer Veronique Vial of male celebrities just waking up. In her book of essays, *A Little More About Me*, published in 1999, Houston writes of her globe-trotting adventures across five continents in places such as Bhutan, Bolivia, and Traverse City, Michigan during a five-year period in her life. In this text, she also muses on topics such as body image, the right of dogs to be free, her addiction to adrenaline, and the importance of close friends. A dynamic reader and gifted teacher, Houston appears often on talk shows and teaches at writing conferences. Houston lives on a 120-acre ranch in southwestern Colorado outside Durango.

Plot Summary

Section 1

In the first section of "The Best Girlfriend You Never Had," Lucy O'Rourke introduces Leo, her best friend with whom she spends the entire day, and Guinevere, a Buddhist weaver Leo loves. The setting is the gardens of the Palace of Fine Arts in San Francisco, a romantic place and popular for weddings. Architect Bernard R. Maybeck designed the palace for the 1915 Panama-Pacific International Exposition, making his theme for the work a Roman ruin. The gardens of the palace are lush, filled with ponds, and surrounded by Greek-style buildings. After eating a breakfast of "flannel hash" (i.e., bacon and beets), Leo and Lucy read poems to each other, and Lucy snaps photographs of a wedding, though she is not being paid for it. "I always get the best stuff when nobody's paying me to shoot," she says.

Section 2

In this section, Lucy recounts the reasons she left Colorado and came to San Francisco, suggesting that she was losing her sense of identity to the landscape and to her friends. This is what she means when she says she felt sandwiched between Josh and Thea and was turning into "something shapeless like oil." Lucy believed the city of San Francisco could restore order to her life. She is proud when she recounts being surprised by a man in a wheelchair who urinates on her while she is walking in the city, likening it to a baptism. The Mission, where Lucy walks and shoots pictures during her first few weeks in San Francisco, refers to the Mission District, a gritty yet vibrant home to more than sixty thousand residents, many of them Hispanic. The name alludes to Mission Dolores at 16th and Dolores Streets, the oldest structure in San Francisco.

Lucy introduces Gordon in this section as well, describing him as a cunning and brilliant young man who knows how to work the system and manipulate people.

Section 3

In this section, Lucy returns to the present tense, continuing the description of her day with Leo. During a discussion about dating and options, Leo rhetorically asks Lucy, "Aren't I the best girlfriend you never had?" Leo is referring to the quality of the time they spend together, the subjects they discuss, and the intimacy they share, all of which are stereotypically associated more with friendships between women than with those between men and women. During their discussion, readers learn that Leo wants to have children and that Lucy fears admitting she is afraid.

Section 4

In this section, Lucy digresses from the present tense and recounts her history with Gordon and an encounter with Guinevere. When she says, "It took me less than half a baseball season to discover my oversight [about Gordon]," she means she found out that he was not the man for her in about three months. His fits of jealous rage poisoned their relationship.

Lucy confides in Guinevere things about Gordon that she cannot even tell Leo, such as his emotionally abusing her in public and her begging him not to leave her. Guinevere consoles Lucy, offering her a cookie and Kleenex, and tells her that she no longer strives to please men to the neglect of herself.

Section 5

In this short section, Lucy recalls an event when she was twenty-five and brought home a boyfriend, whom she thought was her future husband, for her parents to meet. She picked a type she believed her father would like, but her father told her, "Lucille . . . I haven't ever liked any of your boyfriends, and I don't expect I ever will." After that incident, Lucy stopped trying to please her father.

Section 6

Lucy recounts the first time she was mugged in the city, after seeing a show at the Castro Theater. The Castro Theater, a historical landmark and film house built in 1922, is in San Francisco's Castro District, the center of gay nightlife. Lucy's response to her mugger underscores her toughness and unwillingness to show fear.

Section 7

Lucy returns to describing her day with Leo. It is now mid-afternoon, and they lunch on seviche at a Mexican restaurant. Seviche is a spicy Spanish fish dish. Lucy describes the fog rolling "down the lanyard side of Mount Tamalpais," saying that it glistens "like Galilee." "Lanyard" is a nautical term for a short rope or gasket used to secure rigging, which is often on the leeward side of the ship. Here, it refers to the side of the mountain facing the wind. Galilee refers to the Sea of Galilee, a large fresh-water lake located in the northern portion of Israel. According to the Bible, Jesus recruited several of his disciples there, and also walked on its waters.

While telling Leo about her fight with Gordon, she mentions John Lennon. Lennon was a member of the Beatles, a famous rock and roll group of the 1960s and early 1970s. Lennon was murdered in New York City by a mentally ill fan in 1980. When Leo takes Lucy's hands and tells her, "I love you . . . I mean, in the good way," he means as friends, which in Leo's mind ranks higher than as lovers.

Section 8

In this section, Lucy recalls an event from her childhood when she accidentally topples a seven-hundred-pound urn on her legs, breaking both her femurs. She calls the six weeks she spent in the hospital recuperating "the best of my childhood," as doctors, nurses, candy stripers, and her parents lavished her with attention. Lucy says for the rest of her childhood she fantasized about "illnesses and accidents."

Section 9

In this long section, Lucy elaborates on the history of her relationship with Gordon, describing a time when, in a fit of jealous rage, he attempted to abandon her at a trailhead. Instead of being angry, Lucy begged not to be left there. She also lists a number of incidents from her childhood, such as the time a ten-year-old girl "rescued" Lucy from her parents, who were arguing. These incidents are meant as explanations for the adult Lucy's behavior. This is also the first time in the story when the narrator explicitly addresses the reader, showing an awareness of what their perceptions of her might be.

Leo recounts his own story of being mugged in this section, adding to the idea that San Francisco can be a dangerous place. A man who has been shot, and who introduces himself as "Bill," forces Leo to take money out of an automated teller machine at the grocery store and then makes Leo swear that he will call the man's girlfriend to tell her he is okay. Lucy is more interested in Bill's girlfriend's motivation for staying with him than she is in any potential harm done to Leo.

In the last part of this section, Lucy describes her split with Gordon, how he flew into a jealous rage when she talked to another man in a bar. Instead of inviting Gordon into her place when he dropped her off, she told him, "I want you to make your own decision." Gordon drove away in a fit and stalked Lucy afterwards, leaving messages on her door, tearing up her mail, and putting syrup in her gas tank.

Section 10

In this section, Lucy returns to the present tense and Leo. They are now drinking "late-afternoon lattes," and Lucy is talking about how overwhelmed she is with "want" and how she fears "that even if you changed everything right now it's late already to ever be full."

Section 11

Lucy returns to the past and an experience she had with her parents in Phoenix, Arizona, when they all met to attend a New Year's Eve college football game. Lucy was stopped by the police for running stop signs, speeding, and making an improper turn. She did not have her driver's license nor is she wearing her glasses. Her father, slightly drunk, berated Lucy while she interacted with the police officer, and her mother berated the father, yelling at him, "Okay now, on three, daughter, I wish you had never been born." Officer Jenkins felt sorry for Lucy and let her go with a warning, saying, "There's nothing I could do to you that's going to feel like punishment." At the party the family attended later that night, Lucy had another disconcerting experience with her father.

Section 12

In this section, Leo and Lucy borrow Leo's friend's sailboat and go for a ride. Lucy takes the tiller and races a much larger boat to the Golden Gate Bridge. When they sail under the bridge, Leo gives Lucy "an America's Cup hug." This refers to an annual sailboat competition. Lucy addresses herself in the second person throughout a good part of this section, saying things like, "You might forget, for example, that you live in a city where people have so many choices they throw words away, or so few they will bleed in your car for a hundred dollars." She's summarizing much of the information she's already presented, trying to calm herself, telling herself she's not really afraid. At the end of the section, she turns to Leo and admits, "I'm scared."

Section 13

This short section recounts an experience from Lucy's childhood when her father threw her in the ocean to see if she would sink or swim. Lucy's mother was hysterical, and two lifeguards charged to the rescue, but Lucy passed "the flotation test," and her father held her on his shoulders.

Section 14

Leo and Lucy return to the Palace of Fine Arts. Leo stays in the car while Lucy shoots a few photographs of the swans and of the "rose petals bleeding on the sidewalk." She fantasizes about being married under one of the palace's arches. In the final paragraph, Lucy says, "I'm scared" louder, admitting her fear to herself, feeling like the admission signals the beginning of possibility.

Characters

Bill

Bill is the person who mugs Leo, forcing him to drive to a Safeway and withdraw money from an automatic teller machine. Suffering from a gunshot wound, Bill makes Leo swear that he will telephone Bill's girlfriend to tell her Bill is all right. This mugger and his girlfriend play a role in Lucy's imagination, as Lucy wonders "what it was about her that made her stay with a man who ran from the law for a living." Lucy never meets Bill, but hears about him often, as Leo likes to recount the story of his mugging.

Gordon

Gordon is Lucy's former boyfriend. The son of "poor people, strawberry pickers in the Central Valley," Gordon, whose real name is Salvador, is a childhood prodigy, receiving a doctorate in literature from the University of California at Berkeley before he turned twenty and a tenure-track teaching job there before he turned twenty-one. Gordon, who craves attention from his unwilling mother, is obviously brilliant, and he and Lucy often spend their time reading poems to each other. However, he "had a jealous streak as vicious as a heat-seeking missile and he could make a problem out of a paper bag." After Lucy breaks up with him, he terrorizes her to the point that she believes it is entirely possible that he will kill her.

Media Adaptations

- Houston reads stories from *Waltzing the Cat* on an audiocassette of the same name, published in 1998 by Publishing Mills. The same company has released a tape of Houston reading stories from her first collection, *Cowboys Are My Weakness* (1992).

Guinevere

Guinevere is a Buddhist weaver who lives on Belvedere Island. Leo is in love with her but she scarcely pays him any attention. She, in turn, is in love with a man from New York City "who told her in a letter that the only thing better than three thousand miles between him and the object of his desire would be if she had a terminal illness." Guinevere lives an austere and disciplined life, believes that "choices can't be good or bad," and is through with making compromises to please men. She is also friends with Lucy, who confides in Guinevere that she is in love with Gordon.

Jeffrey

Jeffrey was Lucy's boyfriend when she was twenty-five. He comes from a good family, is cultured, has a masters of business administration degree from Harvard University, plays golf in exclusive clubs, and is the type of boyfriend that Lucy believes her father would like.

Josh

Josh is another of Lucy's former boyfriends and is mentioned only briefly in the story. Lucy describes him as someone "who didn't want nearly enough from me," suggesting that the failure of their relationship to develop is partly responsible for her leaving Colorado for San Francisco.

Leo

Leo is a thirty-six-year-old witty, yet slightly depressed architect and Lucy's best friend. He ut-
ters the words that become the story's title, at one point asking Lucy, "Aren't I the best girlfriend you never had?" Like Lucy, he grew up on the East Coast, "eating Birds Eye frozen vegetables and Swanson's deep-dish meat pies on TV trays next to our parents and their third martinis, watching television and talking about anything on earth except what was wrong." Leo and Lucy spend a great deal of time together, discussing love and relationships. Although Lucy sees Leo as a potential mate, Leo sees Lucy as more of a sister. Like Lucy, Leo is also looking for someone to love. He considers suicide at one point after a relationship does not work out and claims that he wants to have children. However, he is antagonistic towards marriage, calling the bridegroom at the wedding he and Lucy watch in the gardens of the Palace of Fine Arts a "sucker."

Lucy O'Rourke

Lucy O'Rourke, a thirty-one-year-old freelance photographer, is the narrator of the story. She is tough, dreamy, and vulnerable, though not naive. In the story's present, she interacts primarily with Leo, an architect to whom she is attracted but who is in love with someone else. O'Rourke's descriptions of her friends, such as Leo and Guinevere, invariably include their inability to find lasting love. O'Rourke views almost every male as a potential partner, sizing up his suitability as soon as she sees him. She moved to San Francisco from Colorado a year before the story opens, writing, "I thought there might be an order to the city: straight lines, shiny surfaces and right angles that would give myself back to me." O'Rourke envies others who have found love, such as the Asian couple whose wedding she photographs. Her own relationships tend to end badly. For example, her months-long relationship with Gordon ends because she loses patience with his fits of jealousy and his inability to communicate. O'Rourke suggests that her relationship with her father, an emotionally immature man who does not support his daughter, plays a large part in her inability to find an appropriate partner.

Lucy's Parents

Lucy's father is a stubborn, selfish, slightly sadistic man who dislikes all of his daughter's boyfriends and who does not show Lucy affection or give her the support that she craves. He drinks, smokes cigars, and is generally unpleasant and bitter. Lucy's mother, born in the Rocky Mountains, is protective of Lucy, loves to sing torch songs, and disdains her husband's resentment of their daughter.

Topics for Further Study

- Collect personal advertisements from local newspapers and online sources, and then analyze them. Consider how women describe themselves and how men describe themselves, and then how women describe the man they are looking for and how men describe the woman they are looking for. In class, make a chart of the similarities (if any) and differences, and discuss.

- Look at one or more family snapshots and, using these snapshots as a catalyst for memory, tell the *true* story of your childhood. Focus on the discrepancies between what the photograph implies about your childhood and what you remember the case to be.

- In groups, discuss the character with whom you most identify in Houston's story, and why. Name a member of your group as note taker and another member as spokesperson who will report highlights of the group's discussion to the class.

- Assume that Lucy O'Rourke's story doesn't end where it does but continues for a few more pages. Write those pages. What "next steps" does Lucy take after admitting her fear?

- Design a questionnaire to discover your classmates' attitudes towards marriage, then photocopy it and distribute it to the class. Make sure respondents can answer anonymously. Summarize the data from the questionnaire, analyze your findings, and then report them to your class.

- Read the rest of the stories in *Waltzing the Cat*, paying close attention to how Houston develops the characters from "The Best Girlfriend You Never Had." As a class, discuss which characters seem to be most "fully drawn," that is, believable. Make sure to support your choices with specific reasons.

- Houston has received criticism from some women for the way she unabashedly describes her love for men. Are there ways in which Lucy O'Rourke can be considered a feminist (according to your own understanding of that term)? Discuss your answers as a class.

- Compare and contrast the dangers that Lucy faced in the city and the wilderness. Do her responses differ, and if so, how? Write a short essay arguing that Lucy demonstrates courage or cowardice. Be sure to provide examples from the text to support your claim.

- Do you believe that people are attracted to a particular "type" of person? On the board, brainstorm a list of characteristics of the type of man Lucy is looking for and the type of woman Leo is looking for, and then discuss whether or not you believe their desires are realistic.

- Some reviewers have called *Waltzing the Cat* a novel. In a short essay, argue for or against the idea that Houston's book is a novel.

Themes

Chaos and Order

With their relentless activity, constant noise, and swarms of people, large cities can be overwhelming, and city dwellers often move to the country for its peace, its trees and rivers. Lucy, however, does just the opposite: she leaves the country and moves to the big city, saying she "couldn't keep separate anymore what was the land and what was me." Her move to the city, then, ironically becomes a move to find order in the chaos her life has fallen into. "I thought there might be order to the city: straight lines, shiny surfaces and right angles that would give myself back to me, take my work somewhere different, maybe to a safer place," she says. Lucy's desire for order is also a desire for balance, a quality she admires in Guinevere and a term that appears frequently in her conversations with Leo. As an adventurer and photographer whose work takes her to dangerous places, Lucy has come to love fear too much. By moving to the city, she seeks to balance her emotional life.

City life, however, proves as chaotic as country life. Lucy falls in love with the wrong kind of man *again,* is attacked by a mugger, urinated on by a wheelchair-bound man, and remains as emotionally lost as she was when she came to the city. Only after she admits her fear to herself and to Leo is she able to face the chaos of her own desires and see the possibility of order in her future.

Self-Esteem

The idea of self-esteem is a particularly American one, rooted in a kind of pop-psychological understanding of the self. Columnists, school counselors, and even politicians are fond of claiming that a person's lack of self-esteem is cause for a variety of phenomena including laziness, aggression, divorce, crime, bad hygiene, etc. Houston describes Lucy as someone who suffers in her relationships because she lacks self-esteem, a lack she developed during her childhood. The anecdotes about and references to Lucy's father's mean-spiritedness and refusal to give young Lucy the attention she needs are meant as precursors to her craving as an adult woman to please men, particularly men who treat her poorly. Lucy's refusal to admit her fear of being alone and her toughness in meeting danger head-on mask her own lack of self-worth. By the end of her day with Leo, Lucy arrives at an insight about herself, finally able to accept the person she has fought so hard not to become.

Romantic Love

For the last few hundred years or so, romantic love has become inextricably linked in the Western imagination to ideas of marriage and to a person's sense of fulfillment. Lucy's desperate attempts to find romantic love contribute to the bad choices she makes in potential mates, and colors her perceptions of others. When she recounts an experience with others or describes people, she invariably focuses on whether or not that person is in love or what that person's prospects are for love. When Leo tells Lucy about an event during which a mugger held a gun to his stomach, all Lucy can think about is the mugger's girlfriend and what about the mugger made her love him.

The very setting of the story, the gardens of the Palace of Fine Arts during a wedding ceremony, has Lucy mesmerized with dreams of finding a husband. In the last scene of the story, she actually fantasizes about ''bow[ing] to . . . [her] imaginary husband'' in the gardens. Houston juxtaposes Lucy's longing to find lasting romantic love with her friendship with Leo. Ironically, this friendship proves more durable and substantive than any of the romantic relationships in which Lucy finds herself.

Style

Plot

Plot refers to how events and information in a narrative work are organized to achieve particular effects (e.g., suspense, arousing fear or apprehension, etc.) and to provide a way in which the author can develop her themes. Houston employs an episodic structure, incorporating flashbacks into her description of a day Lucy spends with a friend, Leo. Only six of the fourteen sections are in the present tense. By selecting flashbacks detailing Lucy's relationships with men and her parents, Houston asks readers to make connections between Lucy's present dilemma and her past. Plot is different than ''story,'' in that events do not have to be presented chronologically. Although the present tense sections of the story *are* ordered chronologically, the flashbacks are not.

Symbol

Symbolic imagery is imagery that carries with it a wide range of associations through its repeated use in specific contexts. For example, Houston uses the image of swans at the gardens to symbolize monogamy and lasting romantic love. Swans usually have one partner and mate for life, the same thing that Lucy desires. Bridges, although a part of the San Francisco landscape, also have symbolic associations, as they represent a safe way to cross dangerous territory. Lucy is looking for just such a bridge in her quest for meaning and love. Houston uses other symbols as well, such as naming the street Lucy lived on as a child ''Worth Avenue,'' signifying the very thing that the adult Lucy needs.

Setting

Setting refers to the place, time, and milieu in which a story takes place. The present-tense setting of the story at a wedding at the gardens of the Palace of Fine Arts is the most obvious symbol in the story, highlighting the very thing that Lucy wants but cannot seem to achieve. Instead of being the bride in a wedding party in one of the most romantic places in the United States, Lucy merely photographs the wedding, marginalizing her as a voyeur.

Historical Context

1990s

While Houston was chronicling Lucy O'Rourke's quest for love in the 1990s and recounting episodes from her dysfunctional childhood, the American family was changing. According to Stephanie Sado and Angela Bayer of the Population Resource Center, the median age for first marriage in the late 1990s was twenty-seven for men and twenty-five for women. But an increasing number of people were forsaking marriage to cohabitate. From 1990 to 2000, the number of unmarried couples living together soared from 3.2 million couples in 1990 to 5.5 million couples in 2000. However, the divorce rate declined during that time, from 4.8 per 1,000 to 4.2 per 1,000 in 1998. For dating, single men and women (and some married ones) increasingly turned to the "Personals," the classified section of newspapers and magazines in which people advertise for mates. Some women turned to books on dating strategy, such as Ellen Fein and Sherrie Schneider's bestselling *The Rules: Time Tested Secrets for Capturing the Heart of Mr. Right* (1996). In an affront to many feminists and progressive thinkers, Fein and Schneider provide a list of dos and don'ts for women who want to "catch" a husband, reinscribing traditional gender roles and forms of behavior in their advice.

The turn toward adopting more traditional gender roles was symptomatic of 1990s America, which, even though it had elected a Democratic president, was developing more conservative social policies. In 1992, while George Bush senior was still in office, Vice President Dan Quayle made a speech in which he criticized single mothers. Though many condemned his remarks, experts agreed that broken families play a large role in the disaffection of youth. In his essay, "Alienated Affection: The Ties That Bind," Walter Kirn notes that during the 1990s, "As the backlash against divorce progressed, state legislatures . . . called for a rollback of no-fault divorce laws and even for premarital waiting periods." During this time, Houston herself married a former safari guide from South Africa, Mike Elkington, whom she subsequently divorced.

Houston's book about O'Rourke's outdoor adventures was one of a number of books on adventuring published during the late 1990s. Jon Krakauer's 1997 *Into Thin Air,* for example, chronicles a catastrophic expedition up Mount Everest in 1996 during which eight people died. Sebastian Junger's first book, *The Perfect Storm: A True Story of Men Against the Sea* (1998), tells the story of the *Andrea Gail,* a swordfishing boat caught in a fierce storm in 1991 off the Grand Banks, and the fishermen aboard her who fought in vain to survive. The American public's hunger for outdoor adventure stories can, in part, be attributed to the increasing amount of time Americans spend indoors, often on the Internet. Houston's O'Rourke seeks a balance in her life between outdoor adventure, frequently putting her own life at stake shooting rapids and climbing mountains, and emotional stability. Though she pursues the former with passion, vigor, and grace, she cannot seem to achieve the latter.

Critical Overview

Reviewing *Waltzing the Cat* for *The New York Times Book Review,* Karen Karbo notes the stories' affinity with Houston's previous collection, *Cowboys Are My Weakness.* Karbo gives the collection a lukewarm appraisal, arguing that it is a "little shaky." Karbo writes:

> Half the stories are gems; another quarter seem as if they could use one more spin through the word processor . . . and a few are as slack as one of Houston's beloved rivers at the end of a dry summer.

Sybil Steinberg and Jonathan Bing, writing in *Publishers Weekly,* praise Houston's prose, claiming, "Houston describes Lucy's sporting adventures with cinematic detail, conveying both her technical prowess and the exhilaration of physical daring." These same reviewers, however, note that some "readers may become exasperated at the number of selfish, foolish, posturing men who wander into Lucy's path." Writing for *Booklist,* Donna Seaman describes Lucy O'Rourke as a "smart, funny, and fearless tough gal," arguing, "Nature is Lucy's solace, and men are her downfall, but Houston still infuses her transported readers with the belief that Lucy's willingness to embrace life will eventually lead her to love." Joanna M. Burkhardt, in *Library Journal,* highly recommends the collection, saying, "Houston speaks to Everywoman." Burkhardt writes, "The dialog, the decisions, the choices, the questions—all are crafted with preci-

The Palace of Fine Arts in San Francisco, California, creates the setting for Pam Houston's ''The Best Girlfriend You Never Had''

sion and with intricate and accurate detail.'' Yahlin Chang of *Newsweek* expresses a similar opinion, calling the collection ''wonderful.'' Houston hasn't been writing long enough for her work to garner the kind of academic critical attention other writers have, but that could well change if she keeps writing with the kind of energy and passion she has thus far shown.

Criticism

Chris Semansky

Semansky is an instructor of English literature and composition who writes about literature and culture for various publications. In this essay, Semansky considers Houston's characterization of Lucy O'Rourke in ''The Best Girlfriend You Never Had.''

The process of creating characters in fiction varies from writer to writer, but key ingredients of characterization include a character's physical appearance, how she talks and interacts with others, her thoughts, and her personal history. Houston charac-

terizes Lucy O'Rourke largely through her dialogue, behavior, and thought, but she also characterizes her through her personal history and her profession—photography. Lucy's passion for taking pictures is more than just a profession; it is a way of seeing the world, and it is integral to the way that Lucy tells her story.

The structure of Lucy's story resembles a photo album. In between her descriptions of the day she spends with Leo, Lucy sprinkles verbal ''snapshots'' of herself as a two-year-old child, as a teenager, as a young adult, and as a thirty-one-year-old newly arrived resident of San Francisco. Photo albums are intensely personal in nature and often are structured to tell a story—about an individual, a couple, a family, etc.—in pictures. The person compiling the photos chooses, consciously or not, photographs that illustrate how the subject changes over time. Conventionally, photo albums contain ''happy snaps,'' that is, snapshots showing the subject in the best light, smiling during a birthday party or goofing around with the family at the beach during a summer vacation. Photographs of unhappy moments or of events that undermine the idea of a less-than-content childhood or less-than-perfect family are rarely taken. Lucy's life, however, is recounted

What Do I Read Next?

- Critics often compare Houston's stories to those of Richard Ford. Both write about the American West and the complexities of love. Ford's *A Multitude of Sins* (2002) collects stories and a novella on these topics.

- *Cowboys Are My Weakness* (1992), Houston's first collection of stories, established her reputation as a serious writer. Houston writes about failed relationships and her adventures in the wild in this well-received volume.

- Many of Houston's stories take place on rivers. *The Whitewater Sourcebook: A Directory of Information on American Whitewater Rivers* (1990), by Richard Penny, is one of the most comprehensive coast-to-coast whitewater reference books available.

- Houston wrote the text to accompany Veronique Vial's black-and-white photographs in *Men before Ten A.M.* (1996). All of the photographs are of men as they wake up in the morning, including celebrities such as Peter Falk, Robert Altman, Kiefer Sutherland, Lou Diamond Phillips, Gary Oldman, Wim Wenders, and John Singleton.

- John Updike and Katrina Kenison co-edited *The Best American Short Stories of the Century* (2000), in which Houston's "The Best Girlfriend You Never Had" appears.

---

as a photo album chock full of just such moments and events. She remembers them because they illuminate her emotional impasse.

Four of the fourteen sections in the story are verbal snapshots of Lucy interacting with her parents. Like Houston, Lucy is an only child. These interactions help to characterize Lucy, giving readers a glimpse into her personal history. They function as a kind of explanation for why Lucy is the way she is. In all four sections, Lucy focuses on her father and the ways in which he withholds love from her. When she describes her parents together, they are fighting. Perhaps the most telling snapshot, if you will, is of a time when Lucy was four years old and she accidentally toppled a large urn onto herself, breaking her legs. She writes about her six weeks in the hospital, exclaiming that they "were the best of my childhood." Lucy loved the attention, "I was surrounded by doctors who brought me presents, nurses who read me stories, candy stripers who came to my room and played games." What's telling about this memory is that Lucy begins her story of the accident by writing that she was *told* this had happened. Her "memory" of the event wasn't so much triggered as it was *instilled* by years of hearing the story told over and over again by her

parents or other family members. This is similar to the way in which photographs construct memory by focusing readers' attention on what they see. What is excluded is forgotten. By having Lucy retell the event in the context of the larger story, Houston uses Lucy's personal history to create an image of the character in readers' minds.

Lucy's memories, however, can't be so easily dismissed. She is a credible narrator who presents the facts as they appear to her. Houston establishes Lucy's credibility both through Lucy's own self-deprecation and through the ways in which other characters respond to her. For example, when Lucy is stopped by Officer "Mad Dog" Jenkins for driving erratically while squiring her parents around Phoenix, and he witnesses the parents bickering about Lucy, he lets her off with a warning, remarking, "There's nothing I could do to you that's going to feel like punishment." Lucy's admissions about her consistently bad choices in men and her desperate need for male approval help both to establish her character *and* to establish trust with readers. By describing the incident at Point Reyes in which Gordon humiliates her and she lets him, Lucy presents herself as someone who is unstable but who cannot help herself. This kind of apparent

> " Lucy's profession as photographer is apt if one considers that by her own admission, she has difficulty separating herself from the objects she shoots and the men she loves."

honesty is heart-winning, as many readers are drawn to vulnerable characters that acknowledge their own flaws.

It makes sense that, as a photographer, Lucy thinks in images, so instead of telling readers that she has endured emotional abuse as a child and has repeated the pattern by seeking out a similar kind of abuse in the men she dates as an adult, Lucy *shows* this information to readers through description. The order in which she presents scenes describing her past is thematic rather than chronological. That is, she doesn't present episodes starting with her childhood and then work her way up to the present. Indeed, the last flashback she offers, near the end of the story, is of herself as a two-year-old. This kind of storytelling is organic; that is, Lucy presents the material as it comes to her, similar to the way that she "looks" for things, people, and situations to photograph. This kind of narration resembles the way that memory works, triggered by particular incidents in the present that have resonance with events from the past.

Lucy's profession as photographer is apt if one considers that by her own admission, she has difficulty separating herself from the objects she shoots and the men she loves. Photographs "freeze" action and in that way order the world, which is just what Lucy was looking for when she moved to San Francisco. Lucy writes that in Colorado she was becoming lost in the very things she photographed: "I had taken so many pictures by then of the chaos of heaved-up rock and petrified sand and endless sky that I'd lost my balance and fallen into them." Of San Francisco, she writes, "I thought there might be an order to the city: straight lines, shiny surfaces and right angles that would give myself back to me." Ironically, Lucy's practice of letting

her photographic subjects choose her, instead of choosing photographic subjects herself, means she has not yet learned to impose order on the world. She is drawn to her photographic subjects because they signify for her the life that she wants, but that has thus far eluded her. In San Francisco, she falls into what she photographs, just as she did in Colorado. At the wedding party, she snaps a photo of the groom kissing the bride, and later she takes a shot of swans swimming in pairs and rose petals on the sidewalk. These photographs become icons of sorts for the lasting love Lucy desperately seeks. In "An Interview with Pam Houston," which is part of the "Reading Group Guide" included in *Waltzing the Cat*, Houston, an amateur photographer, says she made Lucy a photographer so she could "use the metaphor of photography for talking about writing." Houston says:

> The two art forms seem similar to me in terms of framing, the way everything depends on what you leave in and what you leave out. I often construct stories as if they're a series of photographs, a series of sharp and particular images, a physical landscape that will stand in for the story's emotional landscape, that will carry and convey the story's emotional weight.

Lucy's desperation gives her story a sense of urgency. Even though very little happens in the present tense, the accumulated details of her history create a portrait of a woman on the brink of a breakdown or a breakthrough. These details result from Lucy's self-interrogation, and by "confessing" to them, she is taking part in the process of healing herself. The popularity of "The Best Girlfriend You Never Had" is directly related to *how* Lucy tells her story, for it shows readers a character capable of self-understanding and change. It assures them that second chances, and third and fourth and fifth chances, can happen, and that change is possible.

Source: Chris Semansky, Critical Essay on "The Best Girlfriend You Never Had," in *Short Stories for Students*, The Gale Group, 2003.

Susan Sanderson

Sanderson holds a master of fine arts degree in fiction writing and is an independent writer. In this essay, Sanderson examines the character Lucy O'Rourke and discusses how images of pairs in "The Best Girlfriend You Never Had" reflect aspects of Lucy's interior and exterior life.

"The Best Girlfriend You Never Had" is the first in a series of linked short stories about Lucy O'Rourke that make up Pam Houston's book *Waltzing the Cat*.

The story serves as a kind of introduction to Lucy and her life; Lucy remembers her childhood, her life as a young adult before she moved to the West Coast, her experiences in the San Francisco area, and her inclination toward dangerous activities and environments.

Lucy's character is a study in dichotomies. Images of pairs abound as Houston draws Lucy as a young woman caught in the struggle between her interior and exterior lives and between a life that is orderly and one that is frantically out of control. The movement and disarray that define Lucy's life prevent her from confronting the fears she has. The recurring double images are particularly poignant given that Lucy is in her thirties and gloomy over her prospects of ever finding the right romantic partner.

Lucy's exterior world is defined by couples, some successful and others less so. When the story opens, she and her friend Leo are sitting in a San Francisco park reading love poems out loud to each other and watching Asian couples celebrate their weddings amid beautiful black swans. This is an activity the two friends pursue on a regular basis. In fact, before they come to the park on the weekends, they typically have breakfast at a restaurant named for a couple, ''Rick and Ann's.''

But in Lucy's social circle, pairing off is not simple or perfect. She observes that she lives in a community where ''all the people you know— without exception—have their hearts all wrapped around someone who won't ever love them back.'' Leo loves Guinevere, a woman who can hardly remember his name when she sees him. Guinevere loves a man living on the East Coast who once told her, Lucy remembers, that ''the only thing better than three thousand miles between him and the object of his desire would be if she had a terminal illness.'' Though Lucy is dating a dangerously jealous man, Gordon, she is ''a little'' in love with Leo, who is emotionally unavailable and tells her he is ''the best girlfriend you never had.'' Lucy desperately wants her parents to love her, but they are too self-involved and drunk most of the time to connect with each other, let alone to be of any comfort to their daughter. One of the few happy memories of childhood for Lucy involves being in the hospital after an accident and having a cadre of caring doctors and nurses focused on her well-being.

Lucy's persona is split into two parts, as well, and much of the story is focused on her attempts to

> **"** Images of pairs abound as Houston draws Lucy as a young woman caught in the struggle between her interior and exterior lives and between a life that is orderly and one that is frantically out of control."

resolve the divisive inner issues that are apparent through her actions. It is as if there are two voices speaking to Lucy and, despite her exterior bravado, she does not know what she really wants or understand what she really feels. In ''The Best Girlfriend You Never Had,'' Lucy obliquely refers to an episode during which she failed to listen to her own fears about rafting a wild Colorado river and nearly drowning. The event is explored in more depth in the collection's second story, ''Cataract,'' where it is revealed that, though Lucy is an experienced river guide, she let a less experienced partner talk her into doing something she knew in her gut was foolish and dangerous.

The skirmish between Lucy's exterior life and her interior voice continues after she has moved to Oakland. Here, too, she has trouble listening to her own feelings and admitting when she is afraid. At the park, Lucy and Leo examine a flyer that warns of a car-jacking epidemic in the city and urges motorists to drive to a convenience store to exchange information with anyone who bumps their car from behind. Leo doubts that Lucy could ever follow this advice, because it would mean she would have to appear frightened. ''You're the only person I know who'd get your throat slit sooner than admit that you're afraid,'' he charges.

Lucy's desire for dangerous situations is evident in Oakland: ''I'd walk even the nastiest part [of Oakland], the blood pumping through my veins as hard as when I first saw the Rocky Mountains,'' she notes, and she gleefully recounts to her friends how she was ''baptized'' in one of those tough neighborhoods by a man urinating in public. The city streets provide her with the rush of adrenaline she needs—

"all those lives in such dangerous and unnatural proximity." Even when she is mugged, Lucy does not let on that she experiences fear.

Chaos surrounds Lucy, as indicated by her history as well as by her choice of men. By the time she is fifteen years old, Lucy has survived sixteen car accidents. When she is eighteen, Lucy is stopped by a police officer who says, after tailing her for a few miles and observing her break nearly every code of safe driving, "I really don't know where to start." The photographs Lucy took while living in Colorado are filled with disorder, and she remembers, "I had taken so many pictures by then of the chaos of heaved-up rock . . . that I'd lost my balance and fallen into them." She mentions to Leo that she can't blame men for not wanting to commit to her, because "if I saw me coming down the street with all my stuff hanging out I'm not so sure I'd pick myself up and go trailing after."

Lucy is a woman always in motion; before moving to California she lived in Alaska, in Colorado, and on the East Coast, and, as noted in the collection's other stories, she has pursued numerous physically challenging and often risky adventures around the world. Even when she decided to leave her rural life in Colorado for what she perceived as the stability of the city, her decision seemed rash. She packed up everything she owned for the trip to the West Coast but then "left behind everything I couldn't carry." Her move is an attempt to recreate a life away from the chaos and the danger. "I thought there might be order to the city: straight lines, shiny surfaces and right angles that would give myself back to me, take my work somewhere different, maybe to a safer place," she reflects.

Lucy's attraction to dangerous situations and her inability to listen to her gut feelings get her into difficult situations with the men she dates. For example, not only is Gordon insanely jealous, but he also displays a chilling violent streak after Lucy attempts to break up with him. He leaves messages made from cut-out letters taped to her front door and hangs scarves tied to look like nooses in her trees. Thinking back on Gordon's early declaration that "I take the people close to me and try to break them," Lucy wonders why "I could hear and didn't hear what he was saying, the reason why I thought the story could end differently for me." Lucy's interior voice—the one that comes from her gut—is speaking here, but she chooses not to listen to it. She has not had much experience paying attention to the self-preserving interior voice that advises her to run

to safety, choosing, instead, the bravado that has helped her face down a mother bear and her cub, a mugger, dangerous rapids, and a fractured family. The skills she learns from these experiences, however, ultimately cannot help her successfully deal with an abusive boyfriend or understand why she feels so alone.

But Houston has not created a character who is completely beyond self-awareness and the promise of a better life. Lucy is a very sympathetic protagonist precisely because of her many quirks and faults, and her eventual redemption—or, at least, the moment when she decides to push beyond the noise and distraction of her exterior life and listen to some of the very smart things going on in her head—is hinted at in the story. In a series of admissions, Lucy lets on that she has a vulnerable side. She begins by asking Leo if he is ever afraid "that there are so many things you need swirling around inside you that they will just overtake you, smother you, suffocate you until you die?" She goes on to admit that she is worried that her life has progressed too far to ever change.

Lucy's emotional breakthrough, of sorts, occurs when she realizes the substantial yet artificial dichotomy between her interior and exterior lives. After experiencing the thrill of winning an impromptu sailboat race, Lucy notices that she is "still so high . . . that I can tell myself there's really nothing to be afraid of." Suddenly, she knows that this is a lie—there *are* things to be feared in life—and she begins to list the things she has until now tried to forget: her car wrecks, the fact that she is without a loving relationship, and that Gordon might be waiting for her at her house with a gun, for example. At that moment, Lucy begins to see how she has used the chaos and constant movement of her exterior life to cover up the fact that her interior life is in shambles. When she tells Leo "I'm scared," he says he cannot help her. But when Lucy returns to the park where she watched the weddings earlier in the day and says again, "I'm scared," she is saying it to herself, "stronger, almost like singing, as though it might be the first step . . . toward something like a real life."

Source: Susan Sanderson, Critical Essay on "The Best Girlfriend You Never Had," in *Short Stories for Students,* The Gale Group, 2003.

Erika Taibl

Taibl is an English instructor and a writer. In this essay, Taibl examines how the episodic struc-

ture of Houston's story illuminates the story's larger meaning.

In Pam Houston's second full collection of short stories *Waltzing the Cat*, readers are introduced to Lucy O'Rourke, a landscape photographer with a penchant for failed relationships. Throughout the series of interlocking stories, Lucy's character is revealed as if by snapshots, where each story is a separate moment in Lucy's life. The episodic form the collection adopts, in which the stories remain separate yet loosely connected, allows for, as Randall Osbourne says in the introduction to his 1999 *Salon* interview with Houston, the voice of a dawning wisdom, the kind you find and lose repeatedly, and then begin to find more often. By the end of the collection and many of the stories, Lucy is finding wisdom more often and revealing it to the reader. Houston uses the snapshot effect in the collection to build Lucy's life but also in several individual stories to build a story's individual meaning.

Through these short, narrative interludes that resemble in words what photographs reveal through images, Houston ties together a day-in-the-life of Lucy O'Rourke with a smattering of other stories that ultimately give shape to Lucy's future. Together, the snapshots within the story portray much about how individuals learn about themselves—often little by little as a composite of experiences build into self-understanding. The composite Lucy is left with at the end of ''The Best Girlfriend You Never Had'' helps her to accept her single life and define a life as one that is not bounded by failed relationships with others but defined by a healthy relationship with herself.

Just as the photographer works with negative images to create a positive image, the brief, illuminating and factual narratives that comprise ''The Best Girlfriend You Never Had'' tell just enough about a situation in order to imply something more. In her interview with Osbourne for *Salon,* Houston talks about photography as the one visual art form she has any talent for. She says, ''It translated very well into what I was trying to talk about with stories and the way you make or save or erase your life with the stories you tell.'' In ''The Best Girlfriend You Never Had,'' the narrator, Lucy, chooses to recall certain stories or snapshots that illustrate her life. Some are destructive narratives. Some are victorious stories. Together, the stories help Lucy see herself in a new frame of reality. What have been negative images of her past life become positives.

> **" Together, the snapshots within the story portray much about how individuals learn about themselves--often little by little as a composite of experiences build into self-understanding."**

And what is not shown, to herself or the reader, but implied becomes as important as what is shown and explicit. The resulting image shows Lucy an accurate picture of herself and provides for a new image of the future.

What is explicit from the onset is Lucy's present—the one day in her life spent with her best friend, Leo. Glimpses of this day appear throughout the story and act as a frame for the various other recollections. Leo and Lucy spend their day, a perfect day in the city, acting out the perfect date. They begin by watching elegant weddings at the Palace of Fine Arts, an icon of romance in America. They read poetry and sail a boat. They almost torture each other by acting out an ideal that they know is not possible for them. Not only do they watch picture-perfect weddings with the knowledge that they are a seemingly impossible dream, they also dream impossible dreams about the people in their lives. Leo says, for instance, ''The only Buddha I could love is one who is capable of forgetfulness and sin.'' That desire is an inhibited one for Leo, since he loves a woman who does not love him but who loves another man—another man who thinks it would be ideal if she had a terminal illness. Here, illness is used as a great tease, a way to accentuate the romantic obstacles that enflame desire. Why such an emphasis on what cannot be had—the impossible? For Leo and Lucy, it just makes life easier. Being in love with the impossible is much easier than living through the risk that real love entails. The only big problem with desiring the impossible is that it creates a cycle of emptiness without fulfillment, what Lucy later calls, that *want* that won't let go of you. When Lucy begins to understand the dichotomies of her desires, for instance, how deeply she fears both love and the absence of love, she begins to understand the toll of unsatisfied wants and that satisfaction resides in herself and not in her relationships with others.

Leo, the best girlfriend Lucy never had, helps Lucy define a healthy relationship with herself. As the girlfriend, Leo is the one who shows Lucy what she is afraid of, what they need to and can be for each other, and what Lucy needs to be for herself. Their relationship is not complicated by sexual attraction and confusion; they are friends. He is the one to hold up the mirror and tell her, ''you're the only person I know who'd get your throat slit sooner than admit you're afraid.'' When Lucy finally admits, ''I'm scared,'' Leo is the one who says that he cannot help and implies that now she needs to help herself. By not having the answers, Leo is the best kind of friend, the kind that listens but does not give advice, the kind that supports and cheers without leading, the kind that lets the mistakes happen and is around to help pick up the broken pieces.

The best girlfriend Lucy has never had, though, is really herself. Sure, Leo is the best kind of girlfriend on the perfect day in the city. But, Lucy is the one who has been missing from her own life for all this time. Lucy admits she is afraid twice in the story. Once, she admits it to Leo, who not only tells her he cannot help her but implies that she must help herself. The second time, she admits her fear to herself in the park. Ultimately, Lucy is the one who must believe she is afraid and learn to cope with the consequences. The fact that the conclusion of the story implies that she is going to begin to live an honest life full of fear, as well as real possibilities instead of impossibilities, suggests that she is becoming the best girlfriend that she has never been.

Interspersed throughout this day with Leo are stories recalled from two sources, Lucy's own past experience and the lives of friends and strangers. Stories from Lucy's past reveal both moments she is sure to want to forget and moments when strength and courage are revealed to her in surprising ways. Sometimes, these are one and the same. Embarrassed, she remembers begging Gordon to take her back, and then she proudly remembers telling a would-be burglar to get lost. She remembers the story of her father and mother fighting in the car and her mother's suggestion that her father hates her. Then, she remembers surprising both him and herself as a young child by swimming far and fast. After confronting stories of rejection and disappointment in relationships that can perhaps never be healed and realizing that she's been waiting for

everything to fix itself and that maybe, just maybe, that isn't going to happen, she decides to integrate the lessons the stories of rejection and the stories of victory are telling her. She learns that she is capable of surprising herself and that she may be stronger than she perhaps believes.

The stories from friends and strangers also fuel Lucy's growing revelations. Guinevere tells Lucy about her own failed relationships and serves as an example of living life on her own terms. When Guinevere pulls a new age card from the deck that she disagrees with—one that suggests weakness or submission—she tosses it in the garbage. She is not taking the cards that have been dealt her; she is taking control of her own story. Guinevere is one of the characters to whom Susan Salter Reynolds, in her *Los Angeles Times Book Review* article, could be referring when she says that Houston's stories are full of useable wisdom. Guinevere is the one who tells Lucy, ''You only get a few chances to feel your life all the way through.'' She also gives Lucy permission to escape her choices. Lucy recalls her saying, ''Choices can't be good or bad.'' There is only the event and the lessons learned from it. Similarly, the story's use of episodes or snapshots mirrors this piece of wisdom as each narrative avoids passing judgment on characters or situations and presents the scene or situation as a photograph is presented—as image without commentary.

Toward the end of the story, the stories of others really help Lucy define her own story's future path. Lucy wonders about the girlfriend of the robber who kidnapped Leo. ''I wonder how she saw herself,'' she says, ''as what part of the story, and how much she had invested in how it would end.'' Lucy is realizing, at this point, that she is invested in her own story. The composite image that the snapshots are slowly revealing to her is helping her to really see herself. In her own voice, she says, ''I could tell you the lie I told myself with Gordon. That anybody is better than nobody.'' Here, Lucy starts to see herself clearly enough to become her own best girlfriend. Her sage advice is imparted through her own story. She admits that she lied to herself and implies that she did so because she was afraid to be alone.

The final episodes share common themes of survival and victory, and bring together the three types of stories that illuminate Lucy's future: those of strangers, of past life, and of the present. One story that Gordon told her recalls two suicidal bridge jumpers who meet up there on the walkway and find out they are both survivors of a previous jump. She doesn't tell us what this means for her, but the power of definition is implied. When one is suddenly found to be a survivor rather than a possible victim, life changes. The power of definition changes perceptions in life, and the implication as Lucy begins to change the definitions in her life is that she is changing into a survivor, too. The second story from Lucy's childhood recalls a story where Lucy's father threw her into the surf and waited to see her sink or swim. She swam like a pro, surprising herself and her father. This story implies that Lucy is capable of surprising herself and others— that this is still possible. The final scene returns to the present and the stories of brides. Lucy returns to the site of the weddings to take photos of the swans. Here, even the swans have paired up. Symbolically, Lucy bows to an imaginary husband and admits that she is scared. She is alone, finally and truly, and for the first time, she feels like she has a real life, something true, and wise, and lasting. The relationship in the end that defines all others is Lucy's relationship with herself. The composite image left after all the snapshots is a future with and as her true self. Echoing Karen Karbo's *New York Times Book Review* article, the story, like the collection, is far from perfect, but then, so are the characters and themes in Lucy's messy life. In a struggle for identity, future path, and happiness, self-knowledge is the gem that Houston unearths and polishes using a click of the camera shutter to reveal the self frame-by-frame until the whole, true picture is revealed.

Source: Erika Taibl, Critical Essay on "The Best Girlfriend You Never Had," in *Short Stories for Students*, The Gale Group, 2003.

Sources

Burkhardt, Joanna M., Review of *Waltzing the Cat,* in *Library Journal,* Vol. 123, No. 15, September 15, 1998, p. 112.

Chang, Yahlin, "Book Marks," in *Newsweek,* Vol. 132, Issue 16, October 19, 1998, p. 85.

Houston, Pam, "The Best Girlfriend You Never Had," in *Waltzing the Cat,* W. W. Norton & Company, 1998, pp. 15–45.

Karbo, Karen, "Out of the Wild," in *New York Times,* October 11, 1998, Section 7, p. 35.

——, Review of *Walzing the Cat,* in the *New York Times Book Review,* Vol. 103, October 11, 1998, p. 34.

Kirn, Walter, "Alienated Affection: The Ties That Bind," in *Time,* Vol. 150, No. 7, August 18, 1997, p. 57.

Osborne, Randall, "Kissing the Cowboys Goodbye," in *Salon.com,* January 8, 1999, http://www.salon.com/books/int/1999/01/08int.html (last accessed September 2002).

Reynolds, Susan Salter, Review of *Waltzing the Cat,* in *Los Angeles Times Book Review,* November 15, 1998.

Sado, Stephanie, and Angela Bayer, "Executive Summary: The Changing American Family," at http://www.prcdc.org/summaries/family/family.html (last accessed September 2002).

Seaman, Donna, Review of *Waltzing the Cat,* in *Booklist,* Vol. 95, No. 1, September 1, 1998, p. 64.

Steinberg, Sybil, and Jonathan Bing, Review of *Waltzing the Cat,* in *Publishers Weekly,* Vol. 245, No. 28, July 13, 1998, pp. 59–60.

Further Reading

Houston, Pam, "Creating Your Own," in *O, The Oprah Magazine,* Vol. 2, Issue 12, December 2001, p. 169.
In this nonfiction piece, Houston describes how she has cultivated a "rotating family" of friends as a substitute for the large family she never had.

——, *A Little More about Me,* Washington Square Press, 2000.
Houston's autobiographical collection of essays describes her globe-trotting adventures in places such as Botswana, the Grand Tetons, and the Himalayan kingdom of Bhutan.

——, "Redneck Chic," in *Los Angeles Magazine,* Vol. 41, No. 7, July 1996, pp. 90–100.
In this nonfiction piece, Houston describes activities in Los Angeles that are often associated with rural life.

Williams, Linda, and Jamie Jensen, eds., *Eyewitness Travel Guide to San Francisco and Northern California,* DK Publishing, 1994.
This travel guide provides numerous pictures and graphics explaining the architecture of popular buildings in San Francisco, helping readers visualize many of the places Lucy O'Rourke visits and names.

A Conversation from the Third Floor

Mohamed El-Bisatie

1994

Mohamed El-Bisatie's "A Conversation from the Third Floor," like most of his writing, is more like a painting than a typical short story. He creates a scene, then populates it with only essential and simple characters whose gestures speak almost as loudly as their few words. Denys Johnson-Davies, in the translator's introduction to *A Last Glass of Tea and Other Stories*, in which this short story was published, states: "While there is drama in his stories it is never highlighted: the menace lurks almost unseen between the lines." El-Bisatie, Johnson-Davies continues, "is a 'writer's writer'—which is to say a writer who makes no concessions to the lazy reader."

"A Conversation from the Third Floor" is a brief story, almost as short and succinct as the conversation that takes place within it; and it is as stark as the barren environment that encompasses its setting—a prison that sits at the edge of a desert. This makes it read more like a poem, in that every word, every gesture is laden with meaning. Just as in a desert a small patch of green grass screams with color, so too do the quick remarks and the subtle movements in this short story. A small shadow moving across the street toward one of the main characters suddenly becomes a threat, a potent omen.

Describing his inspirations and motives for writing, El-Bisatie, in an article written by David Tesilian for *Al-Ahram Weekly,* stated that he was "interested in the dehumanization of the individual

by circumstances.'' He also said that he writes about people who live in small villages where life is slow and "always the same, and if things happen at all, they happen beneath the surface." "A Conversation from the Third Floor" is an exemplary illustration of these sentiments. The careful reader who takes the time to dig down below the surface of this seemingly simple story will discover that El-Bisatie is not only a master of the written word but also a master of deception.

Author Biography

Mohamed El-Bisatie was born on November 19, 1937, in the Nile Delta in a place called el-Gamalia, Dakahlia, in Sharqiya Province, Egypt, a setting that dominates most of El-Bisatie's writings. He came into this world on a stormy night, as he informs his readers in his autobiography, *Wa ya'ti al-Qitar* (And the train comes, 1999), born to Ibrahim, his father, who was a teacher, and Insaf Rustum, his mother. His mother later told her son that the rain, lightning, and thunder of that birthday storm marked his personality, making him very curious about life and a bit troublesome. He was so difficult as a young boy that his mother at one point attached a rope around his waist, then tied the other end to a stake in the middle of the yard to keep him from causing further problems.

While he was still very young, an epidemic of cholera bore down on his village, and one of its victims was El-Bisatie's father. His grandfather moved into the family home upon El-Bisatie's father's death to help raise the young boy. El-Bisatie had the chore, as a teenager, of boosting his grandfather up onto the family donkey every time the patriarchal figure ventured away from home.

Later, in his teens, El-Bisatie moved away from his family in order to attend the University of Cairo, from which he graduated in 1960 with a bachelor's degree in commerce and accountancy. Although the Nile Delta area where he grew up figures in all his writing, El-Bisatie has never returned there. As his translator, Johnson-Davies, writes in the article "Village Life from Within" for the publication *Al-Ahram Weekly*, El-Bisatie has created such a vivid picture of his birthplace through his writing that "he does not want to risk having the canvas he has painted for himself in any way distorted by reality."

In the early 1960s, El-Bisatie began sending out his short stories to various publications. By 1968, he had written and published enough stories to have them collected in his first book, *Alkibar wa al-sighar* (The old and the young). Subsequently, El-Bisatie has published several more short story collections, including *A Last Glass of Tea and Other Stories* translated by Johnson-Davies in 1994, in which appears the focused story "A Conversation from the Third Floor." He has also written several novels, of which only one has been translated into English, namely *Houses Behind the Trees*, translated by Johnson-Davies in 1998. El-Bisatie is known in Egypt as one of the group of writers called Gallery 68, a reference to a literary magazine of the same name, known as a publisher of avant-garde writers.

After graduating from college, El-Bisatie began a thirty-six-year career as an auditor with Egypt's Government Auditor's Office, finally retiring in 1997. He also served as undersecretary of state in Egypt for three years, from 1994 until 1997.

In 1970, El-Bisatie married Sanaa Abdel Aziz, and together they had three children: Rasha, Hisham, and Yasser. The family currently lives in Cairo, Egypt.

Plot Summary

The story begins with the word "she," and the reader does not know this female character's name until her husband shouts it from inside the prison, where she has come to visit him; but this does not happen until later in the story. At first, the reader does not even know where the woman is standing. All that is told is that this woman has been here once before and that there is a policeman sitting atop a horse outside a long yellow wall. Inside the wall is a long building, and the policeman is trying his best to ignore the woman, who finally begs him to allow her to speak to someone. Who this someone is, where he is, and why the woman wants to talk to him remain a mystery.

When the policeman continues to ignore her, the woman adds, "You see, he's been transferred . . ." No further information is given, as the narrator then describes the weather and the time of day, and adds one more character to the picture, that of a small child, whom the woman carries. Then the woman is described as "quietly" moving away, without protest. She finds a pile of stones and sits down, staring at the building inside the wall. She sees a line of laundry hanging from the "bars of the windows." These bars are the first hint that the building might be some kind of prison. The clothes, hanging motionless by the sleeves and legs, are the second hint, suggesting lifeless as well as incarcerated images of their owners.

The woman stares at the dried mud on her feet and attempts to get rid of it by rubbing her feet together. The mud implies that she has walked a long way. Then she looks up at the third floor, an indication that she knows someone who might be there. Meanwhile, that narrator introduces another figure into the story, a soldier in a tower, confirming that the woman is standing outside a prison building.

Suddenly a man is shouting from a third floor window: "Aziza! Aziza! It's Ashour." The woman, Aziza, sees only two arms at first. She focuses harder and can just barely make out a face in between two bars. Other faces appear in the window as well.

The voice rings out again, calling her, asking her several questions in succession. Ashour asks about a letter he sent to her: did she get it? He asks about their children, identifying each by name. He also asks if she has been taking care of the property: has she pruned the date trees? Through his questions, the reader feels the emotions of this man, who misses being the husband of this woman, the father of his children, the caretaker of his home.

It is now Ashour's turn to focus, this time on the child whom Aziza is holding. Who is the child? Which of his children? Then he wants her to lift the child up, turn him to the sun, so he can see him better. When the child begins to cry, his father is joyful in hearing the young, wailing voice; he is also amused by the sound, "The boy's crying! The little so-and-so! Aziza, woman, keep him crying!" This sound must be like music to the father's ear. In the company of only frustrated men in the jail, the sound of his son is soothing.

Ashour continues to question his wife. He also asks why she is not speaking. Aziza tries to answer his questions with her hands or with nods of her head. Finally, at Ashour's prompting, she vocalizes a response. "Louder, woman," Ashour replies, and Aziza complies. She confirms that she brought the cigarettes that he requested, and Ashour disappears

from the window. In his absence, other men take his place. They are crude men who make obscene gestures at Aziza.

Aziza steals a glance at the policeman on his horse. She has spoken, despite, the reader can assume, a rule that denied her this privilege. The policeman seems oblivious, as does the soldier, who "had taken off his helmet." The heat of the day seem to have affected them, making them sleepy and uninterested in the conversation that is taking place.

Ashour reports to Aziza that instead of the five packets of cigarettes, he has only found three. He questions her, criticizes her, then steps away from the window momentarily and returns to apologize. "Never mind," he tells her, "a couple got taken, it doesn't matter." But of course it does. He needed five packets, but he understands that in prison, he has no choice but to acquiesce to others who have power over him. He tries to regain his composure; tries to calm her in an attempt to calm himself. To do this, he brings up another topic. Did she build the wall, he asks. When she tells him that she did not, he tells her that's alright, then reminds her to be careful on the tram. He next remembers that he is being transferred. Did she know? He does not know where they will take him, but he commands her not to return to this place. His last words to her are only to call out her name. He then gestures for her to move away, and he disappears from the window.

Aziza sits back down on the pile of stone and nurses her child. While sitting there, she notices a shadow coming toward her as the sun begins to set. When the shadow touches her toes, she draws them back. Time is passing. The laundry on the line that once was motionless is now flapping in the breeze. Earlier, Aziza had concluded that the laundry was wet and that was why it did not move in the breeze. Although she makes no comment about it now, the fact that the clothes are moving indicates that they must now be dry. When she looks back down at her feet, she sees that the shadow has "clothed the tips of her toes." She then stands up.

Before leaving, Aziza looks back once more at the window, but it is empty. She glances at the soldier in the tower but only sees the tip of his boot. When she reaches the policeman on his horse, he again appears to be sleeping. In some ways, the scenery has not changed from the beginning to the end of the story. Aziza leaves the scene, walking "down the narrow passageway toward the main street."

Characters

Ashour

Ashour is Aziza's husband. He is in prison for some unexplained crime. He is excited to see his wife. He shouts out her name, saying, "Aziza! Aziza! It's Ashour." The fact that he has to tell her who he is indicates how far away he is from the street where Aziza is standing. He must also ask who the child is that she has brought with her. The child is still nursing, so Ashour has not been in prison for very long. It is only that he is so removed from the street that he cannot tell for sure which of his children is with his wife.

It is obvious that even though Ashour has been in prison for a while, he is used to giving Aziza specific orders. He asks if she has pruned two date trees. He asks why she did not bring their two other children with her. He tells her to lift the child up high so he can see him; to turn the child toward the sun. When the baby begins to cry, Ashour tells Aziza to let him cry, then he tells her to quickly cover him to protect him from the heat. Next, Ashour chastises his wife for only sending him three packets of cigarettes when he had asked for five. Later he softens his tone when he realizes that someone inside the prison has taken the other two packs. Although Ashour's presence is felt throughout the story, his appearance is small and removed, just as he must have appeared to Aziza from the street.

Aziza

Aziza is the wife of Ashour. She stands at the outer perimeter of the wall that surrounds a prison in which her husband is incarcerated. She has come to talk to him. However, she is not allowed inside the wall. She has received a message that her husband is to be transferred, but she does not know where he will be taken.

She pleads with the policeman, but he pays little attention to her. In frustration but without giving up hope, she walks to the other side of the street and sits down. She carries a small child with her and waits in the heat outside the prison, hoping to communicate with her husband.

Aziza is quietly defiant. Although the policeman outside the prison wall does not give her permission to talk to her husband, in a short while Ashour appears at one of the windows. Aziza disregards the policeman and answers her husband's questions. She has brought the cigarettes that he requested, but she has not completed some of the chores at home that he asked her to do. She does not explain herself. She lets her husband come to his own conclusions about why she has been unable to do what he has asked of her. When he tells her, at the end of the story, to go away, she remains, but only for a short time.

Although defiant, Aziza accepts her role. She pushes the limits only slightly and only in desperation. She pleads with the policeman but does not demand. She has walked a long distance, carrying a baby in her arms in order to bring the cigarettes to her husband. There is no sense of complaint in her. She merely asks where her husband will be transferred, leaving the reader to assume that if she found out, it would be only so she could also walk to the new prison to deliver yet another package. She shows very little emotion. The only time that the reader can sense her feelings is in the few words that she says to the policeman: "Sergeant, please just let me say two words to him." Every other action and response that Aziza makes appear as if she does them by rote. She waits, she listens, she responds, then she walks away.

Themes

Disillusionment

El-Bisatie's "A Conversation from the Third Floor" is saturated with expectation. Unfortunately, most expectations lead to disillusionment. There is the wife, Aziza, who travels all the way to the outskirts of some barren land to visit her husband, who is in jail. She is told, when she arrives, that she is not to speak to him. She must visit with him while he is three floors above her and a wall and wide courtyard apart from her. She expects to see him, to talk to him, but the most that she receives is a glimpse of parts of him: his hands, his arms, his nose, part of his face. In order to talk, she must shout. In order to share her children with him, she must lift her baby over her head and expose him to the hot sun. Aziza came to find out where her husband would be transferred, but she was forced to leave without knowing.

Ashour expected to see all of his children but had to satisfy himself with seeing only his baby, the

Topics for Further Study

- Most of El-Bisatie's stories take place in small villages in rural Egypt. The author was born in el-Gamalia, Dakahlia, a small village bordering Lake Manzalah in the Nile Delta. Find as much information as you can about this area, the people who live there, and the way they live. Write a paper on your findings and make a presentation to your class, using as many illustrations as you can (maps, charts, slides, etc.).

- El-Bisatie moved to Cairo as a young adult and has lived in this capital city ever since. Research the history of this ancient city and write a paper that incorporates some of the more significant elements of its long history. Some questions you might want to consider are: Who were some of its most important leaders? How has the architecture changed over the years? What role has religion played in the political aspects of this city? How does the culture differ from U.S. culture?

- Ashour, one of the main characters in El-Bisatie's story, is imprisoned, but the reader is never told what his crime is. Research the political atmosphere, the judicial system, and the correctional systems of modern Egypt and then create a crime for Ashour. How might he have been tried? Would he have had a lawyer? What are the prospects of his ever being released? What is his life like inside the prison?

- El-Bisatie is often described as a painter who uses words to create his pictures. After reading ''A Conversation from the Third Floor,'' create a picture of the main scene of this story—that of Aziza outside the prison, looking up at her husband on the third floor. Include all the elements that El-Bisatie describes. Try to paint or draw them in a very simple style that reflects the way El-Bisatie writes.

---

one he knows least, and he sees the baby only from a far distance. His expectations are so meagerly met that he rejoices when he hears the baby cry, the only emotional response that he will receive. He also expected that Aziza would have trimmed their date trees at home and built a wall. Neither of these chores has been completed. When he asks about the cigarettes that he requested, he hurriedly rushes off to find the package after Aziza confirms that she did indeed bring them. He asked for five packs of cigarettes, but when he finds the bundle that Aziza had brought to him, there are only three packs left. Someone has taken two of them, a price that must be paid when someone is in prison.

As El-Bisatie has stated, one of the main focuses of his storytelling is to explore human disillusionment. As a writer, he never has his characters bemoan their disappointments. They experience them and accept them, as they are a part of their lives that they sense will never go away.

Lack of Authority

El-Bisatie intrudes into the situation of his story as the police officer sitting on his horse interferes on the actions of the people around him. Both are present but only in the most subtle of ways. El-Bisatie is of course the author, having created the characters and the scene. However, he appears to control very little of what is happening. He presents his characters but does not come to any conclusions. He presents the story only in the sense of a witness. He does not impute meaning to their actions; does not present interpretation that might explain what his characters are feeling or thinking.

Likewise, as a mirror-image of the author, the policeman on his horse represents authority. He sits above the people passing in the street, such as Aziza, who must look up at him when she pleads with him to allow her to talk to her husband. Although readers are not privy to a possible prior conversation, they can assume that the policeman has told Aziza that she is not allowed to talk to her husband. However, when she does finally talk, the policeman keeps his eyes shut, as if he were not there. He also does nothing when cell mates shout out of the window and make obscene gestures directed at Aziza.

The soldier in the tower is also ineffective. He paces a bit, shows signs of being affected by the heat, but he makes no motion toward Aziza or the prisoners when they are obviously breaking some rule. Also, for the prisoners inside the jail to be able to gather at the window, shout, and struggle with one another, there must also exist a lack of authority inside. Thus, the whole story is imbued with this sense of no one really being in charge. El-Bisatie writes as if life proceeds on its own course with little intervention, or maybe little opportunity to change it.

Style

Setting

The setting of El-Bisatie's story is very deserted. He makes it appear that there is little to describe. Readers learn of a yellow wall, a tower, a pile of stones, a string of laundry, a few faces at a couple of windows. There are only a few characters in the story, and all through the course of narration, the reader gets the feeling that no one else ever passes by on the street. The land is dry and lacking in vegetation, the village is lacking in structures, and the story is lacking in details. This creates a setting in which the reader senses a wide expanse of space, much like the space between Aziza and Ashour.

This sense of space in the setting also invites an impression of simplicity and where there are few people, few buildings, and few plants, one notices more subtle things. When an author describes his story in simple form, for instance, the nuances of shadow and light take on more importance. The simple calling out of Aziza's name conveys more passion.

If El-Bisatie's story were a painting, one might be reminded of Georgia O'Keefe's works, her scenes of the desert and the sun-bleached bones of cattle. El-Bisatie presents his stories in much the same way. He creates a setting with only the bare bones of construction. He hints at the surroundings and then allows the reader to fill in the images. He tells the reader that the wall is yellow, but he does not relate

what kind of yellow. He does not compare it to the sun, or a flower, or a fruit. It simply is yellow. Neither does he convey details about the type of materials that make up the wall or how high the wall is. This leaves the reader with a vague picture, one that is simple, because only simple facts and words were used to describe it. The setting, like the story itself, is presented as a somewhat incomplete picture, hinting at what is there without fully illustrating it.

Passage of Time

Time is presented not by hours on a watch but by natural occurrences. ''The sun had passed beyond the central point in the sky,'' writes El-Bisatie. Later, there is mention of the laundry that hangs outside the barred windows. Although there is a breeze blowing, the clothes on the line do not move. Aziza concludes that the laundry must be too heavy to move, thus it must be wet. Toward the end of the story, she notices that the clothes are flapping in the breeze and now must be dry. The reader does not know how much time has elapsed from beginning to end, but time has surely moved from one point to another. Likewise, there is mention of the shadow that the wall forms. First it is a thin line at the bottom of the wall. Later, the shadow creeps across the street. Finally, the shadow touches Aziza's feet as she sits and nurses her baby. Time, in this story, is measured only by the progress of the sun, either in its movement across the sky or in its ability to dry the newly washed laundry.

Imagery

The image of the laundry hanging out on the line not only portrays the passage of time, it also becomes a portrait of the prisoners' status. The men in jail, too, are hung up, entrapped, stuck in one place, waiting for time to pass, for someone to finally release them. They have been sent to jail to be ''cleaned'' of their crimes. In prison, they live out their time much like their newly washed shirts and pants; they are suspended, heavy, and lifeless. Once their time is done, they will once again flap in the breezes and be released.

The shadow that creeps across the street and finally encroaches onto Aziza's feet is likewise an image of time but it also has secondary representations. It is time as seen as darkness. Aziza's life without her husband is difficult. She must assume not only her role as mother and nurturer but also his role as provider and maintainer of the home and field. As time is heavy for Ashour, it is also depressing for Aziza. She waits, not knowing how long her husband will be in jail, how long she will have to wait for him, how long she will have to walk the many miles to see him, work the long hours. She watches the shadow, and every time it nears her foot, she moves away from it. When she can no longer avoid it, she gets up and walks away. The shadow is the approaching end of day. She must return home before complete darkness. She has no man to walk at her side. She must face the night alone.

Historical Context

Brief Political History

Egypt has one of the longest histories of all known civilizations, with records going back to about 3200 B.C. Situated as it is on the northeastern corner of Africa, with a land bridge connecting it to Asia, its prominence in the Mediterranean made Egypt a natural center of trade. The Nile River, which bisects the country, has a fertile delta that made it conducive to agriculture. These elements helped Egypt develop an early, as well as an enduring, civilization. These factors also made it ripe for invasion.

In 641 A.D., Muslim Arabs invaded and conquered Egypt, and ever since, Egypt has been a Muslim country. Despite several other invasions, which led to Egypt coming under the control of the Ottoman Empire (1805 to 1849) and later the British Empire (1882 to 1952), its official name today is the Arab Republic of Egypt.

The Land

Only one-tenth or less of Egypt's 626,000 square miles (slightly more than three times the size of New Mexico) are settled or cultivated. The rest is desert. Most farms and villages are located in the valley of the Nile, in isolated oases, or on land along the Suez Canal. Cairo is located just south of the mouth of the Nile, where the river splits into the Rosetta and the Damietta. To the east of Egypt is the Gaza Strip and Israel; to the west is Libya. To the south is Sudan. Conditions of weather and other natural occurrences make living in Egypt challenging. Besides hot, sultry summers in the delta, there are threats of periodic droughts, frequent earth-

quakes, flash floods, landslides, volcanic activity; hot, driving windstorms called *khamsin* occur in the spring, as well as dust storms and sandstorms. There are no forests or woodlands. Date palms are one of the few indigenous trees that grow in the delta, valley, and oases areas.

Environmental Issues

In an attempt to provide electricity for Egypt's growing population, the Aswan High Dam was built in 1970. One of the effects caused by the dam is that it has slowed the flow of the Nile and has trapped the rich silt that has, since antiquity, fertilized the Nile Valley. The waters of the Nile, upon which the entire population depends for drinking water and for irrigation, are becoming progressively more polluted.

The loss of silt, compounded by the spread of urban areas, has decreased the amount of agricultural land. To help boost the economy, Egypt has promoted tourism. However, the increased traffic, the construction of new hotels, and the subsequent increased pressure on the sewage system, have created their own set of problems.

The People

Egypt has a population of over seventy million people, and with most of them concentrated in the Nile Valley, there are, on average, almost five thousand people per square mile, with 45 percent of the population living in urban centers. Cairo and Giza, its sister city on the west bank of the Nile, have a joint population of almost seven million people.

Although there is a standardized Arabic language, only well-educated people can understand it. The rest of the population speaks a colloquial Egyptian Arabic, with a small portion speaking other ancestral languages, such as Berber.

Almost everyone in Egypt is a Sunni Muslim. Since the 1980s, a militant group, the Islamic Jihad, has been active in promoting the establishment of a government based on strict Islamic law. Traditionally, education was received through religious establishments. However, since the early nineteenth century, a public, state-run system has been in operation. Due to economic stress today, many classrooms are overcrowded and ill supplied. Although school is compulsory for children between the ages of six and fourteen, many children are forced to work to help supplement the family income. Only half of the population of Egypt is literate, with the highest rate of illiteracy, over 70 percent, among the adults.

There are two major socioeconomic groups in Egypt. The wealthy upper class and the Western-educated upper-middle class make up one group. The other group consists of the peasants, the urban lower class, and the working class. This second group encompasses the majority of Egyptians and represents Egypt's most grave social problem—that of poverty.

The Literary Arts

Ancient Egyptian literature dates back to 2755 B.C. and includes stories, instructive literature known as wisdom texts, and poems, among other things. Even in these early writings, such literary devices as simile, metaphor, alliteration, and punning are found. In more contemporary times, at the turn of the twentieth century, the Egyptian *Nahda* (Renaissance) began. Egypt experienced a revival of the literary arts, partially influenced by European journalists who brought more modernized views on the arts to Egypt. It was during this time that the short story and the novel form were introduced.

Egyptian literature was recognized worldwide when the author Naguib Mahfouz won the Nobel Prize for literature in 1988. Mahfouz is often referred to as the father of the Egyptian novel; however, many contest this claim. Mahfouz was responsible for popularizing the form. Book reading is not as popular in Egypt as it is in the United States. This, plus problems of illiteracy, variations in colloquial languages, and massive poverty, means book sales do not generate much income for writers. The difficulty in translating Arabic languages into English and other European languages impedes the popularity of Arabic authors on the international level.

Critical Overview

While El-Bisatie is a prolific writer and well recognized in his homeland, only two of his books have been translated into English. His minimalist style of writing, which is visually stimulating but lacking in drama, makes his works feel, to the general English-speaking public, somewhat incomplete. Despite this, many reviewers have praised his collection of short stories for their visual appeal. Most reviewers have enjoyed reading El-Bisatie's works. Their main complaint is that they want more.

David Masello, in the *New York Times Book Review,* describes El-Bisatie as a "generous host," although Masello refines his statement by adding that, in contrast to El-Bisatie's generosity, "his portraits of the people and places of the Nile Delta give only tantalizing tastes of this little-known region." Masello continues by referring to El-Bisatie's writing as being like "allegorical paintings," a reference that many critics use when describing the Egyptian writer's style of writing simple prose, describing the scene without interpreting what is happening in the story.

Brevity and simplicity are traits that El-Bisatie has mastered. His writing style differs not only from that of English-language writers but also from other writers of his own culture. As Johnson-Davies writes in the article "Village Life from Within" for *Al-Ahram Weekly,* El-Bisatie's writing makes "no attempt to either dramatise or romanticise the situations." Instead, El-Bisatie stands aside and allows his characters' "actions and cryptic conversations to speak for them and to provide the only commentary." Johnson-Davies comments that the subject matter of most of El-Bisatie's writing is the same, the "daily comings and goings of these [village] people and the small dramas and comedies of their lives." In another article, "Tasteful Fare," written for the same publication, Johnson-Davies comments, "Peasants are almost wholly invisible in Arabic literature and it is only in modern fiction that the peasant comes into his rightful own in . . . the writings of Mohamed El-Bisatie."

Writing for *Publishers Weekly,* Sybil S. Steinberg continues along the same line in describing El-Bisatie's writing. She states that these stories "follow a logic that is more visual than dramatic and portray a world whose rhythms are more cyclical than narrative."

Commenting for *World Literature Today,* Ibrahim Dawood calls El-Bisatie's book "a striking collection." Dawood adds, "The fact that Mohamed El-Bisatie grew up in the Nile Delta contributes to making his collection representative, documentary, and implicitly satiric of this region's lifestyle and problems." Dawood also points out that this collection of short stories "bears witness to the strict social customs and unbending rules which dominate life in the region in which the stories are set."

This small prison in Egypt sets a scene similar to the one portrayed by the narrator in "A Conversation from the Third Floor"

In describing El-Bisatie's writing in general, reviewer Sophy Proctor, for *Egypt Today,* states that the strength of his style "is its sparsity, its economy of language, detail and explanation." However, Proctor also finds that these same qualities can be "its weakness." Readers have to work when reading El-Bisatie's stories. Or, as some critics put it, El-Bisatie is not for lazy readers.

Criticism

Joyce Hart

Hart has degrees in English literature and creative writing, and she focuses her writing on literary themes. In this essay, Hart explores the drama that El-Bisatie so skillfully hides beneath his seemingly simplistic text.

Mohamed El-Bisatie's stories, such as his "A Conversation from the Third Floor," are often described as paintings. This description aptly fits El-Bisatie, who likes to create scenes to which only

the barest form of narration is applied. In other words, his narration is used to fill in the setting as a painter might use a brush to paint a picture. His sparse narrative is journalistic, in a sense, making El-Bisatie appear more as a reporter than a storyteller. His stories are told from what he sees, not from what he feels, and what the reader must do, in order to fully grasp and appreciate what is going on in the story, is pay attention to the intricate and subtle details that El-Bisatie offers. His stories may appear deceptively simple, but a studied reading reveals the depth that the author intended.

In the opening lines of "A Conversation from the Third Floor," El-Bisatie offers two descriptive sentences. In them, he conveys the message that a woman (whose name is not revealed) has come to some place (unnamed) and stands in front of a policeman. This is the basic information of these first two sentences, but there is a lot more being said here. First of all, El-Bisatie mentions that this is the second time that this woman has come. With the mention of this circumstance, the woman's intent grows a bit more serious. The fact that she has no name creates an atmosphere in which the reader looks at her much as the police officer sees her, as a nameless peasant woman. The details that this po-

What Do I Read Next?

- Kahlil Gibran (1883–1931) was born in Lebanon and later emigrated to the United States. Although he considered himself a painter, he is remembered most for his writings. His most famous work is a book called *The Prophet,* first published in 1923, which contains a series of philosophical essays on topics such as love and marriage. His *Broken Wings: A Novel* was retranslated in 1998, demonstrating a style of writing similar to El-Bisatie's. It was this novel that had the most profound effect on Gibran's fellow writers in Lebanon. Also by Gibran is *The Storm: Stories & Prose Poems,* retranslated in 1997, in which Gibran explores issues such as injustice dealt to the poor and the tender innocence of young love.

- For a female perspective on Egyptian culture, Miral Al-Tahawy's *The Tent* offers a glimpse into the lives of Bedouin and peasant women, exposing elements of their private lives. This novel is set in the desert and explores the sometimes abusive and oppressive nature of a dominant patriarchy. The author Al-Tahawy received her degree in literature at Cairo University. This is her first novel.

- Like El-Bisatie, Said Al-Kafrawi focuses on the short story form for his writing. Al-Kafrawi was also born and raised in a village in the Egyptian Delta, and his writing reflects his memories of those experiences. *The Hill of Gypsies and Other Stories* (2000) is his first collection of short stories to be published in English.

- Only two books written by El-Bisatie have been translated into English: *A Last Glass of Tea and Other Stories* (1994), in which ''A Conversation from the Third Floor'' is contained, and his novel *Houses behind the Trees* (1998). The novel is set in a small Egyptian village in which everyone knows everyone else and their most private secrets. In this story, El-Bisatie explores the impact of these conditions on the villagers' psyches when there is no running away from the past.

- In 1988, Naguib Mahfouz was awarded the Nobel Prize for literature. Born in Cairo in 1911, Mahfouz is considered one of Egypt's best writers. *The Cairo Trilogy: Palace Walk, Palace of Desire, Sugar Street* (2001) is an epic trilogy covering Cairo's history during its years as an English colony and demonstrating its effect on a Muslim family living in Cairo in the early part of the twentieth century. The story traces the lives of three generations. For a sampling of Mahfouz's short stories, *The Time and Place: And Other Stories* (1992) is a good place to start.

---

liceman is sitting atop a horse and is looking down at her give the reader the woman's perspective. She is not only nameless in this simple introduction, she is also belittled.

Next, El-Bisatie's narrator conveys a glimpse at the landscape and setting. The woman and policeman are in the middle of a long street that has a yellow wall running along it. Inside the wall is a nondescript building with windows ''that looked more like dark apertures.'' The overall feeling of this next section is that of unrealized tension. Why is the building surrounded by the long wall? Why is the woman standing so close to the policeman's horse? Why does the officer allow his horse to move so undirected while the woman is standing there? And, of course, why does the narrator describe the windows with the foreboding image of dark holes? In contrast to this underlying tension is the seeming nonchalance of the officer, who closes his eyes as if to sleep.

The woman then moves even closer to the horse. The horse responds by bending one of its forelegs, which gives this moment a sense of expectation. What will the horse do next? Will it move toward the woman in an aggressive manner to impede her progress? The narrator relieves the

" In order to find out more about her husband's welfare, Aziza must suffer the vulgarity of the men's reactions to her, just as she must bear the heat, the mud, and the journey to and from the prison."

tension by having the horse replace its hoof back on the ground. The horse, like its rider, is somewhat uninterested in this woman, who next offers the first words spoken in this tale. She begs the officer, not to see or touch her husband, but only to speak "two words to him." The policeman says nothing. He does not even look at her. She is of no significance to him.

The narrator never tells the reader that the woman is standing in front of a prison. However, the reader is able to deduce this fact from the barbed wire on top of the wall and the guard who stands somewhat idly in a wooden tower at the end. The tension of the story increases with the woman's second comment to the officer that whomever she has come to see will soon be transferred. This adds an element of urgency to her mission. Her sentence also ends on a note of incompletion, with an ellipsis, a hint of resignation or perhaps a loss of hope. This person inside the jail that she has come to see is important to her. She wants to know where he will be sent, when he will go, how she will find him on her next attempted visit. All these questions are implied, but never stated.

With a couple more strokes, the narrator turns up the heat of this story. The woman is carrying a small child. The afternoon sun is hot. The policeman's face is sweating. The woman walks away from the officer "quietly." She is carrying a heavy burden, but she does not want to irritate the officer who is uncomfortable in the afternoon sun. She has not given up, but she must protect her child.

When she looks up at the windows of the jail, she notices laundry hanging out to dry. This is the first glimpse she has of the prisoners, or at least a representation of them, hanging suspended above the ground, entrapped by the clothespins that fasten them to the line, "hung by the arms and legs." She fixes her gaze on one *gallabia,* a long, usually white shirt-like garment, possibly her husband's. The *gallabia* is usually worn in the country by peasants, so with the mention of this type of clothing, the narrator is providing more information about the characters of this story.

Everything in this part of the story appears still. Even the clothes do not move in the breeze. There is no mention of any passersby on the street. There is only the woman, who is now sitting on a pile of stones, her eyes half-closed, the police officer half-asleep on his horse, and the guard who leans against the wall of his tower, lazily scanning the sky and the rooftops of nearby houses. In this silence, the cry of one of the prisoners rings out, piercing the seemingly tranquil scene, not only with his yell but also with his emotion. "Aziza! Aziza! It's Ashour." Suddenly there is recognition, not only between the characters, but among the readers. The woman has a name, and it is Ashour whom she has come to see.

In a rush of questions, Ashour fills in many of the gaps of this story. This must be the woman's husband. He knows the names of their children. He knows the layout of the home they once shared, the chores that must be done. He mentions that he is being transferred. This is the same information that the woman mentioned to the policeman. Ashour also feels the tension of moving away to some unknown place. He flings his arms out of the window as far as he can to grab her attention, in a mock attempt to reach and touch her. He is hampered and ridiculed by his fellow inmates, who mimic his cries, his gestures. They press into him, invading his attempted privacy with his wife. He must fight them, push them away. He finally notices the baby in Aziza's arms and asks who it is. He's been away so long he does not recognize his own child. The child has grown, and his father does not know him. As he struggles to see his child, the inmates again hassle him. He is pulled away from the window. Other faces appear where he once stood. Again he must fight to see the child. When he makes it back to the window, he rejoices in hearing his baby cry, as if the child were speaking to him. He is so deprived of the voices of his children that even a cry is welcomed.

Ashour continues to question Aziza, who tries desperately to obey the commands of the policeman not to speak. She is torn between the authority of the officer and the authority of her husband, who shouts at her, telling her to talk. Without glancing over at the policeman, Aziza finally gives in to Ashour and answers not through gesture but with her voice. At first she speaks softly, but Ashour cannot hear her, so she is forced to shout.

When Ashour leaves the window to check on a package that Aziza has brought him, Aziza must endure abuse; a prisoner remaining at the window "makes an obscene movement in the air with his hand," and another man calls out her name and then lifts his *gallabia* and exposes himself to her. Her reaction is to smile, then look quickly at the policeman, then the guard, both of them oblivious to the insults as well as to her having broken their rules and spoken. She is caught between the crude remarks and her need to communicate with her husband. She must not draw too much attention to herself or demand too much of the situation. In order to find out more about her husband's welfare, Aziza must suffer the vulgarity of the men's reactions to her, just as she must bear the heat, the mud, and the journey to and from the prison. As more men call out her name, she nervously looks at the guard, concerned that the commotion will force him to tell her to move away.

Then there is the issue of the cigarettes. Ashour requested five packs, and Aziza has brought them as he wished. However, only three packs are in the bundle. By using this incident, El-Bisatie further illustrates the frustration, the lack of authority, the humiliation that Ashour must face. His wants are quickly diminished. Ashour, like Aziza, must resign himself to the particulars of his present situation. He is not a free man. Even his smallest desires will not be fulfilled. His wife, who has spent her precious money on the cigarettes, has done so, as it turns out, in part to please the guards, or whoever stole the missing cigarettes. This incident also illustrates a more general fact of all peasants' lives, who must bend their will to the landowners, always accepting less than their dreams. Finally Ashour laughs at the missing cigarettes, just as Aziza smiled at the obscene gestures. With their laughs and smiles, Ashour and Aziza demonstrate their lack of power to change their situations. In the social position in which they both live, it is better to make light of the abuses they experience. To scorn them is useless. Complaining would only bring more of the same.

As Ashour and Aziza say good-bye to one another, it is curious that El-Bisatie inserts the question: "Anything you want?" This question is not specifically attributed to either one of them. It is like a general question that either of them could have asked. The answer is "No," although the reader can surmise that the real answer would be so long that it would be impossible to delineate. Of course there are things that both of them want. They want to know where Ashour will be transferred. They want to know when he will be able to come home. They want to know how they are going to endure their separate circumstances—Ashour's inhumane existence inside the jail; Aziza's struggle to maintain her home, to care for and feed her children. They do not, probably in consideration of one another, offer any of these answers. It is simpler to respond with "no," although both know that the other is needy.

Then there is silence in the story as the two of them stare at each other's faces. The last voice heard is the simple cry "Aziza!" as Ashour wraps his arms around the bars of the window, a poor substitute for wrapping his arms around his wife and children. The narrator does not supply background information or interpretation that might convey the emotions of his characters. There is no need. The simple cry of his wife's name is filled with yearning. The cold, rusted bars that he hugs reveal his desperate emotional hunger.

Although Ashour tells Aziza to move away, she must linger. She has a baby to feed. As she sits on the pile of stones, a shadow from the wall slowly makes its way across the street to her feet. She recoils from it until she can move no more. Then she stands up and walks away so the shadow cannot touch her. This shadow is reminiscent of the description of the prison windows as dark apertures. A darkness fills the hole through which Ashour looks out at the world. A similar darkness attempts to fall across Aziza, but she does not let it.

The story ends as it began, with Aziza near the horse and the sleeping policeman. She again is walking quietly. The horse is again motionless, as Aziza escapes through a narrow passageway, returning, once again, to her world.

Source: Joyce Hart, Critical Essay on "A Conversation from the Third Floor," in *Short Stories for Students,* The Gale Group, 2003.

Carey Wallace

Wallace is a freelance writer and poet. In this essay, Wallace explores the way in which Mohamed El-Bisatie uses his description of the exterior setting to reveal his story's inner truth.

At first glance, it's tempting to think that almost nothing happens in Mohamed El-Bisatie's short story "A Conversation from the Third Floor," which first appeared in his 1994 collection *A Last Glass of Tea and Other Stories*. The plot is hardly complex: a woman, carrying a child, walks to the fence which surrounds a prison, asks for and is refused permission to enter, has a brief conversation with a man, who is forced to shout at her from the third floor, then departs. Even the characters themselves are arguably flat: readers are given almost no description of the woman, the man, and their history, and minor characters, like the policeman and the soldier, are so quickly drawn that they barely constitute sketches—El-Bisatie gives not one single detail to set them off in any way from any other policeman or soldier.

On closer inspection, however, "A Conversation from the Third Floor" is actually a story in which something of great importance happens: a woman sees her husband and the father of the child she holds for what may be the last time. It is the kind of meeting that people retain in their minds in unnatural detail and that she will remember, word by word, and incident by incident, for years. It is an incident to which the child will also return again and again, hoping to find clues to himself and his current problems in what he's been told and remembers about the encounter, whether he's really old enough to remember it or not.

El-Bisatie tells the story of "A Conversation from the Third Floor" in all the detail that the woman, with the acute memory of momentous happenings, will retain and that the child may wish for in days to come. The details El-Bisatie chooses to use, like the details our minds preserves, are initially strange: he spends far more time describing the barren landscape than the face of the man the woman has come to see. But at a second glance, we often discover that our memory has picked details for us that are far more telling than what we might have chosen consciously, and the same is true with El-Bisatie's choices: through his extremely detailed description of the setting, he subtly reveals far more about the underlying emotional truth of the encounter than the surface events of the story do. In fact, in El-Bisatie's world, the characters' surroundings often overpower them to such an extent that, in many cases, the setting actually begins to represent character.

"A Conversation from the Third Floor" opens with a brief depiction of a woman addressing a policeman, then moves into a very detailed description of the building beside them, in particular the "small, identical windows." Initially, this seems like a digression from the conversation between the policeman and woman. But, as the one-sided conversation continues, it becomes clear, through another detailed description of the barbed wire which lines the wall, that they stand before a prison and that the woman is trying to get contact with a prisoner—and suddenly, the windows he might be standing beyond become significant.

Still, not much is obviously happening. Everything in this landscape is static: the policeman who closes his eyes and refuses to respond to the woman's pleas, the shade which lies at the bottom of the wall, even the prisoners' laundry, which hangs limp on the line despite the breeze. Only the woman acts against this backdrop, imploring, moving the child from shoulder to shoulder. Even after the policeman makes it clear that he is going to ignore her request, and she sits down helpless, she continues to fidget, both physically and mentally, even making up a reason for the eerie stillness of the washing: it "must be wet."

To the reader, however, the lesson begins to be clear: this is a world in which, both literally and metaphorically, the overwhelming setting overpowers everything. Obviously, the walls of the prison have enormous power, separating the woman completely from her husband. But it's not just the prison that makes it difficult to move in El-Bisatie's story. The entire environment, inside and out, is oppressive and overwhelming—to the extent that some human beings, like the unmoving policeman, seem to lose their humanity and turn into scenery. In this world, it is the scene that matters. The human beings are just details, even to other human beings. This is driven home especially clearly by El-Bisatie's description of the soldier who, glancing out the window, looks at "the sky . . . the roofs of the houses . . . the street"—but doesn't take notice of any of the people in the landscape.

But the woman has a partner in her attempts to act in this suffocating setting. Just when she has run out of options, there's a shout from one of the windows El-Bisatie mentions in the very first paragraph of his description of the setting. It is the man the woman came to see, who has probably been alerted to her presence due to the delivery of the package she left on her earlier visit. Even here, however, he's no match for his surroundings: locked securely inside the prison, all he can do is shout and wave one arm out the window. In fact, this window already seems to have taken his place, to some degree, in the woman's mind. Sitting pensively outside the wall, she looks up, not to see his face but "at the windows of the third floor." And once she hears his call, she stares, not at him, but "at the window."

Still, the man manages to shout both his name and hers, for the first time giving them personal identity beyond "man" and "woman" and separating them from the more generic "policeman" and "soldier," who are dangerously close to disappearing entirely into the scenery. But even as he speaks, the man reveals that he, too, shares El-Bisatie's, and the story's, obsession with physical setting. His first concern is a change of scene: he's going to move from this place to another, he tells her. And then he asks about the physical conditions at the place he's left: "Did you prune the two date palms?" And when he finally begins to ask about human beings, his concern is still with place: he asks not how, but where, they are: "Where are Hamid and Saniyya? . . . Where's Hamid?"

For a moment, his speech seems to conquer the setting with humanity. The woman can see his face and even discern the other faces around him. When she looks around, she sees not scenery but human beings: "the policeman on the horse . . . the soldier in the tower." The man is able to catch a glimpse of the child. And even the inflexible soldier, who is closely associated with the rest of the oppressive scenery, withdraws inside the tower momentarily. But it's a short-lived victory, perhaps because the man himself continues to worry about the scenery, or the physical world he's leaving. He asks again about the date palms and then, in a gesture that seems at first to be motivated by humanity, tells the woman to give his regards to a friend. In the next sentence, however, he reveals that he sends the greeting in hopes that the friend will prune the palms for him.

Despite the man's concern with setting rather than humanity, the man and woman do achieve at least one more small bit of human contact. In her earlier visit, the woman was apparently able to smuggle some cigarettes to him. And this contact even seems to affect the landscape. Just after describing the delivery of the cigarettes, El-Bisatie adds that the soldier has taken off his helmet, allowing the woman a partial view of his head and making him solidly human, if only for a moment. But the soldier quickly puts his helmet back on, and

> " Through his speech, the man destabilizes everything that currently comes between him and the woman, letting her know that, although he may soon be interred somewhere else, the walls that separate them . . . are not eternal."

the woman's small accomplishment is clouded by disappointment: all five packets didn't make it to the man, as she intended. The setting, specifically the prison itself, has taken its portion. Frustrated, and perhaps angry at the man's remonstrances, the woman turns to go. The man calls after her, but when she turns back, it is not to him but again to the far less personal "window."

Again, however, his speech brings his face into focus. The woman can see him smile, and they steal a few more lines of conversation. Still, the man is concerned primarily with setting, asking, "Did you build the wall?" and giving her the details of his transfer. But it is in this exchange, when, in passing, he lets the woman know that "they're pulling down the prison," that the setting, until now all-powerful, shows its vulnerability. Through his speech, the man destabilizes everything that currently comes between him and the woman, letting her know that, although he may soon be interred somewhere else, the walls that separate them, the policeman and the soldier, and perhaps, by extension, even the blazing sun that beats down on her, are not eternal. And this revelation, that the seemingly all-powerful setting can be changed, leads to another, deeper revelation, the key to his concern about the tree and the wall at home: in this world where physical surroundings create such insurmountable obstacles, these small domestic details are his chance to change the scene, to build a wall which is not the prison's but his own. And just after this revelation that their physical surroundings are not as impenetrable as they seem, for the first time, El-Bisatie reveals not just the names of the man and the woman but their human relationship, naming the man as her "husband" for the first time.

Of course, the man is a prisoner, and his hopes for a change of scene at home still don't allow him to leave the prison walls at the close of this story. He disappears back into the cell, and his wife is again left ''looking up at the window.'' But as she did before, she continues to insist on her focus on humanity rather than scenery, stretching out her leg and suckling her child. As she does so, a remarkable change takes place in the surrounding scene, which is no longer static or impossible to act in. The shadow moves across the street. The laundry has begun to sway in the breeze. The soldier and the policeman, who have aligned themselves too closely with the now-vulnerable, paralyzed setting, now appear just as frozen in space as a wall or a tree— and seem helpless, rather than invincible, due to their lack of movement.

Perhaps most important, El-Bisatie finally breaks the connection in his language between the man and the window. In all previous references, the woman has looked up at ''the window'' as if it were, in fact, her husband in some way, as if the seemingly unchangeable setting had changed him into nothing more than an opening in a prison wall. But as she looks back for the last time, she sees that ''the window was empty.'' And in this seemingly desolate statement, El-Bisatie actually offers a note of victory. The man has not been overcome by his surroundings. He is more than a slot in a prison wall. He is a man, moving about somewhere inside the building which will soon be pulled down, full of his own plans for the change of scene he wants to create in the future for his wife and family.

And in the final line, the woman stages her own small rebellion against the oppressive, seemingly unchangeable setting in which she was forced to meet with her husband: she changes it completely, simply by walking away.

Source: Carey Wallace, Critical Essay on ''A Conversation from the Third Floor,'' in *Short Stories for Students,* The Gale Group, 2003.

Allison DeFrees

DeFrees is a published writer and an editor with a bachelor's degree in English from the University of Virginia and a law degree from the University of Texas. In the following essay, DeFrees discusses how short story writer El-Bisatie conveys the experience of Egyptian village life by focusing on external detail in favor of internal character development.

When encountering literature from another country, a reader may well expect to learn something more about a place and culture than he knew before: the food the people eat, the houses they live in, the customs they observe, the way they converse. In skilled hands, such details immerse the reader in a new world and provide the feeling of having traveled to a far-off place. Too many details, however, and the spell is broken—the story becomes a lecture, and the narrative sags under the weight of a travelogue. In order to involve the reader, a writer must strike a careful balance between what is described and what is left out. Of course, this is a balance that all writers of fiction must strike. In a sense, even a story set in the reader's hometown is inviting him to a place he's never been, and convincing him of that place's reality is no less difficult. The unfamiliar scenes the reader encounters when reading a foreign writer's work simply remind him all the more clearly of the task that any work of fiction must undertake.

Egyptian writer Mohamed El-Bisatie sets his short story ''A Conversation from the Third Floor,'' like most of his work, in a small village on the Nile Delta. In its few pages, however, it offers little in the way of geographical or cultural context. The simple title is a straightforward summary of what happens in the story: a woman arrives in front of a prison and talks to her husband, who yells down to her from the window of his cell. The title gives no hint of what the conversation is about, but then, what the couple discusses does not seem particularly important. They talk about their two date palms, and some cigarettes that she has sent him. Even the most potentially dramatic piece of information they exchange—that the husband will soon be transferred to a different prison—does not make much of an impact. As the title suggests, this is just a conversation, not much different from any other conversation.

Why, then, does El-Bisatie bother to describe it? He seems deliberately to have left out the very details that would capture the reader's interest. He never reveals, for example, why the husband is in jail or if he will ever be released. More important, he never reveals how either of the pair feels about the husband's imprisonment. Like the ever-present sun, the wall that separates them and limits their communication is just a fact to be accepted without comment or explanation. Even the husband's captors fail to provide excitement. As the story opens, the woman encounters a policeman on horseback, whom she must pass to get to the prison:

The woman stood a few paces away from the horse. The policeman looked behind him at the windows, then at the woman. He placed both hands on the pommel of the saddle and closed his eyes. After a while the horse moved and came to a stop crossways in the street. Then, a moment later, it made a half-turn and once again stood at the top of the street.

Here El-Bisatie sets the stage for conflict. It would seem that the policeman has the power to decide if the woman talks to her husband or not. And indeed, a few lines later she asks his permission. But the policeman is utterly passive. He barely moves, and when he does it seems to be his horse's decision. The woman's request goes unanswered and she heads to the prison anyway. What seemed to be an obstacle is no obstacle at all. What might have been an opportunity to learn something about the woman—is she brave? angry? sad?—is left unexplored. And so it goes for the rest of the story. El-Bisatie scrupulously avoids drama at every turn. The husband's cigarettes have been stolen, but he shrugs it off; the woman greets the rude catcalls of the other prisoners with a smile.

Having noted the lack of either emotional or physical action in "A Conversation from the Third Floor," it is a wonder that the story has any power over the reader at all. And yet it does. What El-Bisatie withholds about the characters' personal history and emotions does not seem to cheat the reader or make the story incomplete. Rather, it focuses the reader's attention all the more sharply on the simple visual details in which El-Bisatie economically grounds his story: the lines of sweat on the policeman's forehead, the dried mud on the woman's toes, the faces pressed against the prison window's bars. This effect may be found in many of El-Bisatie's stories, and it has led critic David Masello to say that they are more like paintings than stories. Reviewing El-Bisatie's short story collection, *A Glass of Tea and Other Stories* (which includes "A Conversation from the Third Floor") for the *New York Times Book Review,* Masello writes that the stories "allow the reader to witness scenes rather than become involved in them; often one learns more about the harsh landscape than about the people within it."

This is certainly true of "A Conversation from the Third Floor." But El-Bisatie's painterly interest in the surface does not mean his characters have no depth. He may not state explicitly what the wife is feeling, but his careful description of the "harsh landscape" she inhabits reveals her to the reader in a different way. "It was afternoon," the story states

> The story's narrow focus keeps the reader in the moment, and the reader must surrender to the rhythm of a life different from his own."

at the start. "The sun had passed beyond the central point in the sky, but the weather was still hot." The sun beats down on the wife but not on the husband, and the story repeatedly refers to the sun to underscore their isolation from each other. The woman has brought their child, whom she lifts up toward her husband's cell. He instructs her to "face him toward the sun so I can see him." She does so, and the child closes his eyes and begins to cry. The sun that lets the husband see his son blinds the child, and eventually he tells the woman to cover him. When the conversation stalls for a moment—the husband has forgotten what he wanted to say—the woman turns away her head from the dark cell window "so that part of her face was against the sun." At the beginning of the story, the prison wall casts a narrow shadow on the ground. By the end, this shadow has grown: "The shadow advanced halfway across the street. She saw that its fringe was touching her foot. She drew her foot back a little." This small gesture suggests as much about her character as the few words she says. Of course, as the afternoon wears on the shadow will lengthen, and eventually cover the woman, if she stays still. Her acknowledgment of this seems to prompt her departure. "When she looked at her foot again, she saw that the shadow clothed the tips of her toes. She stood up." It is as if the sun's movement in the sky governs the conversation, rather than anything the man and woman have to say to each other.

In an essay in *Al-Ahram Weekly,* Egyptian critic Nur Elmessiri says that in El-Bisatie's work "everything is there for the reader to see. But what the reader sees, what comes starkly into view, is the impermeability, the utter opacity of things." This is a good description of the deceptive simplicity of "A Conversation from the Third Floor." There is nothing mysterious or hidden here. The characters do not seem to have any secrets. That, however, is precisely what keeps the reader engaged. Much like the woman, who scans the mass of arms and faces in the prison window, trying to pick out her husband, the reader pores over the details El-Bisatie presents in search of some larger meaning. The woman will never see inside the prison, but is instead at the mercy of what the window reveals to her. Similarly, the reader's understanding of the people and culture here represented wholly depends upon a few seemingly insignificant details: the prisoners' laundry, the soldier's helmet, the mundane topics of the conversation. The reader finds himself in an alien place, and El-Bisatie does not provide a guidebook. On the one hand, this thrusts the reader all the more immediately into the woman's life. All of the background information that is lacking, all that is not known about her and her situation, is precisely what she takes for granted. The reader is thus forced to experience this conversation at the prison as she does—as an unremarkable part of a larger routine. The story's narrow focus keeps the reader in the moment, and the reader must surrender to the rhythm of a life different from his own. If El-Bisatie's decision to withhold more specifics results in a less-than-comprehensive knowledge of what life is like in the Egyptian countryside, at least it prevents the reader from falling into the trap of false understanding. The reader is never allowed to forget that he is a tourist here.

Source: Allison DeFrees, Critical Essay on "A Conversation from the Third Floor," in *Short Stories for Students,* The Gale Group, 2003.

Sources

Dawood, Ibrahim, Review of *A Last Glass of Tea and Other Stories,* in *World Literature Today,* Vol. 73, No. 2, Spring 1999, pp. 383–84.

ElmessiNur, "In Full View," in *Al-Ahram Weekly,* Issue 529, April 12–18, 2001.

Johnson-Davies, Denys, Review of "Tasteful Fare," in *Al-Ahram Weekly,* Issue 529, April 12–18, 2001.

———, "Translator's Introduction," in *A Last Glass of Tea and Other Stories,* Lynne Rienner Publishers, 1998.

———, "Village Life from Within," in *Al-Ahram Weekly,* Issue 429, May 13–19, 1999.

Masello, David, Review of *A Last Glass of Tea and Other Stories,* in the *New York Times Book Review,* June 28, 1998.

Proctor, Sophy, "Private Lives," in *Egypt Today,* August 1, 1997.

Steinberg, Sybil S., Review of *A Last Glass of Tea and Other Stories,* in *Publishers Weekly,* Vol. 245, No. 10, March 9, 1998, p. 50.

Tresilian, David, "Summer Reading, á la Française," in *Al-Ahram Weekly,* Issue No. 485, June 8–14, 2000.

Further Reading

Botman, Selma, *Engendering Citizenship in Egypt,* History and Society of the Modern Middle East series, University Press, 1999.

Beginning with the early years of the twentieth century, when Egypt won independence from British rule, Botman studies the effects of an evolving Egyptian culture in which women's social inferiority has been mandated by a dominant patriarchal political, legal, and social system.

Fahmy, Khaled, *All the Pasha's Men: Mehmed Ali, His Army and the Making of Modern Egypt,* Cambridge University Press, 1997.

Most historians consider Mehmed Ali Pasha (1769–1849) the founder of modern Egypt. He was an Albanian officer who helped the Egyptians in their fight to rid their lands of the British forces and gain their independence. Pasha is credited with helping to modernize Egypt, building factories, railroads, and canals, and with bringing in European architects and technicians to create a more modern Cairo.

Foster, John L., *Ancient Egyptian Literature: An Anthology,* University of Texas Press, 2001.

Foster has collected poems, stories, prayers, and wisdom texts from ancient Egyptian writings, making this an excellent introduction to the literature of an ancient land. Foster has been collecting and translating texts from Egypt for more than thirty years. This is a culmination of some of his best work.

Malek, Jaromir, *Egypt: Ancient Culture, Modern Land,* University of Oklahoma Press, 1993.

Covering the vast period of five thousand years, this book uses essays, photographs, maps, and diagrams to illustrate the natural environment, the culture, the economy, religion, and everyday life in Egypt from ancient times to the present.

Rodenbeck, Max, *Cairo: The City Victorious,* Vintage Books USA, 2000.

Rodenbeck is a noted journalist who has spent most of his life in Cairo. This book has been described as a travel book, as a popular history, and as journalism. The reader is given a tour of Cairo, both past and present, through the eyes of this reporter.

Weaver, Mary Anne, *Portrait of Egypt: A Journey trough the World of Militant Islam,* Farrar, Straus and Giroux, 2000.

Torn between the governmental secular forces which have ruled Egypt for many decades and the rising power of the militant Islamic clerics, Egypt is becoming a country in crisis. Weaver explores this conflict through exclusive interviews with militants, generals, and politicians. She concludes with her own views on how this struggle affects the Western world.

The Eye

Paul Bowles

1976

Paul Bowles's short story "The Eye," written in 1976, initially appeared in the *Missouri Review* in 1978 and was reprinted in the *Best American Stories of 1979* and *Ellery Queen's Mystery Magazine* (1981). It is included in Bowles's story collection *Midnight Mass* (1981) and in the *Stories of Paul Bowles* (2001). Like many of Bowles's stories, "The Eye" concerns encounters between foreigners, in this case a Canadian man and the narrator, and Moroccan culture. Bowles uses the encounter to underscore the gap between the belief systems of the West and the Arab world, and to highlight the inscrutability of human existence. As an expatriate who spent most of his life in Tangier, Bowles is intimately familiar with his subject matter.

The story itself, only two thousand words, is accessible and rewarding, giving Western readers a glimpse into a culture with which most are unfamiliar. An unnamed narrator's curiosity is aroused when he hears about the death of a man he has never met, and he sets out to investigate the circumstances behind the man's death. Bowles's spare style and straightforward prose mask a more complicated structure, as the narrator, also an expatriate, tells a story about his attempt to understand another story. The title derives from the spell that the Canadian's Moroccan cook believes he cast on her daughter. Critics have commented on ideas of morality, intention, and crime in "The Eye."

Author Biography

One of the twentieth century's most enigmatic writers, Paul Frederick Bowles was born December 30, 1910, in New York, New York, the only child of dentist Claude Dietz Bowles and poet Rena (Winnewisser) Bowles. Bowles learned to read early and showed a passion for music as a child, studying piano and music theory before composing an opera when he was just nine years old. Apart from his reading and music, however, Bowles described his childhood as a lonely time spent in the company of eccentric adults. His father, a disciplinarian, took his parenting strategy from people like nutritionist Horace Fletcher, who claimed that chewing food until it lost its flavor would cure one of everything from acne to indigestion. Bowles's father forced the boy to chew each mouthful at least forty times before swallowing. Inappropriate swallowing resulted in a slap across the face. When she was not teaching her son to meditate, Rena Bowles would read her son Edgar Allan Poe's stories. Bowles's great-aunt, Mary Robbins Mead, was the most eccentric adult in the family, holding weekly seances from her hilltop home, where she purportedly summoned the spirits of local children.

At nineteen, Bowles dropped out of the University of Virginia and moved to Paris, where he met famous expatriates such as Gertrude Stein, Jean Cocteau, and André Gide. After studying with composer Aaron Copland in Berlin, Bowles toured North Africa and moved with Copland to Tangier, Morocco, in 1931. During the 1930s and 1940s, Bowles traveled widely and wrote scores for numerous plays including Orson Welles's *Horse Eats Hat* (1936) and *Love's Old Sweet Song* (1940), and Tennessee Williams's *Glass Menagerie* (1944). Tired again of New York City, Bowles again moved to Tangier in 1947, then a quasi-anarchic city of intrigue and mystery, and began writing stories. On the strength of these stories, he was commissioned to write a novel, which turned out to be the work for which Bowles is best known, *The Sheltering Sky* (1949). During the 1950s and 1960s, a number of American writers associated with the Beat movement visited Bowles, some of them staying in Tangier for extended periods. These writers included Jack Kerouac, Gregory Corso, William Burroughs, Allen Ginsberg, and Brion Gysin, among others. Many of them came for inspiration, spiritual renewal, and to experiment with readily available drugs such as *kif* and *majoun,* made from cannabis, which Bowles himself used frequently while writing.

Paul Bowles

In addition to his other novels, *Let It Come Down* (1952), *The Spider's House* (1955), and *Up Above the World* (1966), Bowles wrote numerous short stories, collected under titles such as *A Hundred Camels in the Courtyard* (1962), *Three Tales* (1975), and *Midnight Mass* (1981), which includes the haunting story "The Eye." Bowles also wrote operas, poetry collections, and an autobiography, *Without Stopping* (1972), in addition to translating numerous Moroccan stories. *The Stories of Paul Bowles* was published in 2001, two years after Bowles died of a heart attack, November 18, 1999, in Tangier.

Plot Summary

In the first section of "The Eye," the narrator introduces the main character, Duncan Whitelaw Marsh, an expatriate from Vancouver, Canada, whose story he will seek to unravel. Like Marsh, who died ten or twelve years ago, the narrator lives in Tangier, Morocco. During the 1950s and 1960s, Tangier was an exotic and lawless place that many Westerners visited to indulge appetites that would be frowned upon in their own countries. Living there was inexpensive, and drugs were readily available. Before it gained independence in 1956, Morocco was divided among a French protectorate, a Spanish protectorate, and the international Zone of Tangier. The overwhelming majority of Moroccans are Arab or Berber and the dominant religion is Islam.

The narrator admits that he never saw Marsh and only knows of him through cocktail party gossip and expatriate "myth-making." He heard that Marsh moved into a furnished house and hired a teenage Moroccan as night watchman. A few months after dismissing the cook and gardener, who had come with the house, and hiring his own, Marsh became ill with a stomach disorder. He flew to London for treatment, returned, and eventually succumbed to the illness. The narrator notes that many people assumed his death was a case of slow poisoning by the employees. But the narrator is also intrigued by the marks found on the soles of Marsh's feet and by the rumor he heard that Marsh had given the watchman a paper providing him with a monthly allowance for as long as Marsh lived.

The narrator recounts how five years ago he learned that the watchman's name was Larbi and that he was a waiter in a local restaurant. The narrator visits Larbi and convinces him to show the narrator the paper Marsh gave him. Larbi shows him a simple note signed by Marsh that promised Larbi a hundred pounds a month. His curiosity piqued, the narrator sets up a meeting with Larbi at Marsh's former residence, now empty save for a guardian.

Larbi and the narrator meet at the house, now guarded by a man in a "brown *djellaba*." A *djellaba* is a hooded cloak traditionally worn by Moroccan men. Larbi recounts the story of what happened to Marsh to the narrator, who sits expressionless. Larbi says that Marsh, who hated noise, complained that his cook's daughter was too noisy. Trying to scare her, Marsh snuck up and "frowned so fiercely that she began to scream." That night the child fell ill and could no longer walk. Thinking that Marsh had put a spell on her daughter (i.e., "the eye") and that the only way that her child would be able to walk again would be to remove it, Meriam enlisted the help of a *fqih,* a kind of holy man and sorcerer. The *fqih* held a ceremony in front of the little girl during which he drew signs on a sheet of paper. Soon after the ceremony, men from Meriam's family dragged Marsh from his sickbed, holding him over a well while they carved these signs into the soles of his feet so the blood would fall into the water. Larbi's response is inscrutable when the narrator asks him if

he sees a connection between the signs and Marsh's death. Larbi says, "He died because his hour had come." The narrator ends the story by meditating on the relationship between a crime and intention.

Characters

The fqihs
A group of wise men who advise on the child's condition.

Dr. Halsey
Dr. Halsey arranged for Duncan Marsh's body to be taken to the airport from his house. Halsey is the first person to notice the crude incisions on Marsh's feet, which deepen the narrator's curiosity.

Larbi Lairini
Larbi Lairini is Marsh's Moroccan night watchman and the person who relates the story of his former employer's death to the narrator. Larbi works as a waiter at Le Fin Bec, a small restaurant. He understands English well but speaks it poorly. Marsh hired a relative of his, Meriam, as his cook shortly after moving into his house on the slopes of Djamma el Mokra. Larbi shows the narrator the piece of paper on which Marsh promised him a hundred dollars a month but says that it is useless now because he is dead. He represents himself as an innocent in the affair, professing that he had nothing to do with Marsh's death and that he did not know that Marsh was being poisoned. When Larbi recalls seeing men from Meriam's family coming to perform the ritual that would lift the spell, he says, "I got onto my motorcycle and went into the city. I didn't want to be here when they did it. It had nothing to do with me." Larbi's refusal to answer the narrator when he asks if he called the doctor as Marsh asked suggests that Larbi contributed to Marsh's death through his inaction.

Duncan Marsh
Duncan Whitelaw Marsh is an expatriate from Vancouver, Canada, who moved to Tangier about a dozen years before the story opens. He rents a house on a mountain outside the city, dismisses the gar-

dener and cook, and hires a night watchman and a new cook, Meriam. Marsh, an intensely private man who values quiet, makes a face at Meriam's young daughter because she is making too much noise, and soon after the daughter falls ill and loses the ability to walk. Meriam slowly poisons Marsh, believing that her employer has cast a spell on her daughter. He flies to London seeking a cure for his stomach and kidney ailments and then returns to Tangier. Marsh suspects that he is being poisoned by Meriam and enlists Larbi's help, promising the watchman a hundred dollars a month for as long as Marsh lives. However, Marsh's condition only worsens, and he dies when men from Meriam's family drag him to a well, make incisions in his feet, and hold him over the water, attempting to break the spell.

Meriam

Meriam is Marsh's cook and a relative of Larbi, the night watchman. After her daughter comes down with a fever, almost dies, and then becomes paralyzed, she consults *fqihs,* who tell her that Marsh has put "the eye" on her daughter. They recommend she administer "substances" to Marsh to break the spell, which she does, slowly poisoning him. When men from her family bring Marsh back to the house after taking him to the well, Meriam refuses to clean him or touch his body. When he dies, Meriam moves to another town with her daughter.

Narrator

The unnamed narrator has lived in Tangier for five decades. He speaks Arabic, French, Spanish, and English, the languages of the city, and considers himself well versed in native culture. Though he pretends to be objective about the story he relates, in fact, he has already made a judgment, saying at the start, "What happened [to Duncan Marsh] was in no way his fault, notwithstanding the whispered innuendos of the English-speaking residents." He acts as a conduit for Marsh's story, relaying information that has come to him from various sources such as Dr. Halsey and Larbi Lairini, whom he seeks out after being told by an American that Larbi works in a restaurant in town. After Larbi shows the narrator the piece of paper on which Marsh agreed to pay him a set amount of money, the narrator remarks, "I no longer understood anything." More than the details surrounding Marsh's poisoning or the moral ambivalence of Larbi, it is the narrator who remains the story's central mystery.

Media Adaptations

- Jennifer Baichwal directed the documentary *Let It Come Down: The Life of Paul Bowles* (1999), featuring Paul Bowles, William Burroughs, and Allen Ginsberg, among others. Bowles discusses his relationships with some of the twentieth century's most celebrated and notorious writers including Gertrude Stein, Jack Kerouac, and Truman Capote.

- Bowles's novel *The Sheltering Sky* was adapted into a film in 1990. Directed by Bernardo Bertolucci, the film stars Debra Winger and John Malkovich.

- Bowles reads "Allal" and other stories from his home in Morocco in *The Voices of Paul Bowles* (1989), an audiocassette published by the Wexner Center for the Arts, Columbus, Ohio. The cassette also includes early music compositions and field recordings of traditional Moroccan music by Bowles.

Themes

Human Condition

In "The Eye," Bowles presents human beings as the victims of circumstances over which they have little control. He spells out this idea in the plot of the story, as Marsh is unaware of the source of his poisoning and, once he suspects its source, is incapable of stopping it. Larbi represents the idea that Marsh was unable to stop his death because it was his time to die. He sums up this notion in the word, *suerte.* In Spanish, this means "luck." However, in Tangier's Arabic culture, the narrator says, it takes on the additional meaning of "fate."

Colonialism

Colonialism entails not only the physical occupation of one country by the people of another but also a psychological occupation. Morocco has a history of being occupied by others, and Bowles

Topics for Further Study

- Research the history of Tangier and present it to your class. Pay particular attention to how the French, Spanish, and Arab populations have contributed to the city's culture.

- Starting with Italy, research the tradition of magic and sorcery in at least two other cultures. Look for spells that involve "casting the eye" on someone. What similarities and differences do you see between the other cultures' understanding of the spell and Morocco's? Discuss as a class.

- Write an epilogue to the story, explaining what happens to Meriam and her daughter after they move away from Tangier. Read it to your class.

- Compare the expatriate writers and artists in Paris in the 1920s with those in Tangier in the 1950s and 1960s. A good place to read about the former is in Gertrude Stein's *The Autobiography of Alice B. Toklas.* Does one group or another appeal to you more? Support your answer with detailed reasons.

- Many of the American expatriates who moved to Morocco in the 1950s did so to escape what they perceived as the stifling conformity of American life. Does such an atmosphere exist in the United States today? Research where people who are disillusioned with American life move to today.

- Bowles presents Larbi as a passive character who does nothing to stop Marsh's death. Argue for or against the idea that Larbi's inaction constitutes a crime.

---

alludes to both French and Spanish influences on Moroccans. However, Europeans of all stripes moved to Morocco during the middle part of the twentieth century for the inexpensive housing and "exotic" local color. The narrator and Marsh, both expatriates from the West, display the colonial attitude in their condescension towards Moroccans. Marsh has to pay for anything he wants, including his own life. By offering to pay Larbi to keep an eye on the cook, whom he suspects is poisoning him, Marsh illustrates the imbalance of power between the colonizers and the colonized. Although the former appear to have the upper hand because of their formal education and wealth, in reality the latter control events because colonizers depend on them for their very survival. The narrator illustrates his own colonial mindset in the way he characterizes Moroccans as superstitious and ignorant.

Crime

"The Eye" can be read as a detective story, with the narrator acting as investigator seeking to unearth the details and the motives for Marsh's murder. And indeed, the story was published in *Ellery Queen's Mystery Magazine,* a publication known for its detective stories. In the first section of the story, the narrator outlines what he has heard of the "crime," and then he proceeds to learn as much as he can from the person he considers to be the culprit, Larbi Lairini. The narrator cagily tries to extract information from Larbi and then resorts to paying him for details of Marsh's death. However, the more he learns, the less satisfied he is and the less able he is to assign guilt to any one person. He ends the story asking, "What is a crime? There was no criminal intent—only a mother moving in the darkness of ancient ignorance."

Style

Point of View

Point of view refers to the perspective from which a story is told. Bowles uses a first-person point of view in "The Eye," meaning that readers see events through the narrator's eyes. This narrator, the "I" in the story, is never named, but through information he provides the readers know that he is also an expatriate and a long-time resident of Tangier. First-person narrators can be either central to the action or peripheral to it. Bowles's narrator is somewhere in between. He acts as a detective, seeking out information about Duncan Marsh's death, initiates contact with Larbi, and comments on the story that Larbi tells about Marsh. However, he is not a participant in Marsh's story itself and never even met the man.

Setting

Setting refers to the time, place, and culture in which the action of a story takes place. "The Eye" is set in Tangier, a city in Morocco that Westerners flocked to during the middle of the twentieth century for its liberal atmosphere and exoticism. Bowles's descriptions of places in individual scenes, such as Le Fin Bec restaurant and Marsh's house, underscore the mystery inherent in Tangier *and* in the events surrounding Marsh's death. The narrator's inability to comprehend Moroccan culture also adds to the sense that things are never as they seem in Tangier.

Plot

Plot refers to how a story's events are arranged and how they relate. It emphasizes causality and offers a framework for fictional elements such as characterization, conflict, and theme. The way in which Bowles's narrator releases information—slowly and through the words of other people such as Larbi—creates suspense and emphasizes the gap between the story's details and the narrator's inability to comprehend the broader picture or the motivations of those involved.

Historical Context

Turmoil in Morocco

In the mid-1970s, when Bowles wrote "The Eye" while living in Tangier, Morocco was in turmoil. After Morocco became an independent monarchy under Muhammad V in 1956, the country struggled against republican opposition, and King Hassan, who succeeded his father in 1961, fought off attempted military coups and assassinations. Accused of corruption and incompetence, Hassan tried to deflect attention from his administration and consolidate support for the monarchy by pressuring Spain to withdraw from the Moroccan Sahara, a phosphate-rich area. In 1976, Spain, Morocco, and Mauritania signed a treaty dividing the land among the countries. The Polisario Front, a rebel group aligned with the indigenous Saharawis, embarked on a guerrilla war to oust the three countries. They succeeded in forcing Mauritania and Spain out and proclaimed the Saharan Arab Democratic Republic. However, Moroccan troops remain, having built a series of desert walls to demarcate their territory. King Hassan signed a cease-fire in 1991, with the fate of the region to be decided by a United Nations-sponsored referendum. The conflict remains unresolved.

Civil Rights for Native Americans

As the Polisario Front fought for independence in Morocco, Native Americans fought for it at home. In 1975, Congress passed the Indian Self-Determination and Education Assistance Act. This Act encourages Native Americans to take control of their own education and promote their tribal customs, and requires the Secretary of the Interior to enter into self-determination contracts with tribal organizations to plan and administer programs. The law concretizes the federal government's responsibility to individual Indians and tribes. The Act came on the heels of the public's deepening suspicion of the United States government.

American Political Disillusionment

In 1973, Vice President Spiro Agnew resigned under threat of impeachment after being charged with corruption and income tax evasion, and in 1974, President Richard Nixon, who had been battling allegations that he knew more about the Watergate affair than he admitted, resigned. The Watergate affair centered around a burglary of the Democratic Party's National Committee offices at the Watergate Hotel in 1972.

Many Americans became disillusioned with politics as a result of the Watergate affair and lost faith in the government's ability to run the country. Hurt by double-digit inflation and a rising unemployment rate, the American economy fell into its deepest recession in forty years. Not surprisingly, crime also increased during the 1970s, with the violent crime rate alone skyrocketing 30 percent between 1970 and 1977. A soaring crime rate, however, did not dampen the desire of people to make the United States their home. The Hart-Cellar Immigration and Nationality Act of 1965 amended previous policies that favored Western Europeans, abolished immigration quotas by country, and encouraged family reunification. As a result, Asian

Compare & Contrast

- **1970s:** Average annual gross domestic product growth reaches 5.4 percent in Morocco.

   Today: Average annual gross domestic product growth hovers between 3.5 and 4 percent in Morocco.

- **1970s:** Numerous demonstrators protesting the policies of King Hassan are jailed in secret detention centers. Many of them disappear or are killed.

   Today: In 2000, hundreds of former political prisoners and activists in Morocco protest outside a former secret prison to condemn past human rights abuses and to demand trials for those responsible for the detentions, deaths, and disappearances of ex-prisoners.

- **1970s:** Morocco is involved in an inconclusive desert war in the former Spanish Sahara with Mauritania and the Polisario Front. By the end of the decade, Mauritania withdraws, leaving only Morocco and the Polisario Front, which in 1976 proclaims the region the Saharan Arab Democratic Republic.

   Today: Although the United Nations has agreed to sponsor a referendum on the disputed territory, the issue remains unresolved.

and Latino peoples poured into America, dramatically altering the makeup of the workforce in a number of industries.

Critical Overview

Midnight Mass has not received the critical attention of Bowles's other writing because it was published by Black Sparrow, a small but well-respected press. Writing for the *Dictionary of Literary Biography,* Allen Hibbard notes that many of the stories in the collection ''taken together, represent certain stylistic and thematic shifts.'' These shifts, Hibbard claims, ''depend more on the movement of memory than actual physical movement.'' Writing for *Harper's,* Francine Prose zeroes in on Bowles's darkness, the darkness that befalls most characters in his stories. Prose argues, ''Paul Bowles's obsessive subject is the tragic, even fatal mistakes that Westerners so commonly make in their misguided and often presumptuous encounters with the mysteries of a foreign culture.'' Noting how the opening sentence of ''The Eye'' could have been written by ''other writers who have focused on the confrontation between East and West,'' Prose observes, ''But as the opening paragraph progresses, we can watch Bowles part company with his colleagues and enter territory that he has claimed as uniquely his own.'' In her essay for *Critique: Studies in Modern Fiction,* ''Paul Bowles and the Characterization of Women,'' Linda Wagner focuses on Bowles's representation of women in his later stories, arguing that stories from *Midnight Mass* display ''the tendency to set character against character, to create a dialectic that somehow informs the reader.'' In ''The Eye,'' Wagner writes, Bowles emphasizes the ''darker side of woman's power.'' Gena Dagel Caponi agrees with Wagner that Bowles is attempting to teach the reader something. In her study, *Paul Bowles,* however, Caponi contends that morality, not women's power, is the central issue in the story, writing, ''Bowles seems to ask the reader, are we all not moving in the darkness of ignorance of one sort or another?''

Criticism

Chris Semansky

Semansky is an instructor of English literature and composition who writes about literature and culture for various publications. In this essay, Semansky considers the narrator's self-delusion in Bowles's story.

In his study of the West's representation of Arab culture, Edward Said writes that Orientalism "is an ideology born of the colonizers' desire to know their subjects to better control them." Although Said is referring to the way in which historians have represented the Orient, his characterization also applies to the ways in which fiction writers represent it. Said argues that Westerners have depicted Arab cultures as dishonest and irrational and that their writing about the Orient is a form of political propaganda of which the writers themselves are not even aware. Said says, "This is the culmination of Orientalism as a dogma that not only degrades its subject matter but also blinds its practitioners." In "The Eye," the narrator attempts to present information about Arab characters in an objective manner, as if his representations of events are inseparable from the events themselves. However, his desire (like that of others in the Anglo community) to fathom the motivations of the Moroccans involved in Marsh's death illustrates how expatriates think like colonizers in their drive to know the people in whose country they live.

From the story's opening, the narrator positions himself as separate from, yet part of, the expatriate community in Tangier. He believes himself to be an outsider who can objectively view newcomers and natives alike. He begins his tale of Duncan Marsh, writing, "What happened to him was in no way his fault, notwithstanding the whispered innuendoes of the English-speaking residents." Such an attitude illustrates the narrator's own stance towards the event he is about to investigate. He further attempts to set himself apart from both communities when he writes:

> These people [the English-speaking residents] often have reactions similar to those of certain primitive groups: when misfortune overtakes one of their number, the others by mutual consent refrain from offering him aid, and merely sit back to watch, certain that he has called his suffering down upon himself.

He does not mention who those primitive groups are, but his representation of Moroccans in the story certainly suggests that he has them in mind. What is interesting about the narrator's comparison is that he himself is a watcher, or, more accurately, a listener, who does not know Marsh but attempts to put together his story out of curiosity and what

This 1960s view of Tangier, Morocco, sets the scene for Paul Bowles's "The Eye"

appears to be sympathy for the man. He freely admits that he knows no one who ever saw Marsh, and that the information he has heard is the result of "irresponsible residents . . . [who feel] at liberty to indulge their taste for mythmaking."

The narrator says that he has heard other similar stories, suggesting that the story about Marsh could well have been an urban legend. An urban legend is a kind of contemporary folklore that revolves around an issue or a person and circulates through word of mouth, in this case, the cocktail party gossip of expatriates. Often, urban legends function as cautionary tales for a group or groups of people. The narrator's desire to investigate Marsh's story, then, is also a desire to confirm its veracity. Of the other stories he has heard, the narrator notes: "On each occasion it has been said that the European victim had only himself (or herself) to blame, having encouraged familiarity on the part of a servant." Though he positions himself as not sharing the general sentiments of the European community, the narrator takes pains to point out that Marsh confided in Larbi, his night watchman, promising him financial aid for his help keeping an eye on the cook.

What Do I Read Next?

- Critics consider Bowles's 1949 novel *The Sheltering Sky* to be a classic of existential literature and one of the finest novels of the twentieth century.

- William Burroughs, who also lived in Tangier for a while, was a friend of Paul Bowles and a leading voice of the Beat movement. Burroughs's novel *The Naked Lunch* (1959) is a classic of Beat literature.

- Michelle Green's *The Dream at the End of the World: Paul Bowles and the Literary Renegades in Tangier* (1991), is a gossipy chronicle of the expatriate community in Tangier in the 1950s.

- Palestinian-American Edward Said's *Orientalism* (1978) is one of the foundational texts of postcolonial studies. Said critiques Western representations of the East, arguing that Western scholars since the nineteenth century have depicted "Arab" cultures as irrational, anti-Western, primitive, and dishonest.

- *The Autobiography of Alice B. Toklas* (1933), actually written by Gertrude Stein, is the story of Stein's life in Paris among expatriate writers and artists. When Bowles lived in Paris, he attended many of Stein's salons and mingled with the literati.

The narrator maintains his pattern of self-delusion throughout the story, professing objectivity one moment and then in the next making presumptions. For example, after listing a number of details surrounding Marsh's death, the narrator presents the detail about the knife marks found on the dead man's feet, stating, "It was this last bit of information which, for me, at least, made the story take on life." However, rather than influencing his theory about who committed the act, the narrator writes, this new information only complicated the motive of the crime. He is still convinced, "The boy [Larbi] was guilty."

The narrator's care in representing himself as an impartial observer has fooled at least one critic. In discussing "The Eye," Wagner, for example, writes, "As in several other of these late stories, Bowles has used an objective narrator." Objective narrators, however, are narrators most often associated with an omniscient or a third-person point of view. That is, they have access to the thoughts and motivations of *all* characters, or they "simply" present action and dialogue without commenting on them. Many of Ernest Hemingway's short stories employ objective narrators, for instance. However, in "The Eye," Bowles's narrator has neither an omniscient or third-person point of view.

Rather, the narrator foregrounds his own bias in his interactions with Larbi. Trying to identify him at Le Fin Bec, the restaurant at which Larbi works, the narrator says, "I studied the three waiters. They were interchangeable, with wide black moustaches, blue jeans, and sports shirts." Lumping all the waiters together into a stereotype of Arab appearance highlights the narrator's deficiencies of perception, which is surprising considering that he claims to be a fifty-year resident of Tangier. The narrator displays his powers of manipulation in his discussions with Larbi, baiting him by saying, "I thought by now you'd have a bazaar or some sort of shop." He continues his detective-like routine, convincing Larbi to show him the notarized letter he received from Marsh and extracting a promise from the waiter to accompany him to his former employer's house. After exerting considerable effort to track down Larbi, the narrator then tells readers, "I had no intentions then. I might return soon or I might never go back." Deciphering the narrator's ambivalence becomes the reader's primary task.

Caponi links this kind of ambivalence in the narrator to a sense of surrender in Bowles's stories of the 1970s. In her study of Bowles's fiction, *Paul Bowles*, Caponi includes "The Eye" with Bowles's "late colonial fiction," writing that it "displays a more passive resignation to circumstances than do his earlier works.'' Caponi continues: ''In his later fiction the European characters of postcolonial North Africa learn to acquire the fatalism of the Muslims and the Berbers, because they are living in a world beyond their control.''

It is easy enough to see how Marsh displays this fatalism. Though still ill, he returns from a London hospital to Tangier, suspecting that his cook is poisoning him. However, instead of dismissing her, he enlists Larbi, a relative of Meriam, to watch her. Meriam displays her fatalism in believing that Marsh cast a spell on her daughter and by believing that the only way to remove it is by administering certain ''substances'' prescribed by the *fqih*. When Larbi warns her that she is killing Marsh, she responds, ''I've done what I could. It's in the hands of Allah.'' Larbi's fatalism is also apparent in his reactions, both to the men who come to perform the ritual on Marsh and to the narrator's questioning. When the narrator asks Larbi if he called the doctor when Marsh begged him to from his bed, Larbi changes the subject. Later he says that Marsh died ''because his hour had come.'' The narrator displays his own fatalism while reflecting on his chances of ever comprehending what happened. Inside Marsh's house, he writes, ''The absurd conviction that I was about to understand everything had taken possession of me; I noticed that I was breathing more quickly.'' Though the narrator is quick to describe his own physical responses to what he is about to hear, hiding his disapproval by making his face ''entirely expressionless,'' he is oblivious to the ways in which his responses betray his sense of superiority, the way his ''objectivity'' masks his judgment.

Source: Chris Semansky, Critical Essay on ''The Eye,'' in *Short Stories for Students,* The Gale Group, 2003.

Susan Sanderson

Sanderson holds a master of fine arts degree in fiction writing and is an independent writer. In this essay, Sanderson examines the narrator and his transformation.

''The Eye'' is a story that includes elements of numerous genres. Its most immediate access is as a detective story, in which the narrator searches for the person responsible for the poisoning and ultimate death of Canadian expatriate Duncan Marsh. On another level, it can be read as an adventure tale or as a cautionary tale of Europeans venturing into exotic places better left unexplored. Bowles in-

> ''Deciphering the narrator's ambivalence becomes the reader's primary task.''

vokes this genre when he opens the story by describing Marsh as ''a man who would have done better to stay away.''

The story can also be seen as the narrator's anthropological examination of two cultures clashing: Western and North African. In his opening comments about the actions of the English-speaking expatriates living in Tangier, the narrator speaks as someone who studies the behavior of people and cultures, such as an anthropologist. He compares the English speakers to members of ''certain primitive groups'' who, ''when misfortune overtakes one of their number, the others by mutual consent refrain from offering him aid.'' They simply watch from afar, convinced that the misfortune is due to something that person has done, and he becomes ''taboo.'' The narrator makes clear that he does not subscribe to a common perception among the expatriates that Western culture is superior to non-Western cultures.

The narrator, though defined purely by his anonymity and his curiosity about the events of Marsh's death, is of central interest in Bowles's tale. The author gives him no name, no background or profession, and no definite gender—although, an argument can be made that the narrator is a man, given the ease with which he seems to move through the Moroccan streets and back alleys in his quest for Marsh's alleged murderer. The only thing that is certain about him is that he is not a native Moroccan but has lived in Tangier for about fifty years. Even his interest in the events surrounding Marsh's death is unexplained; he never met Marsh, nor does he ''know anyone who claims to have seen him,'' and the death took place some ''ten or twelve years ago.''

There is a reason, however, for the narrator's interest in the case, and it is this reason, finally, that defines the type of story Bowles has written. More than an adventure tale or a mystery or a story of colliding cultures, Bowles has written a story of one man's philosophical and personal transformation— the account of a man moving from a set of beliefs

> More than an adventure tale or a mystery or a story of colliding cultures, Bowles has written a story of one man's philosophical and personal transformation. . . ."

that define the world as a place where order rules and guilt can be assigned to the belief that people live their lives and make decisions in a world that is without structure or constraints and that events often happen for no apparent reason. Duncan Marsh's death was the catalyst that set the narrator upon this philosophical journey, so that he eventually came to see the world as place with no predictable patterns or reliable rules.

The issue of who is guilty of Marsh's death is a constant one throughout the story. Early in his investigation, the narrator dismisses the city's English-speaking population's assumption that Marsh brought this calamity upon himself, and he quickly points the finger at a young night watchman, Larbi. According to the narrator, Larbi was responsible for finding the cook who worked for Marsh, a woman named Meriam. In addition, Marsh had arranged for the young watchman to be supported financially. The narrator therefore hypothesizes that Meriam and Larbi planned Marsh's murder by slow poisoning, something the cook could accomplish without attracting attention, so that the two could be free of their employer and share the ongoing income that Marsh had provided for Larbi. "There could be little doubt that the boy was guilty," the narrator surmises early on in his investigation. Someone must be to blame, the narrator believes, if a man dies under mysterious circumstances.

Underlying the search for Marsh's killer is the narrator's assumption that the events surrounding the Canadian's death can be, and must be, understood. The narrator even refers to his contemplations about the case as his "feasible hypotheses" and acknowledges that he has thought about Marsh for many years after his death. There are, however, a number of things about the case that confound him and challenge the possibility that he will be able to

assign blame entirely. The first is the fact that the doctor who tried to help Marsh when he was near death found deep incisions formed into "crude patterns" on the soles of his patient's feet. The narrator learns another bewildering piece of information when he reads the contract outlining the financial arrangement between the Larbi and Marsh, noting that the payments were to continue only as long as Marsh remained alive. In fact, when the narrator saw the document, he recalls, "I no longer understood anything." He had taken the pieces of information he had and arranged them in a certain way that seemed to solve the puzzle of Marsh's death. But these new pieces do not fit: Why would Larbi be interested in killing his employer if Larbi's income depended upon Marsh's being alive?

Even after this experience, the narrator insists that there must be order and reason surrounding Marsh's death. If money is no longer a likely motive, then there must be some other motive or logical reason why Marsh died when he did and an explanation for the strange marks on the soles of his feet. The narrator eventually begins to believe that "if only I could talk to the watchman, in Arabic, and inside the house itself, I might be in a position to see things more clearly." He behaves as if he is a police investigator, strong in his conviction that returning to the scene of the crime will somehow either force a confession from Larbi or reveal some small bit of physical evidence to show who is responsible for the crime. Every effect has an identifiable cause, he still believes, and if he works hard enough he will uncover it. Walking through Marsh's shuttered house, however, the narrator has a moment of icy self-realization: "The absurd conviction that I was about to understand everything had taken possession of me."

The information the narrator *does* eventually receive from Larbi is no less perplexing and inexplicable than the facts he already knows. In truth, even though the narrator learns about the unkind manner in which Marsh treated Meriam's young child, how the child became seriously ill after Marsh purposely frightened her, and how a group of local wise men, or *fqih,* agreed that the "eye" had been put on the child and instructed Meriam to give Marsh a certain concoction to loosen the spell's grip, the narrator still has no one to blame. Even if the concoction prescribed by the *fqih* played a role in Marsh's death—and it may or may not have—the men were guilty of nothing; they sought only to help a child, not to harm Marsh. The narrator leaves the house "with a vague sense of disappointment," realizing that he "had not only expected, but actually hoped, to find someone on whom the guilt might be fixed."

The narrator receives little satisfaction in exchange for his hard work tracking down the events and people associated with Marsh's death, primarily because Marsh is as responsible for his death as are Meriam, Larbi, and the *fqih;* no single person's actions weigh more heavily than another's, the narrator realizes. Everyone involved made benign or benignly intended choices, yet a man died. "There was no criminal intent," the narrator decides, "only a mother moving in the darkness of ancient ignorance," referring to Meriam's desire to see her sick child well again by consulting the *fqih.*

The narrator, at the story's end, is beginning to look at the world in a new way—this is what he gains for all of his trouble. He has moved from being a man convinced of Larbi and Meriam's guilt, and of the importance of understanding events and assigning guilt, to a man who is aware of the possibility that his understanding of life is limited and flawed.

The question remains at the story's end, however, as to whether the narrator is capable of fully embracing a philosophical outlook that challenges the traditional Western concepts of crime and guilt. Bowles's dislike of most European expatriates living in Tangier is barely disguised in the story, and it is obvious that he considers them no better than the "certain primitive groups" with which the story's narrator compares them. They have come to a place where most of them don't belong, and often they suffer for their insistence on living outside of their natural habitat. While Bowles does not overly praise or exalt the local population in his story—and so avoids the pitfalls many writers fall into when they present non-Europeans as noble savages—he does make it clear that they hold some knowledge and understanding of life to which most Europeans have little access. In seven simple words, for example, Larbi speaks a truth about Marsh's death that has eluded the narrator throughout the story: "He died because his hour had come."

Even as the narrator has come to a different understanding of the world than the one he held in the beginning, the fact that he asks Larbi "if he saw any connection between all this and Marsh's death" indicates that he is still grasping for a clear explanation for the expatriate's premature and violent demise. He still longs for neat categories of cause and effect, crime and punishment, that do not exist, at least in the place where Marsh chose to live and where the narrator himself has chosen to live for most of his life. Through his investigation into Marsh's death, the narrator has come to a new understanding of the culture in which he has lived for fifty years and of life in general. It seems that it will take even longer for the narrator to fully accept what he now understands.

Source: Susan Sanderson, Critical Essay on "The Eye," in *Short Stories for Students,* The Gale Group, 2003.

Allen Hibbard

In the following essay excerpt, Hibbard comments on the narrative aspects of "The Eye."

The stories brought together in *Midnight Mass* (1981) and *Unwelcome Words* (1988) have not yet enjoyed the popularity that those in Bowles's *Collected Stories* have, despite the inclusion of many of them in *A Distant Episode: The Selected Stories* (1988). These recent volumes, however, contain many splendid stories, demonstrating the author's versatility and mastery of the genre. Bowles does not simply serve up tried and popular dishes, though familiar flavors are recognizable. He rather offers novel treats, lending both expected and surprising pleasures.

These later stories, consistently sharper than those of *Things Gone and Things Still Here*, depict a more settled mode of life and experience. There are, to be sure, expatriates in many of these stories, yet they tend now, like Bowles himself during this period, to be rather sedentary, and the conflicts that arise generally pertain to managing local help or dealing with property, rather than those arising from more daring wanderings into hostile, foreign terrain. They describe a Tangier beset by the pains of growth and often inscribe the conflicts of values that accompany modernization. Though no more optimistic about the plight of the world, Bowles seems to have adopted more of the wry, ironic wit that sometimes accompanies the resignation to one's fate in old age.

Midnight Mass signals stylistic as well as thematic shifts. Bowles's characteristic sense of sureness and economy is as sharp as ever. Each sentence drives the story a step closer to its logical outcome. The storyteller gives his listeners what they need when they need it. We get not a word more than necessary. These stories, especially those in *Unwelcome Words*, have that pellucid, bonelike quality we associate with Beckett's later work. This the writer achieves in part by abandoning the use of quotation

> Bowles's telling, in the first person, seems to be but one more telling of a well-known tale, heard second- or thirdhand, transformed and embellished in so many retellings."

marks to indicate dialogue, so that speech, description, and the subtle intrusion of the narrator's ironic wit merge fluidly, creating the semblance of a seamless, integrated whole.

Many of these stories, like those in the preceding volume, have a discernible "oral" quality about them; they often give the reader the sense that the storyteller is right there, telling us the story. More frequently than before, Bowles chooses a first-person narrator. Again the writer's involvement with translation projects during this period, particularly in collaboration with Mohamad Mrabet, is probably responsible in part for these stylistic developments.

If there be a central motif in this collection of stories, a figure in the carpet, so to speak, it might be the preoccupation with houses, the structures we inhabit. The pattern and theme of many of these stories supply yet further examples of what Richard F. Patteson identifies as one of Bowles's central concerns: "That which lies outside is presented as potentially hostile and threatening, yet the barriers, the shelters, erected to keep the danger out are insufficient." The titles of two of the stories, "In the Red Room" and "The Little House," point to this emphasis, as does the content of many other stories.

In some instances stories begin with the presentation of a house, which becomes a fragile haven for human life or a contested site of opposing values. In "Madame and Ahmed" Mrs. Pritchard's house, surrounded by impressive gardens, "was at the top of a cliff overlooking the sea; the winds sweeping through the Strait of Gibraltar struck the spot first, and blew harder there." Two worldviews compete with each other under one roof, literally, in "The

Little House," which opens, "The little house had been built sixty or seventy years ago on the main street of what had been a village which seemed several miles outside of town; now the town had crept up on all sides." In either case, the ensuing dramas reveal a strain the structure ultimately withstands only after a reconfiguration of those patterns of life which they contain.

In the title story, "Midnight Mass," a Westerner actually loses possession of his childhood home in Tangier. Eight years after his mother's death, he comes back to Tangier to reclaim the house and finds it "in even worse condition than he had expected it to be. He had naively assumed that because he paid their wages promptly each month, the servants would make an attempt to keep it in order." He should have known better.

At a Christmas Eve party, the man agrees to let a Moroccan painter use a room in the house. This foothold is all the Moroccan needs. The Westerner is squeezed out: "He did not go to Tangier at Eastertime, nor yet during the summer. In September he got word that the painter's very rich and influential family had taken possession of the entire house." His lawyer is unable to evict them. The story symbolically shows the end of a certain kind of European postcolonial presence and the growing determination of Moroccans to conduct their own affairs. The Morocco of the 1980s was far different from that Bowles had first come to, in its colonial period, 50 years earlier.

Both "The Dismissal" and "Madame and Ahmed" are stories involving relationships between Western expatriate home owners in Tangier and their help. Built into the structure of these relationships are not only a difference in culture but a difference in class. Given the value of foreign currency and the very low wage levels in Morocco, most expatriates have easily been able to afford help. In some cases—such as that of the late Malcolm Forbes, one of Tangier's most notorious expatriates, best known for his collection of toy soldiers and the pair of Harleys he kept by the door of his Marshan mansion—the difference was vast indeed.

Naturally, stories about maids, drivers, and gardeners—their level of competence, their mishaps, their cleverness, problems in communication and trust—circulate in the expatriate community. "Madame and Ahmed" tells of one episode in the relationship between a wealthy Western woman and her Moroccan gardener, Ahmed: "She felt that they knew and understood one another in a basic and important fashion, even though Ahmed never had learned to pronounce her name. For him she was Madame.''

When the garden is doing poorly, her friends urge her to get rid of Ahmed, her gardener of 11 years. Ahmed, in order to keep his position, employs his wit when occasion presents itself. One day a man comes and persuades Madame to buy some plants Ahmed recognizes as being from the municipal garden. The man makes no attempt to hide his intention to take Ahmed's position. That night, after the plants have been put in, Ahmed sneaks out and snips the roots off them. The next day Madame notices the plants wilting in the sun, discovers the cause, and blames the thieves, just as Ahmed had hoped she would. To get rid of the thieves when they returned, Ahmed lies, saying Madame knew where they got the plants from and would report them to the police if they ever showed their faces again. ''Ahmed, what would I do without you?'' Madame exclaims in gratitude. When she asks what Ahmed said to get rid of the men, he lies again: ''I told him no true Moslem would play tricks on a woman with no husband.''

The story is rife with deceit. Everyone is guilty of something—Madame for thinking of dismissing her longtime gardener, the peddlers for stealing the plants, and Ahmed for tricking and lying to his employer. Not much harm comes to anyone, however, and we feel that in the end each got what he deserved.

The expatriate in ''The Eye,'' which appeared in the collection of *Best American Stories of 1979*, meets a worse fate than Madame at the hands of his help. We might imagine this story of an eccentric expatriate, Duncan Marsh, to be a popular one with those in the community. Bowles's telling, in the first person, seems to be but one more telling of a well-known tale, heard second- or thirdhand, transformed and embellished in so many retellings. Calling the story ''laconic, chilly, passionless,'' Joyce Carol Oates has noted that it ''reads as if it had no narrator at all, and aspires to a condition of sheer narrative bereft of character—a tale told by no one in particular (its 'hero,' never directly glimpsed, is dead before the story opens), which nevertheless possesses an uncanny suspenseful power.''

''Ten or twelve years ago,'' the story begins, ''there came to live in Tangier a man who would have done better to stay away.'' Members of the English-speaking community, we are told, said he got what he deserved. With a very sharp understanding of how expatriate communities function, Bowles writes, ''These people often have reactions similar to those of certain primitive groups: when misfortune overtakes one of their number, the others by mutual consent refrain from offering him aid, and merely sit back to watch, certain that he has called his suffering down upon himself. He has become taboo, and is incapable of receiving help.'' This sacrificial abandonment no doubt occurs partly because expatriates, especially in places such as Morocco, where manners and customs are so different from their own, live shipwrecked existences and feel they can ill afford to cast a rope to a drowning compatriot without the risk of being pulled along with him into the hostile sea.

Marsh, whom the narrator says he never himself knew, evidently came to Tangier, rented a home in the Djamaa el Mokra area, became ill, and eventually went back on a stretcher to his home in Vancouver, Canada, where he soon died. The scuttlebutt was that Marsh was but ''one more victim of a slow poisoning by native employees.'' Two interesting facts turn the case into a mystery for the narrator. First, Marsh left the nightwatchman with a certificate guaranteeing his livelihood should his employer leave Morocco. Second, the doctor examining Marsh reported curious patterns of incisions on the bottoms of the patient's feet.

The narrator himself becomes a kind of sleuth when he meets, seven or so years after the affair, the nightwatchman, Larbi, now a waiter in a Tangier restaurant. When Larbi lets the narrator see the written document Marsh left with him, he finds it is worded in such a way that the waiter could not collect a cent. Driven by his desire to solve the mystery, the narrator makes it well worth Larbi's while to accompany him to Marsh's vacant villa, where, on the porch, the Moroccan unfolds the story.

All would have been fine, apparently, if Marsh had not decided to replace his cook, Yasmina, who came with the place. Larbi is called in to find a replacement. The replacement brings her baby, whose crying drives Marsh to distraction. One day, in order to try to stop the baby from crying, Marsh gets down on all fours and makes a fierce face at the baby, causing it to burst into hysterics. When the baby becomes ill, of course, everyone concludes it is because this Westerner has put the evil eye on the girl. The incisions cut on Marsh's feet, Larbi says, were part of what was necessary to undo the spell.

Even with a number of the questions answered, the narrator admits ''a vague sense of disappointment'' because he had ''not only expected, but actually hoped, to find someone on whom the guilt might be fixed. What constitutes a crime? There was no criminal intent—only a mother moving in the darkness of ancient ignorance.''

Both the narrative technique and the thematic content of ''The Eye'' call to mind ''Reminders of Bouselham'' in *Things Gone and Things Still Here.* The story, which turns on the belief in the evil eye, reveals sharp differences in worldviews. Beyond this, the story presents the language issue in a way no other story in this volume does. English is the native tongue for the narrator, as well as for Bowles himself, yet in order to draw the story from Larbi, he uses Spanish, establishing a kind of neutral ground, much in the same way Bowles uses Spanish on a daily basis with his own driver, Abdelouahaïd, and with Mohamed Mrabet, who comes in every day to cook Bowles his dinner. When the narrator wants to gain even more trust, he speaks Arabic with Larbi. Bowles, like the narrator, understands and speaks the local Maghrebi dialect, though he does not read or write Arabic.

Source: Allen Hibbard, *''Midnight Mass,''* in *Paul Bowles: A Study of the Short Fiction,* Twayne Publishers, 1993, pp. 102–18.

Sources

Bowles, Paul, *The Stories of Paul Bowles,* HarperCollins, 2001, pp. 466–74.

Caponi, Gena Dagel, *Paul Bowles,* Twayne, 1998, p. 64.

Hibbard, Allen, ''Paul Bowles,'' in *Dictionary of Literary Biography,* Vol. 218: *American Short-Story Writers Since World War II,* Second Series, edited by Patrick Meanor, The Gale Group, 1999, pp. 56–69.

Prose, Francine, ''The Coldest Eye,'' in *Harper's Magazine,* Vol. 304, Issue 1822, March 2002, pp. 60–66.

Said, Edward, *Orientalism,* Vintage, 1978, pp. 1–7.

Wagner, Linda W., ''Paul Bowles and the Characterization of Women,'' in *Critique: Studies in Modern Fiction,* Vol. XXVII, No. 1, Fall 1985, p. 1524.

Further Reading

Bertens, Jonathan, *The Fiction of Paul Bowles,* Costerus, 1979.
    Bertens analyzes Bowles's fiction, focusing on themes of existentialism and postcolonialism.

Bowles, Paul, *Without Stopping,* G. P. Putnam's Sons, 1972.
    Bowles's autobiography is a useful resource. However, some critics have faulted it for being a less-than-candid account of the writer's life.

Caponi, Gena Dagel, *Paul Bowles: Romantic Savage,* Southern Illinois University Press, 1994.
    Caponi's interpretive biography of Bowles provides an exhaustive yet fascinating exploration of Bowles's contributions to music, ethnography, and literature.

Dillon, Millicent, *A Little Original Sin: The Life and Work of Jane Bowles,* Holt, Rinehart and Winston, 1981.
    Dillon makes extensive use of interviews with Paul Bowles for this biography of Bowles's wife. Jane Bowles was an influential part of her husband's writing life.

Pounds, Wayne, *Paul Bowles: The Inner Geography,* Peter Lang, 1985.
    Using the psychoanalytical theories of R. D. Laing, Pounds analyzes Bowles's fiction.

Stewart, Lawrence O., *The Illumination of North Africa,* Southern Illinois University Press, 1974.
    Stewart's useful study examines the connections between Bowles's travels in North Africa and his fiction.

The Fall of Edward Barnard

W. Somerset Maugham

1921

W. Somerset Maugham's short story "The Fall of Edward Barnard" was published in *The Trembling of a Leaf: Little Stories of the South Sea Islands* in 1921 (available from Replica Books). The story is principally about two young men from Chicago, Bateman Hunter and Edward Barnard, who have been friends since their college days. They are in love with the same woman, a Chicago socialite named Isabel Longstaffe. For reasons of business, Edward travels to the South Sea island of Tahiti. He is expected to return in two years and marry Isabel. But after a while, Edward discovers that he likes living on the island, and he has no plans to return. Bateman travels to Tahiti and tries to persuade Edward, whom he believes to be wasting his life, to return to Chicago. But Edward, who has discovered a new set of values in Tahiti, refuses to change his mind. He plans to marry a Tahitian girl and spend the rest of his life in this tropical paradise.

Thematically, "The Fall of Edward Barnard" deals with a clash of cultures between East and West. Maugham uses much irony to ensure that the East, where life is lived closer to nature, is seen in a better light than the materialistic West, as represented by Bateman and Isabel. The story also presents ideas about the role the social and cultural environment plays in shaping human character, and it illustrates Maugham's dislike of conventional morality.

Author Biography

William Somerset Maugham was born at the British Embassy in Paris on January 25, 1874. His mother died when he was eight and his father, an English lawyer, died when Maugham was ten. Maugham was sent to England to live with his uncle, a clergyman, and his aunt in Whitstable. He attended King's School in Canterbury, then spent over a year in Germany. From 1892 to 1897, Maugham attended medical school at St. Thomas's Hospital in London, receiving an M. D. degree. However, he had no desire to practice medicine, wanting instead to be a writer. His first novel, *Liza of Lambeth*, was published in 1897.

The next ten years constituted Maugham's literary apprenticeship. He published four more novels and a collection of short stories, *Orientations: Short Stories* (1899). He also wrote plays, but in that genre he had no initial success. But in 1907 his play *Lady Frederick* ran for over a year in London. It was the first of twenty-nine of his plays that would be produced over the next twenty-six years.

From 1914 to 1915, at the outset of World War I, Maugham served with a British ambulance unit and with military intelligence in Geneva. In 1915, he published what many regard as his finest novel, the autobiographical *Of Human Bondage*, which has twice been made into a movie. The following year, he visited the South Sea islands, which were to inspire several short stories, and in 1917 he was chief agent in Russia for the British and American secret services.

Although Maugham had homosexual tendencies throughout his life, he married Syrie Wellcome in 1917. They had a daughter, but the marriage was not happy, and the couple divorced in 1929.

Maugham's career continued to flourish and plays, novels, short stories and travel books poured from his pen. His major works from this period include three plays, *The Circle* (1921), *Our Betters* (1923), and *The Constant Wife* (1927); three short story collections, *The Trembling of a Leaf: Little Stories of the South Sea Islands* (1921), *The Casuarina Tree* (1926) and *Ashenden* (1927); and three novels, *The Moon and Sixpence* (1919), based on the life of Paul Gauguin, *The Painted Veil* (1925) and the comic novel, *Cakes and Ale* (1930).

Maugham's literary output remained prolific throughout the 1930s. He wrote three more novels, *The Narrow Corner* (1932), *Theatre* (1937), and *Christmas Holiday* (1939), as well as three more short story collections, and *The Summing Up* (1938), an autobiographical sketch.

During World War II, Maugham lived in the United States where he wrote one of his most important novels, *The Razor's Edge* (1944), as well as *The Mixture as Before* (1940), a collection of short stories. He published his last novel, *Catalina* in 1948.

By the 1950s, Maugham was perhaps the most widely read novelist of the century. In his old age he continued to write, publishing two collections of essays, *The Vagrant Mood* (1952) and *Points of View* (1958).

Maugham died at his villa on the French Riviera on December 16, 1965, at the age of ninety-one.

Plot Summary

''The Fall of Edward Barnard'' begins as Bateman Hunter is returning home to Chicago after a trip to Tahiti. He has some vital news to tell Isabel Longstaffe, a young woman he greatly admires, but he is unsure of how to convey it.

Bateman's father meets him at the train station. He asks about Edward Barnard, but Bateman says he would rather not talk about him. When they get home, Bateman calls Isabel, and she invites him to dinner that night. After dinner with her parents, Bateman and Isabel talk alone. She asks whether Edward Barnard is coming back, and he says no.

Then Bateman tells her his long story, and the narrator also gives the reader the background to what happened. Bateman and Edward are old friends, and they were both in love with Isabel. But Isabel chose Edward, and they were engaged to be married. But then Edward's father met with financial disaster, and Edward, who no longer had any money or prospects, arranged to join the business of a family friend named Braunschmidt. Braunschmidt is a South Sea merchant who owns a branch agency in Tahiti. The plan was for Edward to work in Tahiti for one or two years, learning the business, and then return to take up a position in Chicago. Isabel agreed to wait for him.

Before Edward's departure, his father warned him to stay clear of Arnold Jackson, his brother-in-law, who was the black sheep of the family, having served time in prison for financial fraud. Jackson was living now in Tahiti.

In Tahiti, Edward regularly wrote to Isabel. All seemed well, except for the fact that after a while Edward made no mention of returning to Chicago. Isabel was puzzled but not alarmed. Then Bateman heard that Edward no longer worked for Braunschmidt, having been fired for laziness and incompetence. Bateman decided to go on a business trip to Honolulu and return via Tahiti, to find out what was going on with Edward.

When Bateman reached Papeete, Tahiti, he was surprised to find that Edward was known to the locals as Arnold Jackson's nephew. He eventually found Edward, who was working as a salesman at a trading store. Bateman was surprised to find him in such a humble position, but Edward appeared to be perfectly content, happy, and relaxed.

They returned to Bateman's hotel, where they drank cocktails on the terrace. They were soon joined, to Bateman's confusion and alarm, by Arnold Jackson. Jackson invited them both to dinner that night at his house. He said his wife was a good cook, which puzzled Bateman who knew that Jackson had a wife in Geneva. In the conversation that ensued after Jackson left, Edward revealed his admiration and affection for Jackson, to Bateman's further consternation. Bateman resolved to find out why his friend was so attached to a man Bateman regarded as reprehensible. He also noted that his friend's values seemed to have changed.

Jackson's house was on a hill overlooking the Pacific Ocean, and when Edward and Batman arrived, they went bathing. Jackson joined them, wearing a *pareo,* the native dress. As the three men walked back to the house, Edward was also dressed in a *pareo,* but Bateman insisted on wearing his own Western clothes. At the house, Jackson spoke with great idealism and spirituality, and Bateman had to remind himself of the man's unsavory history. Jackson's beautiful young daughter Eva mixed a cocktail for them, and Jackson spoke unself-consciously of his prison days. Bateman was embarrassed and angry. His discomfort increased when Eva placed on his head a garland of flowers that she had made.

After dinner the three men talked on the verandah. Jackson told romantic stories of the history of

W. Somerset Maugham

the island. After Jackson left them alone, Edward told his friend that he was happy in Tahiti and had no plans to return to Chicago. Bateman urged him to rethink, saying that he had succumbed to evil influences. Edward then explained how he had changed since he arrived in Tahiti two years before. At first he had been full of energy and had many ideas for how the island could be developed and modernized. But gradually he came to like life the way it was in Tahiti, with its ease and leisure and its good-natured people. He found he had time to think and read, and he realized that everything he had formerly thought to be important—the bustle and industry of a large city—seemed trivial. Now he valued beauty, truth, and goodness. He said he still admired Isabel and was prepared to marry her if she held him to his promise, but it was clear that this was not what Edward really wanted. Edward then said that Bateman should marry Isabel instead. Bateman was shocked, but he felt some exultation over the idea. Edward went on to say that he planned to marry Jackson's daughter and move to a small island a thousand miles away. Jackson owned the island and had offered to give it to him. Bateman once more was bewildered and perplexed, thinking that his friend was wasting his life. But Edward looked forward with zest to his future. He believed he would live a peaceful and happy life.

After Bateman finishes telling Isabel his story, she realizes that the situation is hopeless. She knows she will not be able to persuade Edward to return, and she declares that Edward is his own worst enemy.

Bateman then blurts out his love for Isabel, and she says she loves him, too. As they embrace, it is clear that they will marry. Bateman thinks of his glowing future in business, and Isabel thinks of all the antique furniture she will be able to acquire and the cultured life they will lead together.

Characters

Edward Barnard

Edward Barnard comes from a well-off family in Chicago and is Bateman Hunter's best friend. But just after Edward becomes engaged to a suitable young lady, Isabel Longstaffe, his father loses his fortune. Edward is left penniless and is forced to do his business apprenticeship in Tahiti, thanks to the assistance of a family friend. Everyone expects great things from Edward, since he is handsome, capable, energetic, and ambitious. But the longer Edward stays in Tahiti, the more his values change. After two years there, he no longer aspires to become a captain of industry in Chicago, or to marry Isabel. On the contrary, he is quite content in a humble occupation in Tahiti, an island he has come to love. He has learned tolerance and understanding. Bateman implores him to return to Chicago and not waste his life, but Edward believes that he can best realize his new ideals of beauty and goodness in the South Seas.

Eva

Eva is Arnold Jackson's beautiful young daughter by his wife Lavina. Edward Barnard plans to marry her.

Bateman Hunter

Bateman Hunter is Edward Barnard's best friend from their college days. They both fall in love with Isabel, but Bateman is magnanimous when Isabel chooses Edward. Bateman remains a loyal friend to both of them, keeping his real feelings for Isabel in check. He does not envy them their happiness. Bateman is ambitious about his career in a conventional kind of way, but his greatest virtue is his loyalty to his friend. When he travels to Tahiti, he has only Edward's best interests at heart, but his encounter with an alien culture reveals some less appealing aspects of his personality. He is rigid, priggish, and stiff, unable to appreciate values and lifestyles other than his own. When faced with life in Tahiti, he is continually uncomfortable. He refuses to wear native clothes and is embarrassed when Eva places a garland on his head. He cannot relax but remains aloof and disapproving. However, Bateman's motivations are impeccable, and he is a man of unshakable integrity. Only when it is certain that Edward and Isabel will not marry does he confess his love for her. He and Isabel seem to have every chance of happiness since they both have the same materialistic values.

Mr. Hunter

Mr. Hunter is Bateman Hunter's father. He is a wealthy Chicago businessman, the owner of Hunter Motor Traction and Automobile Company. He built his own house in the city to resemble a chateau on the Loire.

Arnold Jackson

Arnold Jackson is Isabel's uncle and the black sheep of the family. Many years before the story begins, he had a successful career in Chicago as a respected banker and was a philanthropist and church member. But he was convicted of fraud and served seven years in prison. His crimes involved such consistent and widespread dishonesty that there was nothing to mitigate his disgrace. His relatives never mentioned his name again, and his wife and children had to move to Europe to escape the stigma.

Jackson ended up in Tahiti. When Bateman visits the island, he desperately wants to avoid him but is unable to do so, since Jackson and Edward have become close friends. Jackson turns out to be rather different from the man Bateman imagined him. Bateman expects to find a rogue and a scoundrel, but Jackson is courteous and charming, an engaging storyteller and a perfect host. He speaks of his incarceration without embarrassment and appears to be happy and content. He loves the South Seas and accepts life serenely as it comes to him. Edward regards him as generous and kind, the most agreeable companion he has ever known.

Lavina

Lavina is Arnold Jackson's second wife. She is a native of Tahiti.

Isabel Longstaffe

Isabel Longstaffe comes from one of Chicago's elite families. She is educated, cultured, sophisticated and is a fine conversationalist. She is also slim and beautiful. Her personality is virtuous and upright, with an unyielding sense of honor. But she is also rigid in her judgments which once made, she never changes. Both Bateman and Edward love her. After she and Edward become engaged and Edward departs for Tahiti, she waits patiently for his return. She never doubts his love, but when she hears the bad news about his change of heart, she quickly accepts it and wastes no time on grieving. She is quick to pass adverse judgment on Edward, saying he is his own worst enemy and that he lacks backbone. When she accepts Bateman's marriage proposal, she is happy because she knows she will have a large house with antique furniture (just like the one she grew up in) and will be able to give concerts and have dinner parties with all the most cultured people in Chicago.

Mr. Longstaffe

Mr. Longstaffe is Isabel's father. He advises Edward to avoid any contact in Tahiti with Arnold Jackson, his brother-in-law.

Themes

Culture Clash

Central to the story is the clash between Western and Eastern values and cultures. Bateman sums up the Western way of seeing things when he says, in answer to Edward's question about how a man gets the best out of life, ''By doing his duty, by hard work, by meeting all the obligations of his state and station.'' Bateman, as an embodiment of the Chicago spirit of the 1920s, values money and power. He justifies this by saying that these assets help to create jobs for many people.

In contrast to the eternal hustle and bustle of Chicago, which is emblematic of Western civilization as a whole, is Tahiti. In this haven of the East, the leisurely, relaxed pace of life and the friendliness of the people suggest a completely different set of values. Much of this is shaped by the warm climate and the sheer beauty of the region, which seems to belong less to time than to eternity. For example, this is the view from the verandah of Arnold Jackson's house: ''The full moon, sailing across an unclouded sky, made a pathway on the broad sea that led to the boundless realms of Forever.''

Edward soon finds in Tahiti that the Western values he formerly lived by were pointless. The things that mattered to him before no longer matter, as Isabel astutely deduces from his letters. Edward decides that the city life he has turned his back on is just a monotonous, draining routine of going to an office each day to work until nightfall and pursuing the same trivial round of leisure pursuits. Worldly ambition now means nothing to him, and Chicago seems like a prison.

If in the West there is an emphasis on achievement, progress, and the conquest of nature, the East prefers to live in harmony with nature. In place of the Western notion of progress is the value of acceptance, of taking life as it comes and as it is. But to Bateman's Western mind, living by this alien set of values is nothing more than a ''living death.'' He tries to convince Edward that he has been ''breathing poisoned air.'' Bateman is entirely blind to the irony of an heir of the Hunter Motor Traction and Automobile Company talking to an inhabitant of the unpolluted South Seas about poisoned air (although to be fair to Bateman, few people in the 1920s could have been aware of the ill effects of air pollution by the automobile).

But Edward believes that it is in the Eastern paradise of Tahiti that he can best live according to his new values of beauty, truth, and goodness. Tahiti also stimulates him to a spiritual view of life. He believes that he has discovered his own soul in his life on the island, and he refers to the New Testament passage that says it will not profit a man if he should gain the whole world and lose his own soul. Thus the dichotomy between the cultures of West and East is given a religious dimension—it is the West, of course, (in Edward's view) that gains the world but at the price of losing what is most valuable about life.

Bateman, on the other hand, believes he can find such things as beauty and truth in Chicago. He is himself a man of integrity, and the story does not entirely favor the East at the expense of the West. He and Isabel value great art, for example, although in Bateman's case this is somewhat undermined by his motivations, as he thinks of the great collection he plans to amass. He simply wants to outdo New York, which is Western competitive spirit at its best (or worst, depending on one's point of view). Western art in any case is an artificial creation, quite

Topics for Further Study

- Which is more important in shaping a person's personality: his genetic inheritance or his social environment? In other words, is ''nurture'' more important than ''nature,'' as the story would seem to suggest? If so, are people no more than the products of their environment? How might you be different had you grown up in a different environment?

- Research the topic of intercultural marriage. What are some of the problems typically encountered by people marrying someone from a different culture?

- Do you think that Edward made the right choice or is Bateman right in thinking that he is wasting his life? Can their different sets of values be reconciled, or must a person always choose one or the other? Can one have what Edward wants—beauty, truth, and goodness—as well as the material values of American life?

- Research the effects of the French colonization of Tahiti and other South Sea islands. What were the effects of colonialism? Were the islands helped or hindered by it? What role do the French play in French Polynesia today?

- In 1995 and 1996, there were riots in Tahiti over the issue of French nuclear testing in the region, which had been going on since 1966. Research this issue. What were the rights and wrongs involved?

---

different from the natural, artless beauty of the South Seas, a beauty that even Bateman is forced to acknowledge as he looks out of the window at Jackson's house:

> [Y]ou saw the vast calmness of the Pacific and twenty miles away, airy and unsubstantial like the fabric of a poet's fancy, the unimaginable beauty of the island which is called Murea. It was all so lovely that Bateman stood abashed.

Nature versus Nurture

The story explores the old debate about whether people are what they are because of certain innate qualities (nature) or because they are shaped by the environment in which they live (nurture). The latter is clearly the case. Isabel, for example, is presented as a product of her environment. Bateman believes that ''no city in the world could have produced her but Chicago.'' Bateman and Edward, before Edward leaves for Tahiti, are also products of their environment. Their values and ambitions have been entirely shaped by the big city environment in which they were raised. Chicago is presented as the most important city in America. Although it is crowded, full of traffic and noise, Bateman does not regard this as a disadvantage. On the contrary, he sees it as the embodiment of a strong collective will to develop the city industrially and so create the kind of wealth that his family, as well as Isabel's, enjoys.

It is because of the importance of environment in molding character that Edward undergoes such a profound change after arriving in Tahiti. At first he is the quintessential American, full of plans to bring the blessings of industrial and technological development to a backward portion of the world. But after a while, the climate, the beauty of the island, and the easygoing, relaxed people all work to change him.

Style

Irony

The title of the story ''The Fall of Edward Barnard,'' is ironic. A statement is ironic if its real meaning is different from the one that is asserted on the surface. In this story, the irony unfolds gradually. When the name of Edward Barnard is first mentioned on Bateman's return to Chicago, Bateman's face darkens, and he says to his father, "I'd sooner not speak about him, Dad." At this point the reader has every reason to suppose that something bad has indeed befallen Edward Barnard. But as the hints unfold in Edward's letters, the reader begins to question whether something else may be the case.

At the same time, Maugham sets up another thread of irony in the story, with the introduction of Arnold Jackson. Jackson is another man who has supposedly fallen. Formerly a respected figure in Chicago society, he served time in prison for financial fraud. So when Bateman travels to Tahiti, he is expecting to find a rogue and a scoundrel, someone beyond the pale of civilized society. But the man he encounters does not fit this expectation. Nor does Edward fit into Bateman's expectations of meeting a man who has failed at his profession and been branded lazy and incompetent.

At this point, the irony becomes so pervasive that it amounts to what is sometimes called structural irony. This is where the irony occurs in more than the odd statement or two; it is central to the author's strategy. In this respect, Bateman functions as what is called a naïve hero, because he fails to see what is obvious to the reader. For example, he insists on interpreting Jackson's character from his own previous expectations. He cannot accurately perceive the man who is in front of his face and so is confused by what he sees and hears. He cannot make the mental leap required to reassess the situation. Here, for example, is the description of Jackson and Bateman's reaction: "His voice was deep and resonant. He seemed to breathe forth the purest idealism, and Bateman had to urge himself to remember that the man who spoke was a criminal and a cruel cheat." The reader immediately appreciates the irony of Bateman's obtuseness.

The same is true for Bateman's perceptions of Edward. He cannot see what is obvious to the reader. When he first sees Edward in Tahiti, for example, he notices something is different about him, but he cannot put two and two together and reach the conclusion that Edward is happy in Tahiti: "He [Edward] walked with a new jauntiness; there was a carelessness in his demeanor, a gaiety about nothing in particular, which Bateman could not entirely blame, but which exceedingly puzzled him."

The irony brings into focus Bateman's basic assumptions (and perhaps the reader's) about what is valuable in life, what success might consist of and what the purpose of life might be.

The final irony in the story turns on Bateman himself. As Bateman clasps Isabel in his arms, Maugham clearly intends the reader to see a superficial couple dreaming empty, materialistic dreams about the future. The surface meaning of the words does not necessarily suggest this, but when taken in the context of the story as a whole, the ironic intention is clear. And the final words of the story, "Poor Edward," uttered by Isabel, also have a different, ironic meaning for the reader than they do for Isabel.

Narrative Technique

Maugham utilizes the technique of the frame story. This occurs when there is a story within a story. The frame in this story is the Chicago setting with which the narrative begins and ends. It is largely concerned with Bateman's interactions with Isabel. In between is the story of Edward and his Tahitian adventure. The frame story is a common technique in both ancient and modern literature. The best known example is probably Chaucer's *The Canterbury Tales*.

Point of View

Maugham adopted, for part of the story, the form of the omniscient third-person narrator, who can see into the minds and emotions of all the characters. However, much of the story is told only through Bateman's point of view. This is known as a limited third-person narrator. The reader only knows events and people as they are seen through the eyes of the viewpoint character. During the part of the narrative set in Tahiti, for example, Edward and Jackson are seen entirely through Bateman's eyes, which adds to their mystery and enables Maugham to deepen the irony on which the meaning of the story rests.

Historical Context

Tahiti

Tahiti was first discovered by Europeans in 1767, in the expedition of the English Captain Samuel Wallis. Louis-Antoine de Bouganville fol-

Compare & Contrast

- **1920s:** Because of its excellent harbor, Papeete, the largest town in Tahiti, has been a center of trade since the nineteenth century. Products shipped from Papeete include copra, sugarcane, vanilla, and coffee. The port is also used often by whaling ships, and it is the seat of the French governor.

  Today: With its modern harbor and airport, Papeete is a major tourist destination and a center of transpacific trade. It is also the seat of the Territorial Assembly, which is the legislative body of French Polynesia. The Assembly consists of forty-one members elected by popular vote. French Polynesia is made up of 130 South Pacific islands, which together constitute a French Overseas Territory. Tahiti, the largest island, has been fully in charge of its internal affairs since 1984. The Territory as a whole has benefited from a five-year development agreement with France that from 1994 to 1998 created many new jobs.

- **1920s:** Chicago is a rapidly growing city. In 1920, the population is 2,701,705; by 1930, this figure climbs to 3,376,438. Chicago also gains a reputation as a lawless city, typified by the activities of the gangster Al Capone. During the 1920s, Capone controls the gambling industry, brothels, nightclubs, distilleries, and breweries. His income is reported to be $100 million.

  Today: In 2000, the population of Chicago is 2,896,016. The population had been falling steadily since the 1950s, but it stabilized in the 1990s. The Sears Tower, built in 1973, is the tallest building in North America and the third tallest in the world. It is 1,450 feet tall (a quarter of a mile), with 110 stories. Chicago has three of the fifteen tallest buildings in the world. In addition to the Sears Tower, these are the Aon Center and the John Hancock Center.

- **1920s:** Colonization by European countries of much of Asia and Africa continues to produce literature written by members of the colonizing nations in which they report and reflect on the colonial experience. Writers such as Maugham, George Orwell, Evelyn Waugh, and E. M. Forster make their mark in this field.

  Today: The age of colonialism is over, and a new genre of literature, known as postcolonial literature, has sprung up. The term refers to literature written mostly by African and Asian authors in the period following their nations' independence from the colonizing European powers. Examples of postcolonial literature include Chinua Achebe's *Things Fall Apart,* Salman Rushdie's *Midnight's Children,* Bapsi Sidhwa's *Cracking India,* V. S. Naipaul's *A Bend in the River,* and Vikram Chandra's *Red Earth and Pouring Rain.*

---

lowed in 1768, claiming the island for France. England's Captain James Cook followed in 1769. The island is actually two islands that are joined together by a small isthmus. Papeete, where much of "The Fall of Edward Barnard" takes place, lies on the northwestern coast. It is the biggest town on the island. The island of Moorea (Murea in the story) lies about twelve miles northwest of Tahiti.

Tahiti was ruled by the local Pomare dynasty until 1880, when the French assumed control. (The French influence can be detected in the name of the hotel de la Fleur in the story.) In 1891, the French artist Paul Gauguin (1848–1903) visited Tahiti, and the exotic location gave him inspiration for his art. He remained there for two years and returned in 1895.

Maugham had long read about the South Sea islands and formed a romantic notion of them before his trip there in 1916. When he arrived in Papeete, he noted a strong English and American influence, although there was also a decidedly French flavor, since the island was a French colony. French, as well as English and Tahitian, was spoken by the native people. Maugham noted that the roads were as well kept up as many roads in France and that the marketplace might have been in any French village.

Maugham and his traveling companion, Gerald Haxton, were shown several paintings by Gauguin at a house thirty-five miles from Papeete, one of which Maugham purchased and took back to France. Maugham's novel, *The Moon and Sixpence* (1919) was set largely in Tahiti, with a protagonist modeled on Gauguin.

Maugham also took a boat trip to the island of Murea. This is his description of a native dwelling:

> The native houses are oblong, covered with a rough thatch of great leaves, and made of thin bamboos placed close together which let in light and air. There are no windows, but generally two or three doors.

The Short Story

Maugham was influenced by the short stories of the French writer Guy de Maupassant (1850–1893), whom he read when he was young. Maugham admired de Maupassant because the French author knew how to tell an interesting anecdote and all of his stories had a beginning, a middle and an end, and they did not wander—qualities that Maugham's stories also possess. Maugham did, however, fault de Maupassant for being weak on character development.

Maugham points out in his writings about his own craft how his work differs from that of the Russian writer Anton Chekhov (1860–1904), one of the acknowledged masters of the short story genre. Chekhov was very influential on many writers at about the time Maugham was writing his South Sea stories. Although Maugham admired Chekhov, he thought he was not a good storyteller, since he wrote mostly about character and atmosphere and so his stories do not have well-developed plots.

Maugham himself was not an innovator, and he did not develop the short story in the way that some of his contemporaries, such as Virginia Woolf or D. H. Lawrence, did. In terms of their form, his stories belong more to the nineteenth century.

Literature of Colonialism

In his South Sea stories and others set in the East, Maugham stands in the tradition of the literature of colonialism. The major writers in this mode before Maugham were Rudyard Kipling (1865–1936) and Joseph Conrad (1857–1924). Kipling was a master of the short story, who lived for seven years in India when it was under British rule. He wrote of the problems encountered by the English colonials who lived in India amongst a subject people. Conrad made effective use of his experiences in Malaya and Africa.

Contemporary with Maugham were writers such as George Orwell, Evelyn Waugh, and Graham Greene, all of whom wrote of the colonial experience from a British point of view. E. M. Forster's novel *A Passage to India* (1924) also deals with similar issues.

Critical Overview

"The Fall of Edward Barnard," as well as many of Maugham's other South Sea stories, were originally published in a commercial magazine. The story then appeared as one of six in the collection *The Trembling of a Leaf: Little Stories of the South Sea Islands* (1921). The volume was popular with the reading public and received some critical acclaim. Louise Maunsell Field, in the *New York Times,* admires Maugham's delineation of character, in which "there is a broader sympathy, a deeper, clearer comprehension, a finer tolerance than any shown in his earlier work." Rebecca West, however, is more critical. Writing in the *New Statesman,* she censures Maugham for a "certain cheap and tiresome attitude towards life, which nearly mars these technically admirable stories." She accuses Maugham of being cynical for satirizing the earnestness of Bateman Hunter in "The Fall of Edward Barnard."

During the 1920s and beyond, in spite of the fact that Maugham's works in many genres enjoyed huge popular success, he was relegated by the British literary intelligentsia to second-rate status. For a while it became fashionable to denigrate his achievements. However, Maugham was more highly regarded in French, German, and American academic circles.

Maugham's South Sea stories have withstood the test of time well. They are often rated as amongst Maugham's best work, and some modern critics have commented directly on "The Fall of Edward Barnard." Stanley Archer describes it as an "ironic and lighthearted sequel to Henry James's novel *The Ambassadors*." Forrest D. Burt draws attention to the similarities between three Maugham characters: Edward in "The Fall of Edward Barnard," Strickland in the novel *The Moon and Sixpence*, and Larry in the novel *The Razor's Edge*. All three characters reject "standard morality and traditional success in favor of the naturalness and spontaneity of life in Tahiti." Finally, Archie K. Loss, in *W. Somerset Maugham,* comments that in all of the South Sea stories, "descriptive details are important in establishing both mood and character."

Criticism

Bryan Aubrey

Aubrey holds a Ph.D. in English and has published many articles on twentieth-century literature. In this essay, Aubrey points out some parallels to the themes of Maugham's story in other literary works.

In his evocation of the naturalness of life in Tahiti as contrasted with the seemingly artificial, pointless life led by many in Chicago, Maugham takes the side of his character Edward. Any doubt about this can be eliminated by consulting Maugham's reflections on his life and career, *The Summing Up* (1938). In section fifty-three, Maugham writes of his experience in the South Seas, saying that his encounter with the East supplied him with "a new self." He had been accustomed to thinking that the most important things in life were art and culture (rather like Isabel in the story). But in the South Seas, he entered a new world in which the people were unlike any he had known before. Few of them had any culture, but they had more vitality than people in the West. They lived a more elemental life and did not disguise themselves with the masks of culture:

> They had learnt life in a different school from mine and had come to different conclusions. They led it on a different plane; I could not . . . go on thinking mine a higher one. It was different. Their lives too formed themselves to the discerning eye into a pattern that had order and finally coherence.

This could almost be Edward in the story, trying to explain himself to an uncomprehending Bateman.

In the opposition between nature (Tahiti) and culture (Chicago) that drives the story, "The Fall of Edward Barnard" has many literary echoes. This can be seen not only in the work of other writers of the period who tackled the meeting of East and West (Kipling and Conrad, for example) but also in the themes of the romantic movement in the early nineteenth century. Maugham's back to nature theme

might, for example, be illustrated by William Wordsworth's two poems "Expostulation and Reply" and "The Tables Turned" from *Lyrical Ballads* (1798). These poems, like "The Fall of Edward Barnard," contain a dialogue between two men with opposing opinions. One values culture as preserved in books and counsels hard work. The other, who speaks for Wordsworth, finds his fulfillment not in books but in silent communion with nature. He tells his friend to "Come forth into the light of things, / Let Nature be your teacher."

The debate is couched in different terms by Victorian poet Alfred Lord Tennyson, in his two poems "Ulysses" and "The Lotos Eaters," which were inspired by Homer's epic poem *The Odyssey.* In "Ulysses," the great virtue is active endeavor. Having returned to his home on Ithaca, Ulysses cannot bear to remain idle. Like the ever-questing, ever-expanding, and progressing Western civilization, he longs to seek out new knowledge and adventures. In "The Lotos Eaters," on the other hand, the people drug themselves into a state of passivity with the fruit of the lotos. They forget their homeland, their own civilization, and are content to rest forever in their calm, dreamy paradise. The two poems illustrate two modes of being, the active and the passive, and in that they resemble the Chicago and Tahiti of "The Fall of Edward Barnard." Interestingly, this is exactly the position Bateman takes when he tells Edward that his infatuation with the island is like that of a "dope-fiend." He tries to convince Edward that when he gets back to Chicago and pursues an active life again, he will feel relieved to have weaned himself from the drug.

In his use of a framing device to tell his story, Maugham creates yet another literary echo, this time of a common pattern in Shakespearean comedy. In a number of these comedies, the action begins in the real world of the city or court (the equivalent of Chicago in the story) and then moves quickly to a "green world" in which life is lived in a purer way (the equivalent of Tahiti). Finally, the action moves back to the city. This is the pattern found in *As You Like It,* for example. The green world of the Forest of Arden is a place where the characters are freed from their normal social selves and are able to discover deeper values of life, just as Edward and Arnold Jackson do in the "green world" of Tahiti.

The literary echoes in the story are not confined to earlier themes in English literature. The other

What Do I Read Next?

- Maugham's *Collected Short Stories* (Penguin Twentieth-Century Classics, Viking Press, 1992), contains every short story that he wrote, including the eighteen that resulted from Maugham's travels in the South Pacific and southeast Asia.

- *In the South Seas* (Penguin Classics edition, 1999), by Robert Louis Stevenson, is a travel book that records Stevenson's two-year journey from the Marqueses Islands in French Polynesia to Tahiti, Honolulu, and Samoa in the late nineteenth century.

- *Tales of the South Pacific* (Fawcett, 1989), by James A. Michener, won the 1948 Pulitzer Prize for fiction. Set in the South Pacific during World War II, it shows how the people of the region were caught up in the conflict.

- Rudyard Kipling's classic novel *Kim* (1901, reprinted by Viking Press, 1992), is set in India during British rule. Kipling's portrait of Indian life is sympathetic, and the contrast noticeable in ''The Fall of Edward Barnard'' between the active way of life of the Westerners and the more contemplative, spiritual life of the indigenous population is apparent in Kim as well. The story is about the adventures of Kim O'Hara, who grew up on the streets of Lahore, the orphaned son of an Irish soldier stationed in India.

---

stories in *The Trembling of a Leaf* (the collection of stories in which ''The Fall of Edward Barnard'' appears) also provide valuable commentary, pointing up certain themes in the story, modifying our perception of others. For example, ''The Fall of Edward Barnard'' is the most optimistic story in the collection, and a reader might well suppose that Edward is set for a happy life with his native bride in his South Sea paradise. But reading ''Red'' and ''The Pool'' might lessen the reader's belief that such an intercultural marriage can work. In Maugham's stories, fate does not treat lovers with much kindness, and the ultimate results of the encounters between Western men and Eastern women are rarely happy.

In ''Red,'' a young American sailor named Red deserts from his warship and ends up on one of the islands of American Samoa. Like Edward Barnard in Tahiti, Red is enamored of the island, falls in love with a young native girl, and decides to stay. He and the girl live happily for a while, but when a British whaling ship arrives on the island, Red feels a longing for tobacco. Going onto the ship to obtain some, he is kidnapped by the captain who needs an extra hand on board. Many years later, Red, now ugly and fat, returns to the island for one nostalgic visit to the place where he and his girl used to live. The girl is still there but is now an old woman who does not even recognize him.

''The Pool'' has an even more negative outcome. Lawson, a young Scotsman in Samoa, falls in love with the island and with a half-caste girl named Ethel. They marry and like Red, are happy for a year or so. But when Ethel gives birth to a son who is dark and looks like a native child, Lawson realizes that the boy will be discriminated against by the whites on the island, so he persuades Ethel to accompany him back to Scotland. But Ethel cannot settle down in the cold climate of Scotland, and as soon as she can, she returns to Samoa with her son. Lawson follows, but he cannot find work on the island and becomes an alcoholic. When he discovers that Ethel is having an affair with another man, he drowns himself in the pool where they first met.

In ''Rain,'' one of Maugham's most famous stories, he develops a theme that is also apparent in ''The Fall of Edward Barnard:'' a dislike of conventional morality. In the latter story, Arnold Jackson is a man condemned by his society as a cheat and a felon. But Maugham refuses to go along with this judgment. He presents Jackson as a sympathetic

> In Maugham's stories, fate does not treat lovers with much kindness, and the ultimate results of the encounters between Western men and Eastern women are rarely happy."

figure: kind, generous, and wise. It is the more conventional characters, Bateman and Isabel, who are the object of Maugham's satire.

Maugham's target in "Rain" is the conventional Christian morality of the Davidsons, a missionary couple who are temporarily stranded at Pago-Pago, the capital of American Samoa, on the island of Tutuila. The Davidsons are a dreadful pair. Mrs. Davidson is disgusted by the "natives." She thinks their dancing is immoral, and she and her husband agree that the native dress, a loincloth called a *lava-lava,* is indecent. That too, according to Mrs. Davidson, encourages immorality, and her husband believes that the island will not be Christianized until every boy over ten years old is made to wear trousers. Eventually he cooks up a scheme whereby the natives are fined every time they "sin," and one thing deemed a sin is not wearing trousers. Maugham's biting irony is in fine form here. Interestingly, the same subject comes up in "The Fall of Edward Barnard." Edward and Arnold Jackson feel comfortable wearing the pareo, a loincloth, which is the native costume. But Bateman is embarrassed by the pareo and insists on wearing his high-collared blue serge suit, which seems inappropriate given the local climate. The contrast is part of the nature versus nurture theme. In the more "primitive" society, there is no shame or embarrassment at showing the body, whereas in "civilized" society the body is always covered.

In "Rain," the racism of Mrs. Davidson, who does not trust the natives to do anything right, draws attention to an element that also appears in "The Fall of Edward Barnard," although it is not given great prominence. That element is the disparaging remarks Bateman makes about the native inhabitants of Tahiti. When he notices that the young man who shows him to his hotel has "a good deal of native blood," he involuntarily adopts a haughty manner toward him. Then he refers to one of the customers at the store where Edward works as a "greasy nigger." The racism creeps into little remarks made by Bateman with no ill intent, as when he seeks to reassure Isabel that Edward is a fine fellow: "He's white, through and through." Bateman's racism is unconscious; he has probably never thought much about it. He simply reflects the attitudes that many white people of his time and place shared. They would no more question their belief in white superiority than they would question whether the sun would rise in the morning.

The Davidsons in "Rain" believe in the superiority not only of their race but also of their religion. They also believe in the absolute rightness of their moral principles. But Maugham shows what happens when people get too high and mighty about their own righteousness. The zealous Reverend Davidson is appalled about the presence of a prostitute in the same house where they are staying; he harries and bullies her and cruelly insists that she be put on a ship for San Francisco, even when he knows that she faces a three-year prison term there. He also indulges in long drawn-out prayer sessions with her in order to convert her. But then, one morning, Davidson commits suicide by cutting his own throat. It transpires that in one of his sessions with the prostitute he had himself fallen prey to lust. Afterwards, he could not live with the knowledge that he had betrayed his own code of behavior.

The moral is that often, underneath the veneer of virtue, lie darker forces that will eventually, when circumstances dictate, rise to the surface. A similar truth emerges in "The Fall of Edward Barnard," although it manifests the other way around. Behind the appearance of vice in Arnold Jackson is a more virtuous self, which life in Tahiti brings to light. Appearances, Maugham seems to be saying, are one thing; reality is another.

On balance, the South Sea stories in *The Trembling of a Leaf* reveal more of the perils than the pleasures that lie in wait for the white man who ventures into one of these apparent tropical paradises. The final example is "Mackintosh." Unlike Edward Barnard, Red, and initially Lawson, Mackintosh hates the Samoan island on which he is an assistant administrator. He does not like the heat, which he would willingly exchange for some cold winds in his native Aberdeen, Scotland, and he is tormented by mosquitoes. (How different this is from the idyllic setting of Tahiti.) He feels like a prisoner on the island. When his boss is killed by the natives whom he regarded as his children, Mackintosh cannot bear the guilt he feels, since he allowed the killer to steal his gun, and he shoots himself.

Maugham never forgot his travels to the East which continued to provide material for his fiction. As late as 1944, in his novel *The Razor's Edge*, he returned to the same theme. Larry, an American from Chicago, travels to India in order to find greater meaning in his life. Like Edward Barnard, he rejects materialism and seeks a more spiritual life. But over the long-term, he does not fare well. Perhaps the reader who enjoyed ''The Fall of Edward Barnard'' and sympathized with its protagonist can be glad that Maugham chose to pursue Edward's story no further than his early dreams of happiness in the South Seas.

Source: Bryan Aubrey, Critical Essay on ''The Fall of Edward Barnard,'' in *Short Stories for Students,* The Gale Group, 2003.

John Whitehead

In the following essay excerpt, Whitehead explores thematic elements in the stories in Maugham's collection The Trembling of a Leaf, *calling ''The Fall of Edward Barnard'' ''pure comedy.''*

In the notebooks Maugham brought back from his wartime voyaging in the South Seas were entries relating to other places besides Tahiti, in particular Honolulu and islands in the Samoan group, and these he came to recognize as providing raw material for short stories, a *genre* he had abandoned along with the novel ten years previously on making his breakthrough in the theatre. But the stories suggested by this material would be of a different kind and on an ampler scale than any he had previously attempted. There were eventually six of them, each of between 12,000 and 15,000 words in length, which together made a book about the size of the average novel. *The Trembling of a Leaf* was the first of five volumes published between 1921 and 1932, each containing six short stories of roughly that length. All thirty were issued in one volume in 1934 as Maugham's collected short stories, and they have been included in his subsequent collections; but it is worth stressing at this point how much the reader gains by reading the stories in their original volumes. The six stories in each by supplementing and illuminating one another form a distinct artistic whole, giving a unity of effect which is lost when a particular story is read out of context. In the case of *The Trembling of a Leaf* this effect is enhanced by the stories being prefaced by a sketch of the Pacific and rounded off by an 'Envoi', which do not appear in any of the collected editions. The irony in its sub-title 'Little Stories of the South Sea Islands', which suggests a series of improving tales issued by some missionary society, is only fully borne in on the reader when he has finished the last story.

For Maugham's purpose in these six stories (as well as in those which were to follow) was to explore the extremes of human emotion and behaviour, so that as a matter of course they deal with sex in its less domestic aspects, suicide, and murder. Each has for its skeleton an anecdote with—as Maugham so often insisted—a beginning, a middle and an end; and these bony structures he fleshed out by presenting his main characters in the round against authentically described backgrounds. For equally with Hardy's Wessex fiction they may properly be termed stories of character and environment. There is a further preliminary point to be made. The very readability of Maugham's stories carries with it the inherent risk that the reader will rest content with the superficial pleasures they offer and fail to appreciate their wider points of reference and deeper resonances. 'Mackintosh', the first story in *The Trembling of a Leaf*, furnishes a convenient example of this.

It is set in the fictitious island of Talua in the western part of the Samoan group which, having fallen to Germany's share when Germany and America divided the islands between themselves, was occupied by the British in 1914. It can be inferred that the events described took place two years later, about the time of Maugham's visit to the islands. Despite the story's title its central character is Walker, the 60-year-old, self-made administrator who for a quarter of a century has administered the island with a rough but benevolent paternalism. Under his coarse banter his assistant Mackintosh, a dour Aberdeen Scot, comes to hate him to such an extent that, though he manages to keep himself under control, his hatred grows into monomania. Walker overreaches himself by his high-handed response to the natives' demand for a fair wage for carrying out a road-making scheme dear to his heart, thereby incurring their enmity as well. Mackintosh, appalled at what he is doing, connives at the theft of his revolver by the chief's son who had instigated the natives' demand and is horrified when Walker is

> " The story with its edge of good-humoured satire is deftly constructed by means of unobtrusive flashbacks and has the additional interest that, twenty years after it was written, its three principal characters were to be reincarnated in . . . Maugham's last major novel <u>The Razor's Edge</u>."

later brought in, dying from bullet wounds. Lying on his bed, Walker calls for whisky and tells Mackintosh he has advised the government in Apia that he is the right man to succeed him in the job of administrator. He asks him to treat the natives fairly: they are children, he says; be firm, kind and just to them. He will not have the crowd round his bed turned out and will not allow anyone to be punished for shooting him; Mackintosh is to say it was an accident.

'You're a religious chap, Mac. What's that about forgiving them? You know.'

'Forgive them, for they know not what they do.'

'That's right. Forgive them . . .'

When Walker dies Mackintosh goes out, gets his revolver (which has been silently returned to him), walks down to the sea and, wading out into the lagoon where he had been swimming when the story begins, shoots himself.

The authenticity of background, on which the effectiveness of this and later Eastern stories depends, is achieved by the process of restraint Maugham imposed on himself. He did not attempt to give more than an intelligent traveller's account of the places in which they are set, nor give the natives parts to play in them that would have demanded a greater knowledge of their customs and language than he possessed—in this avoiding the blunder that falsifies much of Conrad's early work.

Maugham's principal characters are European or white American about whom he could write with the authority conferred by sharing a common culture with them; and during his travels he learnt just enough about the places where his stories are located and of their inhabitants to provide the exotic context in which the principal characters could give rein to their idiosyncrasies. As to wider points of reference and deeper resonances, the analogy of the theme of 'Mackintosh', of which sufficient hints are given and which underpins the drama enacted on the island of Talua, is Christ's betrayal by Judas Iscariot. Much of the story's impact is missed if the reader fails to detect this.

No sacred parallel need be sought to the theme of 'The Fall of Edward Barnard' which, in strong contrast to the previous story, is pure comedy. It tells how the beautiful Isabel Longstaffe, a member of a Chicago brahmin family, finding herself rejected by her fiancé Barnard who opts for a lotus life in Tahiti with Eva a half-caste girl—a goddess of the Polynesian spring, expert in mixing cocktails—settles for his best friend Bateman Hunter, a substantial dollar-bringing male virgin. The story with its edge of good-humoured satire is deftly constructed by means of unobtrusive flashbacks and has the additional interest that, twenty years after it was written, its three principal characters were to be reincarnated in Isobel Bradley, Larry Darrell and Gray Maturin in Maugham's last major novel *The Razor's Edge*. It is not until the reader has read a later story in *The Trembling of a Leaf* called 'The Pool' that a doubt as to the permanence of Barnard's idyll with Eva enters his mind, as it is likely Maugham intended it should.

The third story in the volume 'Red' is put together like a Chinese nest of boxes. All that 'happens' in it—the outer box—is that on the arrival of a shabby schooner smelling of paraffin and copra at an unnamed island in the Samoan group, off its usual run between Apia and Pago-Pago, the skipper, elderly and gross, goes ashore and calls on Neilson, a Swede living in a bungalow there, who tells him the story of the people who had lived there before. The skipper leaves to go about his business, and Neilson decides to return to Europe. The next box enclosed by the outer one is an account of Neilson's earlier history, how he had come to the island twenty-five years before for the sake of his health, having been told he had only a year to live, and been so overwhelmed by the beauty of the island that he determined to spend it there. Eying the repellent obesity of the skipper, he asks him if he had known a man called Red but gives him no chance to reply. The third box inside the other two is the story Neilson tells him of Red, 22 years old and a deserter from an American man-of-war, a comely youth who arrives on the island in a dugout from the native cutter in which he had escaped from Apia and is sheltered by Sally, a beautiful native girl. They fall in love and go to live in a hut on the creek where Neilson's bungalow stands. After an idyllic year together Red is shanghai'd aboard a British whaling-ship. Broken-hearted, Sally waits month after month for his return and four months after his disappearance bears his stillborn child. Neilson's thoughts wander back to his own part in the story—the next in smallness of the boxes—for two years afterwards he had fallen in love with Sally and married her, only to learn with anguish that she was still in love with Red and waited only for his return. For many years now they had lived in mutual indifference, she having aged prematurely as native women do. Red should be grateful, he tells the skipper, that fate had separated him from Sally while their love was still at its height. Suddenly suspicious, he asks him his name, and just as the skipper has admitted that for thirty years he has been known in the islands as Red, a stout, grey-haired native woman comes in, makes a commonplace remark to Neilson, glances indifferently at the skipper and goes out. The smallest box at the centre of the story is this moment of truth when Red and Sally are brought face to face and do not know each other.

'The Pool' is Maugham's first attempt to describe what happens when a European—in this case Lawson the manager of an English bank in Apia—marries a half-caste girl. Ethel, one of several children by native women begotten by a Norwegian adventurer, though able to wear European clothes with elegance prefers putting on a mother hubbard and swimming in a pool of the river a mile or two out of town. When Lawson takes her and their dismayingly dark-coloured son to Scotland she soon begins to pine and unable to bear it returns home with the child. Lawson follows, and while Ethel relapses more and more into her native background, he takes to drink, descending from job to job until he is glad to work for a half-caste store-keeper. On hearing she has taken a fat, elderly German American as her lover, he drowns himself in the pool where she is accustomed to swim. In writing the story Maugham moved from first-person-singular to third-person-singular narration and back again, a proceeding so unobtrusively accomplished that it is

not until he has reached the end that the reader finds himself wondering how certain incidents could have been known to the narrator.

Maugham took a chance of a different kind when constructing 'Honolulu', about the bewitching of the English skipper of a small Chinese-owned schooner plying between Honolulu and the islands. It is the first of his stories to open with a leisurely introduction written in the first person singular as if he were embarking on an essay. There follows an account of his being taken on a tour of the city by an American friend who in the Union Saloon (where Stevenson used to drink with King Kalakaua) introduces him to Captain Butler. Having been presented at length with what amounts to a factual travelogue, the reader is the more ready to swallow the tall story of black magic told to the narrator by Butler after dinner that evening aboard his schooner. The story has an effective surprise ending, though the reader who cares to look back to see how Maugham laid the trap will find that he permitted himself to play a trick which in a detective story would be considered against the rules.

The last of the six stories in *The Trembling of a Leaf* (though the first to be written) is 'Rain', which by way of stage and four film adaptations has become one of the best known of all Maugham's stories. In wartime a ship bound for Apia is detained at Pago-Pago because a crew member had contracted measles, a disease often fatal to Kanakas. Among the passengers are Sadie Thompson an American prostitute, who had joined the ship at Honolulu where she had been plying her trade in Iwelei, its Red Light district, and the high-minded missionary Davidson and his wife. Putting up in inadequately furnished rooms in a two-story frame house belonging to a half-caste, the respectable passengers—their nerves already frayed by the incessant rattling of the rain on the iron roof—are outraged by the wheezy strains of a gramophone playing ragtime and the sounds of dancing and popping corks coming from Miss Thompson's room, indicating that she is in business again. The story moves to its climax as Davidson attempts to bring her to repentance, using as his ultimate weapon the threat of having her deported to San Francisco where a three-year gaol sentence awaits her. The last stage of their duel so strongly resembles the inquisitor's struggle for the soul of the Maid in *St. Joan* (written in 1923) that it is difficult to resist the inference either that Shaw was influenced by Maugham's story or that Maugham had some earlier account of St. Joan's trial in mind when he devised 'Rain'. However that may be, an awareness of the parallel gives the story an added depth.

Source: John Whitehead, ''Between the Wars: Far East,'' in *Maugham: A Reappraisal,* Vision Press Ltd., 1987, pp. 80–114.

Sources

Archer, Stanley, *W. Somerset Maugham: A Study of the Short Fiction,* Twayne Publishers, 1993, p. 26.

Burt, Forrest D., *W. Somerset Maugham,* Twayne's United States Author Series, No. 399, Twayne Publishers, 1993, p. 106.

Field, Louise Maunsell, Review of *The Trembling of a Leaf,* in *W. Somerset Maugham: The Critical Heritage,* edited by Anthony Curtis and John Whitehead, Routledge & Kegan Paul, 1987, pp. 148–51; originally published in the *New York Times,* November 20, 1921.

Loss, Archie K., ''W. Somerset Maugham,'' in *Dictionary of Literary Biography,* Vol. 162: *British Short-Fiction Writers, 1915–1945,* edited by John H. Rogers, Gale Research, 1996, pp. 227–39.

———, *W. Somerset Maugham,* Ungar, 1987, p. 78.

Maugham, W. Somerset, *The Summing Up,* in *The Maugham Reader,* Doubleday, 1950, p. 608.

———, *The Trembling of a Leaf: Little Stories of the South Sea Islands,* Replica Books, 2002.

———, *A Writer's Notebook,* Heinemann, 1949, p. 138.

West, Rebecca, Review of *The Trembling of a Leaf,* in *W. Somerset Maugham: The Critical Heritage,* edited by Anthony Curtis and John Whitehead, Routledge & Kegan Paul, 1987, pp. 153–54; originally published in *New Republic,* November 5, 1921.

Wordsworth, William, and Samuel Taylor Coleridge, *Lyrical Ballads,* edited by R. L. Brett and A. R. Jones, Methuen, 1965, p. 105.

Further Reading

Brander, L. *Somerset Maugham: A Guide,* Barnes and Noble, Inc., 1963.

This concise guide to the whole of Maugham's work includes a chapter on the short stories. In his comments on ''The Fall of Edward Barnard,'' Brander emphasizes the return to nature theme.

Curtis, Anthony, *Somerset Maugham,* Macmillan, 1977.

This well-illustrated book attempts to give a broad-brush portrait of the writer and his world.

Morgan, Ted, *Maugham: A Biography,* Simon and Schuster, 1980.

This is the most reliable and complete biography of Maugham. Morgan discusses Maugham's fiction and plays in detail and shows how the events of Maugham's life are reflected in his work.

Raphael, Frederic, *W. Somerset Maugham and His World,* Charles Scribner's Sons, 1977.

This overview of Maugham's life and work contains 110 illustrations.

Whitehead, John, *Maugham: A Reappraisal,* Barnes and Noble, 1987.

Whitehead attempts a close scrutiny of all of Maugham's works, declaring that although many of them are ephemeral, Maugham at his best ranks with the great novelists of the early twentieth century. Whitehead also regards Maugham's Eastern stories as his finest and rates them as highly as Kipling's Indian stories.

Four Summers

Joyce Carol Oates

1967

Joyce Carol Oates's short story "Four Summers," initially appeared in *The Yale Review* in spring 1967 and the next year was included in *The American Literary Anthology*. Subsequently, the story was included in Oates's story collections *The Wheel of Love* (1970), *Where Are You Going, Where Have You Been?: Stories of Young America* (1974), and in *Where Are You Going, Where Have You Been?: Selected Early Stories* (1993). It also appears in anthologies such as *Fiction 100: An Anthology of Short Fiction* (2001). Like many of Oates's early stories, "Four Summers" takes childhood and the family as its subjects and explores the pain and confusion that accompanies a young person's introduction into the adult world. In four short sections, each describing incidents from four summers, Oates chronicles the changes of Sissie, the narrator, as she moves from childhood to adulthood, trying to understand what she should do and who she should be. By using a first-person point of view, Oates gives readers insight into the thoughts and motivations of a young girl who is coming of age. The story's language is spare and accessible, and young women, in particular, will be able to identify with Sissie's responses to events and changing perceptions. Oates draws on her own working-class upbringing in developing her characters.

Author Biography

A celebrated professor at Princeton University and one of contemporary literature's most prolific authors, Joyce Carol Oates comes from humble beginnings. Born in Lockport, New York, on June 16, 1938, to Frederic James Oates, a tool and die designer, and Caroline Bush Oates, a homemaker, Oates began her education in a one-room country schoolhouse, the same one her mother attended decades before her. She developed her interest in storytelling as a child, constructing elaborate illustrated books while still in elementary school. At Syracuse University, where she studied philosophy and literature, she churned out a novel a term, flabbergasting her professors. Her favorite authors during this time included Franz Kafka and William Faulkner. Oates broke into the publishing world in 1959, when she was named co-winner of the *Mademoiselle* College Fiction Award for her short story "In the Old World," which subsequently appeared in that magazine. In 1960, she received her bachelor's degree, serving as class valedictorian.

The turning point in Oates's career came in 1961 while she was studying for her Ph.D. in English at Rice University in Houston, where she had moved to be with her husband, Raymond Smith. After discovering that one of her stories had been cited in the honor roll in the latest volume of Martha Foley's *Best American Short Stories,* Oates decided to quit graduate school and become a full-time writer. She published her first novel, *With Shuddering Fall,* in 1964 and since then has published plays, novels, short story and poetry collections, and critical studies. Though she draws on her childhood experience for much of her early fiction, as evidenced in pieces such as "Four Summers," Oates's subjects in her later work are varied, ranging from boxing to Shakespeare. In interviews, she sometimes describes her writing as a form of daydreaming that she revises minimally. However, critics have praised her technical skills and willingness to experiment with narrative structure as much as they have her intellect and energy.

Since winning the *Mademoiselle* award, Oates has accumulated a mind-boggling number of prizes for her writing, including five National Book Award nominations. In 1970, she won the award for her novel *them.* Other awards include more than twenty O. Henry Awards for individual stories; National Endowment for the Arts grants; a Guggenheim Fellowship; a National Institute of Arts and Letters Rosenthal Foundation Award; the Lotos Club Award of Merit; the F. Scott Fitzgerald Award for Lifetime Achievement in American Literature; the PEN/Malamud Award for Lifetime Achievement in the Short Story; the Bram Stoker Award for Life Achievement; the Bobst Award for Lifetime Achievement in Fiction; and the Rhea Award for the short story. Her books of stories, poems, plays, and criticism have been nominated for scores of other awards as well. Oates's most recent work includes her novel *Beasts* (2002), her story collection *Faithless: Tales of Transgression* (2001), and a collection of poems, *Tenderness* (1996).

Plot Summary

Part 1

"Four Summers" refers to the four summers that Sissie, the narrator, recounts during the course of the story. In this first section, she is with her parents and brothers at a lakefront tavern. It is early afternoon, a parade has recently disbanded, and men in uniforms are all around. The setting resembles that of Memorial Day. While her parents drink beer with their friends from the old neighborhood, the children pester them for a ride in a boat. The boys, Jerry and Frank, play by themselves, and Sissie stays close to her mother. Lenore's cousin, Sue, gives Sissie a sip of beer, which she does not like. The couples discuss people from the old neighborhood such as Duane Dorsey, a "nut" who was always in trouble, and June Dieter, who now has a serious disease. The war they discuss is probably World War II.

At the end of the section, the children see a blackbird flailing in the scum on the water's surface. One of the children pokes it with a stick, and others, including Frank, throw stones at it. Sissie writes: "I watch them throw stones. I am standing at the side. If the bird dies, then everything can die." Sentences like these mark Sissie's innocence and her position as observer.

Much of the dialogue does not have attribution, and so readers have to infer who is speaking from the context. Ernest Hemingway popularized this kind of spare, elliptical writing in his short stories and novels.

Part 2

In this section, Sissy is at the boathouse tavern again with her father and Jerry. Oates marks the passage of time through details about the characters: for example, her mother has had another baby, and Frank is at a stock car race. Jerry is twelve years old, and Sissie says he is "like Dad, the way his eyes look." Jerry says he hates his father, remarking, "All he does is drink." Jerry and Sissie wait for their father to take them on a boat ride to an island in the center of the lake. Throughout the section, Sissie describes the loudness and vulgarity of the tavern and the men who drink there. Sissie's descriptions in this section also focus on her father, whom she both admires and fears. When they arrive at the island, it is different from the way Sissy and Jerry thought it would be. At the end of the section, the children witness their father vomiting into the water, sick from drinking and rowing.

Part 3

In this section, Sissie is fourteen years old and displays all the thinking and behavior of one her age. She is self-conscious, cocky, sarcastic, angry, and hateful towards almost everyone. Lamenting that she cannot attend the show with her friends Marian and Betty, because she has to help her mother take care of her baby sister, she says, "Poor fat Linda, with her runny nose!" The setting is again the boathouse tavern. The characters present include Sissie, her mother and father, her baby sister, and her aunt Lucy and her uncle Joe. In the first part of this section, the adults bicker about how to secure tickets for a game show, with the women speaking admiringly of the emcee, Howie Masterson, and the men claiming he and the show are phony. In the second part, Sissie encounters a man in the tavern who sweet talks her and then attempts to seduce her. Showing her bravado, Sissie walks with him for a bit, and then after he kisses her and becomes sexually excited, she runs away.

Part 4

It is five years later, and Sissie is nineteen years old, married, and pregnant. She and her husband, Jesse, stop at the Lakeside Bar, the same tavern she had come to with her parents in previous summers. Oates uses the proper name of the place now, as Sissie is now an adult. The way she sees the bar is different from the way she remembers it. It is smaller now and "dirtier." Her description is in keeping with the differences between how human beings perceive the world when they are young and when they are adults. Sissie reflects on the times she and her family had come to the bar. She sees a man she thinks might be the same one who kissed her

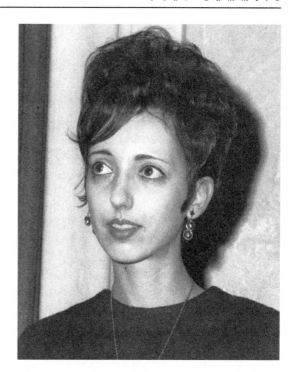

Joyce Carol Oates

when she was fourteen, but she is not sure and so says nothing to her husband. Sissie mixes description of the bar with information about what has happened in the last five years, including a mention of her father's accidental death at the factory. She also compares her own life with her parents' and hopes that Jesse, whom she describes as being like her father, will not turn out like him. At the end of the story, readers are left with an image of a young woman who is still struggling to understand her past, the choices she has made, and what has shaped her desires.

Characters

Duane Dorsey

Duane Dorsey is a former neighbor of Sissie's family. He is frequently in trouble with the law and was recently arrested for breaking windows in his mother-in-law's house. Harry and Sue's husband discuss Duane's antics at the Lakeside Bar.

Frank

Frank is the oldest brother. In the first section, Sissie says he is ten years old and "very big." With

Media Adaptations

- A number of Oates's stories have been adapted into films, including her short story "Where Are You Going, Where Have You Been?" This story was made into the 1985 film *Smooth Talk,* directed by Joyce Chopra and starring Laura Dern and Treat Williams.

- Another adaptation of an Oates's novel is *We Were the Mulvaneys* (2002), directed by Peter Werne and starring Blythe Danner and Beau Bridges.

- Released as a two-part television movie, *Blonde,* an adaptation of an Oates's novel of the same name, was shown in 2001. Joyce Chopra directed the film, which stars Ann-Margaret, Eric Bogosian, and Griffith Dunne.

other children, he cruelly throws stones at a blackbird drowning in the water's muck. During the second summer he is at a stock car race with his friends.

Harry

Harry is Sissie's father. He is handsome, muscular, and suntanned. Sissie describes him as a hard-drinking man who "is always in a hurry to get things done." Although he has a troubled relationship with his sons, Jerry and Frank, he treats Sissie well. Harry works the night shift at the factory, telling Uncle Joe, "I can sleep during the day. What's the difference?" Although he takes Jerry and Sissie for a ride to the island in the middle of the lake during the second summer, he generally ignores his children, spending time at the bar talking with his friends. This is his natural element and the place he is happiest. In conversation, Harry is bitter and angry, saying that his father "is better off dead" and frequently quarreling with his wife. He dies after an accident at the factory, somewhere between Sissie's fourteenth and nineteenth years.

Jerry

Jerry is the middle child who appears in the first two sections of the story. During the first summer he is around eight years old, and in the second he is twelve, with "pimples on his forehead and chin." Sissie says, "Jerry is like Dad, the way his eyes look." And, like his father, he is angry. Referring to his father, Jerry tells Sissie, "All he does is drink . . . . I hate him." After Jerry, Sissie, and Harry row to the island, Sissie and Jerry watch as their father throws up over the side of the boat.

Jimmy

Jimmy is a young soldier who sits and drinks with the two couples at the Lakeside Bar. He is very young but old enough to drink beer. His face is "raw in spots, broken out," but Sissie says he has "nice eyes." His parents, like Harry's, are from the "Old Country."

Uncle Joe

With his wife, Lucy, Joe appears during the third summer. Sissie says he is tired all the time, that he has a gut, a saggy jaw, and a "bald head with the little fringe of gray hair on it," which Sissie claims to hate. Nonetheless, Sissie describes him as "handsome." Joe agrees with Harry that game show host Howie Masterson is a "phony."

Lenore

Lenore is Harry's wife and the mother of Frank, Jerry, and Sissie. In the first summer, she is "pretty" and shows Sissie affection and attention. By the third summer, she is a loud-mouthed drunkard who no longer cares about her physical appearance and who tells her youngest child, Linda, that she was "an accident" and that she did not want her. Like her husband, she is prone to angry outbursts.

Aunt Lucy

Aunt Lucy appears during the third summer with her husband Joe. She has false teeth that Sissie believes make "everyone stare at her." Lucy wrote a letter to Howie Masterson, emcee of a game show, which the couples discuss.

Sissie

Sissie is the narrator of the story, who details events from four summers of her life. These summers depict Sissie's childhood, adolescence, and adulthood. Since Sissie is the narrator, readers never see her outside of her own self-descriptions. The only physical descriptions she provides are in the third section, when she is fourteen years old. Sissie says of herself, ''My legs are too thin, my figure is flat.'' In the last section, she notes, ''My secret is that I am pretty like everyone is . . . . I have a pink mouth and plucked darkened eyebrows and soft bangs over my forehead.''

Sissie's emotional development, while typical in some ways, is heavily influenced by her family dynamics. Her parents are working-class drinkers who ''chose'' the only life they knew. They display the characteristics of people overwhelmed by their circumstances, responding to events rather than initiating them, and settling into a life of lowered expectations, alcoholism, lethargy, and gossip. Sissie's descriptions of her family show an awareness of how she too is being shaped to be like her parents. However, this awareness appears to come too late—after she is pregnant and has married someone just like her father.

Sue

Sue is Lenore's cousin, and she and her husband are with Harry and Lenore at the Lakeside Bar during the first summer. Like the others, Sue is drinking. She is enamored of Sissie, calling her ''cute'' and saying that she wishes she had a daughter like her. From her comment and her husband's response to it, readers can infer that she is perhaps childless. She offers Sissie beer, which disturbs her husband, but Sissie eventually takes a sip after being encouraged by her mother. Sissie describes Lenore as having ''darkish'' teeth, with pale skin and blotches on her red face.

Sue's Husband

Sissie describes Sue's husband as ''a big man with a thick neck.'' A volunteer fireman who just finished marching in the parade, he is loud and at times violent, cursing at his wife and making comments about her appearance and weight. ''His eyebrows are blond, lighter than his hair, and are thick and tufted,'' Sissie remarks. Sue says that he spends most of his weekends drinking in the backyard, leaving the house in disrepair.

Themes

Marriage

Oates questions the possibility that romantic love provides fulfillment for individuals and the idea that romantic love and marriage are necessarily linked. In doing so, she undermines the notion that romantic love, particularly as it is embodied in the institution of marriage, remains both a means and an end to a satisfying life. Sissie's depiction of her own parents' marriage and that of Sue and her husband suggest, instead, that marriages are often more like contractual obligations from which both parties cannot extricate themselves. Sue's husband belittles his wife, while she in turn mocks his laziness and drinking. Sissie describes the relationships between her own parents as one dominated by drinking and quarreling. She even questions her own marriage to Jesse, hoping, against evidence to the contrary, that he will be different from her father. Of her own marriage, Sissie says, ''Like my parents' love, it will subside someday.''

Free Will

Western, and especially American, notions of individuality are built upon the idea that human beings are free to choose their own destinies. Sissie's experience suggests just the opposite. Throughout the first three summers, she describes her parents' marriage and her family in generally unappealing terms. Her father works constantly, and when he is not working, he is drinking. She is not close to either of her brothers, and one of them, Jerry, says he ''hates'' his father. Though she is sympathetic to her mother, she describes her in unflattering terms, writing that she looks ''queer'' and is ''fat,'' with varicose veins darkening her legs. In the third section, the fourteen-year-old Sissie catalogues what she ''hates'' and thinks is ''ugly.'' These things include her baby sister, Linda, the boathouse tavern, and Howie Masterson. Yet, in the last section, Sissie is married and pregnant at nineteen, to a man very much like her father—loud and working-class. Though confused by her ''choices,'' Sissie rationalizes them. Her attitude towards her own life is embodied in her description of her husband's. Of him and of men like him, Sissie writes, ''Their lives are like hands dealt out to them in their innumerable card games: You pick up the sticky cards, and there it is: there it is. Can't change anything.''

Class

Though she never uses the word ''class,'' Sissie's description of her family underscores the idea that human beings are social animals, whose opportunities in life are determined by their socioeconomic status. The activities she describes—beer drinking, card playing, her father's factory work,

Topics for Further Study

- Write a story of your own emotional development from childhood through adolescence or adulthood (whichever is appropriate) following the method laid out by Oates in "Four Summers". Do this by writing about an event or events in four different summers.

- Reflect on your own experiences as a fourteen-year-old. Is Oates's representation of Sissie's thinking and behavior in the third section typical of someone that age? Discuss as a class.

- Compose a list of your parents' character traits, and then compare them with the lists of other students. Do you notice traits in your parents that you feel you want to emulate or escape? Evaluate in groups why or how you might take on or deny certain traits, describing how social and economic conditions have shaped your outlooks and observations.

- Break up into four groups. Each group is charged with adapting one section of Oates's story for the stage and is responsible for writing a script for that section. Make sure that each group member has a role, either writing, acting, directing, or securing and managing props. After each group has performed its scene, discuss the respective performances as a class.

- What are some of the activities you associate with the following terms: "working class," "middle class," "upper class," "blue collar?" Into what class would you place your own family? Discuss as a class.

- Sissie describes her parents as arguing all the time. In groups, discuss some of the possible reasons they argue, supporting your claims with evidence from the story.

- "Four Summers" ends with the nineteen-year-old Sissie married and pregnant, sitting with her husband in the Lakeside Bar. Write the fifth section, picking up Sissie's story five years in the future, when she returns once again to the tavern.

---

and so forth—and the desires of her family, such as wanting to be contestants on a television game show, mark working-class life. Sissie describes the trappings of such a life in stereotypical class terms, focusing on how "loud" her parents talk, their constant bickering, and her father's friends' language (e.g., the bartender's use of the word "nigger"). Though she is obviously repelled by these things, Sissie nonetheless finds herself duplicating the very same kind of life.

Style

Point of View

Point of view refers to the perspective from which a story is told. Oates uses a first-person point of view, as Sissie narrates the events of four summers. In these events, Sissie, the story's "I," is alternately observer and participant. Sissie is not, however, Oates herself but a character Oates creates to relay ideas about growing up in a working-class American family. Sissie is a reliable narrator insofar as her actions, language, and perceptions reflect her age in the story's parts. However, her descriptions must be read in light of her character, which both influences and is influenced by those around her. Other stories in *The Wheel of Love* are told using second- and third-person points of view. In the latter, the narrator presents action without commenting on it and without insight into characters' thoughts; in the former, the narrator uses the pronoun "you" as if addressing the reader.

Plot

Story refers to what happens; plot refers to how the narrator presents what happens. By organizing the action of "Four Summers" into four sections, each of which details events surrounding Sissie during the course of four days in four summers, Oates is better able to develop her subjects and themes. These include the relationship between free will and determinism, the role of social class in shaping human desire, and the emotional development of a young girl. Since each section of the story deals with events from a different summer, readers have to use their imaginations to fill in what happens to Sissie during the intervening years. By using the present tense, Oates gives the story an emotional immediacy that would otherwise be lost.

Imagery

Imagery refers to concrete descriptions of the material world that appeal to readers' senses. Symbolic imagery is imagery that resonates with ideas implicit in the text itself. Oates uses symbolic imagery to emphasize the squalidness of Sissie's childhood years and her disdain for the kind of life her parents led. Her descriptions of adults, her parents, and others, for example, highlight the effect of years of drinking and bad food. Sue's face is "blotched . . . some parts pale and some red," and all the men, except her father, have "big stomachs." In other places, Oates uses symbolic imagery to suggest the situation of Sissie and others like her. For instance, she draws an implicit connection between Sissie and the blackbird trapped in the lake's polluted waters at the end of the first section, writing, "The bird's wings keep fluttering but it can't get out. If it could get free it would fly and be safe, but the scum holds it down."

Historical Context

1960s

When "Four Summers" was initially published in 1967, the United States was in turmoil. Not only were American troops fighting the North Vietnamese, but the government was battling antiwar protesters at home. With 429 major and 2,972 minor military bases around the globe, it had set itself up as the world's policeman, often acting covertly to change the political complexion of countries such as the Dominican Republic and Chile. Not only was the Central Intelligence Agency active overseas but President Johnson had also authorized it to conduct surveillance and compile dossiers on protestors at home. The CIA was joined in its efforts by the Federal Bureau of Investigation, run by J.

Edgar Hoover, a rabid anticommunist who initiated a wiretapping campaign to discredit civil rights leader Martin Luther King, Jr. and directed counterintelligence efforts against government critics. Many of those protesting government involvement in Vietnam belonged to the baby boom generation—those born after World War II. During the 1960s, more than 70 million "boomers" became teenagers and young adults. Those who turned eighteen became eligible for the military draft. It is quite possible that Jimmy, the soldier from the old neighborhood who sits with Sissie's parents at the boathouse tavern in the first section, was drafted.

In the second section of the story, Sissie overhears the bartender of the boathouse use the word "nigger." Such epithets were common in the 1950s and 1960s (and even today) among people who practiced discrimination (consciously or not) against others who were not like them. The Civil Rights movement attempted to change such behavior. Black leaders like Martin Luther King, Jr. and Stokely Carmichael led peaceful protests and sit-ins, often joined by non-blacks, advocating for greater representation and equality in law for blacks. In 1964, the Twenty-third Amendment to the Constitution was ratified, outlawing the poll tax, a measure many southern states used to keep blacks from voting, and in 1965 the Voting Rights Act was passed, abolishing literacy tests and leading hundreds of thousands of blacks to register to vote. However, resistance to greater black participation in Johnson's "Great Society" continued, and during the mid and late-1960s protests and riots erupted throughout the country in major urban centers such as Detroit, Newark, and Los Angeles. Oates lived in Detroit, teaching English at the University of Detroit between 1962 and 1967, and in her 1969 novel, *them*, she provides a fictionalized account of events in this city during the summer of 1967, when hundreds of buildings were burned to the ground in a violent week of rioting. During the late 1960s, the term "black" became an acceptable replacement for the word "negro," as leaders such as Malcolm X preached about black pride and groups such as the Black Panthers advocated black separatism. In 1968, Otto Kerner, head of the National Advisory Commission on Civil Disorders, blamed the racial unrest on institutionalized white power and racism and claimed the country was moving towards two societies.

Working-class families like Sissie's from small towns and rural America, however, were not rioting in the streets. When children finished their school-

Compare & Contrast

- **1960s:** Race riots consumed major American cities such as Los Angeles, Detroit, and Newark as African Americans protested economic and political exploitation and police harassment.

  Today: Most Americans see racial conflict and division as major social issues, though the number of violent protests has considerably diminished.

- **1960s:** Television quiz shows such as *Play Your Hunch, Concentration, Truth or Consequences,* and *The Face is Familiar* appeal to working- and middle-class American fantasies of easy riches.

  Today: Television quiz shows such as *Who Wants To Be A Millionaire, The Weakest Link,* and *The Chair* appeal to working- and middle-class American fantasies of easy riches.

- **1960s:** The minimum wage for Americans is $1.00.

  Today: The minimum wage for Americans in 2002 is $5.15.

work and the adults came home from a day at the factory, they often turned on the television and watched quiz shows, like the one that Sissie's parents and her aunt Lucy and her uncle Joe discuss at the tavern. The possibility of winning "easy money" was irresistible to people like Lenore and Lucy, and shows such as *The Price Is Right, People Are Funny,* and *Do You Trust Your Wife?* capitalized on the fantasies of working-class women.

Critical Overview

The reviews for *The Wheel of Love* were good, though some reviewers had reservations. Writing for *Publishers Weekly,* Barbara Bannon is effusive in her praise, claiming *The Wheel of Love* "May well be Joyce Carol Oates's finest collection of short stories yet . . . the effects on the reader are apt to linger long after he has finished the individual stories." A reviewer for *Kirkus Reviews* writes, "These rich, intent stories . . . have the supra-reality of the bleak hours before dawn as Miss Oates' characters, taut with awareness, suffer the last turn on the wheel of love." In a somewhat mixed review for *The New York Times Book Review,* Richard Gilman calls "Four Summers" one of the best stories in the collection, remarking that it "create[s] a verbal excitement, a sense of language used not for the expression of previously attained insights or perceptions but for new imaginative reality."

Academic critics are paying increasing attention to Oates's work as well. For example, in her essay "Joyce Carol Oates's Craftsmanship in 'The Wheel of Love,'" appearing in *Studies in Short Fiction,* Joanne V. Creighton makes connections between Oates's narrative techniques and the content of her stories, suggesting that Oates's stories fail as often as they succeed. Creighton argues, "The characters of the collection offer a dismal view of the human being's incapacity to enjoy a healthy and wholesome emotional life." In his study *Understanding Joyce Carol Oates,* Greg Johnson notes that *The Wheel of Love* contains a mix of traditional and experimental stories. Johnson writes, "Oates displays the impressive range of fictional technique and subject matter that characterizes all her short story volumes." Johnson praises Oates's ability to "manipulate . . . formal conventions in order to revitalize the genre."

Criticism

Chris Semansky

Semansky is an instructor of English literature and composition who writes about literature and

What Do I Read Next?

- Raymond Carver, like Oates, frequently wrote about his working-class upbringing. His collection of stories *Cathedral* (1983) was nominated for the National Book Critics Circle Award and was runner-up for the Pulitzer Prize.

- Oates's novel *them* (1969) concerns the race riots in Detroit in the late 1960s, when Oates lived in the city. The novel received the National Book Award in 1970.

- In 1987, Oates published the critically acclaimed nonfiction study *On Boxing,* which led to her television appearance as a commentator for a boxing match.

- Oates often discusses her own working-class background and its influence on her fiction. For a clearer understanding of the work world in America, read Studs Terkel's *Working: People Talk about What They Do All Day and How They Feel about What They Do* (1974). Terkel presents the true-life stories of more than one hundred Chicago working people, from the prostitute to the waitress to the rich businessman, taken from interviews with Terkel.

---

culture for various publications. In this essay, Semansky considers the narrator's emotional growth.

Psychologists often chart the development of human beings in stages or phases. Eric Erikson, for instance, lists eight stages of psychosocial development that human beings typically pass through during their lives, including the oral-sensory stage, the stage of adolescence, and the maturity stage. Other psychologists have different models. In "Four Summers," Oates shows Sissie's emotional development through her behavior towards her family and peers, emphasizing both her interconnectedness with others and her quest for individuation.

In the first section, Sissie describes her surroundings in generalities, beginning her story, "It is some kind of special day." Her sentence structure and descriptions are similar to those of a young child. For example, she writes of her mother: "She is pretty when she laughs. Her hair is long and pretty." She refers to her father as "Daddy" and desires to stay by her mother's side rather than play with her brothers Jerry and Frank. Sissie never tells readers how old she is, but she does mention that Frank is ten and "very big." From her descriptions and language, readers can infer that Sissie is around six years old. By primarily using dialogue in this section, Oates dramatizes the action and characterizes Sissie through her responses to what is happening around her. Sue, her mother's cousin, dotes on Sissie, repeatedly calling her "cute," and her father refers to her as "baby." She cannot refuse the adults' desire that she have a sip of beer, remarking, "I have to say yes." The key marker of Sissie's emotional development is her response to the scene at the end of the section, in which her brothers and other children are pelting a drowning blackbird with stones. Sissie remarks, "I watch them throwing stones. I am standing at the side. If the bird dies, then everything can die." This awareness of death and of her own mortality marks Sissie's exit from the world of innocence and her entrance into the world of experience.

The first section of the story establishes the point of view, and in doing so it draws readers into the story. It is hard not to be sympathetic with a young girl, especially one so passive, innocent, and trusting as Sissie. Since readers understand things that Sissie can only describe but cannot comprehend, they feel a kind of paternal empathy towards the girl. This response only deepens as the adults' behavior becomes more unsavory. Oates also does something else in the first section: she withholds information. By setting her story in four days of Sissie's life, each representative of a phase of her

> "Whether the adults are relaxing at a table or the father is rowing the children across the lake, beer is present, lubricating Harry's every moment."

development, Oates creates suspense. Readers become emotionally invested in the story, desiring to discover the trajectory of Sissie's growth.

In the story's second section, readers learn that Sissie has a new baby sister, a fact that will be elaborated on in the third section. Sissie never states her age, but readers can infer that she is younger than her brother Jerry, who is now twelve and "up on the sixth-grade floor." Oates mixes a good dose of Sissie's self-reflection in this section into the dialogue and description. Typical of many ten-year-old girls, Sissie is full of admiration and awe for her father. For example, she describes the men he speaks with at the bar but comments that her father's stomach is not big like the others. She writes, "He has his shirt sleeves rolled up and you can see how strong his arms must be." Sissie dotes on her father, describing how fast he rows and how he smiles. Sissie also notes her older brother Jerry's contempt for their father. Jerry says of their father that, "All he does is drink." When the three are rowing to the island, Harry and Jerry exchange words, and Sissie says her father's face reddens "the way it does at home when he has trouble with Frank." Sissie's father never has a cross word for her, however, calling her "sugar" and generally treating her as his favorite child. Her description of his behavior, however, and of his relationship with her brothers, suggests a dysfunctional family in which open communication is a struggle.

Much of the family's problems stem from the parents' heavy drinking, especially Harry's. For the children, the drinking is a problem; for the adults, it is not. This is typical of how alcoholics view their behavior. Drinking is a regular part of Harry's day, helping him deal with the stress of having four children and a low-paying factory job. In every scene Sissie describes, beer plays a central role.

Whether the adults are relaxing at a table or the father is rowing the children across the lake, beer is present, lubricating Harry's every moment. Not only is compulsive and regular drinking part of the alcoholic's lot but so is drinking to excess, which Harry does in the second section, vomiting into the water once he reaches shore.

The father's anger at his children for needing attention and the children's anger at the father for not providing it are also traits of a family marked by alcoholism. Sissie notes that, already at twelve, Jerry has adopted his father's propensity for anger. Aggressive behavior is common among children of alcoholics, and the boys, and Sissy in the third section, show it. Sissie's observation of her brother's similarity to her father foreshadows her own budding awareness in the last section that her own desires have in large part been shaped by her family dynamics.

In the third section, Sissie is fourteen, displaying all the behaviors and attitude of someone that age. She is obnoxious, obsessed with her body, and contemptuous of adults. Her anger is catalyzed by her rampant hormones and shaped by years of watching her parents drink themselves through the day, fighting. Once again, she is inside the tavern with her mother and father, only this time she can no longer stand it. Sissie says, "Inside me there is something that wants to run away, that hates them. How loud they are, my parents!" Being embarrassed by one's parents is a common enough feeling for young teenagers, but the intensity of Sissie's rage asks readers to look more deeply than to mere adolescent growth pains. One place to look is Sissie's description of her mother, whom she describes as oblivious both to her own personal appearance and to her baby, Linda. Sissie recalls her mother screaming at the baby, "Nobody wanted you, it was a [g——d——] accident." Sissie is no longer the cloying six-year-old she was at the story's opening. She is now beginning to individuate, to see herself as separate from her mother and the adults around her. She says, "I narrow my eyes and watch my mother . . . and think that maybe she isn't my mother after all, and she isn't that pretty girl in the photograph, but someone else." Sissie is also developing an awareness of her own sexuality, flirting with a man she meets in the tavern. Though she is becoming aware of her powers, she is still largely ignorant of her own body, panicking when the man begins to kiss her and asking, "What is he doing? Do they all do this? Do I have to have it done to me too?"

Cut to the last scene in the story, and Sissie is nineteen, pregnant, and married. Oates marks the changes in her perception of the world by having Sissie describe the tavern in detail for the first time. The Lakeside Bar is now "that big old building with the grubby siding, and a big pink neon sign in front, and the cinder driveway that's so bumpy." These details underscore the attention that Sissie now pays to her surroundings as she attempts to make sense out of her life. Like many adults looking back on places of their childhood, the Lakeside Bar does not measure up to her memories. Sissie also pays more attention to herself. In this section, she is consumed with questions about the decisions she has made, and she is tortured by the possibility that she has made a colossal mistake in marrying Jesse. Her responses to the men in the bar, one of whom may be the man she flirted with five years ago, suggest that she is second-guessing her choice of a mate. The paragraphs in this section are the longest in the story and primarily comprise Sissie's thoughts. Rather than delve more deeply into what her responses are telling her, Sissie instead buckles down and attempts to accept her life, to convince herself that all will work out. She says:

> I let my hand fall onto my stomach to remind myself that I am in love: with this baby, with Jesse, with everything. I am in love with our house and our life and the future and even this moment—right now— that I am struggling to live through.

One can imagine her mother doing the same thing when she was Sissie's age.

Source: Chris Semansky, Critical Essay on "Four Summers," in *Short Stories for Students,* The Gale Group, 2003.

Keith Cushman

In the following essay, Cushman provides an analysis of "Four Summers," asserting that Oates is "more interested in psychology than sociology," and finding the story "another version of American Gothic."

Joyce Carol Oates's "Four Summers" is a rich, rewarding, complex story that has received no critical attention. Featured in James H. Pickering's popular anthology, *Fiction 100,* the story is being read these days by a large number of students and teachers. In this essay I will try to account for the story's effectiveness.

Mary Kathryn Grant has pointed out that in "Oates's works three themes—women, city, and community—merge into all-too-real nightmare." All these ingredients are present in "Four Sum-

> The characters in the working-class milieu of 'Four Summers' are trapped by their own limitations and by the conditions of American life. They are poorly educated and unable to communicate meaningfully. They yearn to escape from their empty, dreary lives, but no escape is possible."

mers." The protagonist and narrator, Sissie, is a girl who, like almost all of Oates's heroines, is a victim. The beaten-down characters in the story exist on the periphery of urban life. Community is not possible in such a world; the extremity of Sissie's isolation makes us keenly aware of the absence of community. "Four Summers" contains no overt violence, but the story is sufficiently nightmarish just the same.

The characters in the working-class milieu of "Four Summers" are trapped by their own limitations and by the conditions of American life. They are poorly educated and unable to communicate meaningfully. They yearn to escape from their empty, dreary lives, but no escape is possible. Indeed the abortive effort to escape is a unifying motif in the story.

The social milieu is sharply realized, but social commentary is not the central concern of "Four Summers." Oates feels compassion for the characters in her story and outrage at the system they are part of. Yet she is more interested in psychology than sociology: "Four Summers" is above all a portrait of Sissie. Though she is sensitive and intelligent, she is also unhappy, afraid, and profoundly insecure. In the final analysis "Four Summers"— like so much of Oates's fiction—can be understood as another version of American Gothic. Sissie, an abused, exploited female child, belongs in the same company as such other victimized American heroines as Maisie Verver, Maggie Johnson, and Candace Compson.

"Four Summers" doesn't exactly have a plot. Plot depends on progression and development, but in "Four Summers" people grow older but cannot change. Instead Sissie records four summer outings at the same lakeside tavern. Sissie's compelling descriptions of these four summer days are deeply colored by her anxieties. I will briefly summarize each section of the story here so that I will be able to organize my argument topically and thematically.

Sissie is about five in the first section. The grown-ups sit around playing cards though the children clamor for a boat ride. To amuse themselves Sissie's mother and her mother's friend give the terrified girl a drink of beer. The section ends with one of her brothers, frustrated and angry, and other children stoning a bird caught in some scum while Sissie stands watching. In the second section Sissie's father rows her, now about ten years old, and a brother to a nearby island, but this attempt at parental concern is just as wretched as the neglect in the first section. The island turns out to be a miniature wasteland, and the father, sick from too much exertion after too much beer, starts throwing up. In the third section Sissie is fourteen, rebellious but afraid to rebel. She leaves the tavern, flirts with a man outside, and then runs back into the tavern when he starts to molest her. In the fourth section Sissie, nineteen, married, and pregnant, tries to convince herself that she is happy, but she knows she isn't.

"Four Summers" is bound together not only by its unity of place and mood but also by its careful manipulation of imagery and motifs. Sissie grows in sophistication and self-awareness throughout the story, but at the end she is just as frightened as she was at the beginning. The final section provides resolution only in the sense that after all her yearning to escape from her parents' world, she is now irrevocably trapped by her marriage and pregnancy. "Four Summers" is painful to read because it forces the reader to experience Sissie's entrapment in all its oppressiveness and does so four times over. Even though the reader soon realizes that there is no exit for Sissie, he cannot help hoping that somehow she will escape.

Oates's clever control of point of view is an important element in the story's effect on the reader. Sissie narrates the story of each of the four days. This narration is so convincing in the way it captures both Sissie's character and the world she describes that it is possible to overlook the sleight-of-hand act that Oates is performing.

Consider, for example, that Maisie Verver's developing consciousness is presented to the reader only via James's narrative mediation. James translates his young heroine's thoughts and feelings into his own elevated language. This is often handled for comic effect, but, more importantly, he solves the technical problem of how to present the consciousness of a character too young to create an extended narrative. Mark Twain allows Huckleberry Finn to tell his own story, but often Huck becomes merely a mask for Twain's own voice and sensibility.

In "Four Summers" Oates must convince us that a very young child can tell her own story. It's not even possible to explain logically the relationship between Sissie's words and her audience. She isn't telling her story *to* anyone, nor is there any premise that she is writing it down (which in any case would be impossible except in the fourth section). Neither is the narration a representation of her stream-of-consciousness, for it is neat and coherent. The story is not logically credible as a narrative presented by Sissie unless it is the mature Sissie who is conjuring up in retrospect those earlier days and earlier selves. Sissie the child could not possibly present such polished accounts of her miserable summer days. Furthermore, she is sometimes endowed with a reflectiveness beyond her years. It is not likely that a five-year-old, watching older children throw stones at a bird, could observe that "if the bird dies, then everything can die."

And yet for the most part the reader accepts the narrative without question. Oates relies in part on the conventional nature of first-person narrative and the reader's willingness—and eagerness—to accept that convention. We also accept Sissie's narration because in each section Oates convinces us that she is accurately conveying the sensibility of the growing girl. This sensibility is so strikingly captured that most readers are not apt to notice the violation of credibility. Let me briefly illustrate how Oates registers the consciousness of her young heroine at four different ages.

"It is some kind of special day," the five-year-old Sissie reports at the beginning of the story, articulating the child's dim perception of the mysterious workings of the adult world (and in retrospect making the reader wonder what the ordinary days must be like if this one is special). The diction is understandably at its simplest in this section, and so are the perceptions: "When I run around her chair she laughs and hugs me. She is pretty when she laughs. Her hair is long and pretty." When a courting couple rows up to the dock, laughing together, Sissie—too young to be aware of sexual relationships—simply observes "two people come in, a man and a woman." Sissie is the little sister, tagging along after her brothers with her "bag of potato chips."

Sissie at about ten in section II is more able to generalize about herself and her world. She notices that "Jerry is like Dad." She has a changed relationship with her father, "always in a hurry to get things done," who is now "like a stranger." The fact that her father's appearance "surprises" her reveals her greater awareness. Her mother has changed from "Ma" to "Mommy." Sissie at ten can relate present to past. The men who hang around the tavern "are familiar. We have been seeing them for years."

Sissie at fourteen is in the throes of puberty, worried that "my legs are too thin, my figure is flat and not nice like Marian's." She now has fantasies of running away from her parents, whom she finds embarrassing. Oates masterfully captures the sensibility of the young teen-aged girl at this awkward age: "Where would I rather be? With Marian and Betty at the movies, or in my room, lying on the bed and staring at the photographs of movie stars on my walls—those beautiful people that never say anything—while out in the kitchen my mother is waiting for my father to come home so they can continue their quarrel." She has become openly scornful of family members: "And my aunt Lucy and uncle Joe, they're here. Try to avoid them." Self-conscious and insecure, she crosses "through the crowded tavern, . . . conscious of people looking at me."

Only in the final section has Sissie evolved into full consciousness. Her voice is now mature though self-divided. The completeness of her self-awareness means only that the trap is closed. She is now able to perceive her world with great clarity: "It's the Lakeside Bar. That big old building with the grubby siding, and a big pink neon sign in front, and the cinder driveway that's so bumpy. Yes, everything the same. But different too—smaller, dirtier." Sissie's insights now display a high level of awareness and even poignancy, as when she wonders why the worn-out men in the tavern are "always tired" and why they "flash their teeth when they smile, but stop smiling so quickly." Sissie at nineteen is very much the same person she was at five, ten,

and fourteen, but Oates makes us believe in the growing-up and in the changes in consciousness along the way.

Sissie is finally a very typical Joyce Carol Oates heroine, which means, as Grant has put it, that she is one of those "frustrated, neurotic human beings psychically crippled by the events of their lives and the tragic frustrations with which they cannot cope." Sissie is dominated by her fear and insecurity. Though she wants to act, she is paralyzed by her self-doubt.

Sissie's parents are not cruel people. Instead they are insensitive, too absorbed in their own unhappiness to pay much attention to Sissie, the third of their four children and their first daughter. We never learn Sissie's real name. She is simply "Sissie," most likely a child's diminutive for sister, a detail which suggests her neglect. Sissie's brothers have to fend for themselves too, but since they are boys, this sort of independence receives support. Sissie's lot has always been to tag along: "The boys run out back by the rowboats, and I run after them." Though the brothers tolerate Sissie, "they don't like me, I can see it."

Above all Sissie feels unwanted. At one crucial point she remembers her mother screaming at her little sister:

> "Well, nobody wanted you, kid," she once said to Linda. Linda was a baby then, one year old. Ma was furious, standing in the kitchen where she was washing the floor, screaming: "Nobody wanted you, it was a goddamn accident! An accident!" That surprised me so I didn't now what to think, and I didn't know if I hated Ma or not; but I kept it all a secret . . .

This nightmarish scene must have left a big impact. It resonates against—and contributes to—Sissie's own feelings of being unwanted.

Sissie's personality is dominated by fear that leaves her nearly paralyzed. It is inadequate to remark that she is a detached, isolated outsider and observer: except for the dialogue with the man who paws her in the parking lot, we scarcely even see her talking. Instead we watch her "standing at the side," observing intensely, consumed by her fear.

That fear is everywhere in the story. In the first section as she looks at a man leaning against the railing overlooking the lake, she is "afraid it will break and he will fall into the water." The scene in which the unthinking adults make her drink the beer vividly captures the terror of childhood. She is also frozen with terror as her brother and the other children kill the bird caught in the scum.

Sissie's fear is also explicitly present in each of the other three sections. In the second section as her father rows her and her brother toward the island, she sits "very still, facing him, afraid to move." She is "afraid to look at" the brother "when he's mad." When they reach the island, "the boat bumps; it hurts me. I am afraid." When she sees her father throwing up, she runs after her brother, "afraid." In the third section as she begins to flirt with the man, she tells herself five times that she isn't afraid—heavily underscoring her fear. Just before the man begins to kiss and caress her, she acknowledges that "something frightens me;" he "sees I'm afraid." When the kissing begins, "something dazzling and icy rushes up in me, an awful fear, but I can't move." In the final section the married Sissie thinks she sees the man who had molested her five years earlier. Thrown into the past, she imagines hearing the voices of her parents and aunt. As the man at the bar starts to leave, she is "terrified at being left" by herself with the presences of her family. Sissie's fears are so deep and abiding because of her own lack of inner security. Nothing lasts, nothing is safe.

Sissie's habit of intense, detached observation is related to her fear. Like the young Stephen Dedalus, she is keenly sensitive to the sights and sounds around her. What makes her remarkable is her habit of focusing on the ugliest details available. Even as a small child, when she looks at the boats she observes that "the paint is peeling off some of them in little pieces." She notices the "pink lipstick smudges on the glass" of beer and the "darkish" teeth of her mother's friend.

In the second section as her father rows toward the island, Sissie fixes on his "throat, the way it bobs when he swallows:" "His face is getting red, the way it does at home when he has trouble with Frank. He clears his throat and spits over the side; I don't like to see that but I can't help but watch." That inability to look away is expressive of the inner disturbance. Sissie needs to fix on the ugliness, as if such sights confirm her sense of reality. The second section culminates with the vision of "napkins and beer cans, . . . part of a hotdog bun, with flies buzzing around it" and with her father "throwing up in the water and making a noise like coughing."

Sissie relentlessly seeks out the squalid. The young teenager stares at her aunt's "false teeth" and the "white scalp" beneath her uncle's hair, and

she watches her little sister "sleeping in Ma's lap, with her mouth open and drooling on the front of her dress." In the final section Sissie observes that the ground outside the tavern consists of "bare spots and little holes and patches of crab grass, and everywhere napkins and junk." Inside is no better: "there is a damp, dark odor of beer and something indefinable—spilled soft drinks, pretzels getting stale?" Her husband picks the label off his beer bottle with his "thick squarish fingernails."

The ugliness is not imaginary. People come to the grim, depressing Lakeside Bar to escape for a little while from the treadmill of their lives, not realizing that the tavern is itself a station on that treadmill. Oates is conveying a social reality in her depiction of unattractive people inhabiting the squalid world of the tavern.

But the point is that throughout the story Sissie's state of mind is more important than any objective reality. Though the ugliness is there, the most notable fact is that Sissie's eye always goes right for it and fixes there tenaciously. The squalid world of "Four Summers" is at least half created by its young narrator. Sissie's fixation on ugliness is finally inseparable from her fear.

At the same time the unhappy Sissie is extraordinarily sensitive and self-aware. Though she is perhaps partly self-victimized, she is also acutely intelligent. Only Sissie seems troubled by the world she inhabits and by the clumsy behavior of her family. Only Sissie is able to reflect and make generalizations about life, and in the fourth section these generalizations are particularly perceptive. She yearns desperately to escape her destructive environment, and yet at the end she is trapped, a princess who has somehow not been rescued from the prison of the Lakeside Bar. Why isn't she able to escape?

Sissie above all needs to develop a sense of her own worth, but the story provides no way that this could have happened. The only patterns for emulation available to her are the blighted lives of her parents and their friends. Though Sissie is so conscious of the emptiness and so eager to find something better, she does not know where to turn. The best she can do is marry a man whom she first met when he was "wearing a navy uniform"—a pathetic glimpse of the world beyond the tavern.

Indeed one of the bleakest motifs in "Four Summers" is that of the cyclical pattern of life, repeating mindlessly from generation to generation.

This motif contributes powerfully to the story's feeling of claustrophobia. The more we react against our fathers and mothers and struggle to develop our own identities, the more we become like our fathers and mothers—in fact, the more we *replace* them. When a writer like Tolstoy shows that the important events in a human life, both joyful and sorrowful, happen to everyone, he presents this situation as a triumph for human community. The very commonplace quality of the crucial experiences brings us together. Oates's perception is similar, but her perspective is quite antithetical. We are doomed to repeat our parents' lives and experiences no matter how intensely we attempt to escape.

The courting couple at the beginning of the story is a reminder that Sissie's parents were once a young, handsome courting couple themselves. Sissie's mother even comments that "Sue and me used to come here a lot," though "not just with you two, either." The generational motif is picked up by Sissie's father when he talks about his father's desire to return to Europe:

> He looks as if something tasted bad in his mouth. "My old man died thinking he could go back in a year or two. Stupid old bastards!"
>
> "Your father was real nice. . . ." Ma says.
>
> "Yeah, real nice," says Dad. "Better off dead."

"I hate him, I wish he'd die," Jerry says of his father before the ride to the island. In "Four Summers" each son grows up to hate his father.

In the second section Sissie observes that "Jerry is like Dad, the way his eyes look;" he hates his father, he is becoming his father. A snapshot Sissie talks about in the third section further emphasizes the unhappy cycle of life:

> There is a photograph taken of her when she was young, standing by someone's motorcycle, with her hair long. In the photograph she was pretty, almost beautiful, but I don't believe it. Not really. I can't believe it, and I hate her.

Beautiful Sissie, with the intolerance of youth, cannot accept that her mother was once young and beautiful. Though she hates her mother, she follows in her mother's footsteps in marrying a man much like her father. By the end of the third section, as the man paws her in the parking lot, she must realize that she is trapped in the same cycle: "I think, What is he doing? Do they all do this? Do I have to have it done to me too?" "Girls your age are all alike," the man has observed. This man, like the man Sissie

marries, reminds her of the one man she cannot escape: "His breath smells like beer, maybe, it's like my father's breath . . ."

Sissie at nineteen is all too aware that she has reached the end of the line in marrying a younger version of her father. Jesse drinks beer, just as her father did, and "when he laughs Jesse reminds me of him." When she holds Jesse at night, she thinks of "my father and what happened to him." She prays that Jesse will be different, knowing full well that he won't be.

When Sissie and Jesse were courting, they were simply going through the motions required by that part of the cycle: "Before we were married we went to places like this, Jesse and me and other couples. We had to spend a certain amount of time doing things like that." They had courted as her parents courted, they will become as her parents became: "He still loves me. Our love keeps on. Like my parents' love, it will subside someday." In the first section the grown-ups sit around playing cards instead of taking the children for a boat ride. The card game reappears, climactically and rather too obtrusively, near the end of the story. People are trapped within inherited genes and inherited patterns:

> Jesse is young, but the outline of what he will be is already in his face . . . Their lives are like hands dealt out to them in their innumerable card games. You pick up the sticky cards, and there it is: there it is. Can't change anything . . .

If the cycle of generations functions as a trap in the story, so does the Lakeside Bar. The tavern is dark and stale, and the popular music always playing on its jukebox is a strained, unsuccessful attempt at gaiety. Even when Sissie is outside the bar, there is no escaping the bar. As the children stone the bird caught in the scum—a bird obviously emblematic of Sissie and her fate—Sissie can hear that "inside the tavern there is music from the jukebox." The second section plays off the first, for after staying to play cards in the first section, the father rows his children to the island in the second. But the island, ugly and strewn with garbage and litter, is neither improvement nor escape: "On the other side we can look back at the boathouse and wish we were there."

In the third section Sissie, who now hates "this noisy place and these people," restlessly leaves the tavern. But her attempt at romance leads only to molestation, and she turns to "run back to the tavern." (At least Humbert Humbert takes Lolita away.) The idea of no exit is especially strong in the final section, for Sissie has made her ultimate mistake. As she sits with her husband in the tavern, pregnant and entrenched, she has become the next generation.

The characters in "Four Summers" have nowhere to run. Sissie's aunt fantasizes about a television quiz show host, while at fourteen Sissie tries to lose herself in staring at the photographs of movie stars in her bedroom. Oates presents antisocial behavior as another response to the entrapment these characters feel. Duane Dorsey, the local punk (and obviously admired by Sissie's mother and aunt), has landed in jail in the first section. His offense? "He was breaking windows in his [mother-in-law's] house," clearly an allusion to the motif of attempted escape. Broken windows lead Duane Dorsey not to freedom but to jail.

And of course the men in the story attempt to escape through drink. No recent American story is more awash with beer than "Four Summers," but it's not the sort of story that would sell more Budweiser. The beer the men drink is associated with the futility of their lives and with their entrapment. Usually they drink too much, attempting to blot out the lives they live. The men drink because they are broken and because they have become self-destructive.

It is not every story that has beer as its dominant image. Sissie's mother asks her husband to "leave off drinking" and take the children on the boat ride. There are beer cans on the island, there is beer on the breath of the man in the parking lot, and Jesse drinks beer. Beer is even cunningly associated with death. In the first section the grown-ups cluck their tongues over the "kids or somebody" who "was out in the cemetery and left some beer bottles." Beer and death are unmistakably joined, for the beer drinkers of the story are walking dead men. "Why do they grow old so quickly, sitting at kitchen tables with bottles of beer?"

Beer figures most importantly and ingeniously in the episode in which the young Sissie is forced to drink beer. The mother's bored friend is responsible for this dim idea. Sissie's father angrily protects her, but the women are persistent:

"Who's getting hurt?" Ma says angrily.

Pa looks at me all at once and smiles. "Do you want it, baby?"

I have to say yes. The woman grins and holds the glass down to me, and it clicks against my teeth. They laugh. I stop swallowing right away because it is ugly,

and some of it drips down on me. "Honey, you're so clumsy," Ma says . . .

This is the story's most Gothic moment. The monstrous adults force the terrified child-victim to drink alcohol, they laugh at her, and then they criticize her when she unhappily closes her mouth and some beer spills. The scene is also a cruel ceremony of initiation. The drink the grown-ups give Sissie, however, is no magic potion but rather the liquid of their futility and entrapment. After this rite of passage Sissie is symbolically one of them.

It is rarely wise to speculate about a character's fate beyond the boundaries of the story, but I believe that Oates points us in exactly that direction. Sissie is on her way to spending some fifth summer recuperating from a nervous breakdown. I have already elaborated upon her psychic fragility, her fears and insecurities, her extreme isolatedness, her tendency to seek out ugliness. In the final section not only has her entrapment become irrevocable, but she is also conscious of it. Sissie's good looks have been the only source of her sense of self-worth, but now even this has no value: "My hair is long, down to my shoulders. I am pretty, but my secret is that I am pretty like everyone else." If she is "proud of my legs," she also realizes that she has "little else."

Even worse, she knows her marriage is a mistake. It is five years since the episode in the parking lot, but she thinks she sees the same man in the bar, "wearing a cheap gray suit," looking "tired" and "years older." Sissie must be close to the edge if an encounter with *this* man produces tears and a feeling of lost opportunity. She fantasizes that she could have "gone with him to his car" at the age of fourteen and somehow escaped, somehow broken out of the cycle. It is hard to imagine a more threadbare fantasy.

So Sissie is left trapped inside the bar and inside her life. Her only recourse is to try to pretend that she is happy and that everything will turn out well:

I think of the baby all the time, because my life will be changed then; everything will be different. Four months from now . . . It will be different with me because my life will be changed by it, and nothing ever changed my mother . . .

As hard as she tries to believe this, she cannot:

I let my hand fall onto my stomach to remind myself that I am in love: with this baby, with Jesse, with everything. I am in love with our house and our life and the future and even this moment—right now—that I am struggling to live through.

This young woman is under a great deal of strain. The conflict between the reality of her situation and her fierce desire to transform that reality into something better could lead to a nervous breakdown. At that, the Oates country has its share of nervous breakdowns: think of Clara in *A Garden of Earthly Delights* and Karen in *With Shuddering Fall*.

Critics take Joyce Carol Oates to task for writing too much and too self-indulgently. Often, especially in the recent novels, her urgent need to communicate her bleak vision of contemporary American life has ridden roughshod over artistic considerations. Even the award-winning *them* spins out of control after the brilliant first half. Furious and unrelieved passionate onrush can grow wearisome.

"Four Summers" is an excellent story precisely because the characteristic Oatesian vision has been artistically contained. The despair feels earned rather than imposed. All the emotional power and empathy of Oates at her best are present. The story succeeds, however, not because of the quality of feeling behind it but because that feeling has been controlled by a tightly organized, richly harmonious artistic structure. "Four Summers" seems to demonstrate that for Joyce Carol Oates less can be more.

Source: Keith Cushman, "A Reading of Joyce Carol Oates's 'Four Summers,'" in *Studies in Short Fiction,* Vol. 18, No. 2, Spring 1981, pp. 137–47.

Sources

Bannon, Barbara, Review of *Wheel of Love,* in *Publishers Weekly,* August 10, 1970, p. 47.

Creighton, Joanne V., "Joyce Carol Oates's Craftmanship in 'The Wheel of Love,'" in *Studies in Short Fiction,* Vol. 15, No. 4, Fall 1978, pp. 375–84.

Gilman, Richard, "The Disasters of Love, Sexual and Otherwise," in the *New York Times Book Review,* September 25, 1970, p. 4.

Johnson, Greg, *Understanding Joyce Carol Oates,* University of South Carolina Press, 1987, pp. 92–117.

Joslin, Michael, "Joyce Carol Oates," in *Dictionary of Literary Biography,* Vol. 2: *American Novelists Since World War II,* First Series, edited by Jeffrey Helterman, Gale Research, 1978, pp. 371–81.

Oates, Joyce Carol, "Four Summers," in *Fiction 100,* edited by James J. Pickering, Prentice-Hall, 2001, pp. 1109–21.

Review of *Wheel of Love,* in *Kirkus Reviews,* August 1, 1970, p. 825.

Further Reading

Bastan, Katherine, *Joyce Carol Oates's Short Stories: Between Tradition and Innovation,* Peter Lang, 1983.
  Bastan provides an overview of some of Oates's short fiction, focusing on her style and the relation of her stories to those of other major authors.

Johnson, Greg, *Invisible Writer: A Biography of Joyce Carol Oates,* Dutton, 1998.
  Johnson has written two other critical studies of Oates's work. He was given access to Oates's letters and archival materials for his biography, the only one on Oates.

Matusow, Allen J., *The Unraveling of America: A History of Liberalism in the 1960s,* HarperCollins, 1984.
  Matusow describes the political climate of America during the 1960s, focusing on the major voices of liberal social and economic policies.

Wagner, Linda W., ed., *Critical Essays on Joyce Carol Oates,* G. K. Hall, 1979.
  Wagner collects some of the more important essays written on Oates up until 1978.

In the Kindergarten

Ha Jin

1999

"In the Kindergarten" was originally published in a small magazine, *Five Points,* and was reprinted in *The Best American Short Stories of 1999.* It was written by Ha Jin, a writer who first came to the United States in 1985. This story takes place in Jin's native land, China, a country that has remained isolated from the West even in the modern information age. In this tale, a teacher who is unable to afford food for herself and her mother tricks her students, promising them a delicious meal from the plants she has them pick only to take their harvest for herself. One child, Shaona, who has only been in the school for a few weeks, notices how the teacher has taken advantage of her students and takes revenge against her. American readers will be interested in the subtle ways that the Chinese school is different from Western schools, especially in the relationship between the teacher and her pupils. Even so, the most surprising thing for Westerners might be in how similar the Chinese kindergartners are to the children in all other societies.

In 2000, Ha Jin became the first writer ever to win both the National Book Award and the PEN/Faulkner Award, for his novel *Waiting*. That year, "In the Kindergarten" was included in his collection of stories called *The Bridegroom*. His fiction and his poetry offer quiet, understated insights into what it is like to live in contemporary China, in an ancient society that has been hostile to Western scrutiny and repressive toward its own artists.

Author Biography

Ha Jin was born Jin Xuefei in Liaoning, a province in northeast China, on February 21, 1956. Growing up, he expected to follow a military career like his father. One of the most significant events in China when Jin was growing up was the Cultural Revolution declared by Mao Zedong in the mid-1960s. Because education was considered dangerous to Communist ideology, schools were closed, leaving Jin to piece his education together from whatever few written materials he could obtain. At age fifteen, he entered military service, starting as an artillery gunner and then becoming the operator of a telegraph machine. While he was in the service, stationed at a small town near the Russian border, he began the habit of reading, as books were passed around among the soldiers. In 1974, he left the army and worked as a telegraph operator for the Harbin Railroad Company. Listening to English radio broadcasts, he taught himself the English language.

In 1977, the government allowed the colleges to reopen. Jin attended Heilongjiang University in Harbin, studying American literature and receiving a Bachelor of Arts degree in 1981, the year that he married his wife, now Lisah Bian Jin. He received his master's degree from Shangdong University in 1984. The following year, he came to the United States to study at Brandeis University in Waltham, Massachusetts. His plan had been to go back to China after receiving his Ph.D. from Brandeis, but as the Chinese government became more politically repressive, Jin realized that he would never be able to write honestly if he returned to his home country. Instead, he accepted a position teaching English and creative writing at Emory University in Atlanta after receiving his doctorate in 1992.

In 1996, he published his first book of short stories, *Oceans of Words: Army Stories*. These stories were written while he was a student at Brandeis, and they concerned what life was like in the Chinese army. The book earned Jin the Ernest Hemingway Foundation/PEN award for first fiction in 1997. That year his second short story collection, *Under the Red Flag*, won the Flannery O'Connor Award for Fiction. In early 1999, he published his first novel, *In the Pond*. It received respectable but lackluster reviews. Later that year, though, his second novel, *Waiting*, appeared in print, drawing critical and popular praise. *Waiting* was the first book ever to win both the prestigious National Book Award and the PEN/Faulkner Award, which is the largest annual juried fiction award given in the United States.

"In the Kindergarten" comes from Jin's collection of short stories called *The Bridegroom*, published in 2000. Though most of his fame is based on his works of fiction, Jin considers himself to be a teacher and poet. His most recent book is *Wreckage*, a book of poems that was published in 2001. Most of his work so far has been based on his experiences in China, but he foresees that this is likely to change the longer he lives in America.

Plot Summary

The First Day

"In the Kindergarten" begins during naptime at a kindergarten in China. Shaona, who has only been there less than two weeks, is having trouble sleeping. She listens to her teacher on the phone in the next room. The teacher is asking for three more months to pay the money she owes to a Dr. Niu. She explains that she is weak, that she has lost blood "because of the baby," and that she has to provide for her elderly mother at home. Near the end of the conversation, she begs Dr. Niu not to tell anyone that she has had an abortion. Shaona does not understand much of what Teacher Shen is talking about, why she says a baby weakened her, as if it came out of her body: her mother had a baby a week before Shaona was sent off to school, and she was told that it came from a pumpkin patch.

After the nap, Teacher Shen gathers the entire class together and takes them out to the school's turnip field to pick purslanes, which are weeds that grow between the turnips. She shows the children what purslanes are and explains that they are delicious when cooked, promising that they will have some sautéed for dinner that night if they pick enough. The children turn picking them into a competition, while Uncle Chang, the old man who watches the field, warns them to be careful not to hurt the young turnips. A bully named Dabin gets into a fight with a girl, throwing her to the ground and kicking her. When the teacher asks who started it, Shaona points to Dabin, and he is taken inside to be punished by being locked in a closet.

As they are leaving the turnip field, Shaona is surprised to see Teacher Shen give a large portion of the purslanes they have picked to Uncle Chang. She is further surprised that night to find that there are no purslanes served for dinner. She remembers seeing the teacher ride off at the end of the day with a duffel bag on her bicycle that looked like the one they had collected the purslanes in, but she had thought the teacher was taking her laundry home. She comes to understand that the teacher has left with the plants that the children gathered.

Dabin looks at Shaona throughout dinner, and she knows that he is planning his revenge against her for telling on him. She has some peanuts that her father gave her, so she gives some of them to him as a peace offering. He tells her threateningly that she will have to keep coming up with gifts for him.

At night, Shaona cannot sleep because she misses her family. She eats one of the peanuts her father gave her, even though it is against the rules, and places the shell under her pillow.

The Second Day

The next morning on the playground, Shaona walks past the place where Dabin and the other boys play army games. She plays "court" with the girls. They elect her to be queen because she is good-looking, and for a king they assign Dun, who is the only boy willing to play with them. Shaona is disgusted by Dun because he is weak and mousy and would have made a better courtier than king, so she quits.

While they take a nap after lunch, the teacher takes the children's sweaters and skirts to clean off the mud. Shaona finds the three peanuts that she had left missing, as well as the peanut shell that she had hidden under her pillow the night before. The teacher obviously confiscated them and then looked around the bed for more.

They go out into the turnip field again that afternoon to find any purslanes that they might have missed the afternoon before. Uncle Chang is not at his post. The field is being irrigated, making it muddy. The teacher once again promises them purslanes for dinner, explaining that they were too late turning in the ones they picked the day before. The children dutifully tramp through the mud, trying to find any purslanes that might be left.

When Shaona goes to search through some high grass, a wild rabbit jumps out. The rabbit has an injured leg, and it is confused by the children's noise. Even though she had told them to be careful of the turnips the day before, the teacher is excited

about the possibility of catching the rabbit. She encourages the children, who are slipping around in the mud and ruining the turnip crop, to keep chasing it.

While everyone is concentrating on the rabbit, Shaona goes to the duffel bag where the purslanes have been collected. She urinates in the bag and then carefully covers the wet plants with dry ones.

After the rabbit runs away, the children talk excitedly with one another, but Teacher Shen quickly gathers them together and rushes them back to the school before Uncle Chang arrives and sees how they have ruined the turnip patch.

That night, there are no purslanes at dinner. Shaona is excited about having sabotaged them: she eats heartily and then later plays "soldier" with the boys, "as though all of a sudden she had become a big girl." She is confident that she will no longer cry for her family when she is lying in her bed at night.

Characters

Aili

Aili is a classmate of Shaona. She is first mentioned because her snoring keeps Shaona awake at night. Later, Shaona quits the "court" game that she is playing with the other children, deciding that she does not want to play the queen anymore. When she does, Aili steps in as vice queen to "keep the court from disintegrating."

Uncle Chang

An old, bald man who keeps watch over the turnip field. He allows Teacher Shen to bring her class into the field to pick purslane weeds from between the turnips, but he still keeps a strict eye on the students, making sure that the turnips will not be disturbed. As they leave, Uncle Chang is paid off with a large part of the harvest, almost a third of the purslanes that had been picked. The next day, when the class returns to pick purslanes again, Uncle Chang is absent from his post, and they destroy the turnip crop while chasing after a rabbit.

Dabin

Dabin, described as a "rambunctious" boy, becomes a threat to Shaona during the story. He is competitive, showing off how many purslanes he picked while playing cool about their value: he tells the other children that they taste awful even as the children are excited about picking them. When the teacher catches him fighting with another child, Shaona is the one to point out that Dabin started the fight. He is taken inside and locked in a closet. Later, fearing what he might do to her in revenge, Shaona offers him some of the peanuts that her parents gave her. He takes them and then insists that she will have to continue to be nice to him: ''Remember to save lots of goodies for me, got it?'' he tells Shaona menacingly. On the playground, she is afraid to go near the merry-go-round that Dabin and another boy, Luwen, are playing on.

Dun

Dun is a weak, ''mousy'' boy that the girls in the class do not respect. He is, however, the only boy willing to play with them. When they play ''court,'' he has the part of the king and Shaona is the queen, but she soon quits the game because ''she felt silly calling him 'Your Majesty' and hated having to obey his orders.''

Luwen

One of the boys in the class, Luwen is mentioned a few times in the company of Dabin. He and Dabin play on the merry-go-round, pretending to shoot their toy guns at things. Later, after the children have tried to catch a rabbit, Luwen tops Dabin's claim to have touched the rabbit before it escaped by bragging that he tasted wild rabbit once when his uncle caught two of them.

Dr. Niu

At the beginning of the story, Teacher Shen is on the phone with Dr. Niu, asking for more time to pay her bill and begging the doctor not to let anyone know that she has had an abortion. He does not appear in the story, nor are his words quoted directly.

Shaona

Shaona is the protagonist of this story. She is new to the kindergarten, in her second week there. Three weeks earlier, her parents had a baby boy, but she does not understand the physical process that led to it: Shaona believes what her grandmother told her, that ''babies were dug out from pumpkin fields in the countryside.'' Because she had never tasted the purslane before, Shaona is excited to hear that the children will have sautéed purslanes for dinner once they have collected them from the field, and she plans to pick some for her parents if they are

Media Adaptations

- Jin's short story ''After Cowboy Chicken Came to Town,'' from the same collection as ''In the Kindergarten,'' is read by Patrick Wang on *Best American Short Stories of 2001,* released on audiocassette and compact disk by Houghton Mifflin in 2001. This collection was edited by Barbara Kingsolver.

- Jin's novel *Waiting* is available, unabridged, on a six-tape audiocassette set from Brilliance, read by Dick Hill.

good. This leads to her disappointment when she realizes that the teacher has taken the harvest away and kept it for herself.

Shaona is nervous in the kindergarten. After she gets Dabin in trouble with the teacher by telling on him, she tries to make amends by offering him some of the peanuts that her parents gave her, hoping to avoid more trouble from him. She shies away from the merry-go-round where the boys play, remembering that the one time she'd played on it at length she felt sick for days afterward.

She is good-looking but also strong-headed. After being elected queen while the children are playing court, because she was judged ''most handsome'' among the girls, she walks away from the game because the boy playing the king is weak, and she cannot stand taking orders from him.

When Teacher Shen takes the children's clothes away to clean them, Shaona finds that her peanuts, which her parents gave to her, have disappeared from her sweater pocket. She feels heartbroken, aware that the teacher must have confiscated the peanuts, but she does not say anything about them. Later, though, when the other children are chasing a rabbit, she urinates into the bag of purslanes that have been collected. It is not just an act of impulse, because she is crafty enough to quit at some point so that there will be enough dry plants to cover over the wet ones. Shaona, who is naïve in the beginning of the story when she is listening to Teacher Shen on the telephone, ends up being vengeful and sneaky, driven to take action against her teacher but careful to keep her action a secret. As a result of her devious action, she does not feel like a baby anymore: she plays soldier with the boys that evening, and is sure that she will no longer cry at night.

Teacher Shen

The teacher is a complex adult whom the story's protagonist, Shaona, studies, at first with confusion and then later with anger. The teacher is in desperate need of money, and she is willing to use her children and bribe other officials in order to avoid starvation for herself and her elderly mother. She is young, and rumor has it that she is recently divorced from her husband, who was sentenced to thirteen years in jail for embezzlement.

In the story's opening lines, Shaona hears Teacher Shen on the telephone with Dr. Niu. She talks about having an abortion and about being unable to come up with the money that she owes. Shaona does not understand what she is talking about. Later, Teacher Shen takes her class of kindergartners to the school's turnip field. She tries to get them excited about picking the purslane weeds that grow between the turnips, promising them a delicious meal of purslanes that night. Even the children who have had purslanes but have not liked them are competitive about picking them. Shaona sees Teacher Shen giving some of the purslanes to Uncle Chang, not realizing that this is a bribe for letting them into the field to pick them, and she sees the teacher leave that evening with the rest of the purslanes. The teacher is either selling the plants that the students picked, in order to pay the debt she owes, or she is eating them herself because her debt to the doctor has depleted her food money. She betrays the children by not giving them the delicious meal they worked for.

A mark of the teacher's desperation is that she steals peanuts that Shaona's parents have given her.

The following day, she takes the children back to the turnip field when Uncle Chang is not there. The fields are being irrigated, and it is unlikely that he would allow them to endanger the turnip plants if he knew they were there. The teacher loses all concern about the turnips when someone sees a rabbit and there is a chance of catching it: she tells them to catch it, even though it means tramping the turnips into the mud.

Weilan

Weilan is a tough, scrawny girl who fights with Dabin and sticks up for the teacher. When he says that purslanes do not taste good, she says, ''Teacher Shen told us it tastes great,'' which leads to a bout of obscenities that ends with him pushing and kicking her.

Themes

Loneliness and Isolation

''In the Kindergarten'' is primarily about the suffering that the story's protagonist, Shaona, feels because she is unable to fit into her new surroundings. She is a young child who has been away from home for just over a week. At home, she has been replaced in the family by a three-week-old baby brother. Shaona misses her parents, and she is not even sure whether they love her as they did before, because of the baby.

At school, she finds that she does not fit in with any of the cliques that are already established. She assumes that the rough and tumble play of the boys by the merry-go-round is too much for her to handle, because after having played on the merry-go-round once before, she felt ill for days afterward. The girls accept her and make her the queen in their make-believe court game, but Shaona finds the game too passive for her tastes. Isolated from all factions, she cries through naptime, and in the night she is unable to sleep out of loneliness.

In the end, she becomes socialized by learning a secret behavior that gives her confidence. Spoiling the purslanes that the teacher was counting on rearranges the rules of society in a way that gives Shaona power over her bleak situation, and as a result she no longer fears the aggressive boys on the playground. She steps right into their soldier game and for once feels secure in her bed at night.

Self-Preservation

Teacher Shen behaves in a way that Shaona finds difficult to understand, because the teacher is driven by a knowledge of poverty from which Shaona has been shielded throughout her young life. Shaona expects her teacher to be honest and is shocked to catch her lying, taking home the purslanes that were promised to the students. She does not understand how desperate Teacher Shen's situation is, how her life is threatened by low wages, illness, and the fear that she might lose what little income she has if word of her abortion were made public. Teacher Shen's husband has been sent to prison, and she has to care for her mother, even though she herself is undernourished because of the blood that she lost during the abortion. She does not lie to the students and bribe Uncle Chang because of greed; she does so to save her own life.

Shaona is even more personally affected by the teacher's uncommon behavior when she finds that her peanuts are missing. To Shaona, the peanuts have a sentimental significance because her parents gave them to her. It is a sign of just how starved the teacher is that she would steal from one of her students out of a compulsion to nourish herself.

Teacher Shen tries throughout the story to behave in a responsible manner, even when it is obvious that she is desperate. In the end, the sight of the lame rabbit and the possibility of actually having meat to eat drives her into such a wild frenzy that she forgets her job and her responsibility to the students. The fact that Uncle Chang is not in the turnip patch on the second day is an indication that the class's presence there is probably inexcusable, and so Teacher Shen is taking a great risk to bring them in to pick purslanes. It is a chance that she is apparently willing to take. If entering the turnip patch is dangerous to her, then destroying it is certainly cause for dismissal, if not imprisonment. Still, she is so hungry that she cannot focus on the obvious consequences, and she encourages the children to catch the rabbit at all costs, regardless of what their childish efforts will mean in the long run.

Gender Roles

The attitudes that the people in this story have toward the different genders are very much like typical American attitudes. The kindergarten teacher caring for children is a woman, whereas the guard of the turnip field is a man, although, because the field is not in much danger, the job is given to an old, retired man. Shaona's father apparently cares about his daughter enough, but he is overjoyed when a boy is born into the family.

In the kindergarten, the traditional gender roles are followed: the boys play soldiers and make pretend guns out of anything they can find, and they aggressively threaten and intimidate the girls; the girls play court, but the strongest and smartest of them is expected to take orders from the weakest, dimmest boy, who plays the king.

Topics for Further Study

- Research the songs that would be sung in a Chinese kindergarten. Prepare a tape of them for your class, including translations of the lyrics.

- Find purslanes in your local grocery store. Look up a recipe for them, and sample what they taste like.

- Research what school life was like in China before the Communist government came to power in 1949, and report on how this story would have been different if it had taken place then.

- Assign sides to debate the ethics of what Uncle Chang does in this story. Is it right for him to allow the kindergarten children into the turnip patch to pick purslanes that no one was going to eat anyway, or is it just a case of needlessly endangering the turnips that he is supposed to protect?

- Write a short story about the one memory of your early school experience that most closely resembles what happens in this story.

There are signs that the traditional expectations are changing in the world of this story. One is the fight between Dabin and Weilan. When Weilan disagrees with Dabin, she stands up for herself, and she matches his obscenities with her own of equal strength. Still, she does not fight against Dabin when the conflict turns physical. At the end of the story, though, Shaona does break the line that separates boys from girls by playing soldier with the boys. It is because she is fulfilled and no longer repressing her aggressive, unladylike side that she is able to sleep comfortably.

Growing Up

As the title of this story indicates, ''In the Kindergarten'' belongs in the category of stories about young people who learn to develop independent identities, separate from those of their families. In this particular case, readers are not directly shown the family situation that Shaona, the main character, comes from but are only given hints in the scattered memories she has of her mother and father. Still, the importance of her family is clear from the way that she finds herself unable to sleep, distracted by thinking of them. Having been taken from her family and put into the kindergarten means that she must grow up quickly, because she does not have a chance to follow the gradual process of maturation that she might follow if she had stayed at home.

One harsh reality of the world that Shaona is faced with is the fact that her teacher, whom she trusts as a substitute for her parents, is untruthful. Shaona is in a position to understand this like none of the other students. She is the one who hears Teacher Shen on the phone, begging for time to pay her debt; she is the one who sees the teacher ride away on her bicycle with the bag of purslanes; and she is the one whose peanuts are stolen by the teacher. When she is convinced that Teacher Shen cannot be trusted, Shaona is forced to grow up quickly and to face the ugliness of the world that her parents shielded her from. Deciding to sabotage the purslanes is an immature way to deal with the situation, but it is the fact that she takes action at all that makes it possible for Shaona to think that ''all of a sudden she had become a big girl.''

Style

Point of View

''In the Kindergarten'' is primarily told from Shaona's point of view. The story is told in the third person, which means that the narrative voice refers to Shaona as ''she'' or ''Shaona,'' rather than saying ''I'' as it would if Shaona were telling the story to the readers. Still, the information that is given to the reader is mostly limited to information that would have passed through Shaona's mind. For instance, when Teacher Shen is on the telephone at the beginning of the story, readers are given her exact words just as Shaona would have heard them, and the reader is also given the child's interpretation of what Shaona would have thought. The exact reasoning behind the teacher's behavior—whether she is taking the purslanes for her own consumption, for instance, or is taking them to sell—is never specifically explained, because Shaona does not

have access to what goes on in Teacher Shen's mind. She can only interpret what she sees of the teacher's behavior.

Although most of the story is told from Shaona's point of view, it sometimes slips and gives information that Shaona could not know. Some of the story's information, such as the fact that the teacher used to sing a lot, seems unlikely to be from Shaona's consciousness: she is new to the kindergarten and would not know much about the teacher's former behaviors, although it could be explained as something that she heard from a classmate. Similarly, she could have heard that the teacher divorced her husband when he was sent to prison for embezzlement, but that is a fairly complex idea for kindergartners to be gossiping about. In some cases, the narrative clearly shifts out of Shaona's point of view to that of Teacher Shen. One example is when the readers are told that when Teacher Shen is cleaning the children's clothes, she ''was unhappy because she couldn't take a nap.'' Another example is when she rushes to leave the turnip field at the end because she is ''fearful that Uncle Chang [will] call her names.'' These breaks from Shaona's point of view are extremely rare.

Symbolism

In literary works, symbols are items that have both a specific function in the reality of the story and also refer to a larger, abstract concept. For instance, characters in a story or novel might have to cross a bridge to get from one place to another, but the bridge, in addition to its logical place in the tale, might also be seen as a symbolic ''bridge'' between the estranged people or hostile cultures that it helps bring together.

''In the Kindergarten'' makes much of the purslanes that Teacher Shen has the schoolchildren gather from the turnip field. In reality, purslanes are trailing weeds that are sometimes cooked and eaten, just as they are presented in the story. Symbolically, they tell readers much about the teacher's situation. Turnips are considered lowly roots that are eaten in poor cultures, but the purslanes here are so much lower in status than turnips that they are seen as an annoying clutter in the turnip patch. In the story, they grow so wildly among the turnips that a significant amount can be found on the second day of looking for them. As a symbol of Teacher Shen's starved desperation, the purslanes show that food can always be found if one lowers one's standards and seeks with enough effort.

Similarly, the wild rabbit can be considered a symbol of the children that Teacher Shen is trying to control. Even though the teacher would like her students to conduct their search for purslanes in an orderly way, disrupting as little of the turnip field as possible, she becomes excited about the rabbit and encourages the children to run around the turnip patch just as recklessly as the rabbit does. The fact that the rabbit is lame is a realistic element, in that this would be the only kind that the kindergarten children would have a chance of catching; it can also be considered symbolic of Teacher Shen's poverty, showing that she is so poor that even her fantasy meal is not anything grand—just a sick, injured animal.

Setting

The kindergarten setting of this story presents readers with a universal situation for childhood alienation. Children all over the world know that going to school for the first time marks a child's separation from the closed family society that he or she has known since birth. In this particular case, the familiar situation is magnified by the fact that the Chinese kindergarten is a boarding school, so that the children are forced, at the same time that they are socialized during the day, to deal with spending their nights in a strange place. Placing the story in this setting gives Ha Jin an opportunity to explore Shaona's subconscious fears, which she faces while trying to sleep, in addition to exploring the traditional fears of a child thrown into a social setting for the first time.

One other aspect that marks this setting as distinctive is the school's close association with the turnip field. American schools do not mix commerce and education together in the same place, but in rural China the students would learn the value of tending crops at the same time that they learned more academic pursuits. Because the turnip field is part of the school, the children are familiar with Uncle Chang, and they see nothing unusual about being brought to the field to pick weeds. The fact that the school grows its own produce helps convince Western readers of the poverty that affects people in the story, showing this school to be a small, basic, rural one that does not buy all of the food that it serves its students. Set at another type of boarding school, the students' destruction of a field might be seen as a cause for some discipline: in this setting, though, readers are led to believe that the loss of the turnip crop will hurt the school significantly.

Historical Context

Starvation

In general, Americans know little about China. For most of the time since China adopted a Communist form of government in 1949, it has been closed to visitors from the West. Travel in China has been restricted, and information about government workings has not been as accessible to journalists working there. The Chinese government is actively involved in the lives of its citizens, determining such matters as where individuals will work or go to school or how many children a family may have. The government is faced with the imposing task of caring for one and a quarter billion people, with more than a fifth of the world's total population living within China's borders. Three quarters of the country is rural, living in conditions that Americans would consider below the poverty level.

In trying to handle a population of that size, the Chinese government has made some drastic policy decisions that have had traumatic effects. One of the great catastrophes in modern Chinese history was the economic program called the Great Leap Forward. Initiated in the late 1950s, it was intended to quickly increase the country's economic capacity. The Great Leap Forward entailed consolidating small farms into huge labor cooperatives and moving over 100 million citizens into new positions. In the first few years, 1956 and 1957, the program appeared to be an astounding success, far beyond what anyone could have anticipated. Agricultural production increased greatly, in some areas shooting up ten times what the farms had previously been able to produce. Plans for distribution of food were made, and purchases from other countries were cancelled. Only gradually did the sad truth become known: the reported figures were nowhere near the actual production figures. Pressured by the bureaucratic system, local commune leaders had exaggerated reports to their superiors, who had in turn added their own exaggerations to those reports on each level up the chain to the federal government. Additionally, economists and statisticians who would have realized that the reported increases were impossible had been fired from government positions for being critical of the government. Having planned for grain that did not exist, the country plunged into a famine of staggering proportions. Between 1959 and 1962—a period when Ha Jin, born in 1956, would himself have been in kindergarten—over 20 million people starved to death in China.

In the early 1980s, the government began to accept the fact that a purely communist economy could not feed all of China's citizens. The agricultural sector was restructured, and the large communes were broken down. Under the new system, each household was responsible for growing and then providing a certain quota of crops; anything that was produced over that quota could be sold on the open market, which "In the Kindergarten" implies Teacher Shen may be doing with the plants that she has her students gather.

Reproductive Policies

Even throughout the periods of food shortage, China's economy grew immensely throughout the last half of the twentieth century. Between 1949, when the Communist government was installed, and 1990, the population grew from 540 million people to more than twice that number. Recognizing that overpopulation was a serious threat, the government instituted a policy in 1971 restricting each family to only one child. In cities, where there is a stronger police element, families have become accustomed to this and tend to follow the law, even though it has never been popular. In rural areas, families depend on having boys, who can work harder in the fields. Because these areas are not as well scrutinized, the "one child" law is frequently ignored. In a 1998 book about her ten-year experience as a foreign journalist in China, Linda Jakobson discussed her surprise at entering a country village and finding it populated with big families:

> There seemed to be at least three or four kids in every household. I knew that the so-called one-child policy had, even officially in many rural areas, become a two-child policy. I also knew that, as a result of rising incomes, some families were prepared to pay the heavy fines for having more than the officially sanctioned number of offspring. But I had thought that these were exceptions.

This would explain why, in "In the Kindergarten," Shaona's family is able to have a second child.

Because of the limit on children and the importance of male children for physical labor, there have always been rumors about female babies being abandoned or murdered at birth and mothers being forced to undergo abortions or sterilization. The government denies these rumors, making them difficult to confirm, although the country does have a high rate of infant girls who are put up for adoption annually. One fact that is clear is that abortion in China does not carry the social stigma that it does in the United States, where it is treated as a religious issue. In China, abortion is a practical issue. Having an abortion is treated like any other necessary medical procedure, so the ethics of it is not brought into question. A schoolteacher like the one in this story would not face the questions about her morality and would just have to face the financial burden of paying her doctor's bill.

Critical Overview

Ha Jin has been considered a major American fiction writer ever since the publication of his first book of short stories, *Oceans of Words*, in 1996. His work has won major writing awards, including the PEN/Hemingway prize, the Flannery O'Connor Award for Fiction, the National Book Award, and the PEN/Faulkner Award for Fiction. His books have been reviewed in academic journals such as *World Literature Today*, and in popular magazines with widespread circulation like *Entertainment Weekly*. In less than a decade, Ha Jin has earned a reputation as one of the most important voices in Sino-American literature.

His most successful book to date has been his second novel, *Waiting*, a love story about a Chinese army doctor who returns to his home village every year for seventeen years to beg for a divorce from his wife so that he can remarry. That book was the first ever to win both the National Book Award and the PEN/Faulkner Award. John McNally, writing in *The Progressive*, noted its combination of literary antecedents and cultural insight when he explained that *Waiting* "appears as if from a time capsule: It's a novel of manners in the tradition of Henry James, except that the backdrop is New China, and the manners are prescribed (and often enforced) by the Chinese government." McNally recognized the weakness of *Waiting* as being that it "sags under the weight of cliché. Letters bring rays of hope; characters' faint smiles play around their lips. The result is a world that can be read about but never fully experienced—which is a pity, since Jin's world is a complex and fascinating one."

In *World Literature Today*, Jeffrey C. Kinkley saw *Waiting* as a part of the "Ha Jin phenomenon." Kinkley compared it to Jin's one earlier novel, *In the Pond*, noting that it lacked the "irony and bitter humor" of the earlier book and that it was "unpretentious." In the end, Kinkley characterized it positively but unenthusiastically as "a good read."

''In the Kindergarten'' was published in the collection *The Bridegroom* in the same year that *Waiting* came to national attention. Reviewers generally commented on the stories' deadpan prose style, a mark of simplicity used to draw attention to the complex lives led by Jin's characters. A review in *Publishers Weekly,* for instance, notes that the stories in *The Bridegroom* ''attain their significant cumulative effect through sparse prose penetrated by wit, insight and a fine sense of irony.'' That review pointed out the way Jin's characters ''illustrate the ways in which hardship, lack of living space, inflexible social rules and government quotas thwart happiness.''

Nancy Pearl, writing in *Booklist,* noted that *The Bridegroom* would be welcomed by ''fans of *Waiting* because the two books present similar styles and themes. Altogether,'' Pearl concluded, ''this is a fine collection, sure to be in demand by fans of literary fiction.'' A brief review by Bianca Perlman in *Entertainment Weekly* gave *The Bridegroom* a rating of ''A,'' pointing out that ''Ha Jin's spare prose, subtle wit, and surprising plot twists make for a read that is both quick and memorable.'' *Library Journal* reviewer Shirley N. Quan recommended *The Bridegroom* for ''most larger public, academic, and Asian literature collections,'' noting that ''Jin uses this collection to exhibit his strong writing and storytelling skills with his laconic use of words.''

Criticism

David Kelly

Kelly is an instructor of creative writing and composition. In this essay, Kelly makes the case that the effectiveness of ''In the Kindergarten'' is diminished by the story's inconsistent point of view.

Ha Jin's short story ''In the Kindergarten'' gives readers in-depth information about two main characters. One is five-year-old Shaona, who has been sent away to school recently, when she was replaced in her home by the birth of a baby brother. The other is her teacher, Shen, who is recently divorced from her husband and is recovering from an abortion. Both characters are fascinating in their own right, especially to Western readers who want to understand more about everyday life in China. Unfortunately, this story simply is not big enough to carry all of the information that is packed into it. It has one main character, Shaona. It explains her confusion, follows her growth, and ends with her taking control of her situation. The excessive information given about Teacher Shen's life drains power from what readers think of Shaona's predicament, and it diminishes the success of the story overall.

Success is relative, of course, and judging the success of any work of art is linked to understanding what the work is trying to do. The observation that a short story has multiple points of view only becomes a criticism after the question of how many it rightly should have has been settled. In this story, there are at least three distinct perspectives, and possibly more.

The most conspicuous point of view is Shaona's. Readers see most of the story through her eyes, from the first sentence when she is having trouble sleeping to the last when she realizes that sleeping will not be a problem for her anymore. Between these points, the story follows the range of her consciousness. Shaona is confused as she tries to understand what an abortion is; cunning, in offering two peanuts to her nemesis, Dabin, and hiding the rest in her sock; betrayed when she realizes that Teacher Shen has stolen the class's purslanes and, more personally hurtful, Shaona's peanuts; and triumphant when it strikes her that covert destruction gives her power over the kindergarten bureaucrat that took advantage of her. The story tells Shaona's emotions directly to its readers, explaining what she thinks but does not say aloud, such as that she knows Dabin will take revenge and that she misses her parents. There is no indication anywhere in the story that this is meant to be anything other than a chronicle of Shaona's experiences.

By contrast, Teacher Shen's life is revealed with inconsistent vigor, giving readers spurts of her life story and flashes of her thought. Most of the information given about her is out in the open, where it is entirely believable that the facts readers know are ones that Shaona has acquired from her experiences of the teacher. The clearest example of this is in the story's opening segment. Readers find out that Teacher Shen has had an abortion, that she cares for her elderly mother, that she is so poor that she cannot afford eggs, and that she is in a panic about the prospect of word of her abortion leaking out, and it is all conveyed without the narrative having to enter Teacher Shen's mind. This early part of the story clearly establishes the pattern that makes the story Shaona's, with no need for any

What Do I Read Next?

- Jin's most popular work to date is his novel *Waiting* (1999). Like most of his works, this one deals with Chinese citizens trying to reconcile their basic human instincts with the requirements of a powerful government, as a doctor in the Chinese army returns to his village year after year to ask his wife for a divorce so that he can marry the woman he truly loves.

- Samplings of works by most major Chinese writers of the twentieth century are included in the *Columbia Anthology of Modern Chinese Literature,* edited by Joseph S. M. Lau and Howard Goldblatt and published by Columbia University Press in 1996.

- Lulu Wang's acclaimed novel *The Lily Theater* is about a young girl growing up in China during the Cultural Revolution. The book looks at the class system that the government tried to dismantle and how it endured. The book was published in English translation by Anchor Press in 2001.

- Jung Chang's book *Wild Swans: Three Daughters of China,* published by Anchor World Views in 1992, traces twentieth-century Chinese history through the lives of Chang, her mother, and her grandmother and shows how they reacted to the political changes from the Boxer Rebellion to the Tiananmen Square Massacre.

- *Daughter of the River,* Hong Ying's autobiographical account of growing up in China in the 1960s through the 1990s, is loved by some readers for its simple honesty and rejected by others for its lack of formal structure. Unlike many memoirs written by intellectuals, Ying is a child of the Chongquing slums, and her book reports a difficult life of poverty. It was published by Grove Press in 2000.

- In 1983, Jian Ma quit his job in Beijing and took off traveling to the small outreaches of China that Western visitors rarely see, recording his encounters with a pen and a camera. The book of his journey, *Red Dust: A Path through China,* reminds many American readers of the spirit of Walt Whitman. The first American edition was published by Pantheon in 2001.

- Maxine Hong Kingston is a well-respected Asian-American author. Her book *The Woman Warrior: Memoirs of a Girlhood among Ghosts,* published by Vintage Books in 1989, is a semiautobiographical work based on the stories her mother told her about how girls and women were treated in China.

---

other point of view, since the story is willing to let Shaona gain knowledge through overhearing things, even when it is unlikely.

The pattern that is established in the story's first few pages is broken, however, when the narrative gives readers direct access to Teacher Shen's thoughts. The most flagrant example of this is when the children are asleep and the narrative explains that the teacher is unhappy about not being able to take a nap herself: this is not an observation of her behavior; it is a direct statement of what is going on inside of her mind. Another obvious case of entering the teacher's consciousness is when the story says that she was "fearful that Uncle Chang would call her names." There is no reference to anything she has said or done to indicate that Shaona is just guessing that she harbors this fear. It is the story's narrative telling readers that this is how she feels, presenting Teacher Shen's thoughts directly to the reader.

There are a few instances when the story's narrative attempts to explain how Shaona would know what other characters are thinking. For example, she knows how the absence of purslanes affects her classmates because "[e]very one of her classmates *looked* upset" (emphasis added). She knows that Dabin is pleased about the peanuts that she has given him because it is easy to interpret his response: "His eyes glittered and his mouth twitched like a rabbit's." Descriptions like these allow readers to see how Shaona might reasonably know how others feel, but there are other instances when information that comes from beyond Shaona's direct experiences is harder to explain. In one case, the narrator explains that Teacher Shen "used to sing a lot." Since Shaona has only been at the school for a week and a half, readers can only put this information in her mind if they assume that other students would have mentioned it to her. Likewise, readers can only explain a statement like "The sight of the irrigation made their teacher hesitate" if they presume that Shaona put together the irrigation with a certain, unexplained look on the teacher's face, in order to interpret what was going on within her mind.

There is a third point of view in this story, one that makes observations that cannot be attributed to either Shaona or Teacher Shen. It is this unidentified perspective that tells readers, "It was said that [Teacher Shen] had divorced her husband the previous summer because he had been sentenced to thirteen years in prison for embezzlement." No one in the story could be considered to have come up with this thought: Teacher Shen certainly would not have thought it, and it is highly unlikely that any of the kindergartners would include such obscure details as "embezzlement" and "thirteen years" in their gossip. The same adult narrative perspective later tells readers, "Whenever their little skirts or caps were full, they went over to unload the purslanes into the duffel bag from which their teacher was picking out grass." Since Teacher Shen is referred to as "their teacher," it is not her thought, and yet this line apparently comes from an adult perspective that would see the kindergartners' clothes as "little." There are no other adults in the scene: the story has added a new point of view.

There are short stories that work quite well without holding firmly to one narrow point of view. Some are told from an omniscient perspective, which is one that allows the narrative voice to tell readers anything that happens anywhere at any time, skipping unapologetically from one character's mind into another's, from one locale to another, or even through different time frames. Other stories establish a pattern of changing points of view, focusing first on one character's experience and then shifting to another's. Still others can tell their tales from nonhuman perspectives, viewing the action from the point of view of a building or an

> 'In the Kindergarten' starts out clearly, firmly presenting the world from Shaona's point of view, but through the course of the story it changes. It violates the rules that it establishes for itself, with no deliberate pattern and for no good artistic reason."

abstract concept like a community. These works can all be successful by sticking consistently to one method throughout. "In the Kindergarten" starts out clearly, firmly presenting the world from Shaona's point of view, but through the course of the story it changes. It violates the rules that it establishes for itself, with no deliberate pattern and for no good artistic reason.

The problem with this kind of inconsistency is that it distracts readers from the story's main point and dilutes its effect. The information that the story gives to readers that does not come through Shaona's point of view may be interesting, but, given that this is Shaona's story, it is mainly irrelevant. Teacher Shen's abortion, her husband's jail sentence, and her fear that Uncle Chang might call her names might all be significant points, if this were a different kind of piece. It is a short story, though, and as such its space is limited: some information might be considered interesting but still does not deserve to be covered here. Once this is established as a conflict between Shaona's understanding of the world and the reality that she has found around her, there is an artistic responsibility to stay with that vision. This starts out as a story about Shaona's naïveté, as she tries to make sense of what the teacher says about babies in terms of what she herself knows about them. To bring in other points of view makes the style of those early pages irrelevant. If an artistic piece cannot keep consistent, it needs to show why it should be inconsistent. If not, it just presents readers with a worldview that is not as thoroughly imagined as it could be.

These irregularities of point of view do not make "In the Kindergarten" any less interesting, nor do they detract from its value as a peek into what life is like in communist China, which is probably the aspect that most readers want from it anyway. The extra knowledge about Teacher Shen and comments that come from no discernible source enrich readers' understanding of the facts of the case, even as they weaken the story's artistic purity. The uneven handling of this story's point of view does not ruin the story, and for many readers it will not even be noticeable. Still, the story starts out with an established point of view, and it could have and should have finished what it started.

Source: David Kelly, Critical Essay on "In the Kindergarten," in *Short Stories for Students*, The Gale Group, 2003.

Carey Wallace

Wallace is a freelance writer and poet. In this essay, Wallace explores Ha Jin's meditation on what children are taught and what they really learn.

From the time a child is very young, everyone—parents, teachers, other children—tries to teach him or her something. The things others say don't always make sense to a child; sometimes the message gets horribly scrambled in translation. Children are further confused when parents, teachers, and other children offer wildly different opinions on the same subject. And then there's a whole other category of information for children to deal with: things that nobody tells a child but that they can't help seeing—the way people really act despite what they say, the way things really are despite what people claim. In Ha Jin's "In the Kindergarten," originally published in *The Bridegroom* (2002), Jin meditates on what children are taught and what they really learn, through the eyes of his young protagonist, Shaona.

In her second week of kindergarten, Shaona, who has left home for the first time for her schooling, is still an innocent. And she'd like to stay that way, as Jin implies in the first line: "Shaona kept her eyes shut, trying to sleep." Shaona's sleep, and her innocence, is cut short, however, by an abrupt introduction to a very grown-up world. During her restless naptime, she hears her teacher on the phone, begging someone to extend her terms on a loan that she apparently took out in order to have an abortion performed. Still uncomprehending, Shaona is nonetheless jolted entirely out of her child's sleep: "Those words made Shaona fully awake." And once awake, in a pattern that will continue throughout the story, she proves an eager learner as she strives to understand her world, straining "her ears to listen."

In a speech that tragically illustrates the broken continuum of family life, the teacher fully reveals her secret, mentioning her family responsibility to her own mother at home and that she needs to eat eggs (which are also symbols of fertility) to replace the blood that she lost along with the baby. For the first time in the story, what Shaona learns from her teacher comes into conflict with what she learned from her family. Her grandmother has told her that babies come from pumpkin fields. But if so, "Why did her teacher sound as though the baby had come out of her body? Why did she bleed for the baby?"

Teacher Shen then introduces a new word to Shaona's vocabulary: "abortion." Her mind racing, Shaona tries to make sense of this new term within the context of her innocent world. "Is it something that holds a baby?" she wonders. "What does it look like?" But at the same time, she is already drawing conclusions from the information she has to work with, understanding from the rest of the conversation that it "must be very expensive." Her teacher slams the phone down, ending the conversation, but her student, unbeknownst to her, has just learned an incomplete but somehow horrifying lesson, which puts an end to her child's slumber. "Shaona couldn't sleep anymore"—despite the fact that, yawning "sleepily," she clearly still needs rest. She wishes that she could return to the safety of her parents' home, but even there, she remembers learning another hard lesson—probably her first—upon the birth of her baby brother. Whether she learned it directly or indirectly, Shaona knows that male babies are more highly valued than girls, and she wonders if her parents "would love her the same as before" after her brother's arrival.

After Shaona's sleepless nap, through which the other students slumber peacefully, the children are led outside to pick purslanes, which their teacher tells them they'll enjoy for supper that night. Along the way, Shaona continues to take in and attempt to process the information the world gives her and to bring it into harmony with the information her teachers have given her. Spotting a plane up in the sky, she wonders how "a pilot could fit inside those planes, which looked as small as pigeons."

On the way to the purslane field, however, another category of information surfaces as well:

the pieces of information that students exchange among themselves. Watching the teacher, Jin lists Shaona's own observations of her teacher but then adds something Shaona has heard: "It was said that she had divorced her husband" because he had been imprisoned for embezzlement. But the teacher quickly breaks into Shaona's young meditations by introducing some more official information, giving her class a quick biology lesson on how to tell purslanes from turnips. It's a lesson that quickly turns practical: seconds later she has each child assigned a row to harvest.

During this activity, another student, Dabin, takes it upon himself to teach Shaona another lesson. He asks her to compare bundles of purslanes, notes that hers is smaller, and draws an immediate conclusion: "You're no good." It's a personal lesson that he follows up with a more informative lecture to the whole group, asserting that purslanes "taste awful" and backing his claim up with a perhaps fabricated story about being forced by his parents to eat the herb as a cure for diarrhea. Another girl challenges him, calling on the teacher's authority and reminding him that Teacher Shen has told them that purslanes are delicious. At this point, the children are stymied. At this young age, they have no equipment for deciding who is wrong and who is right when authority figures come into conflict. "How can you know?" Dabin asks the girl. "I just know it!" she says. Dabin then proceeds to teach the girl a far more profound lesson than his opinion on Shaona's worth, or purslanes. In the absence of meaningful debate, he descends into personal insult. And when his female classmate returns in kind, he responds with force, pushing her to the ground and winning the argument—for a moment, until Teacher Shen reasserts control, hustling him off to a punishment room.

But Teacher Shen, although she makes some attempts to fulfill her role as teacher, reminding the children of a traditional proverb about hard work, is about to teach the children some lessons of her own. Shaona gathers several puzzling bits of information from her: as they leave the field, the teacher gives almost a third of the children's hand-picked dinner to grouchy Uncle Chang, without explanation. She then leaves the school with a strangely overstuffed duffel bag. But at dinner, even these aberrations are overshadowed when the children sit down to find no purslanes on their plates. At this moment, the information Shaona has been gathering all day coalesces in her head. "Now she understood," Jin writes. "Their teacher took their harvest home."

> **" She's not just imitating behavior she's seen at this point, not just following a previously observed script; instead, she's come to her own conclusion: her teacher's authority and the rules she's made are corrupt and don't have to be obeyed."**

The new lesson is a hard one to swallow, and it ruins Shaona's dinner. The extracurricular lessons she's been learning from her teacher have already interrupted her sleep. This one makes it difficult to eat. Furthermore, she's got another problem: Dabin is now out of the punishment room and looking for revenge. Shaona must now do something to deal with him.

Her actions prove how quickly she's picked up on her teacher's lessons. Her teacher had offered Uncle Chang a bribe to avoid his wrath, and Shaona quickly offers Dabin some special peanuts, sent to her by her parents, to fend off Dabin's. This mollifies him but brings up another dangerous question: are their more? Again Shaona pulls forth a new tool, borrowed from her teacher's arsenal: lying; she tells him no.

That evening, Shaona again has difficulty sleeping, and to comfort herself, she makes yet another leap as a pupil, by breaking the rules and eating one of her contraband peanuts. She's not just imitating behavior she's seen at this point, not just following a previously observed script; instead, she's come to her own conclusion: her teacher's authority and the rules she's made are corrupt and don't have to be obeyed. Still, Shaona straddles the two worlds, crying quietly about the loss of her womblike family bed and the safe innocence of nestling against her mother's belly.

The next day, it becomes clear that eating the peanut was only the first step in what becomes a full rebellion for Shaona. She's disobeyed the high authority of her teacher and school, and at recess that day she throws off the rules of her fellow students, creating havoc in a play court by refusing to play queen to a "mousy" king. In this act, she's not only breaking free from peer opinion but is also taking a stand in opposition to the very early lesson she learned at the birth of her brother, that boys are more important than girls. Interestingly, it is perhaps one of the only positive lessons modeled by her teacher, when the teacher unexpectedly punishes Dabin for his violence against his female classmate.

Rebellion is pleasantly exhausting, and for the first time in the story, no longer kept awake by anxiety, Shaona falls asleep at naptime, "the moment her head touched her pillow." When she awakes, she's presented with another mystery: her clothes, which had been dirty when she went to sleep, are now clean. This is delightful, a throwback to her innocent days in her family home. But she's quickly reminded again that those days are over: her peanuts, which she had hidden in a sweater, are missing. Shaona cries like a child over the loss, but she doesn't waste any time with childish wondering about their fate. Immediately, she comes to the adult conclusion that "her teacher must have confiscated the peanuts."

When the students return to pick more purslanes that afternoon, all but Shaona are duped by their teacher's claim that the cook wasn't able to make them in time on the previous evening. Shaona alone is sulky, though Jin adds in a line that is telling, both literally and metaphorically, that "she never stopped searching." But when the rest of the students are distracted by the sighting of a crippled rabbit and run off to chase it, Shaona is given the chance to further rebel against the teacher's system. She needs to use the bathroom, and the place she chooses to relieve herself is the bag of purslanes. The rebellion isn't complete—Jin writes that she "dared not empty her bladder altogether," but the act is powerful nonetheless. The other children return, still arguing amongst themselves with unverifiable information as in the previous day, but Shaona has been busy making a completely different set of far more sophisticated calculations—and acting on them.

Were they correct? Shaona suffers a moment of terrible self-doubt, worrying that, if she was wrong, their dinner will include the soiled purslanes. But when she is proved right, she is delighted—in contrast to the other students, who are disappointed—and eats multiple portions of all the offerings. That evening finds her making her stand against the teacher's lessons, her peer's opinion, and even

society's roles for men and women, again on the playground. Instead of simply refusing to play in the girls' silly games, Shaona actually rejoins her young society among the boys, playing soldier and carrying a water pistol, "as though all of a sudden she had become a big girl." This line, still in Shaona's voice, is perhaps slightly misleading, since the young child has no vocabulary yet to describe her true transformation. She has not just become like "a big girl"—she has become adult, on her own terms, within her small society, and she has done it while flouting her society's strict notions of what it means to be a "boy" and what it means to be a "girl." But although Shaona doesn't yet have the words to express her evolution, she knows something has changed. And with her newly adult mind, she forms a concrete and telling conclusion about what the result will be: "From now on, she would not cry like a baby at night again."

Source: Carey Wallace, Critical Essay on "In the Kindergarten," in *Short Stories for Students,* The Gale Group, 2003.

Joyce Hart

Hart has degrees in English literature and creative writing, and she focuses her writing on literary themes. In this essay, Hart examines the layers of deception in Ha Jin's short story.

Ha Jin's short story "In the Kindergarten" is filled with deceit, which is used for several different purposes. Characters manipulate one another for personal gain, to ease sorrow, to avoid social persecution, and in order to seek revenge. Some characters fabricate stories in an attempt to preserve someone else's innocence. Some are subtle in their deception, whereas others carelessly expose their dishonesty in their haste to meet their needs. Even the narrator cannot be fully trusted, as the reader is led to make certain assumptions that upon closer examination turn out to be false. By the end of the story, the reader is left to ponder if Jin's short story is a morality tale or merely a statement of fact: people just tend to lie.

"In the Kindergarten" begins with little Shaona being unable to sleep at naptime. Unlike her fellow classmates in her kindergarten, Shaona's mind is active with thoughts about missing her home and wondering if her parents' love has been withdrawn from her since the recent birth of her baby brother. As she lies awake on her cot, she overhears her teacher talking on the telephone. The voice is fuzzy in the background, however, and Shaona must press her ear to the wall so she can hear better. Teacher Shen is upset, but Shaona is not sure why. Her teacher is using words that Shaona does not understand. The words that Shaona does understand are used in ways that do not make sense to her. For example, Teacher Shen is referring to a loss of blood in connection to having a baby. This conflicts with the image that Shaona has in her head. Shaona's grandmother had told her that babies come from pumpkin patches. Surely, her grandmother would not lie.

When the students finally wake up, they go outside, where the sweet smell of dichlorvos greets them. The potent pesticide will rid the city of flies, fleas, and mosquitoes. Could it be that something with such a pleasant fragrance could be so deadly? Then Shaona sees two jet fighters drawing a long double curve in the sky. Her eyes tell her that the planes are no bigger than pigeons. If this is true, how could a pilot fit inside them? Could her own eyes be deceiving her?

Teacher Shen follows the children outside. She has conceived of a plan. She will treat her students, who trust her completely in their innocence, to a day outside of the isolating walls that surround their school. She will take them to the turnip field behind their kindergarten, where they will learn to recognize and pick purslane, a tasty salad green that grows like a weed in the garden. In order to persuade her students that the work they will be doing in the hot sun is worthwhile, Teacher Shen accentuates the tasty meal of purslane, which she has promised them at the end of their toil, smacking her lips and saying, "It tastes great, different from anything you've ever had. Tell me, do you all want to have purslanes for dinner or not?" Of course they do. Their normal meal is bland and boring. Anything new added to the menu would be exciting, even if they have to work in the noonday sun to get it, instead of playing during their recess. Teacher Shen would not lie to them.

Teacher Shen herself, however, has also been lied to. She used to be more fun, Shaona reflects. She used to sing and smile. Recently, however, she has become sullen. Rumor has it that she divorced her husband because he was sent to jail for embezzlement. Poor Teacher Shen: she has a liar for a husband.

As the children continue to work in the garden, Uncle Chang reminds the students from time to time, from his reclining position under the broad, shady leaves of a tree, not to step on the young

> **"**What Teacher Shen did not reveal to her students was that she had secretly altered the proverb for herself, adding just a small phrase of her own at the end: 'Many hands provide great strength <u>for me</u>.'"

turnip plants as they pull out the purslanes. Uncle Chang is in charge of several gardens in the area. He must be smiling at the children and especially at Teacher Shen, who has figured out a way to weed the garden for him for free. Sneaky Uncle Chang: in the end, not only will he receive a long noontime nap and a weed-free garden but he will, in effect, take home the students' portion of the bounty to enjoy with his dinner meal.

One slightly bright boy, named Dabin, recalls that he once ate purslanes and that they tasted "like crap, more bitter than sweet potato vines." He was forced to eat it for medicinal reasons and would not have done so if his mother had not insisted. His memories can't be true, of course, because the children around him recall that Teacher Shen just told them that it tastes great. The young boy must be a liar. When a fight breaks out between the boy and one of his accusers, Shaona is the final judge of who will be punished. She points to Dabin, who is taken away and put into isolation to mull over his deceitful attitude. Shaona knows that once he is set free, he will seek his revenge on her. She will have to create a scheme to protect herself. However, first she must complete the prodigious task before her, that of filling the large duffle bag with purslanes, a task that will eventually take the children one and a half hours of concentrated work. The exertion is worth it, though, or so they think. To keep them on task, Teacher Shen keeps reminding them (where is her conscience?) of a proverb they had recently learned: "Many hands provide great strength." What Teacher Shen did not reveal to her students was that she had secretly altered the proverb for herself, adding just a small phrase of her own at the end: "Many hands provide great strength *for me*."

Dabin is released from his solitary confinement and glares at Shaona all through the children's purslane-free evening meal. Shaona, fearing Dabin's nasty revenge, decides to trick the young boy. She offers him two of the six peanuts that her father had given her as a treat the last time she left home. Dabin is impressed. After eating the two peanuts, he requests more. Shaona, in a stance of mock innocence, lowers her eyes and tells Dabin that those were the only peanuts that were left. Dabin searches her clothing but finds nothing in her pockets because she has hidden the other peanuts in her socks. Later that night in bed, to soothe her sorrows, Shaona retrieves one of the peanuts and eats it, though it is against the rules. She carefully hides the shell under the pillow so she will not be caught. Does that mean that Shaona is a liar?

The next day, good Teacher Shen comes to the rescue of the children after they soil their clothes in the mud. After admonishing them for creating extra work for her, Teacher Shen washes and dries their clothes during their morning nap. Teacher Shen probably believes that her theft of Shaona's remaining peanuts was justified by the extra work that the children had caused her.

Upon awakening from their nap, the kindergarten students are once again ushered toward the turnip garden next door. To raise their spirits, Teacher Shen has the children sing a song as they march toward the fields. The song is about happiness and playing games, things that children should be experiencing. Is Teacher Shen trying to make it appear that the children are playing a fun game while working in the field? Is she trying to make them forget that they did not receive their prized purslanes the night before? Is she hoping that they will fall for her same lies today? "Aunt Chef couldn't cook those [purslanes] we got yesterday because we turned them in too late," Teacher Shen announces, "but she'll cook them for us today. So everybody must be a good child and work hard." Silly, innocent children: they buy Teacher Shen's lies. Even though Shaona does not quite swallow the misinformation that her teacher is feeding them, she nonetheless does not know how not to follow her teacher's instructions. She works, although sullenly.

Upon the sight of a handicapped wild rabbit, Teacher Shen demands that the students chase it. Teacher Shen's mind is working as quickly as a calculator. Her bill owed to Dr. Niu would be nicely decreased if she could just get that rabbit in her hands. Whereas she was very careful to direct her students while Uncle Chang observed her, in Chang's absence she allows the youngsters to trample the young turnip seedlings and destroy the garden in their exuberance to harness the rabbit. Uncle Chang is, after all, nowhere to be seen. How can he prove that it was her students who destroyed his crop? If he asks, well, Teacher Shen will probably tell him a white lie. She wouldn't want Uncle Chang to think that she had taken advantage of him or that she was not grateful for his help.

Teacher Shen is a sly one; but she is not so sly that she has completely fooled Shaona. Shaona can relate. She knows that, in a tough situation, it is all right to lie or sneak or do whatever one has to do to get revenge. Yes, the same sweet little Shaona that the narrator introduced as an innocent babe, so innocent she still believes that babies come from pumpkin patches and that an abortion is something a mother uses in which to carry her baby, this same young girl is peeing into the duffel bag of the collected greens. Can it truly be that that is what she is doing? She keeps her bottom carefully hidden so no one can tell. She also does not completely empty her bladder so that the moisture will not wet the bag. She then delicately places fresh purslane leaves over the dampened ones so the odor will not be readily apparent. Then, after her task is complete, with a kicking heart she runs back to her group to pretend nothing unusual has just happened. The deceit has lifted her previously sullen mood. Her revenge has lightened her spirits. Her heart is throbbing in victory. She has outdone her teacher in deception.

How does this morality tale end? The narrator describes Shaona as if she has successfully completed a rite of passage. It is as if all of a sudden she had become a big girl. She feels that from now on she will not cry like a baby at night. Shaona, through her deceit, has somehow miraculously grown up. She has learned the ways of the adult world, a world in which deceit usually ends with a reward. Forget the teacher's husband who ended up in jail. Maybe he had lied a little too much. He was a fool. Smarter people know that one must control the size of their untruthfulness if they are to get along in this world. One must judge the situation and manipulate it. One must keep one's eyes open, adjust the ancient proverbs to fit one's own needs, and outsmart one's fellow companions.

Or could it be that this conclusion is a bit misleading?

Source: Joyce Hart, Critical Essay on "In the Kindergarten," in *Short Stories for Students,* The Gale Group, 2003.

Sources

Jakobson, Linda, *A Million Truths: A Decade in China,* M. Evans and Company, Inc., 1998, p. 122.

Kinkley, Jeffrey C., Review of *Waiting,* in *World Literature Today,* Vol. 74, No. 3, Summer 2000, p. 579.

McNally, John, Review of *Waiting,* in the *Progressive,* March 2000, p. 44.

Pearl, Nancy, Review of *Bridegroom,* in *Booklist,* Vol. 97, No. 2, September 15, 2000, p. 216.

Perlman, Bianca, Review of *Bridegroom,* in *Entertainment Weekly,* Issue 562, October 6, 2000, pp. 80f.

Quan, Shirley, Review of *Bridegroom,* in *Library Journal,* Vol. 125, No. 14, September 1, 2000, p. 254.

Review of *Bridegroom,* in *Publishers Weekly,* Vol. 247, No. 36, September 4, 2000, p. 81.

Further Reading

Jie, Zhang, and Li Xiaobing, eds., *Social Transition in China,* University Press of America, 1998.

   This book collects essays from eleven Chinese scholars working in America, offering their assessments of how the country has changed in recent years.

Roberts, J. A. G., *Modern China: An Illustrated History,* Sutton Publishing, 1998.

   This British publication provides readers with a comprehensive overview of Chinese history throughout the nineteenth and twentieth centuries.

Weich, Dave, "Ha Jin Lets It Go," in *Powells.com Interviews: 22 Authors and Artists Talk about Their Books,* iUniverse.com, 2000.

   This interview with Jin covers his influences, his artistic views, and his feelings about having left China forever.

Wong, Jan, *Red China Blues,* Doubleday/Anchor Books, 1996.

   Wong, a Canadian of Chinese descent, went to China in the 1960s during the Cultural Revolution and then returned in the 1980s as a journalist. In this book, she offers an unparalleled look at the people and the culture.

The Indian Uprising

Donald Barthelme

1968

In Donald Barthelme's short story "The Indian Uprising," the unnamed narrator tells of a battle between his troops and a group referred to as "the Comanches." Interspersed between scenes of battle and the torture of a captured Comanche are the narrator's memories of past events and people, conversations with his girlfriend, Sylvia, and sessions with a teacher named Miss R. Ultimately, the narrator's soldiers find themselves overrun by the enemy; the narrator has been betrayed by Sylvia and fooled by Miss R., both of whom reveal that they have sided with the Comanches. At the story's end, the narrator is taken prisoner and presented to a "Clemency Committee," thanks to Miss R., with the Comanches in attendance.

Some critics and scholars have considered Barthelme a writer of metafiction; that is, writing that draws attention to the fact that it is an artifact, not naturally occurring, in order to bring up questions about reality and its relation to fiction. Critics have also called Barthelme a writer of postmodern fiction, which is variously defined as fiction written by anyone after 1945, fiction that blurs the line between high and popular culture, or fiction that questions previous literary forms (the definitions of postmodernism are multiple and often contradictory).

In this story, as in most of his work, Barthleme experiments with word usage, syntax, narrative flow, and time to create a collage of images rather than a traditionally structured tale. Very little is

revealed about the action's location or the characters' backgrounds, but the images Barthelme paints are rich with the curious detail of everyday material items and popular culture. Some critics have noted that the story, written in the 1960s, reflects the televised terrors of the Vietnam War and its protesters, as well as the historical violence of the American West. Others have focused on the story's warlike representation of male-female relationships.

"The Indian Uprising" was one of Barthelme's earliest stories, first published in the *New Yorker*. In 1968, Barthleme included it in his collection of stories, *Unspeakable Practices, Unnatural Acts.*

Author Biography

Donald Barthelme, considered one of the twentieth century's leading writers of experimental short fiction and novels, was born in Philadelphia on April 7, 1931. His parents—Donald Barthelme Sr., an architect, and Helen Bechtold Barthelme, a teacher— reared him and his four younger siblings in Houston, Texas. Three of his brothers (Frederick, Peter, and Steven) have also become writers.

Donald's studies at the University of Houston were interrupted in 1953, when he was drafted into the United States Army to serve in Korea and Japan. Upon his return, Barthelme worked as a reporter for the *Houston Post.* As he recounted in a 1982 *Partisan Review* interview with Larry McCaffrey, "it seemed clear that the way to become a writer was to work for a newspaper, as Hemingway had done." He also held various public relations jobs at the University of Houston. Between 1961 and 1962, Barthelme was the director of Houston's Contemporary Arts Museum, after which he moved to New York City to become the editor of *Location* magazine. Once he began publishing and receiving awards for his writing, Barthleme taught at such universities as Johns Hopkins and City College of New York. He returned to the University of Houston in the early 1980s to teach in its writing program. Barthelme was married four times and had one daughter.

Barthelme published many of his early stories during the 1960s in various literary magazines. His short story "The Indian Uprising" first appeared in the *New Yorker,* and it opens Barthelme's second collection of stories, *Unspeakable Practices, Unnatural Acts,* published in 1968. He won numerous awards for his work, including a Guggenheim fel-

lowship in 1966 and a 1972 National Book Award for children's literature for *The Slightly Irregular Fire Engine, or the Hithering Thithering Djinn.* He also received a PEN/Faulkner Award for Fiction and the *Los Angeles Times* Book Prize for *Sixty Stories* in 1982. He died of cancer on July 23, 1989, in Houston.

Plot Summary

"The Indian Uprising" is told with a limited plot, consisting primarily of the observations, memories, and insights of an unnamed narrator involved in an urban battle against a group called the Comanches. Woven throughout the descriptions of the battle and other war-related events are the narrator's comments and memories of different women.

When the story opens, the narrator is describing the city as it looked during the battle with the Comanches, when he and his compatriots "defended the city as best we could." The city is barricaded and festooned with protective wire, and it features streets with such names as Rue Chester Nimitz and George C. Marshall Allée. The narrator's troops have captured a Comanche and are interrogating and torturing him.

After this, the narrator shifts to describe a variety of situations and details sometimes connected with the interrogation and sometimes unrelated. First, he remembers sitting with a woman named Sylvia and "getting drunker and drunker and more in love and more in love." The narrator also remembers that he has made some tables out of hollow-core doors (cheap doors, usually used for interior rather than exterior doors, that are made by fastening sheets of thin wood together, leaving a hollow space in the center of the door) and wonders about how a person he refers to as "you," most likely his film actress girlfriend Sylvia, felt while filming movie scenes naked. He remembers the tables made from hollow-core doors that he has built for the numerous women with whom he has lived.

He begins describing the barricades he and his fellow soldiers erected against the Comanches. The barricades consisted of numerous unrelated items, which the narrator lists: a bottle of red wine, ashtrays, plates, a poster, and a flute, for example. He mentions that he decided then that he "knew nothing."

The next scene begins in a hospital where the wounded received treatments, "the worth of which was not quite established." Again, the narrator mentions that he "knew nothing." His friends put him in touch with an "unorthodox" teacher, Miss R., who is "excellent with difficult cases." Miss R. is a sort of taskmaster, belittling the narrator and reminding him that he knows nothing. He wants to speak of a woman named Jane who has just been beaten up by a dwarf, but Miss R. will not let him.

As the next scene begins, the narrator is thinking of Sylvia. He remembers being with Sylvia and asking her to call off her "braves," indicating that she was with the other side in the battle. At that time, she ran down the Rue Chester Nimitz, "uttering shrill cries." As it turned out, the Comanches had infiltrated the ghetto of the city; however, the people living there welcomed them. In turn, the narrator's side "sent more heroin into the ghetto," addicting the residents, including Sylvia.

The narrator shifts the scene to Miss R.'s house, where they sat in chairs across from each other while people watched. He remembers his friend Block and their discussion about the progress of the battle. They spoke of Sylvia and a man named Kenneth who owned a large coat that, at different times, had hidden both Sylvia and a knife-wielding Comanche. The narrator remembers asking Sylvia, "Which side are you on . . . after all?" after seeing her wear a muffler in the colors of his side. Miss R. belittled the narrator and said, "The only form of discourse of which I approve . . . is the litany." She explained how she organizes words while the narrator "sat in solemn silence."

After remembering a moment from the battle, the narrator returns to the Comanche who is being tortured. Under duress, the Comanche has admitted that his name is Gustave Aschenbach and that he was born in Silesia. Various memories and thoughts flood the narrator's mind, including those of a visit to Sweden and Jane's run-in with the dwarf. He remembers that he condemned Jane for having an affair with a man named Harold and then comments on the loose organization of the narrative, saying:

> Strings of language extend in every direction to bind the world into a rushing, ribald whole.

The narrator notes that the Comanches "smashed our inner defenses on three sides." He remembers a variety of other moments, including one when he was in bed with someone, most likely Sylvia. They had a quarrel, and there were "white, raised scars" on her back.

The narrator says that his side killed many of the Comanches during the battle but discovered that they were mostly children and that many more were coming from all directions. Miss R. then informs him that he is in front of the "Clemency Committee" and that he must remove his belt and shoelaces. He does what she asks, and the story ends with him looking at the Comanches watching him with "their savage black eyes, paint, feathers, beads."

Characters

Block

Block is one of the narrator's fellow fighters in the battle; he enters the story carrying flowers, bread, and weapons. The narrator calls him "friendly, kind, [and] enthusiastic." Block shares information about the battle, noting that the narrator's troops hold various parts of the city but that the "situation is liquid." He also assures the narrator that Sylvia does not love Kenneth, only his coat.

Captured Comanche

After being tortured by the narrator's troops, the captured Comanche reveals that his name is Gustave Aschenbach. He was born at "L—, a country town in the province of Silesia," a region in Eastern Europe currently shared by Poland and the Czech Republic. His father was a judicial official and all of his relatives were government officials, according to the narrator.

Jane

Jane is one of the narrator's friends. Early in the story, the narrator hears that Jane has been beaten up by a dwarf in a bar, and later he comments that this event doesn't sound like something she would be involved in. On one occasion, the narrator reflects upon Jane's affair with a married man, Harold, and questions her "values." According to the narrator, Jane is attractive and desirable; he describes her leg as "tasty and nice-looking."

Kenneth

Kenneth is one of the narrator's compatriots in the war. He owns a large coat that Sylvia likes, but Block assures the narrator that this does not mean that she is in love with Kenneth. Kenneth mentions at one point that he would like be Jean-Luc Godard, a French film director who was prominent during the 1960s for his nontraditional and nonlinear approach to telling a story through film.

Narrator

The narrator, while never named in the story, is a leader of the troops trying to prevent the Comanches from taking over the city. He is in love with Sylvia but has lived with a large number of other women at various times in his life; he mentions Nancy, Alice, Eunice, and Marianne. There is a sense that he struggles in his relationships with women and may even have employed violence in these relationships; at the end of the story, he says, "the sickness of the quarrel lay thick in the bed. I touched your back, the white raised scars." He is also involved in violence when he participates in torturing the captured Comanche.

His friends urge him to see Miss R. for instruction in an unspecified subject. He tries to remain impassive when she belittles him, but he admits that he finds it exciting when she pushes him into a room where he knows people will be watching the two of them during his instruction.

Miss R.

Miss R. is an "unorthodox" teacher, somewhat plain in appearance and abrupt in her language. Her office is sparsely furnished and has no books. The narrator's friends suggest that he seek out her services, as she is "successful with difficult cases." While it is not exactly clear what she is teaching the narrator, she treats him with disdain and physically pushes him around. She tells him that he knows "nothing" and dictates the topics he may discuss and how he may speak of them.

Miss R. appears to be on the same side of the battle as the narrator until the end of the story, when she reveals that she is with the Comanches. At this point she announces to the narrator, "This is the Clemency Committee," asks for his belt and his shoelaces, and makes him a prisoner of the Comanches.

Sylvia

Sylvia is the narrator's girlfriend and a film actress who has appeared naked in her films. The narrator loves Sylvia and desires her presence on a number of occasions during the battle.

Sylvia eventually betrays the narrator, running to the side of the Comanches during the battle. On one occasion, though, the narrator is confused when he sees Sylvia wearing a long, blue muffler, an accessory that typically signifies to the narrator "the girls of my quarter." He calls out to Sylvia, "What side are you on . . . after all?" Later, she mentions to the narrator that he gave her heroin "first a year ago." This is related to the fact that the narrator's side sent heroin into the ghettos when they found out that the residents were beginning to side with the Comanches.

Themes

Male-Female Relationships

There are no successful relationships between men and women in Barthelme's short story, even between the narrator and his girlfriend Sylvia. The ground between men and women in the story reflects the ongoing battle between the Comanches and the narrator's troops.

Twice the narrator indicates that he is "getting drunker and drunker and more in love and more in love," indicating a certain amount of pain surrounding his feelings for Sylvia. In another scene, Block quickly assures the narrator that Sylvia is not in love with Kenneth, highlighting the narrator's anxiety over his and Sylvia's relationship. Sylvia is shown, ultimately, as a deceptive woman, lying to him about which side in the battle she has chosen. When the narrator remembers lying in bed with her at the story's end, he winces over "the sickness of the quarrel" he has had with her, and his fingers touch "white, raised scars" on her back, calling up images of violence and pain.

The narrator's relationships with other women in the story are also failures. He has lived with a number of women—at least four in addition to Sylvia—indicating that he has had difficulty staying in a relationship. Even his relationship with Miss R. is fraught with pain and anxiety. When he seeks her out for help with an unnamed problem, she belittles and shames him. He responds with passivity and silence. In the end, Miss R. betrays him by assisting with his imprisonment.

Violence

The story opens and closes with impressions of violence achieved and violence to come, and throughout the text there are glimpses of brutality. The characters never remark upon or even notice the violence, as if it has become a normal way of life—

Topics for Further Study

- Donald Barthelme does not provide extensive backgrounds for the characters in his story. Choose two characters from the story and create past and future lives for them. Where are they from? What kind of education do they have? What kinds of jobs did they hold before the battle? What are their families like? What will happen to them after the battle is over?

- Critics have considered whether the Vietnam War, the antiwar protests, and the history and legends of America's West might have influenced Barthelme's writing of this story. Research the history of one of these events or periods and write a brief persuasive essay on whether it

contributed to the story, supporting your argument with examples.

- There are two scenes of torture in the story. Investigate which countries are believed to use torture to interrogate prisoners and what international organizations, such as the United Nations, have to say about what constitutes torture.

- Some critics have argued that Barthelme's story is about the tensions between men and women and their struggles to maintain successful relationships with each other. Investigate the most recent psychological findings and theories on male-female relationships, and present them in a short essay with references.

---

possibly an authorial comment on the constant presence of violence in American society and the limited value words have against violence and in accurately describing violence. The war motif in the story has prompted critics to consider whether Barthelme's story refers to the violence of the Vietnam War, the antiwar demonstrations that were frequently turning American streets into battlegrounds, or the nation's long history of violence against Native Americans.

At the story's start, the narrator is busy torturing a captured Comanche by tilting his head back and pouring water into his nostrils. In response, the Comanche's ''body jerked, [and] he choked and wept.'' Later, the Comanche is forced to speak when the narrator's troops place electrodes on his genitals. During neither torture scene does the narrator, or anyone else, note what is happening. In fact, the narrator's mind habitually wanders off to another place and time.

When the narrator admits that his troops have killed children, he finishes the thought by noting that ''more came from the north and from the east and from other places where there are children preparing to live.'' This flat and emotionless refer-

ence to the deaths of many children and to the fact that many more were coming to replace the dead reflects the narrator's lack of sorrow. The narrator nearly has an emotional response to a quarrel with Sylvia, but when he takes notice of the scars on her back, he does not express concern or explain their source. His casualness about the scars and the previous torture scenes suggest that the narrator is a man who lives comfortably with violence.

Deception

The world in Barthelme's story is filled with deception and lies, and the surface images of things and people often do not accurately reflect what lies beneath. This creates an atmosphere of disorder and confusion in the story and contributes to the story's plotless and nonlinear narrative. There are surprises around almost every corner, but they are surprises that disturb rather than delight.

Sylvia and Miss R. betray the narrator, and ''girls hid Comanches in their rooms.'' When the captured Comanche is tortured, he says that his name is Gustave Aschenbach and that he is from a town in Silesia, a region spanning the Czech Republic and Poland—a rather odd name and origin for an American Indian. A friend's blue coat turns into a hiding place from which a Comanche jumps out and stabs the narrator's leg. A hospital uses a treatment "the worth of which was not quite established." Tables are actually hollow-core doors with wrought iron legs attached, barricades are made up of everyday items, such as a flute or a bottle of vodka, and a friend has an affair with a married man. The deception in the story creates a world in which most things have lost their normal meaning.

Style

Barthelme's story is set in a city during an unspecified modern period. The unnamed narrator is telling the story primarily in the past tense. To tell the story, the author uses a nonlinear and plotless narrative with unusual word choice and sentence structure.

Nonlinear Narrative

"The Indian Uprising" does not read like a traditional story in which there are characters with relatively well-defined roles and backgrounds who appear in a linear or chronological plot with a definable beginning and end. The story's lack of structure is echoed by the "destructuring" activity going in the story: the narrator is involved in a battle that is destroying his city while he witnesses the dissolution of his relationship with Sylvia.

Several times the narrator says to himself, "I decided that I knew nothing," indicating a deep sense of chaos and loss of meaning. This chaos is reflected in the continuous parade of unrelated objects and events that appear in the story. The barricades created to hold back the narrator's enemies are made up of the detritus of everyday life, such as a blanket, window dummies, ashtrays, pillows, a flute, corkscrews, and can openers. In the city, there is a dwarf who has attacked one of the narrator's friends, an "inexplicable shell money lying in the grass," a hundred thousand hyacinths sent to the ghetto, and "a sort of muck running in the gutters." This collage of images further enhances the story's sense of disorder.

Miss R. attempts to impose order when she states that "I believe our masters and teachers as well as plain citizens should confine themselves to what can safely be said." Her attempt, however, becomes farcical when she claims that a list of

unrelated words she has organized into a hierarchical list holds some meaning. In Barthelme's story, only the illogical is meaningful.

Atypical Syntax

The story also features sentences that do not seem to make sense, paragraphs in which the sentences jump from one topic to the next, and sentences that do not use traditional punctuation. For example, after describing a Comanche knife attack, the narrator continues in the same paragraph with a sentence that does not follow typical standards of narration or punctuation:

> Not believing that your body brilliant as it was and your fat, liquid spirit distinguished and angry as it was were stable quantities to which one could return on wires more than once, twice, or another number of times I said: "See the table?"

At times, Barthelme uses a word that does not seem to fit the occasion, as when he tells of receiving information about his friend Jane: "Jane! I heard via an International Distress Coupon that you were beaten up by a dwarf in a bar on Tenerife." A reader might typically expect the word "signal," "frequency," or "call" instead of "coupon." In this manner, Barthelme disrupts the expected flow of a sentence, creating tension, confusion, and questions.

Because of these constructions, only limited glimpses or snapshots of the action are available, and a mood of unease and apprehension quickly settles over the story. Instead of telling the reader about this mood, or having the characters talk about feeling this way, Barthelme uses unconventional syntax and language patterns to communicate the atmosphere he desires.

Historical Context

The Vietnam War During the 1960s

Barthelme wrote "The Indian Uprising" in the 1960s, during the Vietnam War, one of the longest wars in U.S. history. In fact, critics have argued that the battles against the Comanches in the story echo images of that war.

American involvement in Vietnam began in the late 1940s and early 1950s, when the United States contributed resources to help the French create an anti-communist regime in their colonial territories of Indochina, as the region was then called. Eventu-

Compare & Contrast

- **1960s:** The United States military drafts about 1.8 million young men to serve as soldiers during the Vietnam War. A man can qualify for a student deferment from the draft if he is a full-time student and able to show satisfactory progress toward a degree.

  Today: The United States no longer relies on the draft but fills the ranks of its military with volunteers of both genders. However, men between the ages of eighteen and twenty-five must still register with the Selective Service System in case of a national military emergency.

- **1960s:** About 80 percent of those fighting in the Vietnam War are from working-class or poor backgrounds. There are disproportionately high numbers of African Americans serving as combat troops.

Today: In the all-volunteer Unites States military, minorities account for nearly 35% of the personnel, and African Americans account for 20%.

- **1960s:** On April 15, 1967, more than 200,000 protesters gather in New York City and San Francisco to register their displeasure with American involvement in the Vietnam War.

Today: While protesters against the war in Afghanistan are less numerous and vocal than their 1960s antiwar antecedents, they do exist. Scattered demonstrations erupt in October and November of 2002 after the United States begins a military offensive against the al-Qaeda organization in Afghanistan.

---

ally, the French gave up their control over Vietnam, and the country was partitioned into North Vietnam, led by Ho Chi Minh, a communist, and South Vietnam, ruled by a government somewhat friendly to the United States and Europe.

In an effort to stem what was seen as the rising tide of communism in the region, and to help South Vietnam defend itself against North Vietnam, President John F. Kennedy significantly increased U.S. support to South Vietnam in the early 1960s. By 1963, the United States had approximately sixteen thousand soldiers stationed in South Vietnam. A series of events led President Lyndon B. Johnson to authorize sending some eighty thousand troops to defend U.S. airbases in South Vietnam and to engage in limited fighting in April 1965. By the end of 1965, there were 185,000 American soldiers in South Vietnam; that number grew to 500,000 by the end of 1967.

Support for the war began to erode by 1966, with many Americans not fully confident that President Johnson was making progress in helping the South Vietnamese resist communism. President Rich-

ard M. Nixon further escalated the war after his election in 1968, much to the dismay of many Americans, provoking an increasing number of antiwar demonstrations. By January 1975, the American military had removed most of its troops; by April of that year, the North Vietnamese effectively took over South Vietnam.

The Vietnam War created deep and lasting divisions in American society and entirely changed the way the United States looked at committing its troops overseas. The war cost America much more than the $170 billion in material expenditures; more than 58,000 Americans died, and about 23,000 veterans of the war were permanently disabled.

Antiwar Protests During the 1960s

With its images of urban battles and barricades, Barthelme's short story evokes a period during which thousands of Americans took to the streets to protest the Vietnam War. In the mid-1960s, college students and others began organizing demonstrations to show their increasing displeasure with a U.S. government that looked to be supporting a corrupt government in South Vietnam and was sending their friends, brothers, husbands, and sons to a faraway country to fight for a questionable cause. Most of these demonstrations were peaceful, but some erupted in violence.

Students for a Democratic Society (SDS) was one of the most prominent groups organizing antiwar demonstrations during the 1960s. They began in 1960 when a group of students associated with the Socialist Party organized to support the civil rights movement. By 1964, prompted by increased American military activity in Vietnam, SDS began organizing campus demonstrations. At that time, all men between eighteen and twenty-five who were not enrolled in school were required to register for the military draft. SDS circulated a ''We Won't Go'' petition among men of draft age, encouraging them to resist induction into the military and to burn their draft cards.

Teach-ins also began on the nation's college campuses by the mid-1960s. During the teach-ins, faculty and students, often eschewing their regularly scheduled classes, held discussions and information sessions about the war. On March 24, 1965, more than 3,500 attended a teach-in at the University of Michigan in Ann Arbor, sparking similar events at college campuses across the nation that spring. These culminated on May 15 of that year when groups at 122 universities held the ''National Teach-In.''

Also in 1965, an SDS-sponsored demonstration brought more than twenty thousand antiwar protesters to Washington, D.C. Other major rallies against the Vietnam War occurred during this period, including the 1967 March on the Pentagon that attracted more than one hundred thousand, and a violent multi-day demonstration outside the 1968 Democratic Convention in Chicago. By the late 1960s, even mainstream religious, labor, and professional organizations began voicing their opposition to the war.

Critical Overview

Critics have both lauded and condemned Barthelme for the way he used language and reordered the traditional structure of stories. While some have accused Barthelme of being lazy and careless and of intentionally subverting language, most have written of their delight when encountering his experi-

ments with the written word, appreciating the challenge that exists within a Barthelme story.

Soon after Barthelme's death in 1989, John Barth wrote an appreciation of the author in the *New York Times Book Review,* comparing him with another short-story writer, Raymond Carver. Barth wrote that Barthelme shared with Carver ''an axis of rigorous literary craftsmanship, a preoccupation with the particulars of, shall we say, post-Eisenhower American life, and a late-modern conviction, felt to the bone, that less is more.'' According to Barth, Barthelme was ''the thinking man's—and woman's—Minimalist,'' a proponent of a style of art and music originating in the 1960s that emphasized simplicity and straightforwardness. Francis Gillen, writing in *Twentieth Century Literature,* credits Barthelme for alerting modern man to the presence of a world abundant in many things that are, nonetheless, devoid of value and meaning. Gillen praises the author for exploring the ''full impact of mass media pop culture on the consciousness of the individual who is so bombarded by canned happenings . . . that he can no longer distinguish the self from the surroundings.''

''The Indian Uprising'' has generally received high marks from most critics. Neil Schmitz, for example, writing in the *Minnesota Review,* calls ''The Indian Uprising'' a ''brilliantly conceived collage.'' Schmitz praises Barthelme's use of nonlinear narrative as well as everyday objects to develop satire in his work. He notes that Barthelme has, ''with the insane coolness of a TV commentator,'' created a ''Vietnamized world lurching toward an apocalypse by juxtaposing in quick flashes all its profuse objects, events and language.'' Maclin Bocock calls Barthelme ''an original and important writer'' in *fiction international.* He is particularly interested in Barthelme's treatment of the male-female relationship in his work, arguing that much of Barthelme's writing is concerned with ''the failure of a man to achieve a satisfactory and lasting relationship with a woman.'' This theme is present in ''The Indian Uprising,'' Bocock notes, even though it is ''concealed by a cover of complicated language.'' The story, he asserts, is ''an extended metaphor of war,'' meant to represent the painful breakup between the narrator and his girlfriend, Sylvia. The Comanches in the story therefore signify the words Sylvia uses to attack him; by the end of the story, the narrator is beaten down, and his ''emasculation . . . is complete.'' According to Bocock, the hero as a failed lover is common theme in Barthelme's fiction.

Some critics do not take pleasure in Barthelme's experimental prose, however. While John W. Aldridge generally praises Barthelme's *Unspeakable Practices, Unnatural Acts* in the *Atlantic Monthly,* he also has complaints about a few of the stories in it. Some of them, he argues, "strike one as exercises in free association and automatic writing or as descriptions of bad dreams jotted down . . . for the benefit of one's analyst." Walter Sullivan is not impressed by Barthelme's unique style, claiming in the *Sewanee Review* that the author is "apparently devoid of ideas." This has forced Barthelme, he asserts, to use clichés and to write down "whatever ridiculous things occur to him."

Webster Schott agrees with Aldridge that Barthelme's writing is dreamlike, but he considers this a positive feature. Commenting in *Book World— The Washington Post,* Schott finds Barthelme to be "one of the half dozen truly interesting American writers" of the time as well as "original" and a "genuine artist." But he also acknowledges that the author's work can be "tedious, inflated, repetitious, and a bit depressing." Other critics have expressed similarly contradictory feelings about Barthelme's work. For example, Earl Shorris, reviewing Barthelme's 1972 short story collection *Sadness* for *Harper's,* enjoys the uniqueness of the author's writing but is also pained by the impact his words and sentences can have. According to Shorris, Barthelme has "located the square on which we are cowering, and he has assembled the comedy of our activities on that square, our lives, into an instrument of discomfort." On the other hand, he praises Barthelme for being able to "turn the most ordinary events into beautiful language; he is often a poet; he makes sculptures of words; art is alchemy."

Criticism

Susan Sanderson

Sanderson holds a master of fine arts degree in fiction writing and is an independent writer. In this essay, Sanderson examines Donald Barthelme's use of historical figures and events in his short story.

Numerous critics have noted that Donald Barthelme's stories are filled with the everyday bits and pieces of modern life. Tony Tanner summarizes this phenomenon well in his book *City of Words: American Fiction 1950–1970,* noting that Barthelme's writing is "packed with the detritus of modern life: it seems like an unbroken stream of the accumulations and appurtenances which we see around us" and that, somehow, Barthelme is able to turn these familiar collections into "strangeness."

Yet, in his short story "The Indian Uprising," Barthelme moves beyond this effort to expose the material garbage heap of our lives; he has his eye set on our accumulated history as contemporary Americans. According to Barthelme, we are the result of more than two hundred years of collected violence, wars, brutality, and generally rotten behavior toward one another. Thankfully, he delivers this accusation with a bit of black humor. The story presents a collection of historical wreckage gathered into a pile, holding as little meaning and substance as the material bits and pieces of modern life that litter the text. Barthelme's treatment of the references to history in "The Indian Uprising" call to mind the condemnation Russian revolutionary Leon Trotsky leveled against his enemies in 1917: "You are pitiful isolated individuals: you are bankrupt; your role is played out. Go where you belong from now on—into the dustbin of history!"

The city in "The Indian Uprising" is portrayed as a heap of modern junk. Barricades made up of the small bits of everyday modern life—blankets, ashtrays, flutes, and liquor bottles—protect the city streets from the Comanches. There is even an "officer commanding the garbage dump;" indeed, Barthelme makes a number of allusions to the city's military past during this accumulation process. Streets are named for famous military men, and the whole atmosphere of the battle against the Comanches has a familiar cast to it, as if the battle had jumped from the pages of a slightly irregular textbook on the American West. Add to these textual features the fact that Barthelme wrote this story during a period when many Americans were demanding civil rights for African Americans and thousands of young men were leaving to fight in one of America's most controversial and unpopular conflicts, the Vietnam War, and it becomes clear that the author wishes his readers to consider the effects of history.

All of the streets in the story bear the name of a renowned military man who had an impact on American history. Boulevard Mark Clark is named for an American general who served in both World War II and the Korean conflict. In fact, Clark is noted for being the first U.S. commander at that time to sign documents ending a war that the United States did not win as well as for being a protégé of George C. Marshall, the inspiration for George C.

What Do I Read Next?

- Barthelme's first novel, *Snow White* (1967), is a satiric and humorous retelling of the famous fairy tale, complete with dwarves and set in New York City's Greenwich Village neighborhood.

- John Barth's writing has been described as similar to Barthelme's in that Barth, too, pursues uncommon ways of telling a story and using language. In 1968, Barth published a collection of short stories entitled *Lost in the Fun House: Fiction for Tape, Print, Live Voice,* considered by many to be a major work of experimental fiction.

- Robert Coover is another writer who experiments with the content and structure of fiction. In his 1997 novel *Briar Rose,* Coover deconstructs and retells the story of Sleeping Beauty from the heroine's point of view. Coover plays with language and narrative and also offers readers a parody of literary scholarship.

- *Postmodern American Fiction: A Norton Anthology* (1997), edited by Paula Geyh, Fred G. Leebron, and Andrew Levy, covers five decades of postmodern American fiction—a term which typically denotes writing that rejects the traditional narrative format. The volume includes sixty-eight stories, novel excerpts, creative nonfiction pieces, cartoons, and other experimental forms of writing.

- Thomas Pynchon is another experimental writer whose books feature black humor and wild flights of imagination. His 1973 novel *Gravity's Rainbow* is a story set during World War II involving rocket scientists and American soldiers; it won the 1973 National Book Award.

Marshall Allée in the story. Marshall was a World War II general and the main force behind the Marshall Plan, which helped repair Europe's economy after the war. Skinny Wainwright Square in the story is named for Jonathan Wainwright, another American general who served during World War II and spent more than three years in Japanese prisoner-of-war camps. There are more similarly named streets, and by the time the story is over their names are more a humorous aside to the action than a memorial to a war hero. As he does with the story's accumulated material items, Barthelme succeeds in piling up the generals to such a degree that their conventionally historic meaning has been lost.

Barthelme uses the name of a tribe of Indians celebrated for their skills in war, the Comanches, as the narrator's foes in the story. In fact, the Comanches are said to have killed more white settlers in proportion to their own numbers than any other tribe during America's westward expansion. Eventually, though, continued wars with the settlers and the United States military destroyed their society. By giving the captured Comanche a European name and by having stereotypical Indian artifacts appear in unexpected and odd places in his prose—the narrator, for example, finds an arrowhead in a piece of mail and has his way to the post office lit by ''fire arrows''—Barthelme twists this piece of American history in a darkly comic fashion that succeeds in erasing the actual role the Comanches held in history. The narrator of the story even states that the Comanches ''had infiltrated our ghetto and the people of the ghetto instead of resisting had joined.'' At the story's conclusion, Barthelme pulls off the ultimate historical reversal by making the Comanches the winning side in the battle against those in charge in the city.

Barthelme published this story during a period of great upheaval in the United States: vocal opposition to the Vietnam War was increasing, and the civil rights movement had already staged a number of important demonstrations. Barthelme's battle descriptions in the story are evocative of the protests in many American cities during the mid-1960s. In the story, barricades, earthworks, and hedges ''laced with sparkling wire'' circled the city, ''Patrols of

> "According to Barthelme, we are the result of more than two hundred years of collected violence, wars, brutality, and generally rotten behavior toward one another. Thankfully, he delivers this accusation with a bit of black humor."

paras and volunteers with armbands guarded the tall, flat buildings," and "Red men in waves like people scattering in a square startled by something tragic or sudden" filled the streets. These words echo the actual images of people in the streets during the 1960s, protesting the treatment of African Americans or demanding an explanation for America's involvement in an unpopular war.

War protesters and civil rights marchers had one thing in common that would be important for Barthelme in writing this story: both groups rejected the status quo and demanded that, despite what had gone on before, life in America was going to change. Barthelme captures that feeling of disorder and reorder in this story by introducing a nonlinear narrative, chaotically listing material items, and disrupting sentence structure. But perhaps most important to Barthelme's process of reorganizing historical garbage is his success in removing the authority and power from historical events and figures.

By the story's end, the leaders of past wars whose names identify the city's avenues are almost forgotten, and traditional representations of authority have been toppled. "The city officials were tied to trees. Dusky warriors padded with their forest tread into the mouth of the mayor," the narrator notes. When he asks a fellow soldier who he wants to be, the answer is not one of the decorated historical figures whose names have appeared in the story but Jean-Luc Godard, the experimental French film director who became famous in 1959 when he made a movie showing only the beginnings and ends of scenes. Godard was involved in the very same effort

to disrupt traditional storytelling patterns that so engaged Barthelme. History had failed the characters in Barthelme's story and was of little use to them. Increasing numbers of Americans during the 1960s were feeling the same way.

Source: Susan Sanderson, Critical Essay on "The Indian Uprising," in *Short Stories for Students,* The Gale Group, 2003.

Chris Semansky

Semansky is an instructor of English literature and composition who writes about literature and culture for various publications. In this essay, Semansky considers Barthelme's technique.

Attempts to read Barthelme's "The Indian Uprising" as a conventional short story are doomed to failure and inevitably complicate an already challenging text. The most productive strategy for reading the piece is to focus on its medium rather than its message—to look at how it is put together instead of what it means. Barthelme was the consummate postmodernist who, like many postmodernists, believed that literature had exhausted itself, and that the role of the writer was to recreate it by literally destroying the foundation upon which it rests.

Barthelme's text is an attack on the notion that language *reflects* reality. However, rather than arguing against this notion or having one of his characters argue against it, Barthelme embodies the attack in his writing. Most fiction writers attempt to create a world that is recognizable to readers and resonates with their experience. Conventionally, stories include plots that may or may not unfold in chronological order, characters that interact with other characters and are largely driven by identifiable human desires, and details presented in a more or less coherent manner. In short, conventional fiction writers attempt to represent a plausible world and populate it with engaging characters. Barthelme exposes all of these conventions *as* fictions, suggesting that language is a closed circle, and the "real" world that words signify is first and foremost the world of language.

Barthelme foregrounds this statement on language by stitching together disparate word-elements, some from other people's writing, and by imitating the style of writers such as James Joyce in his liberal use of irony, wit, and verbal play. These techniques are called "collage" and "pastiche" respectively. By using them, Barthelme undermines the idea, popular in art and literature, that the primary ingredient for great work should be originality. One way Barthelme builds his text is by lifting bits and pieces of material straight from someone else's story. For example, the reference to Gustave Aschenbach during Comanche's torture session comes from German writer Thomas Mann's novella *Death In Venice,* for which Aschenbach is the emotionally tortured narrator. By having Comanche confess to being Aschenbach using Mann's own words, Barthelme satirizes both the idea that human beings have coherent identities and the idea that texts, especially "classics," exist beyond the pale of influence, historical or literary. The *way* in which Barthelme incorporates Mann's description is also very funny.

In art, "collage" often refers not only to the mixing of elements from different sources but the mixing of various media in a particular work. For example, a collagist might include paint, wood, metal, and photography to create a work. Barthelme literally cannot do this with words, but his narrator does reference various art forms in "The Indian Uprising," including painting, sculpture, music, woodworking, film, and architecture. This suggests a parodying of collage, the very technique he is using; parodies poke fun at a particular style or author through imitation, and Barthelme pokes fun at his own reputation as a postmodernist throughout this piece.

Part of that poking fun is the narrator's references to the very techniques he is using in the text of "The Indian Uprising." For example, directly after passages in which he shifts from describing the torture of the captured Comanche to explaining how to touch a woman, to recounting the cheering of Swedish children over liver paste, to accusing Jane of bad behavior, the narrator writes, "Strings of language extend in every direction to bind the world into a rushing, ribald whole." Another time, he reports the words of a Miss R. who praises the form of the litany, using a litany as part of her praise. This relentless self-reflexivity further underscores the idea that the world "out there," the sensory world beyond language, the world of trees, and rocks, and blood, and bodies is never knowable except as it is mediated through language. Communication is always an act of representation and therefore always an interpretation, Barthelme's story seems to suggest. And if you do not believe that, just try to read his story *as* a story.

Inherent in communication is an audience or an addressee. Barthelme undermines this convention as well, as his narrator shifts addressees often,

> **" This relentless self-reflexivity further underscores the idea that the world 'out there,' the sensory world beyond language, the world of trees, and rocks, and blood, and bodies is never knowable except as it is mediated through language."**

sometimes addressing an unnamed "you," sometimes Jane, and sometimes others. Not only does the audience shift but the tone of the writing does as well. One minute it is grave and the next comic. "What is the situation?" the narrator asks Block. "The situation is liquid," he replies, once again commenting on the composition of the text. The shifts in tone and audience are partly a result from other shifts, shifts brought about through liberal use of anachronisms and surrealist imagery. An anachronism is the representation of something outside of its appropriate time. For example, the narrator places Comanches, Native Americans who lived on the Southern Plains in the United States and were fierce warriors more than one hundred years ago, outside a French city, attacking its barricades. Rooted in the unconscious, this surrealist imagery is dreamlike and frequently juxtaposes unlike items. For example, take the narrator's report of Kenneth's response when asked who he want wants to be, "He said he wanted to be Jean-Luc Goddard but later when time permitted conversations in large, lighted rooms, whispering galleries with black-and-white Spanish rugs and problematic sculpture on calm, red catafalques." The seeming randomness of events, imagery, and discourse mimics a kind of dream logic in which the narrator is a helpless witness to himself rather than a master of his circumstances. In an interview with Larry McCaffery in *Partisan Review,* Barthelme discusses his writing process, commenting that he often looks for an "awkward" rather than a beautiful sentence with which to begin:

> Then a process of accretion occurs, like barnacles growing on a wreck or a rock. I'd rather have a wreck

than a ship that sails. Things attach themselves to wrecks; strange fish find your wreck or rock to be a good feeding ground. After a while you've got a situation with possibilities.

This is not to say that Barthelme's "wreck" is without unifying features. It has a first-person narrator throughout and uses repetition such as the phrase "I knew nothing" as a kind of thread to hold the wildly varying parts together. Some critics such as Maclin Bocock, in his essay, "'The Indian Uprising' or Donald Barthelme's Strange Object Covered with Fur," even provide ingenious and coherent readings of the story. Bocock argues that ultimately "The Indian Uprising" is about the failure of romantic love, writing, "The narrator himself is the city under siege and the Indians are the words with which Sylvia is attacking him." By the end of the story, Babcock writes, "The hero descends a little lower until finally he touches bottom, defeated, no longer able to summon either memory or fantasy to sustain him."

In the end, "The Indian Uprising" says as much about the process of reading and creating meaning as it does about the process of writing. By subverting the conventions of stories in a mosaic of words, Barthelme creates a new code for new readers, a code that asks them to work harder and to be more aware of their participation in how language in general and stories in particular shape their desires and ideas.

Source: Chris Semansky, Critical Essay on "The Indian Uprising," in *Short Stories for Students,* The Gale Group, 2003.

Walter Evans

In the following essay, Evans views "The Indian Uprising" within the context and formula of the Western, asserting that, rather than reflecting on the genre, Barthelme instead "directs outward, at contemporary society."

Donald Barthelme's bizarre, innovative short story "The Indian Uprising" involves a group of sophisticates beseiged in some contemporary city by a band of wild redskins who finally triumph. How must we respond to the story? A historical interpretation might tempt many—one statement by the narrator could recall Viet Nam to some readers: "We hold the south quarter and they hold the north quarter." But Barthelme published the story in 1965 before antiwar materials were at all in vogue, and he's taken care not to limit the associations to any one conflict. Perhaps it's more generally a

story of the haves versus the have-nots (those in the ghetto do join the Comanches). Perhaps the "red" men actually represent the Communists and Barthelme offers a Marxist (though certainly not a social realist) story of Western decadence and fall? Such possible readings seem to me too partial, too incomplete, hardly preferable to those which see all Barthelme's work as somehow subliterary. Maclin Bocock has provided the closest and most substantial reading of the story heretofore, discussing it in Freudian terms as a kind of phallic fantasy involving the narrator's personal failures with his girlfriend Sylvia. Bocock is the very first to treat the piece as truly serious fiction rather than as some sort of postmodern allegory or as a rather trivial jeu d'esprit. Her analysis seems to me limited, however, in considering the failed relationship as the story's central and single theme rather than as another contributing element to a more comprehensive theme.

The key to the story seems to me the elements of Western parody. Parody, however, may be the wrong term. Barthelme himself carefully distinguishes between parody and short story and if parody means simply to mock or ridicule elements of a formula, then "The Indian Uprising" depends on parody of the Western no more than Borges's "The Garden of Forking Paths" depends on parody of the spy formula or *Lolita* depends on parody of a murderer's legal deposition. The Western formula offers a vehicle, not an object, for Barthelme's critical commentary. The Western provides a convenient nexus of themes and values which Barthelme directs outward, at contemporary society, not backward to reflect on the genre itself. Extended allusion might better describe the relationship, but in fact it might be most accurate to describe the story as a postmodern Western and let it go at that.

Certainly a full understanding of the story demands a full understanding of the formula it participates in. The finest and most complete analysis of the Western as formula appears in John Cawelti's *The Six-Gun Mystique.* Cawelti points out that "there are three central roles in the Western: the townspeople or agents of civilization, the savages or outlaws who threaten this first group, and the heroes who are above all 'men in the middle,' that is, they possess many qualities and skills of the savages, but are fundamentally committed to the townspeople."

The first of Cawelti's fundamental elements is the town, which "offers love, domesticity, and order as well as the opportunity for personal achievement and the creation of a family, but it requires the repression of spontaneous passion.'' In this regard the story's opening sentence reverberates powerfully and clearly: ''We defended the city as best we could.'' It is not love, domesticity, and family, not wives, children, even themselves that the narrator and his circle focus on defending, but ''the city.'' And here ''the city'' represents the hyperbolic extremes Western civilization has reached in luxurious material superfluity, effete sensuality.

In the opening paragraph Barthelme rhetorically offers as the narrator's conception of the ''good life'' allusions not to religion, ethics, duty, family, love, the sorts of things that make the town valuable in Westerns, but allusions to pleasant private experiences in which the self-oriented narrator may privately indulge himself: ''apples, books, long-playing records.'' Barthelme loads the rest of his story with sophisticated, self-indulgent luxuries. He describes, for example, some typical ''barricades'' erected against savagery, i.e. against the red men. These barricades consist of ''window dummies, silk, thoughtfully planned job descriptions (including scales for the orderly progress of other colors [racial minorities?]), wine in demijohns, and robes.'' Another ''barricade'' contains, among other materials, ''two-litre bottles of red wine; three-quarter-litre bottles of Black & White, aquavit, cognac, vodka, gin, Fad #6 sherry; a hollow-core door in birch veneer on black wrought-iron legs,'' and so on.

To these ''civilized'' materials of sensual indulgence, of material sophistication, Barthelme intimately relates esthetic-intellectual sophistication. The narrator's people, mediating all through their highly cultivated minds, react even to an Indian uprising by ''trying to understand.'' At the height of the uprising they discuss Gabriel Faur's ''Dolly,'' the narrator ''nonevaluates'' remarks ''as Korzybski instructed,'' they quote Valéry, listen to concerts of ''Gabrieli, Albinoni, Marcello, Vivaldi, Boccherini,'' converse with a tortured Indian who identifies himself as Gustave Aschenbach (protagonist of the thematically quite relevant *Death in Venice*), and so on. Surely a more sophisticated, more ''civilized'' group never faced hostile Comanches.

What is the effect (one might almost say the purpose or function) of civilization or sophistication in the material, sensual, intellectual terms with which Barthelme here identifies it all? Certainly one effect, for Barthelme's story the chief effect, involves muting genuine and spontaneous emotion,

> ❝❝ Barthelme's narrator fails as hero precisely because he remains unable, for himself or for the city, to mediate between the extremes as the Western formula demands.''

limiting and controlling and ordering once perhaps strong but now depleted subterranean forces. Cawelti describes the second of the ''three central roles in the Western'' in terms which Barthelme's story heartily endorses: ''The savage symbolizes the violence, brutality, and ignorance which civilized society seeks to control and eliminate, but he also commonly stands for certain positive values which are restricted or destroyed by advancing civilization.''

In the opening paragraph the narrator responds to (or defends against) the violent uprising by seeking to initiate a calm discussion. When denizens of the ghetto join the uprising the civilized forces initiate a quite characteristic attempt to quell this new threat by calming, by drugging the emotions: ''We sent more heroin into the ghetto, and hyacinths, ordering another hundred thousand of the pale, delicate flowers.''

Cawelti observes that in the Western, the town or civilization ''requires the repression of spontaneous passion.'' The narrator unemotionally mentions participating in torturing at least one, perhaps two captured Comanches; he relates to torture not with warm emotions of either disgust or pleasure, but coolly, with a distanced intellect. A little later, with a friend, the narrator relates ''a little of the history of torture, reviewing the technical literature quoting the best modern sources.'' He consistently relates to the world intellectually rather than emotionally. Even at the height of a crisis he describes his companion dispassionately: ''Block was firing a greasegun from the upper floor of a building designed by Emery Roth & Sons.'' Completely devoid of any emotion, lacking passion, fear, excitement, the narrator here again drifts into intellectualization, identifying an architect. When captured, the narrator and his friends react characteristically; either lacking emotions or still repressing them, they revert to tired intellectual games: "'Who do you want to be?' I asked Kenneth and he said he wanted to be Jean-Luc Godard." Godard, of course, is an "artist" who "intellectualizes" revolution.

What effect has this subversion of emotion? One effect, that which seems most to interest Barthelme, is a corruption of values. The narrator's disinterested use of torture on the Comanche foreshadows a late, neutral report on an ineffective campaign:

> We killed a great many in the south suddenly with helicopters and rockets, but we found that those we had killed were children and more came from the north and from the east and from other places where there are children preparing to live.

Significantly, Barthelme never associates the redskins with the savagery and brutality of the citizens; indeed, at the conclusion the narrator and his friends are neither killed nor tortured (as they so richly deserve), but turned over to the Clemency Committee.

The narrator recalls his Sylvia performing in a movie which, to me at least, sounds pornographic:

> And when they shot the scene in the bed I wondered how you felt under the eyes of the cameramen, grips, juicers, men in the mixing booth: excited? stimulated? And when they shot the scene in the shower I sanded a hollow-core door working carefully against the illustrations in texts and whispered instructions from one who had already solved the problem. I had made after all other tables, one while living with Nancy, one while living with Alice, one while living with Eunice, one while living with Marianne.

Of course the narrator can make a table from a door while men film Sylvia in the shower; he has made lots of doors for lots of women and understands the technique. The implicit question is, How could he do it? The implicit answer focuses on knowledge of technique, not on any moral or emotional dimension. Like the door, the narrator has a hollow core; only the surface finish matters.

The narrator's moral values explicitly appear in the story only once. Near the end the narrator addresses a lane in the second person: "Your affair with Harold is reprehensible, you know that, don't you, Jane?" Harold is married and has children. "I think your values are peculiar, Jane!" Barthelme here intends, it seems, for us to add an egocentric hypocrisy to the narrator's faults. When are the narrator's values ever superior? Apparently the narrator himself seeks to renew a liaison with Jane;

earlier he addresses an unnamed someone in the second person (here employed with Jane): "it is you I want now . . . It is when I am with you that I am happiest . . . "

Is the narrator capable of such an emotion as love? He claims so in the second paragraph, sitting with Sylvia while the city's forces defend against the Comanches: "And I sat there getting drunker and drunker and more in love and more in love." Later essentially the same sentence reappears; Barthelme makes certain no reader can take the statement at face value. It is only nine lines later than the first of these statements that the narrator remembers fashioning at least his fifth hollow-core door/table for his fifth woman while this same Sylvia is in the shower for a pornographic film.

In the opening paragraph, describing the uprising, Barthelme's narrator tells us: "People were trying to understand." Shortly thereafter he twice in four lines repeats the phrase: "I decided I knew nothing." When, on the advice of others, he consults the teacher, Miss R. (who wears a "blue dress containing a red figure" [an Indian?]; is she Miss Redskin?), her response seems quite unironic: "'You know nothing,' she said, 'you feel nothing, you are locked in a most savage and terrible ignorance, I despise you.'"

Miss R.'s speech should lead us to see that the narrator knows nothing *because* he feels nothing. He is "locked in a most savage and terrible ignorance" because his sophistication has locked him away from natural, genuine, spontaneous emotion. In seeking to "know" intellectually he locks himself (a hollow-core door with a shiny veneer) further and further from the emotional key. With tremendous irony, Barthelme uses this "savage and terrible ignorance" to identify the narrator with the negative aspects of—at the same time it distances him from valuable dimensions of—the cliché redskins. Cawelti's analysis of the Western formula clearly outlines the terms and conditions of the protagonist's failure:

> In the simplest Westerns, the townspeople and the savages represent a basic moral opposition between good and evil. In most examples of the formula, however, the opposition is a more complex one, a dialectic of contrasting ways of life or psychic states. The resolution of this opposition is the work of the hero. Thus, the most basic definition of the hero role in the Western is as the figure who resolves the conflict between pioneers and savages . . . the hero is a more complex figure because he has internalized the conflict between savagery and civilization. His inner

conflict . . . tends to overshadow the clash between savages and townspeople.

Barthelme's narrator fails as hero precisely because he remains unable, for himself or for the city, to mediate between the extremes as the Western formula demands. The narrator's ignorance, and Barthelme's condemnation, persist through the conclusion. The last words describe the protagonist still failing to relate to the Comanches with any emotion; his conclusive response, watching them, is an emotionless (though the Indians have emotions) catalog of material phenomena; he looks into "their savage black eyes, paint, feathers, beads."

Barthelme compels us to condemn the artificial world, so clever a distortion of our own, which he reflects. The narrator's initial doubts as to whether theirs is a good life or not provokes Sylvia's unambiguous response: "No." Nothing in the pages which follow the introductory paragraph's indictment modifies that condemnation.

Cawelti's comments on the contemporary Western bear special relevance:

> . . . from the point of view of social ritual, the meaning of the Western formula's pattern of plot and character is that of offering the hero a choice between civilization and its ideals of progress and success and anarchistic savagery with its spontaneity and freedom.

> Though the Western remains officially on the side of progress and success, shifting formula patterns in the twentieth century reflect an increasing disillusionment with these ideals . . . as we approach the present, the ritualistic affirmation of progress and success becomes more and more ambiguous and strained . . . it seems that we have come to a point where it is increasingly difficult to imagine a synthesis between the honor and independence of the Western hero and the imperatives of progress and success. In such a pattern, the ritual action reaffirms the inevitability of progress, but suggests increasing disillusionment and uncertainty about its consequences.

In Barthelme's world, as in many modern Westerns, "civilization" has gone too far. Emotion, energy, spontaneity too long and too forcefully repressed rise up to reassert their place in the human scheme of things. It is this "uprising" which provides the story's subject. In the final sentence Barthelme describes a purely natural phenomenon, rain (often, Frye reminds us, a symbol for the life force): "shattering from a great height the prospects of silence and clear, neat rows of houses in the subdivisions."

Source: Walter Evans, "Comanches and Civilization in Donald Barthelme's 'The Indian Uprising,'" in *Arizona Quarterly*, Vol. 42, No. 1, Spring 1986, pp. 45–52.

Sources

Aldridge, John W., "Dance of Death," in *Atlantic Monthly*, July 1968, p. 89.

Barth, John, "Thinking Man's Minimalist: Honoring Donald Barthelme," in the *New York Times Book Review*, September 3, 1989, p. 9.

Barthelme, Donald, "The Indian Uprising," in *Unspeakable Practices, Unnatural Acts*, Bantam, 1969, pp. 1–13.

Bocock, Maclin, "'The Indian Uprising' or Donald Barthelme's Strange Object Covered with Fur," in *fiction international*, No. 415, pp. 134–45.

Gillen, Francis, "Donald Barthelme's City: A Guide," in *Twentieth Century Literature*, January 1972, pp. 37–44.

McCaffery, Larry, "An Interview with Donald Barthelme," in *Partisan Review*, Vol. 49, No. 2, 1982, pp. 184–93.

Schmitz, Neil, "Donald Barthelme and the Emergence of Modern Satire," in *Minnesota Review*, No. 1, Fall 1971, pp. 109–18.

Schott, Webster, "Dreams of the Body Neurotic," in *Book World—The Washington Post*, November 5, 1972, p. 3.

Shorris, Earl, "Donald Barthelme's Illustrated Wordy-Gurdy," in *Harper's*, January 1973, pp. 92–96.

Sullivan, Walter, "'Where Have All the Flowers Gone?': The Short Story in Search of Itself," in *Sewanee Review*, Fall 1970, pp. 531–42.

Tanner, Tony, *City of Words: American Fiction 1950–1970*, Harper, 1971, pp. 403–404.

Further Reading

Barthelme, Donald, *Not-Knowing: The Essays and Interviews of Donald Barthelme*, edited by Kim Herzinger, Vintage Books, 1999.
　　Originally published in 1997, this book includes essays written by Barthelme and interviews with him on such topics as his and others' writings, art and architecture, music, film.

Barthelme, Helen Moore, *Donald Barthelme: The Genesis of a Cool Sound*, Texas A&M University Press, 2001.
　　Helen Moore Barthelme is an English professor at Texas A&M University, but between 1956 and 1965, she was the writer's wife. In this memoir, she offers personal insights into the writer's early writings and a description of their life together in Houston.

Friedman, Ellen G., and Miriam Fuchs, eds., *Breaking the Sequence: Women's Experimental Fiction*, Princeton University Press, 1989.
　　This book features nineteen essays devoted to exploring postmodern fiction written by women. The writers discussed include Virginia Woolf, Jean Rhys, and Joyce Carol Oates.

Hudgens, Michael Thomas, *Donald Barthelme: Postmodernist American Writer,* Studies in American Literature, No. 43, Edwin Mellon Press, 2001.

This scholarly book covers Barthelme and his role in postmodern literature. The author relates Barthelme's work to examples of other postmodern literature and art.

Powell, James N., *Postmodernism for Beginners,* Writers & Readers, 1998.

This book posits that postmodernism ''is not a bunch of meaningless intellectual mind games'' but a reaction to the failure of the philosophy of the nineteenth century. The book is written using text matched with graphics and comic book–like features.

The Killers

Ernest Hemingway
1927

"The Killers," Ernest Hemingway's story about two hit men who come to a small town to kill a former prizefighter, was first published in the March 1927 issue of *Scribner's Magazine*. Hemingway was paid two hundred dollars for the story, which was the first of his mature stories to appear in an American periodical. His original title for the story was "The Matadors." Hemingway included the story in his 1927 collection *Men Without Women*, and it also appears in *The Nick Adams Stories* (1972). "The Killers" remains one of Hemingway's most anthologized stories because it is representative of Hemingway's style and the subjects that would occupy his work throughout his career. These subjects include the meaninglessness of human life, male camaraderie, and the inevitability of death, and Hemingway explores them using his signature short sentences, slang, and understatement.

Hemingway claims to have written the story in a frenzy of inspiration on May 16, 1926, before lunch. Like many of his short stories, "The Killers" features Nick Adams, a typical Hemingway hero, one in a long line of Hemingway's fictional selves. Hemingway introduced Nick Adams in his first collection of stories, *In Our Time* (1925). Nick is an adolescent in "The Killers," and critics have argued that Nick's experience with the hit men marks his initiation into adulthood and his introduction to evil and violence.

Author Biography

Ernest Hemingway is one of the most influential American writers of the twentieth century. His influence extends not only to novelists and short story writers but also to journalists, playwrights, critics, and filmmakers. Four decades after his death, biographies about him continue to appear. Born July 21, 1899, in Oak Park, Illinois, Ernest Miller Hemingway was the second child of Clarence Hemingway, a doctor, and Grace (Hall) Hemingway. Hemingway's middle-class upbringing was conventional, and after graduating in 1917 from Oak Park High School, he joined the *Kansas City Star* as a reporter. In 1918, Hemingway joined the Red Cross, driving an ambulance in Italy during the waning months of World War I. He was struck with shell fragments from an exploding mortar in July and had more than two hundred pieces of mortar removed from his leg. Over the next four years, Hemingway honed his writing skills as European correspondent for the *Toronto Star* and contributed "color pieces" (feature articles also known as "slice of life" pieces) to other publications. During this period, he also met American expatriate Gertrude Stein, a writer and wealthy art collector who held gatherings in her Paris apartment, during which artists and writers could mingle and "talk shop." Stein, along with American writers Ezra Pound and Sherwood Anderson, were indispensable to Hemingway's early career, providing him with contacts and recommending his work to various editors.

In 1925, Liveright released Hemingway's first widely distributed book, *In Our Time*, a collection of short stories featuring Nick Adams, an autobiographical character who would also appear in future Hemingway stories. His second collection, *Men Without Women* (1927), contained many of what would become Hemingway's most popular and anthologized stories, including "The Killers" and "Hills Like White Elephants." In these stories, Hemingway perfected his spare, elliptical style, using dialogue almost exclusively to develop characters and drive his plot. His early novels, however, cemented his popularity and established Hemingway as the leading voice of his generation. *The Sun Also Rises* (1926) and *A Farewell to Arms* (1929) both address the emotionally debilitating effects of World War I on characters that were fictional projections of Hemingway.

The quality of Hemingway's work diminished after he had established an international reputation, though he did produce two critical and popular successes with his novels *For Whom the Bell Tolls* (1940) and *The Old Man and the Sea* (1952), the latter of which helped Hemingway win the Nobel Prize in literature in 1954. While alive, Hemingway was a popular and much-admired celebrity, a man's man, who cultivated a brawling, hard-drinking, hard-loving image. In 1961, his emotional and physical health deteriorating, "Papa" Hemingway, as he had become known, committed suicide by shooting himself at his home in Ketchum, Idaho. Hemingway's father had also committed suicide. Posthumous works include *A Moveable Feast* (1964), which recounts Hemingway's years in Paris in the 1920s and a number of reissued story collections and novels pieced together by editors, including *Islands in the Stream* (1970), *The Nick Adams Stories* (1972), and *The Garden of Eden* (1986).

Plot Summary

Section 1

"The Killers" begins with two men walking into Henry's lunchroom and discussing what they want to eat. Max and Al bicker over what menu items are available with George, the counterman who had been talking with Nick Adams, the only other customer. Some confusion occurs over the correct time. The clock says 5:20, but George tells the men it is twenty minutes fast. The men finally order eggs with ham and bacon and then taunt Nick and George, sarcastically calling them "bright boys" and making fun of their small town, Summit. Al and Max order George to tell the cook, Sam, to come out of the kitchen, and then Al takes Nick and Sam back into the kitchen. They call Sam "nigger," a much-used epithet for African Americans in 1920s' America.

Max announces that they are at the lunchroom to kill Ole Andreson, a Swede who usually eats dinner there at six o'clock. It is obvious the men have been hired, as Max says they have never seen Ole before. "We're killing him for a friend. Just to oblige a friend," Max says. Al and Max continue with their banter, taunting Nick and Sam. At one point, Al says, "The nigger [Sam] and my bright boy [Nick] are amused by themselves. I got them tied up like a couple of girl friends in the convent.'' Referring to the two as ''girl friends'' is tough talk and meant to belittle the men's masculinity.

A customer comes in at a quarter past six, but George tells him that the cook is not there, and the man leaves. A few other customers come in. George makes one of them a sandwich and tells the other one that the cook is sick. At five minutes past seven, the two men leave, shotguns bulging from their overcoats.

Section 2

George watches the men leave. Nick and Sam come out from the kitchen, and Nick removes the towel that had been stuffed in his mouth. George tells Nick that he better go tell Ole Andreson that the two men are looking for him, but Sam warns him to ''stay out of it.'' After Nick says he is going to tell Ole, Sam remarks, ''Little boys always know what they want to do.'' This remark underscores Nick's youth and his innocence. In this section, it becomes clear that Nick has become the protagonist of the story.

Section 3

In this section, Nick visits Hirsch's rooming house, where Ole lives. Mrs. Bell, the rooming house manager, lets Nick in. Ole is lying on the bed, dressed, staring at the wall. Nick tells Ole about the two men, but Ole says, ''There isn't anything I can do about it.'' He refuses Nick's offer to tell the police, remarking, ''I'm through with all that running around.'' Ole speaks with a ''flat'' voice, meaning that he shows no emotion. Ole thanks Nick for coming.

Section 4

In this last section, Nick walks back to Henry's and tells George about Ole: ''He's in his room and he won't go out.'' Sam opens the kitchen door, says, ''I don't even listen to it,'' and shuts it again. Henry says that Ole ''must have got mixed up in something in Chicago.'' Chicago was a hotbed of crime and gangster activity in the 1920s, so it is conceivable that, as George tells Nick, Ole ''double-crossed somebody. That's what they kill them for.'' Nick is shocked at what happens and says he can't bear to think of Ole waiting in his room to get killed. He vows to ''get out of this town.'' George's response to Nick is not to think about it, underscoring George's own ambivalent attitude towards the situation.

Ernest Hemingway

Characters

Nick Adams

Nick Adams is sitting at the lunch counter at Henry's talking to George when Al and Max walk in. Nick is a teenager, whom Al and Max refer to as ''bright boy.'' Hemingway readers know Nick from Hemingway's short story collection *In Our Time*, which introduces Nick as a vulnerable teenager thrust into a world of violence and meanness. Nick is a typical Hemingway hero who is learning ''the code.'' Hemingway's ''code hero'' is someone who is honorable, courageous, and adventurous and who exhibits grace under pressure. He distinguishes himself from others by his ability to endure and to face death with dignity. Such traits define the code hero's manhood. In short, Nick is learning the code of how to be a man, according to Hemingway's idea of what constitutes manhood. In their essay on Hemingway's story, Cleanth Brooks, Jr. and Robert Penn Warren argue, ''it is the tough man . . . the disciplined man, who actually is aware of pathos or tragedy.'' Such a man, the two argue, ''has learned that the only way to hold on to 'honor,' to individuality, to, even, the human order . . . is to live by his code.'' Nick is still developing the code. His experience with the killers marks his initiation into a world

Media Adaptations

- Director Robert Siodmak's 1946 film *The Killers* is the first adaptation of Hemingway's story for the screen. It stars Burt Lancaster, Ava Gardner, and Edmond O'Brien and is available at most video stores and many libraries.

- Director Donald Siegel's 1964 film *The Killers* also adapts Hemingway's story. Siegel's version stars Lee Marvin, Clu Gulager, John Cassavetes, Angie Dickinson, and Ronald Reagan and is available at most video stores and many libraries.

of brutality and random events. Critics often argue over the real protagonist of "The Killers." In his book *Hemingway's Nick Adams*, Joseph Flora claims, "Hemingway indicates that Nick is to be the central character of the story by making him the only character in the opening scene to be given a whole name." Flora also observes that this story is the last of Hemingway's stories in which Nick appears as an adolescent, and it is the only one not set in Michigan.

By the end of the story, Nick is a changed person. His discovery of the evil in human beings shocks him, and he announces that he is going to leave town after he returns from seeing Ole. Flora writes, "Even though the world is a darker place than Nick had before guessed, he is not in Andreson's frame of mind—merely waiting for the end."

Al

Al is one of the two hit men who come to Henry's to kill Ole Andreson. His face is "small and white and he had tight lips," and like Max, he wears a derby hat and a black overcoat. The narrator describes the two as "a vaudeville team." And, indeed, they often act like comics performing a routine rather than behaving as hit men. Al forces Sam and Nick to the kitchen where he binds and gags them, holding a shotgun on George. He appears as the leader of the two, telling Max at one point to "Shut up" when Max tells George they are going to kill Ole "Just to oblige a friend." The narrator describes both Al and Max as "little."

Ole Andreson

Ole Andreson is a Swede and a former heavyweight boxer who lives in Hirsch's rooming house. He usually eats at Henry's lunchroom around six in the evening but does not show up the day Al and Max come to kill him. When Nick visits him to warn him about the men, Ole is lying on his bed facing the wall. Ole thanks Nick for telling him but is resigned to his fate. He tells Nick that he has not been able to get out of bed and go outside and that he is "through with all that running around." Mrs. Bell, the house manager, calls him "a very nice man." Nick and George speculate that Ole "got mixed up with something in Chicago" and that Al and Max had come to settle a score. Martin sees an irony in Ole's largeness, when compared to Al and Max's small stature. Martin writes that Ole, unlike Nick, knows that telling the police about the men will do no good. Martin argues, "Ole knows better; he knows that his mass is relative to other things such as guns and the mob."

Mrs. Bell

Mrs. Bell runs Hirsch's rooming-house and takes Nick to Ole Andreson's room. Nick mistakes her for Mrs. Hirsch when he leaves, and she corrects him, saying that she just "looks after" the place for her. She tells Nick that Ole is "a very nice man."

George

George is the counter man at Henry's lunchroom, who waits on customers. It is unclear whether or not he is also the owner. Max keeps an eye on him as Al ties up Nick and Sam in the kitchen. George is matter-of-fact in his responses to the men and does not appear cowed by their machismo. When Max tells him they are there to kill Ole, George asks, "What are you going to kill Ole Andreson for? What did he ever do to you?" As Al and Max leave the restaurant, readers see them "pass under the arc-light and cross the street" through George's eyes. George convinces Nick to warn Ole, and when Nick returns and reports that his visit was useless, George speculates that Ole is probably a target of Chicago mobsters. Nick wonders what Ole did to deserve being killed, and George answers, "Double-crossed somebody. That's what they kill them for." When

Nick says, "I can't stand to think about him waiting in the room and knowing he's going to get it. It's too damned awful," George responds, saying, "you better not think of it."

Max

Max is Al's partner and is dressed identically to him. He waits at the counter for two hours while Al guards Sam and Nick in the kitchen, taunting George, calling him "bright boy," and saying he "would make some girl a nice wife." Many critics claim Al and Max perform a kind of vaudeville routine and are little more than caricatures of gangsters. A typical exchange between the two occurs after Max tells George they are killing Ole for a friend in Chicago:

> 'You talk too damn much,' Al said.
> 'The nigger and my bright boy are amused by themselves. I got them tied up like a couple of girl friends in a convent.'
> 'I suppose you were in a convent?'
> 'You never know.'
> 'You were in a kosher convent. That's where you were.'

Sam

Sam is the black cook at Henry's and, along with Nick, is tied up and gagged by Al, one of the hit men. Al and Max refer to him as "the nigger." Sam is obedient, never responding to Max or Al except in the affirmative. He also wants nothing to do with warning Ole. When Nick says he is going to warn the boxer, Sam replies, "Little boys always know what they want to do," underscoring the fact that he, Sam, sees himself as a man who has learned through experience not to become involved in other people's business, especially if it is dangerous.

Themes

Masculinity

Hemingway, known for his representations of manly men who live by a code of honor, parodies his own image of masculinity by making the hit men, Al and Max, clownish figures. The men look the part of stereotypical gangsters, wearing derby hats and tight overcoats and keeping their gloves on when they eat. They also talk tough, announcing

their plans to kill Ole, using slang, answering questions with questions, and mocking the masculinity of George, Sam, and Nick. For example, Max comments about George: "Bright boy can do anything. . . . He can cook and everything. You'd make some girl a nice wife, bright boy." Al describes Sam and Nick, gagged and bound in the kitchen, as "a couple of girl friends in the convent." Al and Max are counterpoints to Nick Adams, an innocent, who believes he can do something to change the situation by telling Ole about the men. This story marks Nick's initiation into the world of men and its attendant violence, chaos, and strategies for survival.

Crime

Societies have laws to ensure a safe environment for their citizens, to maintain order, and to instill a sense of justice in the populace. The blatant flouting of laws, as in Hemingway's story, suggests not only that society has deteriorated but also that there is nothing to be done about it. Al and Max do not fear being caught and, indeed, claim to have no stake in killing Andreson, saying they are doing it "to oblige a friend." Sam's response to the events, to have nothing to do with any of it, underscores the sense of resignation informing the story. George's response is that addressing crime is someone else's responsibility and tells Nick to visit Ole. Nick's response is one of disillusionment and shock and a desire to run away from the town rather than accept its random dangers. These reactions represent a range of responses that Chicagoans had towards criminal activities in the 1920s. The sense of resignation, in large part, stems not only from Hemingway's own dark view of human nature but from the knowledge that many of the Chicago crime bosses had bought off the police, ensuring that law and order became a privilege for the few rather than a right of the many.

Chaos

Hemingway's plot is laden with irony and with characters misreading one another, suggesting that the world is not as it seems. For example, although Max and Al come to town to kill Ole Andreson and know that he eats at Henry's at six o'clock, they ask George the name of the town, and then when George tells them, Max says he never heard of it. Henry's, though referred to as a "lunchroom," is actually a made-over saloon. A similar confusion of identity occurs when Nick addresses Mrs. Bell as Mrs. Hirsch because he assumes that she is the owner of

Topics for Further Study

- In groups, research the history of crime in Chicago in the 1920s, paying particular attention to Al Capone and Dutch Schultz. Report your findings to your class, and then discuss any contemporary parallels. For example, is there a city like Chicago today with individuals like Capone or Schultz controlling illegal industries?

- At the end of "The Killers," Nick says he is going to leave town. In two pages, write where he goes and what he does next. Try to use Hemingway's own spare style.

- Read other stories about Nick Adams in Hemingway's collection *The Nick Adams Stories*, and then discuss how his character in "The Killers" is similar to and different from his portrayal in other stories.

- Film historians claim that film noir emerged from the gangster films of the 1920s and 1930s.

In class, view the 1931 gangster film, *Public Enemy,* starring James Cagney, and then view the 1946 adaptation of "The Killers," starring Burt Lancaster. After researching film noir, discuss how Hemingway's film illustrates or departs from elements of the gangster movie or film noir.

- Hemingway's story is constructed like a play. Divide the class into four groups, assigning each group one "scene" of the play, using the divisions in the plot summary. Have each group perform one of the scenes for the class. Afterwards, discuss choices each group made in staging and performing.

- In pairs, write a short dialogue in which a student tries to convince her teacher she deserves a better grade. Use the short, conversational style that Hemingway uses in "The Killers," and then perform the dialogue for your class.

---

the rooming house. The men come to a town called "Summit" to kill on a "nice fall day," compounding the irony. These glaring differences between the world as it is and the world as it seems affect Nick the most, whose own world up until that point more or less conformed to his expectations as an orderly place.

Style

Dialogue

Dialogue, the conversation between two or more characters, is a primary tool of characterization. Writers create characters through shaping their speech in ways that reflect their desires and motivations. In addition to physically describing Max and Al as stereotypical gangsters, Hemingway has them

talk like gangsters as well. Their speech is peppered with insults, wisecracks, and slang, and they never answer a question directly. They speak like characters out of a Dashiell Hammett novel, in terse bursts. Hammett was popular for his detective stories and his character, Sam Spade, a wisecracking antihero. Dialogue also characterizes the other players in the story as well. For example, when Sam speaks, he makes it clear that he does not want to be involved in any way, and when Nick speaks, he expresses his youth and innocence through his incredulity.

Plot

Plot refers to the arrangement of events in a story. Hemingway tells the story largely through dialogue, as if it were a play. He uses description sparsely, to create atmosphere or to signal a change in scenes. When he describes Max, for example, he writes: "His face was small and white and he had tight lips." When the scene shifts, Hemingway describes the action, using it as a transition: "The two of them went out the door. George watched them, through the window, pass under the arc light and cross the street.''

The triviality of the subjects the characters talk about undercuts the insidious nature of the act the killers are about to commit. Hemingway sums up his spare style in his book on bullfighting, *Death in the Afternoon*:

> If a writer of prose knows enough about what he is writing about he may omit things that he knows and the reader, if the writer is writing truly enough, will have a feeling of those things as strongly as though the writer had stated them. The dignity of movement of an iceberg is due to only one-eighth of it being above water.

Many twentieth-century writers adopted Hemingway's spare elliptical style as their own, including Raymond Carver and Pam Houston.

Narrator

The narrator refers to the speaker through whom the author tells the story. Sometimes it is a character in the story and sometimes it is not. The kind of narrator the author uses is intimately related to the story's point of view. Hemingway uses an "effaced" narrator in "The Killers." This means that the narrator is practically invisible. An effaced narrator does not have access to characters' thinking, which is revealed solely through their dialogue. However, in his essay "Point of View in the Nick Adams Stories," Carl Ficken points out:

> Hemingway is ... able to place Nick sufficiently forward in the account so that the meaning of the story has to do with Nick's discovery of what life is like through those killers and Ole Andreson's reaction to them.

Hemingway popularized this method of narration for short story writers and novelists in the twentieth century.

Historical Context

1920s

When Hemingway wrote "The Killers" in 1926, the United States was at the height of the Prohibition era, and criminal activity, particularly in Chicago, was rampant, with gangsters such as Al Capone and Dutch Schultz controlling the bootlegging industry and a good part of the police force as well. In 1919, Capone had come to Chicago from New York City, where he had worked for crime boss Frankie Yale. In Chicago, he worked for Yale's old mentor, John Torrio. Capone took control of Torrio's saloons, gambling houses, racetracks, and brothels when Torrio was shot by rival gang members and left Chicago. Historians estimate the income from Capone's interests from illegal activities at $100,000,000 a year between 1925 and 1930. This is the image readers had in mind in 1927 when they read that Ole Andreson "got mixed up in something in Chicago."

However, Hemingway wrote the story in Madrid, Spain. Like many American writers and artists, Hemingway became disillusioned with the values of post-World War I America and relocated to Europe. Writers such as John Dos Passos, Henry Miller, and F. Scott Fitzgerald moved to Paris, as did Hemingway for a time, and led bohemian lives, drinking heavily, having affairs, and experimenting with new subject material and style. Gertrude Stein, a controversial writer and a wealthy art collector, held salons at her house at 27 rue de Fleurus in Paris, where many artists and writers met to drink, discuss their work, and receive advice from Stein. It was Stein who coined the term "a lost generation" to refer to Hemingway and his contemporaries, describing their spiritual isolation, cynicism, and amorality. It was at one of Stein's salons in the early 1920s that she met Hemingway, who presented her with a letter of introduction from American writer Sherwood Anderson. Stein urged Hemingway to quit journalism and become a full-time writer. Other writers associated with the "lost generation" include expatriates such as Malcolm Cowley, Ezra Pound, and Archibald MacLeish.

As a result of World War I, in which Hemingway served as an ambulance driver, and the catastrophic loss of human life (tens of millions killed and wounded), many people lost faith in God, ideas of nationhood, even reality itself. Theories by intellectuals and scientists such as Sigmund Freud, Henri Bergson, Sir James George Frazer, Werner Heisenberg, and Albert Einstein presented the world as a place of uncertainty and chaos in which appearances are not what they seem. In his essay on "The Killers" for *The Explicator,* Quentin E. Martin argues that these new theories are useful in understanding Hemingway's story. Citing character confusion in the story, Martin claims, "'The Killers'

Compare & Contrast

- **1920s:** Al Capone runs a murderous gang in Chicago, trafficking in alcohol and illegal gambling houses.

  Today: Organized crime is still widespread, but it is also more diffuse and less concentrated in particular cities. Authorities believe they have largely destroyed the ''Mafia'' when they put New York City crime boss John Gotti behind bars for life in 1992.

- **1920s:** The life expectancy for American males is 53.6 years and for females 54.6 years.

Today: The life expectancy for American males is 73.1 years and for females 79.1 years.

- **1920s:** A crime wave sweeps the United States, as Prohibition helps spawn the bootlegging industry and increases in prostitution and gambling activities.

  Today: Alcohol is legally sold throughout the United States, and legal gambling, in the form of state lotteries and casinos, is widespread.

---

can be seen as a concise and dramatic representation of certain aspects of Einstein's theory of relativity and Heisenberg's principle of indeterminacy (or uncertainty).'' Other writers consciously applied these theories to their work as well, helping to shape literary modernism. T. S. Eliot's poem *The Wasteland* (1922), for example, deploys allusion, symbol, and fragments to describe a world that had literally fallen to pieces. In her novel *To the Lighthouse* (1927), Virginia Woolf uses a stream-of-consciousness narrative to prioritize subjective experience over the depiction of an objective world, drawing from ideas popularized by philosopher Bergson.

Expatriates in Europe were not the only ones producing lasting literature during the time between the world wars. In America, writers such as Zora Neale Hurston, Sterling Brown, James Weldon Johnson, W. E. B. DuBois, Langston Hughes, Jean Toomer, Countee Cullen, and Alain Locke wrote about the African-American experience, giving white America a glimpse into the lives and cultures of a historically oppressed people. Harlem, in uptown New York City, became a magnet for African-American poets, artists, writers, musicians, and playwrights. Representative literary works of the Harlem Renaissance include Johnson's 1927 poetry collection *God's Trombone: Seven Negro Folk Sermons,* one of the more popular works of the era which used the speech patterns of an old black preacher to capture the heart of the black idiom; Claude McKay's novel of working-class blacks, *Home to Harlem* (1927); and Jean Toomer's story of poor southern blacks, *Cane* (1923).

Critical Overview

''The Killers'' is one of Hemingway's most anthologized and analyzed stories. The single most influential critical essay on the story was written by Cleanth Brooks and Robert Penn Warren for their short story anthology, *Understanding Fiction.* Brooks and Warren argue that the story belongs to Nick, not Ole or the gangsters, and that through his experiences with the killers, Nick discovers evil. R. S. Crane argues against some of the claims made by Brooks and Warren in his book *The Idea of the Humanities and Other Ideas Critical and Historical,* writing that Nick is only an ''impersonal messenger . . . a utility character in Hemingway's rendering of an action with which Nick has nothing essential to do.'' In his essay ''Some Questions About Hemingway's 'The Killers''' in *Studies in Short Fiction,* Edward Stone notes many of the peculiarities of the story and contends that it is Al and Max's ''surrealistic appearance'' that shocks Nick, not the pervasiveness of crime or Ole's response to his circumstances. For Stone, the story belongs to Ole, not Nick. Charles Owen, in "Time and the Contagion of Flight in 'The Killers,'" says that the story belongs neither to Nick or Ole but to readers, who, like Nick, retain "faith in expedients, a faith that makes him representative of a whole tradition in American culture."

More recent criticism on the story has focused on myth and literary traditions. For example, John Reardon, in his essay "Hemingway's Esthetic and Ethical Sportsmen," sees the story as one in which characters such as Nick must "measure his status as a man" against the "destructive forces" represented by the killers. In "'The Killers' as Experience," W. J. Stuckey argues that the story is a mixture of romance and realism and that with the "terrifyingly irrational" appearance of the killers, Hemingway introduces into the "tradition of realism that element of romance, danger, that the conventions of realism have banished or forced into exile."

Criticism

Chris Semansky

Semansky is an instructor of English literature and composition who writes about literature and culture for various publications. In this essay, Semansky considers the idea of waiting in Hemingway's story.

Rife with images of waiting, "The Killers" embodies a range of Hemingway's ideas on the human condition, from his notion of "nada" to his code of manly behavior. By foregrounding waiting, Hemingway creates suspense, develops characters, and suggests themes that lesser writers might take twice as many pages to accomplish.

Inextricably bound up with notions of time and human behavior, the act of waiting creates expectation and suspense, while providing a framework for the story's events. The first image of waiting occurs when George tells Al and Max that the dinner they want will not be available until six o'clock. But there's confusion about the time. Although the clock reads 5:20, George tells the men it is twenty minutes fast. Instead of awaiting the hour for dinner, the two men settle for egg dishes. After they eat, the men order the cook out of the kitchen, and Al takes Nick and Sam back into the kitchen. George next looks at the clock after Max has revealed that the

Burt Lancaster and Ava Gardner in the 1946 film adaptation of "The Killers"

two are there to kill Ole Andreson. When the motorman comes in for supper, it is 6:15. But readers are not told whether or not 6:15 is the actual time or the "fast" time. This confusion exacerbates the suspense, as Ole usually comes to dinner at six. A few lines later, readers are told it is 6:55, and George says, "He's not coming." Al and Max leave at 7:05.

Critics have zeroed in on the function of clock time in the story. Owen, for example, notes that "at the very moment when the suspense is the greatest," when Ole might be hauling his body through the lunchroom door, Hemingway "disrupts the time sequence." He does this in a long (for Hemingway) paragraph explaining what had happened between 6:15 and 6:55. Martin, on the other hand, sees in the discrepancies of clock time "the relativity of time," asking, "What clock have they followed and how reliable is it? The clock, like the menu, is unreliable." Such indeterminacy not only illustrates Hemingway's perception of the world as an unruly and objectively unknowable place but it also colors the varying responses that Sam, Nick, and George have toward the events.

Al and Max show their disdain for clock time, suggesting that it, like the men in the lunchroom, is

What Do I Read Next?

- Raymond Carver is just one modern writer who was influenced by Hemingway's style. Carver's collection of stories *Cathedral* (1983) was nominated for the National Book Critics Circle Award and was runner-up for the Pulitzer Prize.

- Hemingway chronicles the life of Nick Adams, who appears in ''The Killers,'' in his story collections *In Our Time* (1925) and the posthumous *The Nick Adams Stories* (1972).

- *The Complete Short Stories of Ernest Hemingway* was published by Scribner's in 1987. This volume contains all of Hemingway's stories, including some previously unpublished pieces. The foreword is written by Hemingway's three sons.

- Critics often call Pam Houston a kind of modern-day Hemingway. Her story collection *Cowboys Are My Weakness* (1992) describes her female narrator's adventures in the wilderness, including whitewater rafting, hunting, and mountain climbing.

- Maxwell Perkins was Hemingway's editor for years. *The Only Thing That Counts: The Ernest Hemingway/Maxwell Perkins Correspondence 1925–1947,* edited by Matthew Joseph Bruccoli, collects letters the two men wrote to each other. Perkins was also F. Scott Fitzgerald's editor.

- In *The Autobiography of Alice B. Toklas* (1933), Gertrude Stein discusses her friendship with Hemingway, as well as with a number of Hemingway's cohorts, including Sherwood Anderson and Maxwell Perkins.

---

merely something to manipulate for other ends. After George explains that the clock is fast, one of them says, ''Oh, to hell with the clock,'' demonstrating impatience with the very thing that controls their purpose in the restaurant. Al and Max ''kill'' time waiting for Ole through performing a kind of vaudeville routine, insulting each other and the three men. Before radio was invented, vaudeville was the primary form of entertainment in America. Most cities and towns had their own vaudeville house, in which traveling entertainers would perform comedy, juggling, clowning, acrobatics, singing, mime, dancing, and music. Many of the comedy routines were improvised, as performers turned awkward situations into jokes, often at another person's expense. A popular routine for vaudevillian comedians was a sketch in which a ''city slicker'' meets a ''country bumpkin,'' and the slicker exploits the naivete of the bumpkin. Though the setting—a diner in the small town of Summit outside the big city of Chicago—of Hemingway's story provides an opportunity for such a routine, Al and Max interact very little with the three men. Mostly, they perform *for* them, treating them literally as a captive audience. Their ''routine'' lasts approximately an hour—about the length of a show—and then they leave.

George has a role to play as well, performing appropriately for customers who come in so that Nick and Sam remain unharmed. It is George who looks at the clock, waiting patiently for the killers to leave, knowing that other people's lives, as well as his own, depend on his actions. Like Sam, George appears used to violence and has developed a strategy for responding to and surviving it. Though Summit is outside Chicago, Hemingway suggests that George and Sam have seen big-city crime before.

Ole himself, of course, the object of the killers' waiting, waits, face turned towards the wall, resignation deep. In his belief that death will come to him and there is nothing he can do about it, the ex-boxer illustrates Hemingway's nihilism, his idea of the meaninglessness of human existence. This idea, encapsulated in the Spanish word ''nada,'' or nothingness, crops up often in Hemingway stories and most pointedly in his short story ''A Clean, Well-Lighted Place.'' In this story, from Hemingway's collection *Winner Take Nothing* (1933), reprinted in *The Short Stories of Ernest Hemingway* (1938) and numerous anthologies, an older waiter, talking to himself as he prepares to leave the cafe, recites this prayer:

> Our nada who art in nada, nada be thy name thy kingdom nada thy will be nada in nada as it is in nada. Give us this nada our daily nada and nada us our nada as we nada our nadas and nada us not into nada but deliver us from nada; pues nada. Hail nothing full of nothing, nothing is with thee.

Ole could just as well have been reciting the prayer himself as he waited for the killers to come get him or for the energy to leave his room and meet his death. He is not a typical Hemingway hero, not a man of action but rather one who is exhausted and "through with all that running around." Though he accepts the fact that he will die, and soon, he still cannot bring himself to face his killers. Waiting, for Ole, both embodies the idea of nada, as Ole illustrates the futility of motion, and it underscores his refusal to believe that acting will make any difference to the ultimate outcome of his life.

Nick waits for the events to cohere into some understandable whole. As an adolescent waiting to grow up, Nick also waits for some kind of explanatory sign, but none appears. Arthur Waldhorn, however, argues that Nick's encounter with Ole does signal a watershed point in Nick's development. In *A Reader's Guide to Ernest Hemingway*, Waldhorn writes:

> Though he fails, Nick's short journey from the diner to the boarding house marks an important milestone in his educational progress. The diner is not Nick's first sight of the world but through Ole he has his first full glimpse of how a man lives and dies in it.

The best advice George can offer Nick is not to think about Ole waiting in his room for his death. Not thinking about it, however, is not a choice for Nick, who says he is going to leave town. Nick's decision to leave is also a decision not to accept the fact of his own inevitable death, a fact that Hemingway suggests George and Sam have accepted through their own actions.

Those who wait most are the readers of Hemingway's story. They wait, like the three men in Henry's, for Al and Max to decide what to do with them; they wait for Ole to come through the door; and they wait, like Nick, for meaning to cohere. They wait while they think about the story's implications for their own lives.

> " In his belief that death will come to him and there is nothing he can do about it, the ex-boxer illustrates Hemingway's nihilism, his idea of the meaninglessness of human existence."

Source: Chris Semansky, Critical Essay on "The Killers," in *Short Stories for Students,* The Gale Group, 2003.

Quentin E. Martina

In the following essay, Martina relates "The Killers" to breakthroughs in physics happening at the time of the story's creation.

"The Killers" can be seen as a concise and dramatic representation of certain aspects of Albert Einstein's theory of relativity and Werner Heisenberg's principle of indeterminacy (or uncertainty). In general and simplified terms, relativity argues that time and mass are relative, not absolute, measurements, and that therefore seemingly fixed things, such as the motion of clocks and the shape of tables, are in fact dependent on their actual motion (as through space) and the perspective of the viewer. Lincoln Barnett explains that "there is no such thing as a fixed interval of time independent of the system to which it is referred" and that "the mass of a moving body is by no means constant."

The principle of indeterminacy, introduced by Heisenberg in the same year that "The Killers" was first published (1927), asserts that it is "impossible to determine with precision both the position and the momentum of a particle;" specifically, one cannot, at the same time, determine both the location and the speed of an electron because both measurements depend on each other and involve a small, though constant, margin of error. The more accurately one determines location, the less accurately one can determine speed, and vice versa. As the British physicist Sir James Jeans explained, "the specifications of position and motion lie in two different planes of reality, which cannot be brought simultaneously into sharp focus."

> **"** Furthermore, as time, mass, motion, and other concepts are discovered to be unfixed, relative, and indeterminate, so too are moral precepts; the ability to judge whether something is evil is part of the positivistic, determinable, Newtonian universe."

The theory of relativity, the principle of indeterminacy, and other breakthroughs in modern physics made even more untenable the positivistic determinism of most nineteenth-century science. Indeed, "The Killers" appeared in the midst of a scientific revolution: Louis de Broglie's discovery of wave mechanics (1924), Erwin Schrodinger's "probability waves" (1926), Heisenberg's "uncertainty principle" (1927), and Niels Bohr's "principle of complementarity" (1928). These and other discoveries proved that it was

> basically impossible to know simultaneously the precise position and the speed of a minute body and . . . that what had been taken until then to be reality was no more than a mirage.

The commonsensical Newtonian world of straight lines, fixed contours, and determinable locations and motions no longer obtained. As Alfred North Whitehead said in a 1925 lecture, "[R]egarding material, space, time, and energy, . . . the simple security of the old orthodox assumptions has vanished." In 1930, Jeans proclaimed that Heisenberg and others had shown that "nature abhors accuracy and precision above all things."

These notions of modern physics suffuse "The Killers." Yet in all the commentary on the story—by critics from Edward Sampson to Joseph Flora, who have indeed noted many of the confusing aspects of the story that I will discuss here—this connection between Hemingway and Einstein, Heisenberg, and other physicists has never been made. These confusing aspects have thus never

properly been explained or understood. (Michael Reynolds makes the same claim in his Einsteinian reading of Hemingway's 1932 story, "Homage to Switzerland.")

The relativity of time is stressed early in the story. When the killers read the menu card, they discover that it contains items that are not available because of the time of day; and when the killers and George, the counterman, refer to the clock, more confusion ensues. The clock reads twenty minutes past five o'clock, but it is really—according to George at least—only five o'clock. He says that the clock is twenty minutes fast. Why the clock is fast is unexplained, but if it is not just a faulty clock and has been purposely set ahead—as is often the case, to hasten closing time for the sake of the employees—then why does George not use that faster time, the 5:20 time, in his discussion with the killers about when the dinner items will be available? Also, several references are made later in the story to specific times (for example, "George looked up at the clock. It was a quarter past six"), but it is uncertain what time is being referred to: the actual time or the faster time. Such questions have direct bearing on the killers' plan because they know that Ole usually comes into the restaurant at six o'clock. How do they know this, when presumably they do not wear watches? What clock have they followed and how reliable is it? The clock, like the menu, is unreliable, which leads the "first man" to say, "Oh, to hell with the clock."

Many of the characters present equally puzzling, if not deceptive, fronts. The two killers' appearance is so similar that they lose any individuality at all—both are "about the same size," and they are "dressed like twins." When they walk away from the restaurant, they are described as looking "like a vaudeville team." Furthermore, they do not even resemble what they are supposed to be—killers. At one point they ask an intentionally rhetorical question: "Do we look silly?" The apparently unneeded answer is "No," for these are two cold, fearsome hit men carrying sawed-off shotguns. But the real answer is "Yes," they do look silly, with their identical dress, derby hats, tight-fitting dark overcoats, and gloves—looking indeed like a vaudeville team.

This deceptiveness of appearance holds for other characters too. Sexual identity in particular is ambiguous and uncertain. Max tells George, after watching him "cook and everything," that "you'd make some girl a nice wife, bright boy." Earlier,

Max has told Nick to "go around on the other side of the counter with your boy friend." Al, too, jokes about their victims' sexual identity; he tells Max, "I got them [Nick and Sam] tied up like a couple of girl friends in the convent."

Ole also presents a confusing front in that his personal size does not have the expected significance. The two killers are repeatedly described as little men, yet Ole, who is so big that he cannot fit in a standard-sized bed, is helpless against them. Big Ole, relative to the power of the seemingly silly little killers, is really a small man. Nick wants to believe that a big, tough boxer such as Ole can "fix it up some way," but Ole knows better; he knows that his mass is relative to other things such as guns and the mob.

Along with the people in the story, physical settings are also presented in indeterminate ways. This lunchroom is not really a lunchroom, for it "had been made over from a saloon into a lunch-counter." And the name of the town, Summit, is obviously ironic and unsuitable for the place where these events occur. Additionally, the murder will take place on a "nice fall day." But less-obvious confusion also involves this town. Early in the story, the killers ask George, "What do they call it [the town]?", and even after being told its name, they say they have never heard of it. But presumably they have followed or somehow traced Ole to the town; they even know where he usually eats. Would they then not know the name of the town he is in, especially if they had been informed about it? And to add to the confusion, they later insist, "We know damn well where we are." Do they or don't they?

Further confusion surrounds the physical settings. The story opens at "Henry's lunch-room"—but who is Henry? No one by that name appears in the story. The apparent owner or manager, George, is, it must be deduced, just an employee of this Henry, though his position is never made clear, like the indeterminate position of an electron. A more prominent example of the confusion of names and places occurs when Nick goes to the boarding house where Ole is staying. It is called "Hirsch's rooming-house," and when Nick talks to the landlady after seeing Ole, he assumes she is Mrs. Hirsch:

"Well, good-night, Mrs. Hirsch," Nick said.

"I'm not Mrs. Hirsch," the woman said. "She owns the place.

I just look after it for her. I'm Mrs. Bell."

George and Mrs. Bell—despite outward appearances and the assumptions of others—do not even run their own businesses. They are mere employees, as the killers are, with Mrs. Bell's name perhaps suggesting her status as an echo of something else.

In the confusion about Mrs. Bell, Nick resembles the reader, who assumes things concerning the reliability of time, locale, appearances, sexual distinctions, etc. but discovers that those "positivistic" assumptions are either incorrect or simplistic, that things are more complex and indeterminate than they seem. The story's purposeful confusion, then, is emblematic of a post-Newtonian scientist who has to discard seemingly solid, commonsensical principles and find his or her way in a mirage-world. "The new situation in the thought of today," Whitehead said in that 1925 lecture, "arises from the fact that scientific theory is outrunning common sense." Nick encounters new things in this story, from the literal newness of having a towel in his mouth to a more involved and troublesome newness. Cleanth Brooks and Robert Penn Warren famously identified the newness as the discovery of evil, but to be more precise, the discovery is really of a modernist indeterminacy that derives in part from the scientific revolution brought about by Einstein, Heisenberg, and others.

Furthermore, as time, mass, motion, and other concepts are discovered to be unfixed, relative, and indeterminate, so too are moral precepts; the ability to judge whether something is evil is part of the positivistic, determinable, Newtonian universe. The black cook's refusal to get involved is perhaps a more "real" perception of this modern world than Nick and George's decision to do the presumably right thing and warn Ole. The cook's comment about Nick and George's decision to get involved and warn Ole is revealing: "Little boys always know what they want to do." Big boys, who have been in the complex, shifting, uncertain modern world awhile, are not always so sure.

Source: Quentin E. Martina, "Hemingway's 'The Killers,'" in *Explicator*, Vol. 52, No. 1, Fall 1993, pp. 53–57.

George Monteiro

In the following essay, Monteiro identifies elements in "The Killers" that serve as a metaphor for bullfighting.

After an earlier unsuccessful attempt to write the story, Hemingway was finally able to set down

"*The Killers*" on a day in which he was confined to his Madrid hotel room because the San Isidro bullfights were snowed out. He originally entitled the story "The Matadors." In some ways, it is a pity that he dropped this title, for this is a story about a killing that does not take place only because the human being marked for death does not play his part that day. If one considers it as a planned, if not quite ritualized, killing in which the "animal's" own habitual behavior (each day he comes to Henry's lunchroom at the same hour) will bring him to his death at the hands of "professional" killers whose duty is to perform this task for hire, we have license to draw certain analogies between bullfighting and the events in Summit.

The bullring has become Henry's lunchroom, the matador(s), "the killers," Max and Al. Replacing the bull is "the Swede"—the prizefighter Andreson, whose first name is, suggestively, Ole. The matador's *banderillas* served up from a case and his sword mantled in cloth have their analogue in the killers' sawed-off shotguns covered up by their tight-fitting overcoats. To say this much stretches the analogies as far as it is useful to take them. What is more interesting, however, once these broad analogies are suggested, is to see how what takes place in Henry's lunch room differs from what takes place in an arena in Madrid. It is by indirection that "The Killers" parodies the bullfight itself. Because Ole Andreson is not killed "around 6 p.m." on this particular day in Henry's lunchroom, and because Nick Adams discovers that Ole Andreson has no fight left in him (he knows his fate and is resigned to being killed if not now, then later, if not in that place, then elsewhere), the horror of his predetermined fate (even though the killing is itself deferred) gradually suffuses the story. Even if the would-be hit has turned out "sloppy" (Al's word) and the "ritual" has been aborted, the ordered killing ("ordered" both because somebody has commanded it or put in an order for it and because it is to be carried out in an "orderly" fashion) reveals that these men have gone beyond the brutes in that, unlike in the bullfight, their passion has been removed from the act of killing.

Their very competence as professionals, moreover, is impugned from the start. Al and Max are "dressed like twins"—derby hat, black overcoat buttoned across the chest, silk muffler, gloves. The overcoats are "too tight." They eat with their gloves on. In fact, "In their tight overcoats and derby hats they looked like a vaudeville team." To resume the bullfighting analogy for a moment, Al

and Max, acting as a team, recall the comic bullfights thrown into an overall program of bullfighting called the "Charlots" or "Charlie Chaplins." The difference, of course, lies in the threat posed by the sawed-off shotguns loaded to kill.

The widespread acceptance of the Brooks and Warren reading of "*The Killers*" as a story characteristically pointed toward Nick Adams's reactions, has often kept readers from seeing that this story is also about psychological and physical domination and that much of the horror the story evokes comes through the reader's recognition that something even more powerful than fear for his safety or the naked instinct for self-preservation and survival has overtaken and defeated the ex-prizefighter. Ole Andreson lies on his bed as if his affections have been sedated, as if he has been caught in a trap that he no longer tries to escape. His morale crushed, he has turned his face and body to the wall even, as figuratively, he has turned his back on life.

By failing to leave his bed, let alone his room, Andreson has chosen his place to die, whether today or some other day. A bull will often establish a *querencia,* a place in the ring, where he becomes especially dangerous because the matador must go in after the bull rather than getting the bull to charge over terrain chosen by the bullfighter. Yet without their ever laying eyes on him, let alone confronting and shooting him, Al and Max (because they merely represent the notion and idea of "the killers" who have already "killed" his will to live) have already won the contest.

Were it not for what we learn from Nick's visit to Mrs. Hirsch's boardinghouse and his discussion with Andreson, the appearance of Al and Max, professional killers, would have constituted nothing more than an ugly, if threatening, interruption in the daily doings in Henry's lunchroom. The two hours or so in which Al and Max take over the restaurant, tie-up and gag both Sam the cook and Nick the customer, and keep a gun trained on George, who runs the place, is a monstrous interlude in a day that has, until that moment, promised to be no different from any other day. And after the killers have left, it's back to business as usual. There is no indication that anyone has called the police, and while it is George who suggested that Nick go to Mrs. Hirsch's boardinghouse to warn Andreson, George seems not to have been much affected by the events in his lunchroom. Even as Nick tells him about how he cannot stand the fact that Andreson will neither fight back, nor run away from his killers, we watch

George performing the same old tasks: he "reached down for a towel and wiped the counter." He is not far from the mark, probably, when to Al's question about the townspeople in Summit, "What do you do here nights?" Max answers, "They eat the dinner . . . they all come here and eat the big dinner."

Of course, by their very presence and the arrangements they make to facilitate their conduct of business, the two killers pervert the lunchroom routine on which the restaurant's customers depend. Yet the success of their plan depends to some extent on their maintaining the semblance of the usual routine in George's responses to customers that come in and to his own movements. George is their front man, whose presence and behavior, even if he cannot deliver the usual dinners at six o'clock (the cook is tied up), give him enough credibility to keep customers from suspecting that on that day something is amiss in Henry's lunchroom. And yet, to maintain the tone of their total domination (and to amuse themselves, claims Max) they work from the start to upset the routine. They ask for items from the dinner menu, even after being told that what is listed on the dinner menu will not be ready until six. When the two plates of eggs are served—one with ham, the other with bacon—Al eats Max's order and Max eats Al's. Their running conversation keeps them amused, George under control, and the overall tension from mounting up. They are so successful in this that when Andreson fails to show up, they just walk away. They are, in Max's words, "through with it." They do no further harm. After all, they haven't even done enough damage to be charged with attempted murder, and they are sure enough of themselves to walk away with their shotguns under their coats. As they go out, they direct one last remark at George, hinting that things could have turned out much worse. "You got a lot of luck," they tell him, "you ought to play the races, bright boy."

Source: George Monteiro, "The Hit in Summit: Ernest Hemingway's 'The Killers,'" in *The Hemingway Review,* Vol. 8, No. 2, Spring 1989, pp. 40–42.

Ron Berman

In the following essay, Berman explores the role vaudeville plays in the action and philosophy of "The Killers."

Kenneth S. Lynn's biography of Hemingway states that

> behind "The Killers" lay some obvious influences: Hemingway's firsthand acquaintance with petty crimi-

By failing to leave his bed, let alone his room, Andreson has chosen his place to die, whether today or some other day."

nals in Kansas City, his close observation of the men entering the back room in the Venice Cafe, and the steady attention he paid in the 20s to journalistic accounts, in European as well as in American newspapers, of the blood-drenched careers of Chicago hoodlums.

Behind the story also is Hemingway's acquaintance by 1926 with vaudeville and with the idea of vaudeville. The connection has long been noted: in 1959, Cleanth Brooks and Robert Penn Warren mentioned the "vaudeville team" of Max and Al, and the "gag" and "dialogue" that remind the reader of their "unreal and theatrical quality." The essay is, however, only the briefest of sketches on the subject.

By the mid-1920s, entertainment had become part of visual and literary art. Music hall scores echoed in the work of T. S. Eliot; the lyrics of Broadway hits were reprinted in the pages of F. Scott Fitzgerald; and revues and Follies were described in fascinating detail in the essays of Edmund Wilson. The expression "the seven lively arts," coined by Gilbert Seldes, was meant to include comics, dancers, and Krazy Kat—and to displace such bourgeois delights as grand opera. It was the fate of one of those lively arts, vaudeville, to wax and wane with modernism.

To be useful to Hemingway as a subject in 1926, two things had had to happen to vaudeville: the first was its permeation of the social world, the second its recognition by the intellectual world. We know that the first of these happened because from W. C. Fields to Eddie Cantor and even to Ed Sullivan, vaudevillians not only dominated the Palace and the Ziegfeld Follies—hence the imagination of much of New York—but also went on to radio and the movies. The second happening was a consequence of the first. A brief chronology: in 1922, vaudeville became "The Great American

> **To be useful to Hemingway as a subject in 1926, two things had had to happen to vaudeville: the first was its permeation of the social world, the second its recognition by the intellectual world."**

Art'' for the *New Republic,* in which Mary Cass Canfield wrote that it need not apologize for comparisons with Robinson and Frost, Masters and Sandburg. In fact, she thought it held its own with the work of Mark Twain as a kind of artistic reaction to our native social repressiveness:

> Grotesque or not, vaudeville represents a throwing away of self-consciousness, of Plymouth Rock caution, devoutly to be wished for. Here we countenance the extreme, we encourage idiosyncrasy. The dancer or comedian is, sometimes literally, egged on to develop originality; he is adored, never crucified for difference. Miss Fannie Brice and Sir Harry Lauder are examples of vaudeville performers who have been hailed, joyfully and rightfully, as vessels containing the sacred fire, and who have been encouraged into self-emphasis by their audiences . . .

Equally important was the fact of universal intellectual acceptance:

> Darius Milhaud, George Auric and the others write ballets and symphonies in which may be heard the irresponsible ''cancan'' of ragtime. John Alden Carpenter, perhaps the most vivid talent among our own composers, will occasionally shift from cooly subtle disharmonies, illustrating poetic or lyric subjects, to write a Krazy Kat Ballet.

Vaudeville was for the intellectual world equal to other forms of artistic composition. And it seemed to gain meaning when it was compared to the modes of modernism.

Throughout 1923, Edmund Wilson produced a barrage of pieces on vaudeville ideas and personalities, and on the meaning of dance, jazz, comic scripts, and revues. He identified some of the leading comics and mimes, among them Bert Savoy, Johnny Hudgins, and Bert Williams. He speculated on the satire of vaudeville and especially on its urban modernist meanings. Wilson thought that the Ziegfeld Follies were inherently part of his and Fitzgerald's literary world:

> Among those green peacocks and gilded panels, in the luxurious haze of the New Amsterdam, there is realized a glittering vision which rises straight out of the soul of New York. The Follies is such fantasy, such harlequinade as the busy well-to-do New Yorker has been able to make of his life. Expensive, punctual, stiff, it moves with the speed of an express train. It has in it something of Riverside Drive, of the Plaza, of Scott Fitzgerald's novels.

Not for the last time, Wilson thought of vaudeville as an equivalent of Dada. He was especially tuned to vaudeville's depiction of anxiety, writing of Williams as a kind of walking Freudian dream, finding Eddie Cantor and Gilda Gray to be mental incarnations of New York ''in terms of entertainment.'' They expressed the city's ''nervous intensity to the tune of harsh and complicated harmonies.'' He thought that Bert Savoy was an exceptionally able interpreter, through impersonation, of the styles and aspirations of upper-middle-class Manhattan life. Wilson thought, finally, that vaudeville was a modernist urban art full of reflections of current experience. He was especially tuned to its staccato delivery and to its own self-conscious sense of authorship. In Wilson's canon, Bert Savoy mattered as much as any textualized idea.

In 1924 Seldes, a friend of Wilson's and known to both Fitzgerald and Hemingway, published *The Seven Lively Arts.* This book gave intellectuals much to think about. Aside from cataloging the great and the good performers, it moved into the heady realms of modernist theory. Wilson thought that the book was chaotic, sometimes out of control, and he was right. But Seldes made some important points for the writers who came after him. He did not originate the argument that Chaplin and other comics belonged with Joyce and Eliot (Eliot himself made that point), but he argued consistently that the ''lively'' arts belonged with so-called higher forms of visual and textual arts. He thought that Bert Savoy belonged in the same world as Remy de Gourmont and James Joyce, and in the same sentence with Charles Dickens. Most important, at least as far as Hemingway is concerned, was the series of manifestos with which the book subsided. Seldes provided an enormous amount of material to anyone inclined to think that conventional American values—and the writings exemplifying them—were bogus.

Seldes took certain modernist beliefs about the unwinding of respectable culture and restated them in terms of comedy, jazz, and even cartoons. For example, Ring Lardner and Mr. Dooley are ''more important than James B. Cabell and Joseph Hergesheimer'' because they say more about present attitudes toward the present moment. This may now be self-evident, but even Mencken, full of pieties for the groaning earnestness of realism, resisted such ideas. Seldes thought that Florenz Ziegfeld was better than David Belasco, and that the circus was better than grand opera. Edmund Wilson thought the last was an exaggeration, but Hemingway might have found the thought more than casually amusing.

It will be useful to cite the last three of Seldes's principles of art because they seem to reappear persistently in Hemingway's thought:

> That there exists a ''genteel tradition'' about the arts which has prevented any just appreciation of the popular arts, and that these have therefore missed the corrective criticism given to the serious arts, receiving instead only abuse.

> That therefore the pretentious intellectual is as much responsible as any one for what is actually absurd and vulgar in the lively arts.

> That the simple practitioners and simple admirers of the lively arts being uncorrupted by the bogus preserve a sure instinct for what is artistic in America.

Perhaps the best account is Wilson's long review of 1924 in which he placed Seldes within ''America's new orientation'' on culture begun by Van Wyck Brooks in 1915. Wilson thought that the Seldes book had identified an important strand of modernism. The ''inconsecutive'' and even ''pointless'' comic art of vaudevillians like Joe Cook, Charlie Case, and James J. Morton could be compared to Jean Cocteau and understood as a parallel to Dada. The art of vaudeville was above all an accurate response to the postwar world and ''the bewildering confusion of the modern city.'' The disconnected and often resentful vaudeville script (in some ways a preface to Hemingway) shows the way the world is and the way our *''own minds are beginning to work.''*

Finally, in 1925, a year before the writing of ''The Killers,'' an article appeared in *The Drama* on the subject of ''The Vaudeville Philosopher'' (which may be the right category for Max and Al). It decried the new sensibility of national ressentiment:

> There are certain standard subjects that are used almost every night on vaudeville stages through the country. An audience, composed of many persons mentally fatigued after a day's work, learns a philosophy that embraces such precepts as: marriage is an unfortunate institution to which the majority of us resign ourselves; women are fashion-crazy, spend money heedlessly and believe that their husbands are fools; politics is all bunk. Prohibition should be prohibited . . . marital infidelity is widespread; clandestine affairs of most any sort between at least one married person and another of the opposite sex are comical; and finally ''nothing in life really matters. The main thing to do is get all the money you can and keep your mother-in-law as far off as possible.''

A few years later, writing about the social mood of the mid-20s, Fitzgerald described ''a widespread neurosis'' and a significant change in American character. He ascribed the change to the boom, not the bust. Vaudeville seems to have picked up the various kinds of national resentments—many of them in the world of ideas.

To some extent this kind of ''philosophy'' had always been there because of the daily collision on stage between comic values and what Fitzgerald and others described as our ''Victorian'' social habit of hypocrisy. Modernism aside, before and during the Great War the national cultural audience had signified a great deal about its sensibility. For example, Willie Hammerstein's Victoria Theatre consciously changed the sentimentality of the music hall. It featured hard-edged discourse on the conflicts of domestic life. It fed off events reported by newspapers and had a symbiotic relationship with them. At the Victoria, comedy was generated out of class, marital, and racial conflict; unrepressed anger and anxieties; and current ''sexual scandals . . . and suffragists.'' Hammerstein's Victoria had put ''newsmakers'' on its stage: chorus girls with very public private lives, speech-making suffragettes, and the occasional celebrities who fired shots at their lovers. This is how Joe Laurie, Jr., describes Hammerstein's pursuit of the new public consciousness: ''he played the killers and near killers.''

As early as 1914, the public had become accustomed to seeing the connection between social resentment and theatrical aggression. By the 20s, vaudeville had become increasingly associated with the techniques and values of modernism. Edmund Wilson and Gilbert Seldes among others emphasized the values of nontextual and impermanent arts. As Wilson put the matter two decades later, these were better than ''our respectable arts.'' The new icons of culture—Joe Cook, Charlie Chaplain, Florenz Ziegfeld, Ring Lardner, Krazy Kat, Al Jolson, and Irving Berlin—had an important role in ''the liquidation of genteel culture.'' Vaudeville was a concurrent form of intellectual style. Hemingway came to the subject in mid-decade with a well-defined map of ''culture'' and of the ways in which comic representation looked at the unrealities of real life.

When Max and Al walk into Henry's lunchroom they are in a confined, lighted, and stagy space with doors for exits and entrances. A running gag begins about not knowing what they want—the gag is at this point merely absurd. Max and Al keep asking each other questions as they go through the formalities of what vaudeville historians call ''The Two-man Act.'' This ''was usually the comedy standout of the bill'' because ''talking routines'' had taken precedence over song, dance, acrobatics, and other forms of insurance for comedians. Hemingway follows one specific vaude tradition: ''usually it was a straight man with a Hebrew comic.'' Max is gentile; Al, who could only have come from a kosher convent, is not. The key, however, is that they really are what they are.

Two-man acts were relentlessly ethnic, and aggressive beyond anything dreamed today. Olsen and Johnson or Smith and Dale or Weber and Fields did ''The Sport and the Jew'' or ''Irish by Name but Coons by Birth.'' The scripts that remain indicate that no punch was pulled, no insult spared. As vaudeville developed, insult gave way to wit. Slapstick was dropped: beginning with belly-laughs, the two-man act after the turn of century utilized ''more rational stuff.'' The costume and demeanor of modern comics indicated a new sophistication, hence the displacement of red noses, checkered coats, and circus shoes by good suits, ties, and stock collars. The two-man act often wore (Hemingway noticed this) city-slicker gray derbies. The act developed ''routines'' that were highly verbal, demanding interpretation.

The straight man had the most status—he was sane in a world of eccentrics—and he had some pretensions to ideas, education, and even style. Both Max and Al like to play the straight man, and they alternate in the role. When they first enter, the dialogue is unfocused because they are free-wheeling, ad-libbing on the clock and menu. But they are strangely aggressive and bring into the story attitudes that the story itself does not account for. Some of these attitudes are (so to speak) professional, but others have to do with the genre. All straight men know that the world is composed largely of fools who must be suffered.

Here are two parallel scripts for an opening gag. The first is from Hemingway:

''This is a hot town,'' said the other. ''What do they call it?''

''Summit.''

''Ever hear of it?'' Al asked his friend.

''No,'' said the friend.

''What do you do here nights?'' Al asked.

''They eat the dinner,'' his friend said. ''They all come here and eat the big dinner.''

The second passage suggests that Hemingway borrowed liberally from vaudeville lore. Scripts that were older than he was provided him with one of his central themes: urban sophistication poised against rural idiocy. A ''well-dressed'' man (he is in fact an actor) from the big city meets one of the local rubes:

''What's the name of this town?''

[. . .]

''Centertown.''

''Where is the theatre?''

''I don't know,'' says the native.

Then the actor looks at him as though he were an idiot.

Hemingway has appropriated the rube's line about not knowing much; he will reverse it, make it into a problem of philosophy. He has exaggerated the free-floating resentment and aggression of comedy, making that the essence of his story.

Max and Al don't like bright boys—the phrase is repeated more than any other in the story. In one of the two-man acts, ''The Sport and the Jew,'' the straight man says to Cohen (whose name has a certain resonance in Hemingway), ''You're a pretty smart fellow.'' He means the opposite. Al and Max are gangsters, satirists, philosophers, and vaudes, but they are above all ironists (Donaldson). Almost everything they say means its opposite. And one of the great resentments in their dialogue is intellectual. The dialogue is economical to a degree— minimalist—conveying the meaning not only of statement but also of predisposition.

Max and Al enter the text with attitudes about a number of things. As professionals, they have ideas about the job, but as comedians they have ideas about life. Their problem is not really Ole Andreson but the yokels they have to deal with—after all, these people have been cluttering up the vaudeville stage past living memory. There is no reason to expect them to behave correctly now.

The repetition of one phrase tells us about scripts and other realities:

"You're a pretty bright boy, aren't you?"

"Sure," said George.

"Well, you're not," said the other little man. "Is he, Al?"

"He's dumb," said Al. He turned back to Nick. "What's your name?"

"Adams."

"Another bright boy," Al said. "Ain't he a bright boy, Max?"

"The town's full of bright boys," Max said.

The vaude tradition pits knowledge against ignorance, so that it should not be surprising that at this point the story becomes comic epistemology. As always, the straight man is right—these hicks are dumb enough to believe that the facts of their daily lives correspond to a larger order, that there is a relationship between what they believe and the *actual* context for any belief. This point is large enough to be the story itself, and I will return to it in detail. Here we should sense a kind of intellectual pace: beginning with the usual resentments of comic dialogue, we are now moving swiftly to a series of revelations that validate them.

Max catches George looking at him—or perhaps not looking at him—and begins to deliver his philosophical punch lines. They seem at first to be, in the phrase of Edmund Wilson, "pointless"—but pointlessness has a special meaning in the mid-20s. It illuminates "the way the world is beginning to seem." That goes substantially beyond the fact that the two-man shows had for a long time in their subversive way "ridiculed middle-class ideals of conduct" (Snyder 138). This one will ridicule middle-class confidence in a grounded moral world:

"What are *you* looking it [sic]?" Max looked at George.

"Nothing."

"The hell you were. You were looking at me."

"Maybe the boy meant it for a joke, Max," Al said.

George laughed.

"*You* don't have to laugh," Max said to him. "*You* don't have to laugh at all, see?"

"All right," said George.

"So he thinks it's all right." Max turned to Al. "He thinks it's all right. That's a good one."

"Oh, he's a thinker," Al said. They went on eating.

The fundamental breach of decorum is for the rube to laugh—after all, he is the joke, not the audience for it. A more serious violation: George is guilty of thinking that anything in the world is "all right." And of wanting "to know what it's all about." He is guilty of being an American after the age of idealism.

There is a splendid remark in Henry F. May's history of thought about the prewar years: progressive idealists were destined to disappear as an intellectual force because "two things seemed to bother them in the world of Fitzgerald, Hemingway, and Faulkner: real frivolity and real pessimism." They never understood Hemingway, but he certainly understood them. They represented to him the imposition of morality and politics on criticism and literature. The world he understood was tragic, not idealistic. It can to some extent be understood through its opposites. For example, in "The Killers" we see a world of small-town loyalties and, in some ways, even of heroism. More important, as a brief, sharp, and deeply philosophical passage shows, it is a world understood through certainties:

"What's the idea?" Nick asked.

"There isn't any idea."

This might indicate a philosophical problem in any system, and it has to be understood within and opposed to an American tradition of thought. American idealism and the public philosophy had the deepest concern for grounding action on logical belief. Recent American philosophy had become known for certain kinds of essays on the order of personal and social life: "How to Make Our Ideas Clear" (Charles Sanders Peirce); "Loyalty to Loyalty, Truth, and Reality" (Josiah Royce); and "The Moral Philosopher and the Moral Life" (William James). There was, one hoped, or should be such an order. In the last of these social statements, we see what George and Nick wish to believe: "ordinary men . . . imagine an abstract moral order in which the objective truth resides."

Nick, George, and Sam are ordinary men with an a priori sense of objective truth. They have never examined their own premises because daily life rarely makes one do that. But this story forces them not only to become conscious of their beliefs but also to change those beliefs. It forces them to change their idea of logic, which is in some ways a harder task than changing ideas about morality. Much of Hemingway's best work is built around questions that force issues. In this story, the questions are of two kinds, tactical and epistemological, both verging on the metaphysical. The tactical questions are about time and the menu, about obeying irrational orders, about going to the movies. There are more than 50 such tactical questions in this story. But they edge into questions of a different order of magnitude, about the nature of things social and universal, about awareness of reality, about the fully human condition. The literature of the first quarter of the century was famous for such questions. Here are some of them as phrased by Josiah Royce: "What do we live for? What is our duty? What is the true ideal of life? What is the true difference between right and wrong? What is the true good which we all need?" Not only are these answerable questions in Royce, *but answering them is itself a moral activity.* The opposite is true in Hemingway, who warns us here and elsewhere that these questions are so difficult—so unreal—that we ought not to think about them. Or, as Sam the cook says in a parable of another sort of wisdom, "You better not have anything to do with it at all." Sam, who is underrated, is intellectually ahead of Nick and George.

Nick and George begin to understand that the two kinds of questions imply each other. When they separately ask "what's the idea?" they mean the idea for doing as they are told; but the reader, a party to the dialogue, will understand that the idea refers more to Plato than to Ole Andreson. The idea referred to is the idea of meaning in action, and also of meaning in life. That there should be no "idea" for moving behind the counter is an intellectual irritant, but if there is no "idea" for doing or explaining anything or coping with fate, then the problem is much larger. It undercuts the basis for their lives. But their lives have been both moral and unreflective, which is why Max and Al are so contemptuous of bright boys who are thinkers.

Max and Al, themselves far more intelligent than they appear, know that one kind of question implies the other. To want to know something implies that something is to be known, that a given course of action has a universal consequence, that all parties look at the issue in more or less the same way—although William James, wryly brilliant and in a Hobbesian mood, understood

> what the words *good, bad,* and *obligation* severally mean. They mean no absolute natures, independent of personal support. They are objects of feeling and desire which have no foothold or anchorage in Being, apart from the existence of actually living minds.

It would be a safe bet that Max and Al know this "idea."

One of the great passages in the story moves with stunning clarity from one form of the same question to its metaphysical shadow:

"Well, bright boy," Max said, looking into the mirror, "why don't you say something?"

"What's it all about?"

"Hey, Al," Max called, "bright boy wants to know what it's all about."

"Why don't you tell him?" Al's voice came from the kitchen.

"What do you think it's all about?"

"I don't know."

By the time this part of the dialogue finishes, Nick realizes that the here and now may not be related to any universal. That particular problem is part of a much larger problem about intelligibility. In 1925, a short time before this story appeared, John Dewey had suggested in an essay on "Nature, Ends and Histories" that the historically naive mind began "with a ready-made list of good things or perfections which it was the business of nature to accomplish." And so it is for what James called the mind of the ordinary American who expects to see in the world the order he has so confidently but wrongly imposed on it. But not for those like Max and Al—messengers from modernism—who know that decision, action, and consequence are relative. Perhaps there is no meaning in life, no morality for causation, no guiding universal. As to the last, reality being purely situational, *there are certain things you never know at the time.*

As Dewey put the matter, it would be deeply confused to think that expectations matched actualities. It would be splendid if the American social order reflected a good and moral universe—but rather a lot of hard work remained to make the world what one hoped it was. One might fail, at that. Also in 1925, in "Existence, Ideas and Consciousness," Dewey argued that "events which brutely occur and brutely affect us" must be converted into meaning, must have "probable consequences." Otherwise, "philosophy finds itself in a hopeless impasse." Wilson seems to have been purposive and contextual in choosing to state outcomes in terms of their "pointlessness." Max and Al may not have been reading either John Dewey or Edmund Wilson, but Hemingway knows about that impasse.

Certain phrases in the story become magnified through repetition and allusion: there is a continual echoing of "what it's all about" and "what's the idea." Readers are intended to recognize that the tactical can become the metaphysical, intended, I think, to move from *what* to *why.* Let us start with a very small and limited *why,* the reason for Max and Al's taking bloody murder very much in stride but being offended by ignorance. Is there something visibly characteristic of American life in the provinces that engages them in a way that their work does not? They find a laughable disparity between mind and material reality. They suggest that Nick and George may be bright—but that they remain boys. Like most straight men, they are adults in a world of children.

Max and Al refer to a subject later mentioned by Walter Lippmann in *A Preface to Morals* about one persistent aspect of our national character: Americans simply did not want to be aware of the way things actually were; they preferred, in fact, to remain deluded about what "the idea" was for anything. Lippmann thought that Americans generally failed to explain the facts of their lives. We wanted to see an orderly moral world, so we invented one. We ascribed "everything which happens" to "the duty of the universe" toward us. But the idea that "the universe is full of purposes utterly unknown" seems utterly unknown to Americans. A phenomenon like, let us say, the advent of Max and Al to the town of Summit is a kind of philosophical demonstration that accepted ideas have no authority. Yet, in the terms used by Lippmann, what Max and Al represent *"is in the nature of things."* Lippmann was to conclude that few Americans could bear to analyze their experience because that would mean the acquisition of a sense of evil (emphasis added). If "The Killers" had a moral, that would be it.

Evil has many forms. Hemingway's dialogue quickly enters the realm of moral imponderables. Movies, which are entertainment, are in fact explanations. Andreson is going to be killed as part of a professional, hence moral, obligation. Fate is circumstance:

> "All right," George said, "What are you going to do with us afterward?"

> "That'll depend," Max said. "That's one of those things you never know at the time."

Rather small and colorless words carry burdens too large to assess: *do, afterward,* and *depend* mean decisions made as Joseph Conrad imagined them, with one's feet not touching the earth. They do not refer themselves to any "idea:" certainly not to justice or meaning, but only to circumstance. Max says that he likes George, and he probably does. But Al may yet blow his head off. Why has all this been revealed? "We got to keep amused, haven't we?"

The dialogue keeps circling back to the premises of the two-man act, which has more to say here than the hoarded sum of western moral thought.

We recall that throughout Hemingway's lifetime, beginning with William James and continuing with John Dewey, there had been a great, self-conscious, and enormously effective attempt to ground the life of democracy precisely *in* those western moral meanings. That was clear to Mencken, who understood that James had defined the meaning of American moral life in a "long and glorious" philosophical reign over the reading audience. And Dewey was to be described by Henry Commager in *The American Mind* as the arbiter of national, ethics: "for a generation no issue was clarified until Dewey had spoken." One silent conclusion of this story is that moral explanations of the kind they had so richly provided for America had failed. That is why such explanation is either absent or ineffective, and why the premises of idealism and pragmatism are so intensely ridiculed. Outside the story, for its readers, there is the enormous moral authority of those who have defined for us the nature of social life—but inside the story they are invisible. The rather large sequence of ideas that George and Nick address—on the meaning of logical action, on universal meaning itself, on the relationship of value to act—have been silently negated. Max and Al replace philosophy. As Edmund Wilson had stated a very short time before, the art of the "pointless" is central to the cultural moment.

Both Wilson and Hemingway developed this idea as a conscious part of the not-especially loyal philosophical opposition. They understood that the relationship of reality to idea was that of perception to composition. They knew what they opposed: Dewey "insisted that the world was a world of meaning, not just a world of flatly unintelligible cause and effect connections." It is impossible to understand "The Killers" without reference to that (supposed) fact. However, when we posit order or nonpointlessness in the world, "it is we who are doing all the intellectual work." Max and Al know this; George and Sam and Nick must become painfully educated.

There are few other works of fiction in which meanings are so impacted. A single word implies heroism, as when George, who is asked if Ole Andreson eats here, simply says "sometimes" and risks his own life. The word *afterward* means the difference between life and death. "They're all right" is nothing less than a special dispensation: it means that George and Nick and Sam will all stay alive because Max knows that they have become realists. George gets the exit line, a rube who has become a straight man: ''you better not think about it.''

The last line of the story may not be Heidegger, but it is definitely philosophy. It ought to be read against an important passage about American provincial life in Royce, in which we are told that ''all of us first learned about what we ought to do, about what our ideal should be, and in general about the moral law'' from ''our teachers, our parents, our playmates, society, custom, or perhaps some church.'' But belief does not matter because of its source alone. It remains for us to validate it: ''What reason can I give why my duty is my duty?'' What makes us human is not what is handed down but the way the mind works under pressure to ''furnish the only valid reason for you to know what is right and good.'' That is what Nick and George and Sam are asked to deny, and what Max and Al conclude they will deny.

In the single best-known statement of recent American philosophy, *Pragmatism,* William James had referred to a notorious crime involving murder and suicide. He understood plainly that this was both a philosophical and a religious issue. James cited the reaction of a drastically empiricist mind that saw in this crime ''one of the elemental stupendous facts of this modern word'' that ''cannot be glozed over or minimized away by all the treatises on God, and Love, and Being, helplessly existing in their monumental vacuity.'' Such crimes or existential facts, James writes, constitute a ''dilemma'' for the American mind, whose sense of the verities of daily life is based on intangibles and unprovables.

The governing ''idea'' of the town of Summit is typical of small towns in the mid-20s, and was evident in the best-known of them all: the assumption that ''the world is good, God is good, and His spirit wherein men are to live is love's spirit'' becomes embodied in ''an elaborate system of beliefs, prohibitions, and group-sanctioned conduct.'' But even inside *Middletown* we are always aware that some of the beliefs of this system are impossible to accept literally, ''without lying to yourself.''

From this dilemma came James's famous statement about American tough-mindedness, a quality that seems to me to describe Hemingway's philosophical stance. The tough-minded were empirical, and in rejecting any systems they rejected not only explanation but also the ''idea'' of explanation. It

may have been only fitting that in 1926 Hemingway too should turn to murder as a philosophical test. James knew that all theories, empiricism among them, and all stances, tough-mindedness among them, were what he called remedies for the world of facts. I believe that Hemingway understood that, but his fiction needed what it found in radical empiricism, which is disguised here as vaudeville philosophy. Or rather, it takes on the appropriate form of vaudeville philosophy.

Source: Ron Berman, ''Vaudeville Philosophers: 'The Killers,''' in *Twentieth Century Literature: A Scholarly and Critical Journal,* Vol. 45, No. 1, Spring 1981, pp. 79–93.

Sources

Brooks, Cleanth, Jr., and Robert Penn Warren, '''The Killers,' Ernest Hemingway: Interpretation,'' in *Understanding Fiction,* edited by Cleanth Brooks Jr. and Robert Penn Warren, Appleton-Century-Crofts, Inc., 1943, pp. 306–25.

Crane, R. S., '''The Killers,''' in *Idea of the Humanities and Other Essays Critical and Historical,* University of Chicago Press, 1967, pp. 303–14.

Ficken, Carl, ''Point of View in the Nick Adams Stories,'' in *Short Stories of Ernest Hemingway: Critical Essays,* edited by Jackson J. Benson, Duke University Press, 1975, pp. 93–113.

Flora, Joseph, *Hemingway's Nick Adams,* Louisiana State University Press, 1982, pp. 92–104.

Hemingway, Ernest, ''A Clean, Well-Lighted Place,'' in *Short Stories of Ernest Hemingway,* Charles Scribner's Sons, 1938, pp. 379–83.

———, *Death in the Afternoon,* Scribner's, 1932, p. 192.

———, ''The Killers,'' in *Men without Women,* Charles Scribner's Sons, 1927, pp. 45–56.

Martin, Quentin E., ''Hemingway's 'The Killers,''' in the *Explicator,* Vol. 52, Issue 1, Fall 1993, pp. 53–58.

Owen, Charles, ''Time and the Contagion of Flight in 'The Killers,''' in *Forum,* No. 3, 1960, pp. 45–46.

Reardon, John, ''Hemingway's Esthetic and Ethical Sportsmen,'' in *University Review,* No. 34, 1967, pp. 12–23.

Stone, Edward, ''Some Questions about Hemingway's 'The Killers,''' in *Studies in Short Fiction,* No. 5, 1967, pp. 12–17.

Stuckey, W. J., '''The Killers' as Experience,'' in *Journal of Narrative Technique,* No. 5, 1975, pp. 128–35.

Waldhorn, Arthur, *A Reader's Guide to Ernest Hemingway,* Farrar, Strauss, Giroux, 1972, p. 284.

Further Reading

Baker, Carlos, *Ernest Hemingway: A Life Story,* Charles Scribner's Sons, 1969.

Baker's authorized biography is heavily detailed and well documented and remains one of the best biographies of Hemingway written.

De Falco, Joseph, *The Hero in Hemingway's Short Stories,* University of Pittsburgh Press, 1963.

De Falco provides readings examining the psychological dynamics of Hemingway's short stories.

Griffin, Peter, *Along with Youth: Hemingway, the Early Years,* Oxford University Press, 1985.

Griffin's study, which contains a foreword by Hemingway's son, Jack Hemingway, includes previously withheld materials, including letters and stories, to document Hemingway's life through the 1920s.

Hemingway, Mary Welsh, *How It Was,* Ballantine, 1977.

Mary Welsh was Hemingway's fourth and final wife. This book is a diary-driven account of her time with him.

Wagner, Linda Welshimer, *Ernest Hemingway: Five Decades of Criticism,* Michigan State University Press, 1974.

This volume collects essays on Hemingway's novels and stories and contains George Plimpton's 1958 *Paris Review* interview with Hemingway in which the writer discusses his craft.

Young, Philip, *Ernest Hemingway,* Pennsylvania State University Press, 1966.

Young believes that Hemingway's writing is the working through of a physical wound he received in World War I. This is a serious and controversial work of criticism.

A Map of Tripoli, 1967

Marlene Reed Wetzel

2000

Marlene Reed Wetzel's "A Map of Tripoli, 1967" is a story of love between two people from very different worlds who are surrounded by portents of war and violence. The story is set in Tripoli, Libya, in the months before the 1967 Six Day War between Israel on one side and Egypt, Jordan, and Syria on the other. Wetzel noted in an interview on the Amazon.com web site that the origins of the story came from her experiences living in Libya in the 1960s and meeting a Jewish crystal salesman named Mantini. The rest of the events in the piece are fiction, according to Wetzel, although she did hear about the final incident in the story after leaving Libya.

Author Biography

Marlene Reed Wetzel was born April 5, 1937, and reared on a small, isolated ranch north of Mile City, Montana, but has also lived and worked in the Middle East. She graduated from the University of Tulsa with a bachelor's degree in English and is currently a freelance writer in Oklahoma.

Wetzel's "A Map of Tripoli, 1967" won the 2000 PEN/Amazon.com Short Story Award, an effort by the national association of literary writers and the online bookseller to discover unpublished writers. Wetzel's story was chosen the winner from among more than twelve thousand entries. Though

the events of the story are based on her experiences living in Libya in the 1960s, Wetzel did not begin writing the piece until the late 1990s. Referring to the origins of the story in an interview on the Amazon.com web site, Wetzel noted, ''The politics and grudges of the Middle East were part of my experience.'' She remembers buying a set of Baccarat stemware from a Jewish shop owner named Mantini, and she remembers hearing, after leaving Libya, about the incident that closes the story. The rest of the story is ''pure fiction,'' according to Wetzel. As part of the prize, ''A Map of Tripoli, 1967'' was published in *The Boston Book Review.*

Wetzel reported that winning the PEN/Amazon prize was ''totally unexpected'' and has generated numerous contacts from major publishing houses and agents. But, in an interview in *The University of Tulsa Magazine,* Wetzel added that some of the attention was ''not entirely positive'' and that some agents have told her that she must ''write a certain type and style of material to be marketable.'' She hastened to note, though, that some of the agents and publishing representatives have encouraged her to follow her ''natural process as a writer . . . and keep in touch.'' While ''A Map of Tripoli, 1967,'' rewritten ''at least twenty times'' according to the author, is one of her first efforts at fiction, she has since published a short story in the *Seattle Review* entitled ''Nikolas'' and set in Montana.

Plot Summary

Section 1

''A Map of Tripoli, 1967'' opens in the city of Tripoli, Libya, in the months before the Six Day War between Israel and Egypt, Jordan, and Syria. Mantini, the Jewish shopkeeper, is opening his crystal store with the help of his shop boy, Mohammed. The American woman Carla has been in town for barely a month and is navigating the narrow streets of Tripoli in her Volkswagen, searching for Mantini's shop.

While maneuvering through the streets, Carla remembers when her husband, Ben, who works at the United States Embassy, picked her up at the airport a month earlier and then immediately rushed off to an assignment in Egypt, leaving her to settle in by herself. Her husband had changed his way of speaking and his looks since Carla last saw him, and this disoriented her. She also remembers Moham-

Marlene Reed Wetzel

med coming to her house, on loan from Mantini to iron Ben's shirts. Mohammed suggested then that Carla look for crystal at Mantini's shop.

When Carla finally finds Mantini's shop, he is gracious, and she finds him charming. They talk about what crystal she is interested in buying, and he mentions Lucia. Carla expresses her sympathy for Lucia's death. Mantini sends Mohammed out for coffee, and when she drinks it Carla becomes faint from its strength. Mantini is tender with her, placing her head in his lap and putting ice cubes wrapped in a cloth on her forehead. He tells her a little about his life, how he has moved from Italy and from place to place, and how he understands how hard that is. Mantini tells her to come to him whenever she needs a friend and arranges to have her driven back to her house.

Section 2

Mantini returns to his home, Villa Cappellini, and notes that the entire household seems to be waiting for Lucia's return. Mohammed is also there, cleaning pans.

Mantini reminisces about how Ben flirted shamelessly with Lucia at a dance. At that time, Lucia was just barely pregnant, Mantini remembers. She generously sent Mohammed over to Ben's house to iron his shirts, since Carla had not yet arrived. Mantini considers Ben a "barbarian" and "affected." Now, he realizes that Ben's wife, Carla, has enlivened him after Lucia's death, and has him wanting to send flowers again.

Section 3

Ben and Carla are going to dinner at a restaurant. Ben argues with the block watcher, who asks for a few coins to watch the car while they are in the restaurant, and Carla marvels that even though Ben has lived in Tripoli for almost a year, he still does not understand that sometimes the way to get things done is through a little monetary tip, called *baksheesh*. She asks him why he has asked her to come to Tripoli since he is never around, and he answers, "It's my job." When they return to the car, a hubcap is missing.

Section 4

Carla is now having a love affair with Mantini. Once a week they meet above his shop and spend time together. He is an attentive lover and showers her with affection. One time, Mantini talks about how Lucia, after giving birth to their daughter, died the very day she came home from the hospital. He blames the doctor, Vollmer, for leaving a piece of the placenta inside her, causing her to bleed to death. Much to Mantini's dismay, Lucia's mother came quickly after Lucia's death to take the baby back to Italy.

Suddenly there is a crash in the store below, and Mantini realizes that he has forgotten to lower the gate protecting the store's windows. On one intact window the Arabic word for Jew is scrawled, and Carla asks whether this is "the beginning." Mantini responds, "No . . . It's probably the end." Carla asks whether he will leave because of the mounting tensions between the Jews and the Arabs, and he says no—but he is sure that she will leave eventually.

The next week Carla is in her car returning from Mantini's when a threatening crowd surrounds her, but the police soon come and run off the crowd. When she gets home Ben is there, to her surprise. She tells him what has happened, but he is not very sympathetic to her wanting to leave Tripoli. He asks what she was doing in that part of town and then pushes her down to the ground, scratching her wrist and causing her to bleed. "You'd better think twice before ruining my career," he says. Ben gives her a map of the city, with evacuation plans and a secret route to the airport, in case of an emergency.

Section 5

Mantini comes to Carla's house only once and asks her to leave Ben and live with him. She thinks the arrangement sounds complicated; she would have to deal not only with Mantini and Mohammed, but also with Lucia's mother in Italy, as well as the difficulties of being Ben's wife. Later, she and Mantini go to the beach.

Section 6

The Six Day War begins, and Carla is evacuated from Tripoli on a military plane. Before she leaves, she puts money in an envelope, places it on her car, and writes a note asking whoever finds it to tell Mantini that she is safe.

Section 7

Carla is now in Rome with the rest of the embassy families and other Americans living in Tripoli. She meets with Ben, who suggests that they get a divorce. She agrees.

Section 8

Back in Tripoli, Mantini leaves the Villa Cappellini, drives to his shop with a small suitcase, and has breakfast. He sits in the room above his shop, where he and Carla used to make love, and waits for the crowd to descend upon his shop.

Section 9

The time is a bit later after the evacuation, but Carla is still in Rome, working at the American Embassy and unsuccessfully attempting to get a visa to return to Libya. She goes to a dinner, where she hears someone talk about Mantini, and how a mob ransacked his crystal shop.

Characters

Ben

Ben is Carla's husband and is working in Tripoli with the U.S. Embassy. When he leaves abruptly after picking Carla up at the airport, she wonders if he is a spy "or someone who thinks he is a spy." Carla notices that some of his mannerisms have changed since she last saw him, including his style of speaking, and he sports a new moustache.

Ben is a cold man, and he and his wife do not get along very well in Tripoli. He ignores Carla and dislikes what she wears. He may also be a bit of a philanderer, as, according to Mantini, Ben made advances toward his wife, Lucia, during a party, and showed a great deal of interest in her. He is pushy and extracts an invitation from Lucia to come to Villa Cappellini for horseback riding.

Through the eyes of those around him, Ben does not seem to be comfortable living in Libya. Mantini comments that Ben "ate oysters like a barbarian," and Carla notes that he refuses to pay the "block watcher," whose practice of watching their car for small change is an accepted local custom. After Carla is evacuated from Tripoli, Ben asks her for a divorce before he returns to Washington.

Mohammed ben Massud

Mohammed is Carla and Ben's houseboy, "on loan" from Mantini for one day a week. On the other six days of the week, he works in Mantini's house and shop. He disappears from Villa Cappellini just before the Six Day War starts, but Mantini remarks that he does this occasionally—to visit his family, Mantini guesses.

Carla

Carla is the protagonist of the story, and much of it is told through her eyes. She lives in Tripoli with her husband, Ben, who is stationed there with the U.S. Embassy. When she arrives in Tripoli, she is more disturbed by what has changed with her husband than by the newness of the culture in Libya. Carla does not fit in with the other "embassy wives" and spends most of her time alone at the beach or in shops where there are no Americans.

Soon after meeting Mantini in his crystal shop and nearly passing out after drinking his strong coffee, she begins an affair with him. They meet once a week in a small room above his shop.

Carla wants to leave Tripoli when tensions mount due to the impending war between Israel and its Arab neighbors, but Ben refuses to let her, saying that her departure would harm his career. Finally, wives and families are evacuated from Tripoli to Rome, where Ben meets her and asks for a divorce. She agrees to it and stays in Rome, hoping for a way to return to Tripoli.

Gianni Mantini

Mantini, also called Il Signore, is the Jewish owner of the Cristalli crystal shop in Tripoli and Carla's lover. He is originally from Italy, but his family fled when the fascists came to power before World War II. He has lived in many countries and he speaks many languages. Before Carla's arrival in Tripoli, his wife, Lucia, died of complications after delivering their child. Lucia's mother subsequently took the child back to Italy. He lives at the Villa Cappellini with his servant, Mohammed ben Massud, and also makes wine.

From the moment Mantini meets Carla, he is very attentive and sympathetic toward her, wanting to use expensive cream on her rough hands, serving her coffee, taking care of her when she becomes faint, and offering suggestions about living in Tripoli. He dresses well and comes to Carla for their weekly tryst after his barber appointment, smelling of "the Orient."

When Arab-Israeli tensions mount in Tripoli, Mantini says he will not leave, having left where he was living too many times already in his life. During a party in Rome after she is evacuated from Tripoli, Carla hears someone speaking of how a crowd ransacked Mantini's crystal shop, and she assumes that he was most likely killed in the process.

Lucia Mantini

Lucia was Mantini's wife, who died after delivering their child. She is portrayed in the story as younger than Mantini and very attractive. Mantini tells Carla that Ben attempted to flirt with her but that she did not reciprocate. She was a generous person, as she sent her house servant, Mohammed, to Ben so that he could have his shirts ironed. The entire household still mourns Lucia's death, and she is never far from Mantini's mind.

Vollmer

Vollmer delivered Lucia and Mantini's child, and Mantini blames him for his wife's death. Mantini warns Carla not to go to him, calling him the "Nazi" because he has been in "hiding" in Tripoli since World War II.

Themes

Love and Intimacy

Carla and Mantini pursue a love affair. Their affection for each other is apparent in their actions and in what they say to each other. They keep their weekly appointment with each other to meet above Mantini's shop and spend the afternoon together, making love, listening to music, and simply being with each other. Mantini is affectionate and caring

Topics for Further Study

- There are many things the author does not reveal about the main characters in this story. Choose one of the characters and write a five-hundred-word biography covering his or her life up to the time of the story.

- Create a timeline that shows the major events occurring between Israel and its Arab neighbors from Israel's official inception as a state in 1948 to the present day. Then, create a timeline that tracks the major events in the women's rights movement from the 1960s to the present day. See how these two major historical themes from the story relate chronologically.

- Find a map of Tripoli from the 1960s and locate as many landmarks from the story as you can (the airport, Ben and Carla's house, Mantini's crystal shop). Are the street names mentioned by the author factual? Trace how Carla might have driven from her home to Mantini's shop and from her house to the airport when she evacuated the city. If you are not able to find a map from the 1960s, find a current one and see if it matches the author's descriptions or if the city has changed a great deal.

- During the 1960s, the Libyan monarchy welcomed American oil companies and other businesses. Since the 1970s, when Colonel Muammar al-Qaddafi began ruling Libya, relations between the United States and his country have seriously deteriorated. Do some research to learn the current state of U.S.-Libyan relations. Write a one-page summary of your findings.

---

toward Carla, as seen by the way he touches her, acknowledges early in their relationship that she makes him want to send flowers, and shares details of his life with her. Mantini's love helps Carla exchange her anger for "a surge of affection" for things as varied as "smiling Nubian goats" and "the decrepit king and his palace."

Mantini also remembers the love he felt for Lucia, his deceased wife. "We were very much in love," he tells Carla, and he remembers how possessive he felt when Ben once flirted with Lucia. The story opens with Mantini trying to decide whether or not to spend the day reminiscing about Lucia, and his household almost aches with her absence.

Memory and the Past

While the crux of the story takes place in the months just before the Six Day War, both Mantini and Carla spend time remembering past events. Mantini thinks about his wife almost constantly before he falls for Carla, and Carla remembers her life with Ben in the United States, when their life seemed normal. Wetzel writes, "She remembers him in the States, helping her chop onions for the stew, planting dahlias. *Jesus.*" But, as she soon begins to realize, Ben is not the same man she remembers him to be; he has changed his way of speaking, his appearance, and how he acts with her.

Rootlessness

Both Carla and Mantini have moved around quite a bit; Mantini originally because he was an Italian Jew when the fascists came to power, and Carla because she is the wife of an American official who works overseas. In the story's beginning she has a headache from "trying to concoct yet another household." At the end of the story, Carla must again leave her home when she is evacuated to Rome, and Mantini, who refuses to leave even when the conflicts over his being a Jew in an Arab country reach the boiling point, sits above his shop waiting for the angry mob to come for him.

Carla seems to be traveling lightly when she arrives in Tripoli, having brought very little with her from the United States. The furniture she buys for the empty house, "a puzzle of found material," is from a variety of places—"Scandinavian sofa, Italian floor lamps, and a rug from the Fezzan"—and she purchases the pieces with a casualness connoting no feeling of permanent ownership. One of the few things she does bring with her from America, window drapes, are not the right size, and a crate of household items brought by Ben still sits outside the house, unopened.

Carla's sense of rootlessness is heightened by her feeling that her husband has "abandoned her in this place resembling the set of a French Foreign Legion movie." When the story opens, she is lost, and she never attaches herself to anyone in Tripoli except Mantini, another rootless soul. She avoids the other wives at the embassy, having no interest in their shopping trips and tours. Her husband is always off on secret trips to unknown places, and the map that he gives her in case of an evacuation puts her on unfamiliar roads. When the evacuated wives and families arrive in Rome, they are "dropped like baggage," and when Ben sees her he acts as if Carla's having to leave another home is no big deal.

Relations between Arabs and Jews

Mantini mentions to Carla when he first meets her that he is Jewish and had to leave his native Italy when the fascists came to power before World War II. The fact that he is a Jew living in an Arabic country during a period of tense relations between these two groups creates major conflict in the story. While he and Carla are in the room above his shop one afternoon, he hears the sound of breaking glass and realizes that someone has smashed the front of his shop and written the Arabic word for Jew across the one window that was not destroyed. Mohammed has told him he should leave, but Mantini refuses to, citing the number of times he has already had to flee to another country.

The story ends with Mantini sitting in the room above his shop and waiting for the mob to destroy his shop and probably to take him as well.

Marriage

Carla and Ben's marriage is in trouble in Tripoli. She does not recognize Ben as her husband, thanks to the changes he has made in his behavior and appearance. He is cold to her almost immediately upon greeting her at the airport and unapologetically leaves her alone in a strange city while he goes to Egypt on business. His primary concern seems to be his career, and he expresses no empathy for the stress Carla is experiencing in a new city where tensions are running high.

Through Mantini's reminiscences, Ben's attentions to another woman are revealed. Whenever Ben speaks with Carla it is only to demand that she do something for or with him, as a matter of obligation. Carla tries to engage him in any kind of conversation, even an argument, but she is unsuccessful. When she considers Ben and his behavior in Tripoli, she thinks of him as acting like "he's trying to shed one skin and grow another." They are strangers to each other, and the only time they seem at peace is outside Tripoli, after the evacuation, when they have decided to divorce.

Mantini, on the other hand, seems to have had a strong and loving marriage with Lucia. He obviously adored her, for example having prepared the house with lilies and roses when she returned with their new baby.

Grief

Mantini is grieving for his wife almost immediately as the story begins. He ponders whether he will "spend the day thinking about Lucia or not thinking about Lucia" as he opens his crystal shop. His entire household is still in a deep state of grieving over Lucia's death. When he returns home after work, he notes that the horse "with animal patience . . . awaits Lucia's return." He has not removed from his bedroom the bassinet that once held his infant daughter, now in Italy with his mother-in-law. Even Mohammed joins Mantini in his grieving, hoping that "somehow they'll enter a room and Lucia's perfume will be there again."

Carla, as well, experiences grief and longing in the story. She has lost her marriage and seems to mourn for the man she thought she married, noting that Ben is the "one thing she'd expected to be reliable." Carla's grief alternates with anger, and she wonders why Ben has brought her to Tripoli. Mantini tells Carla that Ben's experiences have separated him from her.

When Carla must leave Tripoli and Mantini, she begins to grieve for those losses, as well. As she leaves the city, Carla feels as though she would like to "melt through the floor of the plane and fall spinning, down and back," already missing the place she called home for a short time. When she hears of Mantini's death, her grieving for her former lover begins, as "Her heart gives several faltering twists."

Style

Narration

The narration in Wetzel's story shifts primarily between the points of view held by Mantini and Carla. The two characters are not telling the story in first person, but the nearly omniscient narrator allows many of their thoughts to be revealed, as well as their outer actions.

In the beginning of the story, for example, the narrator describes a street scene, then narrows the view down to Mantini's as he opens his shop for the day. Finally, Mantini's desire for a "deep, cold winter to curl up in" is revealed, something that cannot be understood simply by looking at him.

In the next scene, the narrator moves a few yards away to where Carla is standing in the street, trying to figure out the location of Mantini's shop. Again, the narration describes the character's outer behavior and then moves in deeper to look at her thoughts: "The foreign woman tells herself she's not lost." The entire story is told in the third person through the eyes of Carla and Mantini; a scene is never described while looking through Ben's eyes or Mohammed's.

Foreshadowing

Wetzel uses foreshadowing to move the action along in the story and to help tie together disparate scenes. Before Carla has met Mantini, the narrator comments that a man she has not yet met will call her "my flower" in Italian. Later in the story, when they are lovers, he gives her a red hibiscus.

Throughout the story there are allusions to danger and violence, beginning with Mantini's metal gate that protects his shop. When Ben leaves abruptly for Egypt, Carla wonders if he is a spy or "a person who thinks he's a spy." After Mantini forgets to lower his shop's protective gate, and the windows are smashed, he admits to Carla that Mohammed has suggested he leave Tripoli. And when Carla comes home after having her car rocked by a crowd on the street, her husband meets her with instructions on how to leave the city in case an evacuation is necessary. Ultimately, a war erupts between Israel and Arab countries, forcing Carla to leave Libya hurriedly.

Use of a Foreign Language

In a number of places the author uses Italian or Arabic words to foster an exotic and foreign atmosphere in the story. Mantini often speaks Italian to Carla, and those words are included in the text. Because Carla knows Italian, she uses Italian words occasionally, such as when referring to the *farmacia* (a pharmacy) and when she needs to tell Mantini that she is *malato* (sick).

Arabic words for common things are often used, and Arabic and Italian place names are frequently employed. Instead of simply writing, for example, that Mantini's shop is on a street, Wetzel gives the street a specific name, Giaddat Istiklal. And when Mantini hears a prayer from a mosque, it is not just any mosque, but the Karamanli mosque.

Structure

The story is divided into nine sections. Each one, except the fourth, contains primarily one scene. The fourth section is a turning point of sorts and moves from Mantini's room, where he and Carla meet; to the street, where Mantini's storefront is destroyed; to the moment when Carla's car is surrounded by a mob; to her confrontation with Ben afterwards when she begs to be allowed to leave Tripoli. In section 5, Mantini asks Carla to leave Ben and live with him, and after that the pace of the story quickens with the onset of the Six Day War and Carla's evacuation from Libya.

Historical Context

Tensions in the Middle East during the 1960s

Hostilities between Israel and its Arab neighbors have a long history, but the more recent tensions can be traced to 1948, when Israel became a nation in an area that Palestinian Arabs claimed as their own. Fighting almost immediately ensued, culminating in the 1956 Suez-Sinai War, when Israel overran parts of Egypt. Egyptian President Nasser vowed to avenge Arab losses and mobilized Arab states against Israel. Israel preempted a joint Arab attack by launching the Six Day War on June 5, 1967, against neighboring countries Egypt, Jordan, and Syria. Almost immediately Israel gained huge amounts of territory, and by the time the war ended on June 10, Israel had captured the Sinai Peninsula and the Gaza Strip from Egypt, East Jerusalem and the West Bank from Jordan, and the Golan Heights from Syria. In a matter of a few days the capitals of all three Arab nations found Israeli troops perilously close, precipitating a quick end to

Compare
&
Contrast

- **1960s:** Many women in the United States begin to question their traditional roles in society as strictly wives and mothers. Women consider careers in areas previously dominated by men, such as medicine, law, and politics. The percentage of female medical school students in the United States increases from 5.8 percent in 1961 to 10.9 percent in 1971.

  Today: Women make up slightly more than 45 percent of the entering class in U.S. medical schools. By 2010, the American Medical Women's Association predicts, the figure will reach at least 50 percent.

- **1960s:** King Idris I, along with an elected parliament, rules Libya. The Libyan oil boom is beginning, and Libya encourages American and other foreign companies to enter the country to drill for oil.

  Today: Libya's full name is the Great Socialist People's Libyan Arab Jamahiriya. It is ruled by Colonel Muammar al-Qaddafi, who has decreed that all businesses must be owned by Libyans. The country's relationship with the United States has deteriorated in the past twenty years, and the United States no longer has an embassy in Tripoli. The country's principal resource is still petroleum.

- **1960s:** In 1967, Israel fights the Six Day War against Egypt, Jordan, and Syria, seizing large amounts of land from each of its three adversaries.

  Today: Tensions still exist between Israel and the Arab nations, and violent clashes erupt on a regular basis between Israeli forces and Arabs living in the areas annexed after the Six Day War.

the fighting. Israel more than doubled her original territory, and Israeli military swiftness and strength left an indelible impression on the Arab world.

Advances in Women's Rights in the 1960s

After many years of effort in securing equal rights, including advances during the 1800s and early 1900s resulting in women's right to vote in 1920, American women made substantial gains in the 1960s. Many refer to the 1960s as the second wave of advances in women's rights and the acceptance of feminism. In 1963 Betty Freidan published her landmark book, *The Feminine Mystique.* For this book, Friedan surveyed her female college classmates twenty years after graduation and discovered a world in which educated, middle-class women were being emotionally and intellectually oppressed. The book's popularity was said to have ignited women in their search for meaning beyond the role of homemaker. In 1966 a group of women, including Freidan, established the National Organization for Women (NOW). NOW and other similar organizations created in the 1960s sought to change laws and customs that promoted discrimination against women in areas such as property rights, employment and salaries, and sex and childbearing.

In the 1960s, many women like Carla were rethinking their roles in society, in their families, and in their marriages. Various phenomena, such as sit-ins, protest marches, consciousness-raising exercises, and groups such as NOW, challenged the commonly held idea that a woman's primary function in life was to follow her husband and accept a life focused primarily on providing a home for him. This atmosphere encouraged women to consider the possibility of pursuing independent lives and careers.

Libya in the 1960s

During World War II, Libya was the scene of intense fighting between Italian and German troops and Allied forces. After the war, the country was governed jointly by the British and the French, and it received its independence in 1952. King Idris I, along with an elected parliament, ruled Libya throughout the 1950s and 1960s.

In the 1950s, oil was discovered in Libya. The oil boom forced profound changes on the Libyan economy and society, and by the late 1960s oil production reached eighty-five million barrels a month.

In 1953, Libya joined the Arab League, an association of Arabic speaking countries whose stated purpose is to strengthen the ties between Arab countries and promote their common interests. While Libya was not a participant in the Six Day War, the country strongly supported Egypt, Jordan, and Syria in opposition to Israel after the war, through its membership in the Arab League. In fact, Libya provided financial assistance to Jordan and Egypt to help rebuild their economies after the war.

On September 1, 1969, a group of army officers overthrew King Idris' monarchy and established the Libyan Arab Republic. Colonel Muammar al-Qaddafi began his control of the Libyan government that continues today.

Criticism

Susan Sanderson

Sanderson holds a master of fine arts degree in fiction writing and is an independent writer. In this essay, Sanderson examines how Wetzel uses sense-laden prose to create a vivid setting for her short story and to delineate the choice Carla must make between her previous life and a new life.

From the first sentence of Marlene Reed Wetzel's "A Map of Tripoli, 1967," the setting of Carla's crumbling marriage and concurrent romance with the exotic Mantini is firmly foreign. The tale opens with a symphony of street sounds: "horns and radios, bicycle bells, the voice of a rooster that the pots-and-pans man keeps as a pet. . . . the call to prayer from the Karamanli mosque hangs in the air." This is a scene full of life and activity, echoed a few paragraphs down, when Carla's first appearance in the story is heralded with colors and strong images: "White light glances off buildings . . . Shadows fall thick, full of substance. . . . she's the color of a figure in a Titian painting . . . a blood-red

hibiscus in her hand." This robust use of sensual language tells the story of Carla's evolution from a woman who follows her husband, "trying to concoct yet another household," to a woman who knows she is "attractive and clever at making connections."

The scenes featuring Ben, Carla's husband, are in striking contrast to those with Mantini, her lover. The two men are almost perfect opposites. Ben's scenes are almost free from any life-affirming material, a far cry from Mantini's scenes that are played out in colors and sounds vibrant enough for a Technicolor, wide-screen movie. Despite her few protestations against Ben's dictums, all indications are that Carla, before coming to Tripoli, has played the role of the good wife. Ben's neglectful treatment of her, and the intense feelings she experiences (with and without Mantini) after coming to Tripoli, push Carla toward reconsidering her life and future. How Wetzel describes the two men in her life, and their surroundings, makes clear the choice Carla must make in order to find out who she really is.

When Ben first appears, he is meeting Carla at the airport. They have not seen each other for quite some time, but the atmosphere around their meeting is nothing short of dismal. Carla arrives in Tripoli "needing a toilet, in a room filled with ragged cats, unclaimed people and bags, an abandoned cage of birds." No doubt, she identifies with her fellow travelers in this landscape: ragged, unclaimed, and abandoned. Though there is a bird in this scene, it does not sing. Even after she finds Ben, Carla is "disoriented and dizzy," clutching her handbag and passport "desperately." Wetzel writes with a heavy hand in this passage, and there is no joy between the husband and wife, seeing each other after a long period of separation; no gentle touches or soft words are exchanged.

Compared to her lifeless meeting with Ben, Carla's first meeting with Mantini is exuberant and animated. Here, when Wetzel uses the image of cats, they are not "ragged," but are applied to describe Mantini's "graceful" way of walking. When he sees Carla he takes both of her hands in greeting, and then, "as he holds onto her arm, he thinks how nice it would be to rub her rough hands and feet . . . with something perfumed, something expensive in a beautiful jar from Paris." Carla notices Mantini, as well, "an attractive man in a suit tailored by a genius." Her senses go into overdrive, taking him in as "Dark and Levantine . . . surrounded by a lemony fragrance. . . . so unself-consciously *physical.''* The only clue as to Ben's looks is Carla's note that he has a new moustache that looks fake and as if it is going to fall off.

The images of the interiors belonging to each man also differ. In a letter to Carla, Ben has described their home in Tripoli as an exotic villa, but when she actually sees the place its reality does not match up. ''The truth,'' Carla notes, is that the villa is a ''white flat-roofed house . . . very empty.'' One of the few pieces of furniture it does contain is a rocking chair, a homey icon that mocks Carla and her lack of a stable and loving family life.

In contrast, nearly every place Mantini inhabits is alive with color and scents and sounds that connote life. When Carla enters Mantini's crystal shop, Cristalli Imports, she is greeted with the smell of sandalwood and music from a radio. At her house there does not seem to be any sound of life; the houseboy, Mohammed, chooses to bring his own radio when he comes once a week to iron Ben's shirts. Mantini's shelves are filled with ''shimmering glass,'' and when he speaks the name of a brand of crystal, ''The word rests on Carla like a jewel in a décolletage. She sees svelte women, parties, and expensive wines served in Baccarat.''

The room above Mantini's shop, where he and Carla meet each week to pursue their love affair, is also a feast for the eyes, ears, and nose. Their bed is covered with a fringed Pakistani spread, ashtrays ''overflow half-smoked Dunhills,'' a radio plays songs with such titles as ''Moonlight in Vermont'' and ''The Pines of Rome,'' and red geraniums and hibiscus ''tumble out of clay pots.'' When Mantini is with Carla in the room he smells like ''the Orient'' and tastes like almonds.

Mantini's home, Villa Cappellini, is also described in somewhat vivid terms, but they are more subdued. This is because, when Mantini first meets Carla, he is still in mourning for his wife, Lucia, who died after the birth of their daughter. But, despite the respectful air that imbues Villa Cappellini, Wetzel still paints the household with careful animation. Banana trees ''rustle,'' and the house is busy with animals and Mohammed and vivid memories of Mantini's deep love for Lucia.

Exterior scenes associated with Ben continue to be lifeless and dull. When he and Carla eat at a restaurant, the moment is riddled with images of sickness and failure. Ben argues with a man who, according to custom should be allowed to watch their car, and when they return to the car a hubcap is

> " Despite her few protestations against Ben's dictums, all indications are that Carla, before coming to Tripoli, has played the role of the good wife."

missing. Carla sees a cat that is ''crusty-eyed'' and tries to feed it, only to have Ben kick it out of the way. They are too early for dinner at the restaurant, and are alone and ''forlornly American.'' Not sufficiently nourished while eating with her husband, Carla rummages around their refrigerator at home only to find mayonnaise, leftover chicken, and ''Clorox-rinsed now-brown lettuce.''

On the other hand, her excursions with Mantini are almost luscious in comparison. They eat marinated squid, bread, and tomatoes, and drink red wine at a ''protected lagoon.'' Afterward, they dig for treasures and Roman artifacts at the water's edge, coming up with such finds as ''a piece of iridescent glass. . . . looking like a little breast.''

After months of seeing the differences between the two men, Carla moves from being a woman who is simply a helpmate to one who acknowledges her sensuality and sexuality and her power and value as an individual. She is no longer a woman who walks behind her husband, ''Middle Eastern style,'' but a woman who can, at least mockingly, call herself ''a player.'' At the end of the story she moves through a cocktail party by herself with a sense of assurance. Although she is pained by the discovery that Mantini's shop has been destroyed by a mob, and that he is most likely dead, there is a sense that she has found new strength.

Source: Susan Sanderson, Critical Essay on ''A Map of Tripoli, 1967,'' in *Short Stories for Students,* The Gale Group, 2003.

Candyce Norvell

Norvell is an independent writer who has published short fiction and often writes about literature. In this essay, Norvell discusses how the characters in Wetzel's story reflect the pre-feminist period in which the story is set.

Marlene Reed Wetzel's story is set in 1967, a few years before the modern feminist movement began gaining momentum in the 1970s. One of the things that makes Wetzel's story coherent and successful is that its characters are unfailingly true to their time. They are thoroughly and consistently pre-feminist in their attitudes and behaviors. Today's reader does not read them as modern characters, although they were created less than forty years ago and appear in a story that seems modern in many other ways, from its global air travel to its unblinking portrayal of adultery and divorce. As different as Carla, Ben, and Mantini are from one another, they have one thing in common: The idea that a woman might have as much social and economic independence as a man—as much control over her own life—never occurs to any of them.

Ben, of course, is the least sympathetic of the three. He has summoned Carla to live with him in Tripoli because it will be good for his career to have his wife at his side, in addition to being convenient to have her to oversee the house, laundry, and other domestic matters. He has not called her because he misses her, and he has not given any thought to whether she wants to live in Tripoli, what her life there will be like, or even if she will be safe there. She asks, "Exactly why am I here?" and he answers flatly, "It's my job." Her wishes and feelings are not considered, because she is a wife, which means that her life revolves around her husband's desires and his career. If the story were set today, Carla might not be free to move to Tripoli because of her own career commitments, or she might simply decline to move because of her own concerns about boredom, loneliness, or a lack of safety. Such possibilities, however, are not part of the world in which Carla lives.

Instead of introducing Carla to local culture himself, Ben gives Carla the telephone number of the embassy where he works and tells her, "They'll tell you anything you need to know." Not only does Ben not treat Carla as an equal, he does not treat her as a treasured family member or even as a valued guest. He treats her as a functionary who is there to serve him but not to inconvenience him. He shows no concern for her safety in a foreign country that is on the verge of violence, much less for her comfort or happiness.

It's not that Ben is too shallow and self-centered to realize that he cares for Carla; he truly does not care about her. When she is attacked by a mob and saved just in time by the police, Carla, under-standably, tells Ben that she wants to leave Libya. The fact that she is obviously in danger has no impact on Ben whatsoever. His answer is, "You'd better think twice before ruining my career."

Ben treats Carla rudely and callously, and Carla dislikes and disrespects him. Yet it is Ben, not Carla, who initiates their divorce. In this, as in all else, Ben leads, and Carla follows. It seems that she would have stayed with him indefinitely, regardless of how she was treated or how she felt about him, if he had not divorced her.

Mantini is a very different kind of man. He genuinely cares for Carla, as he did for his recently deceased wife. His speech and his manner are as sweet as Ben's are bitter. Mantini calls Carla *cara* (dear) the first time he meets her, and when he notices that her hands show that she has been scrubbing, he wants to rub lotion on them. When Carla becomes ill, he refuses to let her drive and provides a carriage to take her home. In direct contrast to this, Ben gives Carla a map to follow in the event of emergency evacuation. Ben predicts, correctly, that neither he nor the hired driver will be available to help Carla. He expects her to be submissive and dependent when it suits him but independent enough to take care of herself when she would otherwise be an inconvenience to him.

While Mantini's approach to Carla is gentle, warm, and caring, he, like Ben, immediately and automatically takes an authoritarian tone and position toward her. Upon first meeting her, he gives her unasked for advice that is personal and borders on being intimate, saying, "Don't go to the beach in a tiny swimsuit. . . . If you need a lady's doctor, don't go to the Nazi." He also takes physical liberties with her, putting her head in his lap when she is ill. Here his concern takes a rather brazen form. Mantini's actions clearly telegraph that he expects to do as he pleases with Carla. From the beginning, he is seducing her with complete assurance that she will be compliant. And Carla, far from being offended by his taking advantage of her vulnerability while ill and using it as an occasion for sudden physical intimacy, experiences Mantini's attentions as healing. "Her heartbeat steadies, surely due to the infusion of civility," Wetzel writes. Carla does not mind that Mantini is making all the choices in their relationship and ignoring normal social boundaries, because such behavior is what she is accustomed to. The fact that Mantini's treatment of her is based at least partly on appreciation for her is enough to make him seem a refuge in her eyes. At least

Mantini, when he looks at her, sees a human being, acknowledges and acts upon her feelings, and shows that he takes delight in her. That his behavior is inappropriate and driven partly by his own loneliness and lust is far outweighed, in Carla's mind, by his kindness.

Mantini's concern for Carla's needs and feelings is limited, however. Later in the story, Mantini encourages Carla to leave Ben and come live with him. She asks if he is proposing marriage, and he says that he is not. He explains that if he were to marry Carla, this would affect his right to see his daughter. Once again, Carla is expected to subject herself to a man's other commitments and his needs. She is expected to accept a relationship without the possibility of marriage because this is in his best interest. Interestingly, the narrator reports that Carla's response to this is not that it sounds unfair or unacceptable but that "it sounds complicated." It is as if in some vague, unarticulated way, she knows that something is not quite right here, but she is so accustomed to being a mere accessory in men's lives that she does not fully understand her discomfort.

It is easy for Carla to grasp that Ben's treatment of her is degrading, because he is cold, uncaring, and blatantly disrespectful. Mantini, though, is not as easy to read. He offers warmth and caring, yet Carla understands her position in his life enough to suspect that, if she agreed to live with him, she might end up "taking care of Mantini and Mohammed. Maybe she'd have to wash all of those heavy pots while they smoked out on the loggia." She has enough life experience to know that, whether a man is kind or unkind, her role in his life will be essentially the same.

At the end of the story, Carla is in Rome. Ben has told her of his intention to divorce her and has left. Carla has gotten a job at the embassy in Rome. A modern reader might expect that Carla has finally declared her independence—that she has decided to make a career and a life for herself. But the narrator reveals that she is remaining in Rome only in hopes of getting a visa to return to Mantini in Tripoli. When her husband leaves her, the only path Carla can see is one that leads back to another man. This, in spite of the fact that Mantini does not offer marriage and lives in an unstable, violent country far from her own—a country to which she did not want to go in the first place.

Mantini's death at the end of the story represents more than just the loss of a lover for Carla; it is

> **"** The story's abrupt ending is an apt metaphor for the void into which Carla fell when Mantini was hurled from his balcony."

the loss of the hub around which she had hoped to rebuild her life. As Mantini's appearance had steadied her heart when they met, his loss now causes her heart to give "several faltering twists." Carla is alone in a world that has not yet heard feminism's renewed call for women to be mistresses of their own fates. Her ability to maintain her balance and to find her direction in life depends on a connection to a man, because in her world a man is the source of a woman's direction. The story's abrupt ending is an apt metaphor for the void into which Carla fell when Mantini was hurled from his balcony.

Source: Candyce Norvell, Critical Essay on "A Map of Tripoli, 1967," in *Short Stories for Students,* The Gale Group, 2003.

Carol Johnson

Johnson is an instructor of creative writing, composition, and literature. In this essay, Johnson considers Wetzel's story in relation to the long-standing Middle Eastern conflict.

Marlene Reed Wetzel's "A Map of Tripoli, 1967" is the story of a woman coping with a dying marriage and a budding love affair set in a politically unstable region.

The discord of the region is reflected in the triangle of Carla, Mantini, and Ben. Just as Arabs and Jews struggle over property, Ben and Mantini struggle for its human counterpart, Carla. Woman as a commodity is nothing new in literature, and is clearly seen in "A Map of Tripoli, 1967" on the night Mantini and Ben first meet. Ben manages to move his chair close to Lucia Mantini and engages her in conversation. After dancing with her, he returns her to the table where her husband waits. Mantini then "deliberately put his hand on the back of his wife's neck. His fingers played with the gold chain against her warm, fragrant flesh to show his possession, to make the American envy him more."

"A Map of Tripoli, 1967" takes place as tensions in the Middle East lead to the 1967 Six Day War

Immediately following this statement and reinforcing the notion of women as property, the author says, "Now no one owns Lucia. She rests where he can't follow." This ironic statement also foreshadows Mantini's own death.

Multiple reminders of the trio's foreignness serve the dual purpose of foreshadowing—or providing the reader with subtle clues of events to come—future incidents in their lives and representing the adversarial positions in which many ethnic and cultural groups in the Middle East found themselves. Of the three, Carla is the person most foreign to Libya. She is foreign by nationality, by religion (we can assume that she is neither Islamic nor Jewish), and most of all, by gender. Her difference is emphasized repeatedly early in the story. As she makes her way to Mantini's crystal shop, she is referred to as the "foreign woman." Conflicting sights and sounds assault her senses, reminding her that she is a stranger in a strange land. She parks her car "behind a string of camels tied up near Cathedral Square." The incongruity of this combination is reinforced when Carla marks her return path by observing a red bidet (an apparatus much like a toilet, designed for washing one's genitals) showcased in a shop window. While seeing a bidet

in the bathroom of a home or hotel would not be unusual, seeing one (and a red one at that) in a shop window is. Because red is associated with passion and a bidet is associated with genitals, we can interpret the sight as foreshadowing the affair Carla and Mantini will soon embark upon. The city is also a cacophony of sounds that seem out of place to Carla. A discordant mix of "horns and radios, [and] bicycle bells" would pass unnoticed in most urban areas, but the distinctive sound of a rooster crowing in the city would be unusual.

In addition to what Carla sees and hears, her foreignness is apparent physically. The author describes her as being the color of a "titian" painting in a land of darker skinned people. Titian was a sixteenth century painter known for his use of color. Because Mantini cautions her against the sun, her skin is probably quite fair. Carla's behavior marks her as foreign also. In a country where women are treated more like men's property than their equals, she does what other women do not—she travels around the city alone. Her solitude is emphasized by Wetzel's description of the "embassy wives who travel as one sun-hatted flock." Her difference is again emphasized as she makes her way to Mantini's shop for the first time. One of the Arab men who "squat against shop fronts, smoking" notes her passing by making wordless clicking sounds. These sounds can be construed as disapproving or disrespectful since they precede the description of her as being light skinned.

Ben is also foreign, but he occupies a particular niche in that he is male and in the country in an official capacity. He apparently changes personalities with places, developing an accent here, growing a mustache there. He lives in Libya as if the Libyan people were there to serve him, or at the very least, as if they should adapt to his ways. His tunnel vision is illustrated when he and Carla go to the *Ristorante Piemontese.* Although he has been in the country far longer than Carla, he refuses to play by the rules natives have set down. In order for his car to be protected while he and Carla dine, he needs to give a small amount of money to the "block watcher." He refuses, and as a result returns to find a hubcap stolen. Further evidence of Ben's foreignness is in Mantini's observation that he "ate oysters like a barbarian." It seems that Ben does not so much adapt to the country as he adapts to an image of himself in that country. Again seen through Mantini's eyes, Ben is a man "working at being more interesting than he really was, affected, wearing an Englishman's tidy little mustache."

Ben's behavior and his relationship with Carla foreshadow violence. Sometimes this foreshadowing is in the form of language synonymous with fighting. For example, when Ben argues with the block watcher at the *Ristorante Piemontese,* we see his "hands . . . in the air quarreling." Shortly afterward, Carla "wants to pick a fight [with Ben], better in her estimation than silent hostility." The silent hostility between the two is echoed by the fermenting antagonism in the Middle East.

It is ironic that Mantini, who is male and more closely resembles the Libyan people, is the character who dies. He is a Jew, however, and it is that difference that will result in his death. Wetzel illlustrates Mantini's foreignness and the danger inherent in it in subtle ways. First, Carla sees his masculine appeal and notes that he is "unselfconsciously *physical,*" a trait she attributes to his Mediterranean background. Libya, too, is on the Mediterranean, but we know Wetzel associates Mantini's sexuality with his Italian background because he has been speaking to Carla in Italian. Second, when Carla makes her initial visit to the crystal shop, she wears a dress with a rooster on the

"
'A Map of Tripoli, 1967' illustrates the reality of the personal and the global: There are no easy solutions."

front. The sexuality and fertility represented by the rooster connect it to Mantini, but it is also representative of Mantini's difference. Just as the rooster Carla heard earlier seemed out of place in the city, Mantini, a Jew, is out of place in an Arab country. Regardless of how long he might remain, he will always be Jewish, never Arab. The association between Mantini and the rooster is cemented at the end of the story when Carla hears of Mantini's death and pictures him as an "elegant rooster."

Mantini's occupation as a Jewish shopkeeper who sells crystal also foreshadows coming violence. The merchandise he sells evokes images of the Holocaust, the attempted extermination of the Jewish people by the Nazi regime prior to and during World War II. The beginning of that tragic period in history is traditionally traced to an event referred to as *Kristallnacht,* or Night of Broken Glass, when all the synagogues in Germany were set on fire, windows of Jewish shops were smashed, and thousands of Jews were arrested. *Kristallnacht* is echoed when Mantini's window is smashed and the word "Jew" written on the remaining window.

Mantini provides another important element that suggests impending war when he gives the novel *Exodus* to Carla. Published in the 1950s by Leon Uris, *Exodus* details the relationship between an American woman and an Israeli freedom fighter during the struggle for Palestine. The word "exodus" is generally synonymous with flight from oppression and danger. More specifically, it is a term for the flight of Jews from Egyptian slavery, as told in the Old Testament book by the same name. The title not only foreshadows Carla's own flight from Tripoli but also brings to mind Mantini's previous flights from persecution.

Each character in the story exhibits some degree of the stealth and deceit necessary in any planned act of violence. Both Mantini and Carla comment on Ben's underhanded manner. Carla knows Ben would rather attack from behind than talk face to face about their problems. In addition, although Ben's letters to her describe a villa, what Carla finds is a "white, flat-roofed house with high ceilings." Mantini tells Carla of his first meeting with Ben, describing the way Ben insinuated himself into Lucia's good graces, whispering secrets to her and "stealthily maneuvering his chair closer to Lucia." In a different conversation, Mantini places Ben's deceptiveness in a larger context when he surmises that the American "learned state secrets, yes? He probably knows every detail of the Libyan government. . . . Certainly about Israel." Ben is also compared to a serpent, the original Judeo-Christian deceiver. He is pictured as snake-like, "trying to shed one skin and grow another;" related to this image is Carla's belief that her husband is "wearing someone else's personality." She wonders if Ben is a spy or perhaps just "a person who thinks he's a spy," thus deceiving even himself.

Carla and Mantini deceive Ben as they conduct their love affair, but Mantini, like Ben, is guilty of self-deception. In Mantini's case, however, this deception is far more dangerous than Ben's. As part of a family forced to flee persecution more than once, he should be aware of the dangers of being Jewish in an Arab country. Nevertheless, he refuses to leave, even going so far as to "laugh and laugh" at the suggestion. His self-deception not only cost him his life, but that of his wife. He no doubt knew about Nazis from World War II, yet he allowed his pregnant wife to be treated by a Nazi physician, who failed to perform an essential task in delivering a child—making sure the placenta had been completely removed. Finally, Mantini has a metal gate designed to protect his shop and merchandise, yet he sometimes neglects to put it in place.

Wetzel, in "A Map of Tripoli, 1967," has created a work that is intricately constructed and resistant to over simplification. She has avoided placing blame for the troubles in the Middle East and also avoided placing blame for the demise of Ben and Carla's marriage. In the same way Jews and Arabs must take equal responsibility for violence past, present, and future, Mantini, Carla, and Ben must each bear a certain amount of responsibility for the breakup of a marriage. "A Map of Tripoli, 1967" illustrates the reality of the personal and the global: There are no easy solutions.

Source: Carol Johnson, Critical Essay on "A Map of Tripoli, 1967," in *Short Stories for Students,* The Gale Group, 2003.

Sources

Fishback, Doug, "On the Map," in the *University of Tulsa Magazine,* Winter 2000, pp. 28–29.

Wetzel, Marlene, "A Map of Tripoli, 1967," at *Amazon.com,* http://www.amazon.com/exec/obidos/tg/feature/-/44460/suspensenet/002–0069686–1784843 (last accessed November 5, 2002).

Further Reading

Faqih, Ahmad, ed., *Libyan Stories,* Kegan Paul International, 2000.
    Ahmad Faqih has collected thirteen stories by various prominent Libyan writers, which were published during the 1970s and 1980s in the London magazine *Azure.*

Mattawa, Khaled, *Ismailia Eclipse: Poems,* Sheep Meadow, 1997.
    Khaled Mattawa immigrated to the United States from Libya in 1979, when he was fifteen years old. His poetry is rooted in both United States and Arab cultures.

Vandewalle, Dirk, *Libya since Independence: Oil and State-Building,* Cornell University Press, 1998.
    This book supplies a detailed analysis of Libya since 1951 based on the author's work in Libya and on interviews with some of the country's most important officials.

Naming the Names

Anne Devlin

1986

''Naming the Names'' appears in Irish writer Anne Devlin's collection of short stories, *The Way-Paver*. Like much of Devlin's work, the story is set during the recent conflict in Northern Ireland. In 1969, a civil rights campaign by Catholics, who are in the minority in Northern Ireland, led to riots in Derry and Belfast. The British Army was sent to both cities to keep the peace between Catholics and Protestants (who form the majority). The Irish Republican Army (IRA) began a terrorist campaign to force the British out of the province and unite the north of Ireland with the Republic of Ireland in the south. Nearly three decades of violence has ensued.

In ''Naming the Names,'' the protagonist is Finn, a young Catholic woman in Belfast who gets caught up in the sectarian conflict. When she forms a friendship with a young Englishman who is studying the history of Ireland, her romance tragically intersects with her commitment to the republican cause. ''Naming the Names'' is a story about love and betrayal and the complex web of history that draws so many people into murderous conflict. Ultimately, Finn is forced by her own conscience to face up to her own guilt and take responsibility for the death she caused.

Author Biography

Anne Devlin was born to a Catholic family in Belfast in 1951. She is the daughter of Paddy Devlin, a member of Parliament for the Social Democratic and Labor Party. Devlin was raised in Belfast, lived for a short while in Andersonstown, Northern Ireland, and then left Northern Ireland for England. She was visiting lecturer in playwriting at the University of Birmingham in 1987, and a writer in residence at the University of Lund, Sweden, in 1990.

Devlin's work includes short stories and plays, most of which center on the lives of Catholic women during the period of civil disturbance in Northern Ireland which began in 1969. Devlin's short stories were first published in the early 1980s, and nine of them were collected in *The Way-Paver* in 1986. The collection includes the story "Passages," which won the Hennessy Literary Award for Short Stories in 1982. Devlin adapted this story for BBC television as *A Woman's Calling* (1984), and she won the Samuel Beckett Award for Television Drama in 1984.

The Way-Paver also included "Naming the Names," which Devlin adapted as a radio play in 1984 and for BBC television in 1987. It has been shown on public television in Canada and the United States. Devlin also wrote the television plays, *The Long March* (BBC 1984) and *The Venus de Milo Instead* (BBC 1987). She adapted D. H. Lawrence's novel, *The Rainbow* for BBC television (1988), and Emily Brontë's novel, *Wuthering Heights,* for Paramount Pictures (1991).

During the 1980s, Devlin also had success as a playwright for the stage. In *Did You Hear the One About the Irishman* (1981), a Protestant girl and Catholic boy conduct a love affair in spite of death threats from paramilitary forces. *Ourselves Alone*, about the lives of Irish women involved with Irish Republican Army (IRA) men, opened at the Royal Court Theatre Upstairs, London, in November, 1985. The title is a translation of Sinn Féin, the name of the political wing of the IRA. The play was acclaimed by critics in England and was produced in the United States in 1987 at the Kreeger Theatre/ Arena Stage in Washington, D.C. It won the Susan Smith Blackburn Prize and the George Devine Award in 1985.

Heartlanders, a community play to commemorate Birmingham's centenary, followed in 1989 at the Birmingham Repertory Theatre. *After Easter* opened at the Other Place, Stratford, in 1994. It has been called a feminist drama; it features an Irish woman who has religious visions and believes she can stop the violence.

Devlin's most recent work is the screenplay *Titanic Town* (Company Pictures, 1998). The screenplay is adapted from a novel by Mary Costello and is set in the Belfast back streets of the 1970s.

Plot Summary

"Naming the Names" begins on a late August day in Belfast, Northern Ireland. The narrator, Finn, arrives at her place of work, a used bookstore in the Falls, a Catholic area of the city. She is late and is thinking about the fact that a young man she knows has not called her in three weeks. Her supervisor Miss Macken gives her a job to do; it is just a routine day at the store.

A flashback follows, as the Catholic Finn recalls how she first met this young Protestant man. He was a graduate student at England's Oxford University, and he was doing research in Irish history. Finn helped him to obtain the books he needed. They became friends and used to meet twice a week in a café. They eventually began a tentative love affair, even though Finn had a boyfriend, Jack, and the young man had a girlfriend, Susan, in Oxford.

Back in the bookstore in the present, Finn hears the latest gossip from her co-worker Chrissie, who gets it from Mrs. O'Hare, the cleaner, who appears to know everyone's business. Mrs. O'Hare alludes to the sectarian troubles in the city when she tells them that a Protestant employee is being transferred from their area to somewhere else. Chrissie disapproves of this because she thinks it will start to create a Catholic ghetto.

On her own again, Finn reflects on her relationship with Jack, whom she has not seen for a long time. He is an English journalist and is currently visiting the United States.

Next, Finn hears that her young historian friend has called her and left a message with Chrissie. Finn calls him back. Then she recalls the first time she took him back to her house.

That evening, Finn meets her friend in the park. She is nervous and her stomach is in a knot. He explains why he did not call for a while. Because he lived in England, he thought their relationship was not very satisfactory and he did not want to be unfair to her. He tells her he is getting married at the end of the summer. Finn walks away from him and goes home, wishing she had ended the romance earlier.

The next morning at work, Miss Macken and Chrissie discuss the news that a man was murdered in the neighborhood the previous night. The victim was Finn's young English friend. At lunch time the police arrive and question Finn. Finn tells them that on the afternoon of the previous day, she told a man she knew who came to the bookstore that she could ''get him to the park.'' The implication is that the person she refers to is the murdered man, her own friend. The police escort her past her bewildered co-workers and interrogate her at the police station. She refuses to give the names of her accomplices, responding only with a list of place names. She does tell the police, however, how she got involved in terrorist activity.

She first goes back to what happened when the troubles in Belfast began, in mid-August, 1969. She was showing Jack around the Falls Road area. There had been a riot the previous night as Protestants and Catholics clashed. The following night, the riots were worse. Stores were set on fire and several people were killed. As Catholics and Protestants massed for further violence, Finn discovered that her grandmother, with whom she lived, had been hurt by flying glass in her house on Conway Street. She visited her in the hospital, and the following morning she saw that the British Army had arrived to keep order.

Finn was shaken by this but she did not get involved in a terrorist organization until two years later, in 1971. She was on vacation with Jack in Greece when she heard that the British had introduced internment of suspected terrorists without trial and for an unlimited period. When she returned to Belfast, she visited a man she knew and asked if there was anything she could do. Her first job was to help deliver money to the wives of the men interned.

However, Finn will give the police no information about others who may have been involved in the murder. At one point, she faints and dreams of her grandmother. When she recovers, she is questioned again about the names but she just gives a list of the street names of West Belfast.

Jack visits her and says he cannot forgive her for what she has done. The police interrogate her

again, but her response is always the same. She will not name the names, and it may be that she does not know any.

The story ends with a hint that Finn feels some guilt about what she has done, and she does not try to evade responsibility for her acts.

Characters

Chrissie

Chrissie is one of Finn's co-workers at the bookstore. Talkative and clothes-conscious, she is in charge of the crime, western, and romance exchange section.

Eileen

Eileen is one of the down-and-outs who congregate at the bookstore. She and Isabella quarrel and fight.

Harry

Harry is a drunk from the St. Vincent de Paul hostel who often takes refuge in the bookstore. Miss Macken throws him out.

Isabella

Isabella is one of a group of down-and-outs who kill time in the bookstore. She wears black fishnet tights.

Miss Macken

Miss Macken is Finn's boss at the bookstore.

Sharleen McCabe

Sharleen is a young girl who goes to the bookstore to borrow murder mysteries for her grandmother.

Jack McHenry

Jack McHenry is Finn's English boyfriend. He is a newspaper journalist. Finn first met him in 1969, when Jack was reporting on the riots in

Media Adaptations

- "Naming the Names" was adapted for BBC television in 1986 and starred Sylvestra Le Touzel as Finn McQuillen.

Belfast. Jack is a practical man and does what is necessary to take care of Finn, but they do not seem to communicate on a very deep level. Finn says she never talks to him about anything important, and she does not appear to have much romantic feeling for him. They drift apart. Jack goes to the United States on what is supposed to be a six-month trip, but tells Finn he does not expect to come back. Ever practical, he offers to send her some money if she needs it. After Finn is arrested and in police custody, Jack returns and visits her. He reproaches her for what she has done. This appears to be the first time he has ever criticized her.

Finn McQuillen

Finn's name is an abbreviation of Finnula. She appears to have been raised largely by her grandmother, even though her parents were still alive. When she is asked why she lived with her grandmother, she replies that her parents' house was too small. Her father died when Finn was eight or nine years old, and she left school when she was about sixteen. This was in 1969, after the riots and after meeting Jack. Before that, she admits that she led a promiscuous lifestyle. It was clearly not a happy childhood.

In 1971, the Catholic Finn became involved with the terrorist organization, the Irish Republican Army, because she was shocked at the British government's internment without trial of suspected terrorists. Her first job was to deliver money to the wives of the men who were interned. By then she had found a job in a used bookstore, where she became the Irish specialist, knowing every book in that section.

Finn is a quiet, introverted woman and does not reveal much to her friends or co-workers about her personal life. Her young English friend calls her a dreamer. Sometimes she drifts off into her own world—childhood memories often—and people think she is not listening to them. She goes through the summer hardly noticing what is going on around her. Since her grandmother died, she appears to have had no family life at all, and she still lives in her grandmother's house, which she has kept mostly unchanged.

She gives no reason why she betrayed her friend, although she does seem to feel guilty about it. She was faced with a conflict between loyalty to a political cause and loyalty to a friend, and she chose the former.

The Murdered Man

The young man who is murdered is never named. He is tall and fair with dark eyes; Chrissie says he looks like a girl. He is writing a thesis on Irish history at Oxford University, and he spends the summer in Belfast. He meets Finn when he goes to the bookstore searching for books for his studies. Finn begins to feel romantically towards him, and he appears to reciprocate, even though they both have romantic attachments elsewhere. In his behavior towards Finn, the young man is straightforward, open, accepting, and kind. He says he loves Finn, even though he is to marry Susan, his girlfriend. The young man is singled out for murder because his father is a judge, and this means that in the eyes of the Irish nationalists, he represents the British authorities.

In the television adaptation of the story that Devlin wrote for the BBC, the young man is named Henry Kirk, but this name does not appear in the story.

Mrs. O'Hare

Mrs. O'Hare is the cleaner at the bookstore who is also the town gossip.

Themes

Cultural Loss and Preservation

Finn regrets the loss of her childhood world. The Belfast that she once knew has vanished, and she recalls it in loving detail. She remembers the candy store where she bought a tin of barley sugar as a present from her grandmother for her father. She recalls the color of the tin and how it was wrapped. She also recalls her days spent playing in the park; the sights and sounds of the bacon shop where she waited for someone to escort her across the road; and the skipping song which named the streets of west Belfast.

Those streets contained the whole world for her. As the police walk her down a block where there used to be a babyclothes store and an undertaker, she observes: ''Everything from birth to death on that road. Once. But gone now—just stumps where the buildings used to be—stumps like tombstones.'' The destruction of the world she remembers is a partial explanation for why she feels so lost and disconnected from life. It is a manifestation of a desire to escape from the complexities of the present.

Finn's ploy of reciting street names to her interrogators rather than the names of others in the terrorist organization is therefore at once a way of deflecting their questions and also preserving, at least in her own mind, a familiar but now vanished world. The litany of street names, of places rapidly disappearing, is a lament for and a protest against the devastation of a close-knit community by the twin forces of civil conflict and modernization: ''Redevelopment. Nothing more dramatic than that; the planners are our bombers now. There is no heart in the Falls these days.''

Loyalty and Betrayal

The story explores the theme of loyalty and betrayal at several levels: the personal, the familial, and the political. The core conflict is between Finn's affection for her unnamed English friend and her loyalty to the cause of Irish nationalism. Although she chooses the latter, it causes her some distress. This is shown by how she feels in the park on the night she betrays him. Her stomach is in knots and she confesses that she is in love with the man. She is touched by his romantic words to her (something she probably never received from her boyfriend Jack), and refers to him as her ''last link with life.'' After she leaves the park, she tries to forget, to make her mind blank and shut out what she knows is going to happen. Perhaps part of her reason for betraying him (which she may not even admit to

Topics for Further Study

- Research the history of Ireland in the twentieth century. Much of the conflict has been over the question of whether Britain should retain control of Northern Ireland, or whether there should be a united Ireland under Irish control. What are the arguments for and against a united Ireland?

- Can terrorism ever be justified? What makes people resort to terrorism? Why did terrorism emerge in the early 1970s in Northern Ireland, and why did it decline in the mid-1990s?

- Research the British policy of internment without trial of suspected terrorists in Northern Ireland, from 1971 to 1975. What are the similarities and differences between internment as practiced by the British and the detainment of suspected terrorists linked to the al-Qaeda network by the United States? In either case, was or is internment without trial, evidence, or conviction justified?

- By refusing to name her accomplices, Finn shows more loyalty to them than she did to her friend whose murder she brought about. Why do you think this is? Is Finn a very mixed up kid or a young woman with high ideals?

---

herself) is that she is piqued by the fact that he allowed three weeks to go by without calling her. If so, it was her petty resentment rather than her political idealism that cost her friend his life.

Another form of loyalty is to the family and its traditions. Finn is pulled in two directions here also. Although she chooses to act in solidarity with a political cause she believes in, and which seems to be in keeping with her Catholic family heritage, she seems also to want to reject that heritage and be free. This is seen in her dream of her grandmother, who seizes hold of her and will not let her go, in spite of Finn's struggles to free herself. This suggests an unconscious rebellion against her grandmother that is not otherwise apparent. Everything else in the story suggests Finn's loyalty to her. For example, she keeps the house much as it was when her grandmother was alive, complete with its Catholic artifacts. It was also through her grandmother's stories that Finn learned of the Irish history that she now desires to shape.

Style

Imagery

When Finn's friend visits her house, he notices a large spider's web that stretches all the way from the geraniums in the window to a pile of books and then to the lace curtains. Finn tells him that according to her grandmother, a spider's web was a good omen: ''It means we're safe from the soldiers.'' She may be referring to the web of social support (safe houses and the like) that the Catholic republican activists and terrorists received from the local population. If a wanted man disappeared into the web of houses in the Catholic areas of Belfast, he was not likely to be found by the British authorities.

The image of the spider's web also suggests the way in which everyone in Belfast, Protestant and Catholic, young and old, the politically committed and the politically indifferent, are caught up in the web of conflict. This web embraces the innocent as well as the guilty, which is why the young Englishman, who bears no responsibility for anything that happens in the province, can still fall victim to warfare.

When Finn dreams of her grandmother, and there is a fierce struggle between them, she may be trying unconsciously to escape this destructive web. But it appears that she cannot. The spider's web image returns twice at the end of the story. Alone in the police cell, Finn watches a spider spinning a web in the corner of the room. Then in the final paragraph, as Finn reflects on how she came to be in this situation, the implications of the image are made explicit: ''The gradual and deliberate processes weave their way in the dark corners of all our rooms.''

Narrative Technique

The story is not told in a straightforward linear fashion. It consists of short sections, many of which are flashbacks to earlier times in Finn's life. For example, the story begins in the bookstore, then flashes back to Finn's first meeting with her English friend, then returns to the present and the bookstore, then flashes back again to Finn's relationship with Jack, and so on. This back and forth rhythm continues for most of the story.

Because of the convoluted form of narration, the story may sometimes seem disconnected, but eventually all the parts are seen to be linked into a whole, like many threads of a web. Since the image of the spider's web is central to the story, this may well be one of the reasons that Devlin chose to tell the story in this form.

Historical Context

Ireland and Home Rule

Catholic Ireland had been dominated by Protestant England since the sixteenth century. In the first third of the 1600s, the English sent out one hundred thousand Protestant settlers who were loyal to the British crown. The settlers colonized mostly the northern part of Ireland, and are the ancestors of today's Protestants who wish to maintain their link with Britain. English dominance of Ireland was secured in 1690, when the Protestant English king, William of Orange, was victorious over the Catholic James II at the Battle of the Boyne. James had been trying to regain the English throne.

In the nineteenth century, there was a strong movement towards home rule for Ireland. The Irish leader in this campaign was Charles Stewart Parnell. Parnell, who was himself a Protestant, headed a group of Irish members of the British parliament who pledged themselves to the repeal of the Act of Union between Britain and Ireland that had been passed in 1800.

The British prime minister, William Ewart Gladstone, supported home rule for Ireland and prepared Home Rule Bills in the 1880s. But these failed to pass into law. In the story, this is the period of Irish history that Finn's young English friend is researching at Oxford University.

After the failure of the movement for home rule, nationalist feeling in Ireland continued to grow. In 1916 came the Easter Rising. Irish nationalists in Dublin proclaimed the Irish Republic and for five days fought against British troops before being forced to surrender. Fifteen leaders of the rebellion were executed.

Compare
&
Contrast

- **1970s:** The sectarian conflict in Northern Ireland is at its height. A political power-sharing agreement between Protestants and Catholics collapses. The IRA conducts bombing campaigns in England, and also assassinates Lord Mountbatten, Queen Elizabeth II's cousin, in August 1979 by blowing up his fishing boat. The same day, a bomb explodes in South Armagh, Northern Ireland, killing eighteen British soldiers. It is the largest death toll in one day since the troubles began. Protestant paramilitary groups carry out acts of terrorism against Catholic targets.

  1980s: In 1981, IRA prisoners in Belfast's Maze Prison begin a hunger strike. They demand to be classified as political prisoners, with prisoner of war status. During the hunger strike, one of the strikers, Bobby Sands, is elected to the British parliament. The British government refuses to yield to the strikers' demands and ten of them die, including Sands. The strike causes anti-British feeling internationally, particularly amongst the Irish community in the United States. American donations to the IRA triple. An Anglo-Irish agreement in 1985, which gives the Irish Republic a limited role in the affairs of the north, fails to stop the violence, which flares up on both sides again between 1987 and 1989.

  Today: After faltering movements towards peace in the mid-1990s, a peace agreement is finally signed in 1998. A new 108-member Northern Ireland Assembly is created, with responsibility for running the province. A North-South Ministerial Council is created made up of leaders from Northern Ireland and the Irish Republic, to discuss matters such as the environment, tourism, and transportation. The Irish Republic gives up its territorial claims to Northern Ireland. The peace agreement meets with many obstacles, but remains intact. In 2001, a momentous step is taken when the IRA finally begins to decommission its weapons, as called for under the agreement.

- **1960s:** Education in Northern Ireland is almost entirely segregated. Protestants who control the local education boards insist that the compulsory instruction in religion should be Protestant. Catholics boycott the state system, and 98 percent of Catholics attend Church schools. Compared to Protestant schools, these schools are underfunded, have high teacher/student ratios and produce inferior results.

  1980s: Inspired by the All Children Together Movement, which was founded in the late-1970s, the first integrated school in Northern Ireland is established in 1981. By 1989, there are ten integrated schools.

  Today: In January 2002, there are forty-six integrated schools throughout Northern Ireland. However, the fourteen thousand students who attend them comprise only 4 per cent of the school population. The vast majority of children still attend segregated schools.

- **1960s:** Protestants dominate political life in Northern Ireland in part because of the practice of gerrymandering (manipulating electoral boundaries to favor one group over another). Gerrymandering occurs for example in the local government of Londonderry, the city that will later change its name to Derry. Although Protestants are in the minority, boundaries are drawn so that Protestants hold a majority on Derry City Council.

  1970s: The British government reorganizes local government in Northern Ireland. Elections are held in 1973 to elect 526 councilors to the 26 new District Councils. Voting is by the system of proportional representation, which ensures representation according to the proportion of the vote won. In Derry, Catholics win a majority on the City Council.

  Today: In Northern Ireland's new 108-member National Assembly, Protestants are allocated sixty-six seats, while Catholics get forty-two seats. This is in proportion to their numbers in the population. However, the Assembly can make no decision without the support of the majority of Catholics and Protestants.

However, strife with the British continued. In 1920, Britain sent a force known as the Black and Tans to assist the Royal Irish Constabulary in suppressing Irish nationalism. The Black and Tans were a makeshift force composed largely of unemployed World War I veterans. Numbering two thousand men, they were ill-trained for the task they were asked to perform and gained a notorious record for brutality. The memory of the Black and Tans has been passed on generation after generation in Ireland, which is why in the story Finn hears about them from her grandmother.

In 1922, Ireland finally won its independence, although this did not include the entire island. Ireland was partitioned into the mostly Catholic Irish Free State in the south and Ulster in the north. Ulster was predominantly Protestant, and remained part of the United Kingdom.

In 1932, Eamon De Valera, who had been one of the leaders of the Easter Rising, became president of the Irish Free State. In 1937, the Free State changed its name to Eire, and in 1949 it became the Republic of Ireland.

Northern Ireland and "The Troubles"

In 1967, the Northern Irish Civil Rights Association was set up to counter discrimination against Catholics in employment, housing, and political representation. In the shipyard in Belfast, for example, only four hundred of ten thousand employees were Catholics. Nonviolent protest marches were held, but in Derry in 1968 the marchers were subject to attacks by Protestants and the Royal Ulster Constabulary (RUC). Rising tensions finally exploded in August, 1969, when rioting erupted in Derry following the annual Protestant Apprentice Boys parade. The ensuing conflict between Catholic residents and the RUC, as well as Protestant loyalists, went on for two days and became known as the Battle of the Bogside. The following day, riots broke out in Belfast. Many Catholics (including Finn's grandmother in the story) were forced from their homes. After two days of disorder in which many people were killed and injured, British troops were sent to Derry and Belfast to keep the peace.

In September, 1969, a "peace line" was constructed between Catholic and Protestant areas of Belfast to try to prevent rioting. This is the peace line referred to early in the story (the library administrators do not want their staff crossing the peace line when they go home at night). Later, a more

substantial "peace wall" was built. It separated the Protestant Shankhill Road area from the Catholic Falls Road in west Belfast.

In December 1969, there was a split in the Irish Republican Army (IRA). The splinter group became known as the Provisional IRA, which was abbreviated to the Provos, as Chrissie refers to them in "Naming the Names." The original IRA became known as the Official IRA. It was the Provos who carried out most of the terrorist attacks that were soon to follow. The aim of the IRA was to force the British out of Northern Ireland and create a unified Ireland.

In August 1971, the British government introduced internment in Northern Ireland. This meant that suspected terrorists could be arrested and jailed indefinitely without trial. In "Naming the Names," this event so shocks Finn that she begins to help the IRA. On the first day of internment, 342 men, almost all of them Catholics, were rounded up and imprisoned. Internment, however, did nothing to quell the violence. Riots immediately broke out in Derry, Belfast, and other towns in Northern Ireland, and within three days twenty-two people had been killed. Internment also created a groundswell of sympathy for the IRA cause among the local Catholic population. It also helped the IRA to raise funds.

The following year, 274 people were killed in violence related to the political situation. Britain increased its troops in the province to 22,000. In one incident on January 30, 1972, British troops fired on demonstrators after an anti-internment rally in Derry. Fourteen civilians were killed, none of whom was armed. The tragedy became known as "Bloody Sunday." Two months later, Britain suspended the Northern Irish parliament and imposed direct rule on the province from London.

Critical Overview

In general, Devlin is better known as a writer of plays than of short stories, and *The Way-Paver*, the volume in which "Naming the Names" appeared, did not attract much critical attention. However, "Naming the Names" became Devlin's best-known story when she adapted it as a play for BBC television in 1987. Since then, assessments of it have cropped up in a number of books and articles about the work of contemporary Irish writers. In her book *The Living Stream: Literature and Revisionism in Ireland,* for example, Edna Longley noted that the story focuses on Finn's "mixed familial, sexual and political emotions" and that "Her mantra of street names . . . represents a lost childhood stability." In *Fortnight,* Elizabeth Doyle, reviewing the television adaptation, also commented on the naming of streets in the story: "The naming is a creation through language of the Belfast of her childhood, which is being dismantled all around her by the bombers and planners." And Susanne Greenhalgh, in "The Bomb in the Baby Carriage: Women and Terrorism in Contemporary Drama," offered the view that the streets of Belfast that Finn recites "themselves commemorate an imperialistic military past and encode the maze of a violent history from which there seems no escape."

The subject and themes of "Naming the Names" are also typical of Devlin's work as a whole. All the stories in *The Way-Paver* feature a young first-person female narrator, and several are concerned in some way with the Irish situation. Like "Naming the Names," they also deal with romance and intimate relationships. In many of them, dreams play a part, as they do in "Naming the Names."

The conflict in Northern Ireland and its effect on women is also the subject of many of Devlin's plays. In her 1981 play, *Did You Hear the One About the Irishman,* a Protestant girl and Catholic boy fall in love, and *Ourselves Alone* (1987) features three women who are involved passively or actively with the IRA.

Criticism

Bryan Aubrey

Aubrey holds a Ph.D. in English and has published many articles on twentieth-century literature. In this essay, Aubrey analyzes Finn as a woman pulled between two worlds and also discusses the involvement of women in the Irish Republican Army during the conflict in Northern Ireland.

In her article, "Women, War and Madness," Elizabeth Doyle states that "Ambiguity about identity is a constant preoccupation in [Devlin's] work." The question of identity is particularly apparent in "Naming the Names." In a time of civil unrest, Finn, the protagonist, is a confused young woman, pulled in different directions by sexual, romantic, familial,

political, and religious pressures that disturb her deeply and eventually lead her astray.

The odds are stacked against Finn from the beginning. For some reason that she never satisfactorily explains, she was raised by her grandmother, even when her parents were still alive. This may in part have been due to that fact that her grandmother and her father were involved in a feud over her father's choice of wife. But this also is unexplained.

Whatever the circumstances of her early life, at the age of about fifteen or sixteen, Finn was clearly unhappy. She sought security and love in sexual relationships. Until she met her boyfriend Jack, she was, as she puts it, "screwing around like there was no tomorrow." She left school at the age of sixteen, when she might have been expected to stay on for two more years. The fact that she received six "O-level" passes suggests her intelligence. (O-levels, an abbreviation for Ordinary Levels, were the exams taken by all British schoolchildren of that era at the end of the equivalent of tenth grade in an American school.)

Perhaps the most significant thing about Finn's childhood was the fact that her grandmother had strong connections to Irish nationalist history. She passed this on to her granddaughter, awakening in Finn a strong interest in Irish history. Her grandmother told her of how she met Eamon de Valera, one of Ireland's greatest freedom fighters, and she passed on stories of the hated British Black and Tans. After her grandmother's death, Finn retained in her house a framed photograph of Countess Markievicz. Markievicz was one of the leaders of the Easter Rising in 1916, and she served several prison terms for her involvement in the nationalist cause. Finn's grandmother visited Markievicz in prison.

Thus is the link created between Finn and Irish history. She herself gets a reputation at the bookstore for her knowledge of the subject. But the burden of it, the weight of the accumulated past, proves too much for her to carry. She feels the enclosing, stifling pressure of living in a city that is so beholden to the past, a city that nurses such ancient grievances. Much of this comes out in an unconscious way. Most significant is her nightmare, in which her grandmother grabs her hands and tries to pull her out of her bed. Finn resists fiercely and there is a desperate struggle between them. It is as if she is wanting to escape the world in which she was

The 1969 riots in Belfast set the scene for Anne Devlin's ''Naming the Names''

born and raised, and yet she cannot acknowledge this in her conscious mind. Later, when she is left alone in the police cell, she remembers the dream, and even the memory of it is powerful enough to cause her to faint.

This is clearly a young woman who is pulled between two worlds. The other world that tugs at her is the one that might be expected. Like any young person, Finn wants romance and love; she responds like any girl would when her lover says things like, ''Your soul has just smiled in your eyes at me—I've never seen it there before.'' But what Finn failed to realize when she first took up with this young Protestant man from England was that her two worlds would soon, inevitably, be on a collision course. She was already assisting the IRA, but what that organization would eventually ask her to do (or perhaps it was even she who instigated the plot) was not then within the bounds of her imagination. Indeed, she thought she was safe in other ways too. Since both she and the young man had lovers, she thought there would be no complications in their relationship.

Given the stifling and dangerous world in which Finn lives, it is clear that she does not have the maturity to navigate her way through it successfully. Much of the time, Finn is closed in on herself,

emotionally speaking. She does not confide much in others, or say a great deal, even to her lovers. She is introspective and good at controlling her feelings—at least it must appear that way to an outside observer—but she is also given to violent outbursts in which she throws things across the room (as she does in her quarrels with Jack for example). And she sleepwalks through the summer of her romance virtually unaware of what is going on around her. She is ''like one possessed.''

Finn drifts inevitably to the fateful moment when personal loyalty, love, and affection are thrown aside in one terrible act of betrayal; the social and political cause in which she believes is given priority over the individual right to live. Although Finn makes a victim of her lover, who has nothing to do with the Irish conflict except in his misfortune of having an English judge for a father, it is hard to escape the conclusion that Finn is a victim too. As Susanne Greenhalgh puts it in her article, ''The Bomb in the Baby Carriage: Women and Terrorism in Contemporary Drama,'' ''[Devlin's] women characters are depicted as passive victims of a history they cannot control, even when they are themselves agents of terrorism.''

After she is tried and no doubt convicted of conspiracy to murder, Finn will join the many

What Do I Read Next?

- *Ourselves Alone,* first produced in 1987, is Devlin's best known play. Set in Northern Ireland, it explores the lives of three Catholic women who are involved with IRA men. The women are presented as being capable of much richer lives than the men, many of whom are unfaithful, abusive, and emotionally immature.

- Seamus Heaney, a Catholic born in largely Protestant Northern Ireland, is Ireland's foremost contemporary poet. His *Opened Ground: Selected Poems, 1966–1996* (1998) contains many poems that allude to the violence in Northern Ireland, especially the selections from *North,* his 1975 collection.

- In *Belfast Diary: War as a Way of Life* (1995), Chicago journalist John Conroy gives a vivid account of what it was like living in Belfast during the violence of the 1980s. Conroy lived there during this period, among the people most

affected by the conflict. He gives clear explanations of what the "Troubles" are all about, and why they have their roots deep in history.

- *Hope against History: The Course of Conflict in Northern Ireland* (1999), by American journalist and historian Jack Holland, describes how the conflict that began in 1969 eventually produced a perception on both sides that violence was counterproductive and had to stop. Holland credits Protestant, Catholic, and IRA leaders, as well as President Bill Clinton, for their contributions to the peace settlement of 1998.

- William Trevor's story "Lost Ground," in his collection of stories, *After Rain* (1996) gives insight into the deep divisions that exist between Catholics and Protestants in Northern Ireland. It revolves around a Protestant boy who believes he has been visited by a Catholic saint.

---

women who were imprisoned in Armagh Prison for Women during the Northern Ireland troubles. The involvement of women with the IRA was not especially unusual at the time. Although the actual job of planting bombs and killing was usually carried out by men, there were exceptions. One was the practice, alluded to in the title of Greenhalgh's article, of placing a bomb under a baby in a carriage. The woman who volunteered for this task would then push the carriage through an army checkpoint. Since soldiers were unwilling to rummage around inside the baby carriage, they let the woman pass. She would then grab the baby and make a run for it, leaving the bomb to go off. Elizabeth Shannon, who reports this risky tactic in her book, *I Am of Ireland: Women of the North Speak Out,* points out acidly that usually it was not the woman's own baby whom she pushed through the checkpoint.

Even the way Finn arranged her lover's death was not too dissimilar to a number of incidents that took place in the early 1970s. Some of the first

British Army deaths in Northern Ireland came when four soldiers were lured to a Belfast house by four Irish women they met in a pub. The unspoken promise was that the women would make themselves available for sex. Once the unsuspecting soldiers were in the bedroom, a male accomplice of the women emerged from a closet where he had been hiding and shot all four soldiers dead.

Some of the women who were imprisoned emerged unrepentant after completing their prison sentences. Shannon interviewed Mairead Farrell, who came from Belfast and served ten years in prison, from 1976 to 1986, for possession of explosives and membership in the IRA. Farrell told Shannon that she "would bomb or kill again in a minute if called upon to do so."

Although "Naming the Names" does not follow Finn through the years of her imprisonment, it seems unlikely that she would echo Farrell's statements. She may have been able, after her fatal

> " Finn drifts inevitably to the fateful moment when personal loyalty, love, and affection are thrown aside in one terrible act of betrayal; the social and political cause in which she believes is given priority over the individual right to live."

meeting with her friend at the park, to return home "without looking back," but eventually look back she must. Her conscience will not let her rest, and the moving conclusion to the story suggests that she is ready to face up to what she has done. When she comes to examine "the gradual and deliberate processes [that] weave their way in the dark corners of all our rooms," she does not fully understand what drives them. She does not understand how or why history, including the history in which she was caught up, takes the shape it does, why the web is spun the way it is, but she does know that "when the finger is pointed, the hand turned, the face at the end of the finger is my face, the hand at the end of the arm that points is my hand." And she is also ready to admit, "I only know for certain what my part was, that even on the eve, on such a day, I took him there." In other words, Finn now seems willing to accept her guilt as an individual who wronged another individual, rather than to justify her behavior as being in service of a political ideal.

Today, when terrorism is very much in the public mind and there are people, in the Middle East and elsewhere, who are ready to place their political cause above the rights of innocent individuals to go about their lives undisturbed, "Naming the Names" seems especially relevant. Occasionally, real life stories of terrorists and their victims echo the ending of Devlin's story. American journalist Laura Blumenfeld, for example, in her recent book *Revenge: A Story of Hope*, tells of how she wrote to a Palestinian terrorist who shot and wounded her father in a random attack in Jerusalem in 1986. The terrorist, who was serving a prison sentence in

Israel, at first justified his act as part of a legal attack on what he called the Israeli occupation. Like Finn, he felt that the rightness of his cause justified the killing of an innocent civilian. But later, after Blumenfeld visited him, he dropped his ideological and political justifications, apologized to Blumenfeld and promised never to commit a violent attack again. Like Finn, he too must have seen the finger pointing, not at an external enemy, but back towards him, the doer of the deed, the one who must answer for it.

Source: Bryan Aubrey, Critical Essay on "Naming the Names," in *Short Stories for Students,* The Gale Group, 2003.

Joyce Hart

Hart has degrees in English literature and creative writing, and she focuses her writing on literary themes. In this essay, Hart explores the sometimes transparent, sometimes concealed foreshadowing of events that appear throughout this short story.

In some ways, Anne Devlin has created her short story "Naming the Names" in the form of a murder mystery, inviting the reader to take on the role of the detective. She throws hints along the way, enticing readers to answer all the questions. These clues, however, are not easily detected even during a careful first reading. Most readers will have to make their way to the end of the story before the clues to the final outcome become fully comprehensible, thus making a second reading even more deeply appreciated.

The foreshadowing commences with the first line of the story. If the reader is to believe the protagonist, Finn McQuillen, the list of names presented represents the names of streets. This may be true. However, there is hidden meaning in the street names. Whether this is a coincidence or a conscious plan by Devlin is not clear; but by choosing these specific streets, a certain complex shadow casts itself on the reader's mind, providing clues as to the state of Finn's mind even before her clandestine activities are disclosed.

For instance, the first group of names includes Abyssinia, Belgrade, and Bombay, three names that bring to mind British colonial rule. Alma and Balaclava are names of British military regiments. Bosnia, of course, brings images of ethnic cleansing. Later names include Gibson, Granville, Garnet, and Grosvenor, which one character mentions as being names of people involved with British foreign policy. The name Theodore could refer to the Abyssinian king who fought against the British army.

Names are very significant and very prominent in this story, but there are also more subtle clues and references throughout this story. For instance, Finn mentions that the used bookshop had at one time been an old cinema and that the only movie she remembers seeing there was *A Town like Alice.* This movie is about a British woman who becomes a prisoner of war during World War II. It is also a love story, a love torn apart because of the war, thus possibly referring to Finn's own love affair. The message of the film is that one woman discovers that she can make a difference in the world, a theme that Finn might use to justify her involvement in the rebellion.

Another subtle foreshadowing involves the young girl who comes into the bookstore in search of murder mysteries. ''I want three murders for my granny,'' the girl states. Since Finn mentions her own grandmother several times in this story, there is an association between this young customer and Finn. When the girl chooses the book *Murder in the Cathedral,* she is told that it is not, in fact, a murder mystery but rather a book about martyrdom. How else would Finn describe her own role in the IRA other than to use the term ''martyrdom''?

One more subtle clue, cited in the same part of the story, is a statement by Miss Macken, the manager of the bookstore. She yells out to Finn, ''Finnula, the Irish section's like a holocaust! Would you like to do something about it.'' Of course, Miss Macken is referring to the book section on Ireland. The books are probably out of order. However, her statement is right on target with Finn's life. Finn probably believes that the British involvement in Ireland is like a holocaust, and she is determined to do something about it. This is not known by the reader at this point of the story; but it is as if, through incidents such as these, that Devlin projects Finn's most inner thoughts onto the external reality, allowing the other characters to fill in the void created by Finn's silence about what she is doing.

Finn's political involvement is also foreshadowed with the mention of two books on orangeism, a movement throughout the United Kingdom that promotes Protestantism and an adherence to British

> Of course, in this story, Finn turns out to be the spider. She spins her web then lures the young man into it, where he is finally captured and sacrificed for the cause."

rule. Orangeism is at the heart of the conflict between Catholics and Protestants in Ireland. Finn's first contacts with the young man, with whom she will become most intimate in this story, involves his search for two classic works on orangeism. Finn volunteers to hunt down these books.

It is during this same part of the narrative that Finn makes a curious statement, a statement that makes no sense until later on, closer to the end of the story. As she and the young man are negotiating the purchase of these books, she says, ''I looked at the name and address [of the young man] again to make sure.'' On first reading, one might either miss this statement or might ask what she meant by ''I looked at the name and address again to make sure.'' What is she making sure of? The young man's name and address have nothing to do with the books, except that she might have to mail them to him. However, why would she have to make sure of his address to send books there? She's not asking him to repeat his address to confirm it, she's merely re-reading it. Of course, at the end of the story it is revealed that she recognized the address as being the residence of the young man's father, a judge—a man the IRA was after. Her making sure of the address implies that she wanted there to be no mistake that the young man standing in front of her was the judge's son.

In future meetings between Finn and her young man (who is never given a name), it becomes obvious that they each favor a different side of the conflict between Irish Catholics and Irish Protestants. He mentions his research work on William Gladstone, who fought for but lost home rule for the Irish, the defeat of which the young man describes as a rational one on the part of the Protestants, and she mentions Eamon De Valera, an Irish hero who fought against British colonial rule. Later, she also mentions Countess Constance Markievicz, a woman who fought for Irish independence. Although the surface narrative appears to be bringing the young man and Finn closer together, linking them first in a sexual relationship and eventually showing Finn becoming emotionally involved with him, the undercurrent between them exposes that they live on opposite poles of the political world in which Finn is immersed, thus foreshadowing the events that will soon unfold.

At one point, one of the clerks at the bookstore where Finn works responds to the young girl who is still trying to locate murder mysteries for her grandmother. ''This is just too, too grisly,'' Chrissie said, examining the covers. ''Do they always have to be murders? Would you not like a nice love story?'' The young girl replies, ''She doesn't like love stories. . . . She only likes murders.'' These statements, upon a second reading of this short story, appear somewhat prophetic. Finn is given a chance to love. She falls for the young son of the judge and is momentarily torn between her love and her commitment to the IRA. If the young man had loved her in return, maybe his life would have been spared. Maybe he did love her, but not enough, for in spite of his feelings for Finn, he is to be married to another woman. Upon his telling her that he is to be married, Finn turns her back on him, thus also choosing murder over love.

Finn also talks about a previous affair that she had with a young man named Jack. She describes him:

> Jack was always extremely practical: if you killed someone he would inform the police, get you legal aid, make arrangements for moving the body, he'd even clear up the mess if there was any—but he would never, never ask you why you did it.

Finn's reference to her being involved in a murder could also foreshadow the murder of the other young man in Finn's life. There is irony in her statement, however. Not only is Jack not there when Finn gets involved in the murder, but when he does show up, he does none of the things that Finn had predicted he would do. He does not try to help her by getting her legal aid, and the only reason he reappears is to ask her why she did it.

After meeting the judge's son at the bookstore, Finn takes the young man to her apartment, where he notices an enormous spider web. ''Good Lord. Would you look at that web; it looks like it's been there for donkeys!'' he comments. Finn tells him that she likes spiders. ''My granny used to say that a spider's web was a good omen. It means we're safe from the soldiers!'' Of course, in this story, Finn turns out to be the spider. She spins her web then lures the young man into it, where he is finally captured and sacrificed for the cause. She justifies her actions, believing that she is helping to make Ireland safer from the British soldiers, just as her grandmother had justified keeping the webs as a good omen.

Close to the end of the story, on the day of the young man's murder, Finn is walking to the park, where she had met him in the past, when she hears footsteps. She states ''I always listened for footsteps.'' This is the statement of someone who is either a bit paranoid, or someone who is leading a secretive life, a life in which she does not want to be followed. At this point in the story, it is not yet revealed that she is involved with the IRA, so her fears foreshadow events yet to come. ''I'd walked all through those streets at night but I had never been afraid until that moment'' she relates. This statement sets up the tension of the moment. Things unmentionable are lurking in the dark. Things that she is aware of but, in some way, does not want to know about and definitely does not want to tell.

Finally, there is the scene in which she is running away from him. She's thinking that it all should have ended before she became so involved with him. The words ''should have ended'' predict his death, not the break-up of their relationship. Her words, ''He was my last link with life and what a way to find him,'' are understood only after the realization of who he is and of what the consequences of his death imply. Then she describes his murder, though the reader remains unaware of the significance of the images that she is depicting:

> a car screeches to a halt: a lone dog barks at an unseen presence, the night walkers pause in their walk past— the entry. Whose is the face at the empty window?— the shadows cast on the entry wall—the shape in the darkened doorway.

Immediately following this passage, she awakes from a dream to the sound of screeching brakes that mimic a human voice calling her name in anguish ''Finn!'' Her young lover is dead, a fact that the reader will not know until later in the story, when most of the shadows will be illuminated, at least partially. Although Finn mentions that she was awakened by the screeching brakes, she remains lost in her dream, connected only by a thin thread to the world around her; through the naming of names, not the names of her fellow terrorists but rather by naming the names of the streets, ordinary things, on the surface only.

Source: Joyce Hart, Critical Essay on "Naming the Names," in *Short Stories for Students,* The Gale Group, 2003.

Allison DeFrees

DeFrees is a published writer and an editor with a bachelor's degree in English from the University of Virginia and a law degree from the University of Texas. In the following essay, DeFrees discusses Irish author Anne Devlin's shifting use of time to create foreshadowing in her short story.

Like a dream or an unsolved mystery, Anne Devlin's story, "Naming the Names," demands that her readers fill in the blanks. Devlin creates suspense through the omission of detail, by flipping back and forth through time, offering eddies of information that must be parsed together to understand the full picture. She does not bury the reader in detail; instead, she hints at the historical background of the play, allowing it to frame the story with a whisper. It is a subtle telling of a tale, in which every instance of dialogue, each seemingly innocuous detail of a person, place, or time takes on significance as the story progresses. By the end, Devlin has woven a web so intricate that it is only by reexamining the story that the reader begins to peel back the layers of the narrator's tale.

The story is a delicate marriage of language and shifting time, and by manipulating time, Devlin is able to manipulate her reader, as well. The first person narrator meanders through vignettes from her past in a seemingly unrelated, stream-of-consciousness sequence. But, as the story progresses, the reader begins to see that it is a carefully constructed story and that the narrator is parsing out information in an attempt to delay the admission of a crime. Finn chooses what to tell, and when to tell it; the facts are bundled into non-linear units, as discrete details that keep the reader in suspense. It is as if she wants to create sympathy before admitting what she has done, or at least, to give her reader the full story, so as to judge her on the merits of the facts as she chooses to present them.

The story begins with a list of names, written in alphabetical order. The next two lines place the reader in proximity of three different time periods: "It was late summer—August, like the summer of the fire. He hadn't rung for three weeks." Immedi-

> ❝ It is a subtle telling of a tale, in which every instance of dialogue, each seemingly innocuous detail of a person, place, or time takes on significance as the story progresses."

ately, the reader is sensitive to the importance of time. These three time frames become the three periods between which the narrator jumps as she relates her version of the story. The first time period is ostensibly the present—the end of summer, August—which encompasses the days leading up to her capture and questioning by the police. The second time period—the summer of fire—invokes memories of the narrator's past, specifically, her former lover, her grandmother, and the history of her involvement with the IRA. And, the third time period—suggested by the phone call three weeks prior—covers the period during which she met and fell in love with the English journalist whom she later leads to his death. How these three time periods weave together and build to the climax becomes the unifying thread of the story.

After placing the reader in a specific time, the narrator enters the story, talking about the late summer referenced a few sentences earlier. The narrator, who we soon learn is a woman, Finnula McQuillen, describes various employees and patrons of the second-hand bookstore where she works, in West Belfast. She goes into great detail about characters who are later to have little or no import to the main thrust of the plot. However, they offer clues about the historical backdrop of Finn's story and also create a present time, so that Finn has a starting point from which to diverge and piece together, at will, her story. After greeting her coworkers and noting some of the vagabonds who regularly populate the bookstore, Finn and some of coworkers take a break. As they walk along the street, they gossip about the neighborhood.

> 'Quincey's being transferred to Ballymacarrett when the library's reopened.'
> 'Och, you don't say?'

'It's the new boss at Central—that Englishwoman. It's after the bomb.'
'But sure that was when everybody'd gone home.'
'I know but it's security, you know! She doesn't want any more staff crossing the peace line at night. Not after that you—but wait till you hear—he won't go!'
'Good for him.'
'He says he's been on the Falls for forty years and if they transfer him now they might as well throw the keys of the library into the Republican Press Centre and the keys of the Royal Victoria Hospital in after them.'
'He's quite right. It's ghettoization.'

In the span of a short conversation, Devlin creates a vivid picture of the political backdrop of the story. A bomb blew up the local library. Peace is a loosely-held commodity. The women talking are anti-English and anti-Republican, and they fear they are being forced into poverty and despair. Finn states that the events occurring are ''inevitable,'' but Chrissie retorts, ''It's not inevitable, it's deliberate.'' Finn then notes that ''security works both ways,'' intimating that where the Republicans enforce security measures on them, they will retaliate. The conversation ends, but the tension is left hanging in the atmosphere of the story.

Finn makes it clear that the women she knows are loquacious, lower-class, and gossipy. ''There was little on Falls Road that Mrs. O'Hare didn't know about.'' ''After that, Chrissie left us to go down the yard to renew her suntan.'' ''Oh here! You'll never guess what Mrs. McGlinchy at the bakery told me—.'' These women talk almost constantly when they are present in the text. Thus, the fact that, when Finn whispers to a customer, ''I think I can get him to the park,'' they say nothing, hints at ominous events. And later, when police are escorting Finn away from the bookstore for questioning, all of the people in the store and along the street see her with the officials and grow silent, again, the reader senses that something serious is about to be relayed. But what that thing, or event, is has only been proffered in hints and whispers. There are no answers; only questions and conjecture.

When describing her first encounter with the journalist with whom she falls in love and whom she later betrays, Finn writes: ''Senior: Orangeism in Britain and Ireland; Sibbett: Orangeism in Ireland and throughout the Empire. Ironic. That's what he was looking for the first time he came in.'' Finn tells us that the fact that he is looking for a book on orangeism is ironic, but offers nothing more. The reader is left to wonder at the possible political

ramifications of his interest in orangeism, and at Finn's possible relation to it, and to read on. Finn meets the journalist at a café to deliver the book a few weeks later. He is effusive with thanks, and Finn tells the reader, ''And so it started.'' Just what started is not relayed. Both of them are dating other people, ''[s]o there didn't seem to be any danger.'' There didn't seem to be any danger of what? The paragraph seems to hint at the beginning of a love affair, but only vaguely does the reader gain a sense, later elaborated, that Finn is actually describing the beginning of events that would culminate in the British journalist's death.

Finn returns to the chance meeting with the journalist throughout the story, describing bits and pieces of their ensuing relationship. This story is scattered between Finn's telling of the events of the present day, through a series of flashbacks. One strain of the story describes how Finn offers to betray the journalist for the Irish Republican Army and lures the journalist to a park the next night, where, after she admits her love for him and is rejected, she walks away, leaving him to his death. Interspersed between these segments are memories of Finn's time with the journalist—how they met to talk about books and life, how they shared their first kiss, when she first brought him to her home. She also hints, and later, more explicitly explains to the police investigators after the journalist's body is discovered, that a love affair between them had ensued. What she does not tell the investigators, but hints at to the reader, is that the affair lasted even until the last night of the journalist's life.

Was Finn's betrayal an act of revenge? A political act? Her story makes it difficult to discern, but based on the version of history that Finn offers her readers, it appears that the act was inevitable—because the British journalist's father was a judge, he was a target of the political group of which Finn was a part, and he was destined to be murdered, whether or not Finn had a hand in it. She tries to convince the reader that she actually aided his life, rather than his death, when she writes: ''I could not save him. I could only give him time.'' And again, when she is being questioned by the police, she explains that it was not her choice to have him killed. One of the investigators asks her, ''Why did you pick him?'' She replies, ''I didn't pick him. He was chosen.'' From this, it becomes clear that Devlin had foretold the journalist's death earlier in the story, when the women at the bookstore were all gossiping about a dead body that was discovered that morning. Chrissie, another employee, pointedly says, "Oh, Finn, it's awful news," and later says, "[w]e knew him. . . . That young man. The one who looked like a girl. . . . They said it was because he was a judge's son." Devlin reintroduces the women from the bookstore to both reflect on and foreshadow events. The fact that Chrissie addresses Finn with condolences hints that Finn had personal knowledge of the man who died; however, a page later in the story, the reader learns that Chrissie had been present when Finn had told the customer at the bookstore that she could lure the man to the park. Suddenly, it is not clear what Chrissie is intimating when she says, "Oh, Finn, . . ." as she is turning to look at Finn. And earlier in the story, Finn described the journalist when she first saw him: "a young man, tall, fair, with very fine dark eyes, as if they'd been underlined with a grey pencil. . . ."—very much the picture of "one who looked like a girl." Finally, Chrissie connects the death of the young man everyone is discussing with Finn when she mentions that he was a judge's son; a few pages later, Finn tells the police investigators, "It was his father they were after. He's a judge." The reader knows that the British journalist is the man who died; that Finn led the journalist into the park, where he was later killed; and that she voluntarily approached the IRA man with the information that "I think I can get him to the park." But there the clarity ends, and a mass of contradictions make it difficult to discern truth, motive, or facts. As Finn writes at the end of the story:

> The gradual and deliberate processes weave their way in the dark corners of all our rooms, and when the finger is pointed, the hand turned, the face at the end of the finger is my face, the hand at the end of the arm that points is my hand, and the only account I can give is this: that if I lived for ever I could not tell: I could only glimpse what fatal visions stir that web's dark pattern, I do not know their names. I only know for certain what my part was, that even on the eve, on such a day, I took him there.

It is difficult to trust the narrator because she slyly deceives the reader at every turn, hinting at what is to come but never, even at the end, divulging the whole story. That she led the journalist to his death is certain, but because the narrator is not omniscient, the reader only gains a single perspective on the situation, and so is left to pursue final judgment through inferences and conjecture. Was Finn guilty of a political crime, a crime of passion, or both? The adage states that "only time will tell," but Devlin seems to be making the case that, when trying to discern what is real, and what is true, not even time reveals the answers.

Through her narrator's tale, Devlin eloquently points out that it is difficult to ever know the truth of things, to ever be able to sit down and write a history that "tells the whole story." There is no whole story, only tales, bits and pieces, versions of facts, and the inevitable passage of time.

Source: Allison DeFrees, Critical Essay on "Naming the Names," in *Short Stories for Students,* The Gale Group, 2003.

Sources

Anderson, Lisa, "Anne Devlin," in *Irish Playwrights, 1880–1995: A Research and Production Sourcebook,* edited by Bernice Shrank and William W. Demastes, Greenwood Press, 1997, pp. 93–96.

Blumenfeld, Laura, *Revenge: A Story of Hope,* Simon & Schuster, 2002.

Doyle, Elizabeth, "Women, War and Madness," in *Fortnight,* No. 334, December 1994, pp. 37–39.

Greenhalgh, Susanne, "The Bomb in the Baby Carriage: Women and Terrorism in Contemporary Drama," in *Terrorism and Modern Drama,* edited by John Orr and Dragan Klaic, Edinburgh University Press, 1990, pp. 160–83.

Longley, Edna, *The Living Stream: Literature and Revisionism in Ireland,* Bloodaxe Books, 1994, p. 93.

Shannon, Elizabeth, *I Am of Ireland: Women of the North Speak Out,* rev. ed., University of Massachusetts Press, 1997, p. 122.

Further Reading

Brown, Terrence, *Ireland's Literature: Selected Essays,* Barnes & Noble Books, 1988.
    The most relevant chapter in this collection of essays is the final one, "Awakening from the Nightmare: History and Contemporary Literature," in which Brown discusses how Northern Ireland's poets and writers have interpreted the recent phase of their country's history. In the work of Frank McGuiness, Stewart Parker, and Brendan Kennelly, Brown sees signs of an openness to new interpretations of the past.

Devlin, Bernadette, *Price of My Soul,* Knopf, 1969.
    Devlin took part in the early civil rights protests in Derry and became the youngest person ever to be elected to the British parliament. She was twenty-one when elected in 1969. Her vivid autobiography covers the early days of the civil rights movement in Northern Ireland.

Lojek, Helen, "Difference without Indifference: The Drama of Frank McGuiness and Anne Devlin," in *Eire/Ireland,* Vol. 25, No. 2, Summer 1990, pp. 56–68.

Lojek analyzes Devlin's play, *Ourselves Alone,* as an example of radical feminism which posits the superiority of female values.

Sales, Rosemary, *Women Divided: Gender, Religion, and Politics in Northern Ireland,* Routledge, 1997.
The focus of this book is on the interrelation between gender and religious inequalities in Northern Ireland. Topics covered include the impact of the conflict in Northern Ireland on women; labor market inequalities; women and politics; and women and the peace process.

Sternlicht, Sanford, *A Reader's Guide to Modern Irish Drama,* Syracuse University Press, 1998.
This volume contains a useful introduction to Irish history and its literary and theatrical traditions. It features short articles on twentieth century Irish plays and playwrights, including the work of many contemporary dramatists, such as Devlin.

Nightfall

Isaac Asimov

1941

In 1941, John W. Campbell, Jr., editor of the premier science fiction magazine at that time, asked one of the fledgling writers he mentored an intriguing question: What would happen if people saw the stars only once every thousand years? He postulated that people would go mad and asked twenty-one-year old Isaac Asimov to write a story about it. The result was ''Nightfall,'' now one of the most famous science fiction stories of all time. Originally published in *Astounding Science Fiction* in 1941, it now appears in dozens of anthologies, but is perhaps most easily found in *Nightfall and Other Stories* or another of Asimov's own anthologies *The Best of Isaac Asimov*.

To describe a population to whom the appearance of stars would be a rare phenomenon, Asimov created the planet Lagash where there are six suns and perpetual daylight. With no nighttime, the stars cannot be seen and therefore are not known. Astronomical science has not yet reached the point of being able to look beyond the suns. The concept of darkness is mysterious and frightening. However, scientists at Saro University are predicting a total eclipse of all the suns at once. They are aware, based upon archaeological studies, that civilization seems to have been destroyed about every two thousand years, the same time period of the occurrence of the eclipses. If the two are related, will the darkness once again cause a hysteria that will destroy the world? As the scientists prepare for calamity, they are joined by a newspaper reporter, and all hope to

save future generations from fear through a record of factual knowledge. However, a religious cult is also predicting the phenomenon as a judgment against evil. "Nightfall" is a psychological thriller as scientists fight ignorance, zealotry, madness, and their own fears of the unknown.

Author Biography

Born in Russia on January 2, 1920 to Judah and Anna Rachel Berman Asimov, Isaac Asimov and his family moved to Brooklyn, New York, when he was three. He became a naturalized citizen in 1928. His parents owned a series of candy stores where Asimov worked until he left college. Having taught himself to read before he was five, Asimov voraciously read all the magazines the store carried. An extraordinary student, he graduated from high school when he was only fifteen years old. He sold his first story when he was eighteen. Graduating from college with a degree in chemistry in 1939, Asimov then received a master's degree in 1941 and a Ph.D. in 1948, all from Columbia University. During World War II, he worked in the U.S. Naval Air Experimental Station, and then served from 1945 to 1946 as a corporal in the Army.

In 1941, Asimov wrote "Nightfall," the story that was later voted best science fiction story of all time by the Science Fiction Writers of America. By 1958, he virtually retired after nine years of teaching biochemistry at the Boston University School of Medicine to devote his time to writing. However, he maintained a lecturing position at the university and was granted a full professorship in 1979 in recognition of his contributions to science education through his publications.

In his lifetime, Asimov published over 500 books and numerous articles on a wide variety of subjects including science fact and fiction, mystery, history, autobiography, poetry, and even guides to Shakespeare, Gilbert and Sullivan, and the Bible. He was noted for a unique ability to translate complex subjects into understandable language for the average reader, and he wrote for every level from preschool through college. It was Asimov who, with his editor John W. Campbell, Jr., formulated the three laws of robotics that dominated his robot and science fiction detective stories and influenced the image of robots throughout science fiction.

Included among numerous awards that Asimov received are: a Special Hugo Award (the highest honor from the World Science Fiction Convention) in 1962 for his articles in Fantasy and Science Fiction, another Hugo for Best All-Time Series in 1966 for his Foundation Trilogy, a Hugo and a Nebula (Science Fiction Writers of America) Award in 1973 for *The Gods Themselves*, a Hugo and a place on the New York Times Best Seller List in 1982 for *Foundation's Edge*, a Hugo and a Nebula in 1977 for best short story for *The Bicentennial Man* (later made into a movie starring Robin Williams), and a Hugo in 1995 for best non-fiction book for *I, Asimov*.

Asimov married Gertrude Blugerman in 1942. They had two children, David and Robyn, but were divorced in 1973. That same year, Asimov married Janet Jeppson, a psychiatrist who collaborated with him as a writer. A compulsive writer, he usually worked seven days a week from 7:30 a.m. until 10:00 p.m. Asimov died of heart and kidney failure on April 6, 1992.

Plot Summary

"Nightfall" is a story about a planet that does not experience nightfall except once in every 2,049 years. With six suns, Lagash otherwise exists in perpetual sunlight. In the course of describing the last four hours before darkness covers all, Asimov explains how a rare eclipse is able to blot out all the light and why the event always results in universal chaos. This feat he achieves by placing the story in the Observatory of the scientists who are able to predict the coming phenomenon. Aton 77, the aged director of Saro University and chief astronomer, is preparing to try to record the eclipse and whatever follows so that there will be scientific evidence to explain what has happened.

On a planet where darkness is unknown, the expectation is that everyone will go insane from fear and claustrophobia, and that in their fear they will try to burn anything that will catch fire in order to produce light. Archaeological evidence has shown that about every 2,000 years, on at least nine different occasions, whole civilizations have disappeared. The assumption is that the fires get out of hand and everything is destroyed in the chaos of madness. To prevent the panic and help people prepare so that they might survive the next eclipse, the scientists are determined to leave proof of the real reason for the coming of the darkness. In the meantime, a group of Cultists has also predicted the loss of the sunlight, but as a night of reckoning and fire produced by stars. The astronomers have never seen stars because of the brightness of the suns. They think that stars are just a myth perpetuated by religious fanatics to scare people into moral behavior.

Besides the team of astronomers, a faculty psychologist named Sheerin 501 and a newspaper reporter, Theremon 762, wait in the Observatory. They review the research that has led to the prediction of the eclipse and the subsequent madness. It was discovered, only ten years after the Universal Theory of Gravitation was finally formulated and accepted as law, that the expected orbit of Lagash is not in accord with the mathematics of the theory. This observation led to the conclusion that the law was valid, but there was an unknown factor pulling on Lagash, probably another planetary body. When Beta is the only sun in the sky and this moon passes in front of it, the total eclipse occurs.

In addition to the scientific evidence Sheerin has accumulated, he has also been through a fifteen minute tunnel ride of total darkness designed to amuse tourists that actually resulted in death and mental illness for many. However, an experiment by two of the astronomers, Yimot 70 and Faro 24, that tried to simulate the appearance of stars failed to produce any psychological ill effects. While they discuss these findings, they are interrupted by a disturbance caused by a Cultist who has come in an attempt to destroy the telescopic equipment and cameras that he regards as blasphemy. He believes that the salvation of his soul depends on seeing the stars and is thereby forced to remain quiet while the other participants threaten to lock him in a closet where he cannot see the stars when they appear. He occupies himself during the long wait by chanting scripture from his Book of Revelations.

Sheerin is supposed to ride out the terror of the night in a specially-prepared Hideout where a number of people from the university community have taken refuge with supplies and some crudely-made torches for light. Instead, his curiosity gets the better of him, and it is Sheerin and Theremon, both beginning to feel the first effects of the claustrophobia, who bolt the entrances of the Observatory against the crazed mob coming up from the city at twilight.

Isaac Asimov

The story ends as the night begins. The city goes up in flames, and the stars come out in terrifying multitudes.

Characters

Aton 77

Director of Saro University, Aton 77 is the elderly leader of a group of astronomers who are determined to leave a record of the night of darkness. A stern and stiff leader, Aton arranges the swap of information between the astronomers and the Cultists that leads to the discovery of the impending eclipse. It is Aton who expresses the moral to the story when he cries out at the end that they "didn't know that they couldn't know."

Beenay 25

Beenay, a "husky telephotographer," is the character who brings the reporter to the Observatory and catches the Cultist. He is also the character who

Media Adaptations

- *The Best of Isaac Asimov,* a collection of short stories containing "Nightfall," has been recorded by Books on Tape; read by Dan Lazar, it is unabridged on 8 cassettes running 720 minutes.

- *The Complete Stories Volume 1,* produced by the Voyager Company of Santa Monica, California, is computer software on disk in both Windows and Macintosh versions that allows the reader to search, make notes, mark text, and so on.

- Read by various performers, "Nightfall" was recorded by Conde Nast in 1976 on a 33 1/3 rpm phonographic record.

- NBC radio did a presentation of "Nightfall" on its show *Dimension X* on September 29, 1951. It is now available on *The Greatest Old-Time Radio Shows from Science Fiction,* a CD or cassette recording, presented with an introduction by Ray Bradbury; published by Radio Spirits, Inc., in April 2001.

- A movie adaptation of "Nightfall," with some plot relationship to the novel version, was made in India and released in 2000 starring David Caradine and Robert Stevens, directed by Gwyneth Libby.

---

comes up with some interesting theories about the universe. While he is right about the idea that the stars are actually other suns positioned too far away to have gravitational pull on their planet, he is wrong in thinking that there is not enough room in the universe for more than a dozen or so stars. He also thinks that life on a planet with just one sun would be impossible. Asimov uses Beenay and his theories to point out how mistaken even the best scientists can be, given limited knowledge.

Faro 24

Faro is part of the team that will stay in the Observatory during the eclipse to record the phenomenon. He and Yimot are late in arriving because they have been attempting to simulate the appearance of darkness and stars in their own experiment. Their fake stars fail to drive them mad, so Sheerin theorizes that the stars do not cause the madness; rather, the madness causes one to imagine stars as a way to fight the darkness.

Latimer 25

The Cultist who breaks into the Observatory and tries to stop the work of the astronomers,

Latimer is an adjutant of the third class to Sor 5, his leader. Latimer is forced by Sheerin to give his word that he will not interfere further out of fear of being locked away and unable to see the stars when they come. The salvation of his soul depends on being a witness to the stars, and he cannot risk that. However, in the end, the blasphemy of the scientists trying to turn the judgment of sinners into a natural phenomenon is more than he can bear, and Latimer makes one last attempt to destroy the cameras just as the darkness sets in and the stars become visible. It is also Latimer who recites scripture from the Book of Revelations, thus giving the reader a glimpse of the cult's beliefs.

Sheerin 501

A portly psychologist at Saro University, Sheerin leaves the safety of the Hideout to join the astronomers in the Observatory for the final day. He is too curious to miss the experience. As the only person without a job to do in relation to the recording of the expected phenomenon, Sheerin is free to explain to the news reporter, Theremon, the information that he (and the reader) needs to understand the situation of the story. His expertise in psychology also enables Sheerin to provide insight into the reasons for the expected universal madness once the planet goes dark.

Sor 5

Referred to as ''his serenity,'' Sor 5 is given only brief mention as the leader of the Cultists.

Theremon 762

A reporter for the Saro City *Chronicle,* Theremon dared to come to the observatory to cover the story of the predicted last day despite the fact that he had ridiculed the work of the astronomers for two months in his column. Theremon's conversations with Sheerin and others provide the background and the explanation of the science involved in the story for the benefit of the reading audience. Usually possessed of ''an ample supply of coolness and self-confidence,'' Theremon boasts that he will be fine when the darkness comes. Yet, he and Sheerin seem to take turns at being affected by the claustrophobia and fear. Together, however, they bolt the doors of the Observatory against the mob. It is through the character of Theremon that readers witness the final moments.

Yimot 70

One of the two young astronomers who arrive late at the Observatory because they were experimenting with the concept of stars. The failure of Yimot and Faro's artificial stars to produce madness evokes a conversation between Sheerin and Beenay about other possible explanations for the stars. Yimot operates the huge solarscope while the others are all assigned to cameras.

Themes

Darkness and Light

The whole story is built around the concepts of darkness and light. On a planet with perpetual sunlight, darkness is inconceivable. The story presents an interesting theory about the effects of darkness on a people who have never experienced it. Asimov's editor believed that such people would go mad in darkness, even though the stars would become visible. So, Asimov wrote a story based on that supposition.

Deprivation and Need

Being deprived of light is the worst fear of the people of Lagash. After 2,000 years of light, they are genetically in need of light. Darkness is an unthinkably terrifying concept. Thus, the conflict in the story is the problem of how to respond to a crisis when one of the most basic needs of existence disappears. Cleverly, Asimov provides a psychologist as one of the main characters in the story in order to discuss and analyze the situation.

Vulnerability

Knowing that they are dependent on light, the scientists understand that the impending darkness makes them vulnerable to insanity. Each person in the story is trying to come to grips with this vulnerability because survival depends on being able to overcome it. Asimov provides some telling lines in the story about falling victim to this vulnerability; for example:

> Gamma, the brightest of the planet's six suns, was setting. It had already faded and yellowed into the horizon mists, and Aton knew he would never see it again as a sane man; He [Theremon] was going mad and knew it, and somewhere deep inside a bit of sanity was screaming, struggling to fight off the hopeless flood of black terror. It was very horrible to go mad— to know that in a little minute you would be here physically and yet all the real essence would be dead and drowned in the black madness.

Initiative

Aton and his team of astronomers take the initiative to save those in the future rather than just succumb or concentrate on personal survival. Aton also takes the initiative to ask the Cultists for their data that might help his research. The scientists also show initiative by inventing the torches to provide light once the darkness came, thus possibly helping to prevent the terrible consequences of total darkness. Initiative is an important theme to Asimov who believed strongly that humans create their own problems and are therefore the only ones who can solve them.

Madness and Sanity

Obviously, the preservation of sanity and the avoidance of the products of madness is the main concern of the characters in ''Nightfall.'' The presence of a psychologist in the story allows Asimov to discuss how the mind works and why the darkness could cause insanity. Sheerin says: ''Your brain is going to be presented with the phenomenon outside its limits of comprehension. You will go mad, completely and permanently! There is no question of it!''

Topics for Further Study

- Asimov was considered one of the three greatest writers of science fiction in the 1940s along with Robert Heinlein and A. E. Van Vogt. Read a work by each of these other two authors and comment on the science fiction of this time period.

- The climax of "Nightfall" is a total eclipse. Research this phenomenon and write a report on the frequency of occurrence on Earth and the folklore surrounding a total eclipse of the sun.

- Asimov was an atheist and a secular humanist whose skepticism about religion can be seen in his fiction, including "Nightfall." Define secular humanism and comment on its effect on modern culture.

- Asimov believed that the world's greatest prob-

lem was over-population. Research Asimov's writings on this subject and summarize his proposals for solving this problem.

- Asimov formulated the "Three Laws of Robotics." What are the three laws and how do they apply to any of the books or stories or movies that you are aware of that employ robotic characters?

- There exists a subgenre of science fiction called social science fiction that deals with the impact of technology on humanity. Asimov is one of the primary writers within this subgenre. Identify other writers of social science fiction and explain the interaction between science fiction and social concern they are focusing on.

Style

Character

The characters in this story are not aliens with four eyes and antennae. They are human. They may have numbers for last names, but they are physically the same as humans and use contemporary language. Asimov wanted the story to be a metaphor for life on earth, so he wanted his readers to be able to identify with the characters. Consequently, he has a "tubby" psychologist, a redheaded newspaper reporter, a white-haired pedantic director, and a cast of otherwise "just-like-us" characters who may be able to give the reader some insight about how to handle a crisis that calls for initiative and self-sacrifice.

Climax and Denouement

The whole story is aimed at the point at which the eclipse will be total and the planet will be plunged into unaccustomed darkness. The true climax comes when the stars come out. It is their existence that was most debated, and their effect that was most feared. The denouement is the few

minutes it takes after Theremon sees the stars to go mad. The reader experiences the last rational thoughts of Theremon and Aton, and then knows that, indeed, "The long night had come again."

Point of View

The point of view is third person omniscient. Even though the character of Theremon is used to ask questions and get explanations for the reader, the story is not presented by him. The reader is allowed to view the whole scene and, after watching Theremon go mad, to observe the world of Lagash going up in flames outside the Observatory windows.

Setting

A common method of writers who want to comment on their culture without making direct references is to provide an otherworld setting. Asimov may be describing a situation on the planet Lagash, but he intends for the lessons in the story to be taken to heart by the readers on Earth. This task requires inventing the elements of the other place in appearance, dress, activities, technology, and so forth. In a short story, Asimov did not have to go into any great detail, so the only truly differentiating factor is the perpetual daylight caused by six suns. After that, Lagash could be Earth, but that one factor is what causes the unique catastrophe facing Lagash.

Suspense

The overriding characteristic of ''Nightfall'' is the suspense of waiting for the darkness and the stars to come. The astronomers are preparing their equipment for that moment. The people in the Hideout are probably experiencing great tension from the suspense of not knowing whether they will succeed in surviving, and what they will do with what's left of their world if they do. Every person in the story is trying to deal with the anticipation of impending madness. Of course, Asimov succeeds at building suspense when the reader can hardly wait to find out if the Cultists will manage to break in, if Latimer will break his word, if indeed everyone will go mad or if some of them will overcome their fears and genetic conditioning and maintain sanity.

Historical Context

''Nightfall'' is set on a fictional planet at an indeterminate time. Consequently, there can be no discussion of the context of the times depicted in the story. However, written in 1941, ''Nightfall'' was created at an important time in the life of its author and in the history of the world

At the time of this story's publication, Asimov was only twenty-one years old, but he had already been writing for a few years, publishing about a dozen stories, and was finishing his master's degree in chemistry at Columbia University in New York City. Asimov himself admits that ''Nightfall'' ''was a watershed in my professional career.'' His payment for the story was the most he had ever received. ''What's more, I was suddenly taken seriously and the world of science fiction became aware that I existed. As the years passed, in fact, it became evident that I had written a 'classic.''' Asimov went on, of course, to become one of America's most prolific and diversified writers of fiction and nonfiction. He received awards in a number of genres and activities. Yet ''Nightfall,'' his youthful work written as something of an assignment by his editor, retained the reputation as the best science fiction story ever written.

The world of science fiction in 1941 was hot. It was a popular genre that had developed out of what was called scientific romance. The label, science fiction, was coined in 1929 by Hugo Gersback whose magazine *Amazing Stories* touted the works of Jules Verne and H. G. Wells as examples to follow. Until Asimov raised the bar for science fiction, it was the stuff of pulp magazines, and they existed in abundance, but mostly in the United States. It was in 1939 that Orson Welles caused panic with his broadcast of one of science fiction's most famous works, *War of the Worlds.* The tone of the early stories was largely that of social optimism about a future filled with technology. The readers were typically young males otherwise not interested in literature, but very interested in science, space, and mechanical gadgetry. Science fiction clubs flourished. Asimov attended his fist meeting of the well-known Futurians in 1938. Legend has it that Asimov was often thrown out for being loud and opinionated.

Most of the science fiction magazines died out during World War II because, of course, the war preoccupied everyone, and the main audience for the magazines went off to fight. Nonetheless, the famous writer and editor John W. Campbell, Jr. held things together at *Astounding Stories* and mentored new authors such as Asimov. The result was that, despite the interruption of the war, the 1940s became what is known as the Golden Age of science fiction.

In 1941, America was just pulling out of the Great Depression. This was one of the most difficult and revolutionary times in American history. The stock market had crashed, and the banks had failed. One fourth of the labor force was out of work. People were broke and desperate and began questioning the role of government. A number of people explored the merits of communism and other social and political alternatives to fix the failures of democracy. This inquiry later proved detrimental to their reputations during the McCarthy era.

However, on the positive side, government did respond with numerous social action programs that put people back to work and guaranteed certain rights for the workers. It was in this period of social re-examination that Asimov injected the element of social responsibility into science fiction. Science fiction was no longer just ''What if'' but ''What if, and how will it affect humans?'' ''Nightfall'' is a perfect example of this questioning attitude. Asimov

Compare & Contrast

- **1941:** Despite Asimov's anti-religious assertions in "Nightfall," American culture is steeped in religion, mostly Christian, and atheists are looked upon with suspicion.

  Today: Society is secularized with prayer removed from public events and schools.

- **1941:** Despite the probable presence of cults since the beginning of religions, cults are generally rare and secret, so the idea of a cult is a strange one used by Asimov in "Nightfall" to represent the worst effects of religion.

  Today: The creation and profusion of cults is a well-recognized facet of modern culture that has gained notoriety with the Jim Jones group suicide and the Branch Davidian catastrophe in Waco, Texas.

- **1941:** Knowledge in the field of astronomy seemingly does not extend much beyond that of Asimov's imaginary world in "Nightfall." However, in the real world, it is known that there are other suns beyond the solar system, rocketry is in

its infancy, and in 1938 Grote Reber had received short waves from the Milky Way.

  Today: Knowledge of the universe expands virtually daily as various probes, the space station, space flights, and telescopes like the Hubble send back information and pictures.

- **1941:** On December 7, the United States enters World War II after being attacked by the Japanese at Pear Harbor.

  Today: The United States is once again at war after the World Trade Center in New York City and the Pentagon in Washington, D.C., are attacked by terrorists.

- **1941:** Asimov's "Nightfall" has only male characters, although women are mentioned as being in the Hideout.

  Today: When Asimov rewrites *Nightfall* as a novel in 1990, he adds female characters and eliminates the part of the sentence about the Hideout that said they need "strong, healthy women that can breed children."

---

questions the validity of sacred scriptures and the motives of religion and asserts that science will provide the only real hope for the future. It was a precursor to cultural concerns in the latter half of the twentieth century

Critical Overview

On the whole, Isaac Asimov is greatly admired as one of America's most prolific and accomplished writers across a broad spectrum of subjects and genres. While some may argue that Asimov's most notable contributions are in the field of science fiction, others make a strong case that his remark-

able ability to clearly explain complex issues in science for the lay reader left an important legacy in the public's understanding of modern technology.

The science fiction of the 1930s tended to be soap operas set in space with lots of gadgets. Asimov created science fiction that focused on people and the social and historical changes that affected them and their moral decisions. Mervyn Rothstein said in his obituary for the *New York Times* that Asimov was "a pioneer in elevating the genre from pulp-magazine adventure to a more intellectual level that dealt with sociology, history, mathematics and science."

Epitomizing this new direction is "Nightfall," the story that made Asimov a star among science fiction writers when it was published in 1941. As L. David Allen said in his article for *Science Fiction*

Writers, "The concept behind the story evokes the sense of wonder that has been one of the hallmarks of the best science fiction." Allen also listed several other elements of "Nightfall" that made it so successful:

> Although the characters in "Nightfall" are necessarily one-dimensional, the characterizations are sharp and cover a range of human reactions to an unusual situation. The background is carefully presented and made plausible. The opposition of science to mythology adds depth to the story. The suspense is built step by step to a powerful climax. There is a kind of poetry in the story. . . . the kind of poetry that arises when the idea and development of a story merge and flow forth. It is the way that all of the elements work together, rather than any single element, that gives "Nightfall" its lasting impact.

Allen's comments about the background of the story coincide with the observations of other critics as well. They note that Asimov is able to set up a credible explanation for the rare appearance of stars on Lagash: a 2049 year cycle of eclipses. From that situation, all the other elements of the story beautifully evolve: a population accustomed only to constant light and therefore having an inherent and deep fear of darkness, the potentially disastrous results of plunging the world into darkness without explanation or preparation, and the interpretations of archaeological and religious evidence of previous occurrences of the darkness. In addition, the critics note, Asimov provides believably advanced technology for a world so accustomed to perpetual light that people do not even know how to make a decent torch or candle.

Michael Stanton, in an article about Asimov for the *Reference Guide to American Literature* touched on two of the same points made by Allen about the power of the concept of Asimov's story and about the characters. Although speaking in general terms about all of Asimov's stories, Stanton felt that Asimov "was at least as interested in idea as in character." Since the idea for the story was suggested to Asimov by his editor, one might say that he built the story around the idea and, therefore, the idea is more important. However, a study of critical material about Asimov reveals that, although the idea for the situation presented in the story was intriguing, it was the reaction of the people in the story to their situation that was most revealing. After all, Asimov's editor not only set up the background of the story and asked him what he thought would happen in that situation, but also Campbell opined that he thought the people would go mad. Asimov's response to Campbell's opinion

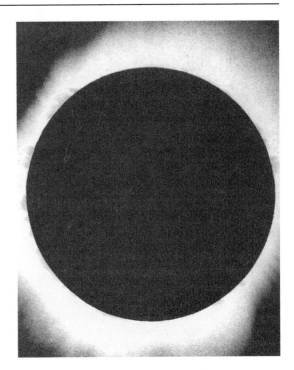

A total eclipse is the source of destruction for the planet Lagash in "Nightfall"

was to insert another element that critics have found in much of Asimov's work: a hope that science would overcome human frailty.

Some critics, and Asimov himself, were perturbed by the idea that one of his earliest stories would be considered his best. As Asimov wrote in 1969 in the introduction to his collection *Nightfall and Other Stories,* "It seemed to me, after all, that although I know no more about Writing now than I knew then, sheer practice should have made me more proficient, technically, with each year." Nonetheless, in 1970, "Nightfall" was voted the best science fiction short of all time by the Science Fiction Writers of America, and it is now one of the most anthologized of science fiction stories.

Criticism

Lois Kerschen

Kerschen, a former teacher, is now the executive director of a children's charity and a freelance writer. In this essay, Kerschen examines the simi-

What Do I Read Next?

- *Nightfall and Other Stories* is a collection that Asimov published in 1969 so that his most famous story would appear in his own anthology. All the stories are presented in order of publication date so that readers can form their own opinions about Asimov's literary development and whether "Nightfall" is truly the best of his short stories.

- In *The Best of Isaac Asimov* (1974), Asimov provides the collection of short stories with an introduction that explains the history and significance of each of the stories in relation to his career.

- *Nightfall,* the novel published in 1990 by Isaac Asimov in collaboration with Robert Silverberg, is the book-length version of Asimov's most famous short story.

- *The World Treasury of Science Fiction,* edited by David G. Hartwell with an introduction by general editor Clifton Fadiman, is a huge collection in one volume of over fifty complete works from all over the world. It ranges in scope from the 1930s until its publication date in 1989, and its stories run the gamut of science fiction topics and authors.

- *Age of Wonders* by David G. Hartwell, published in 1984, describes the origins of science fiction and discusses the components of the genre.

---

larities to Earth culture that permeate the alien world found in Asimov's most-admired short story.

"Nightfall," one of Isaac Asimov's earliest and best-known short stories, presents an alien world in crisis. Lagash has six suns and perpetual daylight, yet it is populated by humans, and they are struggling to confront the unknown and survive. Through the story, Asimov champions science and rational behavior as the only viable vehicles under such circumstances. Endowing life on Lagash with many of the same characteristics as that on Earth, the message is hard to miss that Asimov is commenting on what he sees as helpful and harmful to his own world's civilization.

Michael Stanton, in an overview of Asimov for the *Reference Guide to American Literature,* says that Asimov "is notable for a straightforward and unadorned style. The meaning of his fiction is very much on the surface and, while important themes run throughout his stories, symbol-hunting generally goes unrewarded." Examples of Earth-like touches include the use of the name Johnny Public for the common person even though the other names in the story are alien sounding. The newspaper in the story has the very familiar name of the *Chronicle.*

Similar to Earth culture, Lagash has a "World Expo" called the Jonglor Centennial Exposition, complete with amusement rides. Also familiar to modern readers is the concept that news reporters are annoying and will do anything to get a story, that "putting a spin" on a story is a negotiable practice.

Asimov actually refers to the Earth by name at the end of the story: "Not Earth's feeble thirty-six hundred Stars visible to the eye; Lagash was in the center of a giant cluster." While it may seem a slip to mention Earth, Asimov was probably trying to impress the reader with the enormity of the change in the sky by providing a comparison that the reader would understand. Despite all the similarities to Earth, Asimov included sufficient differences to remind the reader that "Nightfall" is set in another world. For instance, the characters have numbers (family codes he called them in the novel version of the story) instead of last names, and currency called credits, a term used by a number of other science fiction writers, too.

Besides a few familiar terms, Asimov draws parallels between Earth's history and that of Lagash. There is evolutionary development from a Stone Age—one in which people "were little more than rather intelligent apes.'' Just as Earth has had Incas, Aztecs, and Mayans, Lagash has had whole cities and cultures at their height mysteriously destroyed with ''nothing left behind to give a hint as to the cause.''

While archaeologists are discovering a regular cycle of progress and destruction in the history of Lagash, the astronomers are busy calculating applications of the Law of Universal Gravitation. This law is a recent conclusion, and Asimov copies Earth history to describe its development. Sheerin explains that ''After Genovi 41 discovered that Lagash rotated about the sun Alpha rather than vice versa— and that was four hundred years ago—astronomers have been working.'' The mention of Genovi 41 is an allusion to Earth's Galileo and the similar discovery that Earth rotated around the sun rather than the sun around Earth.

Sheerin goes on to explain that twenty years earlier it was demonstrated that the law accounted for the orbital motions of the six suns. But ten years ago, the law and the orbit observed did not coincide. ''Either the law was invalid, or there was another, as yet unknown, factor involved.'' Was the law really a scientific law, or back to being just a theory? Asimov is making the point that even universally accepted facts should be questioned and tested because there is always the possibility of an unknown factor. In this case on Lagash, the Law of Universal Gravitation does hold up, and the problem is indeed something unknown.

The extent to which humans can guess wrong based on inadequate information is demonstrated repeatedly in the story. Yimot 70 and Faro 24's experiment shows how primitive and misdirected the science can be when people are trying to figure out something never experienced. Beenay is correct when he theorizes about ''suns that are so far away that they're too dim to see.'' But then Beenay blows it when he concludes that there would be only a dozen or two, maybe. ''There just isn't any place in the universe you could put a million suns—unless they touch each other.'' This thinking is as limited as the IBM executive who turned down the idea of building personal computers because he could not imagine that anyone would want a computer in the home.

Beenay's next idea further emphasizes how wrong seemingly logical conclusions can be when based on ignorance. Beenay says: ''Supposing you had a universe in which there was a planet with only one sun.'' The idea is so foreign to Sheerin that he

asks doubtfully: ''But would such a system be dynamically stable?'' Although Beenay is able to say that it would be stable based on mathematical calculations, he goes on to say that ''life would be impossible on such a planet. It wouldn't get enough heat and light, and if it rotated there would be total Darkness half of each day. You couldn't expect life—which is fundamentally dependent upon light— to develop under those conditions.''

Such a conclusion gives the reader a good laugh. Obviously, life on such a planet is possible. The ironic point is, of course, that people on Earth are possibly making the same mistakes about life and conditions on other planets. In addition, Beenay's educated, intelligent, but totally wrong assumptions illustrate the moral of the story as expressed by Aton's final words: ''We didn't know it all. We didn't know anything.''

The idea for ''Nightfall'' was suggested to Asimov by his editor who quoted Ralph Waldo Emerson's *Nature:* ''If the stars should appear one night in a thousand years, how would men believe and adore, and preserve for many generations the remembrance of the city of God?'' However, they felt that they had to reverse Emerson's romantic notion that the stars were proof that there is a God and that they would therefore be comforted by the awesome sight of the stars. In this story, the possible existence of stars is interpreted by the religious to be an awe-filled and awful avenue to salvation. To the non-religious, the stars are a terrifying sight that turns out to be proof only of the limited knowledge of humans.

The fact that Aton had to call upon the Cult to get data that he needed may seem to give some credit to religion. Asimov, an atheist, was only admitting that there is some basis in fact for the beliefs of the religious. Otherwise, he makes sure to include statements such as Sheerin's "Of course they mix all this up with a lot of religio-mystic notions" and Theremon's "I've been laughing at that sort of thing all my life."

It is remarkable that Asimov wrote this story in 1941 because so many of the comments he makes about religion seem to come from the culture of the latter part of the twentieth century. For example, Theremon says, "This is not the century to preach 'The end of the world is at hand.' . . people don't believe the Book of Revelations any more." The Book of Revelations is, of course, an allusion to any of the religious texts such as the Bible, the Book of Mormon, the Koran, etc. These writings are interpreted literally by many, but Asimov sees them as mythology of the type the Cultists in the story use to explain the coming darkness—that Lagash enters a huge cave every 2,049 years.

Fundamentalists like the Cultists often give circular arguments. Latimer 25 objects to the attempt to back up the Cult's beliefs with scientific evidence: "There was no need to prove that. It stands proven by the Book of Revelations." The question is, of course, but what proves the validity of the Book of Revelations? To Latimer, the answer is simply "I just know." Just knowing is another way of saying, "I take it on faith; I believe without proof." To someone like Asimov, such acceptance without scientific verification is impossible. Instead, to Asimov, the Book of Revelations and its kin are, as described by Sheerin, formed "on the testimony of those least qualified to serve as historians; that is, children and morons; and it was probably edited and re-edited through the cycles." Consequently, these scriptures "can't help but be a mass of distortion." In contrast, to Latimer and other believers, the work of the scientists is blasphemy: "You made of the Darkness and of the Stars a natural phenomenon and removed all its real significance."

Asimov draws further comparisons to religious practices in his own world. He has Latimer 25 chant scripture in an ancient language, thus alluding to the chanting of many Eastern religions or Gregorian chants in Latin. Borrowing from the shaved heads of the Buddhist monks or the long sideburn curls of Hasidic Jews, Asimov describes Latimer as having a "short yellow beard curled elaborately in the style affected by the Cultists." Just as certain religious leaders on Earth have titles, the head of the Lagash Cult is called "His Serenity."

To Asimov, a belief in a god or gods is a way for people to explain the seemingly inexplicable, just as mythology was a primitive world's way to explain natural occurrences such as the seasons. He also knows that religious leaders can be unscrupulous people who take advantage of the gullible for their own benefit. Thus, in the story, Asimov shows the Cultists taking advantage of the eclipse to promote their cause: "The Cult is in for an hour of unexampled prosperity. I trust they'll make the most of it." He describes the scene in the city as "one gigantic revival" where people suddenly find religion in their fear. Even those who never give much thought to their souls are frantic to redeem themselves when faced with death, just in case there is something to this god thing.

Consequently, "the cultists are active. They're rousing the people to storm the Observatory— promising them immediate entrance into grace, promising them salvation, promising them anything." Since the work of the scientists is considered blasphemous, the attainment of salvation can be achieved by destroying the Observatory. Putting one's soul in jeopardy of eternal damnation is a powerful threat. It worked to get Latimer to give his promise not to interfere anymore, and it worked to get the people to form a mob to storm the Observatory. It seems odd that Sheerin would say "Keep on working and pray that totality comes first." Is "pray" just a figure of speech, or is there a whisper of belief in everyone? Perhaps Sheerin uses the word because "Your brain wasn't built for the conception [of darkness] any more than it was built for the conception of infinity or of eternity. You can only talk about it."

Marian Pehowski, writing about Asimov for *Contemporary Novelists,* remarked that

> Asimov is the writer who most clearly established the science fiction thesis that the future is one of alternatives—good or bad—and that there are choices to be made by beings along the way. . . . his favorite proposal [was] that there is a way to survive, but first there must be a will to do so—the first of all good choices.

As Stanton noted: "Asimov was a scientist and an apostle of rationalism and scientific discipline. He was literally a secular humanist and his fiction, fully cognizant of human folly, celebrated human reason and human possibility." History is cyclical as evidenced by the rise and fall of many civilizations. But, with "Nightfall," Asimov is saying that the cycle can be broken with free will and determination. The scientists at the Observatory have chosen, at the risk of their sanity and their very lives, to try to break the cycle that is inhibiting civilization on Lagash from developing to its full potential. On the grand stage of world history, it is such seemingly minute but powerful actions of heroic individuals that effect change.

Source: Lois Kerschen, Critical Essay on ''Nightfall'' in *Short Stories for Students,* The Gale Group, 2003.

Michael Tritt

In the following essay, Tritt explores similarities between Lord Byron's poem ''Darkness'' and Asimov's ''Nightfall,'' finding both have ''darkness and mankind's reaction to it'' as a central theme.

When Asimov sat down, a sheet of paper in front of him, blank except for Emerson's quotation from *Nature* as a heading, what a great feat of extrapolation was involved in pounding out ''Nightfall'' (1941), one of his best short stories. True, Asimov and his editor Campbell had talked of the Emerson quotation, had even decided together upon the name of the story; but in the end, it was up to Asimov to ''face the empty sheet of paper in the typewriter.'' Without detracting from his imaginative accomplishment, I would like to suggest that Asimov may have drawn not so much on the American poet and essayist as on an earlier work of Byron's, the poem ''Darkness'' (1816). This poem, though not specifically recollected as a source by Asimov, may nonetheless have shaped ''Nightfall.'' The two works are linked by a shared vision of a world become desolate without light. The terrifying destruction of man in the context of this desolation underlines the tenuousness of man's sanity and indeed of his very existence.

Darkness and mankind's reaction to it are at the heart of both Asimov's story and Byron's poem. In ''Darkness,'' the ''bright sun is extinguished,'' while in ''nightfall'' the last of Lagash's suns is eclipsed (''a giant eyelid shutting slantwise over the light of the world''). Both authors paint a blackened landscape which is horrible and frightening. Byron writes:

> . . . and the icy earth
> Swung blind and blackening in the moonless air;
> Morn came and went—and came, and brought no day,
> And men forgot their passions in the dread
> Of this their desolation . . .

Asimov describes Saro City as a place ''where the spires . . . gleamed bloodily on the horizon.'' He also portrays Beta, the sun, as ''dwarfed and evil,'' while Lagash itself is shown to be a ''cold, horribly

> ''**What is presented, then, in both 'Nightfall' and 'Darkness' is a vision of man driven mad and desperate by a blackened planet. Man, the rational creature, becomes bestial, 'howling' and 'clawing.' Where poem and tale differ is in the finality of the vision of destruction.''**

bleak world.'' The two writers describe literally the effects of darkness on the landscape, but they also extend darkness to the level of metaphor, for the darkness without represents a darkness within man which is released by the barren landscape.

In ''Nightfall,'' the cultists maintain a belief that as the darkness comes and the stars appear, men are robbed of their souls and become inhuman: ''. . . the souls of men departed from them, and their abandoned bodies became even as beasts; yea, even as brutes of the wild; so that through the blackened streets of the cities of Lagash they prowled with wild cries.'' This ''religious'' belief is affirmed in the context of the tale as men are driven mad in their desperation. ''He was going mad, and knew it, and somewhere deep inside a bit of sanity was screaming, struggling to fight off the hopeless flood of black terror . . . The bright walls of the Universe were shattered and their awful black fragments were falling down to crush and squeeze and obliterate him.'' Men are reduced to beasts ''crawling'' and ''groping,'' conscious not of each other, but only of a need for light: they ''made for the observatory or fort and assaulted it with bare hands . . .'' Even Aton, the super-rational head scientist, becomes a ''terribly frightened child,'' and the final images of the story include ''someone [who] clawed at a torch.''

Byron likewise describes man reduced by darkness to a beast, lost and terrified: illustrating the ''hideousness'' of a ''fiend.''

> . . . and all hearts

Were chilled into a selfish prayer for light:
The brows of men by the despairing light
Wore an unearthly aspect, as by fits
The flashes felt upon them; some lay down
And hid their eyes and wept; and some did rest
Their chins upon their clenched hands, and smiled;
And others hurried to and fro . . .
. . . and looked up
With mad disquietude on the dull sky,
The pall of a past world; and then again
With curses cast them down upon the dust,
And gnashed their teeth and howled . . .

Man, as he is portrayed in both these visions, is reduced to an irrational beast ''howling'' and ''clawing''; he has moved from sanity to madness, from civilization to primitiveness.

With an all-consuming desire for light to ease the terrors of pervading darkness, men take to burning whatever will create light. In ''Nightfall'': ''On the horizon outside the window, in the direction of Saro City, a crimson glow began growing, strengthening in brightness, that was not the glow of the sun.'' In ''Darkness,'' ''the thrones,/The palaces of crowned Kings—the huts,/The habitations of all things which dwell,/Were burnt for beacons . . .'' The passion for light is futile, for the flames are ''extinguished with a crash'' and there proves to be nothing that can stem the coming of the ''long night.'' Man passes into extinction.

What is presented, then, in both ''Nightfall'' and ''Darkness'' is a vision of man driven mad and desperate by a blackened planet. Man, the rational creature, becomes bestial, ''howling'' and ''clawing.'' Where poem and tale differ is in the *finality* of the vision of destruction. In ''Nightfall,'' the sun is extinguished for but a day; the eclipse will end, and life begin once again. Significantly, the stars, unlike in ''Darkness,'' do not ''Wander darkling in the eternal space'' but rather, ''appear.'' They indicate a universe which is yet alive; Lagash itself will return to life. In ''Darkness'' there is no evidence that life will begin again. The final passages of that poem relate a return to chaos which is eternal; the death is one not only of the earth but of the universe as well:

The waves are dead; the tides were in their grave,
The moon, their mistress, had expired before;
The winds were withered in the stagnant air,
And the clouds perished; Darkness had no need
Of aid from them—She was the Universe.

In the final analysis, one cannot state whether one vision is more effective than another. Surely, Byron's is the more poetic and haunting; what for him was ''not all a dream'' becomes for the reader

nothing less than nightmare. The images he presents are terrifying; the two men who face each other and die of ''mutual hideousness'' remain with us. The image of the dog howling over his dead master blends with Byron's poem as a whole to capture beautifully a sense of utter desolation. Asimov, on the other hand, does not try to be poetic (though at times he may be so); he creates a work of SF in which a world and its inhabitants react to a specific natural catastrophe. He imagines an S-F context, a planet Lagash with six suns. Through this unusual setting, we are able to understand the meaning darkness has for Lagash's inhabitants, and beyond that their ignorance of the existence of stars. Asimov creates ''cultists'' whose religious beliefs explain the wonder and the reverence inspired by the stars, as described in his epigraph from Emerson, and further brings to life all of the characters and other variables which ''glue'' the whole together coherently.

Inevitably, both ''Nightfall'' and ''Darkness,'' unique as they are, must be appreciated on their own terms. Perhaps what is most remarkable about the two works when they are examined together, is that two so very different men, writing in different eras, in different forms, should share similar visions of man driven mad, even to extinction, in a world deprived of light.

Source: Michael Tritt, ''Byron's 'Darkness' and Asimov's 'Nightfall,''' in *Science Fiction Studies,* Vol. 8, No. 1, March 1981, pp. 26–28.

Joseph F. Patrouch, Jr.

In the following excerpt, Patrouch discusses Asimov's ambivalence about the quality of ''Nightfall,'' and analyzes critically elements Asimov had identified as suspect.

Before writing ''Nightfall'' Asimov had written thirty-one stories and sold seventeen (four more would sell eventually). ''Marooned Off Vesta,'' perhaps ''The Callistan Menace,'' and ''Homo Sol,'' along with the robot stories ''Reason'' and ''Liar!'' were the best he had done so far. His own assessment of his career to this point is ''Looking back on my first three years as a writer, then, I can judge myself to be nothing more than a steady and . . . hopeful third-rater.''

Then, on March 17, 1941, he began to write ''Nightfall,'' his thirty-second written story, his sixteenth published, and the story that established him as a frontline science fiction writer.

Science fiction readers and writers are unanimous in their respect and admiration for this story. In 1968–69, for example, the Science Fiction Writers of America voted ''Nightfall'' by a wide margin the best science fiction short story ever written, and in 1971 the readers of *Analog* in an informal poll expressed similar feelings. Whenever the magazines poll their readers for favorite stories, ''Nightfall'' is at or very near the top. For the average reader Asimov and science fiction are synonymous; for the science fiction reader Asimov and ''Nightfall'' (along with the Robot Stories and the Foundation Series) are synonymous. Whenever I use ''Nightfall'' in the classroom, it is inevitably the students' favorite story in the course.

Yet Asimov professes himself to be ambivalent about the story's fame. He feels that the story shows a bit too much its pulp heritage, especially in its language, its characters, and its plotting. He also feels that he has written better stories since, perhaps many better stories. (He usually cites as his favorites from among his works ''The Ugly Little Boy'' followed by ''The Last Question,'' though in *Before the Golden Age* he calls ''The Last Question'' ''my personal favorite of all the short stories I have ever written''.) In *Nightfall and Other Stories* he writes as follows:

> I must say, though, that as time passed, I began to feel some irritation at being told, over and over again, that ''Nightfall'' was my best story. It seemed to me, after all, that although I know no more about Writing now than I knew then, sheer practice should have made me more proficient, technically, with each year.

He decided to bring out a collection that began with ''Nightfall'' and contained nineteen other stories in chronological order, so ''now you can see for yourself how my writing has developed (or has failed to develop) with the years. Then you can decide for yourself why (or *if*) 'Nightfall' is better than the others.'' This looks as if the purpose of the collection *Nightfall and Other Stories* is, at least partly, to destroy the reputation of ''Nightfall.''

But Asimov couldn't really bring himself to do that. The result is a collection of stories that he had not seen fit to anthologize before. There are no stories from the forties, the period immediately following ''Nightfall'' and during which he was composing the Robot Stories and the Foundation Series. Three quarters of the stories are from the fifties, which he had already culled over for *The Martian Way, Earth Is Room Enough*, and *Nine Tomorrows*. The result seems to be that Asimov

> The pace of 'Nightfall's' plot, then, is sustained with a series of interruptions which account for the story's helter-skelter quality. There really is no story. There is instead a continuing revelation of a situation. The 'story' is 95 per cent exposition via conversation.''

wants us to compare ''Nightfall'' with stories that he himself did not really think of as his best. This is a good indication of his ambivalence toward ''Nightfall.''

Let's turn to the story itself. It is headed by a quotation from Ralph Waldo Emerson's essay ''Nature,'' the first paragraph of the first chapter (also called ''Nature''). The remark is an exclamation designed by Emerson to show the powerful effect nature would have on man if it weren't so familiar: ''If the stars should appear one night in a thousand years, how would men believe and adore, and preserve for many generations the remembrance of the city of God!'' In effect, the story converts the exclamation point to a question mark (as was actually done in the editions of *Nightfall and Other Stories*) and answers the question ''Under such conditions, how *would* man remember and adore?'' Asimov divides men into two groups depending on their reaction. The great majority convert to the Cult and react by turning passive: it is God's will that the world should end, and they accept it as God's will. The minority, under Aton and the astronomers, try to do something about it. They react actively, rationally. And Asimov leaves no doubt in our minds as to which side he is on. It's ''Marooned Off Vesta'' in a different form: the hysterics of Mark Brandon versus the reason of Warren Moore, the religion of the Cultists and the masses versus the reasoned planning of Aton and the scientists. Asimov shows that Emerson was right—man would believe and adore— but that man was wrong to do so. He should think rather than merely believe.

Let's move on to the problems Asimov sees in the story, the problems of language, characterization, and plotting. The pulpish quality of the writing can be illustrated by its first two sentences (italics mine).

> Aton 77, director of Saro University, *thrust* out a *belligerent* lower lip and *glared* at the young newspaperman in *a hot fury.*

> Theremon 762 took that fury *in his stride.*

Note that the diction Asimov uses is not simply strong. It is extreme and trite. The thrust-out lower lip, the glaring, and the hot fury are overly familiar to us all, as is taking something in stride. No matter how interesting the content may be, there is no originality or interest in the language.

Very soon after this, "Beenay 25 thrust a tongue's tip across dry lips and interposed nervously." This reuse of "thrust" indicates a paucity of vocabulary. Then "the director turned to him and lifted a white eyebrow." The lifted eyebrow is trite. Follow Aton's actions for a moment: "The director . . . shook it [a newspaper] at Theremon furiously . . . Aton dashed the newspaper to the floor, strode to the window and clasped his arms behind his back. 'You may leave,' he snapped over his shoulder. He stared moodily . . . He whirled. 'No, wait, come here!' He gestured peremptorily . . . Aton gestured outward." An extreme example of this stereotyped pulp diction can be found toward the end of the story: "Theremon cried out sharply and muttered through a blinding haze of pain. 'You double-crossing rat!'" In the pulps any crying out was done sharply, the hero always muttered, a haze of pain was always blinding, and for some reason all rats were double-crossing.

Though the general quality of the writing has this pulpish triteness about it, some flashes of interesting language do get through. In the paragraph immediately following "You double-crossing rat!" we find, "then there was the strange awareness [still pulpy] that the last thread of sunlight had thinned out and snapped." Contrary to what happens in reading the greater part of the story, the interest here is almost solely in the language rather than in what is being described. (Have you ever seen any threads of light snap at sunset?)

And later, "Thirty thousand mighty suns shone down in a soul-searing splendor that was more frighteningly cold in its awful indifference than the bitter wind that shivered across the cold, horribly bleak world." That "shivered" is exactly right here, it is far from trite, and the whole sentence—the thought and the language combined—stimulates the reader. We have hints here of an Asimov who is a writer and knows how to manipulate language rather than simply an Asimov who knows his pulp idiom and how to write salable stories in it.

The characters tend to be pulpish, too. Writers for mass circulation media as old as the pulps and as new as TV quickly realized that certain professions are easier to write stories about because their practitioners can legitimately ask questions dredging up information the reader or the viewer needs to know. A detective, a physician, or a lawyer may ask what you were doing the night before last, but who would believe a plumber who asked the same thing? The point here is not that lawyers are inherently more interesting than plumbers. It is that stories about lawyers are easier to write than stories about plumbers, because the exposition is easier.

Another profession very popular in the pulps, on the radio, and on early TV—though not used so much anymore, perhaps because it has become trite through overuse—is the newspaper reporter. It is perfectly legitimate for a reporter to hear about something interesting and to go out to get the facts. And it is perfectly legitimate for the reader's-listener's-viewer's ignorance of "what happened" to be satisfied while the reporter learns these facts. Theremon is a reporter who goes to the observatory to have questions answered. As Aton and Sheerin answer them, we learn about the setting, the Cult, the conflicts, the eclipse. In other words Asimov in this story makes use of the age-old expository device of the inquiring newspaper reporter. Note how Theremon recedes in importance as the need for exposition diminishes.

Aton is another trite, conventional, unindividualized character. The extent of Asimov's characterization of him is to classify him as an astronomer—and you know how they are: "Astronomers were queer ducks, anyway, and if Aton's actions of the last two months meant anything, this same Aton was the queer-duckiest of the lot."

Only Sheerin comes across as an individual, with his high spirits and his gregarious willingness to help Asimov tell Theremon and us all we need to know to understand the story. He has curiosity. He leaves the Hideout in order to be "where things are getting hot" because he wants to see the legendary "Stars." He has courage. Sheerin leads the way down the dark staircases to bolt the doors against the invading mob from the city. Most important, he has hidden whiskey. "Tiptoeing to the nearest window, he squatted, and from the low window box beneath withdrew a bottle of red liquid that gurgled suggestively when he shook it. 'I thought Aton didn't know about this,' he remarked.''

On the whole, the characters are not people but rather labels for the different parts of the story machine: a newspaper reporter who asks our questions for us, an observatory director who answers some of them, a jolly little tub who answers the rest when the director must get back to work. They exist not as people in their own right, but as counters to keep the story moving for ward. This is the pulp attitude toward characterization. The story is the thing.

Despite the fact that the story is almost entirely conversation, it has a helter-skelter quality about it. One scene tends not to flow into the next, but to be interrupted by the next. In the first scene shift, Sheerin and Theremon simply walk into an adjacent room for some expository conversation. This ends with a ''sudden hubbub that came from the adjoining room.'' This second scene ends in midsentence when ''from somewhere up above there sounded a sharp clang, and Beenay, starting to his feet, dashed up the stairs with a 'What the devil!''' It turns out that a religious fanatic, Latimer, is destroying photographic plates. The interrogation of Latimer is interrupted by Theremon's reaction to the onset of Beta's eclipse: '''Look at that!' The finger he pointed toward the sky shook, and his voice was dry and cracked. There was one simultaneous gasp as every eye followed the pointing finger, and, for one breathless moment, stared frozenly. *Beta was chipped on one side!*'' Sheerin and Theremon's resultant conversation is interrupted by Aton's approach: '''You know why it didn't w—' [Sheerin] stopped and rose in alarm, for Aton was approaching, his face a twisted mask of consternation. *'What's happened?'*'' A conversation between Beenay and Sheerin is then interrupted: ''Sheerin's chair went over backwards as he sprang to his feet in a rude interruption. 'Aton's brought out the lights.'''

Then a pause. Silence. ''After the momentary sensation, the dome had quieted.'' Then a gradual recognition of the ''extraneous noise'' of the townsmen coming to destroy the observatory. ''The silence ripped to fragments at [Theremon's] started shout: *'Sheerin!'* Work stopped!'' Out of the silence Asimov has begun to build his story's climax.

The pace of ''Nightfall's'' plot, then, is sustained with a series of interruptions which account for the story's helter-skelter quality. There really is no story. There is instead a continuing revelation of

a situation. The ''story'' is 95 per cent exposition via conversation. The development—the forward thrust of the reader's interest—takes place in the reader's understanding. When we know what must happen and why and what its effects will be, the inevitable happens and the story is over.

The initial physical situation in ''Nightfall'' is very similar to that in ''Marooned Off Vesta'' in one important way. Both stories rely on a physical arrangement whose occurrence in nature is so highly unlikely that we might as well consider it impossible. A planet cannot have an orbit stable enough for long enough to support life when that planet moves in the midst of six suns. It is highly improbable that a moon the size described would be detectable only once every 2,049 years. It is very unlikely that a race could develop cities—and an urban architecture—without having experienced darkness and developing artificial sources of light on a large scale. Here on Earth the planet Venus is often visible in the daytime, yet we are to believe that Lagash is in the center of a globular cluster of ''thirty thousand mighty suns'' which remain invisible until the exact moment of Beta's total eclipse.

Certain details are vague as well. For example, at the beginning of the story, yellow Gamma is just setting, and red Beta rides high in the sky. As a result, the light is described as orange. Later everything is bathed in the dim red of Beta alone. Note that we have been shown a range of colors from yellow through orange to red (and only two of the six suns were involved). Under these conditions, how can anything on Lagash be said to have *a* color? (Aton's eyebrows, you will recall, were described as white.)

Again, Yimot and Faro perform an experiment intended to simulate the appearance of stars in a dark sky in order to see what effect such an event might have on their psychology, but nothing happens. Despite Sheerin's assertions that he knows why the experiment failed, it turns out his explanation is wrong, and we are left holding a loose thread. And students are always asking, what happened to the people in the Hideout? We are left to assume that there are too few of them to change the shape of history (a theme developed at length in the Foundation Series), but we don't really know when we finish reading ''Nightfall.'' They aren't taken into account by the ending.

In one sense the story ends too soon. It has been Aton's story if it has been anyone's. He has led the efforts to find out what is happening and to preserve that knowledge for the next cycle. He has established the Hideout to help some sanity survive. What is the result of these efforts on his part? It is as if ''Marooned Off Vesta'' were allowed to end with Warren Moore's ''Aha! Why didn't I think of it before?'' We are never told how Aton's efforts turn out. They are subsumed in the larger catastrophe. The extent to which we are not told these things is the extent to which we are left holding loose threads at the end of the story.

After accepting the story for publication Campbell introduced into it one minor flaw and one nice touch. The nice touch was Aton's incoherent speech four paragraphs from the end, ''We didn't know we couldn't know, etc.'' The flaw was the opening phrase of a slightly earlier paragraph: ''Not Earth's feeble thirty-six hundred Stars visible to the naked eye.'' The whole story had meticulously refused to recognize the existence of Earth, yet this phrase added by Campbell violates this important part of Asimov's narrative strategy.

An early critic of ''Nightfall'' has dealt with some of these problems, at least by inference. Ernest Kimoy, in adapting the story for broadcast on the radio program ''Dimension X'' in the early fifties, made two major kinds of changes in the story. One kind was made necessary by the shift in medium from printed page to radio, from eye to ear. The narrative voice, for example, must actually speak aloud on the radio, and in effect this adds another character—the narrative point of view—whom most of us forget about when we read.

But the more important set of changes for our purposes include those made in an apparent attempt to deal with what Kimoy may have seen as flaws in the story. Kimoy the practicing writer is in effect Kimoy the practical critic. For example, he, too, seems to realize that ''thirty thousand mighty suns'' would be visible long before Asimov permits his characters to see them, since he changes the phrase to ''thirty thousand minute suns.'' He also drops the whole Yimot-Faro experiment. One might argue that this was due to limitations of time. ''Dimension X'' was only a half. hour program. Still, cutting the Yimot-Faro experiment shows that it was cuttable. Besides being inconclusive, it did not contribute anything essential to the story.

The most significant difference in the two men's treatment of the same story can be found in their handling of setting. Asimov sets the whole story in the observatory. Thus people must come to the observatory to express their points of view. For example, Latimer, the Cultist who came to smash the photographic plates, is then interviewed at some length. Some things we can only learn at second hand, as when Sheerin tells Theremon that a fifteen-minute-long amusement-park ride through a dark tunnel caused insanity. Kimoy, on the other hand, sends Theremon away from the observatory to interview people directly. In succession he talks with a priest of the Cult, Sheerin, a man in the street called Pallet, and an aged member of the Cult. The priest gives the information presented in the story by the captured Cultist. Sheerin actually takes Theremon to see and listen to a person driven insane on the amusement-park ride. The man in the street takes a very practical attitude toward the whole affair: the world may be ending but he's putting money in the bank just in case. And the old Cultist presents the opposite reaction: he has sold everything that he has and given it to the poor so that he can go to glory with the Stars.

As both men treat the story, it has a great deal of dramatic impact, but Asimov's is the stronger of the two. His single setting gives the story a more unified impact than the diversified interviews in the street. Whether it is accurate or not, the flashing forth of thirty thousand mighty suns staggers us emotionally. It may not be scientifically true, but it is dramatically true, and for a writer effect is what counts. Asimov first made it as plausible as he could. Then he made it right.

What is ''Nightfall'' about, and where does its compelling power lie? In his essay ''Social Science Fiction'' Asimov distinguishes between two kind of fictional reactions to the French and Industrial revolutions: ''Social fiction is that branch of literature which moralizes about a current society through the device of dealing with a fictitious society,'' and ''science fiction is that branch of literature which deals with a fictitious society, differing from our own chiefly in the nature or extent of its technological development.'' In the context of the essay it is clear that Asimov views social fiction as presenting an alternate society with the intent of criticizing contemporary society, whereas science fiction creates an alternate society for its own sake, to show us that things could (not *should* or *ought to*) be different, to accustom us to change. Elsewhere he distinguishes between science fiction and what he calls tomorrow fiction, in which the writer simply tries to show what life will actually be like in a few years. The point in both distinctions is that science fiction must present an alternate society for its own sake rather than comment on contemporary society or attempt to show accurately where we are going.

"Nightfall" presents alternate society for its own sake. It obviously not an attempt to show what life will be like a few years from now, so it is not tomorrow fiction. And though it contains a few satirical touches directed at commonly held contemporary assumptions—for example, Beenay's notion that life as we know it could not exist on a planet revolving about a single sun—still it does not attempt to make us feel in our guts that air pollution is evil or that violent hoodlums have a right to their own identities. "Nightfall" not social fiction.

There is no obvious connection between the characters in "Nightfall" and ourselves. They do not live on Earth past or future, and they are not the remnants of a human colony that ran into trouble. At the same time, we are given no reason to picture them in our imaginations as anything different from ourselves. They have arms and eyebrows. Or at least Asimov uses the language worked out to describe human beings in describing his aliens. Perhaps this is Asimov's use of the "doctrine of accommodation" that Milton scholars talk about, wherein Milton describes his angels—fallen and unfallen—as they were shaped like us and collected sense data like us, though in fact they are not and do not. Milton simply accommodates the angels to human conceptions. Perhaps Asimov's aliens are really alien, but he has accommodated them to our concepts of ourselves so he can talk about them.

Fundamentally, though, it doesn't make any difference. "Nightfall" is about the relationship between consciousness and its environment. The physical apparatus in which that consciousness is embodied is irrelevant. Human-shaped or alien-shaped, the consciousnesses on Lagash are what they are because they developed under six suns and a nightfall that comes once every 2,049 years. Their psychology is different became their environment is different.

"Nightfall" has the powerful effect it does because it convinces us that that's way we would be under those different circumstances. "Nightfall" embodies a cosmic conception: what we are and the way we think are determined by the accident of the environment into which we are born. It figures forth an alternate world and society for its own sake. But that world is not totally irrelevant to our own. It has lessons for us, too. Consciousness, regardless of the environment that shapes it, is sacred. The people of

Lagash are our brothers. When they are destroyed, we are destroyed, because we share consciousness. John Donne wrote, "No man is an island, entire of itself; every man is a piece of the continent . . . Any man's death diminishes me, because I am involved in mankind." "Nightfall" expresses the same sentiments, only on a universal rather than a planetary scale. The sacredness and dignity of life is the message of Donne's Seventeenth Meditation, Asimov's "Nightfall," and science fiction.

Source: Joseph F. Patrouch, Jr., "The Earliest Asimov," in *The Science Fiction of Isaac Asimov,* Doubleday, 1974, pp. 3–29.

Sources

Allen, L. David, "Isaac Asimov," in *Science Fiction Writers,* Charles Scribner's Sons, 1982, pp. 267–76.

Asimov, Isaac, "Introduction," in *The Best of Isaac Asimov,* Doubleday and Company, Inc., 1974, p. x.

———, "Preface to *Nightfall,*" in *Nightfall and Other Stories,* Doubleday and Company, Inc., 1969, p. 1.

Pehowski, Marian, "Isaac Asimov," in *Contemporary Novelists,* St. James Press, 1991, pp. 49–56.

Rothstein, Mervyn, "Isaac Asimov, Whose Thoughts and Books Traveled the Universe, Is Dead at 72," in the *New York Times,* April 7, 1992.

Stanton, Michael, "Asimov, Isaac," in *Reference Guide to American Literature,* 3d ed., edited by Jim Kamp, St. James Press, 1994.

Further Reading

Chambers, Bette, "Isaac Asimov: A One-Man Renaissance," in *Humanist,* Vol. 53, Issue 2, March–April 1993, pp. 6–9.
Written by the President Emeritus of the American Humanist Association, this article reviews Asimov's relationship with the association and his beliefs concerning secular humanism and related issues.

Goldman, Stephen H., "Isaac Asimov," in *Dictionary of Literary Biography,* Vol. 8: *Twentieth-Century American Science-Fiction Writers,* edited by David Cowart and Thomas L. Wymer, Gale Research, 1981, pp. 15–29.
A good review of the life of Asimov and his works, this essay presents a critical analysis, particularly of plot development, of some of the most important of Asimov's works in chronological order of their publication.

Hassler, Donald M., "Some Asimov Resonances from the Enlightenment," in *Science Fiction Studies,* Vol. 15, No. 44, March 1988, pp. 36–47.

One of Asimov's biographers, Hassler discusses in this essay Asimov's use of Enlightenment philosophy in *I, Robot* and the Foundation trilogy. There are two comparisons to ''Nightfall'' concerning its use of a sense of cycles and of a reporter as a device.

Moskowitz, Sam, *Seekers of Tomorrow: Masters of Modern Science Fiction,* World Publishing Company, 1961.

This book presents a chapter on each of the authors generally considered the best writers of science fiction with an analysis of their influence and their most significant works.

Nichols, Lewis, ''Isaac Asimov: Man of 7,560,000 Words,'' in the *New York Times Book Review,* August 3, 1969, pp. 8, 28.

An excellent biographical piece done after a visit to Asimov in his home that describes his work habits and environment.

Touponce, William F., ''Chapter Seven: Asimov's Other Fiction,'' in *Isaac Asimov,* Twayne's United States Authors on CD-ROM, 1997.

This article is a discussion of some of Asimov's novels and his critical reputation.

A Perfect Day for Bananafish

"A Perfect Day for Bananafish" first appeared in the January 31, 1948, issue of the *New Yorker* and was collected as the first piece in *Nine Stories* (1953). The story is the first concerning a member of the fictional Glass family Salinger created, whose members figure in much of his work.

Seymour, the oldest of the Glass children, is Salinger's main character in one of his most elusive pieces of writing. The reader of "Bananafish" learns that Seymour, a veteran of World War II, has had trouble readjusting to civilian life—an understandable problem that thousands of soldiers had to face. However, his suicide in the story's final paragraph shocks most readers and then leaves them scratching their heads, trying to understand why, exactly, Seymour pulled the trigger.

This apparent lack of motive is at the heart of the critical debate on the story. Some readers find Seymour's wife, Muriel, partially to blame, as her self-interest seems to overshadow what should be her wifely concern for her troubled husband. Others view Seymour as something of a guru, a man wise enough to know that his world can only corrupt him and who, therefore, escapes from it. Also plausible is the idea that Seymour is like the bananafish he describes: a man so glutted (with horror *or* pleasure) that he can no longer survive. Multiple interpretations are possible, which makes the story's meaning ripe for debate, a much-disputed point for both professional critics and casual fans. Regardless of

J. D. Salinger

1948

what specific motive a reader assigns to Seymour's suicide, he or she is sure to be involved in Salinger's elaborate game of symbols, colors, and other indirect means of storytelling.

Author Biography

Jerome David Salinger was born in New York City on New Year's Day, 1919. His father, Solomon, was a Jewish cheese importer who hoped that his son would eventually learn his business; his mother, Marie Jillich, was an Irish Catholic whose parents disowned her when she eloped with Solomon. In 1932, the family moved to Park Avenue (as a result of Solomon's success) and Salinger was enrolled at the McBurney School, a private school in Manhattan where he (like his most famous creation, Holden Caulfield) managed the fencing team, wrote for the school newspaper and acted in some drama productions. His failing grades, however, prompted his parents to send him (in 1934) to Valley Forge Military Academy in Pennsylvania, where he edited his class's yearbook and from which he graduated in 1936.

After a brief tour of Europe, Salinger enrolled in Ursinus College in the fall of 1938. After only one semester, however, he dropped out. The following year, he took a course at Columbia University taught by Whit Burnett, the editor of *Story* magazine; Salinger's first piece of fiction, ''The Young Folks,'' impressed Burnett, who published it in a 1940 issue of *Story.* Salinger then sold a number of stories (many now uncollected) to magazines such as *Collier's,* the *Saturday Evening Post* and *Esquire* before he was drafted by the United States Army in 1942. Salinger served with the Army Counter-Intelligence Corps before participating in the 1944 D-Day invasion, where he landed at Utah Beach. In 1945, Salinger suffered some sort of breakdown or illness as a result of the war (the details are unclear) and spent some time at an Army hospital in Nuremberg. That same year, he married his first wife, Sylvia, a woman about whom very little is known. They divorced eight months later, after Salinger had brought her to the United States; she returned to Europe, where she practically disappeared from later biographers.

Despite his failed marriage, Salinger's career as a writer now gained momentum and he enjoyed a long relationship with the *New Yorker,* the magazine that would publish a number of his stories and

longer works: ''A Perfect Day for Bananafish'' was first published in the January 31, 1948 issue. Other works that followed were the stories ''Uncle Wiggly in Connecticut,'' ''The Laughing Man,'' and ''For Esme—With Love and Squalor,'' all of which were later collected in the book *Nine Stories* (1953). In 1950, the first (and only) film treatment of a Salinger work premiered: a version of ''Uncle Wiggly in Connecticut'' renamed *My Foolish Heart.* Salinger hated the film and, to this day, there have been no major film (or stage) adaptations of his work. In 1951, Salinger's most famous work, *The Catcher in the Rye*, was published. He moved to Cornish, New Hampshire in 1953; a year later, he married Claire Douglass, who bore two children, Margaret Ann and Matthew, before her divorce from Salinger in 1967.

Other literary successes followed *The Catcher in the Rye*, in the forms of further narratives concerning the Glass family: *Franny and Zooey* (1961) and *Raise High the Roof Beam, Carpenters and Seymour: An Introduction* (1963). At some point after the appearance (in *The New Yorker*) of the story ''Hapworth 19, 1924,'' Salinger stopped publishing his works, granting interviews and cooperating with would-be biographers. His intense desire for privacy, however, made him even more famous when (in 1987) he had his lawyers challenge the publication of Ian Hamilton's *J. D. Salinger: A Writing Life* on the grounds that Hamilton quoted unpublished letters that he had read at university libraries. Salinger won the case and Hamilton's book was eventually released in a revised form. Since his deposition for the Hamilton case, Salinger has made no public statements of any kind. In 1997, a rumor began purporting that a small publishing house would re-release ''Hapworth 19, 1924,'' but as of 2002, no such book has appeared and Salinger still lives in Cornish, reportedly writing without publishing.

Plot Summary

The story begins in a Florida hotel room, where newlyweds Seymour and Muriel Glass are staying for their vacation. During the first half of the story, however, Seymour is lying on the beach while his wife talks on the telephone to her mother in New York. Muriel's mother repeatedly asks Muriel if she is ''all right,'' which begins to irritate Muriel; her mother's concern arises from a past incident where Seymour apparently tried to kill himself (and possibly others) by driving his father-in-law's car into a tree. When Muriel tells her that Seymour drove to Florida, her mother is naturally anxious; but Muriel says that Seymour ''drove very nicely'' and avoided any ''funny business.'' This does not, however, placate her mother, who asks more questions about Seymour's behavior. Muriel says that Seymour has dubbed her ''Miss Spiritual Tramp of 1948,'' and she tells her mother of Seymour's annoyance that she had not yet read the book of German poems he had bought her (most likely by Rainer Marie Rilke).

Muriel learns that her father had recently spoken to Dr. Sivetski, their family physician, about Seymour's odd behaviors, behaviors which Salinger leaves cloaked in mystery: ''That business with the window. Those horrible things he said to Granny about her plans for passing away. What he did with all those lively pictures from Bermuda—everything.'' Dr. Sivetski told Muriel's father that the Army should not have released Seymour from the hospital and that there is a ''very *great* chance'' that Seymour ''may com*plete*ly lose control of himself.'' Worked into a near panic, Muriel's mother begs her daughter to return. Muriel refuses on the grounds that this has been the first vacation she's had in years. The two then talk about a psychiatrist who is also staying in the hotel: Muriel explains that they spoke about Seymour in the hotel bar, but it was too noisy for them to engage in an in-depth conversation. The talk then shifts to trivial matters of fashion and dinner guests until Muriel's mother asks her once more to come home. Muriel refuses and hangs up.

Meanwhile, the napping Seymour is awakened on the beach by Sybil Carpenter, a little girl of six or seven years who has struck up a friendship with Seymour since his arrival at the hotel. Seymour tells Sybil that he loves her blue bathing suit, despite the fact that it is yellow—a point she vehemently makes as she points to it. She accuses Seymour of favoring Sharon Lipschutz, another little girl at the hotel, since he allowed Sharon to sit next to him on the bench as he played the piano. Seymour calms her by saying, ''I pretended she was you'' and the two of them walk to the ocean.

As Sybil floats on her raft (which Seymour keeps from going out too far), Seymour tells her about the bananafish of the story's title. ''They lead a very tragic life,'' he explains, for they swim into a hole where there are a lot of bananas and then eat as many as they can; however, they then get so fat that they cannot swim back out of the hole, so they die

J. D. Salinger

there of ''banana fever.'' After Sybil says that she saw one, Seymour kisses the arch of her foot and brings her raft back to the shore. Sybil then says ''Goodbye'' and runs to the hotel.

In the elevator he takes to his room, Seymour scolds a woman for looking at his feet (whether or not she actually was looking is unclear). Offended, the woman exits the elevator on the next floor. When the elevator reaches his floor, Seymour exits, enters his room (where Muriel is asleep), takes a hidden pistol from his suitcase, sits down, looks at Muriel and shoots himself in the head.

Characters

Mrs. Carpenter

Sybil's mother appears briefly: after applying suntan lotion to her daughter's back, she tells her to ''run and play'' on the beach while she goes back to the hotel for a martini. Like Muriel, Mrs. Carpenter is more interested in her own pleasures than in truly making contact with the innocent person whom she has been placed in charge.

Sybil Carpenter

As her first name suggests, Sybil is a seer or prophet-like character, who is able to ''see'' the bananafish that Seymour describes to her during their swim. Her opening words (''See more glass'') also suggest her ability to perceive the deeper meaning of experience, a quality that many of Salinger's child characters possess—and one that many of his adult characters lack. (Her mother's reaction to her precocious insight is to tell Sybil things like ''stop saying that'' and then leaving her for a martini.) Her innocence acts as a tonic for the troubled Seymour and her ''sighting'' of the imaginary bananafish confirms, for Seymour, the degree to which the adults around him are unable to ''see more'' of the world's innocence (her last name may, in part, suggest her ''constructive'' role in Seymour's enlightenment). Seymour's kissing of Sybil's foot is a gesture of obeisance and a recognition of those qualities in Sybil not found in characters like Muriel, Muriel's mother, and the woman he meets in the elevator.

Muriel Glass

Muriel Glass, Seymour's wife, is a shallow young woman who faces pressure from her parents to leave her husband in Florida and return to New York by herself. In the story's opening paragraph, the narrator pokes fun at Muriel's annoyance at the long-distance lines being ''monopolized'' by the advertising men staying in her hotel. Her activities while she waits for her mother to call (tweezing a mole, removing a spot from a suit, moving a button on her Saks blouse, polishing her nails) suggest her preoccupation with her own appearance. Her answering the telephone only on the ''fifth or sixth ring'' again accents her vanity.

Muriel's ''defense'' of Seymour while talking to her mother also suggests much about how she views her husband. Her telling her mother that she let Seymour drive suggests a faith in her husband and a willingness to put his past indiscretions (or worse) behind her. When she speaks of the psychiatrist she met in the hotel, however, she reveals what seems to be a lackadaisical attitude toward Seymour's problems: she does not recall the doctor's name (''Rieser or something'') and says that she did not really discuss Seymour's troubles with him because the bar was too noisy. The ease with which she then shifts into a conversation about this year's fashions and her hotel room (which is ''*just* all right'') suggests a lack of empathy with her husband's plight.

Seymour Glass

With his almost nonchalant suicide at the story's end, Seymour has become one of American literature's most enigmatic characters. ''Why did he do it?'' is a difficult question with which many readers and writers struggle; an overview of the story, however, suggests a few possible routes of inquiry about Seymour's past and present problems.

The reader learns (from Muriel's conversation with her mother) that Seymour served in the United States Army and spent an undisclosed amount of time in a veteran's hospital, presumably for psychiatric evaluation or recovery. Since the story was first published in 1948, the reader can assume that Seymour (like his creator) saw action in World War II that affected him in terrible and unspoken ways. The reader also learns that Seymour tried to crash his father-in-law's car into a tree, attempted some ''business'' with a window (also presumably self-destructive), said ''horrible things'' to Muriel's grandmother about ''her plans for passing away,'' tried to do ''something with Granny's chair'' and harmed ''all those lovely pictures from Bermuda.'' Obviously, Seymour is preoccupied with death, a preoccupation that becomes a reality in the final paragraph.

Seymour's war experiences have left him so badly shaken that he searches for some form of purity in what he sees as a dangerous and corrupt world. Thus, his only two friends at the hotel are Sybil and Sharon: two little girls whose innocence amuses and refreshes Seymour. His parable of the bananafish serves as a possible metaphor for Seymour's troubles: like the bananafish, he has glutted himself full of war and death to the point that he can no longer ''get out of the hole again.'' (This, however, is only a partial explanation for the meaning of the bananafish story: another possibility is that Seymour has been so moved by the purity of Sybil that he can no longer return to a world of Muriels and psychiatrists.) His kissing Sybil's foot is a gesture of respect, a gesture that she (in her innocence) cannot understand, and his suicide is an even more dramatic one that, presumably, his wife will not understand.

Muriel's Mother

Like her daughter, Muriel's mother is a woman concerned with Seymour and his problems, but aloof at the same time. On one hand, she voices concern over Seymour's problems and her daughter's safety; on the other, her proposed solutions to these problems involve Muriel abandoning her husband and taking a "lovely cruise" by herself. (Her adding that Muriel's father is "more than willing to pay for it," suggests she feels that solutions to psychological problems can be bought.)

Dr. Sivetski

Dr. Sivetski is Muriel's family physician. Muriel learns that her father spoke to him about Seymour's mental illness and that Dr. Sivetski warned that Seymour may "com*plete*ly lose control of himself."

Woman in the Elevator

When Seymour leaves the beach, he takes an elevator to his room. During the elevator ride, he sees a woman whom he accuses of gawking at his feet. After his accusation, the woman says she "happened to be looking at the floor" and gets off at the next floor. Presumably, this woman is treated so roughly by Seymour because (unlike Sybil) she hides her emotions and thoughts behind a silly excuse.

Themes

Alienation

Almost everything (and everyone) in Seymour's world is tainted by shallowness, vanity, or violence. The most obvious example of this state of affairs is the war, which destroyed a part of Seymour that he is only able to recognize in the two children he befriends at the hotel. Muriel is almost completely self-absorbed: all of her actions in the story's opening paragraph have to do with her appearance (moving a button, cleaning a skirt, polishing her nails, washing her comb and brush, tweezing a mole); when asked by Seymour to read the poems of Rainer Marie Rilke, she mocks Seymour's enthusiasm and instead flips through a brainless article titled "Sex Is Fun—or Hell." (Presumably she has to be told the answer to this riddle.) Despite Seymour's past indications that his mind was collapsing, she brushes aside her mother's concern because this is "the first vacation" she has had "in years." Her coat is of equal concern to her as her husband's troubled mind, and the reader is invited to believe that she let Seymour drive to Florida not out of any great faith in him but because she is not the kind of girl who would drive herself (as the reader is told, she is "a girl for who a ringing phone dropped exactly nothing").

Despite the fact that he married her, there is nothing in the story to suggest that Seymour can make any kind of real contact with his new wife: Salinger never puts them in the same scene until the very end, when Seymour (significantly) does not wake her up before killing himself. The characters with whom Seymour *does* connect, however, are Sybil and Sharon. Sybil's mother reminds the reader of Muriel, for she, too, is more concerned with herself than in protecting her daughter. Seymour can only speak to Sybil because of her innocence and freedom from what he sees as the corruption and phoniness of the world. (This is why Seymour resents the woman in the elevator lying about looking at his feet: a child would simply look at someone's feet without any unease or desire to hide the fact.) After his conversation with Sybil (from which she runs "without regret," leaving the scene without any compunction or need to engage in the kind of false manners that marks the conversation of Muriel and her mother), Seymour quite possibly realizes that such innocence and freedom from the hypocrisy of adulthood has vanished from his own life—which leads to his decision to forsake that life, in favor of a better one elsewhere.

Suicide

Like *The Catcher in the Rye*'s Holden Caulfield, Seymour Glass is a person whose essential innocence marks him as unfit for the world in which he finds himself; while Holden retreats into bouts of near-insanity before his final emotional collapse, Seymour takes much more drastic (and final) action. *Why*, exactly, he takes such drastic action is the central question of the story.

One reason (discussed above) could be that Seymour feels such despair at the thought of his own fall from innocence (a fall made more apparent by his activities in the war) that he kills himself to prevent his soul from becoming more tainted. Seen in this light, Seymour's troubles are a magnification of those felt by millions of veterans who return from any war with the images of its horrors still fresh in their minds. Another possibility is the obverse: Seymour (like the bananafish) has glutted himself with too much sensory pleasure and feels such self-disgust that he commits suicide out of shame after speaking to Sybil. He does not want to become like the self-consumed Muriel, so he kills himself to prevent this from happening. (Of course, if the bananafish story is applied in this way to Seymour, one realizes that it is the nature of bananafish to eat too many bananas, just as Seymour feels it is the

Topics for Further Study

- Research Sigmund Freud's ideas of the *id,* the *ego* and the *superego.* To what degree do Seymour's actions reflect these different parts of the mind asserting themselves?

- Locate a contemporary casebook that details some of the more commonly diagnosed reasons for suicide and apply some of these reasons to Seymour. Can you explain his suicide in clinical terms?

- There is some debate among Salinger scholars concerning the degree to which the Seymour of ''Bananafish'' resembles the Seymour of Salinger's later Glass family fiction. Read some of the other Glass stories and decide if the Seymour

that appears in those pages acts and talks like the Seymour in Salinger's original story.

- Despite Salinger's desire to live as a recluse, a number of biographers have offered theories as to why Salinger, at the height of his popularity, decided to stop publishing his work. Research and compare some of these theories. Do any of them seem psychologically credible, or are they merely sensational conjecture?

- Compose a story that begins the moment after Seymour pulls the trigger. What runs through Muriel's mind when she awakens? What happens to her later in life? How might Seymour's suicide affect her values and assumptions?

---

nature of humans to glut themselves with sensory pleasure.) A third possibility is that Seymour is, at heart, a child—but a child who (unlike Sybil) demands attention from his loved ones, to the point where his suicide is something like a temper tantrum at the injustices of the adult world. (This accords with his outburst in the elevator, his last spoken words to another person.) However, Salinger's leaving the meaning of Seymour's suicide open to such wide avenues of interpretation suggests the ultimate impossibility of fully fathoming the mind of any person who willingly destroys him or herself. (Such fathoming is what Buddy Glass, Seymour's younger brother, attempts to do in Salinger's later fiction.)

Style

Symbolism

Every symbol (in life and in literature) is composed of two parts: the symbol (the actual picture, such as a skull and crossbones) and a referent (the thing for which the symbol stands, such as poison). Writers use symbols as a matter of course: things

like the river in *The Adventures of Huckleberry Finn* or Hester's ''A'' in *The Scarlet Letter* allow readers to better grasp the meanings of each work as a whole.

However, part of what makes ''A Perfect Day for Bananafish'' so intriguing is Salinger's use of symbols where the referents are highly ambiguous. The most notable example of this is the story of the bananafish itself. Seymour says that these imaginary fish lead ''very tragic'' lives, since they are ''very ordinary-looking fish'' until they swim into the banana hole, where they eat so many bananas that they get banana fever (a ''terrible disease'') and then die. This symbolic story of Seymour's is grounds for confusion about the nature of its referents. The bananafish may be symbolic of all people, who (in their fallen state) gorge themselves so much with sensory delights that their souls (or capacity to understand the innocence of someone like Sybil, for example) are figuratively killed by ''banana fever.'' (The sexual symbolism of the story adds weight to this interpretation.) The bananafish may also be symbolic of Seymour himself, who (like many young men) was lured into the ''banana hole'' of war and figuratively consumed so many of the war's horrors that he is now unable to come out of the hole and reintegrate himself into the world of non-combatants. Either way (or even along other routes), Salinger deliberately leaves the referent of Seymour's symbols open for debate.

Other symbolism occurs in Salinger's use of the color blue. Like the bananafish, however, the symbolic importance of these colors is often ambiguous. Blue is a color often associated with innocence and spirituality (hence, for example, the blue material in which the Virgin Mary is often depicted in religious paintings). Here, Seymour wears a blue bathing suit (and tells Sybil that "if there's one thing" he likes, it's a blue bathing suit) and swims with Sybil in the blue waters of the Atlantic (where, presumably, he is moved by the spiritual purity of his young companion). The fact that Sybil's bathing suit is yellow, however, does not faze Seymour, who tells her, "That's a fine bathing suit you have on," and feigns stupidity when Sybil corrects him about the color; to him, Sybil's bathing suit may as well be blue, in light of the innocence she embodies.

Another symbol is found in the story's frequent mention of sunburn. Muriel is burned so badly that she "can hardly move," Sybil's mother is first seen putting suntan lotion on her daughter's back, Seymour keeps his robe closed tightly while he lies on the beach, and the woman Seymour accosts in the elevator has zinc salve covering her nose. All of these examples symbolically suggest that as humans attempt to shield themselves from the dangerous rays of the sun, they likewise have varying degrees of success when they attempt to shield themselves from corruption and superficiality, two aspects of the modern world that are as common as sunlight. Thus, Muriel is the most sunburned because she is the most vain and superficial; the innocent Sybil never burns; the elevator woman's nose is protected, but not her whole self (as seen in her lying to Seymour); and Seymour keeps his robe clenched tightly—Salinger's suggestion that Seymour subconsciously fears the corrupting influences of the world as he fears the damaging rays of the sun.

Historical Context

The Birth of American Postmodernism

Literary movements rarely begin on clear and set dates; the postmodernist movement was no exception. Loosely defined, postmodernism is an artistic movement that experiments with (and often destroys) traditional modes and methods of characterization and narrative. Postmodernists characteristically believe, for example, that what we see and hear is nothing but an artificial structure that does not represent the world accurately. "A Perfect Day for Bananafish," published in 1948, is an early example of a postmodernist story in which the key element of the plot (the motive for Seymour's suicide) is conspicuously missing—it challenges the very idea that a writer can enter the mind of a character and make the workings of such a mind understood by a reader.

American Literature and World War II

On September 2, 1945, Japan's formal surrender to the United States ended World War II, a conflict to which authors and filmmakers continue turning today. Norman Mailer's powerful debut *The Naked and the Dead* (1948), published the same year as "A Perfect Day for Bananafish," made its author a celebrity and sparked a new era in which writers attempted to illustrate the devastating effects of the war on those who served in it. Other works, such as Irwin Shaw's *The Young Lions* (1948), John Hawkes' *The Cannibal* and James Jones' *From Here to Eternity* (1951) explore similar themes. Like Salinger's story, they often depict the veteran as a man scarred by what he has seen and, in some cases, unable to reintegrate himself into civilian life.

The American Short Story and Magazines

The 1940s saw a number of magazines become more prominent as a result of their satisfying readers' desires for short stories. Magazines such as *Collier's,* the *Saturday Evening Post, Harper's* and *Good Housekeeping* offered their readers countless stories by both "hacks" and masters of the craft: writers such as F. Scott Fitzgerald, John O' Hara, and Ernest Hemingway all appeared in popular magazines during their careers.

Two magazines esteemed for their fiction were *Esquire* and (although it had a smaller readership) *Story.* A writer whose work appeared in one of these publications could feel proud of his or her achievement, so impressive were these magazines' reputations. Salinger's first story, "The Young Folks" was published in *Story*'s March-April 1940 issue: a small triumph, considering Salinger's age (twenty–one) and the degree to which the magazine's editor, Columbia University's Whit Burnett, was esteemed. Salinger's next magazine appearance was in the

Compare & Contrast

- **1940s:** Magazine fiction is a hot commodity: a nation of readers seeks entertainment in the pages of periodicals like the *New Yorker,* the *Saturday Evening Post,* and *Esquire.*

  Today: Although the *New Yorker* still stands as the premiere source for cutting-edge short fiction, more and more short story writers find their work first published in specialized literary journals.

- **1940s:** The psychological toll of war on a person's mind is called "shell-shock" or "battle fatigue;" some of those suffering from it are labeled cowards by their superiors or the public.

  Today: What is now known as post-traumatic stress disorder is widely recognized by psychologists and other doctors as a terrible, but treatable, mental illness.

- **1940s:** J. D. Salinger is known by readers of the *New Yorker* and other magazines as an up-and-coming talent.

  Today: Approximately forty years since Salinger stopped publishing his work and withdrew into private life in Cornish, New Hampshire, his name has become a household word and *The Catcher in the Rye* still sells more than 250,000 copies every year.

July 12, 1941 issue of *Collier's:* his story, "The Hang of It" confirmed Salinger as an author to watch. More magazine success followed: "The Heart of a Broken Story" in the September 1941 issue of *Esquire,* "The Long Debut of Lois Taggett" in the September-October issue of *Story,* and "Last Day of the Last Furlough" in the July 15, 1944 issue of the *Saturday Evening Post.* Many other stories appeared in these and other, lesser-known magazines.

While Salinger had conquered the "slicks" (as some writers and editors derisively called mass-market magazines), his work had yet to appear in what fiction writers regarded as the Holy Grail of magazines: the *New Yorker.* The magazine had accepted his story about Holden Caulfield, "A Slight Rebellion Off Madison," in 1941 but had not suggested to him when (if ever) the story would appear. However, Salinger did break into the pages of the *New Yorker* in the December 21, 1946 issue with his (by then) five-year-old story. Its publication marked the beginning of Salinger's long relationship with the magazine: "A Perfect Day for Bananafish" appeared in the January 31, 1948 issue, followed by "Uncle Wiggly in Connecticut" the following March, and "Just Before the War with the Eskimos" in June. For the remainder of his publishing career, Salinger's work (including his

novellas) appeared in the *New Yorker* until his last published work, "Hapworth 16, 1924" appeared in the June 19, 1965 issue.

Critical Overview

In his controversial biography, *In Search of J. D. Salinger,* Ian Hamilton calls "A Perfect Day for Bananafish" "spare, teasingly mysterious, withheld"—surely a deliberate understatement in light of the great deal of ink the critical community has spilled over the story. In his essay "A Critical Perspective on the Works of J. D. Salinger" (collected in Harold Bloom's 2002 *J. D. Salinger,* part of the Bloom's BioCritiques series), Clifford Mills remarks that Salinger's stories may be read as "riddles without any obvious solutions" and points of departure for "thinking, questioning" and "meditating." Knowing the degree to which readers yearn for a solution to the story's mystery, Mills concedes that Seymour's suicide is "one of the central riddles of Salinger's later fiction." In his famous essay, "J. D. Salinger: 'Everybody's Favorite'" (also collected by Bloom), the renowned critic Alfred Kazin praises Salinger's having "done an honest and stimulating professional job" in his stories, which project "emotion like a cry from the stage" and reveal their author's "almost compulsive need to fill in each inch of his canvas, each moment of his scene." However, Kazin also remarks that Salinger is guilty of "cute" characterization and writing laden with "self-conscious charm and prankishness." Still, he admits that "A Perfect Day for Bananafish" does possess a "brilliantly entertaining texture."

There are almost as many opinions about why Seymour kills himself as there are readers of the story, which is why a combination of praise and puzzlement is found in many critical appraisals. For example, in his essay, "J. D. Salinger: Seventy–Eight Bananas" (collected in Harold Bloom's 1987 collection *Modern Critical Views: J. D. Salinger*), William Wiegand attempts to "solve" the riddle of Seymour's death when he argues that Seymour is "a bananafish himself," who has "become so glutted with sensation that he cannot swim out into society again." Wiegand further argues that Seymour's suicide is not the fault of any other character (such as Muriel), but that "the bananafish diagnosis" applies to many of Salinger's characters. Like Wiegand, Warren French (in his book *J. D. Salinger, Revisited*) writes that Seymour is not upset with "the insufficiently appreciative Muriel" as much as with himself for "succumbing to materialistic temptations." Similarly, in Bernice and Sanford Goldstein's appraisal, "Zen and *Nine Stories*" (also collected in Bloom's *Modern Critical Views*), Seymour is described as "the enlightened man rejected by the non-enlightened world," a world he flees through his suicide. In his *J. D. Salinger: A Critical Essay*, Kenneth Hamilton even contends that Seymour kills himself for Muriel's sake and that his suicide is "his way of allowing the true Muriel to escape from the banana hole where she has become trapped through her attitude to marriage." To Hamilton, Seymour "dies physically in order that she may again live spiritually"—a strained conclusion, perhaps, but one that illustrates the degree to which critics will try to wrestle a solution from the story.

Other critics shy away from clear-cut solutions and instead focus on the ways in which the story dramatizes Zen and Buddhist thought, a different manner of thinking than that to which a Western reader is accustomed. In his book, *J. D. Salinger*, James Lundquist quotes the Zen *koan* that Salinger uses as an epigraph for *Nine Stories* ("We know the sound of two hands clapping. But what is the sound of one hand clapping?") and argues that, like the *koan,* the story urges its readers to ponder profound Buddhist issues such as the degree to which a person can truly know him or herself and the ability (or inability) for a person to reach *satori,* a "sudden and intuitive way of seeing into themselves." Lundquist ultimately argues that the story urges its readers to "vomit up the apple of logic" and realize that, in Buddhism, suicide lacks the stigma that it carries in Christianity. Other writers, such as Frederick L. Gwynn and Joseph L. Blotner (whose essay "One Hand Clapping" appears in Henry Anatole Grunwald's *Salinger: A Critical and Personal Portrait*) concur with Lundquist, generalizing (as Gwynn and Blotner do) that Salinger's stories reflect Zen thought to make the reader "aware that the tales present problems which he may or may not solve for himself by supersensory perception." Further application of Zen thinking to Salinger's work has continued over time, as more critics have examined Salinger's later works about the Glass family.

Criticism

Daniel Moran

Moran is an instructor of English and American literature. In this essay, Moran argues that Salinger's story trivializes the very subject it is meant to explore.

> If suicide isn't at the top of the list of compelling infirmities for creative men, the suicide poet or artist, one can't help noticing, has always been given a very considerable amount of avid attention.—Buddy Glass, discussing his older brother in *Seymour: An Introduction*

Partly because of the shock value of its ending and partly because Salinger is an author whose withdrawal from the world gives all his work the stamp of "serious art," "A Perfect Day for Bananafish" is often puzzled over by students and critics with all the reverence of the faithful. Not "getting" why Seymour kills himself is, according to many of Salinger's fans, the whole point, or at least part of the point. Suicide, they contend, is an obscure and intimate business: not everyone kills him or herself like Romeo, Othello, or Willy Loman, with their reasons known to both the readers and themselves. The reader is unprepared for Seymour's suicide, so when it comes, he or she is shocked, which, of course, is part of Salinger's plan. Salinger

"A Perfect Day for Bananafish" first appeared in this volume of the New Yorker *on January 31, 1948*

is then praised for his brilliance in *not* offering a "traditional" motive (love, despair) for suicide, but for depicting it as it "really is."

If that were the case, however, Salinger's story would be markedly different. As it stands, the reader is invited (if not roughhoused) into going back through the story after the report of the pistol. After Seymour pulls the trigger, Muriel, of course, awakens, sees her dead husband and—eventually, readers can assume—begins traveling on the same train of thought as the reader: Why did he do it? What was the origin of this terrible event? Did it just sneak up on him, or was it a long time coming? A reader cannot imagine that Seymour killed himself for reasons unknown, nor will Muriel be able to brush off her husband's death with the same logic. Readers go back over the story and look for what clever critics would call "foreshadowing" or what psychologists would label "cries for help."

As Henry James said, "All reading is rereading," so the second time around, the reader notices more apparent "clues" that might help him or her solve what comes to feel more and more like a murder mystery, as opposed to an examination of a suicide.

What Do I Read Next?

- *The Catcher in the Rye* (1951) is Salinger's most famous work. The novel follows Holden Caulfield, a disaffected prep-school dropout, as he meanders in New York City for three days. Like Seymour, Holden feels alienated from those around him and toys with thoughts of suicide.

- Salinger's two novellas *Raise High the Roof Beam, Carpenters and Seymour: An Introduction* (1963) are both narrated by Buddy Glass, Seymour's younger brother. *Carpenters* tells the story of Seymour and Muriel's wedding, while the *Introduction* is Buddy's attempt to make the reader appreciate his brother's more elusive qualities.

- *Franny and Zooey* (1961) is another of Salinger's extended examinations of the Glass family. While these two novellas do not directly concern Seymour, they do add to the overall literary universe of which Seymour is undoubtedly the center.

- T. S. Eliot's poem *The Waste Land* (1922) is quoted by Seymour; as Salinger's story explores the destruction of a single soul, Eliot's poem explores the destruction in an era and civilization.

- The British poet John Keats's "Ode on Melancholy" (1813) explores the "wakeful anguish of the soul," an anguish that Seymour surely feels.

- Shakespeare's *Hamlet* (1601) contains some of the playwright's most moving and introspective soliloquies; Hamlet's famous "To be or not to be" soliloquy can certainly be read as an argument about suicide and Hamlet himself (with his shifting moods and rejection of those around him) resembles Seymour in a number of ways.

- Like "A Perfect Day for Bananafish," Ernest Hemingway's story "Soldier's Home" (1925) details the inability of a combat veteran to reintegrate himself into society. Here, the protagonist is returning from World War I.

- For those readers who find Seymour's suicide motivated by his love for the world (rather than his revulsion at it), Emily Dickinson's poem "I Died for Beauty" (1890) may be appropriate, since it addresses the same viewpoint.

- Like Seymour, the title character of Edwin Arlington Robinson's poem "Richard Cory" (1897) kills himself for reasons about which the reader is left to speculate.

The first batch of clues comes from the story's number-one suspect: Muriel. Before the first-time reader reaches the end of the story, the scene with Muriel on the telephone with her mother reads like tame, *New Yorker*-brand social satire. The second time, however, the reader is inclined to view Muriel in a harsher light, a light cast by Salinger himself:

> There were ninety-seven advertising men in the hotel, and the way they were monopolizing the phone lines, the girl in 507 had to wait from noon till almost two–thirty to get her call through. She used the time, though. She read an article in a women's pocket-sized magazine, called "Sex Is Fun—or Hell." She washed her comb and brush. She took the spot out of the skirt of her beige suit. She moved the buttons on her Saks blouse. She tweezed out two freshly surfaced hairs in her mole. When the operator finally rang her room, she was sitting on the window seat and had almost finished putting lacquer on the nails of her left hand.

Muriel's "using the time" reflects her own shallowness and vanity and all her activities as she waits for the operator to "finally" ring her room suggest the degree to which she loves herself and her appearance. Salinger's repeated use of "She" followed by a verb draws attention to her actions in order to highlight their apparent meaninglessness. All of her attention is turned inward and the reader begins to suspect that Muriel's shallowness has something to do with Seymour's suicide. (His looking at her before he pulls the trigger adds to the suspicion.)

> "Like a child who has just written his or her full name for the first time and wants his or her parents to hang it on the refrigerator, Salinger constantly calls attention to himself and his precocious intellect."

Other parts of the opening scene invite the reader to look down his or her nose at Seymour's bride. She does not, for example, even recall where she *left* the book Seymour gave her of (presumably) Rilke's poems (the "only great poet of the century," according to Seymour) and instead "uses her time" reading brainless magazine articles like "Sex Is Fun—or Hell." She complains that her room is "All right," but "*Just* all right, though." She refuses her mother's wish to return to New York not because she wants to show her mother how much she trusts Seymour but because she "just *got*" there and this is the "first vacation" she has had "in years." She apparently was not interested enough in Seymour's troubles to pursue a conversation with a psychiatrist staying in the hotel. She complains about her sunburn as if that were worse that the unspecified troubles afflicting her husband. Finally, the faculty with which she moves from the topic of Seymour's mental illness to ones concerning fashion ("You see sequins—everything") cements the reader's opinion of her as "Miss Spiritual Tramp of 1948." Yes, the reader thinks, with that nickname, Seymour is definitely "onto something."

After all, he can *see more.* If Muriel seems somehow blameworthy on a second reading, Seymour seems less so. Knowing that he is going to kill himself causes all of his actions to arouse more sympathy. The same reader who, at first, wondered whether or not Seymour was a pedophile now dismisses his or her initial impressions (and even feels guilty for forming them). Now he or she thinks that Seymour talks to Sybil (and Sharon) because they are more honest and "real" than Muriel. Seymour is now a dead man talking and the reader

naturally harkens to everything he says, again hoping to find some clue that will explain Seymour's actions at the end.

What he says is, of, course, a collection of puzzling things masquerading as wisdom, the first of which involves Sybil's bathing suit. "That's a fine bathing suit you have on," he tells her. "If there's one thing I like, it's a blue bathing suit." After Sybil corrects him ("This is a *yellow*"), Seymour brushes off the joke—but the reader is left wondering why Seymour made the joke in the first place. He or she then thinks of where else in the story the color blue is found, and remembers that Seymour's own bathing suit is "royal blue," that Muriel's coat (from which she had the padding taken out) is also blue, and, of course, that Seymour and Sybil swim in the blue Atlantic. Then the reader recalls what he learned in his or her Introduction to Literature course about colors: red is traditionally associated with passion or blood, white is usually a sign of purity, and blue often suggests innocence.

At this point, one can hear the collective "A-*ha*s!" of a generation of readers. Yes! Seymour's bathing suit is blue because he is innocent—that's why he can only talk to children! And that's why he swims with Sybil in the ocean: it is the sea of innocence, where (like an equally innocent dolphin) Seymour belongs, instead of the corrupt hotel room that smells of Muriel's "new calfskin luggage and nail-polish remover"). That's why Seymour tells Sybil that she is wearing a blue bathing suit: it may *literally* be yellow, but Seymour can *see more* and perceive Sybil's essential innocence. As for Muriel's blue coat, she had the padding taken out, so she is *less innocent.*

Once this kind of thinking begins, there is almost no way to stop it. The whole story becomes a cipher that the reader is meant to decode. But who can blame him or her? Salinger has loaded it with seemingly symbolic words and things, the most obvious being the bananafish story itself: is Seymour the bananafish who has glutted himself with the simple pleasures of life (like swimming with an innocent child) but who then must die because such rapture cannot be sustained? Or is he *afraid* of becoming like the bananafish, making his suicide his only solution for forsaking the sensual pleasures of the world? Salinger purposefully poses these questions and places clues his characters' names: Seymour, as noted, "sees more" than the average person and, like glass, is easily broken. The name Sybil suggests the female prophets of classical mythology: are Sybil's words meant to portend the death of Seymour? Of course, the name Carpenter calls to mind the carpenter who is at the heart of many literary allusions and who, like Seymour, died an innocent man with only a handful of people aware of his divinity: Jesus Christ.

Such reasoning could continue for pages and there are other elements of the story (the various characters' degrees of sunburn or the kissing of Sybil's foot, for example) that could be treated in the same way. But the above paragraph illustrates well enough that Salinger lures the reader into a literary guessing-game of which only Salinger knows (or pretends to know) the answer. Anyone who questions Seymour's actions is placed in the same category as Muriel: a philistine who cannot ponder the big questions that are, presumably, running through Seymour's mind. Seymour is intended to stand as the embodiment of a romantic soul, and the reader is supposed to take his essential and absolute innocence on faith; he is too foolish for this awful world and his suicide is meant to be read as a protest against the shallowness of Muriel, the horrors of World War II, or the state of fallen man who must, inevitably, succumb to his desires—take your pick. Seymour must die because he sees more; he must die because he is too tender; he must die because the world is too corrupt.

Fans of the story tirelessly point out Muriel's self-indulgence, but what could be more self-indulgent than Salinger's authorial activity in this story? To use something as horrifying and distressing as suicide as a forum for showing off one's ability to manipulate symbols and pseudo-philosophical parables is much more self-indulgent than moving a button on a blouse or tweezing a mole. Like a child who has just written his or her full name for the first time and wants his or her parents to hang it on the refrigerator, Salinger constantly calls attention to himself and his precocious intellect. Such activity, of course, only *trivializes* the subject and makes it the occasion for an exhibition of Salinger's powers.

In his exhaustive study *Rousseau and Romanticism* (1919), Irving Babbitt notes that when a romantic such as Seymour discovers that his ideals are incompatible with the real world, he does not blame himself; rather, he "simply assumes that the world is unworthy of being so exquisitely organized as himself." The result of the romantic's ability to "see more" is that he is "at once odious and unintelligible to the ordinary human pachyderm." No reader, of course, wants to count him or herself among the "ordinary pachyderms" (such as Muriel), so, instead, he or she views Seymour's suicide as a very meaningful event instead of the sham that it is.

At another point in his book, Babbitt quotes an observation of Goethe's that might be applied to Seymour: "weakness seeking to give itself the prestige of strength." What a reader not taken in by Salinger's shenanigans sees in "A Perfect Day for Bananafish" is self-indulgence seeking to give itself the prestige of profundity. And what would one call an author who willfully (and enthusiastically) manipulates his readers, luring them into guessing games about a subject of awful importance? To borrow the favorite phrase of Salinger's most famous creation: a phony.

Source: Daniel Moran, Critical Essay on "A Perfect Day for Bananafish," in *Short Stories for Students,* The Gale Group, 2003.

Carey Wallace

Wallace is a freelance writer and poet. In this essay, Wallace explores the mysteries Seymour Glass struggled with on the day before his death.

In some ways, J. D. Salinger's "A Perfect Day for Bananafish" is a mystery story. Its protagonist, Seymour Glass, is married to a beautiful woman. He is on vacation at a tropical resort. He has just spent the day on the beach, having a playful nonsense conversation with one of the hotel's child guests. Why, then, would he end his afternoon by putting a gun to his head?

Some clues can be found in Salinger's other writings, *Franny and Zooey* and *Raise High the Roof Beam, Carpenters and Seymour: An Introduction,* which concern the Glass family, a group of precocious siblings of which Seymour is the eldest. Each of these other stories is in some way about Seymour as well—the other siblings consider him the genius of the family. In fact, it becomes clear from the other stories that Seymour takes it upon himself to educate the family's youngest children in his own special program of readings and meditation, deeply affecting the way they think for years to come. Because Seymour is a larger-than-life figure in the family, his suicide is a constant topic in the rest of the Glass cycle. Was his death an act of cowardice or completion? Should the rest of the siblings follow his example as they followed his other teachings? And, more simply, why did he do it?

Salinger's other Glass writings seem to give clues. Elsewhere in the cycle, Salinger reveals,

> **" ... people who do not have a fear that they are not normal do not go around asserting that they are. . . ."**

for instance, that Seymour's wife, Muriel, looks very much like another precocious young girl whom Seymour knew, and presumably loved, as a child, which might explain his attraction to a woman with whom he seems otherwise very badly matched. And, in *Raise High the Roof Beam, Carpenters* Seymour's younger brother, Buddy, describes Seymour and Muriel's wedding; Seymour and Muriel do not actually attend, electing to elope instead. While the guests are waiting, however, Muriel's family's disapproval and Seymour's eccentric behavior are described in detail, through their comments.

The rest of the Glass Family cycle offers more details, but no true answers. Seymour is too sensitive a man not to have noticed the difference between his childhood love and Muriel long before "A Perfect Day for Bananfish," and probably long before their wedding—that revelation alone cannot be the reason for his death. Salinger gives ample evidence of both Muriel's parents' doubts about Seymour and Seymour's strange habits, within "A Perfect Day for Bananafish" itself. Not only that, but Seymour does not actually appear in any of the other Glass Family stories—he is always a topic, but also always absent: spoken about, thought of, but never really there. So the solution to the mystery of "A Perfect Day for Bananfish" must be within the story itself, the only published story in which Seymour gets to speak for himself.

Salinger sets the stage for his readers through the conversation between Muriel and her mother. In the opening paragraphs, he reveals that Muriel is beautiful; that she is active, as she uses the time she spends waiting for her phone call for all sorts of organization and grooming; that she is married, and, very quickly thereafter, that her mother disapproves of the match and even fears for her daughter's safety with her husband. Muriel is also shallow. When the conversation is in her control, she speaks to her mother mostly about banal details, and she responds to her mother's pleas to leave her husband not with a declaration of fidelity, but by saying that she is not leaving yet because this is the first vacation she has had in ages.

On the other hand, Muriel is by no means a monster. Despite her concern with surfaces, she shows some spark of her own, sarcastically telling her mother that a psychiatrist might be competent even though her mother had never heard of him. Muriel is even capable of loyalty and steadfastness: her mother reveals that Muriel waited for Seymour all through the war, while other women were less faithful to their husbands. And unlike her mother, Muriel seems largely unruffled by Seymour's implied shenanigans: it may not be exactly appropriate, but her response to Seymour nicknaming her "Miss Spiritual Tramp of 1948" is a giggle, not a display of wounded vanity. Several times she defends Seymour against her mother's fears, and she declares that she herself is not afraid of him.

It is Seymour himself, actually, who appears to have the deeper problems. Although Muriel's mother is clearly a hysteric, his behavior, especially the suggestion that he is dangerous to himself and others when driving, is somewhat frightening, as is the suggestion that he had been released too soon from an Army hospital, for an ailment that is clearly mental.

Readers are given a chance to judge for themselves between the two in the story's next segment, in which Seymour is finally seen speaking for himself. What they find is a man in some ways perfectly suited to society, and in others completely incapable of fitting in, a man who both deeply desires and deeply fears love—a mass of contradictions who is at the same time extremely ill-equipped to deal with the contradictions he finds in others and in society in general. His unhappy marriage to Muriel is just a symptom of these larger issues, which will eventually kill him.

From the onset, Seymour's interaction with Sybil is both brilliant and strange. When the very young girl arrives, he greets her as if she were a similarly aged companion, even flirting with her, gently. This, in itself, does not make him crazy; kids love to be treated like grown-ups, so it is a natural way to play with them. But, Seymour's imitation of adult talk, directed at Sybil, has an unmistakable ironic edge. And it reveals something else: although, according to Muriel and her mother, he has been doing a bad job at getting along in society, in a situation in which it is not exactly appropriate, he proves he has actually got all the equipment needed to be a great success in almost any social circle.

He also reveals, for the only time, his thoughts on his wife, in response to Sybil's question about what Muriel is doing. "Having her hair dyed mink," he says. "Or making dolls for poor children, in her room." Seymour's analysis of Muriel is similar to the one that could be gathered from her earlier conversation with her mother: Muriel may not be deep, but she is capable of acts of goodness, and even selflessness. Seymour does not present this as an accusation. Instead, he seems to be struggling with his own ambivalence about her contradictions.

"Ask me something else," he suggests to Sybil, to get off the subject, and immediately he launches into his first bit of nonsense, which can either be interpreted as childish word-play, or as a glimpse into his own slightly mad vision: he tells her how much he likes her blue bathing suit. But her bathing suit, in fact, is yellow, and Sybil is having none of it. She insists on reality as she knows it, repeating twice that what she is wearing is "yellow." In response, Seymour capitulates, then slips back into what would be socially acceptable conversation, if he were in the company of others his age. "I'm a Capricorn," he tells her, launching into one of the oldest pickup lines in the book, and then continues on with a string of eerily grownup responses to her jealousy about his friendship with another little girl. His responses, which sound strikingly like an adult trying to explain a small infidelity, are now thick with irony. Although Sybil does not notice it, for the adult reader, they serve less to throw Seymour's sanity into question than to undermine the sanity of society in general, by pointing out how closely their conversation, if they really were adults, would verge on childish nonsense. But once again, Sybil the pragmatist is unconvinced by his arguments: next time, she says, Seymour should push the other girl right off the piano bench.

Seymour quickly veers away from the adult back into imagination again, however, telling Sybil that he's got a new idea: they should go looking for bananafish. Sybil goes with him down to the water, but she is still staunchly resistant to his nonsense, insisting on her address, even when he playfully tries to destabilize it, and calling him on his lie that he has read "Little Black Sambo," by reminding him that there were only six tigers in the book, instead of the multitudes Seymour claims to have seen. Sybil remains recalcitrant even in Seymour's

opening gambit about bananafish, refusing to join in the game by insisting that she does not see any. Seymour presses on, telling her a lengthy story about the nature of bananfish, who swim into small holes and gorge themselves on bananas, meeting their deaths when they find themselves too sick from "banana fever" to swim back out.

The story is interrupted by a large wave which is about to break on the beach. Sybil points it out nervously, and Seymour responds with yet another line that would function perfectly well in polite society: "We'll ignore it. We'll snub it." With this line, he effectively turns the societal graces that would make him functional in his mother-in-law's eyes into total nonsense, employing them against a force of nature that can be neither snubbed nor ignored. In so doing, he points out the ridiculousness of "snubbing" itself and the society that allows it. And on a deeper level, he speaks to a great tragedy—the sense that the two of them are employing tools that are at best imaginary to beat back a danger with all the force and infinitude of the sea.

For the moment, however, they are successful: the wave crashes over Sybil, but safely, and she screams with pleasure. And, for the first time, she joins Seymour in his nonsense, announcing that she has just spotted a bananafish. She even borrows from the reality she was so attached to before, in order to embellish her imagined sighting, adding that it had six bananas in its mouth, the same as the real number of tigers she contradicted Seymour with earlier. For the first time, she has stepped into Seymour's world with him. In response, Seymour draws the interview to a quick close. A romantic might suggest he does this in order to preserve a perfect moment. But the story allows for, even insists on, several other explanations: that Seymour is troubled to have the girl so close, and perhaps wary of drawing her into his own madness.

His nonsense dialogue with Sybil, however, has had its effect on the way readers now experience "sane" dialogue. Are Sybil's non-sequiturs about eating wax really any different from Muriel and her mother's strange intermingling of fashion gossip with whether Muriel will leave her husband? And this new trouble with "appropriate" interaction is further highlighted by Seymour's encounter with the woman in the elevator on the way back to his room. "I see you're looking at my feet," he says—a direct, childlike statement that would have been perfectly appropriate only minutes ago, with Sybil. Here, however, it throws the woman into a huff—

and Seymour's clever inversion of appropriate and inappropriate conversation leads the reader, initially, to side with him, looking at the woman's confusion as somewhat ridiculous.

In the elevator, for the first time, it is not clear whether Seymour is really in control of the confusion: is he teasing the woman, or has he made a true misstep—confusing his two worlds to the extent that he thought his statement really was acceptable adult conversation? In either case, the "sane" woman who shares the elevator with him is, for some reason, affronted, and finally frightened by his simple statement. In response to her fear and bluster, Seymour finally cracks, swearing at her, somewhat cruelly, that she should not be "such a . . . sneak." And after she disembarks, Seymour's next statement cuts to the heart of his trouble: "I have two normal feet and I can't see the slightest . . . reason why anybody should stare at them," he says. But people who do not have a fear that they are not normal do not go around asserting that they are, and Seymour's outburst does more to reveal his fears that he is not normal, and that people can see it, than it does to save the honor of his feet.

Seymour, it seems, is acutely aware that he is different from the rest of society and caught in what feels to him to be an unbearable tension. He has a great deal of pride, and even joy, in his unique vision. At the same time he is full of loneliness and despair that he may never find someone to share it. And very deep, perhaps entirely buried in the text, lies a fear that he may, in fact, be insane; and finding someone to share his vision would entail dragging him/her with him to insanity—which is why he ends his conversation with Sybil so quickly once she begins to see things as he does, and why he takes such enormous offence at the suggestion that his feet are unusual enough to take a second look at. Seymour is baffled by the contradictions in his wife's character, yes, but his true disease eats much deeper. On the most basic level, he is baffled by, and even fearful of himself, which is a far more desperate situation.

Why does Seymour pull the trigger on returning to his room? To a certain degree, it remains a mystery, which is part of the reason that "A Perfect Day for Bananafish" is such a successful story: instead of providing easy answers, it raises, and refuses to answer, all the same haunting questions any suicide leaves behind him in reality. But the initial sense that nothing in Seymour's life on "A Perfect Day for Bananafish" should have driven

him to suicide holds true even on close examination. Nothing in the world around Seymour is really sufficient to drive him to such a tragic act of violence. Instead, Seymour chooses death because he is unable to deal with the mysteries inside him.

Source: Carey Wallace, Critical Essay on "A Perfect Day for Bananafish," in *Short Stories for Students,* The Gale Group, 2003.

James Finn Cotter

In the following essay excerpt, Cotter shows how the poetry of German poet Rainer Maria Rilke informs the actions of Seymour in "A Perfect Day for Bananafish."

I

J.D. Salinger's short story, "A Perfect Day for Bananafish," employs the traditional device of a surprise ending. Seymour Glass returns to his Miami hotel room, glances at his wife asleep on her bed, takes from his luggage a heavy-caliber German automatic, sits down on his bed, looks again at Muriel, and fires a bullet through his head. Not even Richard Cory's suicide has provoked more critical commentary. Why does Seymour shoot himself?

The number of reasons proposed for this denouement attests to the effectiveness of the surprise. Is Seymour no longer able to cope with the everyday world represented by Muriel and her mother? Is this act a gesture of despair brought on by sexual frustration? Does Seymour want revenge on Muriel and hope by his suicide to win her lost attention? Or does he kill himself because of an inability to reach ideal spiritual perfection? Perhaps, on the other hand, his death is a religious act performed on the perfect day for attaining nirvana? May it not be an heroic deed of self-sacrifice liberating Muriel to her own life at last?

Obviously, the risk of resorting to guesswork pays off with diminishing returns. Turning to Salinger's later work for possible explanations also takes the chance of second-guessing. Whatever evidence exists for Seymour's death must be found within the story. With the reader's indulgence, let us imagine the immediate aftermath of the suicide. Muriel will follow her mother's last instructions: "'Call me the *instant* he does, or *says,* anything at all funny—you know what I mean.'" Mother will probably feel vindicated that her fears were well founded: Seymour proves himself a threat, but to himself and not to her daughter. Muriel, for all her selfish aplomb, will suffer genuine shock. While her mother, like the lady in the elevator, cannot see beyond the nose on her face and may even express relief at the outcome, Muriel loves Seymour enough to look for reasons for his act. Since he left her no suicide note, she must seek elsewhere for some clue. Recently he has again asked her to read a book of German poems which he had sent her from overseas. Both the book and revolver are war souvenirs: perhaps they are connected in Seymour's mind. Muriel has looked for the poetry, but her mother had not packed it in the luggage. She found room, however, for the useless suntan lotion.

These poems have been written, in Seymour's words, "'by the *only great poet of the century*.'" Because they are in German, his wife must find a translation or learn the language, a logical demand that elicits from Mother a typical reaction: "'Awful. Awful. It's *sad,* actually, is what it is.'" She is wrong about so many things in her conversation with her daughter that Salinger obviously intends to whet the reader's curiosity. Muriel has one advantage denied to his audience: possessing the book, she knows its author and title. Whether or not she understands and loves Seymour enough to carry out his wish is at best doubtful. But the volume is her husband's last will and testament for her.

Critics generally agree that the poet referred to is Rainer Maria Rilke. Besides listing him as an author who influenced his development, Salinger sometimes mentions him in his stories. More importantly, some critics discover in Rilke's poem, "The Carrousel," the key to the concluding scene of *The Catcher in the Rye.* The same use of allusion may be at work in "A Perfect Day for Bananafish." Only one critic, until now, has picked up the scent. Gary Lane has suggested that the book involved is the *Duino Elegies.* The parallels he draws, however, are less convincing than those found in an earlier volume of Rilke's, *The Book of Images,* and in one poem in particular, from "The Second Book, Part II": "The Song of the Suicide." This "Song" is one of a series of ten poems entitled *The Voices: Nine Pages with a Titlepage.* In the second part of this paper the question of Salinger's indebtedness to the whole sequence will be examined.

The poem reads first in its original version and then in translation: . . .

The Song of the Suicide

Well then, another minute yet.
Again and again they manage to cut
my rope.
Recently I was so well prepared,
and there was already a little eternity
in my entrails.

> " Since he has now communicated the essential meaning of Rilke's poem--not, unfortunately, to his wife but to another mother's daughter-- Salinger's hero proceeds straight to his death."

They hold out the spoon to me,
that spoonful of life.
No, I don't want, I don't want any more,
only let me vomit.
I know life is well-done and good,
and the world is a full pot,
but with me it doesn't get into my blood,
it only mounts to my head.
Others it nourishes, me it makes sick;
you understand one spurns it.
For at least a thousand years now
I shall need to diet.

In Salinger's story Seymour is literally fed up with the nauseous phoniness of those around him. Like the six tigers in *Little Black Sambo,* people are the victims of their own gluttony and pride. Or, to use his own image, they are like bananafish that are overly greedy. As Seymour explains to his friend and pupil Sybil: "'They [the fish] lead a very tragic life . . . They swim into a hole where there's a lot of bananas. They're very ordinary-looking fish when they swim *in.* But once they get in, they behave like pigs.'" Ordinary people in a Miami or American-dream setting overexpose themselves to the good life: too much sun, drinking, phoning, buying and selling in the midst of their pleasure. Ninety-seven New York advertising men occupy part of the hotel; Muriel is "'so sunburned [she] can hardly move;'" the psychiatrist holds forth "'in the bar *all* day long;'" and Sybil's mother has more time for a Martini than she does for her child.

Despite his mother-in-law's foreboding: "'Seymour may *completely* lose control of himself'"— she repeats it for emphasis—he alone possesses self-control, protecting himself against the sun, playing the piano in the bar instead of drinking, and finding time for profitable conversation with Sybil. He manages the rubber float and his own suicide with equally efficient regard for detail and with dispatch. Even his effrontery toward the woman on the elevator shows a similar economy of behavior. If the woman refuses to look him in the eyes, she must be gazing at his feet, and he reprimands her for her dishonesty, just as he corrects Sybil (more subtly, to be sure) for her treatment of the toy bulldog in the hotel lobby. Like Rilke's Suicide, he will not let life get into his blood because he lives consistently in his head. He can "see more" than anyone else in the story.

But how real is Seymour's control? Is Muriel's mother paranoid or is she justified in worrying about her daughter's wellbeing—even life? Her emphatic references to her son-in-law's behavior in the past indicate an erratic pattern on his part: he has endangered Muriel by his distracted driving, damaging the car while paying more attention to the trees than to the road. Mother summarizes Seymour's problems: "'The trees. That business with the window. Those horrible things he said to Granny about her plans for passing away. What he did with all those lovely pictures from Bermuda—everything.'" She says that Seymour has also tried to do something to Granny's chair. Her conclusion is that the Army released Seymour prematurely from the hospital. How is the reader to take these *"sad"* and *"awful"* horrors?

Surely the mother-in-law's list is not meant to be taken seriously. Muriel offers the correct perspective toward Seymour when she answers: "'Mother, I'm not afraid of Seymour.'" Since Muriel is not threatened by Seymour, the reader too should not be intimidated or drawn into the supposedly normal view of him as expressed by the mother and the psychiatrists. If we suspect that his final gesture in reaching for the gun and preparing to fire it has anything at all to do with a threat to Muriel's life, then we have completely missed the point of Salinger's story. Seymour is in control of his fate. All the trivial details of his previous behavior may add up to what a psychiatrist calls a death wish but what a Buddhist believes is nirvana. At the end, he "fired a bullet through his right temple." The echoes of a religious act in a sacred place must be deliberate on the author's part. Like the Suicide of Rilke's poem, Seymour doesn't "want any more" of this nauseating existence. A phony life only makes him vomit. Muriel's mother finds that the topic of death is a horrible thing to mention to Granny. But Seymour has his own "plans for passing away." For Granny and for everyone—even the mother—such plans are entirely appropriate and necessary. Only Seymour carries his out.

Seymour exercises dietetic self-control by wanting no part of the world's appetite for "a full pot." Through a series of references to the stomach, Salinger establishes this theme. We first meet Seymour on the beach: "He turned over on his stomach, letting a sausaged towel fall away from his eyes." The image of the sausage cleverly fits in with the eating metaphor. Sybil next "looked down at her protruding stomach" and, later, "resumed walking, stomach foremost." In the water, "the young man picked her up and laid her down on her stomach on the float." As a receptive child, Sybil has yet to taste the avarice that fills most grown-up lives; she too can turn away from the spoon held out to her. As Teddy tells Nicholson in the final story of Salinger's collection, people are "'a bunch of apple-eaters.'" The apple represents the archetypal object of man's greed. Teddy says: "'What you have to do is vomit it up if you want to see things as they really are.'" "Only let me vomit," Rilke's Suicide begs. Those who hunger now may yet be satisfied.

The bananafish, on the other hand, do not throw up the forbidden fruit. Seymour relates their fate to Sybil: "'Naturally, after that [eating as many as seventy-eight bananas] they're so fat they can't get out of the hole again.'" As a result, they die of banana fever—"a terrible disease" because those who suffer from it cannot escape their own craving; they "'can't fit through the door.'" Not even death offers them hope of delivery since they remain trapped in the cave, modern counterparts of Plato's prisoners.

In contrast, Seymour's death, which like Teddy's is merely physical, means deliverance and even reincarnation. Since bananafish nourish their bodies but not their souls, their "tragic" death is by rights spiritual and irrevocable. Teddy describes mere dying: "'All you do is get the heck out of your body when you die. My gosh, everybody's done it thousands and thousands of times.'" Like the Suicide of the poem, Seymour is also ready for a thousand-year diet. He too spurns a materialistic life. When Sybil sees the bananafish with six bananas in its mouth, the young man kisses her foot in gratitude because her vision no longer comes from earth but from within. She shares his non-material view. Sybil's diet of candles and discarded olives has already won Seymour's approval: "'Olives and wax. I never go anyplace without 'em.'"

Since he has now communicated the essential meaning of Rilke's poem—not, unfortunately, to his wife but to another mother's daughter—Salinger's hero proceeds straight to his death. Having "already a little eternity / in [his] entrails," Seymour Glass, with his accustomed sense of purpose and self-control, acts according to his hidden schedule without "another minute" lost.

Source: James Finn Cotter, "A Source for Seymour's Suicide: Rilke's *Voices* and Salinger's *Nine Stories*," in *Papers on Language and Literature,* Vol. 25, No. 1, Winter 1989, pp. 83–98.

Gary Lane

In the following essay excerpt, Lane finds the framework of "A Perfect Day for Bananafish" and the key to Seymour's suicide in Rilke's Duino Elegies.

The Suicide of Seymour Glass in "A Perfect Day for Bananafish" has troubled readers and critics alike; despite the considerable attention paid it, its meaning has remained uncomfortably uncertain. Seymour, it is sometimes suggested, "unable to tolerate the everyday sensations of his tiresome, postwar life," has simply "lost his mind." This theory, however, emphasizes unduly the Seymour we hear about from other characters—the kind and gentle man we actually meet on the beach seems eccentric but eminently sane—and fails to explain convincingly, among other things, the clearly allegorical tale of the bananafish. Other critics feel that Seymour, for all his obvious intelligence, remains a child, that he "does many things—intentionally or unintentionally—to disrupt others' composure" and to gain thereby their attention. "He has tried in increasingly conspicuous ways to upset [Muriel, and] . . . finally, as with the child so desperate for the desired attention that it will risk injury, there remains but one thing he can do—he can shoot himself. Then she will have to pay attention; then her iron composure will be disrupted. She will cry and run hysterically about the hotel room—or so he hopes." Again, though, Muriel is given too much credit; surely the psychotic exhibitionist posited here would spend his vacation at the hotel bar, not on the beach by himself. Closest to the truth, still others suggest, is a more complex position: Seymour's suicide is not "merely a rejection of this world of crass superficiality, but it is also—and more significantly—a rejection of the mystical life itself." This explanation, however, derives largely from hints in Salinger's later work—its proponents offer little evidence from "Bananafish" to support it—and thereby leads us somewhat astray. We will do better, I think, closer to home. Indeed, there is

within the story an important though oblique reference, which, tracked down, may tell us a good deal about Seymour Glass, and in the process help show "Bananafish" to be tighter and more careful than has been supposed.

The reference occurs during the story's opening scene. Muriel, on the telephone with her mother, inquires suddenly about "that book he sent me from Germany . . . those German poems." The book is on Seymour's mind: "he *asked* me about it, when we were driving down. He wanted to know if I'd read it." And, since poetry matters to Seymour—we will note later how telling is his wry allusion to "The Waste Land"—he must feel very close to it, for he considers its author "the *only great poet of the century.*" I submit that the poems in question are Rilke's *Duino Elegies.* These last and greatest poems of Rilke, though diverse and difficult, are informed by a basic thematic lamentation over the insufficiency of man and pervaded by a symbolic Angel, the reminder, in his transcendence of human limitation, at once of man's aspiration and necessary failure. The poems are thus reflections about precisely the problems that, as we shall see, oppress Seymour. Indeed, several passages from the *Elegies* correspond so exactly to situations in "Bananafish" that, corroborating other evidence, they furnish a kind of explicative gloss to the story.

We first meet Seymour through the dramatically subjective observations of his wife and mother-in-law. The story begins by introducing us to Mariel, and, significantly, we learn at once that she has been reading an article entitled "Sex Is Fun—or Hell." Far from indicating, however, some sexual problem of Seymour's, this fact gives us an introductory perspective on his wife. As the telephone dialogue unfolds her character, our initial indication is reinforced and amplified; we come to see that, for all her *chic* and poise, Muriel is basically simple—and basically corrupt. She possesses the undisciplined mind of a child, equating things of unequal importance, skipping indiscriminately among conversational topics, and perhaps even expecting to learn something about sex from the knowing writers of women's magazines. Further, she is bored with her mother and her life, baffled but bored with her husband, and complacently, simple-mindedly unconcerned with everyone. It is through this rather dense filter that our first light on Seymour passes, and we must allow for a certain amount of refraction when we hear it implied that Seymour is confusing, crude, and dangerously near the brink of mental unbalance. Of greater importance are the book he

> " The remarks are the
> <u>Kläge</u> of the <u>Elegies</u>, laments
> for man's mortality, for
> Seymour, like Rilke, in
> knowing much becomes
> inextricably entangled in the
> divine web that the limited
> mortal must try to spin."

has sent Muriel and the fact that he will not remove his bathrobe on the beach, and, as will become clear, the former is a key to the latter.

When Muriel's phone call is finished, the scene abruptly shifts, and the import of the change, from hotel room and gossip of Seymour to the beach and the man himself, is heralded at once: here, as the unconsciously oracular Sybil unconsciously announces, we will find the real "see more glass." The man on the beach is kind and brilliant, ironic and questioning, but quite sane. His encounter with the child, during which the decision for suicide is made final, calls to mind first this passage from Rilke's *Fourth Elegy: . . .*

> Who'll show a child just as it is? Who'll place it
> within its constellation, with the measure
> of distance in its hand? Who make its death
> from grey bread, that grows hard,—or leave it there,
> within the round mouth, like the choking core
> of a sweet apple?. . . Minds of murderers
> are easily divined. But this, though: death,
> the whole of death,—even before life's begun,
> to hold it all so gently, and be good:
> this is beyond description!

Seymour, in the story, experiences the same poignant perception of the nearness to death, and hence infinity, that the child's imaginative and self-supporting world attains. To see Sybil in her innocence is to see the incomprehensible goodness of the child, who carelessly allows death to live beside it. Yet even in this goodness, which Seymour loves for its simplicity, there are suggestions of imperfection: on the one hand, it is easily corrupted; on the other, it exists unaware of complexities.

For Sybil, after all, is no Rilkean Angel; the clearer our—and Seymour's—perspective on her,

the more visibly does the tarnish on her innocence spread like the sun-tan oil down "the delicate, winglike blades of her back." Jealous and possessive, she instructs Seymour, should Sharon Lipschutz again sit by him at the piano, to "Next time, push her off." "Ah, Sharon Lipschutz," he replies; "How that name comes up. Mixing memory and desire." Like the polymorphous narrator of *The Waste Land,* Seymour looks longingly back to a time that can no more exist, a time before he understood that Sharons, "never mean or unkind", turn soon into Sybils, who "poke . . . little dog[s] with balloon sticks", and that Sybils, at least spontaneous and honest, grow thence to Muriels. Besides, Sybil's bathing suit is *yellow* and she *lives* in Whirley Wood, Connecticut. Seymour's apparently irrational statements about these things are his ironic recognition that the child's simple, sure mind, if more comfortable than his own, is no more infinite, no more transcendent; it is the very failure to understand that keeps the child close to death. The remarks are the *Kläge* of the *Elegies,* laments for man's mortality, for Seymour, like Rilke, in knowing much becomes inextricably entangled in the divine web that the limited mortal must try to spin.

The symbol of this aspiring but defeating mortality, the constant reminder that . . .

> Yes, the springs had need of you. Many a star
> was waiting for you to espy it. Many a wave
> would rise on the past towards you; or, else, perhaps,
> as you went by an open window, a violin
> would be giving itself to someone. All this was a trust.
> But were you equal to it? Were you not always
> distracted by expectation, as though all this
> were announcing someone to love?

is for Seymour his tattoo, his body. And, though he explains to Muriel that he "doesn't want a lot of fools looking at his tattoo", it is a lonely part of beach he is on, and, as he says to Sybil, "What a fool I am"! It is Seymour himself who does not wish to confront the symbol of what his mind cannot surmount. When at last he removes the robe, faces squarely the insoluble problem of himself as man, Seymour decides that fully realized love is not to be found in life. He has loved Sybil for her bright, child's being, but, realizing her inadequacies, seen in her the seedling of a future Muriel. The remaining way is that which Rilke calls the "less illuminated" side of life, death. The bananafish story is Seymour's parable of his defeat in life and decision for death: Seymour, coming into the world with a rare capacity for love, takes too much aspiration to it, becomes trapped by man's imperfect mortality, and must die.

We can see now why Salinger devised the careful and ominous structural parallel between the second scene and the first. In both we begin with a girl and her mother—each, appearances notwithstanding, basically uninterested in the other—who talk, without communicating or understanding, about Seymour; in both we end with a severed connection and a girl, unregretful and alone. We see clearly the differences between the implied psychotic of scene one and the actual man on the beach, but the structure warns us not to overlook the similarities of the women involved. For when we understand those similarities—and recognize that they represent not Holden Caulfield's adolescent and self-excluding conception of a world of phonies, but the sad and adult realization that all humanity, Seymour self-consciously included, is limited and corruptible—we can see the *cul de sac* from which Seymour would escape.

Salinger emphasizes the universality of this condition with his choice of names. Seymour Glass is the Emersonian poet, the man who "turns the world to glass" and, like Seymour in Florida, "must pass for a fool and a churl for a long season"; he is the sensitive barometer of the weather of human possibility, and the conditions he reacts against are irreversible. Perhaps he is as well Wallace Stevens' "impossible possible philosopher's man,"

> The man who has had the time to think enough,
> The central man, the human globe, responsive
> As a mirror with a voice, the man of glass,
> Who in million diamonds sums us up.

Sybil, bright with innocence but already tarnishing, symbolizes for Seymour the human condition: like the sibyls of old, she is the unconscious oracle through whom prophecy is revealed, the instrument of truth; what she reveals to Seymour is the finality of that unbridgeable gap between human aspiration and human possibility. Seymour's suicide is his summing up.

In part, he would escape the pain that his tattoo, his finite human body, invokes. For this reason Salinger emphasizes it in the final elevator vignette; the lady with the zinc salve on her nose, like Sybil's and Muriel's mothers and like the daughters themselves, is, however worldly, simple in her failure to suffer. And Seymour, who cannot resent this in a child, is understandably offended when the child-woman rudely reminds him of his pain. But the suicide is also a freeing of the self, for death has its Rilkean, life-extending properties. Seymour's final glance at Muriel—with its echo of a relationship that has failed for him because . . .

> One thing to sing the beloved, another, alas!
> that hidden guilty river-god of the blood.

—confirms the hopelessness of his mortal plight; for to love as a man is merely to remind oneself of the limitations of that love. Yet the glance may offer a kind of hope, for perhaps on that shadowy, darker side of life—death—human limitation will give way to infinite possibility. There is little, really, for Seymour to lose. So "he went over and sat down on the unoccupied twin bed, looked at the girl, aimed the pistol, and fired a bullet through his right temple."

Source: Gary Lane, "Seymour's Suicide Again: A New Reading of J. D. Salinger's 'A Perfect Day for Bananafish,'" in *Studies in Short Fiction,* Vol. X, No. 1, Winter 1973, pp. 27–34.

Sources

Babbitt, Irving, *Rousseau and Romanticism,* Houghton Mifflin Co., 1919, pp. 215, 308, 319.

Bloom, Harold, ed., *J. D. Salinger,* Bloom's BioCritiques series, Chelsea House Publishers, 2002, pp. 50–51.

French, Warren, *J. D. Salinger, Revisited,* Twayne Publishers, 1988, pp. 66–67.

Goldstein, Bernice, and Sanford Goldstein, "Zen and *Nine Stories,*" in *J. D. Salinger,* edited by Harold Bloom, Modern Critical Views series, Chelsea House Publishers, 1987, p. 86.

Gwynn, Frederick L., and Joseph L. Blotner, "One Hand Clapping," in *Salinger: A Critical and Personal Portrait,* Harper & Row, 1962, p. 110.

Hamilton, Ian, *In Search of J. D. Salinger,* Random House, 1988, p. 105.

Hamilton, Kenneth, *J. D. Salinger: A Critical Essay,* William B. Eerdmans Publishing, 1967, p. 30.

Kazin, Alfred, "J. D. Salinger: 'Everybody's Favorite,'" in *J. D. Salinger,* edited by Harold Bloom, Bloom's BioCritiques series, Chelsea House Publishers, 2002, pp. 68–73.

Lundquist, James, *J. D. Salinger,* Frederick Ungar Publishing Co., 1979, pp. 78–79.

Mills, Clifford, "A Critical Perspective on the Writings of J. D. Salinger," in *J. D. Salinger,* edited by Harold Bloom, Bloom's BioCritiques series, Chelsea House Publishers, 2002, pp. 50–51.

Salinger, J. D., *Raise High the Roof Beam, Carpenters and Seymour: An Introduction,* Little, Brown and Co., 1963, p. 141.

Wiegand, William, "J. D. Salinger: Seventy-Eight Bananas," in *J. D. Salinger,* edited by Harold Bloom, Modern Critical Views series, Chelsea House Publishers, 1987, p. 8.

Further Reading

Alexander, Paul, *Salinger: A Biography,* Renaissance Books, 1999.

This recent biography is based on newly released material from the Salinger archives; in it, Alexander explores the reasons for Salinger's withdrawal from the public eye and whether it was based on a sincere desire for privacy or an attempt to generate publicity.

Hamilton, Ian, *In Search of J. D. Salinger,* Random House, 1988.

Hamilton's controversial book is partly a biography and partly the story of Hamilton writing the biography: at the last minute, Salinger's lawyers challenged Random House's right to print Hamilton's book and eventually argued their case in federal court.

Kotzen, Kip, and Thomas Beller, eds., *With Love and Squalor: 14 Writers Respond to the Work of J. D. Salinger,* Broadway Books, 2001.

This is a collection of essays in which contemporary authors offer their opinions of Salinger's work and reminisce about what his work has meant to them as students, readers, and artists.

Salinger, Margaret A., *Dream Catcher: A Memoir,* Washington Square Press, 2000.

This much-publicized memoir by Salinger's daughter offers a glimpse into the mysterious author's role as a father and some of the ways his artistic concerns affected his family.

A Point at Issue!

Kate Chopin

1889

Kate Chopin's "A Point at Issue!" appeared, along with "Wiser than a God," in the *St. Louis Post Dispatch* on October 27, 1889. Its publication marked the beginning of a decade of literary work by the author that culminates in her controversial masterpiece *The Awakening*. "A Point at Issue!," which now can be found in her *Collected Works*, announces Chopin's interest in the dynamics of male-female relationships, a subject she would explore in various ways throughout the body of her work.

The relationship at the heart of "A Point at Issue!" is that of Charles and Eleanor Faraday, who pride themselves on their progressive attitude toward marriage. Determined to maintain their independence, they embark on a test of their resolve, which involves a long period of separation. While they are able to withstand the social pressure to conform to traditional gender roles, they ultimately cannot ignore the dictates of their own hearts. Charles and Eleanor's developing relationship illuminates the human desires that inevitably complicate the quest for freedom.

Author Biography

Katherine O'Flaherty was born on February 8, 1851, in St. Louis, Missouri to Thomas and Eliza (Faris) O'Flaherty. Her mother introduced the family to the prominent French-Creole community in

Kate Chopin

St. Louis, a group that would appear later as characters in her daughter's fiction. Her father's successful business ventures as a merchant granted their inclusion in the city's high society. When Katherine was four, her idyllic childhood came to an end after her beloved father's sudden death in a train accident. Thereafter, she was raised by her mother, grandmother, and great-grandmother, whose storytelling enthralled Katherine.

Katherine was an avid reader during her school years. After she graduated in 1868, she was caught up in the social life of St. Louis but maintained her independent streak, which eventually prompted her to question the position of women in her society and time. In 1870, she married businessman Oscar Chopin with whom she would have six children. She and Oscar, whose background was French-Creole, moved to New Orleans, where they gained entrance into the city's social community. Oscar's business collapsed, however, forcing the family's relocation to Natchitoches Parish, Louisiana, which would become the fictional backdrop for many of Chopin's short stories. After her husband died in 1883 of swamp fever, Chopin moved back to St. Louis and began writing in an effort to cope with the loss.

Chopin's first published work, a poem titled "If It Might Be," appeared in the Chicago periodi-

cal *America* in 1889. After being introduced to the work of French author Guy de Maupassant, she published two short stories: "Wiser than a God" and "A Point at Issue!" These works established the subject matter that would dominate her fiction—an examination of the intricacies of male-female relationships. In 1890, her first novel, *At Fault*, was published with mixed reviews.

During the next few years, she wrote over three dozen stories and sketches, many of which were published in magazines like *Youth's Companion, Harper's Young People,* and *Vogue.* In 1894, a collection of twenty-three of her stories appeared under the title *Bayou Folk,* which earned her a reputation as an important writer about local color. Her short story collection *A Night in Acadie* also received strong reviews when it appeared in 1897.

Her most famous and most celebrated work, *The Awakening,* produced a public outcry after its publication in 1899. Readers claimed the novel's focus on the sexual awakening of a young married woman was pornographic and immoral. The negative response, coupled with her inability to publish another collection of short stories due to their controversial subject matter, tarnished her reputation and effectively ended her literary career, although she continued to write. In 1904, she began to have health problems, and on August 22 of that year, she died in St. Louis of a cerebral hemorrhage. Since her death, her literary reputation has grown considerably. She is now considered to be one of the most important American realists.

Plot Summary

"A Point at Issue!" begins with the wedding announcement of Eleanor Gail and Charles Faraday, as printed in the Plymdale *Promulgator,* the couple's local newspaper. Eleanor is not happy with the announcement because she considers it to be "an indelicate thrusting of herself upon the public notice." She had agreed to the announcement as a concession to social rules, hoping that she would not have to make such concessions in the future.

Her new husband, Charles, regards her as the ideal woman; he is happy that she is "logical" and will study subjects with him such as philosophy and science. When Eleanor declares that she wants to learn to speak French fluently, the two decide that she will study in Paris while he spends most of the year in America. After their European honeymoon,

Eleanor rents rooms in Paris and Charles returns to Plymdale, planning to spend the following summer with her. The couple's behavior outrages Plymdale society, which is indignant at the idea that "two young people should presume to introduce such innovations into matrimony." The two write each other regularly.

Charles begins spending his free time with the Beatons, a local family, finding them "all clever people, bright and interesting." Mr. Beaton is a colleague at the university where Charles teaches. Charles thoroughly enjoys the company of this happy family, especially that of their blissful and self-absorbed youngest daughter, Kitty. Charles writes to Eleanor expressing his admiration for the young girl, dismissing as illogical the possibility that his wife would be jealous, but Eleanor does not send back a response with her usual promptness. When a letter finally does arrive, it expresses an "inexplicable coldness" in tone. However, he soon receives several letters from his wife "that shook him with their unusual ardor."

After a winter apart from his wife, Charles leaves for Paris to see her. Before he arrives, there is a description of Eleanor pacing her rooms, obviously disturbed, fighting "a misery of the heart, against which her reason was in armed rebellion." The narrator does not reveal the nature of the misery that causes Eleanor to collapse in "a storm of sobs and tears."

When Charles arrives, he sees only his familiar, idealized vision of his wife, but then notices that she has become more beautiful. As they converse, a housemaid appears, eyeing Eleanor "with the glance of a fellow conspirator" and holding a card in her hand. Eleanor hastily thrusts the card in her pocket and turns toward Charles "a little flustered."

A few days later, Charles interrupts a conversation between Eleanor and a handsome man in her parlor. The narrator notes that "they were both disconcerted" and that Eleanor "had the appearance of wanting to run away, to do any thing but meet her husband's glance." Charles accepts his wife's assertion that her visitor was "no one special." A few days later, however, when Eleanor tells him vaguely that she has an urgent appointment, he begins to question his wife's fidelity.

Unable to rid his mind of "ugly thoughts," Charles walks around Paris. While sitting at a café, he sees Eleanor riding in a carriage with the same man who had come to see her. Both appear in high spirits. Charles's initial reaction is to "tear the scoundrel from his seat and paint the boulevard red with his villainous blood."

When Charles returns to their apartment, he finds Eleanor waiting impatiently for him. She leads him excitedly into the parlor where he meets the handsome stranger. Eleanor presents him to Charles as an artist who has just completed a portrait of her, intended as a surprise for Charles's arrival. She notes that its completion had been delayed, hence the necessity, Charles understands, for their meetings.

As Charles begins his plans to return home, Eleanor asks him whether he believes that she has gained a good command of French, and he answers in the affirmative. She then suggests he book a passage home for two, which fills him with happiness. Then, he inquires about the coldness of the letter she had sent him a few months ago, and Eleanor admits that it was written in response to his declaration of his feelings for Kitty. Eleanor reveals her failure to suppress jealous emotions but insists that she believes that her husband has remained faithful. Astonished at her admitted jealousy, Charles concludes to himself, "but my Nellie is only a woman after all." The narrator closes the story noting the fact that Charles has conveniently forgotten his own jealousy.

Characters

Monsieur l'Artiste

This is the name the narrator gives to the artist who paints Eleanor's portrait as a surprise gift for Charles. Eleanor's actions suggest that she had some romantic feelings for the artist, who is described as quite handsome. He fades, however, into the background when the portrait is completed and Eleanor decides to return home with Charles.

Kitty Beaton

Kitty, the youngest Beaton daughter, has just returned from boarding school when Charles begins his relationship with her family. She is a headstrong young woman, "with a Napoleonic grip . . . keeping the household under her capricious command," described as self-centered. "Her girlish charms" however, coupled with the "soft shining light of her eyes" touch Charles to such a degree that he admits

Media Adaptations

- Penguin Audiobooks has published an excellent cassette tape of *The Awakening and Selected Stories* (June 1996), performed by Joanna Adler, which includes readings of "The Storm" and "Story of an Hour," two of Chopin's most anthologized stories.

---

his desire to kiss her. Yet, while nothing in the story suggests that he ever acts on this desire, his acknowledgement of his feelings toward the young woman stirs Eleanor's jealousy and perhaps her own attention to Monsieur l'Artiste.

Margaret Beaton

Margaret, the eldest Beaton daughter, becomes a representative feminist in the story. Her community views her as "slightly erratic" for her participation in the Woman's Suffrage movement, which includes the wearing of "mysterious" clothes as a statement of solidarity with her sisters and freedom from constraining social custom. The narrator critiques her actions, noting that her clothes produced "the distinction of a quasi-emancipation," which, "defeated the ultimate purpose" of her cause.

Mr. Beaton

Mr. Beaton is a fellow professor at the university where Charles teaches. He is an older man but retains a youthful vitality, which "formed the nucleus around which [his] family gathered, drawing the light of their own cheerfulness." Charles enjoys the company of Beaton and his family in Eleanor's absence.

Mrs. Beaton

Mrs. Beaton, Mr. Beaton's wife, represents the traditional wife and mother. Her "aspirations went not further than the desire for her family's good, and her bearing announced in its every feature, the satisfaction of completed hopes."

Charles Faraday

Charles, a professor of mathematics at Plymdale University, originally falls in love with Eleanor Gail because of her beauty. Later, her logical mind makes her what Charles considers his "ideal woman." Charles creates an ideal vision of marriage, insisting that he and his wife will reject the traditional restrictions on individuality that are typical of the institution. His convictions are strong enough to endure public condemnation, although the critics appear to be harsher in their assessment of Eleanor's behavior than of his.

Charles tempers his wife's earnestness with humor and optimism that prevents their explorations into the ideas of the times from acquiring "a too monotonous sombreness." He has an outgoing and friendly nature that "invited companionship from his fellow beings."

Charles has an active mind and prides himself on his careful thought processes. He comes to conclusions by the slow "consecutive steps of reason." Concluding that Eleanor should have the opportunity to fulfill her desires, he adapts himself quite readily to the long separation from her, resuming his "bachelor existence as quietly as though it had been interrupted but by the interval of a day."

His optimistic vision of his wife and their unconventional marriage, however, blinds him to the realities of human nature. He does not see the danger in his affections for Kitty, nor does he understand that sharing those feelings with Eleanor will cause a very human, jealous response. He also fails to recognize that same fault in his own character when he becomes enraged over his suspicions that Eleanor is having an affair with the handsome Frenchman he sees in her company. Ironically, he quickly falls back into ascribing stereotypes when he faults his wife's jealously, noting that really, she is "only a woman after all" while forgetting his own display of that same emotion.

Eleanor Faraday

Eleanor Faraday enters into a non-traditional marriage with Charles, both respecting the other's sense of individuality and needs. Eleanor is Charles's "ideal woman," intelligent and intellectually curious. She becomes the perfect companion for Charles as the two engage in various programs of study. Although she has a logical mind, "sharp in its reasoning, strong and unprejudiced in its outlook," she also displays a quick intuition, a nice counter to Charles's slower, more methodical thought processes. Her earnestness and intensity are balanced by Charles gentle humor. He also appreciates her confidence, "unmarred by self-conscious mannerisms."

Eleanor has a history of diverging "from the beaten walks of female Plymdaledom," a tendency she exhibits from the start of the story when she complains about having to put her marriage announcement in the local newspaper. This type of public recognition disturbs her and she has previously avoided it. Her refusal to go against her nature and to make expected social concessions has resulted in her being branded a "crank." When she refused to have a pre-announcement of the wedding published, the public "while condemning her present, were unsparing of her past, and full with damning prognostic of her future." Yet, Eleanor stands "stoically enough" in the face of public criticism. For her, "the satisfying consciousness of roaming the heights of free thought, and tasting the sweets of a spiritual emancipation" far outweighed the slights.

Eleanor, like her husband, takes pride in her independence and her sense of reason. Yet, again as is the case with her husband, both qualities are tested during the course of the story and found wanting. Her immediate reaction to Charles's declaration of his feelings for Kitty is jealousy, and perhaps, the narrator hints, an urge to take a lover. Her utter despondency before Charles arrives suggests that she may have entered into a relationship with Monsieur l'Artiste. The narrator never makes the relationship clear and avoids any insight into her motivation, but her actions suggest that she has difficulty accepting Charles's independence and honesty when it concerns his attention to another woman.

Eleanor, however, is able to quickly restore her relationship with Charles when she explains her business relationship with Monsieur l'Artiste and declares that she wants to return to America. Ironically, her honesty in admitting her jealousy over Kitty prompts her husband to regard her in a traditional light, as an emotionally flawed woman.

Themes

Freedom

The story begins with Charles and Eleanor determined to retain their freedom within their

Topics for Further Study

- Read over the passage where Eleanor has an emotional breakdown before Charles arrives in Paris. Chopin never provides enough information for readers to understand what causes this outburst. Rewrite the ending of the story, providing a clear explanation of Eleanor's despair and how it affects the outcome. How does the story's meaning change?

- Compare and contrast the subject of marriage in Chopin's *The Awakening* and "A Point at Issue!" How do the women deal with their positions similarly and differently?

- Create a storyboard outlining each scene for a cinematic version of the story.

- Investigate the women's movement at the end of the nineteenth century. How did it influence American society? What kind of opposition did it face? Was it successful?

marriage, which they insist will not "touch the individuality of either; that was to be preserved intact." Priding themselves on their progressive attitudes, they make an unconventional decision to separate for most of the year while Eleanor pursues her desire to study French. After they part, each feels the pang of separation, but they are confident in the rightness of "a situation that offered the fulfillment of a cherished purpose."

Jealousy

Soon, however, jealousy interferes with the couple's determination to maintain their personal freedom. Charles's loneliness prompts him to seek out the company of the Beatons, especially their young, attractive daughter Kitty. Assuming that reason will temper any other emotion, he tells Eleanor of his attraction to the girl. Naturally, Eleanor cannot contain her jealousy and delays her customary letter to Charles. When the letter finally arrives, it contains "an inexplicable coldness."

Charles experiences his own bout with jealousy when he arrives in Paris. After he comes across a handsome Parisian in the company of his wife, he becomes uneasy. His mood affects his vision of the beautiful city as he finds "the inadequacy of every thing that is offered to his contemplation or entertainment."

His jealousy "drove him to ugly thoughts," which are compounded when he sees Eleanor and the Frenchman in high spirits, riding in a carriage. Incensed, Charles contemplates tearing "the scoundrel from his seat and paint the boulevard red with his villainous blood." He is eventually able to temper his emotions with reason. Yet, the incident prompts him to reevaluate his insistence on freedom in marriage. He admits, "here was the first test, and should he be the one to cry out, 'I cannot endure it.'"

Repression

By the end of the story, the dynamic of Charles and Eleanor's relationship shifts from freedom to repression. Both have already experienced emotions that, they determine, need to be repressed because they are illogical. Yet Charles's suspicions of Eleanor's potential infidelity prompt him "to wonder if there might not be modifications to this marital liberty of which he was so staunch an advocate."

Eleanor also comes to the conclusion that absolute freedom of expression is not appropriate in a successful relationship. When Charles is stunned by her admission of jealousy in response to his feelings for Kitty, she admits, "I have found that there are certain things which a woman can't philosophize about, any more than she can about death when it touches that which is near to her." Ultimately, her desire to strengthen her relationship with her husband supersedes her desire for independence, and she decides to return home with Charles.

Style

Impressionism

In her article for *Modern American Women Writers,* Wai-chee Dimock notes Chopin's impres-

sionistic style in many of her works including *The Awakening.* She argues that "things are transitory in her writings—nothing is fixed, irrevocable, or predetermined." As a result, Dimock insists, "there is no last word in Chopin. Light and shadows play in her fiction; moods come and go. Nothing stands still, and everything could have been otherwise." Chopin uses this technique in "A Point at Issue!" when she focuses on Eleanor's experiences in Paris. The impressionistic vision she supplies never allows the reader to determine the causes of Eleanor's despair or what motivates her to leave Paris. Her relationship with the artist who paints her portrait is also left vague. As a result, readers are unable to judge her actions, which was most likely Chopin's intention. Chopin's narrators rarely comment on characters' behavior, which effectively redirects the readers' attention not to motivation, but to consequences. This stylistic device becomes an appropriate method to employ in her investigations of how morality can become merely a social, not ethical, construct.

Symbolism

Chopin symbolizes the conflicts Charles and Eleanor will face in their marriage when, at the beginning of the story, she describes their wedding announcement in the local paper. The announcement is "modestly wedged in between" an offer to mail the paper to subscribers who will be "leaving home for the summer months" and "an equally somber-clad notice" of a local company's "large and varied assortment of marble and granite monuments." Charles, in fact, will be one of the subscribers who will be out of town when he visits his wife in Paris during the summer months. The reference to gravestones suggests the inevitable death of independence that Eleanor will face by the end of the story.

The Beaton family becomes another important symbol in the story. Mr. and Mrs. Beaton typify the traditional marriage: he holds an important teaching position at a university, engaging his mind and his talents while his wife concerns herself exclusively with the operations of the household. While her sister Margaret has joined a radical feminist movement, Kitty Beaton turns her attentions to more conventional activities, "keeping the household under her capricious command." Her combination of youthful vigor and traditional role-playing obviously attracts Charles, whose conservative slant emerges more noticeably by the end of the story.

Compare & Contrast

- **Late Nineteenth Century:** In 1888, the International Council of Women is founded to mobilize support for the woman's suffrage movement.

  Today: Women have made major gains in their fight for equality. Discrimination against women is now against the law.

- **Late Nineteenth Century:** A new term, the ''New Woman'' comes to describe women who challenge traditional notions of a woman's place, especially the privileged role of wife and mother. These challenges are seen as a threat to the fabric of the American family.

  Today: Women have the opportunity to work inside or outside the home or both. However, those who choose to have children and a career face difficult time management choices due to inflexible work and promotion schedules.

- **Late Nineteenth Century:** Feminist Victoria Woodhull embarks on a lecture tour in 1871, espousing a free love philosophy, which reflects the women's movement's growing willingness to discuss sexual issues.

  Today: Women have the freedom to engage in premarital sex and to have children out of wedlock. The issue of single parenting caused a furor in the early 1990s when then Vice President Dan Quayle criticized the television character Murphy Brown for deciding not to marry her baby's father. Today, however, single parenting has become more widely accepted.

Historical Context

Realism

Realism became a popular form of painting, especially in works by Gustave Courbet, and literature in the mid nineteenth century. Writers involved in this movement, such as Gustave Flaubert, turned away from what they considered the artificiality of romanticism to a focus on the occurrences of everyday, contemporary life. They rejected the idealism and celebration of the imagination typical of romantic novels and instead took a serious look at believable characters and their often problematic interactions with society. To accomplish this goal, realist novelists focused on the commonplace and eliminated the unlikely coincidences and excessive emotionalism of romantic novelists.

The realist movement in America included a conscious turning away from the structure and content of the works of the American Renaissance. Writers like Samuel Clemens discarded the traditional optimism and idealism of Thoreau and Emerson and the romantic forms and subject matter of Hawthorne and Poe. Instead, they chronicled the strengths and weaknesses of ordinary people confronting difficult social problems, like the restrictive conventions under which nineteenth-century women suffered. Writers who embraced realism used settings and plot details that reflected their characters' daily lives and realistic dialogue that replicates natural speech patterns.

Naturalism

Naturalism is a literary movement that emerged in the late nineteenth and early twentieth centuries in France, America, and England. Writers included in this group, like Stephen Crane, Emile Zola, and Theodore Dreiser, expressed in their works a biological and/or environmental determinism that prevented their characters from exercising their free will and controlling their fates. Crane often focused on the social and economic factors that overpowered his characters. Zola's and Dreiser's work include this type of environmental determinism coupled with an exploration of the influences of heredity in their portraits of the animalistic nature of men and women engaged in the endless and brutal struggle for survival.

Literary critics have found elements of realism and naturalism in Kate Chopin's depiction of the difficult struggle women at the turn of the last century faced as they tried to establish a clear sense of self. The realistic struggles in her fiction raise complex questions about how much influence women have over their destinies.

The New Woman

At the close of the nineteenth century, feminist thinkers began to engage in a rigorous investigation of female identity as it related to all aspects of a woman's life. Any woman who questioned traditional female roles was tagged a "New Woman," a term attributed to novelist Sarah Grand, whose 1894 article in the *North American Review* identified an emergent group of women, influenced by J. S. Mill and other champions of individualism, who supported and campaigned for women's rights. A dialogue resulted among these women that incorporated radical as well as conservative points of view.

The most radical thinkers in this group declared the institution of marriage to be a form of slavery and demanded its abolition. They rejected the notion that motherhood should be the ultimate goal of all women. The more conservative feminists of this age considered marriage and motherhood acceptable roles only if guidelines were set in order to prevent a woman from assuming an inferior position to her husband in any area of their life together. This group felt that a woman granted equality in marriage would serve as an exemplary role model for her children by encouraging the development of an independent spirit. Chopin's works enter into this dialogue, exploring a woman's place in traditional and nontraditional marital unions.

Critical Overview

Per Seyersted, in his biography on Chopin, noted that after her first two short stories "A Point at Issue!" and "Wiser than a God" had been published in 1889, editors told Chopin that her stories would continue to be published if she could create more traditional female characters. Luckily, Chopin did not listen. Over the next decade, her works would focus on women who struggled to break away from conventional standards. As a result, the public often found Chopin's work shocking. After

the publication of her masterful novel *The Awakening* in 1899, in which Chopin made her boldest statement on the necessity for personal expression, public outrage eventually resulted in the end of her literary career.

During the ten years between the publication of her first short stories and her novel, Chopin earned a reputation as an important local writer. Her short story collections *Bayou Folk*, published in 1894, and *A Night in Acadie*, which appeared in 1897, gained solid reviews that praised her accurate portraits of bayou life and her concise style. Chopin collected her more radical stories of male-female relationships previously rejected for publication into a third collection, *A Vocation and a Voice*, but she was unable to find a publisher.

The response to *The Awakening* was overwhelmingly negative. Many reviewers attacked the character of Edna Pontiellier, including one in *Public Opinion* who was "well satisfied" by Edna's fate, and another in the *Nation* who complained of the "unpleasantness" of his response to the main character. The book was subsequently banned from many libraries due to its controversial and subversive subject matter. One of the few positive reviews, from a critic for the *New York Times Book Review,* praised Chopin's artistry in the novel and responded to Edna with "pity for the most unfortunate of her sex."

The public's anger over the novel effectively ended Chopin's literary career. As Tonnette Bond Inge notes in her article on Chopin in the *Dictionary of Literary Biography,* Chopin "passed from the literary scene almost entirely unappreciated for her pioneering contributions to American fiction." Yet in the 1930s, a new generation of readers began to appreciate her short stories, and she again earned praise as a describer of local color. In the 1950s, *The Awakening* began to be recognized as an important literary work. Robert Cantwell, for example, wrote in the *Georgia Review* of Chopin's "heightened sensuous awareness" and insisted that the work was "a great novel."

In the 1960s, scholars heralded the complex psychological portraits and sociological themes in Chopin's fiction. Their reviews, coupled with Per Seyersted's definitive biography and edited collection of her complete works, established her reputation as one of the twentieth century's most important authors.

What Do I Read Next?

- *The Columbia Guide to American Women in the Nineteenth Century* (2000) presents a comprehensive history of the conditions of American women in the nineteenth century.

- *The Awakening,* published in 1899, is Chopin's masterful novel about a young woman who struggles to find self-knowledge and inevitably suffers the consequences of trying to establish herself as an independent spirit.

- In his play *A Doll's House* (1879), Henrik Ibsen examines a woman's restricted role in the nineteenth century and the disastrous effects of these limitations on her marriage.

- Kate Millet's *Sexual Politics* (1969) studies the history and dynamics of feminism.

- "Wiser than a God," published along with "A Point at Issue!" in 1889, presents a different view of an unconventional woman who tries to determine her own life and destiny. It is available in Chopin's *Collected Works.*

Criticism

Wendy Perkins

Perkins is an instructor of American literature and film. In this essay, Perkins analyzes Chopin's exploration of the difficulties inherent in the establishment of a nonconventional marriage.

A recurring theme in much of Kate Chopin's work is women's difficult struggle for emancipation. In her article for the *Dictionary of Literary Biography,* Tonette Bond Inge notes that as Chopin explores this theme, she does not avoid "showing the sacrifices and suffering associated with the journey to self-realization." This struggle becomes the main focus of Chopin's masterpiece *The Awakening* as it documents Edna Pontillier's journey from the restrictions of marriage to a discovery of self that affords her a sense, albeit an ironic one, of freedom. As it traces Edna's difficult process of awakening to selfhood, the novel reflects society's determination to force women to conform to expected roles.

As in *The Awakening*, most of Chopin's fiction chronicles the movement of her characters from bondage to freedom, outlining the social obstacles that impede this journey. Yet Chopin's earliest work is not reflective of this pattern. "A Point at Issue!,"

one of her first published short stories, begins with the main character already emancipated. At the beginning of the story, Eleanor, a strong woman with a clear sense of her own desires, has entered into an unconventional marriage with Charles Faraday that affords her the opportunity to express her individuality outside the traditional boundaries of this union. However, while she has been able to withstand social pressure to conform to delineated female roles, she ultimately cannot ignore the dictates of her own heart. As a result, by the end of the story, she has moved from freedom to the bondage of a traditional marriage. In her depiction of Eleanor's journey, Chopin exemplifies the human as well as social limitations that impede the quest for freedom.

Chopin created Eleanor as a reflection of the growing women's movement in the latter part of the nineteenth century, when an increasing number of women questioned traditional notions of marriage and motherhood. As a "new woman" Eleanor clearly rejects the primacy of social judgments of behavior, developing her own sense of her identity. At the beginning of the story, she has agreed to enter into a marriage with Charles Faraday, but only because they have both determined that their union will not restrict either partner's individuality. They idealistically view marriage, as noted by Barbara H. Solomon in her introduction to *The Awakening and Selected Stories,* as "an unfinished, incompletely

> As is the case with many of Chopin's heroines, Eleanor finds the obstacles to her independence overwhelming."

defined institution,'' where husband and wife are continually making ''new decisions'' and not playing ''mechanical roles.''

The first new decision Eleanor makes is to not publish an engagement announcement in the local paper. Eleanor had ''endured long and patiently the trials that beset her path when she chose to diverge from the beaten walks of female Plymdaledom.'' Her overwhelming need to roam ''the heights of free thought, and taste the sweets of a spiritual emancipation'' had given her the strength to endure social condemnation.

Charles appreciates Eleanor's ''clear intellect'' and ''the beautiful revelations of her mind'' and so he encourages her to engage with him in the study of the world around them. They seem well suited to each other, each complimenting and balancing the other's qualities. Her intellectual curiosity piques his own while his humor and optimism temper her earnestness and intensity. She is to him an ideal woman, one who will not reshape her identity into the traditional role of wife. They decide ''to be governed by no precedential methods. Marriage was to be a form, that while fixing legally their relation to each other, was in no wise to touch the individuality of either.'' As a result, marriage becomes for her ''the open portal through which she might seek the embellishments that her strong, graceful mentality deserved.''

Per Seyersted, in his biography on Chopin, writes that Eleanor is not a reflection of the more radical tenets of the emerging women's movement. He notes that Eleanor will enter into marriage with Charles only on an equal footing, but she accomplishes this by cooperating with him ''without any of the antagonism often attributed to her emancipationist sister.'' Seyersted argues that the story promotes real emancipation, ''not the 'quasi-emancipation' [Chopin] authorially attributes to women showing their protest by wearing strange clothes, but the true, inner kind of growth and

independence.'' Eleanor and Charles's union, as the narrator notes, is based on ''trust in each other's love, honor, courtesy.'' Chopin, however, did not ignore the complexities of such a union, especially when human nature intervenes.

As Chopin traces the complications that arise in the couple's marriage, she illustrates her point that the ideal of freedom that Charles and Eleanor envision can never be obtained in any kind of meaningful relationship. When the two are separated by their individual desires for fulfillment, Chopin suggests that human nature will inevitably impede this type of modern redefinition of love and marriage.

Neither Charles nor Eleanor is influenced by social dictates. The couple stoically face up to the public outcry when they decide that Eleanor will study in Paris and that Charles will continue his teaching at home. The society of Plymdale suffers ''indignant astonishment at the effrontery of the situation. . . . that two young people should presume to introduce such innovations into matrimony!'' The gossips incorrectly conclude that ''he must have already tired of her idiosyncrasies, since he had left her in Paris.'' Yet when they question the prudence of Eleanor living alone in Paris (''of all places. . . . Why not at once in Hades?''), they illustrate the possibility of complications that could arise in this ideal marriage, complications that the couple have refused to acknowledge. As a result, the two ignore the gossip and write each other frequent, long letters after they are separated.

Neither, however, had considered the impact of the loneliness and subsequent need for companionship that would result from such a separation. Charles's genial nature prompt him to seek out the company of the Beaton family, who welcomed him frequently into their home. Chopin inserts a note of irony into Charles's relationship with the Beatons, who enjoy a traditional family dynamic, with Mr. Beaton teaching at the nearby university while Mrs. Beaton's ''aspirations went not further than the desire for her family's good, and her bearing announced in its every feature, the satisfaction of completed hopes.'' The comfort Charles finds in their company suggests that his nature is more conventional than he realizes.

His appreciation of the Beaton family extends to their daughter Kitty, whose ''girlish charms'' and ''soft shining light of her eyes'' sexually attract Charles. Determined to promote honesty in his marriage, Charles writes Eleanor of his attraction to the girl, apparently convinced that his wife's progressive thinking and logical sensibility will override any feelings of jealousy. Charles, however, miscalculates, ignoring the strength of this very human emotion.

Chopin suggests that Eleanor responds with jealousy to Charles's attentions to Kitty, as evidenced by her late and cold letter to him. Her subsequent actions, however, are not as clearly drawn. Not long before Charles's arrival in Paris, Eleanor is overcome with "a misery of the heart, against which her reason was in armed rebellion." Eventually she crumbles "into a storm of sobs and tears," a "signal of surrender."

The narrator refuses to interpret the scene, explaining that the reason for Eleanor's despondency "will never be learned unless she chooses to disclose it herself." Chopin only hints at the possibilities: Eleanor may have entered into a romantic relationship with the artist who is painting her portrait and is coming to the painful decision to give him up; or she recognizes that she cannot bear to be separated from her husband and so has decided to give up Paris and return home with him. Either explanation for her outburst involves a very human response. Eleanor could have decided to turn to another in her loneliness, suspecting that her husband was doing the same. Or perhaps she could have come to the realization that her love for Charles was more important than her need for independence, and thus to ensure that Charles would no longer depend on the Beatons for company, she would give up Paris. The only clue Chopin will allow reflects the emergence of Eleanor's humanness during her breakdown: "Reason did good work and stood its ground bravely, but against it were the too great odds of a woman's heart, backed by the soft prejudices of a far-reaching heredity."

As is the case with many of Chopin's heroines, Eleanor finds the obstacles to her independence overwhelming. She has been able to withstand social pressures to conform to traditional notions of a woman's role, but she cannot hold up against the demands of her own nature. By the end of the story, Eleanor retains a small degree of freedom; she, not Charles, makes the decision for the two of them to return home. Yet, Charles's final response to her suggests that their union will deteriorate into a conventional relationship. When she admits that his attentions to Kitty stirred her jealousy, he forces her back into a stereotype, insisting "I love her none the less for it, but my Nellie is only a woman after all." Chopin adds a nice touch of irony in response, noting that "with man's usual inconsistency," Charles had forgotten his own bout of jealousy.

By the end of the story, Eleanor and Charles have given up their idealistic vision of the efficacy of the modern marriage, and Eleanor has relinquished a good measure of her independence. In this bittersweet story, Chopin illustrates a woman's journey from freedom to repression, suggesting that the requirements of the human heart complicate the best of intentions.

Source: Wendy Perkins, Critical Essay on "A Point at Issue!," in *Short Stories for Students,* The Gale Group, 2003.

Allison DeFrees

DeFrees is a published writer and an editor with a bachelor's degree in English from the University of Virginia and a law degree from the University of Texas. In the following essay, DeFrees discusses the early feminist tendencies of fiction writer Kate Chopin.

Can women and men be equal? The question appears prosaic and even simplistic. But it elicits a larger question: what is equality? Is it something that exists in nature, or does it spring from the machinations of society? How Kate Chopin answers that question in her short story, "A Point at Issue!," is a manifestation of both her liberal mindset—especially by mid-nineteenth century standards, which was when the story was written—and of the blossoming of that mindset from within the confines of a society holding fast to the notion that a woman's position in the hierarchy of the household was strictly beneath her husband. Chopin produces a sly retelling of the happy-ever-after wedding tale and sets up for her readers a revolutionary theory of equality within the union of marriage. The ending does not promise that the vows of equality and mutual respect will be lasting, but it does something more: it turns the tables on what were then perceived as conventional patterns of thought about marriage.

In some ways, the story reads like a sitcom: a couple meets; the man and woman fall in love and attempt to set up an arrangement wherein they share their lives as equals; the two separate temporarily to pursue their individual interests; misunderstandings ensue, but all is gilded with a happy ending. On the

> **Despite the young couple's pre-planned, rational approach toward their relationship, when matters of the fidelity impinge upon 'reciprocal liberty,' it is instinct that takes root as intellect takes flight."**

surface, it is almost a tale of manners, a comedy of errors. It is easy to envision any number of television stars—dependant upon the generation of the reader, of course—starring in the televised version of the story, or to imagine a laugh track when Charles trips over his chair as he starts to chase down his wife, who is riding in a carriage with another man. But what Chopin is doing in "A Point at Issue!" is far subtler than the broad comedic gestures of a sitcom. In the span of a short tale, Chopin lays down the tenets of her vision of women's liberation—to be seen as an intellectual equal, and to be given the same opportunities for cerebral advance as men—then layers those desires with societal expectations, exposing the hurdles that stand, even today, in the way of men and women being able to operate on an equal plane. This is a common topic today, but at the time Chopin wrote "A Point at Issue!," the thoughts were revolutionary— so much so that Chopin's early work, such as this story, contains outlines of her later stories that loudly decry the inequality between husband and wife.

The story begins with shame. Eleanor Gail shudders at the sight of her name in the local newspaper's small notice proclaiming: "MAR- RIED—On Tuesday, May 11, Eleanor Gail to Charles Faraday." Although the notice is inobtrusive— "modestly wedged"—to Eleanor, it is an invitation for the rest of society to scorn at her. Eleanor has previously refused to hold a fancy wedding includ- ing members of the community and has made a conscious choice to step away from the expected paths of other young ladies. The narrator explains that Eleanor sees the marriage announcement as

"an indelicate thrusting of herself upon the public notice" and that when she sees the notice, "she was plunged in regret at having made to the proprieties the concession of permitting it." Eleanor chose to "diverge from the beaten walks of Plymdaledom," with "Plymdaledom" representing a marriage to someone in one's own social and economic status. From the first paragraph, the reader knows that Eleanor is different, that she is not afraid of going against societal norms.

In fact, Eleanor knowingly accepts the appear- ance of being "relegated to a place amid that large and ill-assorted family of 'cranks.'" For, regardless of "the disappointed public" she is an "ideal woman" in the eyes of her husband. She expresses regret only for having given any concessions to societal norms at all. The private life she has chosen affords her an equality that cannot be weighted in public terms. While the ladies of Plymdale were "condemning her present . . . unsparing of her past, and full with damning prognostic of her future," Charles Faraday "had caught a look from her eyes into his that he recognized at once as a free masonry of intellect," a woman "able to grasp a question and anticipate conclusions by a quick intuition." Charles and Eleanor's courtship lasted for over a year, and in that time, rather than consider how many children to have or where they should live, they "knocked at the closed doors of philosophy—a field of study not normally open to women. Rather than court each other with family histories and idle chatter, Eleanor and Charles "went looking for the good things of life."

Charles's admiration for Eleanor's intellect did not flag upon the end of their courtship; in marriage, they vowed that "each was to remain a free integral of humanity, responsible to no dominating exactions of so-called marriage laws." As Chopin expounds on the agreement between Eleanor and Charles regarding their relationship, the reader begins to see the full thrust of Chopin's opinions regarding a woman's right to think for herself, whether married or single. The couple scoffed at tradition and de- cided, in their marriage, to be "governed by no precedential methods." Chopin created a new mar- riage contract through Charles and Eleanor, one that, according to Cynthia Griffin Wolff's review in *American Writers,* closely emulated Chopin's own marriage. Individuality was to remain intact, made possible through "trust in each other's love, honor, courtesy, tempered by the reserving clause of readi- ness to meet the consequences of reciprocal liberty."

It is the final statement in that train of thought, with its "reserving clause," that opens the door to the plot, and the ultimate point, of Chopin's story, and foreshadows that there will, indeed, be repercussions to their novel model of marriage. Despite the young couple's pre-planned, rational approach toward their relationship, when matters of the fidelity impinge upon "reciprocal liberty," it is instinct that takes root as intellect takes flight. A test of marital fidelity reaches the bounds of rational thought, and the reader sees doubt take over even the most idealistic minds. Suspicion takes hold, and the "new marriage contract" is tested by the harshest of judges: the jealous heart.

After a long honeymoon, Charles ironically leaves Eleanor in Paris—the city of love—to follow her intellectual interests while he returns to the Unites States to run his business. Though they miss each other when apart, all is well between them while this arrangement ensues, and they carry on their intellectual relationship through letters. They are redoubtable in their powers of rationality and adherence to their modern arrangement, unfettered by envy or uncertainty. But Charles and Eleanor fall prey to the seduction of doubt.

It would seem, accordingly to the plot, that Eleanor is the first to fall jealous. But this line is blurred by Chopin's word choices, which hint at the disdain she feels toward a man so callous as to expect his wife to be always above the caste of jealous society. Regarding the letter that Charles writes to his wife, the narrator explains that "with the cold-blooded impartiality of choosing a subject which he thought of neither more nor less prominent than the next, he descanted at some length upon the interesting emotions which Miss Kitty's pretty femininity aroused in him." What woman would not question the effusive praise and admitted sexual attraction related by her husband about another woman? As the narrator explains: "Reason did good work and stood its ground bravely, but against it were the too great odds of a woman's heart, backed by the soft prejudices of a far-reaching heredity." Here Chopin seems to indicate that a woman is, by her nature, the weaker sex, prone to fits of jealousy. But the events that follow indicate something more profound: when Chopin refers to "far-reaching heredity," it is the heredity of mankind, not just of women. It is the eternal condition of man to be jealous, to want to possess another, and to be certain of one's place in the world. Charles does not think twice about the words of praise he has

related to his wife about another woman because he is faithful, but his fidelity does not make him immune to his own jealousy.

Charles comes to Paris after a long absence, and one day he sees his wife in a carriage, gaily conversing with another man. Charles immediately thinks the worst, but just as he considers leaping from his seat to "follow and demand an explanation," his "better self and better senses [come] quickly back to him." But are these really his better senses and his better self? Had he leapt from where he sat in the Parisian café, bounded to the horse carriage and bellowed in anger at the sight of his beloved carrying on with another man, might not that have been the more honest presentation of his feelings for Eleanor? The reader is left to ponder these questions, for the event never comes to pass. Charles reasons himself out of his state of vengeful anger, and Eleanor never learns that Charles experienced his jealous rage.

Both husband and wife fall prey to the same natural weakness, but the way that they relate their feelings to each other in this regard hints at a rupture in their union that is likely to create a permanent emotional divide. By the end of the story, it could be interpreted that, because Eleanor asks her husband to take her back to the states with him, she has somehow given the power in the relationship to her husband. But it may just as easily be interpreted that, in fact, by evidencing her desire to be with him, and in admitting her jealousy, she has opened her heart, and her soul, to the possibility of true intimacy and equality. When he responds with shock at her belief that he "cared" for another woman, she believes him heartily, and says, "there are certain things which a woman can't philosophize about, any more than she can about death when it touches that which is near to her." Eleanor has brought her humanity to bear on the misunderstandings she and her husband have shared, and it brings out the best in her. Charles, on the other hand, says nothing to Eleanor about his doubts, and instead reduces Eleanor from her status as "pre-eminent" and "his ideal woman" to that of "only a woman," like any other. The reader might at this point agree with Charles that Eleanor has a woman's frailty and that Charles is the stronger of the two, but for the final sentence of the story: "With man's usual inconsistency, he had quite forgotten the episode of the portrait." Charles, in seeing his wife's weakness exposed so clearly, stands tall in his righteousness, forgetting his own identical imperfection.

Chopin seems to be winking at the reader, offering an irony to those sympathetic to her views. Hers is a tentative leaning to the possibility of the intellectual emancipation of women, and a precursor to her most acclaimed work, *The Awakening,* in which she more openly calls for the emancipation of women from the stifling confines of marriage, to which her society clung so tightly. It is unclear whether it was Chopin's deliberate choice to speak subtly about the infidelities of a man's mind in regard to his wife, or the result of a young writer still timid about bearing her beliefs about equality to a public unaccustomed to the notion of a wife as the equal of her husband. In either case, the end result is a delightfully subtle and slyly political reproach of men's refusal to recognize the full potential of their wives. In "A Point at Issue!," Charles may think he has pegged his wife as "only a woman," hypocritically forgiving her for her petty jealousy, but it is actually Eleanor who truly understands the nature of the relationship between man and wife. And, it was Chopin who saw that, for all the whispers of equality in the nineteenth century, women remained placed behind their men.

Source: Allison DeFrees, Critical Essay on "A Point at Issue!," in *Short Stories for Students,* The Gale Group, 2003.

Per Seyersted

In the following essay excerpt, Seyersted examines Chopin's take on feminist issues in her first three stories (as well as a "A Point at Issue!") within the context of Chopin's idea of a modern female.

Kate Chopin was never a feminist in the dictionary sense of the term, that is, she never joined or supported any of the organizations through which women fought to get "political, economic, and social rights equal to those of men." Not only did she shy away from societies and issues in general, but she probably regarded the New World feminists as unrealistic when they so closely allied themselves with efforts to elevate men to their own supposedly very high level of purity; she undoubtedly concurred with the early George Sand, who felt that woman largely had the same drives as man and therefore also should have his "rights."

Though American literary permissiveness was slowly being somewhat extended in matters connected with the senses—we might point to the fact that R. W. Gilder published Whitman and that Reedy's *Mirror* gave space to sex-scientists like Krafft-Ebing and Havelock Ellis—the feminists turned their back on a novel like Sarah Grand's *The Heavenly Twins* because the author dared to combine her plea for a single standard with a discreet mention of male promiscuity and its results. As usual, Kate Chopin was a detached observer, a skeptic who could not share any easy optimism. When a friend praised Mrs. Grand's book, in which there is much talk about women's rights, but no suggestion that females as well as men have sexual urges, she exclaimed in her diary: "She thinks 'the Heavenly Twin' a book calculated to do incalculable good in the world: by helping young girls to a fuller comprehension of truth in the marriage relation! Truth is certainly concealed in a well for most of us."

Just as Mrs. Chopin saw that the problems confronting her sex were too complicated to admit of easy solutions, she was also well acquainted with the manifold tendencies in the women themselves. It seems more than an accident that her three earliest extant stories are each in turn devoted to one of what we might call the three main types of women: the "feminine," the "emancipated," and the "modern" (to use the terminology of Simone de Beauvoir's *The Second Sex*), and that the tension between the two leading components of this triad was to reverberate through her whole *oeuvre.*

"Euphrasie," Kate Chopin's first tale from 1888, is the story of a feminine or traditional heroine, that is, a woman of the kind who accepts the patriarchal view of her role very pointedly expressed, for example, in the marriage sermon of Father Beaulieu of Cloutierville: "Madame, be submissive to your husband . . . You no longer belong to yourself."

In a society where man makes the rules, woman is often kept in a state of tutelage and regarded as property or as a servant. Her "lack of self assertion" is equated with "the perfection of womanliness," as Mrs. Chopin later expressed it in a story. The female's capital is her body and her innocence, and she should be attractive and playful enough for the man to want her, while showing a reticence and resistance which can gratify his sense of conquest, or "the main-instinct of possession," as the author termed it in another tale. What man wishes, writes Simone de Beauvoir, "is that this struggle remain a game for him, while for woman it involves . . . [a recognition of] him as her destiny." In the man's world, woman should accept a special standard for the ''more expansive'' sex, and for herself, she should eagerly welcome the ''sanctity of motherhood.'' As Mme. de Staël's Corinne is told: Whatever extraordinary gifts she may have, her duty and ''her proper destiny is to devote herself to her husband and to the raising of her children.''

Euphrasie is a dutiful daughter, and also a loyal fiancée as she tries to hide even from herself that she has suddenly fallen in love with someone else than the man she is engaged to. In the tradition of the feminine woman, she accepts the role of the passive, self-obliterating object as she makes no attempt to influence her fate, and she is willing to break her heart and proceed with the marriage, even though she considers it immoral to kiss her fiancé when she does not love him. (It is interesting to note that the author, in her very first story, on this point echoes George Sand; she does not openly offend by saying in so many words that Euphrasie should have kissed the other man when it becomes evident that they are mutually attracted, but that is what she implies.) As behooves a feminine woman, she lets the men decide her destiny: When her fiancé learns the truth by accident, he sets her free, thus—in Euphrasie's words—saving her from the sin a marriage to him would have meant to her.

As has been noted before, Kate Chopin put this story aside for a few years and destroyed the next two she wrote. The original draft of ''Euphrasie'' is lost, and we do not know why she titled the tale after the girl's fiancé when she later revised and shortened it. Nor do we know anything about the two other stories, except that the first was set on Grand Isle, and that the second, ''A Poor Girl,'' was offensive to editorial eyes, perhaps because the author already here was too open about untraditional urges in women.

The next of Kate Chopin's tales which has come down to us is ''Wiser than a God.'' It is the story of Paula Von Stoltz, a young woman who works hard to become a concert pianist. She loves the rich George Brainard, but when he asks her to follow a calling that asks ''only for the labor of loving,'' she replies that marriage does not enter into the ''purpose of [her] life.'' George insists that he does not ask her to give up anything; she tells him, however, that music to her is ''something dearer than life, than riches, even than love.'' This is too contrary to George's idea of woman's role; calling Paula mad, he lectures her and declares that

> In the third story we have from Mrs. Chopin, 'A Point at Issue,'--she turns to modern woman, that is, the female who insists on being a subject and man's equal, but who cooperates with the male rather than fighting him, without any of the antagonism often attributed to her emancipationist sister."

even if the one who loved him had taken the vows as a nun, she would owe it to herself, to him, and to God to be his wife. But Fräulein Von Stoltz leaves to become an internationally renowned pianist, and her later constant companion is a composer who is wise enough not to make any emotional demands on her.

Paula largely answers to Simone de Beauvoir's definition of the emancipated woman that is, a female who ''wants to be active, a taker, and refuses the passivity man means to impose on her''; who insists on the active transcendence of a subject, the *pour soi,* rather than the passive immanence of an object, the *en soi;* and who attempts to achieve an existentialist authenticity through making a conscious choice, giving her own laws, realizing her essence, and making herself her own destiny.

The pride indicated in Paula's family name does not manifest itself in a haughty attitude toward her admirer; she is soft-spoken compared to the impetuous, youthful George who insists that she is throwing him into ''a gulf . . . of everlasting misery.'' But she speaks up when she realizes they are in two different worlds, that he represents the patriarchal view of woman, and she the view of Margaret Fuller that women so inclined should be allowed to leave aside motherhood and domesticity and instead use their wings to soar toward the transcendence of a nonbiological career. ''Wiser than a God'' has something of Mme. de Staël's *Corinne* in that

George for a moment believes he can accept a wife who lives not solely for him and his children; unlike the French heroine, however, Paula tells her suitor that life is less important to her than the unhampered exertion of what she considers her authentic calling and her true self.

The self-sacrifice represented by Corinne's suicide to set Oswald free is unthinkable in the Kate Chopin heroines who are awakened to unusual gifts or impulses in themselves and to self-assertion. "Euphrasie" proves that it is not female submission as such which the author leaves out in her writings, but only the concessions to sentimentality and conventionality, the violations of the logic in the various types of heroines. The author combines in these two tales a detachment and objectivity with a tender understanding and respect for both the feminine and the emancipated young lady.

In the third story we have from Mrs. Chopin, "A Point at Issue,"—she turns to modern woman, that is, the female who insists on being a subject and man's equal, but who cooperates with the male rather than fighting him, without any of the antagonism often attributed to her emancipationist sister. Such modern women were not uncommon at the time, and when they married, some decided not to take their husband's name, that sign of ownership, but to keep their own. In 1895, for example, the St. Louis *Post-Dispatch* printed the statements which such a woman and her husband had made when they entered their "advanced matrimony." She not only kept her maiden name, but also declared that she and her suitor entered marriage with the understanding that both should preserve their individuality and that he should not "let this marriage interfere with the life work she had chosen."

Unlike Paula of the previous story, Eleanor Gail of "A Point at Issue" does wed her suitor, Charles Faraday; they decide, however:

> . . . to be governed by no precedential methods. Marriage was to be a form, that while fixing legally their relation to each other, was in no wise to touch the individuality of either; that was to be preserved intact. Each was to remain a free integral of humanity, responsible to no dominating exactions of so-called marriage laws. And the element that was to make possible such a union was trust in each other's love, honor, courtesy, tempered by the reserving clause of readiness to meet the consequences of reciprocal liberty.

The Latin proverb which Kate Chopin gave as a motto for the previous story: "To love and be wise is scarcely granted even to a god," should more appropriately have been put at the head of "A Point at Issue." While Euphrasie disregards the conflict between love and reason because she has been indoctrinated with the idea of leaving the responsibility for her life to a man, and Paula avoids it by devoting herself to art and making her own decisions, Eleanor is the one really to be put to the test, as she, like her husband, believes that she can both love and be wise as they share a life in "Plymdale" as equals.

The two progressive lovers seem well fitted for their venture. Eleanor, who combines her "graceful womanly charms" with a lack of self-consciousness, has chosen to "diverge from the beaten walks of female Plymdaledom . . . [and taste] the sweets of a spiritual emancipation." This strange person is, like her mathematician husband, "possessed of a clear intellect: sharp in its reasoning, strong and unprejudiced in its outlook. She was that *rara avis,* a logical woman." The two are ready to take broad views of life and humanity as they live in the harmony of a united purpose and "a free masonry of intellect." Being more learned, Charles leads the way when they, for example, study science, but with her "oftentimes in her eagerness taking the lead."

Faraday agrees with his wife that she shall spend a year or two alone in Paris learning French. Once he tells her in a letter how a girl had momentarily charmed him, feeling no qualms in doing so as he saw it as unimportant, and, besides, "Was not Eleanor's large comprehensiveness far above the littleness of ordinary women?" While he thinks no more of the matter, Eleanor cannot escape old-fashioned jealousy; nor can Charles when he joins her in Paris for the summer and one day sees her with another man, who later turns out to be a painter doing her portrait. For a moment he wants to kill the "villain," but reason takes over, even before he learns that his jealousy was unfounded.

As a result of these incidents, both retreat one step from their advanced stand. Eleanor rejoins her husband in America, and, being unable to forget how jealousy made her suffer like a "distressed goddess," she has gained insight into her own nature and knows that, as she tells Charles, "there are certain things which a woman can't philosophize about." He has learned nothing from *his* agony, however, while Eleanor's affliction causes him to slip into the traditional attitude of the male when he patronizingly concludes: "I love her none the less for it, but my Nellie is only a woman, after all.'' And the author adds: ''With a man's usual inconsistency, he had quite forgotten the episode of the portrait.''

In her first two stories, Kate Chopin had betrayed a possible involvement with marriage only when she in ''Wiser than a God,'' with what looks like mild irony, speaks of ''the serious offices of wifehood and matrimony'' which constitute all of life to the woman Brainard eventually marries. When there is a somewhat more pronounced suggestion of an engagement in the third tale, it is again on the issue of woman and matrimony. The author by no means makes it clear that she speaks only for Eleanor when she writes: ''Marriage, which marks too often the closing period of a woman's intellectual existence, was to be in her case the open portal through which she might seek the embellishments that her strong, graceful mentality deserved.'' It is interesting to note the surprising juxtaposition of marriage and death with which the story opens when it informs us that the wedding announcement of the Faradays was printed side by side with a ''somber-clad'' advertisement for ''marble and granite monuments.''

The impression we are left with by this tale is that Kate Chopin sympathizes with Eleanor even more than with Euphrasie and Paula and that she wishes the Faradays success in their venture to live as perfect equals. She appears to favor female emancipation, not the ''quasi-emancipation'' she authorially attributes to women showing their protest by wearing strange clothes, but the true, inner kind of growth and independence. She also seems to favor the couple's lack of preconceptions as they attempt to make ''innovations into matrimony'' by introducing a marital liberty. But Mrs. Chopin saw the complexities of this point at issue: ''Reason did good work,'' she observes in connection with Eleanor's fight with jealousy, ''but against it were the too great odds of a woman's heart, backed by the soft prejudices of a far-reaching heredity.'' Among the inherited factors imposing themselves upon even a modern woman and a modern man are fundamental impulses, such as jealousy, and notions, such as that of male supremacy.

The idea of man's superiority is emphasized as Charles falls back into the age-old concept that his wife is ''only a woman.'' It is perhaps a little surprising to find inconsistency attributed to him, a quality which traditionally typifies the so-called

changeable women; how ever, it serves to stress his male overevaluation of himself: As a female, Eleanor is not expected to know much; therefore she can allow herself to feel that ''she knew nothing,'' and at the same time be open for learning. Charles, on the other hand, is a man, thus a superior being, and as such he does not need to be taught anything.

With her three first stories, Kate Chopin had stated her major theme: woman's spiritual emancipation—or her ''being set free from servitude, bondage, or restraint,'' as the term has been defined—in connection with her men and her career. The sensuous is not touched upon in these tales, except in the case of Faraday. His ''stronger man nature'' may refer to expressions of eroticism, and we are told, apropos of the matter dealt with in his letter, that ''it is idle to suppose that even the most exemplary men go through life with their eyes closed to woman's beauty and their senses steeled against its charm.'' The modest success of *At Fault* gave the author a certain encouragement and self-confidence, and seemingly as a result of this, she began, as she entered the second stage of her career, to deal with woman's emancipation also in the field of the senses.

Source: Per Seyersted, ''A More Powerful Female Realism,'' in *Kate Chopin: A Critical Biography,* Louisiana State University Press, 1969, pp. 99–115.

Sources

Cantwell, Robert, Review of *The Awakening,* in *Georgia Review,* Winter 1956.

Dimock, Wai-chee, ''Kate Chopin,'' in *Modern American Women Writers,* Charles Scribner's Sons, 1991, pp. 63–78.

Inge, Tonette Bond, ''Kate Chopin,'' in *Dictionary of Literary Biography,* Vol. 78: *American Short-Story Writers, 1880–1910,* edited by Bobby Ellen Kimbel, Gale Research, 1989, pp. 90–110.

Review of ''A Point at Issue!,'' in the *Nation,* August 3, 1899.

Review of ''A Point at Issue!,'' in the *New York Times Book Review,* June 24, 1899.

Review of ''A Point at Issue!,'' in *Public Opinion,* June 22, 1899.

Seyersted, Per, *Kate Chopin: A Critical Biography,* Louisiana State University Press, 1969.

Solomon, Barbara H., ''Introduction,'' in *The Awakening and Selected Stories of Kate Chopin,* Signet, 1976.

Wolff, Cynthia Griffin, ''Kate Chopin,'' in *American Writers,* Supplement I, Charles Scribner's Sons, 1979, pp. 200–26.

Further Reading

de Saussure Davis, Sara, "Kate Chopin," in *Dictionary of Literary Biography,* Vol. 12: *American Realists and Naturalists,* edited by Donald Pizer, Gale Research, 1982, pp. 59–71.

Davis places Chopin in the realist tradition and discusses how the "unconventional" heroine in "A Point at Issue!" relates to those in her other works.

Rocks, James E., "Kate Chopin's Ironic Vision," in *Louisiana Review,* Vol. 1, No. 2, 1972, pp. 110–20.

Rocks analyzes Chopin's use of irony in several of her works.

Skaggs, Peggy, "Chapter 6: 'Miscellaneous Works,'" in *Kate Chopin,* Twayne's United States Author Series Online, G. K. Hall, 1999.

Skaggs compares "A Point at Issue!" to "Wiser than a God."

Wolff, Cynthia Griffin, "Kate Chopin," in *American Writers,* Supplement I, Charles Scribner's Sons, 1979, pp. 200–26.

Wolff provides an overview of Chopin's work, including a negative assessment of "A Point at Issue!," claiming the story to be "too neatly constructed, symmetrical, and sterile."

Glossary of Literary Terms

A

Aestheticism: A literary and artistic movement of the nineteenth century. Followers of the movement believed that art should not be mixed with social, political, or moral teaching. The statement ''art for art's sake'' is a good summary of aestheticism. The movement had its roots in France, but it gained widespread importance in England in the last half of the nineteenth century, where it helped change the Victorian practice of including moral lessons in literature. Edgar Allan Poe is one of the best-known American ''aesthetes.''

Allegory: A narrative technique in which characters representing things or abstract ideas are used to convey a message or teach a lesson. Allegory is typically used to teach moral, ethical, or religious lessons but is sometimes used for satiric or political purposes. Many fairy tales are allegories.

Allusion: A reference to a familiar literary or historical person or event, used to make an idea more easily understood. Joyce Carol Oates's story ''Where Are You Going, Where Have You Been?'' exhibits several allusions to popular music.

Analogy: A comparison of two things made to explain something unfamiliar through its similarities to something familiar, or to prove one point based on the acceptance of another. Similes and metaphors are types of analogies.

Antagonist: The major character in a narrative or drama who works against the hero or protagonist. The Misfit in Flannery O'Connor's story ''A Good Man Is Hard to Find'' serves as the antagonist for the Grandmother.

Anthology: A collection of similar works of literature, art, or music. Zora Neale Hurston's ''The Eatonville Anthology'' is a collection of stories that take place in the same town.

Anthropomorphism: The presentation of animals or objects in human shape or with human characteristics. The term is derived from the Greek word for ''human form.'' The fur necklet in Katherine Mansfield's story ''Miss Brill'' has anthropomorphic characteristics.

Anti-hero: A central character in a work of literature who lacks traditional heroic qualities such as courage, physical prowess, and fortitude. Anti-heroes typically distrust conventional values and are unable to commit themselves to any ideals. They generally feel helpless in a world over which they have no control. Anti-heroes usually accept, and often celebrate, their positions as social outcasts. A well-known anti-hero is Walter Mitty in James Thurber's story ''The Secret Life of Walter Mitty.''

Archetype: The word archetype is commonly used to describe an original pattern or model from which all other things of the same kind are made. Archetypes are the literary images that grow out of the ''collective unconscious,'' a theory proposed by psychologist Carl Jung. They appear in literature as incidents and plots that repeat basic patterns of life. They may also appear as stereotyped characters. The ''schlemiel'' of Yiddish literature is an archetype.

Autobiography: A narrative in which an individual tells his or her life story. Examples include Benjamin Franklin's *Autobiography* and Amy Hempel's story ''In the Cemetery Where Al Jolson Is Buried,'' which has autobiographical characteristics even though it is a work of fiction.

Avant-garde: A literary term that describes new writing that rejects traditional approaches to literature in favor of innovations in style or content. Twentieth-century examples of the literary *avant-garde* include the modernists and the minimalists.

B

Belles-lettres: A French term meaning ''fine letters'' or ''beautiful writing.'' It is often used as a synonym for literature, typically referring to imaginative and artistic rather than scientific or expository writing. Current usage sometimes restricts the meaning to light or humorous writing and appreciative essays about literature. Lewis Carroll's *Alice in Wonderland* epitomizes the realm of belles-lettres.

Bildungsroman: A German word meaning ''novel of development.'' The *bildungsroman* is a study of the maturation of a youthful character, typically brought about through a series of social or sexual encounters that lead to self-awareness. J. D. Salinger's *Catcher in the Rye* is a *bildungsroman*, and Doris Lessing's story ''Through the Tunnel'' exhibits characteristics of a *bildungsroman* as well.

Black Aesthetic Movement: A period of artistic and literary development among African Americans in the 1960s and early 1970s. This was the first major African-American artistic movement since the Harlem Renaissance and was closely paralleled by the civil rights and black power movements. The black aesthetic writers attempted to produce works of art that would be meaningful to the black masses. Key figures in black aesthetics included one of its founders, poet and playwright Amiri Baraka, formerly known as LeRoi Jones; poet and essayist Haki R. Madhubuti, formerly Don L. Lee; poet and playwright Sonia Sanchez; and dramatist Ed Bullins. Works representative of the Black Aesthetic Movement include Amiri Baraka's play *Dutchman,* a 1964 Obie award-winner.

Black Humor: Writing that places grotesque elements side by side with humorous ones in an attempt to shock the reader, forcing him or her to laugh at the horrifying reality of a disordered world. ''Lamb to the Slaughter,'' by Roald Dahl, in which a placid housewife murders her husband and serves the murder weapon to the investigating policemen, is an example of black humor.

C

Catharsis: The release or purging of unwanted emotions—specifically fear and pity—brought about by exposure to art. The term was first used by the Greek philosopher Aristotle in his *Poetics* to refer to the desired effect of tragedy on spectators.

Character: Broadly speaking, a person in a literary work. The actions of characters are what constitute the plot of a story, novel, or poem. There are numerous types of characters, ranging from simple, stereotypical figures to intricate, multifaceted ones. ''Characterization'' is the process by which an author creates vivid, believable characters in a work of art. This may be done in a variety of ways, including (1) direct description of the character by the narrator; (2) the direct presentation of the speech, thoughts, or actions of the character; and (3) the responses of other characters to the character. The term ''character'' also refers to a form originated by the ancient Greek writer Theophrastus that later became popular in the seventeenth and eighteenth centuries. It is a short essay or sketch of a person who prominently displays a specific attribute or quality, such as miserliness or ambition. ''Miss Brill,'' a story by Katherine Mansfield, is an example of a character sketch.

Classical: In its strictest definition in literary criticism, classicism refers to works of ancient Greek or Roman literature. The term may also be used to describe a literary work of recognized importance (a ''classic'') from any time period or literature that exhibits the traits of classicism. Examples of later works and authors now described as classical include French literature of the seventeenth century, Western novels of the nineteenth century, and American fiction of the mid-nineteenth century such as that written by James Fenimore Cooper and Mark Twain.

Climax: The turning point in a narrative, the moment when the conflict is at its most intense. Typically, the structure of stories, novels, and plays is one of rising action, in which tension builds to the climax, followed by falling action, in which tension lessens as the story moves to its conclusion.

Comedy: One of two major types of drama, the other being tragedy. Its aim is to amuse, and it typically ends happily. Comedy assumes many forms, such as farce and burlesque, and uses a variety of techniques, from parody to satire. In a restricted sense the term comedy refers only to dramatic presentations, but in general usage it is commonly applied to nondramatic works as well.

Comic Relief: The use of humor to lighten the mood of a serious or tragic story, especially in plays. The technique is very common in Elizabethan works, and can be an integral part of the plot or simply a brief event designed to break the tension of the scene.

Conflict: The conflict in a work of fiction is the issue to be resolved in the story. It usually occurs between two characters, the protagonist and the antagonist, or between the protagonist and society or the protagonist and himself or herself. The conflict in Washington Irving's story ''The Devil and Tom Walker'' is that the Devil wants Tom Walker's soul but Tom does not want to go to hell.

Criticism: The systematic study and evaluation of literary works, usually based on a specific method or set of principles. An important part of literary studies since ancient times, the practice of criticism has given rise to numerous theories, methods, and ''schools,'' sometimes producing conflicting, even contradictory, interpretations of literature in general as well as of individual works. Even such basic issues as what constitutes a poem or a novel have been the subject of much criticism over the centuries. Seminal texts of literary criticism include Plato's *Republic,* Aristotle's *Poetics,* Sir Philip Sidney's *The Defence of Poesie,* and John Dryden's *Of Dramatic Poesie.* Contemporary schools of criticism include deconstruction, feminist, psychoanalytic, poststructuralist, new historicist, postcolonialist, and reader-response.

D

Deconstruction: A method of literary criticism characterized by multiple conflicting interpretations of a given work. Deconstructionists consider the impact of the language of a work and suggest that the true meaning of the work is not necessarily the meaning that the author intended.

Deduction: The process of reaching a conclusion through reasoning from general premises to a specific premise. Arthur Conan Doyle's character Sherlock Holmes often used deductive reasoning to solve mysteries.

Denotation: The definition of a word, apart from the impressions or feelings it creates in the reader. The word ''apartheid'' denotes a political and economic policy of segregation by race, but its connotations—oppression, slavery, inequality—are numerous.

Denouement: A French word meaning ''the unknotting.'' In literature, it denotes the resolution of conflict in fiction or drama. The *denouement* follows the climax and provides an outcome to the primary plot situation as well as an explanation of secondary plot complications. A well-known example of *denouement* is the last scene of the play *As You Like It* by William Shakespeare, in which couples are married, an evildoer repents, the identities of two disguised characters are revealed, and a ruler is restored to power. Also known as ''falling action.''

Detective Story: A narrative about the solution of a mystery or the identification of a criminal. The conventions of the detective story include the detective's scrupulous use of logic in solving the mystery; incompetent or ineffectual police; a suspect who appears guilty at first but is later proved innocent; and the detective's friend or confidant—often the narrator—whose slowness in interpreting clues emphasizes by contrast the detective's brilliance. Edgar Allan Poe's ''Murders in the Rue Morgue'' is commonly regarded as the earliest example of this type of story. Other practitioners are Arthur Conan Doyle, Dashiell Hammett, and Agatha Christie.

Dialogue: Dialogue is conversation between people in a literary work. In its most restricted sense, it refers specifically to the speech of characters in a drama. As a specific literary genre, a ''dialogue'' is a composition in which characters debate an issue or idea.

Didactic: A term used to describe works of literature that aim to teach a moral, religious, political, or practical lesson. Although didactic elements are often found in artistically pleasing works, the term ''didactic'' usually refers to literature in which the message is more important than the form. The term may also be used to criticize a work that the critic finds ''overly didactic,'' that is, heavy-handed in its delivery of a lesson. An example of didactic literature is John Bunyan's *Pilgrim's Progress.*

Dramatic Irony: Occurs when the reader of a work of literature knows something that a character in the work itself does not know. The irony is in the contrast between the intended meaning of the statements or actions of a character and the additional information understood by the audience.

Dystopia: An imaginary place in a work of fiction where the characters lead dehumanized, fearful lives. George Orwell's *Nineteen Eighty-four,* and Margaret Atwood's *Handmaid's Tale* portray versions of dystopia.

E

Edwardian: Describes cultural conventions identified with the period of the reign of Edward VII of England (1901–1910). Writers of the Edwardian Age typically displayed a strong reaction against the propriety and conservatism of the Victorian Age. Their work often exhibits distrust of authority in religion, politics, and art and expresses strong doubts about the soundness of conventional values. Writers of this era include E. M. Forster, H. G. Wells, and Joseph Conrad.

Empathy: A sense of shared experience, including emotional and physical feelings, with someone or something other than oneself. Empathy is often used to describe the response of a reader to a literary character.

Epilogue: A concluding statement or section of a literary work. In dramas, particularly those of the seventeenth and eighteenth centuries, the epilogue is a closing speech, often in verse, delivered by an actor at the end of a play and spoken directly to the audience.

Epiphany: A sudden revelation of truth inspired by a seemingly trivial incident. The term was widely used by James Joyce in his critical writings, and the stories in Joyce's *Dubliners* are commonly called ''epiphanies.''

Epistolary Novel: A novel in the form of letters. The form was particularly popular in the eighteenth century. The form can also be applied to short stories, as in Edwidge Danticat's ''Children of the Sea.''

Epithet: A word or phrase, often disparaging or abusive, that expresses a character trait of someone or something. ''The Napoleon of crime'' is an epithet applied to Professor Moriarty, arch-rival of Sherlock Holmes in Arthur Conan Doyle's series of detective stories.

Existentialism: A predominantly twentieth-century philosophy concerned with the nature and perception of human existence. There are two major strains of existentialist thought: atheistic and Christian. Followers of atheistic existentialism believe that the individual is alone in a godless universe and that the basic human condition is one of suffering and loneliness. Nevertheless, because there are no fixed values, individuals can create their own characters—indeed, they can shape themselves—through the exercise of free will. The atheistic strain culminates in and is popularly associated with the works of Jean-Paul Sartre. The Christian existentialists, on the other hand, believe that only in God may people find freedom from life's anguish. The two strains hold certain beliefs in common: that existence cannot be fully understood or described through empirical effort; that anguish is a universal element of life; that individuals must bear responsibility for their actions; and that there is no common standard of behavior or perception for religious and ethical matters. Existentialist thought figures prominently in the works of such authors as Franz Kafka, Fyodor Dostoyevsky, and Albert Camus.

Expatriatism: The practice of leaving one's country to live for an extended period in another country. Literary expatriates include Irish author James Joyce who moved to Italy and France, American writers James Baldwin, Ernest Hemingway, Gertrude Stein, and F. Scott Fitzgerald who lived and wrote in Paris, and Polish novelist Joseph Conrad in England.

Exposition: Writing intended to explain the nature of an idea, thing, or theme. Expository writing is often combined with description, narration, or argument.

Expressionism: An indistinct literary term, originally used to describe an early twentieth-century school of German painting. The term applies to almost any mode of unconventional, highly subjective writing that distorts reality in some way. Advocates of Expressionism include Federico Garcia Lorca, Eugene O'Neill, Franz Kafka, and James Joyce.

F

Fable: A prose or verse narrative intended to convey a moral. Animals or inanimate objects with human characteristics often serve as characters in fables. A famous fable is Aesop's "The Tortoise and the Hare."

Fantasy: A literary form related to mythology and folklore. Fantasy literature is typically set in non-existent realms and features supernatural beings. Notable examples of literature with elements of fantasy are Gabriel Garcia Marquez's story "The Handsomest Drowned Man in the World" and Ursula K. LeGuin's "The Ones Who Walk Away from Omelas."

Farce: A type of comedy characterized by broad humor, outlandish incidents, and often vulgar subject matter. Much of the comedy in film and television could more accurately be described as farce.

Fiction: Any story that is the product of imagination rather than a documentation of fact. Characters and events in such narratives may be based in real life but their ultimate form and configuration is a creation of the author.

Figurative Language: A technique in which an author uses figures of speech such as hyperbole, irony, metaphor, or simile for a particular effect. Figurative language is the opposite of literal language, in which every word is truthful, accurate, and free of exaggeration or embellishment.

Flashback: A device used in literature to present action that occurred before the beginning of the story. Flashbacks are often introduced as the dreams or recollections of one or more characters.

Foil: A character in a work of literature whose physical or psychological qualities contrast strongly with, and therefore highlight, the corresponding qualities of another character. In his Sherlock Holmes stories, Arthur Conan Doyle portrayed Dr. Watson as a man of normal habits and intelligence, making him a foil for the eccentric and unusually perceptive Sherlock Holmes.

Folklore: Traditions and myths preserved in a culture or group of people. Typically, these are passed on by word of mouth in various forms—such as legends, songs, and proverbs—or preserved in customs and ceremonies. Washington Irving, in "The Devil and Tom Walker" and many of his other stories, incorporates many elements of the folklore of New England and Germany.

Folktale: A story originating in oral tradition. Folktales fall into a variety of categories, including legends, ghost stories, fairy tales, fables, and anecdotes based on historical figures and events.

Foreshadowing: A device used in literature to create expectation or to set up an explanation of later developments. Edgar Allan Poe uses foreshadowing to create suspense in "The Fall of the House of Usher" when the narrator comments on the crumbling state of disrepair in which he finds the house.

G

Genre: A category of literary work. Genre may refer to both the content of a given work—tragedy, comedy, horror, science fiction—and to its form, such as poetry, novel, or drama.

Gilded Age: A period in American history during the 1870s and after characterized by political corruption and materialism. A number of important novels of social and political criticism were written during this time. Henry James and Kate Chopin are two writers who were prominent during the Gilded Age.

Gothicism: In literature, works characterized by a taste for medieval or morbid characters and situations. A gothic novel prominently features elements of horror, the supernatural, gloom, and violence: clanking chains, terror, ghosts, medieval castles, and unexplained phenomena. The term "gothic novel" is also applied to novels that lack elements of the traditional Gothic setting but that create a similar atmosphere of terror or dread. The term can also be applied to stories, plays, and poems. Mary Shelley's *Frankenstein* and Joyce Carol Oates's *Bellefleur* are both gothic novels.

Grotesque: In literature, a work that is characterized by exaggeration, deformity, freakishness, and disorder. The grotesque often includes an element of comic absurdity. Examples of the grotesque can be found in the works of Edgar Allan Poe, Flannery O'Connor, Joseph Heller, and Shirley Jackson.

H

Harlem Renaissance: The Harlem Renaissance of the 1920s is generally considered the first significant movement of black writers and artists in the United States. During this period, new and established black writers, many of whom lived in the region of New York City known as Harlem, published more fiction and poetry than ever before, the first influential black literary journals were established, and black authors and artists received their first widespread recognition and serious critical appraisal. Among the major writers associated with this period are Countee Cullen, Langston Hughes, Arna Bontemps, and Zora Neale Hurston.

Hero/Heroine: The principal sympathetic character in a literary work. Heroes and heroines typically exhibit admirable traits: idealism, courage, and integrity, for example. Famous heroes and heroines of literature include Charles Dickens's Oliver Twist, Margaret Mitchell's Scarlett O'Hara, and the anonymous narrator in Ralph Ellison's *Invisible Man.*

Hyperbole: Deliberate exaggeration used to achieve an effect. In William Shakespeare's *Macbeth,* Lady Macbeth hyperbolizes when she says, "All the perfumes of Arabia could not sweeten this little hand."

I

Image: A concrete representation of an object or sensory experience. Typically, such a representation helps evoke the feelings associated with the object or experience itself. Images are either "literal" or "figurative." Literal images are especially concrete and involve little or no extension of the obvious meaning of the words used to express them. Figurative images do not follow the literal meaning of the words exactly. Images in literature are usually visual, but the term "image" can also refer to the representation of any sensory experience.

Imagery: The array of images in a literary work. Also used to convey the author's overall use of figurative language in a work.

In medias res: A Latin term meaning "in the middle of things." It refers to the technique of beginning a story at its midpoint and then using various flashback devices to reveal previous action. This technique originated in such epics as Virgil's *Aeneid.*

Interior Monologue: A narrative technique in which characters' thoughts are revealed in a way that appears to be uncontrolled by the author. The interior monologue typically aims to reveal the inner self of a character. It portrays emotional experiences as they occur at both a conscious and unconscious level. One of the best-known interior monologues in English is the Molly Bloom section at the close of James Joyce's *Ulysses.* Katherine Anne Porter's "The Jilting of Granny Weatherall" is also told in the form of an interior monologue.

Irony: In literary criticism, the effect of language in which the intended meaning is the opposite of what is stated. The title of Jonathan Swift's "A Modest Proposal" is ironic because what Swift proposes in this essay is cannibalism—hardly "modest."

J

Jargon: Language that is used or understood only by a select group of people. Jargon may refer to terminology used in a certain profession, such as computer jargon, or it may refer to any nonsensical language that is not understood by most people. Anthony Burgess's *A Clockwork Orange* and James Thurber's "The Secret Life of Walter Mitty" both use jargon.

K

Knickerbocker Group: An indistinct group of New York writers of the first half of the nineteenth century. Members of the group were linked only by location and a common theme: New York life. Two famous members of the Knickerbocker Group were Washington Irving and William Cullen Bryant. The group's name derives from Irving's *Knickerbocker's History of New York.*

L

Literal Language: An author uses literal language when he or she writes without exaggerating or embellishing the subject matter and without any tools of figurative language. To say "He ran very quickly down the street" is to use literal language, whereas to say "He ran like a hare down the street" would be using figurative language.

Literature: Literature is broadly defined as any written or spoken material, but the term most often refers to creative works. Literature includes poetry, drama, fiction, and many kinds of nonfiction writing, as well as oral, dramatic, and broadcast compositions not necessarily preserved in a written format, such as films and television programs.

Lost Generation: A term first used by Gertrude Stein to describe the post-World War I generation of American writers: men and women haunted by a sense of betrayal and emptiness brought about by the destructiveness of the war. The term is commonly applied to Hart Crane, Ernest Hemingway, F. Scott Fitzgerald, and others.

M

Magic Realism: A form of literature that incorporates fantasy elements or supernatural occurrences into the narrative and accepts them as truth. Gabriel Garcia Marquez and Laura Esquivel are two writers known for their works of magic realism.

Metaphor: A figure of speech that expresses an idea through the image of another object. Metaphors suggest the essence of the first object by identifying it with certain qualities of the second object. An example is "But soft, what light through yonder window breaks?/ It is the east, and Juliet is the sun" in William Shakespeare's *Romeo and Juliet*. Here, Juliet, the first object, is identified with qualities of the second object, the sun.

Minimalism: A literary style characterized by spare, simple prose with few elaborations. In minimalism, the main theme of the work is often never discussed directly. Amy Hempel and Ernest Hemingway are two writers known for their works of minimalism.

Modernism: Modern literary practices. Also, the principles of a literary school that lasted from roughly the beginning of the twentieth century until the end of World War II. Modernism is defined by its rejection of the literary conventions of the nineteenth century and by its opposition to conventional morality, taste, traditions, and economic values. Many writers are associated with the concepts of modernism, including Albert Camus, D. H. Lawrence, Ernest Hemingway, William Faulkner, Eugene O'Neill, and James Joyce.

Monologue: A composition, written or oral, by a single individual. More specifically, a speech given by a single individual in a drama or other public entertainment. It has no set length, although it is usually several or more lines long. "I Stand Here Ironing" by Tillie Olsen is an example of a story written in the form of a monologue.

Mood: The prevailing emotions of a work or of the author in his or her creation of the work. The mood of a work is not always what might be expected based on its subject matter.

Motif: A theme, character type, image, metaphor, or other verbal element that recurs throughout a single work of literature or occurs in a number of different works over a period of time. For example, the color white in Herman Melville's *Moby Dick* is a "specific" *motif,* while the trials of star-crossed lovers is a "conventional" *motif* from the literature of all periods.

N

Narration: The telling of a series of events, real or invented. A narration may be either a simple narrative, in which the events are recounted chronologically, or a narrative with a plot, in which the account is given in a style reflecting the author's artistic concept of the story. Narration is sometimes used as a synonym for "storyline."

Narrative: A verse or prose accounting of an event or sequence of events, real or invented. The term is also used as an adjective in the sense "method of narration." For example, in literary criticism, the expression "narrative technique" usually refers to the way the author structures and presents his or her story. Different narrative forms include diaries, travelogues, novels, ballads, epics, short stories, and other fictional forms.

Narrator: The teller of a story. The narrator may be the author or a character in the story through whom the author speaks. Huckleberry Finn is the narrator of Mark Twain's *The Adventures of Huckleberry Finn.*

Novella: An Italian term meaning "story." This term has been especially used to describe fourteenth-century Italian tales, but it also refers to modern short novels. Modern novellas include Leo Tolstoy's *The Death of Ivan Ilich,* Fyodor Dostoyevsky's *Notes from the Underground,* and Joseph Conrad's *Heart of Darkness.*

O

Oedipus Complex: A son's romantic obsession with his mother. The phrase is derived from the story of the ancient Theban hero Oedipus, who unknowingly killed his father and married his mother, and was popularized by Sigmund Freud's theory of psychoanalysis. Literary occurrences of the Oedipus complex include Sophocles' *Oedipus Rex* and D. H. Lawrence's "The Rocking-Horse Winner."

Onomatopoeia: The use of words whose sounds express or suggest their meaning. In its simplest sense, onomatopoeia may be represented by words that mimic the sounds they denote such as "hiss" or "meow." At a more subtle level, the pattern and rhythm of sounds and rhymes of a line or poem may be onomatopoeic.

Oral Tradition: A process by which songs, ballads, folklore, and other material are transmitted by word of mouth. The tradition of oral transmission predates the written record systems of literate society.

Oral transmission preserves material sometimes over generations, although often with variations. Memory plays a large part in the recitation and preservation of orally transmitted material. Native American myths and legends, and African folktales told by plantation slaves are examples of orally transmitted literature.

P

Parable: A story intended to teach a moral lesson or answer an ethical question. Examples of parables are the stories told by Jesus Christ in the New Testament, notably ''The Prodigal Son,'' but parables also are used in Sufism, rabbinic literature, Hasidism, and Zen Buddhism. Isaac Bashevis Singer's story ''Gimpel the Fool'' exhibits characteristics of a parable.

Paradox: A statement that appears illogical or contradictory at first, but may actually point to an underlying truth. A literary example of a paradox is George Orwell's statement ''All animals are equal, but some animals are more equal than others'' in *Animal Farm*.

Parody: In literature, this term refers to an imitation of a serious literary work or the signature style of a particular author in a ridiculous manner. A typical parody adopts the style of the original and applies it to an inappropriate subject for humorous effect. Parody is a form of satire and could be considered the literary equivalent of a caricature or cartoon. Henry Fielding's *Shamela* is a parody of Samuel Richardson's *Pamela*.

Persona: A Latin term meaning ''mask.'' Personae are the characters in a fictional work of literature. The persona generally functions as a mask through which the author tells a story in a voice other than his or her own. A persona is usually either a character in a story who acts as a narrator or an ''implied author,'' a voice created by the author to act as the narrator for himself or herself. The persona in Charlotte Perkins Gilman's story ''The Yellow Wallpaper'' is the unnamed young mother experiencing a mental breakdown.

Personification: A figure of speech that gives human qualities to abstract ideas, animals, and inanimate objects. To say that ''the sun is smiling'' is to personify the sun.

Plot: The pattern of events in a narrative or drama. In its simplest sense, the plot guides the author in composing the work and helps the reader follow the work. Typically, plots exhibit causality and unity and have a beginning, a middle, and an end. Sometimes, however, a plot may consist of a series of disconnected events, in which case it is known as an ''episodic plot.''

Poetic Justice: An outcome in a literary work, not necessarily a poem, in which the good are rewarded and the evil are punished, especially in ways that particularly fit their virtues or crimes. For example, a murderer may himself be murdered, or a thief will find himself penniless.

Poetic License: Distortions of fact and literary convention made by a writer—not always a poet—for the sake of the effect gained. Poetic license is closely related to the concept of ''artistic freedom.'' An author exercises poetic license by saying that a pile of money ''reaches as high as a mountain'' when the pile is actually only a foot or two high.

Point of View: The narrative perspective from which a literary work is presented to the reader. There are four traditional points of view. The ''third person omniscient'' gives the reader a ''godlike'' perspective, unrestricted by time or place, from which to see actions and look into the minds of characters. This allows the author to comment openly on characters and events in the work. The ''third person'' point of view presents the events of the story from outside of any single character's perception, much like the omniscient point of view, but the reader must understand the action as it takes place and without any special insight into characters' minds or motivations. The ''first person'' or ''personal'' point of view relates events as they are perceived by a single character. The main character ''tells'' the story and may offer opinions about the action and characters which differ from those of the author. Much less common than omniscient, third person, and first person is the ''second person'' point of view, wherein the author tells the story as if it is happening to the reader. James Thurber employs the omniscient point of view in his short story ''The Secret Life of Walter Mitty.'' Ernest Hemingway's ''A Clean, Well-Lighted Place'' is a short story told from the third person point of view. Mark Twain's novel *Huckleberry Finn* is presented from the first person viewpoint. Jay McInerney's *Bright Lights, Big City* is an example of a novel which uses the second person point of view.

Pornography: Writing intended to provoke feelings of lust in the reader. Such works are often condemned by critics and teachers, but those which can be shown to have literary value are viewed less harshly. Literary works that have been described as pornographic include D. H. Lawrence's *Lady Chatterley's Lover* and James Joyce's *Ulysses.*

Post-Aesthetic Movement: An artistic response made by African Americans to the black aesthetic movement of the 1960s and early 1970s. Writers since that time have adopted a somewhat different tone in their work, with less emphasis placed on the disparity between black and white in the United States. In the words of post-aesthetic authors such as Toni Morrison, John Edgar Wideman, and Kristin Hunter, African Americans are portrayed as looking inward for answers to their own questions, rather than always looking to the outside world. Two well-known examples of works produced as part of the post-aesthetic movement are the Pulitzer Prize-winning novels *The Color Purple* by Alice Walker and *Beloved* by Toni Morrison.

Postmodernism: Writing from the 1960s forward characterized by experimentation and application of modernist elements, which include existentialism and alienation. Postmodernists have gone a step further in the rejection of tradition begun with the modernists by also rejecting traditional forms, preferring the anti-novel over the novel and the anti-hero over the hero. Postmodern writers include Thomas Pynchon, Margaret Drabble, and Gabriel Garcia Marquez.

Prologue: An introductory section of a literary work. It often contains information establishing the situation of the characters or presents information about the setting, time period, or action. In drama, the prologue is spoken by a chorus or by one of the principal characters.

Prose: A literary medium that attempts to mirror the language of everyday speech. It is distinguished from poetry by its use of unmetered, unrhymed language consisting of logically related sentences. Prose is usually grouped into paragraphs that form a cohesive whole such as an essay or a novel. The term is sometimes used to mean an author's general writing.

Protagonist: The central character of a story who serves as a focus for its themes and incidents and as the principal rationale for its development. The protagonist is sometimes referred to in discussions of modern literature as the hero or anti-hero. Well-known protagonists are Hamlet in William Shakespeare's *Hamlet* and Jay Gatsby in F. Scott Fitzgerald's *The Great Gatsby.*

R

Realism: A nineteenth-century European literary movement that sought to portray familiar characters, situations, and settings in a realistic manner. This was done primarily by using an objective narrative point of view and through the buildup of accurate detail. The standard for success of any realistic work depends on how faithfully it transfers common experience into fictional forms. The realistic method may be altered or extended, as in stream of consciousness writing, to record highly subjective experience. Contemporary authors who often write in a realistic way include Nadine Gordimer and Grace Paley.

Resolution: The portion of a story following the climax, in which the conflict is resolved. The resolution of Jane Austen's *Northanger Abbey* is neatly summed up in the following sentence: "Henry and Catherine were married, the bells rang and everybody smiled."

Rising Action: The part of a drama where the plot becomes increasingly complicated. Rising action leads up to the climax, or turning point, of a drama. The final "chase scene" of an action film is generally the rising action which culminates in the film's climax.

Roman a clef: A French phrase meaning "novel with a key." It refers to a narrative in which real persons are portrayed under fictitious names. Jack Kerouac, for example, portrayed various his friends under fictitious names in the novel *On the Road.* D. H. Lawrence based "The Rocking-Horse Winner" on a family he knew.

Romanticism: This term has two widely accepted meanings. In historical criticism, it refers to a European intellectual and artistic movement of the late eighteenth and early nineteenth centuries that sought greater freedom of personal expression than that allowed by the strict rules of literary form and logic of the eighteenth-century neoclassicists. The Romantics preferred emotional and imaginative expression to rational analysis. They considered the individual to be at the center of all experience and so placed him or her at the center of their art. The Romantics believed that the creative imagination reveals nobler truths—unique feelings and attitudes—than those that could be discovered by logic or by scientific examination. "Romanticism" is also used as a general term to refer to a type of sensibility found in all periods of literary history and usually considered to be in opposition to the principles of classicism. In this sense, Romanticism signifies any work or philosophy in which the exotic or dreamlike figure strongly, or that is devoted to individualistic expression, self-analysis, or a pursuit of a higher realm of knowledge than can be discovered by human reason. Prominent Romantics include Jean-Jacques Rousseau, William Wordsworth, John Keats, Lord Byron, and Johann Wolfgang von Goethe.

S

Satire: A work that uses ridicule, humor, and wit to criticize and provoke change in human nature and institutions. Voltaire's novella *Candide* and Jonathan Swift's essay ''A Modest Proposal'' are both satires. Flannery O'Connor's portrayal of the family in ''A Good Man Is Hard to Find'' is a satire of a modern, Southern, American family.

Science Fiction: A type of narrative based upon real or imagined scientific theories and technology. Science fiction is often peopled with alien creatures and set on other planets or in different dimensions. Popular writers of science fiction are Isaac Asimov, Karel Capek, Ray Bradbury, and Ursula K. Le Guin.

Setting: The time, place, and culture in which the action of a narrative takes place. The elements of setting may include geographic location, characters's physical and mental environments, prevailing cultural attitudes, or the historical time in which the action takes place.

Short Story: A fictional prose narrative shorter and more focused than a novella. The short story usually deals with a single episode and often a single character. The ''tone,'' the author's attitude toward his or her subject and audience, is uniform throughout. The short story frequently also lacks *denouement*, ending instead at its climax.

Signifying Monkey: A popular trickster figure in black folklore, with hundreds of tales about this character documented since the 19th century. Henry Louis Gates Jr. examines the history of the signifying monkey in *The Signifying Monkey: Towards a Theory of Afro-American Literary Criticism,* published in 1988.

Simile: A comparison, usually using ''like'' or ''as,''of two essentially dissimilar things, as in ''coffee as cold as ice'' or ''He sounded like a broken record.'' The title of Ernest Hemingway's ''Hills Like White Elephants'' contains a simile.

Social Realism: The Socialist Realism school of literary theory was proposed by Maxim Gorky and established as a dogma by the first Soviet Congress of Writers. It demanded adherence to a communist worldview in works of literature. Its doctrines required an objective viewpoint comprehensible to the working classes and themes of social struggle featuring strong proletarian heroes. Gabriel Garcia Marquez's stories exhibit some characteristics of Socialist Realism.

Stereotype: A stereotype was originally the name for a duplication made during the printing process; this led to its modern definition as a person or thing that is (or is assumed to be) the same as all others of its type. Common stereotypical characters include the absent-minded professor, the nagging wife, the troublemaking teenager, and the kind-hearted grandmother.

Stream of Consciousness: A narrative technique for rendering the inward experience of a character. This technique is designed to give the impression of an ever-changing series of thoughts, emotions, images, and memories in the spontaneous and seemingly illogical order that they occur in life. The textbook example of stream of consciousness is the last section of James Joyce's *Ulysses.*

Structure: The form taken by a piece of literature. The structure may be made obvious for ease of understanding, as in nonfiction works, or may obscured for artistic purposes, as in some poetry or seemingly ''unstructured'' prose.

Style: A writer's distinctive manner of arranging words to suit his or her ideas and purpose in writing. The unique imprint of the author's personality upon his or her writing, style is the product of an author's way of arranging ideas and his or her use of diction, different sentence structures, rhythm, figures of speech, rhetorical principles, and other elements of composition.

Suspense: A literary device in which the author maintains the audience's attention through the buildup of events, the outcome of which will soon be revealed. Suspense in William Shakespeare's *Hamlet* is sustained throughout by the question of whether or not the Prince will achieve what he has been instructed to do and of what he intends to do.

Symbol: Something that suggests or stands for something else without losing its original identity. In literature, symbols combine their literal meaning with the suggestion of an abstract concept. Literary symbols are of two types: those that carry complex associations of meaning no matter what their contexts, and those that derive their suggestive meaning from their functions in specific literary works. Examples of symbols are sunshine suggesting happiness, rain suggesting sorrow, and storm clouds suggesting despair.

T

Tale: A story told by a narrator with a simple plot and little character development. Tales are usually relatively short and often carry a simple message. Examples of tales can be found in the works of Saki, Anton Chekhov, Guy de Maupassant, and O. Henry.

Tall Tale: A humorous tale told in a straightforward, credible tone but relating absolutely impossible events or feats of the characters. Such tales were commonly told of frontier adventures during the settlement of the west in the United States. Literary use of tall tales can be found in Washington Irving's *History of New York,* Mark Twain's *Life on the Mississippi,* and in the German R. F. Raspe's *Baron Munchausen's Narratives of His Marvellous Travels and Campaigns in Russia.*

Theme: The main point of a work of literature. The term is used interchangeably with thesis. Many works have multiple themes. One of the themes of Nathaniel Hawthorne's ''Young Goodman Brown'' is loss of faith.

Tone: The author's attitude toward his or her audience may be deduced from the tone of the work. A formal tone may create distance or convey politeness, while an informal tone may encourage a friendly, intimate, or intrusive feeling in the reader. The author's attitude toward his or her subject matter may also be deduced from the tone of the words he or she uses in discussing it. The tone of John F. Kennedy's speech which included the appeal to ''ask not what your country can do for you'' was intended to instill feelings of camaraderie and national pride in listeners.

Tragedy: A drama in prose or poetry about a noble, courageous hero of excellent character who, because of some tragic character flaw, brings ruin upon him- or herself. Tragedy treats its subjects in a dignified and serious manner, using poetic language to help evoke pity and fear and bring about catharsis, a purging of these emotions. The tragic form was practiced extensively by the ancient Greeks. The classical form of tragedy was revived in the sixteenth century; it flourished especially on the Elizabethan stage. In modern times, dramatists have attempted to adapt the form to the needs of modern society by drawing their heroes from the ranks of ordinary men and women and defining the nobility of these heroes in terms of spirit rather than exalted social standing. Some contemporary works that are thought of as tragedies include *The Great Gatsby* by F. Scott Fitzgerald, and *The Sound and the Fury* by William Faulkner.

Tragic Flaw: In a tragedy, the quality within the hero or heroine which leads to his or her downfall. Examples of the tragic flaw include Othello's jealousy and Hamlet's indecisiveness, although most great tragedies defy such simple interpretation.

U

Utopia: A fictional perfect place, such as ''paradise'' or ''heaven.'' An early literary utopia was described in Plato's *Republic,* and in modern literature, Ursula K. Le Guin depicts a utopia in ''The Ones Who Walk Away from Omelas.''

V

Victorian: Refers broadly to the reign of Queen Victoria of England (1837–1901) and to anything with qualities typical of that era. For example, the qualities of smug narrow-mindedness, bourgeois materialism, faith in social progress, and priggish morality are often considered Victorian. In literature, the Victorian Period was the great age of the English novel, and the latter part of the era saw the rise of movements such as decadence and symbolism.

Cumulative Author/Title Index

Nationality/Ethnicity Index

Subject/Theme Index